Challenges to Globalization
Analyzing the Economics

A National Bureau
of Economic Research
Conference Report

Studieförbundet Näringsliv och Samhälle
Center for Business and Policy Studies

Challenges to Globalization
Analyzing the Economics

Edited by **Robert E. Baldwin and L. Alan Winters**

The University of Chicago Press

Chicago and London

ROBERT E. BALDWIN is professor emeritus of economics at the University of Wisconsin at Madison and a research associate of the National Bureau of Economic Research (NBER). He is the author or coeditor of many books including *Geography and Ownership As Bases for Economic Accounting, The Structure and Evolution of Recent U.S. Trade Policy, Political Economy of U.S.-Taiwan Trade,* and *Trade Policy in a Changing World Economy.* L. ALAN WINTERS is professor of economics at the University of Sussex. He is a research fellow of the Centre for Economic Policy Research (CEPR, London), and a senior visiting fellow of the Centre for Economic Performance at the London School of Economics. Among his books are: *An Econometric Model of the Export Sector, Europe's Domestic Market, Eastern Europe's International Trade, Trade Liberalisation and Poverty: A Handbook, Regional Integration and Development,* and *Liberalising Labour Mobility under the GATS.*

The University of Chicago Press, Chicago 60637
The University of Chicago Press, Ltd., London
© 2004 by the National Bureau of Economic Research
All rights reserved. Published 2004
Printed in the United States of America
13 12 11 10 09 08 07 06 05 04   1 2 3 4 5
ISBN: 0-226-03615-4 (cloth)

Library of Congress Cataloging-in-Publication Data

Challenges to globalization: analyzing the economics / edited by
    Robert E. Baldwin and L. Alan Winters.
        p.   cm.
    "A National Bureau of Economic Research conference report"—
    Includes bibliographical references and index.
    ISBN 0-226-03615-4 (alk. paper)
    1. International economic relations. 2. Globalization. 3. Pressure
groups. 4. Income distribution. 5. Human rights. I. Baldwin,
Robert E. II. Winters, L. Alan.

HF1359.C438 2004
337—dc22
                                                                2003056531

Relation of the Directors to the
Work and Publications of the
National Bureau of Economic Research

1. The object of the NBER is to ascertain and present to the economics profession, and to the public more generally, important economic facts and their interpretation in a scientific manner without policy recommendations. The Board of Directors is charged with the responsibility of ensuring that the work of the NBER is carried on in strict conformity with this object.

2. The President shall establish an internal review process to ensure that book manuscripts proposed for publication DO NOT contain policy recommendations. This shall apply both to the proceedings of conferences and to manuscripts by a single author or by one or more co-authors but shall not apply to authors of comments at NBER conferences who are not NBER affiliates.

3. No book manuscript reporting research shall be published by the NBER until the President has sent to each member of the Board a notice that a manuscript is recommended for publication and that in the President's opinion it is suitable for publication in accordance with the above principles of the NBER. Such notification will include a table of contents and an abstract or summary of the manuscript's content, a list of contributors if applicable, and a response form for use by Directors who desire a copy of the manuscript for review. Each manuscript shall contain a summary drawing attention to the nature and treatment of the problem studied and the main conclusions reached.

4. No volume shall be published until forty-five days have elapsed from the above notification of intention to publish it. During this period a copy shall be sent to any Director requesting it, and if any Director objects to publication on the grounds that the manuscript contains policy recommendations, the objection will be presented to the author(s) or editor(s). In case of dispute, all members of the Board shall be notified, and the President shall appoint an ad hoc committee of the Board to decide the matter; thirty days additional shall be granted for this purpose.

5. The President shall present annually to the Board a report describing the internal manuscript review process, any objections made by Directors before publication or by anyone after publication, any disputes about such matters, and how they were handled.

6. Publications of the NBER issued for informational purposes concerning the work of the Bureau, or issued to inform the public of the activities at the Bureau, including but not limited to the NBER Digest and Reporter, shall be consistent with the object stated in paragraph 1. They shall contain a specific disclaimer noting that they have not passed through the review procedures required in this resolution. The Executive Committee of the Board is charged with the review of all such publications from time to time.

7. NBER working papers and manuscripts distributed on the Bureau's web site are not deemed to be publications for the purpose of this resolution, but they shall be consistent with the object stated in paragraph 1. Working papers shall contain a specific disclaimer noting that they have not passed through the review procedures required in this resolution. The NBER's web site shall contain a similar disclaimer. The President shall establish an internal review process to ensure that the working papers and the web site do not contain policy recommendations, and shall report annually to the Board on this process and any concerns raised in connection with it.

8. Unless otherwise determined by the Board or exempted by the terms of paragraphs 6 and 7, a copy of this resolution shall be printed in each NBER publication as described in paragraph 2 above.

Centre for Economic Policy Research

The Centre for Economic Policy Research (CEPR) is a network of 600 research fellows and affiliates, based primarily in European universities. The Centre coordinates the research activities of its fellows and affiliates and communicates the results to the public and private sectors. The CEPR is an entrepreneur, developing research initiatives with the producers, consumers, and sponsors of research. Established in 1983, CEPR is a European economics-research organization with uniquely wide-ranging scope and activities.

The CEPR is a registered educational charity. The Centre is supported by the European Central Bank, the Bank for International Settlements, the European Investment Bank, twenty-three national central banks, and forty-one companies. None of these organizations gives prior review to the Centre's publications, nor do they necessarily endorse the views expressed therein.

The Centre is pluralist and nonpartisan, bringing economic research to bear on the analysis of medium- and long-run policy questions. CEPR research may include views on policy, but the Executive Committee of the Centre does not give prior review to its publications, and the Centre takes no institutional policy positions. The opinions expressed in this report are those of the authors and not those of the CEPR.

Guillermo de la Dehesa, *chair of the board*
Richard Portes, *president*
Hilary Beech, *chief executive officer*
Mathias Dewatripont, *research director*

Swedish Center for Business and Policy Studies

The Swedish Center for Business and Policy Studies (SNS) is an independent network of leading decision makers from the private and public sectors who share a commitment to social and economic development in Sweden. Its aim is to improve the basis for rational decisions on major social and economic issues by promoting social science research and stimulating public debate.

The SNS engages leading academics from universities in Sweden and other countries in its social science research. It has its own publishing house and organizes conferences, courses, and local branch meetings. A private, nonpartisan and nonprofit association, SNS is financed through membership fees, research grants, book sales, and conference fees, as well as annual subscriptions by companies, public bodies, and other organizations.

Executive Board

Carl-Johan Bonnier, *chairman*

Carl Bennet	Stefan Lundgren	Torsten Persson
Ingemar Hansson	Marianne Nivert	Meg Tivéus
Kerstin Hessius	Anders Nyrén	Sten Westerberg

Officers

Stefan Lundgren, *president and chief executive officer*

Research Directors
Göran Arvidsson	Olof Petersson	Hans Tson Söderström
Pontus Braunerhjelm	Stefan Sandström	Birgitta Swedenborg

Contents

V. MACROECONOMICS

Acknowledgments

This volume contains the papers and discussants' comments presented at the seventh International Seminar in International Trade (ISIT). The seminar, jointly arranged by the Centre for Economic Policy Research, London (CEPR), the National Bureau of Economic Research, Cambridge, Massachusetts (NBER), and the Center for Business and Policy Studies, Stockholm (SNS), was held on May 24 and 25, 2002, in Stockholm. Financial support from the Jan Wallander and Tom Hedelius Foundation, NBER, and the U.K. Department for Trade and Industry is gratefully acknowledged.

The seminar, which is a biennial event, brings together economists from North America and Europe to discuss papers aimed at informing those concerned with current public policy matters about relevant empirical economic research on these issues.

We are grateful to Stefan Sandström of SNS who oversaw all the arrangements for the meeting; to Janet Seabrook of CEPR, who coordinated the program and logistics; to Helena Fitz-Patrick of NBER, who coordinated the preparation of the manuscript; and to Alex Schwartz of the University of Chicago Press, who coordinated the publication process.

The manuscript benefited greatly from the comments of referees at both NBER and the University of Chicago Press, to whom we are grateful.

Challenges to Globalization
An Overview

Robert E. Baldwin and L. Alan Winters

Introduction

The failure of the World Trade Organization's (WTO's) 1999 ministerial conference in Seattle was a shock to the traditional trade-policy community. Most member governments and outside observers believed that trade ministers would be able to hammer out an agenda for a new round of multilateral trade negotiation, difficult though this would be and vague or ambiguous the language might be on some points. Instead, not only did ministers fail to establish an agenda or set a date for a new round of trade negotiations, but the meeting revealed deep divisions among governments and private-sector groups concerning the nature of the globalization process as it was being shaped by such public international organizations as the WTO, the International Monetary Fund (IMF), and the World Bank, as well as by multinational private corporations.

Fortunately, as a consequence of much hard work by the WTO director general Mike Moore and the country representatives stationed in Geneva, plus several key compromises by ministers, the ministerial meeting on trade held in Qatar in November 2001 was successful in launching a new round—the Doha Development Agenda—in January 2002. However, one agenda item important for some industrial countries, namely core labor standards, was rejected outright, and negotiations on a number of other

Robert E. Baldwin is Hilldale Professor of Economics, Emeritus, at the University of Wisconsin–Madison and a research associate of the National Bureau of Economic Research (NBER). L. Alan Winters is professor of economics at the University of Sussex. He is a research fellow of the Centre for Economic Policy Research (CEPR) and a senior visiting fellow of the Centre for Economic Performance at the London School of Economics.

key items were postponed until after the next ministerial meeting, and then only if there is "explicit consensus" among members to proceed.

Observers of trade negotiations have long been accustomed to bitter disputes among members on such issues as agricultural liberalization, the appropriate tariff-cutting rule to adopt, and the extent and timing of liberalization obligations on the part of the developing countries. But the run-up to Seattle and the meeting itself highlighted two sets of deeply held beliefs about the WTO and the trading system that industrial-country governments had largely been able to ignore until that time.

First, and most important, most developing countries felt that the benefits they received from the Uruguay Round negotiations fell far short of what they had expected in return for signing the agreements promoted by the developed countries during this round. They concluded, for example, that the adjustment burdens placed on them under the agreements on trade-related intellectual property rights (TRIPs) and trade-related investment measures (TRIMs) were much greater than those imposed on the developed countries in areas such as agriculture and textiles/clothing. The developing countries also felt that the time schedules established for them to implement the obligations assumed in previous agreements were too short and inflexible and that the developed countries were not fulfilling their parts of the bargains struck on such issues as agriculture and textiles/apparel. Furthermore, they were frustrated by what they perceived to be the misuse by developed countries of certain WTO rules for protectionist purposes, especially those related to antidumping. All these views made developing-country governments reluctant to agree to developed countries' proposals to establish new WTO rules in trade-related areas such as competition policy, environmental standards, labor rights, government procurement policies, and foreign direct investment. Moreover, developing countries felt isolated and marginalized in the WTO's internal processes, especially as they worked at Seattle itself. As a consequence of these views, the developing countries were quite prepared to see the Seattle ministerial meeting (as well as the later Doha ministerial conference) fail, unless the agenda included action items that would seriously address their concerns.

Second, as became evident in Seattle from the street demonstrations and the harassment of delegates, many nongovernmental organizations (NGOs) were deeply dissatisfied with certain consequences of the globalization process resulting from the international liberalization of trade, investment, and finance. These groups tended to be mainly concerned about three issues: the environment, human and worker rights, and inequality and poverty, particularly in developing countries (see chapter 1 in this volume by Elliott, Kar, and Richardson). Environmentalists are concerned with such matters as the maintenance of biodiversity and pollution in critical ecosystems. They fear that trade liberalization and the resulting competition for international markets may lead directly to unsustainable consumption of natural resources and excessive pollution and indirectly to a reduction in existing environmental standards. Similarly, according to many worker-rights and human-rights advocates, trade liberalization and unrestrained foreign direct investment in developing countries lead to lower wages; to unhealthy, unsafe working conditions; and, in some instances, to the loss of basic human rights in these countries. The NGOs interested in promoting greater income equality and reducing poverty are also skeptical about the merits of freer flows of goods, technology, and capital in furthering their goals.

As with the views of developing countries, trade officials and interested parties in the private sector had been aware for several years that a growing number of NGOs opposed the international liberalization of trade, investment, and finance. Yet these NGOs did not receive much attention from the governments and international economic institutions that were promoting this liberalization until the late 1990s, when they began to organize large street protests at the meetings of such key trade and financial institutions as the WTO, the IMF, and the World Bank and at the meetings of intergovernmental organizations such as the Group of Eight (G8) and private groups like the World Economic Forum.[1] Even then, the protesters were initially largely dismissed as being anarchists and economically irrational. However, as those who seem bent on violence have been relegated to a less-prominent role and as more and more formal and informal contacts have been established between proponents and opponents of further liberalization of trade, finance, and foreign investment, the anti-globalization movement has become an important force to be reckoned with in public and private decision making in these areas. Nevertheless, the divergence of policy positions between the groups is still very wide.

Given the new willingness of the developing countries to assert their power over the form of international liberalization efforts and the growing influence of NGOs highly critical of previous efforts to increase the worldwide flows of goods, technology, and investment funds, the nature of future globalization is very much in question. An important reason for the continuing disagreement and misunderstanding is both a lack of careful case studies and statistical analyses (in contrast to anecdotal evidence) concerning the effects of various aspects of this process, and a lack of information among many affected by globalization of the knowledge we already have on the subject.

This conference volume aims both at informing those concerned with globalization issues about the knowledge that economists have already gained in studying various aspects of the topic and at providing new knowledge based on the research of the authors. We focus largely on the

1. One exception was the World Bank's attempt to create a dialogue with the NGOs from 1995 onward.

economic effects of globalization over which there is disagreement between pro-globalists and anti-globalists, and then we focus on only a small number of the many points in dispute. We believe, however, that the papers included here cover the issues of greatest interest to policymakers and the general public. Globalization is a large, complex, and relatively new subject, so the papers of the volume do not adopt a standard approach or methodology. Rather, each is tailored to the subject it treats, aiming efficiently to communicate to the reader what is known and not known in the various areas. In some cases we deal with precisely defined research issues whereas in others the need is for a broad account of a topic. The papers are grouped under five headings.

The Critics

The first group of papers deals directly with the critics of globalization, describing them, characterizing their objectives and discussing their views in economic terms.

In chapter 1, Kimberly Elliott, Debayani Kar, and J. David Richardson contrast the "talkers" about globalization—the critics—with the "doers." They describe who the critics are, where they came from, and what they want, and then they ask how economists and others might understand them better and what their views imply for globalization. They note that many critics are themselves strongly internationalist and want to see globalization proceed, but under different rules. Some, particularly the protesters in the streets, focus mainly on what is wrong with the world. But some of them put forward broad alternative visions, while others offer detailed recommendations for alleviating the problems they perceive in the current style of globalization. Most of the critics have their roots in long-standing transnational advocacy efforts to protect human rights and the environment and reduce poverty around the world. What brings them together today is a concern that the *process* by which globalization's rules are being written and implemented is undermining democracy and preventing the benefits from being shared broadly.

Elliot, Kar, and Richardson translate the issues and concerns that motivate the critics of globalization into the terms, concepts, and analytical approach of mainstream economics. They attempt to capture the concerns of Southern as well as Northern critics and to analyze the issues that divide them as well as those that bring them together. The authors find more resonance for the critics' agenda in existing economic analysis than is commonly recognized by either the critics or the "doers" of globalization. Finally, chapter 1 evaluates those issues and alternative proposals on which even globalization enthusiasts and the critics might come together cooperatively.

In chapter 2, Carl B. Hamilton considers directly the charge that globalization undermines democracy. He finds a superficial plausibility to the view, but argues that, in general, it does not stand up to scrutiny. In particular, he reports survey results suggesting considerable support for globalization among the peoples of the world, although certain countries (e.g., France, Australia, Turkey, and Argentina) buck the trend, which is possibly, in the latter pair, a reflection of their recent financial crises. There is, however, a fairly widespread suspicion that globalization is bad for jobs. Hamilton argues from these results that the NGOs' hostility to globalization is not well grounded in popular support. But even if it were, he argues, the NGOs display a marked democratic deficit themselves: They are responsible to no one and are heavily biased toward the rich industrial countries rather than being representative of the South.

In the second part of chapter 2 Hamilton argues that democracy has both an intrinsic and an instrumental value, and that the World Bank, which is now heavily focused on issues of governance, should be less coy about promoting it directly. (He would not make democracy a condition for receiving World Bank loans, however.) He also argues that openness and globalization are positively associated with democracy—either promoting it or resulting from it—and from this he concludes that concerns about the democratic consequences of globalization are exaggerated.

Trade Flows and Their Consequences

Part II of the book considers the extent to which different countries can take advantage of globalization to expand their trade and two sets of consequences for any such expansion—the decline in prices facing primary product producers and the relocation of production to "pollution havens" that permit dirty technologies.

Chapter 3 by Stephen Redding and Anthony J. Venables investigates the determinants of countries' export performance, looking in particular at the role of international product-market linkages. It begins with a novel decomposition of the growth in countries' exports into the contributions from increases in external demand and from improved internal supply. For any exporter, the former is derived from aggregate expenditure in each market deflated by its local prices and its internal trade costs and aggregated over markets using a function of distance between the exporter and the market as weights. The latter (supply) component of export growth reflects the exporter's size (the number of varieties it produces) and its own internal trade costs. Among the notable results of this decomposition is the dominance of supply capacity growth in Southeast Asian exports over 1970–1985, but the importance of market access growth during the subsequent period 1985–1997, with the majority of that access growth coming from within the region. For sub-Saharan Africa, on the other hand, market access growth was below average over the entire 1970–1997 period and supply capacity growth was actually negative.

Building on the results of this decomposition, Redding and Venables move on to an econometric analysis of the determinants of export performance. Their results include the finding that poor market access, poor internal geography, and poor institutional quality contribute in approximately equal measure to explaining sub-Saharan Africa's poor export performance.

In chapter 4, Christopher L. Gilbert and Panos Varangis consider the effects of the trade and marketing liberalizations of the 1980s and 1990s on the West African cocoa producers. They pay particular attention to the "adding up" problem: Although each cocoa producer is small enough to have virtually no effect on world prices individually, if all liberalize simultaneously their aggregate effect is to drive world prices down. Since African exporters account for 60 percent of world production, such global effects are likely to be larger in cocoa than in any other commodity market.

Gilbert and Varangis' results show that a 3 percent reduction in taxes and intermediation costs (internal marketing) results in a 1 percent fall in the world cocoa price. Farmers in the liberalizing countries remain better off (by 2 percent), but developed country consumers also benefit (by 1 percent). Approximately one-third of the cost reduction in the African cocoa-producing countries arises out of efficiency gains and two-thirds from tax reductions. Thus the farmers' benefit is approximately equal to the governments' (and taxpayers') loss, while the benefits of the efficiency gains accrue more or less to developed-country consumers.

None of this implies that liberalization is undesirable, but it does suggest that the calculus of costs and benefits from liberalization is more complex than the proponents of liberalization programs have sometimes suggested. In particular, advocates of liberalization may have insufficiently distinguished the benefits of increased competition in commodity marketing from those of reduced taxation.

Jamie De Melo and Jean-Marie Grether join the debate on globalization and the environment in chapter 5. They ask whether trade and investment liberalization have allowed firms to relocate activity toward countries with low pollution controls, or "pollution havens." If so, there will be more pollution per unit of output and more output since lower abatement costs will induce greater demand. They work with a sample of fifty-two countries over the period 1980–1998, analyzing shifts in production, consumption, and trade in the five most polluting industries.

Globally, de Melo and Grether find that revealed comparative advantage in polluting products fell for developing countries for the five polluting products as a group, as one would expect if the environment is a normal good in consumption. However, this overall result was due to the influence of one important product, namely, nonferrous metals, for which the revealed comparative advantage ratio in developing countries fell significantly.

De Melo and Grether then fit a panel gravity model on bilateral trade data for dirty industries and show that, compared with nonpolluting industries, dirty industries have higher barriers to trade in the form of larger elasticities of bilateral trade with respect to transport costs. These results confirm the intuition that most heavy polluters are both weight-reducing industries and producers of intermediate goods. For these sectors, proximity to users will enter location decisions more heavily than for consumer goods, which are typically high-value products. Thus, they identify natural barriers to trade in the typical heavy-polluting industries as one of the factors accounting for less-than-expected relocation of such industries to the developing countries. Utilizing the difference in per capita income as a proxy for the regulatory gap between countries (the greater the per capita income difference, the wider the regulatory gap) and controlling for several factors that influence the volume of bilateral trade, the authors find little evidence in their statistical analysis that bilateral trade is influenced by regulatory gaps.

Overall, de Melo and Grether conclude that there is only limited support for the pollution-havens hypothesis. They do note, however, that they have examined only manufacturing and hence cannot take into account the resource-extracting industries that may have sought pollution havens.

Factor Markets: Labor

Part III contains three chapters on the labor market, covering the influence of globalization on relative skilled versus unskilled wages, the brain drain, and the economics of sweatshop labor in the developing world.

Increased trade (or potential trade) with developing countries is frequently blamed for the depression of unskilled wages and employment in the Organization for Economic Cooperation and Development (OECD) countries. Many economists have argued, however, that trade flows are not large enough to have had such effects or that commodity prices have not evolved in the way that such a hypothesis requires. Recently, however, research has revealed that vertical specialization—slicing up the value chain to take less-skilled operations abroad—could affect unskilled wages without final commodity price changes or large actual trade flows. Vanessa Strauss-Kahn explores this possibility in France over the period 1977–1993 in chapter 6. She shows that a decrease in trade costs (globalization) modifies the international structure of production toward vertical specialization, and that shifting relative labor demand across countries increases skilled and unskilled wage inequality in a way that is observationally equivalent to skilled-biased technological progress. She evaluates the contribution of vertical specialization in explaining the observed within-industry shift away from unskilled workers in France, using detailed input-output tables and labor data. She finds that vertical specialization, defined as the share of imported inputs in production, rose from 9 percent in 1977 to 15 percent in 1996. Then, regressing industry employment against a scale variable, capital intensity, and the extent of vertical specialization, she finds that the last contributed 11 to 15 percent of the decline in the share of unskilled workers in French manufacturing employment over 1977–1985 and around 25 percent of the decline experienced over 1985–1993.

Chapter 7, by Simon Commander, Mari Kangesniemi, and L. Alan Winters, surveys current thinking on the brain drain, specifically from the point of view of developing countries. Estimates of the relative migration rates of educated individuals show that developing countries (especially small ones) can lose large proportions of their skilled workforces. Large countries, on the other hand, such as China and India, which supply a high proportion of the developed countries' skilled immigrants, lose only small proportions of their overall stock of skills. However, in recent years, migration has been particularly strong among information-technology workers, and the migration of health workers has long given rise to concern, and in these sectors outflows are proportionately significant, even for India.

Early theoretical models of the brain drain hinge around labor market distortions, such as wage rigidity and subsidies to education. They typically suggest negative implications from outflows, and, although these models were rarely tested empirically, their authors frequently advocated strong policy interventions, like taxes, to combat the brain drain. This conclusion ignored the role of remittances in sharing the benefits of emigration as well as the possibility that the improved skills of returning migrants and the business networks created by expatriates could also add to the local benefits of brain drain.

The most telling recent attempts to model the implications of the brain drain stress the formation of human capital and the positive impact that it can have on economic growth. If the chance of working abroad at high wages is related to levels of education, opening up the possibility of emigration raises the expected returns to education, which, in turn, increases the incentives to obtain human capital. Provided that not all the additional human capital so created actually emigrates, there is a possibility that the supply of human capital at home increases, thus leading to higher economic growth. General empirical evidence suggests that there may be a grain of truth in these models: private education has expanded considerably in developing countries. There is a caveat, however. Immigrants to the main receiving countries are carefully screened; if only the best are selected, the increased incentives due to emigration will be relevant only for the individuals with highest ability who would have chosen education anyway. The less able may never qualify for emigration, and so will not have any incentive to undertake additional education. Under this scenario the developing country would lose its best workers but create no additional skilled workers; it would unambiguously lose. Commander, Kangasniemi, and Winters thus argue that such screening must lie at the heart of thinking about the "beneficial brain drain."

A frequently heard charge against globalization is that multinational firms in developing countries are exploiting their workers by paying them low wages and subjecting them to sweatshop working conditions. In chapter 8, Drusilla K. Brown, Alan V. Deardorff, and Robert M. Stern examine the empirical evidence on this issue as well as what economic theory has to say about the effects of foreign direct investment (FDI) and multinational firms on wages and investment. They begin by reviewing the campaign by American students against sweatshop conditions in poor-country firms producing apparel with logos of their universities and colleges and the controversies arising from the efforts to establish codes of conduct and monitoring systems for these firms. This is followed by a brief survey of what economic theory has to say about the effects of FDI and multinational firms on wages and working conditions in host countries. The chapter concludes with an examination of the empirical evidence on wages and working conditions associated with multinationals.

The authors are critical both of the lack of broad consultation in the processes by which many university and college administrators agreed to establish codes of conduct and monitoring systems, and of the practicality of the codes and monitoring systems themselves. They also conclude that whether transfers of capital, technology, or parts of the production processes to developing countries by multinational firms raise or lower wage levels in these countries is basically an empirical question. A theoretical overview of this issue yields ambiguous conclusions. Their review of the empirical studies of the issue finds virtually no solid and systematic evidence that multinational firms adversely affect their workers by paying lower wages than in alternative employment or worsen their working conditions. In fact, the opposite appears to be the case.

Factor Markets: Capital

Part IV of the book turns more directly to the activities of firms. Two chapters consider the behavior of multinational firms and foreign direct investments, and the third considers the implications of the recent wave of mergers and acquisitions.

In chapter 9, Robert Lipsey presents a detailed analysis and appraisal of the empirical findings concerning the home- and host-country effects of FDI. He first summarizes the empirical evidence concerning the effects of FDI on home-country exports and on home-country factor demand and then discusses wages, productivity, exports, and the introduction of new industries on the host-country side.

Debate over the possible substitution of U.S. firms' foreign production for U.S. exports began with worries about the U.S. balance of payments in the 1960s. From his review of the many studies on this issue, Lipsey concludes that concerns over this possibility have mostly dissipated. His suggested interpretation of these studies is that foreign production by a firm or industry has very little influence on exports from the parent firm or its home country since trade is determined by other factors, such as countries' changing comparative advantages in production. Direct investment, he states, is mainly about the ownership of production, not its location. There is some evidence, however, that multilateral operations have influenced the demand for home-country factors of production. Specifically, they have led to a shift in the United States toward more capital-intensive and skill-intensive production, while unskilled labor–intensive production has been allocated to affiliates in developing countries.

Consistent with the conclusions reached by authors of other chapters in the volume, Lipsey finds abundant evidence that foreign-owned firms pay higher wages than domestically owned firms. In part this is because foreign-owned firms tend to be in high-wage sectors of the economy, to hire more educated and better qualified workers than locally owned firms, and to be larger and more capital intensive. There is also some evidence that foreign-owned firms pay a higher price for labor of a given quality, but there are not many studies that include data on worker characteristics. Comparisons of total factor productivity in foreign-owned versus domestically owned firms almost always find productivity levels to be higher in the foreign-owned firms. But evidence of spillovers of the higher foreign productivity to domestically owned firms is mixed. There is general agreement, however, that FDI leads to the introduction of new industries and products in the host-country economy and to an increase in knowledge about demand and world markets and how the host country can find a place in the worldwide allocation of intermediate steps in global production. Finally, inward direct investment is associated with faster economic growth, both through productivity effects and through the introduction of new products. Lipsey points out, however, that faster growth also involves disruptions and the destruction of old skills and production techniques, and some may not find foreign involvement to be beneficial, on balance.

In chapter 10 David Carr, James Markusen, and Keith Maskus examine whether multinational firms transfer production to developing countries largely to take advantage of the low wages of unskilled labor in these countries. They first point out that summary statistics comparing average per capita income in developing countries to average FDI per capita in these countries show FDI per capita to be the lowest in the poorest countries. For a given level of per capita income, they also find that FDI per capita is higher the larger a host country's gross national product. The authors conclude from these relationships that FDI is not aimed solely at exploiting cheap labor for export production and, moreover, that a significant proportion of the existing foreign production in developing countries is intended for local sale.

Carr, Markusen, and Maskus next briefly review recent FDI theory, especially the knowledge-capital model developed by Markusen that allows for motives for both horizontal and vertical FDI. They then utilize data on outward investment from the United States for a large number of developed and developing countries (but, due to lack of data, excluding the least developed countries) over the period 1986–1997 to test hypotheses from this model about the patterns and determinants of FDI flows to developing countries. A feature that differs from their earlier empirical work is the addition to their econometric estimation of a measure of infrastructure quality to accompany such host-country characteristics as size (in terms of gross national product), labor force composition, investment barriers, and trade costs.

Their main conclusion is that U.S. outward investment generally seeks large, skill-abundant countries. However, outward investment in small host countries (both developed and developing) seems to be unskilled labor seeking. As far as production for local sales versus exports is concerned, affiliates in developing countries are not more export oriented than affiliates in developed countries. Inward investment from the United States is also encouraged by high-quality infrastructure and low barriers to investing and discouraged by a country's distance from the United States.

As the authors point out, these findings run completely counter to the contention of some anti-globalists that multinational firms are primarily attracted to countries with low-wage labor. They explain that very low-wage countries receive almost no FDI because branch-plant production (particularly setting up the branch plant) requires a certain minimum level of labor skills that are lacking in the very poorest countries. In addition, the absence of reliable legal institutions and infrastructures in these countries make them unprofitable locations for production.

In chapter 11, Simon Evenett explores the boom in cross-border mergers and acquisitions in the late 1990s. To establish a benchmark, he compares it with its predecessor in the late 1980s. The recent one is found to be at least five times larger (in real terms), to involve firms from more OECD nations, and to include many more service-sector transactions than the earlier one. Even so, in comparison to the size of national stock market capitalizations, foreign acquisitions of domestic firms during this latest wave were small, especially in the Group of Seven leading industrial economies. Thus, concerns that large shares of economic activity in OECD countries are falling into foreign hands are greatly exaggerated.

In the second part of chapter 11, Evenett examines the effect of cross-border mergers and acquisitions on performance in one important service sector, banking. Specifically, he estimates the relative importance of cross-border mergers and acquisitions, domestic mergers and acquisitions, domestic entry and exit, and strategic alliances and joint ventures in explaining changes in interest-rate spreads in thirteen OECD nations. The principal findings suggest that the effects of these firm-driven changes in banking market structure differ markedly between European Union (EU) economies and non-EU industrialized economies. In the EU, cross-border strategic alliances appear strongly to increase spreads—that is, to be anti-competitive—whereas full cross-border mergers appear to reduce them, presumably via efficiency gains. Domestic changes in industry structure seem to have little net effect. Outside the EU, on the other hand, domestic changes have tended to increase spreads while cross-border alliances and mergers have reduced them in almost equal measure. These results highlight the importance of differentiating between types of cross-border inter-firm agreements and the pitfalls of generalizing about the effects of the latest wave of cross-border mergers and acquisitions.

Macroeconomics

Finally, part V of this book considers the effects of globalization in the large—first on financial stability and second on economic growth.

In chapter 12, Joshua Aizenman evaluates the empirical evidence on whether opening up developing countries to short-term capital flows increases the chance of financial crises and then appraises various recent proposals for reducing this possibility.

On the basis of his survey of recent research into financial crises across countries, Aizenman argues that there is solid evidence that financial opening increases the chances of such crises in developing countries. This research also finds tenuous evidence that financial liberalization increases growth over time. Thus, there may be a complex trade-off between the adverse intermediate-run and beneficial long-run effects of financial opening. The core of the problem, he argues, is that we deal with incomplete financial markets, exposing creditors to sovereign risk and moral hazard. But, since greater trade integration erodes the effectiveness of restrictions on capital mobility, financial opening for successful emerging markets that engage in trade integration is not a question of *if*, but of *when* and *how*. Aizenman maintains there is no quick fix to the exposure to financial crises induced by financial opening and, instead, that we should focus on reducing the depth and frequency of such crises.

Aizenman is rather skeptical about the effectiveness of many of the new proposals aimed at reducing the costs of financial crises on the general grounds that any significant reform will change agents' behavior in ways that are hard to predict without a better understanding of the fundamental forces explaining sovereign borrowing and default. For example, he doubts the degree to which such ideas as insurance, which is based only on meeting ex ante conditionality, will survive the time-inconsistency and transparency challenges. Similarly, in view of the greater weight of non-bank lending and the great increase in the number of institutional investors, he expects recent reform proposals dealing with better coordination among creditors and with formation of international bankruptcy procedures to be vigorously tested by coming crises.

In the final chapter, Robert Baldwin reviews and appraises empirical research since the 1950s concerning the manner in which the international economic policies of governments affect the rates of growth of their economies. The first set of detailed empirical studies of the impact of international economic policies on economic growth were undertaken in the early 1970s in response to the growth difficulties faced by a number of developing countries that had seemed to successfully pursue import-substitution policies after World War II. The early widespread support by economists for these policies was based on an extension of the infant-industry argument to the manufacturing sector as a whole and on earlier experiences with protecting home markets in various developed countries. However, case studies of most of the developing countries showed that their levels of import protection measured on a value-added basis were not only extremely high and variable across industries, but also penalized export activities. Later case studies that broadened the policy framework to include monetary, fiscal, and exchange-rate policies further strengthened the argument that import-substitution policies were holding back growth rates and helped to convince many developing-country governments to shift to an export-oriented approach to development.

Stimulated by new theories of endogenous growth and improved econometric techniques in the early 1990s, a succession of large cross-country statistical studies have found a strong positive relationship between outward-looking policies and growth rates of gross domestic product (GDP) or total factor productivity. These studies have recently come under criticism, however, especially by Francisco Rodriguez and Dani Rodrik, on the grounds that the tariff and nontariff components in the authors' broad measures of openness do not by themselves support this conclusion or that they fail to do so in a robust manner under reasonable respecifications of their econometric models.

Baldwin's evaluation of this controversy is that, while we should be grateful to Rodriguez and Rodrik for pointing out that a liberal trade policy alone is not always associated with faster growth rates, these authors adopt an overly narrow policy viewpoint when they contend that the main implication of the studies is that countries should dismantle their barriers to trade. Authors of both the case studies and cross-country statistical analyses almost uniformly argue that a whole set of policies—ranging from sound monetary, fiscal, and exchange-rate policies to responsible government behavior and a transparent legal system—is necessary for raising developing-country growth rates in addition to trade liberalization.

Some Conclusions

The chapters of this book do not examine every criticism that has been made of globalization, but especially on the real (as opposed to the financial) side of the economy they deal with the main ones. The book demonstrates that most of the current complaints have already been addressed by economists in their serious academic research. While most criticisms are valid in theory under some sets of circumstances, and while many of them can be identified to have occurred in specific cases, most turn out not to be major systemic problems. Thus, for example, openness to trade (accompanied by appropriate policies elsewhere) generally assists growth, multinationals do not generally drive down wages or labor standards, and trade does not generally lead to a race to the bottom in environmental standards.

On the other hand, the chapters have confirmed that globalization can cause problems for some people under some circumstances—for example, in reducing the prices of primary exports, reducing competition in sectors subject to mergers and interfirm agreements, and via the emigration of talented workers. In these cases, however, appropriate policy responses can often serve to alleviate or bypass the problems.

The fact that globalization can cause problems for some people, or in some circumstances, sometimes appears to be enough for critics to reject it out of hand. We—and most economists, we believe—would reject that response. Virtually every issue of public policy involves trade-offs of some sort. If a society gains on average from a reform, there is a strong case for making the reform and compensating the losers.

Considering compensation brings us face to face with the issue of the distribution of welfare—not only of income but also of things like human rights and social inclusion. These are important issues on which opinions differ, and it is legitimate for different groups to debate their views and to reach different conclusions about economic policies on the basis of them. Economists as a group have no particular position in these debates, nor expertise in ruling one view better than another. They do, however, seek to be explicit about the value judgments entailed in their models and to distinguish between judgments on issues such as these and positive economic analysis (the way in which the economy operates). It is frequently the case that, once value judgments and analysis are separated, it becomes evident that objectives can be met more effectively by policies that maximize economic welfare than by any others. This is precisely the case for globalization: by maximizing economic activity and organizing it efficiently it becomes easier to achieve the goals to which society aspires.

I

The Critics

Assessing Globalization's Critics: "Talkers Are No Good Doers?"

Kimberly Ann Elliott, Debayani Kar, and
J. David Richardson

1.1 Introduction

In Shakespeare's *King Richard III* (act 1, scene 3, line 351), the Duke of Gloucester hires two men to do away with a rival and encourages them to do it quickly, so the victim will not have the chance to plead for mercy and perhaps "move [their] hearts to pity." The first murderer reassures the Duke, "Fear not, my lord, we will not stand to prate [prattle]; talkers are no good doers."

This paper is about the critics of the "doers" of globalization. A variety of concerns motivate these critics, but the common thread is the belief that the distribution of globalization's benefits is unbalanced and that this is the inevitable result of policies and processes that are undemocratic and, therefore, illegitimate. The critics want the doers to stop and talk. The doers dismiss the critics' concerns as unrelated to economic globalization or as misinformed and misguided; they want to keep doing as they have been doing. This paper describes who the critics are, where they came from, what they want, and how economists, policymakers, and others might understand them better.

Until recently, globalization's critics likely would have sympathized with

Kimberly Ann Elliott is a fellow at the Institute for International Economics. Debayani Kar is a research associate at the Center for Economic and Policy Research. J. David Richardson is a fellow at the Institute for International Economics, professor of economics at the Maxwell School of Syracuse University, and research associate of the National Bureau of Economic Research (NBER).

The authors are grateful for the comments on an earlier draft of Susan Aaronson, Robert E. Baldwin, Harry Flam, Ellen Frost, Robert E. Lipsey, Matthew J. Slaughter, and Alan Winters, as well as the participants in authors' meetings in Cambridge and Stockholm in Spring 2002.

the Duke's intended victim, feeling that they could not get a word in edge-wise before the forces of globalization rolled over them. Many proponents of globalization did not want to talk or even listen. Activists responded by mounting large street protests at each major meeting of the key international organizations—the World Trade Organization (WTO) in Geneva (1998) and Seattle (1999); the International Monetary Fund (IMF) and World Bank in Prague and Washington, DC (2000); the Free Trade Area of the Americas (FTAA) in Quebec (2001); and the Group of Eight (G8) in Genoa (2001). Also because slogans (e.g., "Fifty Years is Enough," "Fix it or nix it," "Dump the debt," "People over profits," "Jobs with justice," or "Another world is possible") fit on posters better than elaborate plans to change the world, their demands often seemed more strident than they are.

Although the protesters in the streets represent a number of different movements, they share, in the words of one critic, "a belief that the disparate problems with which they are wrestling all derive from global deregulation, an agenda that is concentrating power and wealth into fewer and fewer hands" (Klein 2000, 19). Above all else, the disparate elements of this broad "Mobilization for Global Justice," as a major umbrella coalition is called, are held together by a concern that the *process* by which globalization's rules are being written and implemented is undermining democracy at both the national and international levels. Under this umbrella of shared concerns, the various groups tend to cluster around one of three issues as a focus of their particular globalization critique.

- The environment
- Human rights and worker rights
- Inequality and poverty (particularly in developing countries)

Economists and policymakers might recognize some of these concerns as relating to environmental externalities, imperfectly competitive labor markets, or inadequate distributional mechanisms. But when the activists and protesters claimed credit for killing the Multilateral Agreement on Investment in 1998 and for blocking a consensus to launch new multilateral trade negotiations in Seattle in 1999, the initial response from many doers was a backlash against the anti-globalization backlash. In some quarters, there was a tendency to circle the wagons and to reject compromise as the first step down the slippery slope towards protectionism.

One step in moving beyond the dialogue of the deaf is to orient the critics' concerns in terms of potential market failures that economic analysis already recognizes. A second is to recognize that not all of the critics are anti-globalization, some are, but others are not. With the end of the Cold War, some see anti-globalization as a new front in the long-running battle between socialism and capitalism. But other critics, including many with a religious orientation, are strongly internationalist and want to see globalization proceed, albeit under different rules. We will refer to these latter critics as the "*alternative* globalization movement." We will reserve the "movement" for the full spectrum of activists opposed to current globalization trends.

This paper will attempt to identify important groups involved in the alternative globalization movement. It will also attempt to sketch a picture of the key issues and concerns that motivate them in a way that is broadly representative and intelligible to economists.[1] In so doing, we hope to capture the concerns of Southern as well as Northern groups and to analyze the issues that divide as well as bring them together. Finally, we will analyze key elements of the critiques of current globalization and representative alternative proposals, assessing both their merits and weaknesses.

The sections on the roots of the movement and who the critics are cast a rather wide net, but the presentation and analysis of what the critics want focuses on key groups that have offered alternatives, detailed recommendations, or specific critiques. We will address only in passing the true anti-globalizers, those who might be characterized as localists on the left and nationalists on the right.[2]

1.2 The Roots of the Alternative Globalization Movement

Poverty, inequality, human rights, and protection of the environment are hardly new issues. Transnational advocacy on human rights by non-governmental organizations (NGOs) predates World War I, going back at least to the anti-slavery movement of the eighteenth and nineteenth centuries (Keck and Sikkink 1998; Lorenz 2001). The International Labor Organization (ILO), created to protect the peace by promoting social justice, was founded in 1919 and is the only surviving League of Nations institution. The Universal Declaration on Human Rights by the United Nations (UN) dates to 1948. Concern for the environment is a more recent issue for global activists, but it is one that has grown rapidly since the first UN conference on the environment in 1972. The NGO involvement in poverty and development issues has traditionally been more on the operational side,

---

1. Similar efforts include Ostry (2001) and Florini (2002).
2. On the right, anti-globalizers oppose international rules that constrain national sovereignty and power as well as trade or investment that undermines American industry and control. Some of these critics are xenophobic as well. On the left, localists want to maintain maximal independence at the grassroots level and oppose most broader centralization, including the economic homogenization associated with national and global markets and especially, global agreements that impinge on local autonomy. Unlike the nationalists on the right, the localists are not anti-internationalist, and their interests sometimes overlap with the alternative globalization movement, for example, on preserving local or national policy autonomy in the environmental area, but they share with the right the goal of rolling back globalization. On the right, see, for example, Buchanan (2000); on the left, see International Forum on Globalization (2002), Hines (2000), echoes in Korten (1999), and even in Gandhi (1996; see the speech "Economic and Moral Progress" presented to the Muir College Economic Society in 1916).

raising and distributing funds and planning projects, particularly emergency relief. Transnational-policy advocacy on behalf of poor people in poor countries emerged more recently as a result of the debt crisis and increased involvement in development policy on the part of the international financial institutions.

Thus, Mobilization for Global Justice and the similar groups that have been dogging international meetings and summits for the past five years represent a coming together of several advocacy strands that have been operating on largely separate tracks for a number of years. Demands by civil society to be included in international rule making on economic issues emerged as a response to the expanding scope of that rule making into in a broad range of regulatory areas. That is, groups focusing on environmental issues, human rights, and development issues began to come together in the 1990s because they perceived that pro-globalization priorities were impinging upon their own and, therefore, that they had a common interest in challenging both the substance and the process as the rules governing globalization were developed. In addition, the development of communications technology that could handle large amounts of information facilitated the task of transnational and cross-issue organizing. A brief summary of the evolution of each of the strands follows.

1.2.1   The Environment

Since the creation of the UN Environmental Program (UNEP) at the global Conference on the Human Environment in 1972, the UN has been a key institutional focus for transnational advocacy on environmental issues ranging from fisheries, forestry, and other resource management to combating the ozone hole and global warming. Almost from the beginning, NGOs were recognized as playing an important role in the process, in part because many of them bring technical expertise that would otherwise not be available (UNEP 2001). Just a year after UNEP was created, an NGO office was established to oversee civil society participation in its activities. Today, there are roughly 200 multilateral environmental agreements, with representatives of civil society often playing an important role in various aspects of negotiation and implementation.[3]

An ambitious attempt to integrate environmental issues under the sustainable development rubric was made at the 1992 UN Conference on Environment and Development (UNCED) held in Rio de Janeiro, Brazil, with extensive involvement from NGOs. The UNEP estimates that representatives from 800 NGOs from 160 countries were present in Rio, reflecting as well their intense involvement in planning the conference (UNEP 2001). The UNCED resulted in an action plan for addressing a long list of

---

3. For example, see chapter nineteen of Benedick (1998) on the negotiation of the Montreal Protocol on ozone depletion.

environmental problems, dubbed "Agenda 21," as well as the founding of the Commission on Sustainable Development (CSD) to monitor implementation of the (largely voluntary) commitments. In order to facilitate their ongoing involvement, an NGO steering committee was created by the CSD and roughly 400 groups were accredited as of the end of 2001. A decade later, tens of thousands of public- and private-sector representatives are expected to gather in Johannesburg, South Africa, to review (limited) progress and to discuss the next phase of implementation, but planning has been marred by sharp disagreements over the responsibility of developed countries to increase resource transfers to poor countries for development and environmental protection, as well as the relative rights and responsibilities of multinational corporations in sustainable development.

1.2.2   Human Rights and Worker Rights

Like environmental groups, human rights groups have traditionally focused on governments and the UN regarding the promotion of universal norms and standards. In the 1970s and 1980s, however, transnational advocacy groups involved in the fight against apartheid in South Africa, frustrated by the unresponsiveness of governments, turned their attention directly to corporations. After years of futilely pushing governments and the UN to formally impose sanctions on the apartheid regime, activists turned to pressuring multinational corporations operating in South Africa as a second-best conduit for pressuring the government there. At a minimum, activists such as Leon Sullivan hoped that the code of corporate conduct bearing his name would improve the day-to-day lives of black workers under apartheid. Many of the groups that are active today in the anti-sweatshop movement—including the Interfaith Center for Corporate Responsibility, the Investor Responsibility Research Council, and Reverend Sullivan—have their roots in the anti-apartheid movement, as do many of the tactics used today, such as corporate codes of conduct, shareholder resolutions, boycotts, and other market-based campaigns to promote change.

1.2.3   Development and Poverty

Groups concerned with human rights, particularly of indigenous peoples, and the environment in developing countries turned their attention to the international financial institutions in the 1980s, beginning with criticism of the World Bank for ignoring the environmental and human consequences of its large infrastructure projects and for failing to consult with local people affected by those projects. The IMF became a target somewhat later as policies developed to respond to the debt crisis, triggered by Mexico in 1982, failed either to resolve the debt problem quickly or to restore economic growth. In the 1990s, many of these concerns coalesced around the issue of debt relief and Jubilee 2000, which began in the United Kingdom, and became a global phenomenon, fronted by rock stars and consulted by world leaders (Birdsall, Williamson, and Deese 2002). Criticism of the IMF, in particular, escalated sharply in the late 1990s when many mainstream economists were questioning their response to the Asian financial crisis as well as the Fund's earlier push for increased capital-market liberalization in developing countries without prudential regulations in place.

1.2.4   The Trade System and Social Issues

The General Agreement on Tariffs and Trade (GATT) was created in 1948 as a mechanism for contracting parties to multilaterally negotiate reductions in trade barriers. It was regarded by affiliated governments and most observers as relatively effective in unwinding the high Depression-era tariffs that lingered after World War II, but as relatively weak in settling disputes over more difficult issues, such as agricultural protection and nontariff barriers (Elliott and Hufbauer 2001). Thus, for most of its first forty years, it was largely ignored by advocacy groups. In this period, neither governments nor civil society groups particularly challenged the notion that the major constituencies that needed to be consulted about trade negotiations were business and organized labor. The dynamics of trade negotiations changed dramatically in the 1990s, however, particularly after conclusion of the Uruguay Round negotiations, which expanded the scope of trade rules in areas such as product health and safety, drugs and other patents, and instituted a more binding enforcement system under the WTO.

As the Uruguay Round progressed, it appeared to many critics that all of the major international economic organizations were moving in a similar, deregulatory direction, placing more and more constraints on the ability of governments to organize economic activity. In the early 1990s, GATT dispute-settlement panels twice ruled against a U.S. ban on imported tuna, the harvesting of which resulted in the killing of dolphins. The decisions shocked and angered environmental advocates who had lobbied for the Marine Mammal Protection Act to protect the environment and who had no protectionist intent. Around the same time, the United States and Mexico (joined later by Canada) decided to negotiate a "deep integration" trade agreement without accompanying rules on the environment or working conditions.

The decision to negotiate the North American Free Trade Area (NAFTA) seemed to the critics to bring the specter of a race to the bottom right to America's borders and it began to pull together the separate strands of environmental, human rights, and development advocacy into today's movement for alternative globalization (Aaronson 2001; Mayer 1998). Despite vigorous protests from NGOs and only after much debate, Congress approved the NAFTA agreement in November 1993. In deference to concerns of the critics, however, newly elected President Bill Clinton had directed his trade representative to negotiate side deals to accompany the agreement, which was completed by President George H. W. Bush just before the 1992 election. The labor agreement did little to appease labor opponents, but the side agreement on environmental issues was regarded by moderate environmental groups as a positive step forward, and several of them endorsed NAFTA. Within a few years, however, those groups became disillusioned with the implementation of the side agreement and increasingly concerned by corporate challenges to environmental regulations under NAFTA's investment provisions. When renewal of "fast-track" or "trade promotion authority" was debated again in the late 1990s, the environmental community was much more unified in its opposition.

The next target of this growing movement against (corporate-led) economic globalization was the U.S.-led effort to negotiate a Multilateral Agreement on Investment (MAI) in the Organization for Economic Cooperation and Development (OECD). The opposition again centered as much on process as on substance and, in particular, the perception that this was an attempt to *secretly* negotiate rules to further empower global corporations. When the OECD finally admitted failure in 1998, the anti-MAI forces were more than happy to declare victory in defeating it, even though careful analysis suggests that the agreement might well have fallen under the weight of its own contradictions—driven by intergovernmental differences on policy—even without the NGO protests (Henderson 2000; Graham 2000). Regardless, the movement had more than enough momentum to carry it into the streets of Seattle for a WTO ministerial meeting in late 1999 that was intended to launch a new round of multilateral trade negotiations. Like the MAI, the critical differences in Seattle were as much between governments themselves as they were between governments and the protesters, but the "turtle-teamster" coalition and others were more than happy to take credit and to continue riding the wave of momentum.[4]

1.3   Who Are Globalization's Critics Today?

Clearly transnational advocacy is not a recent phenomenon. Nevertheless, just as clearly, the scale of activity has increased sharply in recent years. As of the late 1990s, Edwards (2001, 4) and Florini (2001, 29) cite figures ranging from 15,000 to 20,000 for the number of transnational NGOs, most of them formed since 1970 and many inspired by and focused on UN

4. In 1998, a WTO panel ruled against a U.S. law banning shrimp imports from countries that did not require the use of "turtle-excluder devices" to allow endangered sea turtles to escape from shrimp nets. To highlight what they viewed as yet another outrageous decision, many activists wore turtle costumes during the Seattle protests.

activities in a variety of areas.[5] Of these, hundreds, perhaps thousands, are affiliated with the movement challenging economic globalization, and they cover a broad spectrum of views, from the anarchists of the Black Bloc, who are against all forms of institutional control, to mainstream religious or charitable organizations, such as the American Friends Service Committee and Medecins Sans Frontieres (Doctors without Borders), which won the Nobel Peace Prize in 1999. In-between are groups that fundamentally oppose the capitalist economic model and others that just want to push it in a more humane direction.

The appendix lists roughly 100 coalitions, networks, and groups that work on globalization issues from a critical perspective and that we believe are the most important. Because we cannot identify the full universe of alternative globalization groups, it is difficult to determine the criteria for a representative sample, and, for purposes of creating the appendix, only the most general criteria were used. Groups listed are concerned with the consequences of *economic* globalization and are involved in *advocacy*. This excludes large numbers of *local* community groups concerned about the environment or economic justice; others that are interested in global but noneconomic issues (for example land mines); and some research or development groups that do not also engage in advocacy.

We began with the list compiled for a *Financial Times* series on the counter-capitalist movement (October 2001), then added others with which we were personally familiar and that seem to show up again and again at protests and in the press.[6] In an effort to exclude marginal groups while ensuring that we did not leave out major ones, we turned to the internet search engine Google, which has a toolbar that provides a website's page rank, backward links, and a list of similar pages. Google's page rank purports to show the relative importance of a website, on a scale from one to ten, based on how many other pages link to it, weighted in turn by the relative importance of those pages. Backward links give the number of links from other websites to a particular website. The similar pages func-

5. As of 2001, more than 120 NGOs had general accreditation status with the UN's Economic and Social Council (ECOSOC), meaning that they could send observers to meetings and submit written statements to ECOSOC and its subsidiary bodies; roughly 1,000 had special accreditation status, meaning that they may be consulted and attend meetings on specific issues where they have specific competence; and nearly 1,000 were on the UN's third-tier roster of groups that can be called upon by UN bodies when appropriate. Edwards (2001, 9) notes, however, that less than one-fifth of the NGOs with consultative status are from developing countries. For a list of NGOs with consultative status, see http://www.un.org/partners/civil_society/ngo/n-ecosoc.htm#top. The search function allows visitors to search for particular organizations and then get contact information for them.

6. The first part of the planned series appeared in the *Financial Times* on 10 September, 2001 as part of the run-up to the Bank-Fund meetings at the end of the month. After the September 11 terrorist attacks, the series was put on the shelf until 10 October, 2001, when a new piece on the challenges facing the counter-capitalism movement in the new environment appeared. At the same time, the full series was published on the FT's website at http://specials.ft.com/countercap/index.html.

tion lists roughly two dozen websites that are most similar to the website in question.[7]

Groups that had a page rank of at least 6, the majority, were kept on the list; the highest rank of any group is 8. Besides the two large networking sites at the top of the list, large membership groups with lots of chapters, such as the Sierra Club, Greenpeace, and Amnesty International, generally have the highest rankings in the sample. To put the rankings in perspective, we were unable to find any website that received a rank of 10. The UN, the World Bank, and the White House websites have rankings of 9, while the IMF, WTO, and ILO each get an 8. After culling the low-ranking groups, we selected the highest-ranked groups in each of our functional areas—human and worker rights, the environment, and development—and used the similar pages function to ensure that other important groups were not left out. While there are undoubtedly many other NGOs in the potential universe, we believe we were able to identify the key players in the movement and avoid including any that are unimportant.

1.3.1 Explanation of Categories

The groups in this movement differ in three important dimensions that we have tried to document in the appendix: issues on which they focus; roles they play within the movement; and their advocacy style. We briefly discuss each in turn.

Key Issues

We categorized groups by the broad strands of transnational advocacy discussed above—development, human rights, and the environment—and added a fourth category of multi-issue group or coalition/network for the many groups that advocate broad reforms of global institutions or, even, the system as a whole. This was not easy. Human rights and environmental groups are usually interested in sustainable, equitable, and democratic development as well, and development-oriented groups are obviously interested in human rights and the environment. We tried to assign the groups to categories based on the *lens* through which they approach issues, not the narrowness with which they focus.

Roles in the Movement

The NGOs, collectively and individually, play a variety of roles in the movement, and the assignment of categories was, again, not easy. Some tilt more toward activism and others more toward research; some also provide not-for-profit services, such as emergency relief in crises, monitoring and

---

7. Note that as Google is updating its database of websites and links all the time, the numbers change a bit from day to day. Our numbers are accurate up to 3 May, 2002, the date upon which we ran the Google search and rankings.

verification of corporate compliance with codes of conduct, and legal services in advocacy lawsuits. For reasons of access, we have focused on groups that have websites, as most do today, which means that all groups have some role in disseminating information. Those identified as such here, however, are those that focus on collecting and disseminating information, either of a general nature (Common Dreams) or of particular utility in activist campaigns (CorpWatch). Although they may include briefing papers or articles by group staff on their websites, original research is not the focus of these groups.

Advocacy Style

Morton Winston of the College of New Jersey and Amnesty International has categorized groups working on corporate social responsibility issues into Confronters, who take an adversarial approach to corporations in the belief that only the threat of reduced profits will induce them to improve conditions, and Engagers, who work to help firms do "the right thing" (Winston 2001). Although not all NGOs working on globalization issues fall into one of these two categories, similar labels could be applied to groups working in other areas, such as those seeking to reform the international financial institutions and the WTO. Following Winston's lead, we define these categories based, not on their protest tactics (which may be quite confrontational), but on their willingness to engage with their antagonists, whether multinational corporations (MNCs) or international economic institutions. Thus, those that have explicitly rejected any cooperation with or that have called for the abolition of existing economic institutions are classified as confronters; those that have joined in multistakeholder initiatives that include representatives of all parties interested in an issue, such as the UN Global Compact or the Forestry Stewardship Council, are classified as engagers.

1.4   What Do They Want?

Many of these talkers *are* also doers. The Jubilee movement is perhaps the most successful and uses rock stars, such as Bono, that help thousands of average churchgoers and other activists to put debt relief at the center of development discussions. Oxfam International is now following up that campaign with a new one to "make trade fair" and ensure that the new Doha round of multilateral trade negotiations will be, as promised, a development round. In the Jubilee movement's case, activists were able to focus on broad goals—reducing debt burdens as broadly and deeply as possible and using the proceeds to alleviate poverty—while Oxfam International's trade campaign is based on a nearly 300 page report calling for detailed changes in national and international policies by a variety of actors.

But what of all the other groups in the street in Geneva, Genoa, and Seattle? Is it just cacophony or is there a coherent message? While it is clear from the appendix that this is a "movement of movements" with no single leader or agenda, it is possible to identify common concerns that bring them together. First, the critics reject arguments that growth is both necessary *and* sufficient to spread globalization's benefits equitably. They believe that, under current rules, the well-off and mobile "haves" benefit relatively more than immobile "have-nots"; salaries and dividends have increased while wages in many countries declined or stagnated. And they believe that this is, in part, the result of disproportionate corporate influence on the rule-making process.

Therefore, in order to achieve more inclusive outcomes from globalization, the critics also believe that it is necessary to address the democratic deficit in current globalization decision making and to make it more inclusive (see Hamilton's chapter two in this volume). Almost every group involved in the protests against the IMF, World Bank, and WTO emphasizes *process* as much as substance. The International Labor Rights Fund's Pharis Harvey opposed fast-track trade-negotiating authority for the president in 1991 as much because he thought the process was an end run around democracy as because of what might be negotiated with it (Mayer 1998, 76). Thus, whatever other issues are raised, globalization's critics put increased transparency and accountability at the top of their list of demands for how national governments and the international institutions address globalization issues.

Finally, critics see far more market failure and regulatory imbalance in current globalization than proponents do. They also trust government regulation more, at least in transparent and accountable systems. This, in turn, leads the critics to different conclusions than the enthusiasts regarding which rules and regulations need to be harmonized and in which areas diversity should be respected. Many critics reject current globalization trends and the rules promoting it as homogenizing forces that squeeze out cultural diversity and national and local policy autonomy in many areas. Table 1.1 illustrates some of the differences as they relate to the major international economic institutions. The WTO rules, for example, promote harmonization of product standards while defending diversity in process standards—with the important exception of the agreement on trade-related intellectual-property rights (TRIPs). For the critics, this is evidence that globalization enthusiasts want to promote market integration at the expense of workers, the poor, and the environment. They typically want to preserve more space for national-policy autonomy in these areas, and to harmonize in areas where there are global externalities or public goods. Their exception is support for *global* labor standards and some environmental issues, even where international spillovers are limited, and, on these issues, Northern and Southern critics sometimes part company.

Table 1.1   **Critics' Views of Harmonization and Diversity in the Current International Economic Order**

	Rules That Are Too Constraining (pro-diversity arguments)	Rules That Are Missing (pro-harmonization arguments)
WTO and trade agreements	TRIPs, SPS/TBT, government procurement, trade remedy laws, NAFTA chapter 11, article XX interpretations of national environmental laws	Core labor standards, global tax evasion, climate change, species/habitat loss
Potential areas of rules negotiation	Free trade in public services, rights and responsibilities for foreign investors, S&D in subsidy and other industrial policies for LDCs, relationship between WTO and MEAs, competition policy	
IMF[a]	"Washington consensus" conditionality, macroeconomic austerity, capital mobility (now under review)	"Odious debt" avoidance and relief, financial market volatility (Tobin tax), CLS and environmental protections
World Bank	Structural adjustment lending conditionality	Protection of human (indigenous peoples) rights and the environment in project and sectoral lending, especially in resource extraction

Notes: TRIPs = trade-related intellectual property rights agreement; SPS/TBT = agreements on sanitary and phytosanitary, and technical barriers to trade; S&D = special and differential treatment; MEA = multilateral environmental agreement; CLS = core labor standards.
[a]In implicit collusion with financial markets.

With these common concerns as background, we turn now to some of the specific concerns that motivate different movement groups in our three broad functional areas: development and poverty, human rights and worker rights, and the environment. We begin with the broad-development critique of globalization (as it is currently proceeding) because it is often joined by human rights and environmental NGOs, and thus it is more holistic and, on average, less divisive than some of the narrower issues, such as international labor standards or how to address climate change. We then follow with some of the more specific labor, human rights, and environmental criticisms and then conclude with a summary of a far-reaching proposal from a broad coalition, including representatives from the North and South, for a fundamentally different approach to globalization and economic and social organization.

1.4.1   The Development NGOs' Critique of the International Economic Institutions

Much of the development NGOs' critique of globalization is a rejection of the "Washington Consensus" model of development, which, as promoted by the international financial institutions, is interpreted as requiring macroeconomic austerity, privatization, and a relatively laissez-faire approach to economic management, all of which are alleged to exacerbate unemployment and poverty.[8] Another major target are the large infrastructure projects often funded or guaranteed by the World Bank, which NGOs opposed because they seem prone to corruption, increased indebtedness, and environmental degradation. In advance of the 2002 World Bank and IMF joint meetings in Washington, D.C., the *Mobilization for Global Justice* and its affiliated groups coalesced around four core demands for reform of the two institutions.[9]

1. Open all World Bank and IMF meetings to the media and the public.
2. Cancel all impoverished-country debt to the World Bank and IMF using the institutions' own resources.
3. End all World Bank and IMF policies that hinder people's access to food, clean water, shelter, health care, education, and right to organize. (Such structural-adjustment policies include user fees, privatization, and economic austerity programs.)
4. Stop all World Bank support for socially and environmentally destructive projects, such as oil, gas, and mining activities, and all support for projects, such as dams, that include forced relocation of people.

In addition, many development activists, particularly in the wake of the Asian financial crisis and, more recently, Argentina, are concerned about capital-market volatility and want the Bank and Fund to allow more measures to head off potential financial crises, including measures such as an international Tobin tax or more latitude for countries to impose capital controls. The Association for the Taxation of Financial Transactions for the Aid of Citizens (ATTAC; available at http://www.attac.org/indexen. htm) started with the Tobin tax as its key proposal, both to reduce capital-market volatility and to raise funds for development.

In the run up to the spring 2002 meetings of the Bank and Fund, a U.S. Civil Society Coalition, representing twenty-seven labor, environmental, religious, and other groups, released a proposal for responsible reform of the World Bank.[10] Besides addressing the usual issues of debt relief, transparency, poverty, and environmental-impact statements, the document

8. The term "Washington Consensus" was originally coined by John Williamson in 1990 to describe a set of ten broad policies around which consensus among policymakers seemed to exist regarding the basic reforms needed in the first stages of economic stabilization. The term has since been used to refer to a more specific set of neoliberal—or market fundamentalist— economic policies that go well beyond either consensus or what Williamson himself intended (Williamson 1997).

9. For additional background, see http://www.globalizethis.org/fightback/feature.cfm?ID =37. These demands were originally developed in anticipation of the 2001 joint meetings, which were cancelled following the September 11 terrorist attacks. For the World Bank's response at that time and a counter response by Jubilee USA and nineteen other groups, see http://www.worldbank.org/html/extdr/pb/pbfourdemands.htm and http://www.jubileeusa.org/ jubilee.cgi?path=/learn_more/&page=rebuttal.html.

10. The report is available on the website of the Bank Information Center at http://www. bicusa.org.

also includes specific proposals on worker rights, forest protection, pesticides, gender issues, HIV/AIDS, and water policy. These groups are not against international-financial flows, per se, but they do want to see different rules to govern them.

More fundamentally, many critics of globalization argue that it has not produced the promised growth. The Center for Economic and Policy Research (CEPR), based in Washington, D.C. has published several papers highlighting the lack of growth in many developing countries during a period of rapid globalization under the tutelage of the Bank, IMF, and the WTO. Their papers, "Scorecard on Globalization" and "The Emperor Has No Growth,"[11] point out that, even as the influence of these institutions increased over the last twenty years, growth in many low- and middle-income countries lagged. They see this lack of growth as evidence that the neoliberal Washington Consensus is not benefiting the majority of the world's peoples.[12]

The Fifty Years is Enough (FYIE) organization has taken a more radical stance than these critics, calling for reparations for the effects of structural-adjustment policies and for the social and environmental effects Bank projects; privatization or abolition of Bank entities (the International Finance Corporation [IFC] and the Multilatteral Investment Guarantee Agency [MIGA]) that provide assistance to the private sector; and personal and institutional accountability for Bank and Fund complicity in corruption. Also, FYIE calls for an assessment of the International Financial Institutions' (IFI) future—including the possibility of abolition in the absence of radical reform—but, at a minimum, this group wants to weaken and reduce the funding available to them.[13]

Although FYIE calls for the money to be transferred to other, more acceptable (to them) forms of assistance, the demand to reduce IFI funds, along with differences among some groups over the details of debt relief, have at times divided Northern and Southern NGOs working on development issues (Nelson 2001, 71–72). While largely agreeing with Northern NGO demands to reform IFI programs and conditionality and to restructure the institutions to give client countries more of a say in decision making, Southern NGOs have been more skeptical of demands to shrink these institutions. Jubilee South has also gone further than some Northern-based groups in terms of demanding unconditional debt relief and reparations for slavery, colonialism, and "odious debt" (Collins, Gariyo, and Burdon 2001; www.jubileesouth.net).

Although development-oriented NGOs from both the North and South

---

11. See http://www.cepr.net for links to all of their publications.

12. For other skeptical analyses of growth-globalization links, see Khor (2000), Rodrik (2001a), and Rodriguez and Rodrik (2001).

13. See http://www.50years.org/s28/demands.html; see also http://www.50years.org/about/platform.html.

continue to push for broader and deeper debt relief, they are increasingly focusing on what is needed to restore growth and promote equitable development *after* debt relief. Perhaps inspired by the call in Doha in November 2001 to make the just-launched WTO trade negotiations a development round, many NGOs are now focusing on what they see as inequities in the trading system that discriminate against developing-country exports.

In two publications linked to the launch of the new Doha round or to multilateral trade negotiations, Oxfam International recognizes the potential contribution of international trade and investment to economic development in poor countries, and it criticizes the hypocrisy of rich countries that promote globalization's growth benefits while disproportionately restricting developing-country exports to their markets. The Oxfam reports focus, in particular, on the inequities in the agriculture and intellectual-property agreements that were negotiated during the Uruguay Round. But, unlike World Bank and other traditional trade economists who have written reports with similar titles, Oxfam International has not embraced unconditional free trade, and their vision of "Harnessing Trade for Development" (Oxfam International 2001) couples increased market access for poor-country exports with increased flexibility for those countries to use industrial and trade policies as part of their development strategy. Thus, Oxfam recommends

- "[T]ransition periods for implementing WTO agreements [that are] based on development milestones not arbitrary dates;"
- Replacement of the single undertaking to give developing countries more flexibility in signing on to WTO agreements;
- Reform of the dispute settlement understanding to make it fairer and more workable for the less-developed countries (LDCs) and to ensure that rulings take into account poverty, human rights, and environmental effects (consider joint panels with specialized UN bodies)
- Increased technical assistance and capacity-building for LDCs.
- Decision-making processes that "increase effective participation of developing countries;" and
- Increased access to documents and public scrutiny through "more active involvement of national parliaments and regular consultations with civil society" (Oxfam International 2001, executive summary and policy proposals, 9–10).

In addition, the report underlying the new Oxfam International campaign to make trade fair puts trade into the broader context of national and international development policies, including trade-related conditionality and project selection in the IMF and World Bank, as well as the application of WTO rules to poor countries. But the concluding chapter, "Making Trade Work for the Poor," begins with the *national* policies to improve health and education and to reduce corruption that need to be in place if poor countries are to take advantage of the opportunities offered by globalization.[14]

Finally, an issue that has led to increased criticism of the World Bank in recent years is its support of natural-resource-extraction projects, particularly in institutionally weak and often corrupt developing countries. The NGOs, including many local ones, have criticized these projects for infringing upon human rights (particularly of indigenous groups), degrading the environment, and feeding corrupt, often repressive regimes. Oxfam America recently weighed in on these issues in a policy paper that concludes that heavy dependence on resource extraction fails to reduce poverty in many cases, even if it succeeds in raising growth (Ross 2001). The report calls for international assistance to oil- and mineral-dependent countries to diversify their economies; full disclosure of financial transactions between extractive firms and host governments; international financial assistance to develop extractive sectors *only* if the host governments are democratic and "have demonstrated a commitment to fighting poverty" (Ross 2001, 18); and support only for projects with safeguards to ensure that some revenue goes to poverty alleviation and with independent monitoring to guard against corruption.

One example of efforts to address some of these issues may be found in the guidelines negotiated by the World Bank and other stakeholders when the Bank agreed to support a Chad-Cameroon oil pipeline project (available at http://www.worldbank.org/afr/ccproj). The safeguards include extensive reviews of the potential environmental impacts; dialogue with local people along the pipeline route regarding resettlement, compensation, and a revenue management plan; and independent external monitoring to guard against corruption. While the agreement may serve as a model for these projects, questions about implementation were raised almost immediately when Chad's government appeared to divert some of the project revenues to buy weapons for the military. Additional criticisms followed quickly (e.g., see Friends of the Earth International 2001).[15]

1.4.2 Labor and Environmental Critiques of Globalization

A principal aim of development NGO's critiques of globalization is to increase resource transfers from North to South, and, therefore, Northern

14. "Harnessing Trade for Development" seems a more apt title or slogan for Oxfam's campaign, which includes special and differential treatment for developing countries, than does the more recent and more polemical "Rigged Rules and Double Standards" (Oxfam International 2002). Both reports are available on the Oxfam International website at http://www.oxfam.org. See also Rodrik (2001b; *The Global Governance of Trade as if Development Really Mattered*).

15. At the end of the Clinton administration, the U.S. State Department and the U.K. Foreign Ministry unveiled a narrower initiative involving a set of voluntary principles negotiated with MNCs and NGOs to ensure that security arrangements to protect investments do not result in human-rights abuses, as has been alleged in mining projects in Indonesia and oil extraction in Nigeria (http://www.state.gov/www/global/human_rights/001220_fsdrl_principles.html).

and Southern NGOs are *generally* on the same page. When it comes to labor and the environment, however, the direction of the redistribution of incomes is less clear and divisions between groups—for example, between environmentalists and unions or between North and South—tend to increase. Sometimes the differences are over *ends*, such as whether development of oil resources in the Alaskan National Wildlife Refuge would destroy the environment or create thousands of jobs at acceptable cost. But often the differences are over *means*, such as whether or not trade measures should be used to enforce labor or environmental standards.

The key labor critique of globalization rules is that they protect property rights for investors and for intellectual property owners, but not worker rights. These critics argue that international rules that promote and protect capital mobility while restricting labor mobility skew economic outcomes in favor of capital and against labor, especially low-skilled labor.

Although WTO members have steadfastly refused to discuss labor issues, activist and union pressures on the trade system contributed to the willingness of governments and employer groups to agree to a consensus definition of core labor standards at the ILO. The 1998 Declaration on Fundamental Principles and Rights at Work affirms that all 175 members, regardless of whether or not they have ratified the related conventions and regardless of their level of development, have an obligation to respect and promote

- Freedom of association and the right to organize and bargain collectively;
- Freedom from forced labor;
- Freedom from child labor; and
- Freedom from discrimination.

Differences remain over how to implement these principles in practice, but the declaration establishes the legitimacy of these core standards and creates a follow-up mechanism to monitor countries' efforts to promote them.

While the meaning of freedom of association remains controversial in many countries, particularly nondemocratic ones, the most divisive part of the debate has been over proposals to incorporate labor standards in trade agreements and to give the WTO the major role in enforcing them. While much of the discussion of social clauses has been general and driven primarily by the individual biases of the debater, at least two specific proposals have been made by the International Labor Rights Fund and the International Confederation of Free Trade Unions (ICFTU). Both proposals show sensitivity to the concerns of developing-country governments, trade economists, and MNCs regarding the possibility of protectionist abuse. In the former, the proposal requires that a panel of independent experts must verify that a violation has occurred before any sanction can be imposed, while the latter relies on the ILO to play a similar role. In neither case are individual governments authorized to impose sanctions without independent or multilateral review.[16]

In addition to trying to use trade to strengthen enforcement of core labor standards, labor and human-rights NGOs are also pressing development institutions to be more sensitive to workers' concerns when responding to financial crises or planning development projects. In particular, they argue that IFI concerns about labor-market flexibility should be balanced with concern for protection of worker rights and the adequacy of social safety nets to ease the adjustment of displaced workers. Labor and human-rights organizations are also involved in monitoring corporations (e.g., the Workers Rights Consortium and the Fair Labor Association) and in putting pressure on individual companies to change their practices (e.g., Sweatshop Watch and United Students Against Sweatshops).

Environmental concerns are the most difficult to summarize or distill. The range of issues is broad, the linkages to globalization complex, and the differences between North and South often sharp. Important issues include combating pollution, climate change, species loss, deforestation, preserving ecosystems that are particularly rich in biodiversity, and ensuring adequate food health and safety.

There is a tension within the environmental community, however, between the desire to preserve domestic-policy autonomy and, at the same time, the need to negotiate enforceable multilateral agreements to address global problems—at least when those agreements are not universal. Thus, environmentalists slammed WTO dispute-settlement rulings that appeared to impinge upon domestic-policy autonomy—for example, American clean-air regulations on gasoline or the European ban on hormone-treated beef. Another target is chapter 11 of NAFTA, which allows investors to mount legal challenges to environmental or other regulations that lower the value of their investments. At the same time, many of the same groups have been equally harsh in criticizing other WTO decisions intended to protect other countries' sovereignty by limiting the use of trade measures to enforce environmental laws (e.g., shrimping, tuna fishing, and turtle- and dolphin-protection disputes). In some of these cases there are multilateral agreements, but they are without enforcement rules that address the dispute; in other cases there are no rules at all. The concern is that rules restricting the use of trade measures against nonsignatories to multilateral environmental agreements encourage free riding.

There are also tensions between Northern and Southern groups regarding priorities. The LDCs tend to be more concerned about developed-country regulations, for example, those relating to food safety—that impede their exports and their lack of capacity to develop standards of their own. They also strongly oppose use of trade measures to enforce environmental standards and agreements. There are also differences between de-

16. See Harvey, Collingsworth, and Athreya (n.d.) and ICFTU (1999).

veloping-country governments and Northern groups over the latter's advocacy of increased transparency and access, especially in dispute settlement in the WTO context, because of the asymmetries in capacity between Northern and Southern NGOs and because of the lack of LDC governments' legal capacity in dispute-settlement cases.

Biotechnology is a relatively new source of conflict, sometimes between the North and the South as well as in other cases among developed countries. Some developing-country researchers join U.S. companies and advocates in defending the potential benefits for poor people of disease-resistant strains of subsistence crops, but others oppose patenting of traditional knowledge, which may restrict access while failing to adequately compensate the "inventors." Perhaps the most intense conflicts to date, however, have been between the United States and European Union. There are areas of agreement between environmentalists, economists, and LDC governments in some areas—for example, the need to address market failures in resource pricing or the perniciousness of subsidies to fishery fleets, forestry firms, and other resource sectors. There is also agreement between many environmentalists and economists on agriculture subsidies, but differences arise with small-farm advocates and some developing-country advocates that want protection for small farmers and the rural poor for poverty reasons. There is also often broad agreement on the reality of global commons problems (e.g., global warming and the ozone hole), but there are big differences on the distribution of the costs of addressing those problems and over the relative use of carrots and sticks in implementation.

1.4.3   Globalization from the Ground Up

Ultimately, many critics view current international rules as promoting a particular neoliberal economic model that they reject and clearly do not want to see globalized. Responding to complaints from pro-globalization critics, such as *New York Times* columnist Thomas Friedman, that they have no coherent alternative, the International Forum on Globalization embarked in 1999 on a multiyear, transnational effort to develop a broad, comprehensive proposal for the fundamental reform of the global economy as well as of national and local economies. The preliminary result, published in the book titled *Alternatives to Economic Globalization: A Better World is Possible!*, stresses that supporters and critics of globalization trends have very different views of the direction of those trends—one side believes that globalization is creating growth and spreading prosperity, and the other sees mainly increasing inequality, erosion of community values, and a degraded environment.[17] The IFG is an alliance of sixty leading activists, scholars, economists, researchers, and writers from twenty-five countries, including the United States, Canada, Europe, Brazil, Chile,

17. Though the full report was due for release in Spring 2002, only a summary was available as of early August; see http://www.ifg.org/alt_eng.pdf.

India, Japan, Mexico, Malaysia, the Philippines, South Africa, and Thailand. Their alternative vision tilts relatively more toward anti-globalization than toward alternative globalization because it does not agree that maximizing incomes and growth should be the goal of economic policy and, therefore, rejects the key theoretical arguments in favor of freer trade and capital flows. The central values in this vision are democracy and sustainability, and the key policy approach derived by the IFG is "subsidiarity," an approach to policy that "consciously favor[s] the local," and that redistributes power from "global bureaucracies and global corporations" to local communities and national governments. In this alternative view, "The proper role of global institutions is to facilitate the cooperative coordination of national policies on matters where the interests of nations are inherently intertwined—as with action on global warming" (IFG 2002, 6).

1.5   How Are Economists To Understand It All?

Many economists in universities and think tanks, as well as in policy positions, have been taken aback by the growing scope and intensity of the global protest movement over the past ten years. To them, the recent history of globalization seemed largely to have delivered the once-wishful hopes of the 1960s for development and prosperity.[18] "What's it all about?" is still a common question.[19]

In this section, we try to respond especially to international and some development economists. This presentation may not do full justice to an ideal characterization of the critics' concerns, but it is at least an early attempt to translate the concerns cross-culturally for a tribe who speak a different language. It will also not do justice to diversity within the tribe of economists, but it is intended to highlight work from other fields within economics and from other disciplines that may put the critics' concerns in a new light.

We try here to rationalize the opposition to globalization, using the logic of rational choice, of course, but not of individualistic self-interest nor materialism. Neither self-interest nor materialism is necessary to the discourse of economics, however prevalent.

In every case, we try to explain how an economist might more easily understand the agendas of the critics and, where appropriate, respond to them more constructively. We organize our discussion in three parts: microeconomics, macroeconomics, and "metaeconomics."

18. Three recent and comprehensive articulations of the gains from globalization are made by Lindert and Williamson (2001) and World Bank (2002a, 2002b), which are, respectively, historical, forward looking, and current.

19. One well-known economist recently wrote, "I don't really understand what it is that gets the protestors in the streets," articulating a common bafflement within the profession, though he had several conjectures.

1.5.1 Microeconomic Critiques

Microeconomics is the study of decision-making by various types of agents under various constraints and in various environments. Although identified with individualism, microeconomic agents often represent social groups, such as profit-seeking and not-for-profit firms, households, and governments. This is perhaps the simplest and most fundamental way to understand the critics' agenda. It is often motivated by *social* identity, not individual identity, and sometimes it is motivated by relative social-group objectives (solidarity) in a manner familiar to most social scientists, but less so to economists. In this microeconomic spirit, globalization's critics often emphasize different objectives and preference sets and show greater sensitivity to political as well as market failures that can undermine assumptions about how markets work in some cases.

Different Objectives

Family Preference. Some of today's globalization critics still have at heart the welfare of the national family with whom they identify. To them, family preference is not protectionism any more than is the kind of special treatment accorded to one's own spouse, siblings, and children. It makes sense from this perspective that those outside the family should be tolerantly and justly treated, but not *specially*. To be indiscriminate in one's treatment of family members and outsiders would be just wrong and unloving.

But discrimination in favor of one's family is implicit discrimination against others. And classic free trade is defined as the *absence* of such discrimination or family preference at a national level. This is not popularly understood. The case for open trade (i.e., no border barriers) is *not* the case for free markets *uber alles.* Open trade simply implies no border discrimination against foreign suppliers or demanders. Open trade does *not* imply unregulated markets; only that such regulation be even-handed, applying equally to "us" and "them" (nondiscrimination). Likewise is the case for openness in services and foreign direct investment (national treatment of firms).

Of course, even classical, well-accepted reasons for discrimination and national preference include responsibilities of citizenship (hence migration barriers at the border) and national security, but some critics want a more thorough return to the view that one's nation is one's family and should be treated specially.[20]

Class Identity. Others, however, have emphasized class and other common interests and experience as the grounds for social identity and suspect free traders of having corporate-class interest at heart, whatever their rhetoric.

---

20. See Anderson (1983) for a widely cited, though critical, treatment.

These critics are often themselves internationalist. Some critics emphasize traditional class categories, such as workers, and favor globalized labor relations.[21] Others emphasize religious identity (e.g., Muslim opposition to globalization of secularism) or cultural parallelism (e.g., global opposition on behalf of the world's indigenous peoples), and still others emphasize gender (Cagatay 2001; Heyzer 2001).

With these understandings, economists may see better that what matters most to many critics are the aspects of globalization that economists usually call income-distributional effects and consider less important than the efficiency gains that globalization allows to national families. The critics, by contrast, see the income-distributional effects as *primary*.

Relative Position and Positional Goods. To many critics, furthermore, the relative welfare of one's family or community is just as important or more important than its absolute welfare. They object to the globalization that makes some elite countries and groups *much* better off than others, even if all gain on average. Economists have been willing to accept this from the perspective of national security, and political economists from the perspective of international power. But, increasingly, microeconomists are analyzing the *general* microeconomics of *relative* objectives (e.g., envy, altruism, power, and revenge) and discovering rational behaviors that appear costly and inefficient, yet satisfy deep nonmaterial human and social needs and preferences.[22]

Greater Sensitivity to Values Reflected in "Goods"

Not all goods are "good" in the value schemes of many of the critics. Globalization has facilitated exchange in a number of perceived social "bads" (i.e., bad for me and bad for thee—which is the community of others with whom I identify). Many progressives identify arms trade as bad; many moralists oppose globalized gambling. People of many persuasions oppose global sexual trafficking and trade in drugs, although often for different reasons. Economists traditionally claim to be reluctant to include normative values in their reasoning. Yet when they are included as a type of preference, they have the same foundational character as other preferences, including some nonmaterial preferences that economists have come

21. See, for example, Frank (1999). This is, obviously, one way of rationalizing why I might care about *how* things are made abroad, but production *processes* are not usually admitted by trade economists as a permissible reason to oppose trade (but also see Rodrik 1997).

22. Much of the recent work of Robert Frank represents this view, as does research by Blanchflower and Oswald 2000, for example, and others on whether and when material prosperity correlates with perceptual measures of satisfaction and happiness. See Frey and Stutzer (2002) for a review and Wright (2000) for a readable summary that includes psychology research as well. Recent experimental-economics research (Zizzo and Oswald 2001, as summarized in *The Economist,* 16 February 2002, 69) suggests that the poor are indeed willing to *pay* out some of their scarce resources to reduce the incomes of the rich.

to accept without hesitation (e.g., risk aversion and altruism), and normative preferences can be analyzed using familiar economic methods.

Greater Sensitivity to the Unevenness of Constraints

International economists never tire of showing how global trading opportunities expand the choices available to individuals, groups, and countries. Critics are sensitive both to the gap between those enjoying greater choice and those without it and to the possibility that when the "haves" exercise their expanded choice, the opportunities available to the "have-nots" may actually shrink.

Thus, for example, it is not clear that the world's indigenous peoples or illiterate populations find enhanced choices from globalization, and they may in fact lose.[23] Nor is it clear that globalization enhances choice for the immobile, which are those whose genes or culture make them locally and occupationally stationary relative to others (e.g., women and teachers of tribal languages). Nor is it obvious that those who are geographically immobile (workers of average skills facing migration barriers) gain opportunity as a group from the enhanced choices of geographically mobile skilled workers and owners of capital and other mobile resources.

International economists almost always answer that social redistribution of the overall gains from globalization (compensation) can leave everyone better off, which is of course true. But as public advocates, they rarely argue as strongly for practical diffusion-of-gains schemes within societies as they do for increased openness. "I do international economics, not public or distributional economics," they say implicitly and often boldly, "potential compensation is enough," but that does not satisfy the critics who sense irresponsibility.[24]

It is surprisingly rare for economists to construct comprehensive distributional accounts of a Northern country's gainers and losers from global integration; the identification of such gainers and losers occupies much of the political debate. (There is much more Southern research on these themes.[25]) There is, of course, massive economic research on the functional income distribution[26] and on sectors (appropriate work when there are sector-

---

23. For two classic treatments, see Wood (1994) or Sen (1999).

24. Some economists who leave the issue of actual compensation on the doorstep of domestic government simultaneously criticize government for doing its business wastefully and corruptly. The legitimate core of the argument is that compensation (redistribution) itself may have a resource cost that should be factored into a three-way evaluation of the status quo, deeper integration with compensation, and deeper integration without it. For a more detailed discussion of how economists have struggled with the principle of compensation and how the debate might gain from more cross-disciplinary work, see Kanbur (2002).

25. We have in mind research in development studies on Gini coefficients and on rural-urban differences.

26. Showing that, as a presumption for small- and modest-sized countries, deeper globalization *necessarily* worsens the living standards of some factor owners (Stolper-Samuelson)—unlike other policy trends and reforms.

specific factors). Yet there is little research on the regional effects of globalization,[27] little research on its effects by size distribution,[28] and little research on its effects on income-distribution volatility and mobility (e.g., mobility between quintiles within generations and across generations).

Realism About the Need for Protest

Economists sometimes find conflict and protest, in contrast to negotiation, to be intrinsically baffling.[29] Yet microeconomists who study the economics of contracts are familiar with the "hold-up" problem and its implicit tensions. Applying its insights to explicit or implicit social contracts is perhaps a helpful way to understand the economics of protest from a microeconomic perspective.

The hold-up problem is endemic to contracts. Once negotiated, contracts are usually costly to break. In many cases, the contract's value depends on the sustainability of the relationship among the contracting agents, and the assets involved in that contract have relationship-specific value. In that case, there is an incentive for each agent through opportunistic behavior, including threats, to tilt the distribution of the relationship-specific value in their favor. The natural response of the other agent is resistance and protest, and opportunistic behavior is often provoked by some change in the external environment of the contract that widens global opportunities, for example.

Such opportunism and protest turn out to be more than just a distributional question. Hold-up problems cause microeconomic *inefficiency*—specifically, underinvestment in all relation-specific assets.

Applied to social contracts, commercial opportunism coupled with protest may be more than just a distributional matter, too. It may cause inefficient, economy-wide underinvestment. Economists should perhaps be as concerned as the critics if globalization encourages opportunism and protest, and these problems in turn cause underinvestment in social capital of all kinds, ranging from "hard" infrastructure to "softer" trust in institutions and in each other.[30] This material provides a natural transition to macroeconomic articulations of the critics' concerns.

27. But, see Yusuf, Wu, and Evenett (2000) and McCulloch, Winters, and Cirera (2002).
28. Smeeding and Rainwater (2000), along with others, have pioneered cross-country comparisons of welfare of similar groups at similar positions in their own country's size distribution, but there is not yet enough time depth in the underlying data to do cross-country studies of response to trends such as globalization. International economists who have pioneered continuum-of-goods models of general-equilibrium trade might easily shift their attention and skills to continuum-of-talents models of factor rewards and exhaustively explore the complete distributional effects of globalization. Yeaple (2002) is a recent paper in this direction; Bond (1985) was a start.
29. As always, there are exceptions (e.g., Hirshleifer 2001).
30. A putative example of hold-up opportunism leading to loss of trust in the multilateral-trade context is the history of the TRIPs Agreement and the possible reneging by the rich countries on agricultural and textile/apparel concessions made in the Uruguay Round in return for poor-country acceptance of TRIPs.

1.5.2   Macroeconomic, General-Equilibrium, and Political-Economic Critiques

In a more macroeconomic spirit, globalization's critics often seem to have intuitively sensed thorny problems. They are often skeptics about markets in general, whereas economists are enthusiasts, especially for global and intertemporal (financial) markets. But economists turn out often to share the skepticism of the critics in very specific ways. They recognize and accept familiar shortcomings of markets across time, contingency, and jurisdiction (e.g., local public goods). Unfortunately, in the policy debate over globalization, these amendments to the general model too often get lost.[31] This failure in communication is in part because economists are often skeptics about government intervention, whereas critics are enthusiasts, especially for intervention by accountable, transparent, democratic governments—their preferred polity. But, since many developing-country governments still lack these attributes, it is also odd that the critics focus so little attention on national governments, compared to that focused on international organizations.[32]

Financial Volatility, Dependence, and Debt Relief

Globalization makes available immense gains from intertemporal trade and trade across contingencies,[33] but it also exposes economies to financial volatility and crises of many kinds—bubbles, banking crises, exchange crises, and sovereign-debt crises. Though there is a strong economic consensus on best-practice (and second-best-practice) national institutions and policies designed to modulate and deter financial crises, almost none of these institutions and policies exist at the global level. There is no global-equities regulator, merely informal protocols for difficulties of sovereign debtors (or the private agents that they guarantee) and only primitive, systemic banking regulation (the Basel Agreements on bank capital). But financial and insurance markets have grown at the global level without adequate prudential discipline and insurance against fraud.[34] Under these conditions, international economists might have been more chary than they were about "unprotected" financial globalization and more sympathetic to the critics.[35]

Furthermore, there is a longstanding economics of efficient debt relief on which much of modern bankruptcy law is based (Miller 2002). Without any formal provisions at the global level, there is no guarantee that open global financial markets will avoid inefficient rationing and discrimination,

---

31. Kanbur (2000, 14–15) remarks on the counter-productive tendency for economists who do "policy messaging" to make their recommendations "sharp and hard," out of concern that if they "give [critics] an inch of nuance, they'll take a mile of protection."

32. Oxfam International (2002) is an exception.

33. See Obstfeld and Rogoff (1996), World Bank (2001a), and DeSoto (2000), more popularly.

34. Litan (2000) or Padoa-Schioppa and Saccomanni (1994), presciently.

35. Kanbur (2000, 15) views this as a major policy failure due to the "negotiating mindset" of policy economists that inhibits giving ground.

nor inequitable odious debt[36]—to say nothing of the "bad equilibria" discussed later.

Concerns over Homogenization and Vicious Circles

Critics often oppose both homogenization (Westernization or Americanization) and wasteful diversity (excessive variety and excessive provision of luxury), and they can find support for these concerns in economic models showing the uncertain general-equilibrium optimality of free-entry differentiated-product (monopolistic) competition. From Hotelling's classic example of inefficient concentration of hot dog vendors on a beach to the familiar conclusion that monopolistic competition can sometimes create excess competition and excess capacity,[37] economists have a suitcase full of reasons to doubt the automatic welfare-maximizing character of free trade under differentiated-product monopolistic competition, which is itself a strong candidate for the most relevant and truly global market structure.

Furthermore, critics often worry—more generally than regarding merely debt relief—about poverty traps and vicious circles that might afflict poorer countries and subpopulations. Once again, they can look to economists who have pioneered models of multiple equilibria in spatial and dynamic competition both within and among nations.[38] In such models, some equilibria are demonstrably better than others on the usual welfare criteria. It is not clear that economists should have so reflexive and unyielding confidence that capital markets will assure that the best equilibrium gets picked, since imperfect-information economics shows us so often how capital markets fail to do so and are themselves subject to multiple equilibria (Hoff 2002).

So with these models in mind, economists and policymakers might dialogue with critics more fruitfully if they adopted a more nuanced, pragmatic, and less ideological defense of globalization.

Intertemporal Concerns over Environment, Public Health, and Education

Critics worry over inadequate bequests of environment, durable public goods, educational capital, and other property to the future, and they worry further that globalization increases the rate at which the future is mortgaged to reward those living now.[39] It is ironic that economists cannot reassure them better, often relying instead on models with infinitely-lived actors and on overcasual appeals to the way that history hasn't worked out that way (yet).[40] One reason, of course, is that market solutions seem im-

36. See Kremer and Jayachandran (2002) and Birdsall, Williamson, and Deese (2002) for recent treatments.
37. For example, see Suzumura (1995).
38. Graham and Temple (2001) are just one recent example.
39. Kanbur (2000) discusses differences in the time horizon over which economists and others evaluate; this is not the same point we are making.
40. For example, in reaction to Club of Rome concerns over global resource depletion.

possible when the problem is *missing* markets for intergenerational valuing of durable goods, both public and private. And democratic social-choice solutions do not help if there is the corresponding problem of missing *polities* for voting on relevant policies.

Elementary models of ideal intergenerational equity and sustainable development are, of course, well-established.[41] But such models often involve extra-market ombudsmen and planners with (fiduciary?) responsibility to the future and ignore how such actors should be institutionally situated, for example, on the issue of ideal political scope and accountability. (Should they have local, national, global constituents?) A very practical application of the economics called mechanism design is called for, but, to the authors' knowledge, this does not exist.

Cases in point are easy to identify; these are not just abstract, academic theories. Future generations, for example, are excluded from planning how to cope with global warming and from debating how to manage global-investment markets and worker (hence, taxpayer) migration with an eye to the looming public-pension underfunding of many currently rich Northern countries.

Grassroots and Median Voter Concerns

Critics also worry about whether globalization overempowers elites and what it does to the ordinary citizen and to the poor. Economists should recognize such concerns as relating to medians and "lower tails" of the income and other distributions. But most international economists seem preoccupied instead with aggregate gains from global integration—that is to say, with mean gains, not medians or similar measures.[42] Again, in the context of the policy debate, globalization enthusiasts often seem reluctant to concede that there are any losers at all.

Regarding the policy context, questions about the distribution of the gains should be addressed explicitly. Is globalization less attractive the greater the difference between a nation's *mean* gains from trade and the gains from trade earned by the *median* earner in the distribution?[43] And if the *median* earner actually loses, why would or should a democracy embrace policies that deepen global integration? Should it not resist or protest at least until some explicit provision is made for diffusing the gains from trade more widely (i.e., until potential compensation becomes actual)?

41. For example, either Phelps-Solow "golden-rule" saving, consumption, and growth paths, overlapping-generations models of social insurance, or equitable equilibrium-dynamic price trajectories for nonrenewable resources.

42. McCulloch, Winters, and Cirera (2002) is an exception to this preoccupation and provides earlier references to research in this same distributional spirit.

43. Dutt and Mitra (2002), for example, show this empirically in capital-abundant countries. Most of the earlier economic research on median voters and protection has been narrowly theoretical.

Concerns About Regulatory Capture, Corruption, Checks and Balances

Capture. Critics often complain that the institutional architecture of globalization unduly reflects a corporate agenda. They may have it right with respect to business capture of nascent global regulatory initiatives, such as in the TRIPs Agreement, in the attempt to forge a multilateral investment pact with legal recourse for foreign investors that arguably exceeds that of local firms,[44] and in quasi-official institutions, such as the Transatlantic Business Dialogue, and standards-setting bodies. Economists familiar with the economics of regulatory capture will immediately recognize the potential for global versions of its inefficiencies and inequities.

Corruption. Furthermore, there are many channels by which globalization may facilitate the diversion of public goods, property, and revenues into private gains.[45] Resource-wasting rent seeking and the possible growth of cross-border versions of it are just two examples of how open trade can facilitate trade in perceived bads as well as goods. Since openness can also constrain venality and corrupt policy, however, neither economists nor others ought to rush to judgment over whether the gains of the goods exceed the banes of the bads in any particular case. Measuring the bads ought to be a natural cooperative enterprise of globalization's critics and enthusiasts.

Checks and Balances. Finally it is worth remembering that the WTO and GATT have a peculiar and unique parentage in the Havana Charter for the stillborn International Trade Organization. Whatever one thinks of its merits and demerits, its *intent* was clearly to provide balanced rules for global commerce, including attention to small business and workers. Therefore, why is it so obvious to defenders of status quo globalization that the current boundaries and precedents of the WTO are appropriate and that there are adequate checks and balances to the narrowly commercial interests reflected there? Why not a constitutional convention on the new WTO[46] or on a genuinely new international economic order? As the critics often say, "we don't oppose globalization; we oppose the *unbalanced rules* governing *this* globalization."

Centralization and Subsidiarity Concerns

Last, it is worth remembering that some of the classic (and often complex) economics of fiscal federalism and urbanization have some morphological application to the concerns of globalization critics. Examples are

44. For example, see chapter eleven of the NAFTA agreement (available at http://www.sice.oas.org/trade/nafta/naftatce.asp).
45. See Elliott (1997).
46. Esty (2002) can be read as sympathetic to this view. Barfield (2001) and Howse and Nicolaidis (2001), by contrast, recognize the constitutional problem in the WTO, but think a procedural exercise in constitution-building would be fatal to it.

- The uncertain welfare economics of interjurisdictional tax and infrastructure competition with capital (and other factor) mobility across boundaries;[47]
- The efficiency and equity implications of global and local regulation, the value of local political autonomy (e.g., better information about activities being regulated), and optimal subsidiarity;" and
- Among other considerations, whether burdens of capture and perils of corruption are greater or less when regulation is global versus local.

1.5.3 Metaeconomic Critiques

In addition, there are still broader concerns that we call metaeconomic. Most spring from the fact that commercial rights are being harmonized and globalized steadily—property rights, intellectual-property rights, rights to have local regulatory standards recognized abroad (mutual recognition), rights to local judicial standing and compensation for foreign investors in host countries, and rights to migrate temporarily for skilled business professionals. But is such narrow global momentum on commercial rights self-evidently desirable?

- Is it desirable without equal global momentum on other important human rights, such as freedom from forced labor and freedom of association?[48]
- Is it desirable without renewed debate over whether such rights should be assigned only to individuals or to groups also? If so, what kind of groups would be sanctioned to enjoy rights? Free labor unions, religious and civil-society associations, and indigenous-people groups (i.e., land and resource rights)? This is an issue because global commercial rights increasingly accrue to incorporated firms that are taken all too reflexively to be groups of persons entitled to enjoying such rights. But if so, why not rights for other groups? Historical American jurisprudence validated the identification of American firms as persons with respect to property rights, but the global suitability of such validation has not yet been established.[49]
- Is it desirable without global governance structures that nest those rights within some democratically accountable (possibly global) polity that develops such rights, conditions them, implements them, and enforces them? If the only real human rights (as opposed to hor-

---

47. See Wilson (1996).
48. See Charnovitz (1999), among others, for a sympathetic treatment.
49. For an economic analysis, see Glaeser and Schliefer (2001). More generally, American, German, and other countries' economic, political, and social history is worth studying seriously for possibly global lessons about the "necessary nexus" among single-market deepening, federal political procedure, law and judicial oversight, social mobility, and regulatory protocols and institutions. DeSoto (2000), for example, treats a number of these topics, most deeply for Peru and the United States. Frost, Richardson, and Schneider (2003) treat them historically for the European Union and the United States.

tatory ideals) presuppose nation-states that oversee them,[50] shouldn't international human rights, including commercial rights, presuppose a more serious global political order than is currently embedded in the United Nations?

1.6   Where do We Go From Here?

Having tried to characterize globalization's critics in terms and concepts familiar to its defenders, we finish by asking whether there is any common ground between critics and defenders (rather than just a fight for raw supremacy). Can talkers and doers talk together? Can they do together? What might the doing look like?

Thus far, there has been some working together on issues related to the *process* of international economic policymaking. The World Bank, IMF, and WTO are all more transparent than they used to be and, to varying degrees, also more open to input from a broader variety of stakeholders than before. The NGOs and grassroots groups do not necessarily get a *vote* in these intergovernmental institutions, but the institutions, particularly the Bank, have recognized the value in designing more effective and sustainable projects and in policies of listening to a wider variety of *voices*. Although critics still complain that the consultation process is more rhetorical than real, these organizations accept the need for increased transparency and accountability in Bank and Fund policy development. The WTO remains the least open of the three, but it is releasing more documents more quickly and the appellate body has agreed that it can accept submissions from NGOs in dispute settlement cases. However, the latter remains controversial, and the WTO remains the most government centered of the international economic institutions and the least open to civil society input.

Policy economists and the three major international economic institutions are also responding to the critics by addressing poverty and inequality more explicitly in their analyses of globalization and, to varying degrees, in their programs. While some question whether or not the IMF should be in this area at all, it is shifting the focus of its long-term lending from extended structural adjustment to poverty reduction and growth. The World Bank is funding fewer large infrastructure project and lending more for human resource development. Health and education, which are at the top of the list of millennium development goals developed by the United Nations, along with social protection accounted for nearly one-third of new World Bank loan commitments in 2001 (World Bank 2001b). There is also evidence of changing attitudes at the WTO, the most obvious being that the outcome of the ministerial meeting in Doha, Qatar, which

---

50. For example, see Ignatieff (2001).

launched a new round of trade negotiations in November 2001, is being called the Doha Development Agenda.

The area that remains the most contentious is the *substance* of the rules themselves. What needs to be harmonized, coordinated, or globalized, and what can be reserved to national or local governments? But there are areas upon which pro-globalizers and the critics of current globalization should be able to agree on the need for new rules. Concerns about corruption are broadly shared, although reactions to this issue also underscore the different approaches that fuel the debate over globalization. The critics focus on the alleged role of the international financial institutions in feeding corruption through loans and projects that are diverted for personal gain. The IFIs focus on the need for corrupt and inept national governments to get their own houses in order. Nevertheless, both defenders and critics fundamentally agree that corruption can be a major impediment to development and that steps to increase transparency and accountability are required.

Promoters and critics of globalization might also agree on trade rules in some new areas that could both improve the functioning of markets and make globalization more equitable, environmentally friendly, and politically sustainable. Already, a number of governments, economists, NGOs, and others agree that an unquestionably positive proposal for promoting trade, environmental sustainability, and development would target subsidies for farming and fishing. More controversially, economists and activists might agree that reforms to the TRIPs agreement could balance intellectual-property protection with incentives for diffusion (Richardson 2001). Activists who are concerned about the increased and potentially anticompetitive reach of MNCs might join with economists and others who favor limited competition rules to guard against cartels, for example (Richardson 2001; Oxfam International 2002). The role of corruption in deterring or perverting foreign investment might also logically lead to some agreement on at least minimal rules to protect investors from arbitrary actions by predatory governments and to protect people from human-rights or environmental abuses by corporations that are unregulated by those same governments.

Increasingly, the question that we started with—whether or not the doers willing to stop and talk—is being turned around: Are the critics only talkers or are they also doers? As South African Finance Minister Trevor Manuel said at the IMF World Bank Annual Meeting in Prague in September 2000, "I know what they're against but have no sense of what they're for" ("Protestors Paralyze Prague," *Washington Post*, 27 September 2000, A16). The NGOs are being asked to demonstrate their own legitimacy through increased transparency (e.g., regarding funding) and to be explicit about to whom they are accountable and who they represent. One close observer, who has worked both with NGOs and as a civil-society specialist at the World Bank, notes that it is important to analyze "who enjoys the benefits and suffers the costs of what the movement achieves, especially at the grassroots level" (Edwards 2001, 6)?[51]

Moving forward together will also require some changes in method. After the death of the young man during the G8 protests in Genoa and, particularly, the September 11 terrorist attacks, organizing large protests around each major international economic meeting appears to be reaping diminishing returns. Concrete demonstrations of protest will almost certainly continue to play an important role, but the movement seems ready to move beyond serial protesting or being "a movement of meeting-stalkers, following the trade bureaucrats as if they were the Grateful Dead" (Klein 2000, 20–21). Forgoing large street protests outside the Waldorf Astoria in New York during the World Economic Forum meeting in January 2002 and gathering instead in Porto Alegre to discuss alternatives could prove to be a turning point toward dialogue and toward more constructive interaction between the critics and defenders of economic globalization.

51. See Florini (2001, 39) and Clark (2001, 26) for other recommended NGO reforms to increase transparency and accountability.

Appendix

Table 1A.1   A Sampling of Alternative Globalization Actors

Organization	Key Issues	Roles in the Movement	Advocacy Style[a]	Page Rank	Backward Links
OneWorld London, UK; www.oneworld.net	These sites are a good place to start exploration of the many alternative globalization groups worldwide. One World has more than 1,000 pa lists more than 26,000 nonprofit and community organizations in 153 countries (20,088 in the United States) and is also searchable by topic and location.			8	6,690
Action without Borders New York, NY; www.idealist.org	Multi-issue network or coalition	Organizing, mobilization		8	7,030
Alliance for Responsible Trade Washington, D.C.; www.art-us.org	Multi-issue network or coalition	Organizing, mobilization	Confronter	6	216
Anti-Capitalist Convergence www.abolishthebank.org	Multi-issue network or coalition	Organizing, mobilization		6	446
Focus on the Global South Bangkok, THA; www.focusweb.org	Multi-issue network or coalition	Research		7	2,010
Hemispheric Social Alliance www.asc-hsa.org	Multi-issue network or coalition	Organizing, mobilization		6	322
International Forum on Globalization San Francisco, CA; www.ifg.org	Multi-issue network or coalition	Research		7	1,590
Mexico Solidarity Network Chicago, IL; www.mexicosolidarity.org	Multi-issue network or coalition	Grassroots education, mobilization		6	518
Mobilization for Global Justice Washington, D.C.; www.globalizethis.org	Multi-issue network or coalition	Organizing, mobilization		6	1,180
Peoples' Global Action Ottawa, CAN; www.agp.org	Multi-issue network or coalition	Organizing, mobilization	Confronter	6	2,210
Third World Network Singapore, www.twnside.org.sg	Multi-issue network or coalition	Research		7	4,650

(continued)

Table 1A.1 (continued)

Organization	Key Issues	Roles in the Movement	Advocacy Style[a]	Page Rank	Backward Links
Transnational Institute Amsterdam, NET; www.tni.org	Multi-issue network or coalition	Research		6	2,010
World Social Forum Porto Alegre, BRA; www.worldsocialforum.org	Multi-issue network or coalition	Organizing, mobilization		6	2,260
Adbusters Vancouver, CAN; www.adbusters.org	Multi-issue group	Campaign- and action-information provider		8	2,410
Africa Action Washington, D.C.; www.africaaction.org	Multi-issue group	Organization, mobilization, campaign information		6	2,260
ATTAC Paris, FRA; www.attac.org	Multi-issue group	Organization, mobilization, information provider	Confronter	6	3,650
Center for Economic and Policy Research Washington, D.C.; www.cepr.net	Multi-issue group	Research		7	1,310
Center of Concern Washington, D.C.; www.coc.org	Multi-issue group	Networking, organizing, research	Engager	6	892
Common Dreams Portland, ME; www.commondreams.org	Multi-issue group	Information collection and dissemination (articles, op-eds on globalization and other issues of concern to the left)		7	6,340
Corporate Europe Observatory Amsterdam, NET; www.xs4all.nl/~ceo/	Multi-issue group	Organization, mobilization, campaign information	Confronter	6	1,080
Corporate Watch Oxford, UK; www.corporatewatch.org.uk	Multi-issue group	Campaign- and action-information provider		6	922
CorpWatch San Francisco, CA; www.corpwatch.org	Multi-issue group	Campaign- and action-information provider		7	5,150

Organization	Type	Activities	Role		
Council of Canadians Ottawa, CAN; www.canadians.org	Multi-issue group	Grassroots education, mobilization	Confronter	6	2,170
Essential Action Washington, D.C.; www.essentialaction.org	Multi-issue group	Campaign- and action-information provider	Confronter	6	446
Fair Trade Federation Washington, D.C.; www.fairtradefederation.org	Multi-issue group	Certification, labeling	Confronter	6	862
Global Exchange San Francisco, CA; www.globalexchange.org	Multi-issue group	Organization, mobilization, campaign information, "Reality tour" organizer	Confronter	7	5,210
Institute for Agriculture and Trade Policy Minneapolis, MN; www.iatp.org	Multi-issue group	Research		7	2,100
Institute for Policy Studies Washington, D.C.; www.ips-dc.org	Multi-issue group	Research		7	1,820
Interfaith Center on Corporate Responsibility New York, NY; www.iccr.org	Multi-issue group	Corporate-social-responsibility activism	Engager	7	774
International Centre for Trade and Sustainable Development Geneva, SW; www.ictad.org	Multi-issue group	Information collection and dissemination, dialogue facilitation	Engager	7	2,120
Investor Responsibility Research Center New York, NY; www.irrc.org	Multi-issue group	Corporate-social-responsibility research		6	870
Public Citizen's Global Trade Watch Washington, D.C.; www.tradewatch.org	Multi-issue group	Organization, mobilization, campaign information	Confronter	6	2,600
Protest Net protest.net	Multi-issue group	Campaign- and action-information provider	Confronter	7	3,230
RESULTS Washington, D.C.; www.results.org	Multi-issue group	Grassroots education, mobilization	Confronter	6	644
The Ruckus Society Oakland, CA; www.ruckus.org	Multi-issue group	Protest tactics, training	Confronter	7	1,450

(continued)

Table 1A.1 (continued)

Organization	Key Issues	Roles in the Movement	Advocacy Style[a]	Page Rank	Backward Links
Trade Observatory (sponsored by IATP) Minneapolis, MN; www.tradeobservatory.org	Multi-issue group	Information collection and dissemination (news, articles, and research on trade from wide variety of sources)		6	292
TransFair USA Oakland, CA; www.transfairusa.org	Multi-issue group	Certification, labeling		6	814
Union of Radical Political Economics New Haven, CT; www.urpe.org	Multi-issue group	Research		6	174
United for a Fair Economy Boston, MA; www.ufenet.org	Multi-issue group	Grassroots education, mobilization		6	2,000
AFL-CIO Washington, D.C.; www.afl-cio.org	Human/worker rights	Organization, mobilization, campaign information		6	274
American Friends Service Committee Philadelphia, PA; www.afsc.org	Human/worker rights	General advocacy		7	4,940
Amnesty International London, UK; www.amnesty.org	Human/worker rights	General advocacy	Engager	8	18,900
Campaign for Labor Rights Washington, D.C.; www.summersault.com/~agj/clr/	Human/worker rights	Organization, mobilization, campaign information		6	882
Communication Workers of America Washington, D.C.; www.cwa-union.org	Human/worker rights	Organization, mobilization, campaign information		7	2,430
COSATU Johannesburg, SA; www.cosatu.org.za	Human/worker rights	Organization, mobilization, campaign information		6	1,510
Fair Labor Association Washington, D.C.; www.fairlabor.org	Human/worker rights	Monitoring, verification	Engager	6	418
HealthGAP Coalition www.globaltreatmentaccess.org	Human/worker rights	Organization, mobilization, campaign information	Confronter	6	284

Organization	Issue area	Activities	Role		
Human Rights Watch New York, NY; www.hrw.org	Human/worker rights	General advocacy	Engager	8	16,300
ICFTU Brussels, BEL; www.icftu.org	Human/worker rights	Organization, mobilization, research		7	2,070
International Brotherhood of Electrical Workers Washington, D.C.; www.ibew.org	Human/worker rights	Organization, mobilization, campaign information		7	1,730
International Human Rights Law Group Washington, D.C.; www.hrlawgroup.org	Human/worker rights	General advocacy	Engager	7	690
International Labor Rights Fund Washington, D.C.; www.laborrights.org	Human/worker rights	Coalition building, mobilization, campaign information	Engager	6	624
Jobs with Justice Washington, D.C.; www.jwj.org	Human/worker rights	Grassroots education, mobilization	Confronter	6	758
Lawyers Committee for Human Rights New York, NY; www.ichr.org	Human/worker rights	General advocacy	Engager	7	2,360
MADRE New York, NY; www.madre.org	Human/worker rights	General advocacy		6	860
Maquila Solidarity Network Toronto, CAN; www.maquilasolidarity.org	Human/worker rights	Grassroots education, mobilization, information collection and dissemination		6	988
National Labor Committee New York, NY; www.nlcnet.org	Human/worker rights	Campaign- and action-information provider	Confronter	7	1,750
SEIU Washington, D.C.; www.seiu.org	Human/worker rights	Organization, mobilization, campaign information		7	2,040
Social Accountability International New York, NY; www.cepaa.org	Human/worker rights	Monitoring, verification	Engager	6	728
Sweatshop Watch Oakland, CA; www.sweatshopwatch.org	Human/worker rights	Campaign- and action-information provider		6	1,500
UNITE! New York, NY; www.uniteunion.org	Human/worker rights	Organization, mobilization, campaign information		6	1,370

(continued)

Table 1A.1   (continued)

Organization	Key Issues	Roles in the Movement	Advocacy Style[a]	Page Rank	Backward Links
United Students Against Sweatshops Washington, D.C.; www.usasnet.org	Human/worker rights	Organization, mobilization, campaign information	Confronter	6	552
Workers Rights Consortium Washington, D.C.; www.workersrights.org	Human/worker rights	Monitoring, verification	Confronter	6	560
Amazon Watch Topanga, CA; www.amazonwatch.org	Environment	Grassroots education, mobilization	Confronter	6	1,120
Center for International Environmental Law Washington, D.C.; www.ciel.org	Environment	Research, advocacy		7	1,430
Centre for Science and Environment New Delhi, IND; www.cseindia.org	Environment	Research, advocacy		7	7,230
Environmental Defense New York, NY; www.environmentaldefense.org	Environment	Research, advocacy, legal services		7	4,760
Forest Stewardship Council Oaxaca, MEX; www.fscoax.org	Environment	Monitoring, verification	Engager	7	1,620
Friends of the Earth International Amsterdam, NET; www.foei.org	Environment	General advocacy		7	2,340
Greenpeace International Amsterdam, NET; www.greenpeace.org	Environment	Organization, mobilization, campaign information		8	10,400
International Institute for Sustainable Development Winnipeg, CAN; www.iisd.org	Environment	Research, advocacy (also links to sustainable "web ring")	Engager	6	6,300
IISD Linkages Winnipeg, CAN; www.iisd.ca		Information collection and dissemination (electronic clearinghouse on international environment/development meetings)		7	5,060
International Rivers Network Berkeley, CA; www.im.org	Environment	Research, grassroots campaigning	Confronter	7	2,410
National Wildlife Federation Reston, VA; www.nwf.org	Environment	General advocacy		7	7,420

Organization	Type	Activities	Role		
Natural Resources Defense Council, New York, NY; www.nrdc.org	Environment	General advocacy		7	6,320
Project Underground, Berkeley, CA; www.moles.org	Environment	Grassroots education, mobilization	Confronter	6	2,090
Rainforest Action Network, San Francisco, CA; www.ran.org	Environment	Campaign- and action-information provider		8	4,920
Redefining Progress, Oakland, CA; www.rprogress.org	Environment	Research		7	1,780
Sierra Club, San Francisco, CA; www.sierraclub.org	Environment	General advocacy		8	11,900
Sustainable Energy and Economy Network, Washington, D.C.; www.seen.org	Environment	Campaign- and action-information provider		6	1,160
World Resources Institute, Washington, D.C.; www.wri.org	Environment	Research	Engager	8	7,740
World Wildlife Fund, www.wwf.org	Environment	Research	Engager	8	8,100
Worldwatch Institute, Washington, D.C.; www.worldwatch.org	Environment	Research		7	4,640
50 Years is Enough Network, Washington, D.C.; www.50years.org	Development	Organization, mobilization, campaign information	Confronter	6	2,180
ActionAid, London, UK; www.actionaid.org	Development	Advocacy		7	1,250
Ashoka, Washington, D.C.; www.ashoka.org	Development	Activist capacity building		7	2,530
Bank Information Center, Washington, D.C.; www.bicusa.org	Development	Organization, mobilization, campaign information		7	934
Brazilian Landless Workers Movement (MST), Brasilia, BRA; www.mstbrazil.org	Development	Grassroots education, mobilization	Confronter	6	508
Center for Economic Justice, Washington, D.C.; www.econjustice.net	Development	Coalition organizing, grassroots education, mobilization	Confronter	6	80
Development GAP (Group for Alternative Policies), Washington, D.C.; www.developmentgap.org	Development	Networking, organizing, research		6	754

(continued)

Table 1A.1 (continued)

Organization	Key Issues	Roles in the Movement	Advocacy Style[a]	Page Rank	Backward Links
Doctors Without Borders (MSF) multiple chapters, www.msf.org	Development	Advocacy		7	3,660
Food First/Institute for Food and Development Policy Oakland, CA; www.foodfirst.org	Development	Research		7	2,180
Grameen Bank Dhaka, BAN; www.grameen.org	Development	Development projects		6	276
Jubilee 2000/Plus/Research London, UK; www.jubileeplus.org	Development	Organization, mobilization, campaign information		6	2,980
Jubilee South Quezon City, PHI; www.jubileesouth.net	Development	Organization, mobilization, campaign information	Confronter	n.a.	336
Jubilee USA Washington, D.C.; www.jubileeusa.org	Development	Organization, mobilization, campaign information		6	1,220
Mexican Action Network on Free Trade (RMALC) Mexico City, MEX; www.malc.org.mx	Development	Organization, mobilization, campaign information		6	252
Oxfam International www.oxfam.org	Development	Advocacy		7	3,440
Save the Narmada Movement Baroda, IND; www.namada.org	Development	Networking, organizing, research	Confronter	6	916
Women's EDGE Washington, D.C.; www.womensedge.org	Development	Networking, organizing, research		6	674
World Development Movement London, UK; www.wdm.org.uk	Development	Grassroots education, mobilization, research		6	1,060

Notes: CAN = Canada; UK = the United Kingdom; THA = Thailand; NET = the Netherlands; BRA = Brazil; SA = South Africa; BEL = Belgium; IND = India; MEX = Mexico; BAN = Bangladesh; and PHI = the Philippines. AFL-CIO = the American Federation of Labor-Congress of Industrial Organizations; COSATU = Congress of South African Trade Unions; SEIU = Service Employees International Union; MSF = Medicins sans Frontieres; and RMALC = Red Mexicana de Acción Frente al Libre Comercio.

[a] Where appropriate.

References

Aaronson, Susan Ariel. 2001. *Taking trade to the streets: The lost history of public efforts to shape globalization.* Ann Arbor, Mich.: University of Michigan Press.

Anderson, Benedict. 1983. *Imagined communities: Reflections on the origin and spread of nationalism.* London: Verso.

Barfield, Claude E. 2001. *Free trade, sovereignty, democracy: The future of the World Trade Organization.* Washington, D.C.: American Enterprise Institute.

Benedick, Richard Elliot. 1998. *Ozone diplomacy: New directions in safeguarding the planet.* Cambridge, Mass.: Harvard University.

Birdsall, Nancy, John Williamson, and Brian Deese. 2002. *Delivering on debt relief: From IMF gold to a new aid architecture.* Washington, D.C.: Center for Global Development and Institute for International Economics.

Blanchflower, David G., and Andrew J. Oswald. 2000. Well-being over time in Britain and the USA, Dartmouth College, Department of Economics. Manuscript, October.

Bond, Eric. 1985. Entreprenurial ability, income distribution, and international trade. *Journal of International Economics* 20 (May): 343–56.

Buchanan, Patrick J. 2000. The millennium conflict: America first or world government. Speech presented to the Boston World Affairs Council. 6 January. Boston, Mass.

Cagatay, Nilufer. 2001. Trade, gender, and poverty. Trade and Sustainable Human Development Background Paper, Social Development and Poverty Elimination Division, Working Paper Series no. 5. New York: United Nations Development Program, October.

Charnovitz, Steve. 1999. The globalization of economic human rights. *Brooklyn Journal of International Law* 25 (1): 114–24.

Clark, John D. 2001. Ethical globalization: The dilemmas and challenges of internationalizing civil society. In *Global citizen action,* ed. Michael Edwards and John Gaventa, 17–28. Boulder, Colo.: Lynne Reinner Publishers.

Collins, Carole J. L., Zie Gariyo, and Tony Burdon. 2001. Jubilee 2000: Citizen action across the north-south divide. In *Global citizen action,* ed. Michael Edwards and John Gaventa, 135–48. Boulder, Colo.: Lynne Reinner Publishers.

De Soto, Hernando. 2000. *The mystery of capital: Why capitalism triumphs in the West and fails everywhere else.* New York: Basic.

Dutt, Pushan, and Devashish Mitra. 2002. Endogenous trade policy through majority voting: An empirical investigation. *Journal of International Economics* 58 (October): 107–33.

Edwards, Michael. 2001. Introduction to *Global citizen action,* ed. Michael Edwards and John Gaventa, 1–14. Boulder, Colo.: Lynne Reinner Publishers.

Elliott, Kimberly Ann. 1997. *Corruption in the global economy.* Washington, D.C.: Institute for International Economics.

Elliott, Kimberly Ann, and Gary Clyde Hufbauer. 2001. Ambivalent multilateralism and the emerging backlash: The IMF and WTO. In *Multilateralism and U.S. foreign policy: Ambivalent engagement,* ed. Stewart Patrick and Shepard Forman, 377–413. Boulder, Colo.: Lynne Reinner Press.

Esty, Daniel C. 2002. The World Trade Organization's legitimacy crisis. *World Trade Review* 1 (1): 7–22.

Florini, Ann M. 2001. Transnational civil society. In *Global citizen action,* ed. Michael Edwards and John Gaventa, 29–40. Boulder, Colo.: Lynne Reinner Publishers.

———. 2002. From protest to participation: The role of civil society in global governance. Paper presented to the Kiel Week Conference, Kiel Institute of World Economics. 24–25 June, Kiel, Germany.

Frank, Dana. 1999. *Buy American: The untold story of economic nationalism.* Boston: Beacon Press.

Frey, Bruno, and Alois Stutzer. 2002. What can economists learn from happiness research? *Journal of Economic Literature* 40 (June): 402–35.

Friends of the Earth International. 2001. *Broken promises: The Chad Cameroon Oil and Pipeline Project; profit at any cost?* www.foei.org/ifi/brokenpromises.html.

Frost, Ellen R., J. David Richardson, and Michael Schneider. 2003. Lessons for a globalizing world: European and U.S. experiences in market integration. Syracuse University, Global Affairs Institute. Manuscript.

Ghandi, M. K. 1996. Economic and moral progress. In *The essential writings of Mahatma Ghandi*, ed. Raghavan Iyer, 92–101. Delhi: Oxford University Press.

Glaeser, Edward L., and Andei Schleifer. 2001. The rise of the regulatory state. NBER Working Paper no. 8650. Cambridge, Mass.: National Bureau of Economic Research, December.

Graham, Bryan S., and Jonathan R. W. Temple. 2001. Rich nations, poor nations: How much can multiple equilibria explain? Centre for Economic Policy Research (CEPR) Discussion Paper no. 3046. London: CEPR, November.

Graham, Edward M. 2000. *Fighting the wrong enemy: Antiglobal activists and multinational enterprises.* Washington, D.C.: Institute for International Economics.

Harvey, Pharis, Terry Collingsworth, and Bama Athreya. No date. Developing effective mechanisms for implementing labor rights in the global economy. Workers in the Global Economy Project Papers. Washington, D.C.: International Labor Rights Fund. Available at http://www.laborrights.org/.

Henderson, David. 2000. *The MAI affair: A story and its lessons.* London: Royal Institute for International Affairs.

Heyzer, Noeleen. 2001. *Globalization, gender equality, and state modernization.* Penang, Malaysia: Third World Network.

Hines, Colin. 2000. *Localization: A global manifesto.* London: Earthscan.

Hirshleifer, Jack. 2001. *The dark side of the force: Economic foundations of conflict theory.* New York: Cambridge University Press.

Hoff, Karla. 2002. Solidarity networks in the extended family system. Cornell University, the Moral and Social Dimensions of Microeconomic Behavior in Low-Income Communities project. Working Paper. Available at http://www.aem.cornell.edu/special_programs/AFSNRM/Pew/.

Howse, Robert, and Kalipso Nicolaidis. 2001. *Legitimacy and global governance: Why constitutionalizing the WTO is a step too far.* In *Efficiency, equity, legitimacy: The multilateral trading system at the millennium*, ed. Roger B. Porter, Pierre Sauve, Arvind Subramanian, and Americo Baviglia Zampetti, 227–52. Washington, D.C.: the Brookings Institution.

Ignatieff, Michael. 2001. *Human rights as politics and idolatry.* In *Human rights as politics and idolatry*, ed. Amy Guttman, 3–98. Princeton: Princeton University Press.

International Confederation of Free Trade Unions (ICFTU). 1999. *Building workers' human rights into the global trading system.* Brussels: ICFTU.

International Forum on Globalization. 2002. *Alternatives to economic globalization: A better world is possible!* San Francisco: Berret Koehler.

Kanbur, Ravi. 2000. Economic policy, distribution and poverty: The nature of disagreements. *World Development* 29 (6): 1083–94.

———. 2002. Economics, social science and development. *World Development* 30 (March): 477–86.

Keck, Margaret E., and Kathryn Sikkink. 1998. *Activists beyond borders: Advocacy networks in international politics.* Ithaca, N.Y.: Cornell University Press.

Khor, Martin. 2000. Globalization and the south: Some critical issues. United Nations Conference on Trade and Development (UNCTAD) Discussion Paper no. 147. New York: UNCTAD, April.

Klein, Naomi. 2000. The Vision Thing. *The Nation* 20 July, 18–21.

Korten, David C. 1999. *The post-corporate world: Life after capitalism.* West Hartford, Conn.: Kumarian Press.

Kremer, Michael, and Seema Jayachandran. 2002. Odious debt. *Finance & Development* 39 (2): 36–39.

Lindert, Peter H., and Jeffrey G. Williamson. 2003. Does globalization make the world more unequal? In *Globalization in historical perspective,* ed. Michael D. Bordo, Alan M. Taylor, and Jeffrey G. Williamson. Chicago: University of Chicago.

Litan, Robert E. 2000. Toward a global financial architecture for the 21st century. In *Local dynamics in an era of globalization,* ed. Shahid Yusuf, Weiping Wu, and Simon Evenett, 19–30. New York: Oxford University Press.

Lorenz, Edward C. 2001. *Defining global justice: The history of US labor standards Policy.* South Bend, Ind.: Notre Dame University Press.

Mayer, Frederick W. 1998. *Interpreting NAFTA: The science and art of political analysis.* New York: Columbia University Press.

McCulloch, Neil, L. Alan Winters, and Xavier Cirera. 2002. *Trade liberalization and poverty: A handbook.* London: Centre for Economic Policy Research.

Miller, Marcus. 2002. Sovereign debt restructuring: New articles, new contracts— or no change. Policy Briefs no. PB02-3. Washington, D.C.: Institute for International Economics, April.

Nelson, Paul. 2001. Information, location, legitimacy: The changing bases of civil society involvement in international economic policy. In *Global citizen action,* ed. Michael Edwards and John Gaventa, 59–72. Boulder, Colo.: Lynne Reinner Publishers.

Obstfeld, Maurice, and Kenneth Rogoff. 1996. *Foundations of international macroeconomics.* Cambridge, Mass.: MIT Press.

Ostry, Sylvia. 2001. Global integration: Currents and counter-currents. The Walter Gordon Lecture, presented at Massey College, University of Toronto. 23 May.

Oxfam International. 2001. *Harnessing trade for development.* Briefing paper no. 1, August. Available at http://www.oxfam.org/eng/pdfs/pp0108_Harnessing_trade_ for_development. pdf.

———. 2002. *Rigged rules and double standards: Trade, globalisation, and the fight against poverty.* London: Oxfam. Available at http://www.maketradefair.com/ stylesheet.asp?file=03042002121618&cat=2&subcat=6&select=1.

Padoa-Schioppa, Tommaso, and Fabrizio Saccomanni. 1994. *Managing a market-led global financial system.* In *Managing the world economy: Fifty years after Bretton Woods,* ed. Peter B. Kenen, 235–68. Washington, D.C.: Institute for International Economics.

Richardson, J. David. 2001. Narrow new issues as a natural way forward for the WTO. Syracuse University, Economics Department. Manuscript.

Rodrik, Dani. 1997. *Has globalization gone too far?* Washington, D.C.: Institute for International Economics.

———. 2001a. *Globalization, growth, and poverty: Is the World Bank beginning to get it?* http:/ksghome.harvard.edu/~.drodrik.academic.ksg/index.html.

———. 2001b. *The global governance of trade as if development really mattered.* New York: United Nations Development Program.

Rodríguez, Francisco, and Dani Rodrik. 2001. Trade policy and economic growth:

A skeptic's guide to the cross-national evidence. In *Macroeconomics Annual 2000*, ed. Ben Bernanke and Kenneth S. Rogoff, Cambridge, Mass.: MIT Press.

Ross, Michael. 2001. *Extractive sectors and the poor.* http://www.oxfamamerica.org/pdfs/eireport.pdf.

Sen, Amartya. 1999. *Development as freedom.* New York: Random House.

Smeeding, Timothy M., and Lee Rainwater. 2002. Comparing living standards across nations: Real incomes at the top, the bottom, and the middle. Syracuse University, Center for Policy Research. Manuscript.

Suzumura, Kotaro. 1995. *Competition, commitment, and welfare.* Oxford: Oxford University Press.

United Nations Environmental Program (UNEP). 2001. *Enhancing civil society engagement in the work of UNEP.* Strategy Paper on General Council Decision no. 21/19, October. Available at http://www.unep.org/documents/default.asp?documentid=226&articleid=2955.

Williamson, John. 1997. The Washington consensus revisited. In *Economic and social development into the XXI century*, ed. Louis Emmerij. Washington, D.C.: Johns Hopkins University Press.

Wilson, John Douglas. 1996. Capital mobility and environmental standards: Is there a theoretical basis for a race to the bottom? In *Fair trade and harmonization: Prerequisites for free trade?* Vol. 1, *Economic Analysis*, ed. Jagdish N. Bhagwati and Robert E. Hudec, 393–428. Cambridge, Mass.: MIT Press.

Winston, Morton. 2001. NGO strategies for promoting global corporate social responsibility. In *Justice in the world economy: Globalization, agents, and the pursuit of social good* ed. Robin Hodess. New York: Carnegie Council on Ethics and International Affairs.

Wood, Adrian. 1994. *North-south trade, employment, and inequality: Changing fortunes in a skill-driven world.* Oxford: Clarendon Press.

World Bank. 2001a. *Finance for growth: Policy choices in a volatile world.* Washington, D.C.: World Bank.

———. 2001b. *The World Bank annual report.* Washington, D.C.: World Bank.

———. 2002a. *Global economic prospects for developing countries, 2002.* Washington, D.C.: World Bank.

———. 2002b. *Globalization, growth, and poverty: Building an inclusive world economy.* Washington, D.C.: World Bank.

Wright, Robert. 2000. Will globalization make you happy? *Foreign Policy* 120 (September/October): 55–64.

Yeaple, Stephen Ross. 2002. A simple model of firm heterogeneity, international trade, and wages. University of Pennsylvania, Department of Economics. Manuscript, February.

Yusuf, Shahid, Weiping Wu, and Simon Evenett, eds. 2000. *Local dynamics in an era of globalization.* New York: Oxford University Press.

Zizzo, Daniel J., and Andrew J. Oswald. 2001. Are people willing to pay to reduce others' incomes? *Annales d'Economie et de Statistique* 63–64 (July–December): 39–66.

Comment   Harry Flam

My comments are about the second part of the paper. The first part is a very interesting and useful survey and categorization of the anti-globalization movement, for which the authors should be commended. The anti-globalization movement is—we learn—to a considerable extent *pro*-globalization, but wants globalization to proceed in different ways and with different goals. The authors limit their scope to groups concerned with economic globalization and involved in advocacy. These are placed into four categories: development and poverty, human and worker rights, environment, and multi-issue groups (global reformers).

Economists tend to have a dim and unfair view of the anti-globalization movement and what it has to say, perhaps under the influence of television coverage of violent protests in the streets of Seattle, Genoa, and other places. The second part of the paper seeks to make the arguments understandable and acceptable to economists by using the language and concepts of economics and appealing to well-known imperfections of institutions, markets, and economic policies. I think Elliott, Kar, and Richardson are quite convincing and successful in this. When translated into the language of economists, it is obvious that many of the concerns raised by such groups as Oxfam International make sense. But I cannot avoid a lingering suspicion that as a description of the movement as a whole, much ignorance, misplaced criticism, and nonsense have been left out.

Furthermore, the paper tends to give the impression that most of the issues brought up by the critics have been of no concern to academic economists, while it is possible to argue that the opposite is true. To take one of the most obvious examples: Growth, development, and income distribution, both inside and between nations, have been on the agenda of development and trade research for decades, including research at such institutions as the World Bank (e.g., work by Hollis Chenery in the 1970s). Other examples include the relations among growth, trade, and the environment; the trade and wages debate; various aspects of the world trading system; and the debt crisis. It is perhaps true that economists tend to be more interested in what determines the size of the pie than how it is shared, but I do think that it needs to be emphasized that many of the issues brought up by the critics of globalization are not new.

What is puzzling to mainstream economists like myself is the emphasis of the globalization critics on globalization, international organizations, and multinationals in the context of poverty, underdevelopment, lack of human and worker rights, and environmental degradation. Admittedly, the World Bank can be criticized for putting too much emphasis on large in-

Harry Flam is professor at the Institute for International Economic Studies.

frastructure investments in the past, the IMF for being insensitive to the distributional consequences of stabilization programs, the WTO for giving developed-country firms too strong property rights in the TRIPS agreement, and multinationals for their conduct in poor countries and against weak governments. But the fact is that these institutions have made great contributions to the improvement of living conditions for the world's poor. Developing countries are very actively seeking World Bank loans and are participating in project design. The IMF steps in when national governance and governments have failed. The WTO system provides much-needed rules for world trade and has contributed to a substantial reduction of trade barriers during the last half-century. As for multinationals, most developing countries actively seek and compete for their investments.

One cannot help thinking that the focus on international trade and investment and on international institutions is opportunistic and largely misplaced. The focus should be on national governance and national policies: the lack of democracy, corruption, bad policies, badly protected property rights, privileges for the elite, and so on. The international institutions and globalization serve as scapegoats, when the really important barriers to economic development and well-being lie in the national, not the international, arena.

In fact, one can well argue that globalization has very positive effects in putting restrictions on national governance and policies. National autonomy is often used to pursue bad governance and policies, as in North Korea and Burma (to take extreme examples). Exposure to international trade and factor movements, and participation in international cooperation and institutions tend to prevent government mismanagement. (We do not have to go to developing countries to find examples: the creation of the European Monetary Union has placed much-needed discipline on bad national monetary and fiscal policies.)

It must be pointed out that my misgivings about the anti-globalization movement are not intended as criticism of the paper. They can, however, explain why economists are less than enthusiastic in their views of the movement.

Globalization and Democracy

Carl B. Hamilton

2.1 Introduction

It is for good reasons that many people regard the world as unjust and plagued with poverty. From that observation, one could draw the conclusion that the state of the world is the result of existing international institutions and today's ruling political ideologies. If you take this view, it is hardly surprising that you also protest when international leaders and representatives of fifty-plus long-standing international organizations declare that the recipe is "more of the same"—more and freer trade, stricter and more norm-based fiscal and monetary policies, and the like. In addition, although many of these leaders themselves come from democratic countries, they do not seem to bother too much about the absence of democracy for poor people in many developing countries. Is it surprising that some protest?

This paper takes as its starting point the criticism coming from the anti-globalist movement. Two distinctly different claims are looked into. First, the claim that globalization is undemocratic and, second, that institutions like the World Trade Organization (WTO), the World Bank, and the International Monetary Fund (IMF) should be democratic.

Carl B. Hamilton is adjunct professor of international economics at the Stockholm School of Economics and is also a Member of Parliament.

The author has benefited from comments of participants in The International Seminar on International Trade (ISIT), "Challenges to Globalisation," a CEPR/NEBR/SNS Conference, May 24/25, 2002—in particular those of Kimberly Ann Elliott, Jim Rollo, Alan Winters and Ulrika Stuart—and Jagdish Bhagwati and others at "The Symposium of Globalisation and the Welfare State," May 31–June 1 2002, as well as participants at a SSE seminar, June 2002. Financial support from Svenska Handelsbanken's Research Foundations is warmly acknowledged.

2.2   Globalization, Anti-Globalists, and Democracy.

Following Sen (1999, chap. 6, 152), any country that "is independent, that goes to elections regularly, that has opposition parties to voice criticisms, and that permits newspapers to report freely and question the wisdom of governments policies without extensive censorship" is regarded as democratic. The concept includes not only political rights (like the right to form political parties that openly can compete for and be elected to positions of power in government), but also crucial civil liberties, like personal freedoms, freedom of the press, belief, and association. Countries' level of democracy has been measured by index. One such index has been constructed from the Policy III data set, but there are several other indexes, like the Freedom House index[1] (see Gurr and Jaggers 1995).

The word "globalization" means different things to different people. To limit confusion, here globalization means international trade in goods and services and foreign investment.

Who are the anti-globalists?

> There are strong tensions between organised labour and campaigning non-governmental organisations (NGOs); between people who want to protect national autonomy and those who want to override it; between those who want to save the environment and those whose main aim is development; between those who want to protect traditional ways of life and those who want to upset them; and, of course, those who want reform and those who seek a revolutionary transformation. Some protesters are self-interested. Others are idealistic. (Martin Wolf, *Financial Times*, September 4, 2001)[2]

In the light of this description, is it possible to find a common denominator among the anti-globalist NGOs?

First, many take one of three views: there should be less globalization than there is today; globalization at least should not increase from today's magnitudes, or, if globalization would increase, it should not do so unless there are some additional conditions attached to it. Second, many anti-globalists take a skeptical view of international organizations like WTO, the World Bank, and IMF (the latter two are generally regarded as international financial institutions [IFI]). Of course, it is possible to be positive toward globalization and negative toward the present work of WTO and the IFIs.

2.3   Undemocratic Globalization?

What distinguishes many anti-globalists from others—like scholars and journalists—is that some of them claim that they are able to represent the preferences of others and not just themselves. There are

---

1. The index, methodology, and criteria can be found on http://www.freedomhouse.org.
2. See also Bhagwati (2002a, c).

grassroots NGOs claiming to represent people whose lives and liveli-hood are being directly affected by the actions and policies of the IMF, the World Bank and the WTO. The argument here is that representation in international institutions is imperfect. The emissaries of existing gov-ernments fail to represent many groups' rights and predicament. NGOs acting in international fora are necessary to fill the gap in representation and accountability that results. (Woods and Narlikar 2001, 15)

This argument, as it stands, is not that globalization is necessarily bad, but that not all views are represented when important decisions are taken in international fora on for example, the rules of the multilateral-trading system.

However, implicitly or explicitly, the critique is also that the preferences of those who are *not* represented in international institutions are more neg-ative on globalization than are the preferences of those who are repre-sented. If the preferences of all concerned—the set of which is difficult to define precisely and whose preferences are more difficult than usual to ag-gregate—had been taken into account, then the decisions of the IFIs would have yielded different outcomes and less trade and foreign invest-ment.

Let us consider a claim that the true preferences of peoples of the world on globalization are more skeptical than the preferences reflected in the policies of WTO's member states and of member states and staff of the IFIs.

Can a hypothesis be rejected which states that the present ruling prefer-ences on trade, economic integration, and investment—as reflected in the policies of important rich and poor countries and consequently also in the WTO and the IFI—reflect the views of a majority of the populations in the rich and poor countries?

To discuss the popular preferences on globalization, two approaches are used. Since we want to capture the history of Gatt/WTO rounds during the last forty-plus years, we start off by dividing countries into democratic Or-ganization of Economic Cooperation and Development (OECD) member countries and "other countries." For the subset of OECD member coun-tries, the question is whether or not it is possible that the preferences of the electorate on trade and integration in a systematic way in elections have differed from that of the democratically elected governments' positions? For the other countries, comparative international opinion polls on glob-alization, trade integration, and protectionism are considered. With good polls, one should be able to learn how respondents in different countries look upon globalization and trade. If such polls consistently would yield the result that globalization and free trade are disliked and that respon-dents are inward looking and in favor of protectionism, then the polls would call into question the basis for many member countries' positions and of the policies of the IFIs.

2.3.1   Democratic OECD Countries

Do democratic member countries of, for example, the WTO differ in policy positions from the voters' preferences in a systematic pro-globalization way?

> Even if every government in the world were democratically elected, a large problem of accountability would still remain for international organisations. . . . We have seen that in national politics a government rarely wins or loses an election on a particular issue. Yet rarer would be a government that won or lost an election (or office through some other means) due to a position taken by its representative within an international organisation. Indeed, given that elections do not hold politicians to account on domestic issues, it would be rather ludicrous to assert that they might serve as a mechanism of accountability in the international sphere where voters have even less information, and less motivation to cast their votes on such issues. Clearly elections as a mechanism of domestic restraint on public officials cannot be stretched into an effective mechanism of accountability for international institutions even if every government in the world were democratically elected. Yet this is precisely what the arguments about the traditional structure of governance and representation attempts to do. (Woods and Narlikar 2001, 7)

The authors are hardly correct that "a government rarely wins or loses an election on a particular issue." There are plenty of counter examples unless one defines "issue" in an extremely narrow sense. Apart from this flaw in the quote, the authors are probably correct if one would consider individual decisions in the WTO and most countries at a particular point in time. But do isolated cases of narrowly defined issues constitute the appropriate sample? Our answer is no: The authors seem unlikely to be correct when considering the direction of policy embedded in the large number of successive decisions over some forty years on multilateral trade rounds resulting in lower trade barriers and enhanced economic integration.

Let us consider the OECD countries. To be a member of the OECD, a country must fulfill the requirements of being a pluralistic democracy, enforcing respect for human rights, and having a market economy exposed to international competition. Assuming that *on average* there has been at least twenty-five such members per year since 1960 and that the average period between general elections has been four years, this means that there have been at least 250 general elections among this group. (The true number is higher since the number of members has increased, and the average term is less than four years.) If these governments' decisions to liberalize (manufacturing) trade had been in a systematic conflict with the voters' preferences, it is likely that such a misrepresentation at some points in time had become serious election issues in some of the 250 elections.

Are voters in OECD countries—as a general rule—unmoved by issues like trade, economic integration, and globalization? Trade has on several occasions been an issue in U.S. elections—as reflected in the U.S. handling of the Seattle WTO meeting in 1999 and the U.S. steel protection following the 2000 presidential campaign. Trade has also figured on several earlier occasions in U.S. politics (e.g., see Scheve and Slaughter 2001, chap. 1). The post–World War II history of Western Europe has had many national elections and referenda fought on aspects of economic and political integration. The outcomes of these elections and referenda have sometimes forced governments to resign and have permanently split political parties. From Western Europe we also have the additional experience that democratic countries—through elections and referenda—choose different degrees of integration with the surrounding world. Switzerland has decided to stay out of the European Union (EU), as well as the European Economic Area (EEA). Norway and Iceland are members of the EEA, but they are not members of the EU. Denmark, the United Kingdom, and Sweden are members of the EU, but they have not (yet) adopted the common currency. The United Kingdom is a member of the EU, but not the Schengen agreement on passport-control-free movement of persons. One can also note that over time the European countries have decided, in democratic processes, to integrate more and more.

The hypothesis does not seem possible to reject: The forty-plus years of pro-globalization positions and decisions of OECD democracies represent the preferences of their electorates.

If, on the other hand, it had been a correct description that trade issues seldom have been significant election issues, such an observation does not warrant a claim that voters are unmoved by globalization issues. Precisely for the opposite reason, political parties and governments may try to ensure that trade and integration issues do not become significant ones in elections. They can do this by trying to ensure beforehand that trade and integration policies will be unlikely to cause—from their perspective—disruptive conflicts and undermine efforts to control the agendas of the election campaigns. Then the hypothesis cannot be rejected, of course.

Also, if voters had been opposed to a continued opening up of markets for goods and services and investment, in Europe, for example, nationalistic politicians at times can be expected to have capitalized on such sentiments. Indeed, one has seen inward-looking nationalistic movements in many European countries, but these have typically focused on immigration and asylum seekers and not on trade in goods and services and foreign investment. In several polls, xenophobia does not correlate reliably with the respondents' views on globalization.[3]

The conclusion is that the trend to liberalize in the multilateral trade ne-

---

3. Received by mail from Dough Miller of Ipsos-Reid. The polls can (soon) be found on the home page of the Political Science Department of Queens University, Canada.

gotiations—including exceptions like agriculture and textiles—cannot be said to have been in conflict in a systematic way with the preferences of the voters in the OECD countries. Thus, one cannot reject the hypothesis that some forty years of (pro-globalization) positions and decisions of the OECD democracies have been in line with the OECD electorates' preferences.

2.3.2   Other Countries

With the help of three international and comparative polls, the group of countries is widened to include also important non-OECD ones, including several ones that are not democratic.

Globalization

In October to December 2001, a poll on globalization was taken with representative samples of individuals in twenty-five countries.[4] Some of the questions are seen in the head of table 2.1. The survey results can be said to be within a 3 percent positive or negative range of what they would have been nineteen times out of twenty had the entire population been surveyed. Globalization was defined as international trade in goods and services and in investment. In the table, the countries have been grouped in two classes, richer and poorer ones. The column heads of table 2.1 supply, first, the participating countries' GNP per capita and, second, the three different questions that the respondents were asked.

The (unweighted) averages are strikingly similar (column [2]). Among the OECD countries, Australia, France, and Spain stand out as the more negative ones. Argentina's and Turkey's recent economic crises seem to be reflected in strongly negative attitudes. Note the similar results for the populous countries—China, India, Indonesia, and Nigeria—but also for Qatar, Venezuela, and South Korea. They all report weak negative (column [2]) and strong positive (column [3]) attitudes to globalization. When the results for poorer countries are weighted by population size, the pro-globalization results of the four populous countries dominate. Thus, accounting for some 43 percent of total world population and 51 percent of all low- and middle-income countries' population (in 1998), only some 10–15 percent of the sample regarded globalization as negative. As many as 70–80 percent regarded globalization as positive. One should note in particular the positive Chinese responses to the country's benefits from integration with the world economy (columns [4], [7], and [10]).

Considering the two biggest economies, the United States and Japan, the respondents of Japan were more skeptical to globalization than those of the United States. In fact, the respondents of the United States and the

---

4. See the table 2.1 source and note for reference and some information on the methodology.

Table 2.1 Poll on Attitudes to Globalization, 25 Countries, Representative Samples of 1,000 Citizens, October to December 2001

Country	PPP GNP Per Capita 1998 (1)	Perceived Effects of Globalization on Respondent and Family			"Will the Economy of Our Country Get Better or Worse Because of Globalization?"			"Will the Number of Jobs in Our Country Get Better or Worse Because of Globalization?"		
		Negative (2)	Positive (3)	(3) – (2) (4)	Worse (5)	Better (6)	(6) – (5) (7)	Worse (8)	Better (9)	(9) – (8) (10)
The United States	29,240	21	76	55	27	65	38	45	46	1
Canada	22,814	22	74	52	34	59	25	45	47	2
France	21,214	34	37	3	57	31	–26	72	17	–55
Germany	22,026	20	77	57	37	59	22	70	28	–42
Italy	20,365	22	61	39	21	62	41	29	48	19
The United Kingdom	20,314	22	73	51	25	64	39	43	44	1
The Netherlands	22,325	13	87	74	26	75	49	41	59	18
Spain	15,960	33	36	3	34	39	5	48	24	–24
Australia	21,795	35	60	25	29	63	34	58	33	–25
Japan	23,592	12	32	20	43	40	–3	76	10	–66
Qatar	18,871	11	78	67	11	88	77	21	75	54
South Korea	13,286	21	75	54	36	62	26	52	45	–7
Avg. above	20,984	22	64	42	32	59	27	50	40	–10
Argentina	11,728	48	39	–9	69	24	–45	73	22	–51
Brazil	6,460	27	62	35	41	51	10	54	39	–15
Chile	8,507	20	60	40	30	55	25	42	40	–2
China	3,051	10	75	65	10	83	73	41	49	8
India	2,060	15	79	64	26	69	43	50	43	–7
Indonesia	2,407	16	74	58	57	40	–17	65	33	–32
Kazakhstan	4,317	11	60	49	11	69	58	19	59	40

(*continued*)

Table 2.1 (continued)

Country	PPP GNP Per Capita 1998 (1)	Perceived Effects of Globalization on Respondent and Family			"Will the Economy of Our Country Get Better or Worse Because of Globalization?"			"Will the Number of Jobs in Our Country Get Better or Worse Because of Globalization?"		
		Negative (2)	Positive (3)	(3) – (2) (4)	Worse (5)	Better (6)	(6) – (5) (7)	Worse (8)	Better (9)	(9) – (8) (10)
Mexico	7,450	23	69	46	34	54	20	41	45	4
Nigeria	740	10	70	60	31	61	30	28	59	31
Russia	6,180	13	32	19	17	46	29	26	33	7
South Africa	8,296	18	61	43	46	42	–4	61	28	–33
Turkey	6,594	61	27	–34	43	45	2	13	70	57
Venezuela	5,706	13	87	74	30	65	35	39	55	16
Avg. above	5,654	22	61	39	34	54	20	42	44	2

Source: Data from World Economic Forum "Global Public Opinion on Globalization," conducted by Environics International Ltd. in collaboration with the World Economic Forum, February 2002.

Note: Globalization is defined as increased trade between countries in goods and services and investment. In each country, face-to-face or telephone interviews were conducted with representative samples of 1,000 citizens (for a total of 25,000). Each national poll is accurate to within ±3 percent, 19 times out of 20. The GNP of United Arab Emirates is taken as proxy for Qatar's GNP.

United Kingdom in this poll display very similar preferences on globalization. One can also note the positive attitude to globalization found in Russia. The respondents throughout are more skeptical about the effect of globalization on jobs than on the economy as a whole. This is especially striking for Germany, Japan, and Australia.

Trade and protection

The Ipsos-Reid Global Poll (2000) was taken at about the same time as the previous one (i.e., November to December 2001).[5] It covers twenty countries, some of which overlap with the first poll (see table 2.2). This poll asks about free trade versus protection rather than the more vague concept of globalization. Also, from this poll, it is difficult to nail down any distinct difference in opinions between, for example, rich and poor countries. An open orientation of respondents in China and South Korea is confirmed, and Taiwan can be added as well. Mexicans seem distinctly positive to openness in both polls, while the opposite holds for the Argentineans' attitudes at the beginning of the acute phase of the country's 2001–2002 crisis. Again, France and Australia stand apart as skeptics to trade and globalization. The U.S. respondents seem positive regarding globalization generally, but seem negative toward free trade. This confused attitude is shared with the United Kingdom and Brazil. The second question in table 2.2 tries to capture the response regarding the freedom to shop versus restrictions. Here there is another type of confusion, which is to say that in four countries many respondents seem to prefer freedom to shop and restrictions on imports at the same time (i.e., the United States, Australia, Poland, and Portugal).[6]

Scheve and Slaughter (2001) have looked more deeply into U.S. attitudes. Their polls indicate that Americans think that international trade is beneficial from an overall perspective, but at the same time Americans worry about job destruction and lower wages, in particular among lower-skilled and lower-paid Americans.

The papers by Mayda and Rodrik (2001) and O'Rourke and Sinnott (2001) both use the same database to look into similar questions. The database that they use is the *International Social Survey Program* (ISSP), a sur-

5. See the Ipsos-Reid Global Poll, 20 February 2002. The poll is available from http://www. Thomas.riehle@ipsos-reid.com, and the methodology from http://www.rob.breitzkreutz@ ipsos-reid.com.
6. Given the French respondents' consistently skeptical views on globalization and free trade, it is somewhat surprising in the Ipsos-Reid poll that in no other country—apart from the respondents in Japan and the United States itself—is it more popular to work for an American company than in France. (That part of the poll is not discussed further here.) The polls for France underscores one of France's European dilemma, that is to say, wanting to be the leader and engine of European integration and at the same time often being more skeptical than other European countries about the benefits of international trade, investment, and globalization. It is difficult to have it both ways.

Table 2.2 Poll on Protection Versus Free Trade, 20 Countries, Representative Samples

Country	PPP GNP Per Capita 1998 (1)	Question 1[a]			Question 2[b]			
		Restrict Imports[c] (2)	Do Not Restrict Imports[d] (3)	(3) – (2) (4)	"Good Thing" (5)	"Not Such a Good Thing" (6)	"Doesn't Make any Difference" (7)	(5) – (16) (8)
The United States	29,240	51	41	-10	51	11	36	40
Canada	22,814	43	49	6	48	13	38	35
France	21,214	51	40	-11	25	24	48	1
Germany	22,026	40	49	9	54	12	33	42
Italy	20,365	43	46	3	33	21	41	12
The United Kingdom	20,314	47	41	-6	56	12	31	44
The Netherlands	22,325							
Spain	15,960	40	40		43	20	31	23
Australia	21,795	60	30	-30	44	21	32	23
Japan	23,592	43	53	10	69	8	23	61
Qatar	18,871							
South Korea	13,286	36	58	22	47	28	20	19
Avg. above	20,984	45	45	-1	47	17	33	30
Argentina	11,728	77	18	-59	21	46	26	-25
Brazil	6,460	49	43	-6	45	17	37	28
Chile	8,507							
China	3,051	28	61	33	67	12	19	55
India	2,060							

Country	GNP							
Indonesia	2,407							
Kazakhstan	4,317							
Mexico	7,450	43	54	11	38	42	20	-4
Nigeria	740							
Russia	6,180							
South Africa	8,296	44	47	3	56	12	28	44
Turkey	6,594	37	48	11	36	29	21	7
Venezuela	5,706							
Avg. above	5,654	46	45	-1	44	26	25	18
Colombia	50	48	-2	38	26	36	12	
Poland	56	34	-22	44	25	25	19	
Portugal	49	40	-9	60	7	27	53	
Taiwan	31	51	20	55	7	34	48	

Source: Data from World Economic Forum "Global Public Opinion on Globalization," conducted by Environics International Ltd. in collaboration with the World Economic Forum, February 2002.

Notes: Urban and quasinational samples in Argentina, Brazil, China, Mexico, South Africa, and Turkey. In each country, face-to-face or telephone interviews were conducted with representative samples of 1,000 citizens (for a total of 25,000). Each national poll is accurate to within ±3 percent, 19 times out of 20. The GNP of United Arab Emirates is taken as proxy for Qatar's GNP.

[a] "Which of the following two broad approaches do you think would be the best way to improve the economic and employment situation in your country?"

[b] "Nowadays, multi-national companies sell things, such as soft drinks, television sets, computers, and cars, in this country and worldwide. Do you think that being able to buy such multinational products in this country is a good thing for people like yourself, not such a good thing, or it doesn't make a difference?"

[c] "Protect our industries by restricting imports from other countries?"

[d] "Remove import restrictions to increase international trade with other countries?"

vey that was conducted in twenty-four countries in 1995 to 1996 and concerned countries that can be characterized as old OECD plus Eastern Europe.[7] The sample thus did not cover third-world countries (with the exception of the Philippines) and it was taken five years before the above two polls. In the survey, the respondents were asked how much they agreed or disagreed with the statement that their country "should limit the imports of foreign products in order to protect its national economy." In spite of slightly different methods being used to analyze the data, the two papers arrive roughly at the same empirical conclusion. In a country that is abundant in unskilled labor, relative to most of the rest of the world, the unskilled labor should be in favor of free trade. Mayda and Rodrik (2001, 3) state the conclusion as such: "individual trade preferences interact with country characteristics in exactly the manner predicted by the factor-endowments model. . . . It is a robust result and perhaps our strongest single finding." They later elaborate that "Highly educated individuals tend to be pro-trade in countries that are well endowed with human capital (the USA), but against trade in countries that are poorly endowed with human capital (the Philippines)" (2001, 32). O'Rourke and Sinnott (2001, 5) discuss the result outside the ISSP's sample and the possibility that the conclusion would hold also for a larger sample, including the world's poor countries: "Of course, this is pure speculation on our part: nonetheless, the results we are able to obtain from these data seem entirely consistent with the insights of Eli Heckscher and Bertil Ohlin."

The results of the two polls presented above, if anything, support O'Rourke and Sinnotts speculation that in populous countries, abundant as they are in unskilled labor, the population on the whole would have a free-trade orientation, in line with the predictions of the factor endowments theory.

WTO

In a poll conducted by TEMO in June 2001 in Sweden, the respondents were asked how they regarded WTO. The result was, first, that the WTO was regarded as "very positive" or "positive" by 44 percent, which was much less than for the UN (88 percent), but slightly more than for the EU (40 percent). However, almost half of the respondents answered either that they were neither positive nor negative to WTO, or that they didn't know.[8]

---

7. Specifically, the countries are Australia, West Germany, East Germany, Great Britain, the United States, Austria, Hungary, Italy, Ireland, the Netherlands, Norway, Sweden, the Czech Republic, Slovenia, Poland, Bulgaria, Russia, New Zealand, Canada, Philippines, Japan, Estonia, Latvia, and Slovakia.

8. See *Svenska folket om globalisering* (The Swedish population on globalization), TEMO investigation no. T-21950, 26 June, 2001; see http://www.temo.se. Several questions were asked in addition to the one on WTO. One of these was on child labor: Of the generally free-trade-oriented group of Swedish respondents, no less than 74 percent agreed with the statement that Sweden should not trade with countries allowing child labor.

From these polls, it does not seem possible to reject the hypotheses that when governments and international institutions advocate and promote openness, they reflect the views of the majority of populations of the OECD countries and distinctly poor countries of the world.

2.4   Can Non-Governmental Organizations (NGOs) Fill a Gap in Representation and Accountability?

Suppose that the above conclusions—based on some polls and the revealed record of decades of policy making in democracies—were wrong. Still the question remains as to whether or not NGOs' preferences could be said to be less wrong. To quote a view presented in Woods and Narlikar (2001, 15), is it true that "NGOs acting in international fora are necessary to fill the gap in representation and accountability"? Are the preferences of NGOs focusing on trade and development more representative and more correct as a starting point for decisions on globalization and trade rules than current polls and the revealed positions of the democracies of the world?

First of all, there are many hundreds of NGOs; they do not think alike, and their internal systems of representation and accountability differ. Second, most NGOs have their origin in developed countries and are likely to reflect knowledge of and concerns about development felt in their home countries. These values and priorities need not be same as those of the poor countries, of course: "A long standing concern about these NGOs is that their activities further magnify the voice and influence of industrial countries' peoples and governments in international debates and institutions which already disproportionately represent the industrialised world" (Woods and Narlikar 2001, 15). Of the 738 NGOs accredited to the 1999 WTO-meeting in Seattle, 87 percent were based in industrialized countries (UNDP 2002, 8). The largest Swedish NGO—Forum Syd (Forum South)—is an umbrella organization for all Swedish-development NGOs and it is financed entirely by the Swedish state through its aid agency Swedish International Development Authority (SIDA). The interest of rich countries in poor countries' labor standards and environmental protection is often in those poor countries regarded as a particularly hypocritical form of protection against their exports.[9]

The NGOs are like multinational firms (MNF), trade unions, and farmers' organizations in the sense that they all have roles to play in domestic policy discussions. They can also be invited and included in country delegations since the composition of these is a national decision. An NGO or an individual from a developed country can quite legitimately be made a member of a poor country's team. However, a *formalized* role for NGOs,

---

9. See Bhagwati (1995) and (2002b).

MNFs, trade unions, farmers' organizations, and the like in the international debates, negotiations, and decision making of the WTO or IFIs raises serious questions about representation and accountability. What criteria should be applied when selecting MNFs and NGOs? To state that "such a selection [of NGOs] should be done in collaboration with civil society"—as suggested by Bellman and Gerster (1996, 40)—is not a starting point since it just raises the question of the operational content of the concept of "civil society." Furthermore, there are no guarantees against—but instead the very real risk—that a formal role for MNFs and NGOs would give some countries extra votes. Likewise, there are no guarantees against—but the opposite due to the logic of *realpolitik*—that some NGOs would be funded (and founded) by MNFs, farmers' organizations, trade unions, and other organized interest groups, and operate under the cover of a NGO label.

A typical NGO often starts with concerns for specific projects or issues. Perhaps it is for this reason that most NGOs have developed a microperspective of development. They can be involved in projects focusing on farming in some region; the plight of women, children and education; microcredits; environmental concerns; and so forth. These are all honorable causes, but—from the point of view of representation of views—the overall result is likely to be tilted in favor of distributional issues and "soft" policy stances. There are few, if any, NGOs devoted to "hard" issues, like the enhancement of better and more stringent rules for budget discipline, financial-sector reforms, the reform and abolition of bad banks, a unified exchange rate, a rent-free trade policy, or simply economic efficiency.

There are some particular aspects of the links between democracy, NGOs, and developing countries that merit consideration. First, if a (poor) country is on its way to democracy, it can be risky for an international institution to bypass the fragile democracy and its institutions and instead use an NGO as the institution's channel to the population, even if the NGO is run in an exemplary manner. There need not be a conflict between fragile democracy and an NGO, of course, but there is a clear procedural dilemma.

Second, poor countries have well-known difficulties with participation in the WTO. If well-funded NGOs, MFNs, and so forth are given formalized roles—like the right to be heard or speak in decision-shaping processes (as urged by Bellman and Gerster 1996)—that is very likely to result in a crowding out of poor countries' struggle for attention and influence in WTO. Today, well-funded and capable NGOs already can achieve what many poor countries cannot afford, that is a presence in Geneva and being continuously involved in WTO activities. If scarce resources, like time in the WTO machinery, are spent on presentations of the views of NGOs,

MNFs, and others, such a time allocation will almost certainly be at the expense of weaker parties, like poor countries' and their interests.[10]

A most surprising aspect of Bellman and Gerster (1996) is that they do not seem to recognize that their demand for significantly larger influence of NGOs in WTO would be at the expense of their other major request— a vastly expanded role for national parliaments. Neither do they seem to realize the separation of roles in a parliamentary democracy regarding decision preparation and decision making between the government (executive) and the parliament (their description of the role of parliaments in the formulation of countries' trade policy is not always correct).[11]

In conclusion, it is impossible to give a definite answer for all places and times on the value and a proper role of NGOs. Neither does it seem possible to deliver an answer to the question if NGOs can fill a gap when it exists and properly reflect the preferences of others, like the poor persons of a country. However, in the light of the above, it seems very unlikely that NGOs normally could fill a gap. The burden of proof rests heavily on the NGOs themselves.

2.5   International Institutions, Globalization, and Democracy.

Now the second criticism—the claim that decisions taken in international institutions like WTO and IFI are undemocratic—is considered. It is clearly correct that these decisions are imperfect reflections of the views of the peoples of the world. This is so in spite of a statement like the following from an otherwise excellent book on WTO: "Some would argue that . . . the WTO is probably the most democratic international organisation extant, in that it operates by consensus and, if voting occurs, it is on the basis of one-member-one-vote" (Hoekman and Kostecki 2001, 70).[12] For example, not all of WTO members are democracies (e.g., China and Saudi Arabia), and such member countries' representatives should not be as-

10. Bellman and Gerster (1996) argue for NGO participation in several ways in WTO: In the dispute settlement process (Article 13.2), they suggest that "NGO participation could possibly be enhanced if recourse to [NGO contributions] were to be made compulsory" (37). The WTO and NGOs (jointly?) should undertake systematic "impact assessment studies on development and the environment" (40, 62). In addition, NGOs should have observer status in WTO's Committee on Trade and Development (CTD) and on WTO's Committee on Trade and Environment (CTE). However, Bellman and Gerster (1996) do not suggest that there would be any NGO interest for a role in WTO's Committee on Budget, Finance, and Administration. This reinforces an impression of wanting to play with the angels only.

11. Bellman and Gerster (1996, 50) write, "Parliamentarians are authorized to participate only . . . as observers [in the WTO]." What other role could they possibly take on without replacing the government?

12. Also, the UNDP (2002, 8) takes the view that democracy in WTO would be one country, one vote: "Consider the World Trade Organization. Every member has one vote, which is very democratic."

sumed even to have the representation of the population as their ambition. Furthermore, why should Iceland and India—with 350,000 and nearly one billion inhabitants, respectively—have the same number of votes? If one were thinking about even some imperfect approximation of democracy, it would be reasonable for India to have more votes than Iceland. These remarks do not mean that the issue of representation of preferences in international institutions would be trivial or unimportant—quite the contrary; Demands for more democracy in intergovernmental organizations is more complex than many critics of WTO and the IFIs seem prepared to discuss. One cannot ignore the basic undemocratic feature, namely, that it is the nation-state that has a right to membership of WTO and IFIs.

One would have thought that demands for global democracy, a global parliament, and a world government would be the logical visionary alternative suggested by the critics of today's intergovernmental organizations (e.g., one along the lines suggested by the world federalist movements). But just the opposite seems to be the rule: The anti-globalists seem more local than global in their visions when it comes to political decision making ("glocalism").

Thus, issues on international trade and globalization will likely continue to be handled by governments in intergovernmental organizations and by diplomats and other civil servants. Then, negotiations and decisions are prepared and taken in processes that are not always open and—to be effective—many times cannot be open except with a time lag.[13] This is a classic problem of democratic accountability in foreign and security policy, and it is not specific to WTO and IFIs. The problem is handled in slightly different ways in different democracies, and generally speaking, through parliamentary committees with special rights to secret information, to closed sessions, and to the possibility of being consulted and deciding on negotiating positions. However, compared to a normal parliamentary control of governments' domestic actions, the control of what goes on in international organizations is often weak and indirect and is dominated by the participating governments' agendas and selection of information. Furthermore, it is only in the subset of democratic member states of WTO and IFI that parliamentary control can be exercised.

Moreover, the parliamentary perspective is typically a national one. The economist's interest in the global-welfare effects of trade reform, systemic aspects of the global trading system, and problems of regionalism attract few votes and have few pressure groups working for them. This, of course, just makes economists' contributions on these matters relatively more important.

---

13. The time lag normally can be anything between two hours or a few weeks, and only rarely would it be necessary to last for years.

2.6   Globalization, Democracy, and Poverty Reduction

The democratic deficit that is part and parcel of the intergovernmental form of decision making makes the WTO and IFIs natural targets for many anti-globalists.[14] However, the fact that the WTO and the IFIs are not actually *being run in a democratic way* does not exclude the possibility that they would *advocate democracy* as the preferred mode of government of nations. However, the IFIs are not seen to argue in favor of democracy. Should the IFIs be neutral on the issue? This section looks into the issue both in the light of the anti-globalist critique and the UN's poverty-reduction objective.

It is likely that the anti-globalists' criticism that owners and staff of the IFIs promote globalization from an undemocratic platform would lose ground if the IFIs would argue openly for democracy in member states, but avoiding such criticism cannot be the aim of the IFIs. There is a much more substantive issue, namely whether democracy is instrumental in achieving the IFIs' stated overriding objective (i.e., poverty reduction) in addition to being a desirable objective per se.

Second, the IMF and the World Bank support the UN's Millennium Development Goals. These are, by the year 2015, "to have reduced by half the proportion of people living on less than a dollar a day, and to have reduced by half the proportion of people who suffer from hunger," while improving health, education, and the environment (see the UN website at http://www.un.org/milleniumgoals/index.htlm).

2.6.1   Governance, Poverty, and Democracy

Individuals have preferences not only over outcomes, but also over processes. Thus, measures taken to enhance openness and globalization that have been decided upon through a democratic process are more legitimate and should have a better chance of long-term survival than if the same decisions were arrived at in some other way (e.g., through a dictator's decision, occupation of territory, or external pressures). This is described by the IFIs as the importance to apply "participatory approaches" and for governments to "own" domestic reforms and policies. A democratic process is—among other things—a participatory approach. *Ceteris paribus*, democracy thus seems desirable for the IFIs from a governance point of view.

Of course, the World Bank has for many years been working on so-called governance issues, but the Bank has not seen it proper to argue openly and clearly in favor of democracy.

---

14. After the ISTI conference, the UNDP (2002) published its development report. It contains much material on governance, poverty, and democracy. The UNDP—like the UN, WTO, and the IFIs—is not a democratic organization, of course.

The World Bank has identified three distinct aspects of governance: (i) the form of political regime; (ii) the process by which authority is exercised in the management of a country's economic and social resources for development; and (iii) the capacity of governments to design, formulate, and implement policies and discharge functions. *The first aspect is deemed outside the Bank's mandate.* (World Bank 1994, xiv, our italics)

The Bank at times seems very close to endorsing democracy with a governance motivation, although it never calls for a democratic process or democracy: "It is all about equal opportunity and empowerment for people, especially the poor," as stated by director James Wolfenson (World Bank 2002, iii). The Bank can go to great lengths not to use the word democracy when it describes desirable governance policies.

Exchanging information through open debate creates demand for institutional change by holding people accountable, by changing behaviour, and by supplying ideas for change from outside the community . . . Developing country actors often face too little competition, often because of current institutional structures." (World Bank 2002a, 4 and iv)

Democracy and desirable economic reforms are about power, of course.

The effectiveness of institutional designs adopted by governments will be affected by the political distribution of power. . . . Sometimes policymakers wishing to embark on reforms may have to create new institutions . . . ineffective institutions may exist in part because there are no interest groups pressing for change—not because some interest groups oppose change. (World Bank 2002a, 10)

Against this background of World Bank descriptions of desirable approaches to governance—to reach the objective of reducing poverty by half to 2015—there seems reason for the Bank and its owners to be clearly in favor of democracy from a governance point of view (if for no other reason).

It seems important to note, before leaving the governance argument, to point out that the above conclusion is not a claim that democracy itself necessarily fosters economic growth. There is a fairly large and inconclusive discussion of this different, but related, issue (e.g., Bhalla 1997; Przeworski and Limongi 1993, 1997; Stiglitz 1999) and a brief survey in the United Nations Development Program (UNDP; 2002, 56 box 2.4). Good arguments are put forward both for and against the suggestion that democracy is good for growth. However, in surveys, like UNDP (2002), the observation is made that "democracy appears to prevent the worst outcomes, even if it does not guarantee the best ones" (56).

2.6.2   Famines as Acute Poverty and Democracy

An important example in which democracy provides a channel for information and an early warning system is when there is a risk of famine. Sen and Drèze have focused on this acute form of poverty.

No substantial famine has ever occurred in any independent country with a democratic form of government and a relatively free press. Famines have occurred in ancient kingdoms and contemporary authoritarian societies, in tribal communities and in modern technocratic dictatorships, in colonial economies run by imperialists from the north and newly independent countries of the south run by despotic national leaders or by intolerant single parties. But they have never materialised in any country that is independent, that goes to elections regularly, that has opposition parties to voice criticisms, and that permits newspapers to report freely and question the wisdom of governments' policies without extensive censorship. (Sen 1999, 152)[15]

An interpretation of this result is that the effect of democracy is to reduce variance of economic performance: "One can argue that regimes affect the variance of rates [of economic growth], and specifically, that democracies are less likely to generate both miracles and disasters than dictatorships" (Przeworski and Limongi 1997, 166).[16] Against this background and since the IFIs have as their objective to reduce poverty by half by 2015, the IFIs should be in favor of democracy as an antifamine method, if for no other reason.

2.6.3 The "Democratic Peace" and Poverty Reduction

A second important claim for democracy is that there have been no wars between democracies (the democratic peace). The argument does not apply to wars between democracies and nondemocracies, it does not apply just to self-defense situations, and it does not apply to peace within democracies. The latter is important to note since a large part of today's violence occurs in conflicts within states. The huge discussion in the international relations literature on democratic peace has been summarized as follows.

Although some still argue that the hypothesised impact of democracy on peace is spurious, or that causality runs from peace to democracy rather than from democracy to peace [references], there is a growing consensus that the pacifying effects of joint democracy are real. While some say that it goes too far to claim that the absence of war between democracies 'comes as close as anything we have to an empirical law in international relations' (Levy 1980, 270), no one has identified a stronger empirical regularity, and many make the law-like claim that joint democracy is a sufficient condition for peace [references]. (Levy 2002, 358–59)[17]

15. Sen (1999) also refers to this point in chapters 2 and 6. See also Drèze and Sen (1989).
16. The infant mortality rate is a measure of basic hygiene and health conditions and thus has been used as a proxy measure of poverty. Bhalla (1997) arrived at the conclusion that the increased democracy of a country results in a faster decline in the infant mortality rate.
17. Other references on the democratic peace discussion are Brown, Lynn-Jones, and Miller (1996); Russett (1993); Cederman (2001); Russett and Oneal (2001); and Hegre et al. (2001).

The next question is *why* democracies do not wage war against each other. There are basically two lines of explanations. The first one is ideological and refers to a democratic ethos that is being developed—tolerance, moderation, basic inclination to seek peaceful conflict resolution, and so forth. The other one is structural. A democratic structure implies that there is power sharing, public accountability, and so forth, and this makes it difficult for leaders to convince citizens to go to war. However, for the present purpose, there is no need to have an answer to the debate on the causality.[18] It is enough to conclude that it has a significant value if countries are democracies since it prevents wars against other democracies and reduces poverty that would otherwise have been a consequence of such conflicts. For example, had Africa's nations become democracies after independence, some of the violence on the continent would not have occurred, and poverty and other disasters would have been less widespread. However, the numerous and bloody civil wars (e.g., in Angola, Rwanda, and Burundi) would not necessarily have been prevented—but, on the other hand, it may be that the drawn-out and disastrous civil war in Angola would have been a brief and limited conflict had South Africa, Soviet Union, and Cuba been democracies at the time. There are probably more examples of this kind.[19]

To summarize, starting from the objective of the UN and the World Bank to reduce poverty, which is endorsed by the Bank's owners, there are at least three arguments for the Bank to state that democracy is the preferred mode of government, that is to say, governance, elimination of famines, and reduction in war. This does not mean that the Bank's membership would be limited to democracies only or that only democratic member countries would be allowed to borrow or receive technical assistance from the Bank. However, it would imply that the Bank—to enhance its own poverty-reduction objective—should be crystal clear on the issue that the Bank prefers democracy to other modes of government. A link between democracy and poverty reduction implies also that the Bank should support projects with the objective of enhancing democracy, like fostering and supporting independent media, technical assistance on the practicalities of democracy in the legal system, and so forth.

By analogy, the IMF could consider the same policy on democracy as the preferred form of government.

18. For a recent survey, see chapter 18 of the *Handbook of International Relations,* as quoted by Levy (2002).

19. There seems to be a parallel to the democratic peace, that is, democratic trade liberalisation: Democratic pairs of countries tend to be more likely to cooperate to lower trade barriers and to sign trade-liberalizing agreements than are autocratic ones (Mansfield, Milner, and Rosendorff 1997, 1998).

2.6.4   Openness and Democracy

We now return to the globalization theme. Taking democracy to be the preferred mode of government, and *if* openness—as a suggestion—would enhance democracy, then increased openness would be desirable as an instrument for enhanced democracy and (in the next step) reduced poverty.

What can be said about the relationship between economic openness and democracy?

Is there causality from democracy to openness or vice versa? Milner and Kubota (2001) ask the question of whether or not democracy is conducive to trade liberalization. They find empirical evidence that democracy, in general, and democratization have contributed to the lowering of trade barriers in a number of developing countries since the 1970s (i.e., they find a causality from democracy to increased openness). The model that they test defines democratization as an expansion of the group of actors involved in government.

> Democratisation means a movement toward majority rule with universal suffrage . . . [and] the democratisation of the political system may open up new avenues of support for free trade . . . *and reduce the ability of governments to use trade barriers [and rents] as a strategy for building political support.* . . . Political leaders may have to compensate more voting consumers for the same level of protection [i.e. with the same amount of total rent], and may no longer be able to afford as much protection [rent per supporter]. . . . Hence an increase in the size of the electorate and thus the winning coalition may change political leaders' optimal policy in the direction of freer trade, ceteris paribus. (Milner and Kubota 2001; 6, 19, and 10–11)

Using data for over 100 developing countries in the period 1970–1999, the authors then provide empirical evidence for the hypothesis that more democratic countries have lower trade barriers and are more open economies. However, as the authors themselves acknowledge, they regard democratization as exogenous. "It might be that having a more open trade regime exerts an impact on the type of political regime. Although we lag all our independent variables [in the testing] this could be a longer term effect" (Milner and Kubota 2001, 41).

Two estimates undertaken in this chapter suggest that openness and democracy go together. I do not claim to establish a direction of causality. Since the early 1970s, Freedom House (FH) has evaluated almost all countries' status with regard to political rights and civil liberties in its annual surveys[20] and has constructed a democracy index with a scale running

---

20. The methodology, criteria, and so forth that have been developed over the years can be found on http://www.freedomhouse.org.

from 1 to 8. The lower the number, the more democratic the country. In the 2000–2001 survey, the traditional developed countries, as well as many other countries, take on values below 2.[21] To measure countries' openness, two proxies were used: The first one was countries' simple mean tariff (from World Bank 2002b, table 6.6). The hypothesis is that there would be a correlation between the level of the simple mean tariff at the end of the 1990s (mostly either in 1998 or 1999) and the value of the 2000–2001 democracy index. A standard (Pearson) correlation coefficient yields r^2 = 0.44 for the tariff variable (significant at the 99.9 percent level; n = 91). The hypothesis that openness—measured as a lower mean tariff—is positively correlated with democracy cannot be rejected.

As a second proxy for openness was used for the relative *change* between 1989 and 1999 in trade as share of GNP, that is, $(X + M)$/GNP, measured in purchasing power parity (PPP) terms and calculated from *World Development Indicators 2001*, table 6.1 (World Bank 2002b). The hypothesis is that there is a negative correlation between a change in share of trade in GNP and the value of the democracy index (remember, the more democracy, the lower the index value). Again, a correlation calculation yields r^2 = –0.19, and a significant correlation at just about the 90 percent level between our measure of change in openness and the FH measure of democracy (n = 75). Again, the hypothesis that openness and democracy are positively correlated cannot be rejected.

Finally, one should note one of the poll results of table 2.3 (statement 5). Respondents were asked about the perceived effect of globalization on different aspects of life. Globalization was regarded as much more positive than negative for human rights, individual freedom, and democracy.[22]

In summary, it may be that the character of political regimes has a direct effect on trade policy, and, at the very least, it seems very plausible that openness and democracy go together. If so, it has important implications for the present conflict over the value of globalization. If the causality goes from openness to democracy, and if anti-globalists' demand for less openness and reduced world economic integration was satisfied, it would mean reduced prospects for democratic development. Accepting the positive effect of democracy on governance, famine prevention, and peace, less

21. Examples are Argentina, Belize, Bolivia, Cape Verde, Costa Rica, Mauritius, Panama, South Africa, Surinam, Taiwan, and Uruguay. Most Caribbean countries and also Benin, Botswana, Bulgaria, the Dominican Republic, Ghana, Guyana, India, Jamaica, South Korea, Madagascar, Mali, Mexico, Mongolia, Namibia, Papua New Guinea, the Philippines, and Thailand are found just above the value 2. The least democratic ones take on numbers at the other end of the scale, like Algeria, Angola, Belarus and most other Commonwealth of Independent States countries, Bahrain, Brunei, Burma, Cameroon, China, Cuba, Egypt, Iran, Kenya, North Korea, Libya, Pakistan, Qatar, Saudi Arabia, Sudan, Swaziland, Syria, Tunisia, Uganda, the United Arab Emirates, Vietnam, and Zimbabwe.

22. An aggregate view of the meaning of the other economic variables of table 2.2 is hard to formulate since they seem rather contradictory.

Table 2.3   **The Perceived Relationship between Globalization and Fifteen Variable Conditions for Twenty-Five Countries, October–December 2001 (%)**

	Response		
Statement	Worse	Better	Difference
1. Access to foreign markets	22	66	44
2. Availability of inexpensive products	25	63	38
3. Your family's quality of life	23	60	37
4. Natural cultural life	28	60	32
5. Human rights, individual freedom, and democracy	28	57	29
6. National economy	33	56	23
7. Your income and buying power	27	54	27
8. Economic development in poor countries	36	51	15
9. Quality of jobs in country	39	48	9
10. World peace and stability	38	47	9
11. Workers' rights, working conditions, and wages	40	47	7
12. Economic equality in the world	40	45	5
13. Number of jobs in country	46	42	−4
14. World poverty and homelessness	45	41	−4
15. Environmental quality in the world	47	41	−6

Source: Data from World Economic Forum "Global Public Opinion on Globalization," conducted by Environics International Ltd. in collaboration with the World Economic Forum, February 2002

openness would be negative for poverty reduction over and above the traditional arguments in favor of division of labor through international trade.

If, on the other hand, the causality goes from democracy to openness (e.g., in the developing countries, as suggested by Milner and Kubota 2001), the anti-globalists would have two channels for their argumentation: First, to argue directly against international trade and investment or, second, to argue against the spread and enhancement of democratic rule in poor countries. Alternatively put, the Milner-Kubota result points to a choice that would have to be made with regard to developing countries between either (a) more democracy and more openness or (b) less democracy and less pressure for openness.

2.7   The World Trade Organization (WTO) and Accountability

Anti-globalists criticize the WTO for working without proper democratic accountability and being dominated by a few countries, leaving the others outside. Member governments have handled this criticism by improving transparency, public observation, and openness to the press.[23]

Focusing on the European perspective, the EU Commissioner for Ex-

23. See Sampson (2001).

ternal Trade, Pascal Lamy, in 2001 provided four suggestions to democratize the WTO. First, Lamy suggested more transparency "at home" in member countries; second, "a closer involvement of Parliaments in WTO matters, both in capitals and in Geneva"; and third, "a substantial reinforcement of the rights of the European Parliament [EP] in the formulation and control of trade policy" (Lamy 2001). Finally, Lamy thought that "there is merit in discussing the establishment of a WTO Parliamentary Consultative Assembly" (Lamy 2001). While there seems to be little reason to oppose the first or second proposals (see the following discussion), there are important argument against the last one.[24]

A Parliamentary Consultative Assembly of the WTO would cause constitutional confusion. First, the WTO was set up in the mid-1990s as an intergovernmental organization in which governments and the EU, through its commission, are represented. In such a system, there is no decision-shaping or decision-making role for a parliamentary body. The body would risk being a pseudodemocratic side scene. If so, first, the end result could be just the opposite one to the proclaimed one, that is to say, to discredit the WTO. Second, all delegates would not be elected (directly or indirectly) through a democratic procedure (China and Saudi Arabia, again, are clear examples). Third, "at home" in the WTO's democratic member states, a consultative assembly would cause constitutional confusion about the roles of the executive and legislative branches in the area of external trade policy.

Democratically elected parliamentarians and free media are two of the most important democratic control mechanisms. Considering Lamy's second suggestion, it may well be an advantage for the WTO and for the debate in member states if a larger number of democratically accountable persons learned more about the world trading system—what the WTO can and *cannot* do, since enhanced globalization and WTO-related issues have become increasingly domestic and more important in domestic politics. With regard to parliamentarians, two to three members of a country's parliament, for example, could be attached to the task of following WTO matters more closely. They could do this at home through hearings and investigations in parliamentary committees, as well as through regular *observer* participation in, for example, WTO seminars on specific issues, key countries and country groups, and systemic aspects of world trade. To achieve this enhancement of accountability, there is no need for any new international agreements or bodies, but instead for national decisions by national parliaments to become more active in this area. (Some countries already have such arrangements.)

24. The convention on the future constitution of the European Union suggested 2003 that the EP would have a bigger role in the EU's external trade policy. If implemented, the result is likely to be reduced effectiveness on the part of the EU in international trade negotiations.

2.8   Concluding Remarks: The Globalization Paradox

Globalization in the sense used in this paper, opens up *increased possibilities* for citizens as well as governments through an enhanced global division of labor. Potentially, all citizens can enjoy the fruits of increased specialization, for example, in the form of higher incomes and a larger menu of goods and services to choose from. Governments can exploit a larger tax base and provide more public goods and services as well as transfers. Globalization is also likely to enhance democracy. However, globalization at the same time *reduces governments' room for maneuvering* because of a more intensive international competition and international rules, like those of WTO. This is a paradox of globalization. Unfortunately the global antiglobalist movement seems unable to see anything but the latter part of this paradox, in spite of being a typical product of the globalization age.

References

Bellman, C., and R. Gerster. 1996. Accountability in the World Trade Organization. *Journal of World Trade* (December): 31–74.

Bhagwati, J. 1995. Trade liberalisation and "fair trade" demands: Addressing the environmental and labour standards issues. *The World Economy* 18 (November).

———. 2002a. Coping with anti-globalisation. *Foreign Affairs* 81 (1).

———. 2002b. *Free trade today*. New Delhi: Oxford University Press.

———. 2002c. *In defense of globalisation: It has a human face but we can do better*, forthcoming.

Bhalla, S. 1997. Freedom and economic growth. In *Democracy's victory and crisis*, ed. A. Hadenius. Cambridge: Cambridge University Press.

Brown, M., S. Lynn-Jones, and S. Miller, eds. 1996. *Debating the democratic peace*. Cambridge, Mass.: MIT Press.

Cederman, L-E. 2001. Back to Kant: Reinterpreting the democratic peace as a macrohistorical learning process. *American Political Science Review* 95 (1).

Drèze, J., and A. K. Sen. 1989. *Hunger and public action*. Oxford: Clarendon Paperbacks.

Gurr, K., and G. T. Jaggers. 1995. Tracking democracy's third wave with the polity III data. *Journal of Peace Research* 32 (4):

Hegre, H., T. Ellingsen, S. Gates, and N. P. Gleditsch. 2001. Towards a democratic civil peace? *American Political Science Review* 95 (1): 33–48.

Hoekman, B., and M. Kostecki. 2001. *The political economy of the world trading system. The WTO and beyond.* 2d ed. Oxford: Oxford University Press.

Lamy, P. 2001. Global policy without democracy. Speech presented to the European Union Commission. 26 November, Berlin.

Levy, J. 2002. War and peace. In *Handbook of international relation*, ed. W. Carlsnaes, T. Rissne, and Beth A. Simmons. London: SAGE Publications.

Mansfield, E., H. Milner, and B. P. Rosendorff. 1997. Free to trade: Democracies and international trade negotiations. Paper presented at the Annual Meeting of the American Political Science Association, September, Washington D.C.

Mayda, A. M., and D. Rodrik. 2001. Why are some people (and countries) more protectionist than others? NBER Working Paper no. 8461. Cambridge, Mass.: National Bureau of Economic Research, September.

Milner, H., and K. Kubota. 2001. Why the rush to free trade? Democracy and trade policy in the developing countries. Paper presented at the Annual Meeting of the American Political Science Association, 30 August–2 September, San Francisco.

O'Rourke, K., and R. Sinnott. 2001. The determinants of individual trade policy preferences: International survey evidence. Paper presented at the *Brookings Trade Policy Forum*, 10–11 May, Washington, D.C.

Przeworski, A., and F. Limonge. 1993. Political regimes and economic growth. *Journal of Economic Perspectives* 7 (3): 51–69.

———. 1997. Democracy and development. In *Democracy's victory and crisis*, ed. A. Hadenius. Cambridge: Cambridge University Press.

Russett, B. 1993. *Grasping the democratic peace: Principles for a post-cold war world*. Princeton: Princeton University Press.

Russett, B., and J. Oneal. 2001. *Triangulating peace. Democracy, independence and international organizations*. New York: Norton.

Sampson, G. 2001. *The role of the World Trade Organization in global governance*. New York: United Nations University Press.

Scheve, K. F., and M. J. Slaughter. 2001. *Globalization and the perceptions of American workers*. Washington, D.C.: Institute for International Economics.

Sen, A. K. 1999. *Development as freedom*. Oxford: Oxford University Press.

Stiglitz, J. 1999. Participation and development: Perspectives from the comprehensive development paradigm. Paper presented at the World Bank International Conference on Democracy, Market Economy and Development. 27 February, Seoul, Korea.

United Nations Development Program (UNDP). 2002. *Human development report 2002. Deepening democracy in a fragmented world*. Oxford: Oxford University Press.

Woods, N., and A. Narlikar. 2001. *Governance and the limit of accountability: The WTO, the IMF and the World Bank. International Social Science Journal* 170 (November).

World Bank. 1994. *Governance. The World Bank's experience*. Washington, D.C.: World Bank.

———. 2002a. *World development report 2002: Building institutions for markets*. Washington D.C.: World Bank.

———. 2002b. *World development indicators 2001*. Washington, D.C.: World Bank.

Comment   Kimberly Ann Elliott

The survey of anti- or alternative globalization activists by myself, Debayani Kar, and J. David Richardson (in this volume) finds that critics are as concerned about the legitimacy of the process by which globalization is occurring as they are about the outcome. But process and outcomes are also linked in their minds. Many critics believe that the globalization out-

Kimberly Ann Elliott is a fellow at the Institute for International Economics.

comes they perceive as being unbalanced and unsustainable, both ecologically and socially, result from a negotiation and rule-making process that is also unbalanced and undemocratic.

Carl Hamilton's interesting paper approaches these issues from a variety of angles. He examines survey results to ask whether pro-globalization policies are at odds with public opinion and finds that, in most countries, it does not appear that they are. He then asks whether it is plausible that fifty years of post–World War II liberalization could be fundamentally at odds with voter preferences in democratic countries and, again, concludes that it is not. Hamilton also argues that NGOs do not necessarily make existing institutional arrangements any more representative or accountable and that including them more formally in the process could squeeze out the voices of developing countries with, sometimes, more limited resources and influence. Hamilton concludes that governments do pretty well at representing the interests of their citizens and that existing intergovernmental institutions should remain just that. He does, however, recommend that the international financial institutions embrace democratic governance more explicitly in their work—for both legitimacy and pro-development reasons—and that the WTO consider engaging parliamentarians from member countries more intensively, through observer status and education programs, and encouraging these representatives to learn about and follow WTO activities more closely.

While the call for the IFIs to embrace democracy would clearly be welcomed by globalization's critics, Hamilton's other responses to their concerns are unlikely to sway many. Breaking the analysis down along slightly different lines, however—on the nature of democratic process and the changing nature of the globalization—could help to move the dialogue further along. This comment will focus on three distinctions that could help:

- transparency and accountability as core elements of democracy, which highlights the distinction between having a voice but not necessarily a vote;
- changes in the negotiating agenda, from lowering border barriers to writing rules to govern globalization that potentially conflict with national laws and regulations; and,
- the need to recognize important nuances in the polling data that suggest broad support for globalization is contingent on complementary policies to address the costs.

The Meaning of Democracy

The ultimate measure of effective democracy is a government that is accountable to its citizens. Transparency is a key tool in ensuring democratic accountability. Voting is a means of allowing citizens to express their preferences, but that alone does not deliver democratic governance if corruption, media repression, or other illiberal institutions impede transparency, give certain groups or individuals in a society preferential access, and prevent officials' being held accountable for their actions. This suggests that democratic legitimacy could be improved by increasing transparency, as both the IFIs and the WTO have done in recent years, and by ensuring that all relevant constituencies, and not just privileged ones, have access to the process. This does not mean that NGOs or other representatives of civil society need to have a vote or a veto, but allowing them more access in the form of voice could result in outcomes that are more acceptable and more sustainable.

How this might be done would differ from institution to institution . . . more meaningful consultation with affected populations in World Bank projects? *amicus curae* briefs in WTO dispute settlement? less extensive, detailed IMF conditionality?

Finally, there is another large hole in the argument that governments adequately represent their citizens and that intergovernmental institutions should remain as such. As the WTO membership has expanded, more nondemocratic countries have joined, most notably China, and as developing countries have become more active in negotiations and in decision making, questions about the legitimacy of outcomes have grown. The consensus rule of decision making in the WTO ameliorates this concern to some degree (thanks to Robert Baldwin for pointing this out), but the greater the weight of large and undemocratic regimes in the WTO (China, Egypt, Malaysia, Burma, potentially Vietnam) the more the concern will grow.

Process and the Changing Agenda

Negotiation and ratification rules appropriate for bargaining over border barriers may be less appropriate for writing rules that constrain national and local policy autonomy in areas previously regarded as primarily domestic—food health and safety, services regulation, and professional certification and licensing.

Although there were always import-competing industries that opposed liberalization that threatened their interests, there is a broad consensus that eliminating tariffs, quotas, and other explicit discrimination between foreign and domestically produced goods and services improves national and global welfare. There is no such consensus regarding the appropriate level of regulation for health and safety or other public purposes; and as the WTO has moved from removing de jure discrimination to de facto discrimination, which requires judging the legitimacy of the regulations themselves (e.g., with respect to genetically modified organisms or the use of hormones or antibiotics in meat production), the conflicts have sharply increased.

In these areas, single-undertaking and fast-track (in the United States) rules, which were efficient and effective in promoting trade liberalization and preventing log-rolling in tariff bargaining—may be neither.

Examining the Polling Data More Carefully

General questions about people's attitudes toward globalization do not tell us much. More detailed surveys, such as those conducted or summarized by the Program on International Policy Attitudes (PIPA), show that most people are not opposed to trade per se but that they are concerned about the conditions under which liberalization takes place. While similarly detailed surveys are not (yet) available for other parts of the world, extensive analysis of poll questions on trade by Slaughter and Scheve find that U.S. voters are split right down the middle. They recognize the benefits of trade, in terms of lower costs and greater variety, but they are concerned about the costs and they tend to weigh the costs more heavily than the benefits.

If the costs are addressed, however, (e.g., by providing training or other adjustment assistance to those dislocated by trade), support for further liberalization increases markedly. Respect for minimum labor standards is also widely supported. In sum, most people are supportive of globalization, as long as their other concerns are also addressed. Knowing more about what those concerns are requires international economic institutions to be more open and more willing to listen—and respond—to constituencies beyond the business community and narrowly focused central bankers, finance ministers, and trade negotiators.

II

Trade Flows and Their Consequences

Geography and Export Performance: External Market Access and Internal Supply Capacity

Stephen Redding and Anthony J. Venables

3.1 Introduction

There have been wide variations in countries' export performance over the last quarter century. East Asian countries have seen real exports increase by more than 800 percent since the early 1970s, while those of sub-Saharan African have increased by just 70 percent. Across individual countries, real export growth varies from over 1,000 percent for the top five countries to minus 40 percent or worse for the bottom five. This divergent performance has raised concerns that although some countries are benefiting from globalization, others are, at best, passed by. It has also stimulated a huge debate about what lies behind the differences. Are certain countries excluded from major markets by virtue of their geography, their commodity specialization, or discriminatory trade policies? Is export performance beyond the control of governments, or are poorly performing countries largely responsible for their own fates with weak performance reflecting poor institutions and policies?

This paper investigates some of the determinants of divergent export performance, looking in particular at the roles of external and internal geography. This issue is not only of interest in itself, but, insofar as export

Stephen Redding is a senior lecturer in economics at the London School of Economics. Anthony J. Venables is the Yu Kuo-Hwa Professor of International Economics at the London School of Economics.

This paper is produced as part of the globalization program of the U.K. Economic and Social Research Council (ESRC)-funded Centre for Economic Performance at the London School of Economics (LSE). Redding gratefully acknowledges financial support from a Philip Leverhulme prize. We are grateful to Robert Baldwin, Alan Winters and seminar participants at the National Bureau of Economic Research (NBER)-Center for Economic Policy and Research (CEPR) International Seminar in International Trade (ISIT) and the LSE for helpful comments. Martin Stewart provided able research assistance.

growth is thought to influence economic performance more generally, it is also of wider interest in identifying policy priorities nationally and internationally.[1] Whether or not globalization creates opportunities for all or whether or not some countries benefit more than others is clearly of paramount importance in shaping attitudes to globalization and the political economy of future rounds of international trade negotiations.

Geography may be expected to influence export performance in a number of ways. One way is through external geography—a country's location, in particular its proximity to rapidly growing export markets, and the consequent extent to which it is a recipient of international-demand linkages. For example, countries in Southeast Asia have been at the center of a fast growing region, which creates growing import demand. Given everything we know about the importance of distance as a barrier to trade, the export opportunities created by these growing import demands are likely to be geographically concentrated, creating spillover effects between countries in the region. Our first objective in this paper is to measure the strength of these effects. This we do by developing a theoretical model of bilateral trade flows and using gravity techniques to estimate the model's parameters. Each country's export growth can then be decomposed into two parts. One is based on the country's location relative to sources of import demands, which we call the country's foreign-market access. The other is due to changes within the country, which we call internal-supply capacity.

We find that a substantial part of the differential export growth of various countries and regions since 1970 can be attributed to variations in the rate at which their foreign-market access has grown. Changes in countries' foreign-market access arise because of changes in aggregate import demand from other countries—particularly countries that are close. There may also be particular regional effects arising, for example, from regional integration agreements. We capture these by refining our modeling to allow the intensity of intraregional trade to differ from trade as a whole. These effects are positive for Western Europe and negative for sub-Saharan Africa. They also exhibit significant changes through time, with increasing intraregional intensities in North America and in Latin America.

Having separated out the foreign-market access and internal-supply capacity contributions to export growth, our next objective is to investigate the determinants of each country's internal-supply capacity. We develop a simple theoretical structure to show how this depends on countries' internal geography (such as access to ports), on measures of their business environment (such as institutional quality), and also—in equilibrium—on their foreign-market access. The theoretical structure provides the basis for

1. There is, of course, an extensive debate on the relationship between trade and growth. See, for example, Sachs and Warner (1995) and Frankel and Romer (1999) for the positive case, and Rodriguez and Rodrik (2000) and Rodrik, Subramanian, and Trebbi (2002) for the case in which domestic institutions and policy are more important.

econometric estimation of countries' export performance as a function of these variables, and we find that all three characteristics are significant and quantitatively important. We use our results to explore the performance of different regions, and show how almost all of sub-Saharan Africa's poor export performance can be accounted for by poor performance in each of these dimensions.

The paper is organized as follows. The next section outlines a theoretical framework, and section 3.3 constructs the measures of foreign-market access and internal-supply capacity. The contribution of these measures to regions' export performance is reported, so too are interregional linkages, giving the contribution of each region to the foreign-market-access growth of every other region. Section 3.4 extends the analysis to a more detailed investigation of intraregional trade, showing how the intensity of this trade has changed through time. Section 3.5 endogenises each country's supply capacity. A simple theoretical framework is developed and provides the motivation for the export equation that we econometrically estimate to establish the effects of foreign-market access, internal geography, and institutions.

3.2   Theoretical Framework

A key feature of theoretical models of international trade in the presence of product differentiation and trade costs is the existence of a pecuniary-demand effect across countries. An increase in expenditure on traded goods in one country raises demand for traded goods in other countries, and, because of trade costs, the size of this effect is much greater for neighboring countries than for distant countries. How much of countries' differential export performances can be accounted for by variation in these demand conditions, and how much by differences in internal supply-side characteristics? Our main task in this paper is to separate these different forces and thereby identify the foreign-market access and internal-supply capacity of each country.

Performing this decomposition requires use of bilateral trade information in a gravity model. Gravity models offer an explanation of countries' trade flows in terms of exporter and importer country characteristics and between-country information, particularly distance. The gravity model is consistent with alternative theoretical underpinnings (see, e.g., Anderson 1979; Deardorff 1998; Eaton and Kortum 2002), and here we start by developing one of them—namely, a trade model based on product differentiation derived from a constant elasticity of substitution (CES) demand structure (see, e.g., Fujita, Krugman, and Venables 1999).

The world consists of $i = 1, \ldots, R$ countries whose tradeable-goods sectors produce a range of symmetric differentiated products. For the moment, we take the range of products produced in each country and their prices as exogenous; section 3.5 deals with general equilibrium. Demand for differentiated products is modeled in the usual, symmetric, constant elasticity of substitution way; σ is the elasticity of substitution between any pair of products, implying a CES utility function of the form,

$$(1) \qquad U_j = \left[\sum_i^R n_i x_{ij}^{(\sigma-1)/\sigma} \right]^{\sigma/(\sigma-1)}, \quad \sigma > 1,$$

where n_i is the set of varieties produced in country i; x_{ij} is the country j consumption of a single product variety from this set, and all such varieties are symmetric.

Dual to this quantity aggregator is a price index in each country, G_j, defined over the prices of individual varieties produced in i and sold in j, p_{ij},

$$(2) \qquad G_j = \left(\sum_i^R n_i p_{ij}^{1-\sigma} \right)^{1/(1-\sigma)},$$

where we have again exploited the symmetry of products.

Given country j's total expenditure on differentiated products, E_j, its demand for each variety is (by Shephard's lemma on the price index)

$$(3) \qquad x_{ij} = p_{ij}^{-\sigma} E_j G_j^{(\sigma-1)}.$$

Thus, the own-price elasticity of demand is σ, and the term $E_j G_j^{(\sigma-1)}$ gives the position of the demand curve in market j.

We assume that all country i varieties have the same producer price, p_i, and that the cost of delivery to market j gives price $p_{ij} = p_i t_i T_{ij} t_j$. Trade costs thus take the iceberg form, and t_i and t_j are the ad valorem cost factors in getting the product to and from the border in countries i and j, while T_{ij} is the cost of shipping the product between countries. Thus, t_i and t_j capture internal geography, and T_{ij} the external geography of trade flows.

The value of total exports of country i to country j is therefore

$$(4) \qquad n_i p_i x_{ij} = n_i p_i^{1-\sigma} (t_i T_{ij} t_j)^{1-\sigma} E_j G_j^{\sigma-1}.$$

This equation for bilateral trade flows provides a basis for estimation of a gravity trade model. The right-hand side of this equation contains both importer and exporter country characteristics. The term $E_j(G_j/t_j)^{\sigma-1}$ is the market capacity of country j; it depends on total expenditure in j, on internal transport costs t_j, and on the number of competing varieties and their prices (summarized in the price index). On the supply side, the term $n_i(p_i t_i)^{1-\sigma}$ measures what we refer to as the supply capacity of the exporting country; it is the product of the number of varieties and their price competitiveness, such that doubling supply capacity (given market capacities) doubles the value of sales.[2] We will denote market capacity and supply capacity by m_i and s_i respectively, so

---

2. For further discussion of the concepts of market and supply capacity and the related concepts of market and supplier access introduced later, see Redding and Venables (2003).

(5) $$m_i \equiv E_i(G_i/t_i)^{\sigma-1}, \quad s_i \equiv n_i(p_i t_i)^{1-\sigma}.$$

From equation (4), bilateral trade flows can be expressed simply as the product of exporter supply capacity, importer market capacity, and the term $(T_{ij})^{1-\sigma}$, which measures bilateral transport costs between them

(6) $$n_i p_i x_{ij} = s_i(T_{ij})^{1-\sigma} m_j.$$

Empirically, supply capacity will capture all observed and unobserved characteristics of an exporting country i that affect its bilateral trade with all importers. Similarly, market capacity will capture all observed and unobserved characteristics of an importing country j that affect its bilateral trade with all exporters.

We are concerned with each country's overall export performance, that is, the value of its exports to all destinations, denoted V_i. This can be decomposed between supply capacity and foreign-market access by noting that,

(7) $$V_i = n_i p_i \sum_{j \neq i} x_{ij} = s_i \sum_{j \neq i} (T_{ij})^{1-\sigma} m_j = s_i M_i,$$

where M_i is the foreign-market access of country i,

(8) $$M_i \equiv \sum_{j \neq i} (T_{ij})^{1-\sigma} m_j.$$

This is simply the sum of the market capacities of all other countries j, weighted by the measure of bilateral trade costs of reaching each country.

Analogous to foreign-market access is the concept of foreign-supplier access, S_i, defined as the sum of the supply capacity of all other countries, weighted by the measure of bilateral trade costs in obtaining goods from each individual supplier j.

(9) $$S_i = \sum_{j \neq i} (T_{ij})^{1-\sigma} s_j$$

This measures proximity to sources of export supply, and the total value of imports of country i, Z_i, is the product of its market capacity and foreign-supplier access.

(10) $$Z_i = m_i S_i$$

Given observed values of total exports and imports, V_i and Z_i, and values of bilateral trade costs, $(T_{ij})^{1-\sigma}$, for R countries, equations (7) through (10) comprise a system of $4R$ equations in $4R$ unknowns (m_i, s_i, M_i, and S_i for all i). Solving these gives the required decomposition.[3] In particular, we can find each country's supply capacity, s_i, and foreign-market access, M_i,

---

3. Beginning from initial values for m_i, s_i, M_i, and S_i, we repeatedly solve the system formed by equations (7) through (8) for all R countries. Irrespective of initial conditions, the system rapidly converges to unique equilibrium values of m_i, s_i, M_i, and S_i.

giving the decomposition of exports that we seek, $V_i = s_i M_i$. However, doing this requires that we have values of bilateral trade costs, $(T_{ij})^{1-\sigma}$, as well as exports and imports, and it is to this matter that we now turn.

3.3 Sources of Export Growth: Decomposition

3.3.1 Data Sources and Gravity Estimation

Estimates of bilateral trade costs are derived from gravity estimation. We use data on the value of bilateral trade flows for 101 countries during the period 1970–1997, obtained from the NBER World Trade Database (Feenstra, Lipsey, and Bowen 1997; Feenstra 2001). Since we are concerned with the growth in the real value of countries' exports, the current dollar data in the NBER World Trade Database are deflated by the U.S. gross domestic product (GDP) deflator to obtain a measure of real trade flows. A country's market and supplier access depend on its trade with all other countries, and these trade data have the advantage of being available for a large cross section of countries. It is likely that there are substantial year-to-year fluctuations in bilateral trade flows—particularly for small countries—and we are concerned here with the determinants of long-run real export growth. Therefore, in the empirical analysis that follows, bilateral trade flows are averaged over four-year periods. With twenty-eight years of data, this yields seven periods of analysis. See the appendix for further details.

To obtain measures of bilateral trade costs, we estimate the gravity equation (6), which implies a relationship between bilateral trade, supplier capacity, and market capacity. The equation is estimated using bilateral distance and a dummy for whether or not countries share a common border. Supplier capacity and market capacity are controlled for respectively using an exporter-country and importer-partner dummy.[4] The estimation results are summarized in table 3.1, and we take the predicted values for bilateral trade costs from this equation as our measures of trade costs: Thus, $(\hat{T}_{ij})^{1-\sigma}$ = $\text{dist}_{ij}^{\hat{\theta}} \cdot \exp(\hat{\gamma}\text{bord}_{ij})$, where dist_{ij} is the distance between a pair of countries i and j, and bord_{ij} is a dummy variable that takes the value of 1 if the two countries share a common border.

3.3.2 Export Growth Decompositions

We are now in a position to decompose each country's total exports into the contributions of supplier capacity and foreign-market access. The mea-

---

4. This specification is more general than the standard gravity model in which country and partner dummies are replaced by income and other country characteristics. In particular, the importer-partner dummies capture variation in the manufacturing price index G that is a determinant of market capacity m, and this specification thus controls for what Anderson and van Wincoop (2003) term "multilateral resistance." For a recent survey of alternative approaches to estimating the gravity equation, see Feenstra (2002).

Table 3.1   **Bilateral Trade Equation Estimation (country and partner dummies)**

ln(X_{ij})	(1)	(2)	(3)	(4)	(5)	(6)	(7)
N	9,981	9,981	9,981	9,981	9,981	9,981	9,981
Period (years)	1970–73	1974–77	1978–81	1982–85	1986–90	1990–94	1994–97
ln(dist$_{ij}$)	–0.831	–0.866	–0.882	–0.883	–0.853	–0.866	–0.866
	(0.072)	(0.062)	(0.059)	(0.061)	(0.05)	(0.05)	(0.046)
bord$_{ij}$	0.532	0.494	0.483	0.449	0.528	0.607	0.688
	(0.179)	(0.157)	(0.154)	(0.16)	(0.146)	(0.151)	(0.152)
Country dummies	yes	yes	yes	yes	yes	yes	yes
Partner dummies	yes	yes	yes	yes	yes	yes	yes
Estimation	WLS	WLS	WLS	WLS	WLS	WLS	WLS
F(·)	96.56	106.83	124.23	128.43	172	198.71	212.87
Prob > F	0.000	0.000	0.000	0.000	0.000	0.000	0.000
R^2	0.863	0.85	0.852	0.844	0.897	0.906	0.898
Root MSE	0.879	0.89	0.891	0.954	0.761	0.7	0.723

Notes: Huber-White heteroscedasticity robust standard errors in parentheses; ln(X_{ij}) is log bilateral exports from country i to partner j plus one; ln(dist$_{ij}$) is bilateral distance between countries i and j; and bord$_{ij}$ is a dummy for whether or not the two countries share a common border. All specifications include exporting-country and importing-partner fixed effects. Observations are weighted by the product of country and partner GDP. N = number of observations; Prob. = probability; F(·) = F-statistic; WLS = weighted least squares; MSE = mean square error.

sures of trade costs derived above are combined with data on countries' total imports and exports to solve the system of simultaneous equations (7) through (10) for all countries' market capacities, supply capacities, foreign-market access, and foreign-supplier access. This implies, of course, that the product of each country's supply capacity and foreign-market access exactly equals its actual exports (and analogously on the import side in equation [10]), permitting an exact decomposition of actual export volumes.

An alternative approach would be to use the estimates of the exporter-country and importer-partner dummies obtained from the gravity equation as measures of market capacity and supply capacity. This approach was used in another context by Redding and Venables (2003) but, for the present purposes, has the disadvantage that the decomposition of *total* exports into foreign-market access and supply capacity would not then be exact. In practice, we find a high degree of correlation between measures of foreign-market access and supplier capacity constructed from solving the system of equations for all countries' total imports and exports and those constructed based on estimates from bilateral trade flows.[5]

5. The correlation across countries and over time between the measure of foreign-market access constructed from solving the system of equations for total exports and total imports and the measure based on estimated exporter and importer dummies from the gravity equation is 0.99. The corresponding correlations for market capacity and supplier capacity are 0.98.

The decomposition we undertake is extremely general. Although we derived $V_i = s_i M_i$ from a precise theoretical model, this decomposition holds for any theoretical model that yields a gravity equation of the form in equation (6), where bilateral trade is explained by exporting-country effects, importing-partner effects, and bilateral trade costs.

We begin by examining the evolution of foreign-market access and supply capacity. To provide a broad overview, we aggregate countries to nine geographical regions: Eastern Europe, Latin America, the Middle East and North Africa, North America, Oceania, Southeast Asia, Other Asia, sub-Saharan Africa, and Western Europe. Thus, $R(k)$ denotes the set of countries in region k, and the foreign-market access (FMA) of the region is simply the sum $M_{R(k)} \equiv \Sigma_{i \in R(k)} M_i$. Similarly, the supply capacity of the region is the sum of values for individual countries. The upper two panels of figures 3.1 and 3.2 display the evolution of regional FMA, while the lower two panels graph the time series of supply capacity. To control for regions having different numbers of countries, the figure graphs average values rather than totals. To clarify changes over time, we normalize supplier capacity so that it is expressed relative to its initial value.

At the beginning of the sample period, Eastern and Western Europe have the highest levels of FMA. The Eastern European position is not as surprising as it first seems because of its proximity to the countries of Western Europe. These regions are followed by North America. Looking at the upper right panel (and noting the vertical scale) the initial ranking then proceeds as Southeast Asia, Latin America, Other Asia, sub-Saharan Africa, and Oceania. The obvious features over time are the rapid growth of Southeast Asia and the acceleration of Other Asia in the second half of the sample period.

Turning now to export growth, the proportionate growth rates of supply capacity and FMA compound to the observed growth rate of exports.[6] Intuitively, the decomposition of export growth into these two components reveals the extent to which increases in a country's exports are due to improved own-country performance or external developments in trading partners. Appendix table 3A.1 reports the decomposition for each country, and table 3.2 of the text gives the regional aggregates. The first rows of table 3.2, the benchmark case, report the rate of growth of overall world exports in each period and the growth of supply capacity and market capacity that would be observed if all countries had identical export performance.

A number of results stand out. Southeast Asian countries experience export growth much faster than the benchmark in both periods. In the first period this was driven particularly by supply-capacity growth, and, in the

---

6. This is so because $V_i = s_i M_i$, $(1 + g_i^V) = (1 + g_i^s)(1 + g_i^M)$, where g is a proportional growth rate. When we aggregate to the regional level, this decomposition is no longer exact since $\Sigma_{i \in R(\ell)} V_i = \Sigma_{i \in R(\ell)} s_i M_i \neq \Sigma_{i \in R(\ell)} s_i \Sigma_{i \in R(\ell)} M_i$.

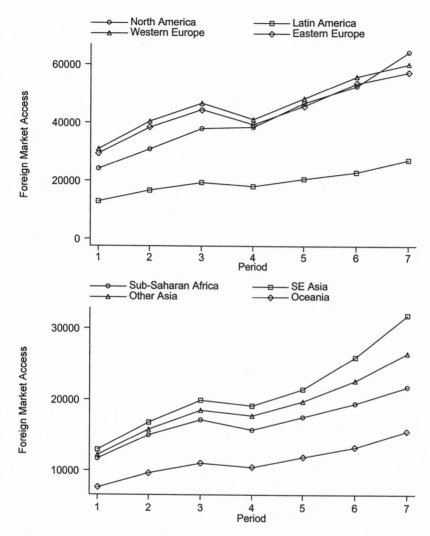

Fig. 3.1   Average regional FMA

second, FMA growth becomes relatively more important. Looking at individual countries in Southeast Asia (table 3A.1) shows that FMA growth was generally faster in the first period than in the second. For some of the earlier developers, supply-capacity growth slowed sharply in the second period (e.g., Japan, Taiwan, and Korea) while the later developers experienced a dramatic increase in second period supply-capacity growth (e.g., the Philippines, Thailand, and Vietnam).[7]

7. For a discussion of the commodity structure of East Asian export growth and its relationship to factor endowments and nonneutral technology differences, see Noland (1997).

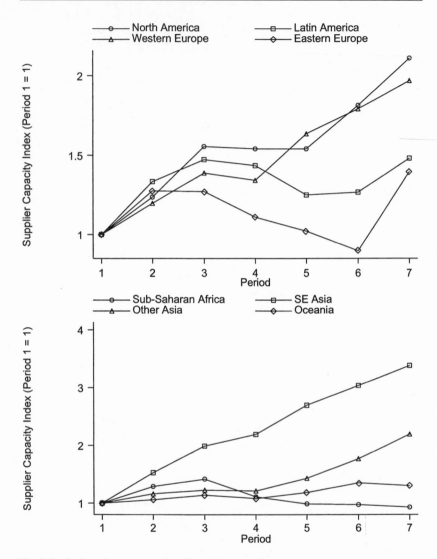

Fig. 3.2   Index of average regional supplier capacity

Other Asia experienced below-world-average export growth in the first period, but this is accounted for by significantly faster than benchmark market-access growth coupled with much slower than benchmark supply-capacity growth. This is in sharp contrast to the second period in which market-access growth close to the benchmark was associated with supply-capacity growth at twice the benchmark, giving overall export growth of nearly twice the world rate.

Latin America shows a different picture. Close to benchmark market-

Table 3.2   **Regional Sources of Export Growth, 1970/1973–1994/1997, Percentage Rates of Growth**

Region	Period (1)	Exports, V (2)	FMA, M (3)	Supplier Capacity, s (4)
Benchmark	Periods 1–7	326.3	106.5	106.5
	Periods 1–4	104.4	42.9	42.9
	Periods 4–7	108.5	44.5	44.5
North America	Periods 1–7	288.99	166.07	110.86
	Periods 1–4	92.74	59.42	54.00
	Periods 4–7	101.82	66.90	36.92
Latin America	Periods 1–7	193.32	110.82	48.11
	Periods 1–4	90.17	40.39	43.45
	Periods 4–7	54.24	50.17	3.25
Western Europe	Periods 1–7	269.37	94.29	96.82
	Periods 1–4	75.05	33.02	34.12
	Periods 4–7	111.01	46.06	46.75
Eastern Europe	Periods 1–7	187.43	94.84	39.62
	Periods 1–4	44.03	33.95	10.95
	Periods 4–7	99.56	45.45	25.84
Sub-Saharan Africa	Periods 1–7	70.38	86.44	−7.24
	Periods 1–4	54.18	34.71	10.80
	Periods 4–7	10.50	38.40	−16.28
North Africa and Middle East	Periods 1–7	189.77	102.82	41.20
	Periods 1–4	245.48	48.38	135.71
	Periods 4–7	−16.13	36.69	−40.10
Southeast Asia	Periods 1–7	826.17	146.35	238.04
	Periods 1–4	233.67	47.88	119.01
	Periods 4–7	177.57	66.59	54.35
Other Asia	Periods 1–7	371.95	117.80	119.31
	Periods 1–4	76.45	45.74	21.01
	Periods 4–7	167.48	49.44	81.23
Oceania	Periods 1–7	166.82	104.30	29.86
	Periods 1–4	48.35	37.34	7.89
	Periods 4–7	79.85	48.75	20.36

Notes: Periods 1–4 = 1970/1973–1982/1985; periods 4–7 = 1982/1985–1994/1997. Regional variables are the sum of those for countries within a region; see appendix for the countries included in each region. Columns (2) through (4) of the table are based on equation (7). Column (2) is the rate of growth of exports; column (3) is the rate of growth of FMA; and column (4) is the rate of growth of supplier capacity. The rates of growth of supplier capacity and FMA compound to the rate of growth of total exports. At the country level, this decomposition is exact. When we aggregate to regions, the decomposition is approximate since $\Sigma_{i \in R_k} V_i = \Sigma_{i \in R_k} s_i M_i \neq \Sigma_{i \in R_k} s_i \Sigma_{i \in R_k} M_i$.

access growth in both periods was associated with close to benchmark supply-capacity growth in the first period and weak growth in the second. Results for the Middle East and North Africa aggregate are dominated by oil exporters, and those for sub-Saharan Africa elaborate on a familiar story. Taking the two periods together, the contribution of FMA to sub-Saharan Africa's export growth was nearly 20 percentage points below the benchmark case, suggesting the importance of geographical location in explaining the region's poor export performance. However, supply capacity grew less fast than the benchmark in both periods, and positive export growth in the second period was achieved by market-access growth offsetting a reduction in supply capacity.

The main messages from this section are that both levels and rates of change of FMA vary widely across countries and regions. Foreign-market access levels in Western Europe are nearly three times those in sub-Saharan Africa. Thus, taking as given supplier capacity, FMA plays an important role in accounting for export performance. In general equilibrium, there will typically also be an endogenous response of supplier capacity to external conditions, and we consider this idea further in Section 3.5. Before doing so, we look in more detail at the regional structure of FMA growth.

3.3.3   Regional Effects

The decomposition of table 3.2 looks at each country's FMA growth, but does not divide the sources of this growth geographically. How much FMA growth do countries receive from the performance of other countries in their own region, and how much do they receive from growth in other regions? Out of these other regions, which ones are the more important?

A country's FMA can be divided according to geographical regions in which the markets are located and expressed as the sum of the access to markets in each region. Thus, if $M_i^{R(k)}$ is the market access derived by country i from region k, then

$$(11) \quad M_i^{R(k)} \equiv \sum_{j \in R(k)} (T_{ij})^{1-\sigma} m_j, \text{ and } M_i = M_i^{R(1)} + M_i^{R(2)} + \ldots + M_i^{R(K)}.$$

Changes in $M_i^{R(k)}$ can be computed for each country, and the final two columns of table 3A.1 report, for each country, the FMA growth contributions from a country's own region and from other regions as a whole.

We concentrate on results not for individual countries, but for their regional groupings. Thus, $M_{R(\ell)}^{R(k)}$ is the market access derived by all countries in region ℓ from region k, given by

$$(12) \quad M_{R(\ell)}^{R(k)} \equiv \sum_{i \in R(\ell)} M_i^{R(k)} \text{ and } M_{R(\ell)} = M_{R(\ell)}^{R(1)} + M_{R(\ell)}^{R(2)} + \ldots + M_{R(\ell)}^{R(K)}.$$

The change in the market access of region ℓ can be decomposed into the contribution of regions k according to

$$(13) \quad \frac{\Delta M_{R(\ell)}}{M_{R(\ell)}} = \left[\frac{M_{R(\ell)}^{R(1)}}{M_{R(\ell)}} \right] \left[\frac{\Delta M_{R(\ell)}^{R(1)}}{M_{R(\ell)}^{R(1)}} \right] + \ldots + \left[\frac{M_{R(\ell)}^{R(K)}}{M_{R(\ell)}} \right] \left[\frac{\Delta M_{R(\ell)}^{R(K)}}{M_{R(\ell)}^{R(K)}} \right],$$

where there are two components to the contribution of each region. Region R_k may make a large contribution to region R_ℓ's FMA growth either because it constitutes a large share of the region's FMA $[M_{R(\ell)}^{R(k)}/M_{R(\ell)}]$ or because there is rapid growth in market demand in the countries making up that region $[\Delta M^{R(k)}_{R(\ell)}/M^{R(k)}_{R(\ell)}]$.

Results are reported in table 3.3, panel A for the period as a whole, and in panels B and C for the two subperiods.[8] Reading across the first row of the tables we see that North America derived virtually all of its FMA growth from itself. This reflects the fact that Canada's FMA is large relative to that of the United States (FMA captures access to markets *other* than one's own), and the United States constitutes an extremely large share of Canada's FMA. Canada benefits much more from being located close to the United States than the United States benefits from being located close to Canada, and own-region FMA growth in Canada thus accounts for over 98 percent of total Canadian FMA growth.

Latin America was much more dependent on FMA growth from outside the region—almost entirely so in the first period. Of these extra-regional sources, North America is far and away the most important. Turning to Europe, Western Europe provides a major source of FMA growth both for itself and for Eastern Europe.

The striking features of sub-Saharan Africa are the negative contribution of the own-region effect and the lack of a dominant external source of FMA growth. Over the period as a whole, North America was the most important, followed by Western Europe, with the Middle East and North Africa playing a noticeable role in the first subperiod.

The Asian figures illustrate two main points. One is the dominant role of intraregional linkages within Southeast Asia, and the other is the growth in the importance of Southeast Asia for Other Asia. This arises partly from the growing import demands of Southeast Asia and partly also from the westwards expansion of economic activity in the Southeast Asia region. It is also interesting to look down the Southeast Asia column in table 3.3, panel A, indicating the contribution of this region to FMA growth in other regions; the region now provides a major potential source of demand for African exports.

3.4   Regional Trade Intensities

In the gravity model used so far, trade frictions between countries are measured simply by distance and whether or not the countries share a common border. In this section, we present a brief exploration of the importance of regional trading by allowing the costs of trading within a region to differ from those of trading between regions.

To allow trade costs to vary in this way, we augment the distance and

---

8. Note that this decomposition of FMA growth shares features with the literature concerned with a shift-share analysis of countries' export growth (see, e.g., Richardson 1971), although it uses our theoretically based measures.

Table 3.3   Percentage Growth Contributions of Partner Regions to the Growth of Foreign Market Access of Each Exporting Region

Exporter	FMA (all regions)	North America	Latin America	Western Europe	Eastern Europe	Sub-Saharan Africa	North Africa and the Middle East	Southeast Asia	Other Asia	Oceania
				A. Periods 1–7 (1970I/1973–1994I/1997)						
North America	166.07	141.42	3.22	9.53	0.29	−0.43	1.30	9.82	0.33	0.59
Latin America	110.82	59.11	19.32	13.99	0.42	−0.86	2.18	14.93	0.55	1.19
Western Europe	94.29	15.49	1.45	61.91	2.01	−0.53	2.90	10.15	0.50	0.41
Eastern Europe	94.84	14.38	1.44	60.67	2.99	−0.57	3.66	11.21	0.60	0.45
Sub-Saharan Africa	86.44	27.24	4.57	23.79	0.75	−2.44	6.00	23.84	1.36	1.34
North Africa and the Middle East	102.82	20.36	2.35	33.04	1.08	−1.08	23.91	20.67	1.65	0.83
Southeast Asia	146.35	19.10	2.18	13.04	0.46	−0.72	3.40	104.67	1.88	2.34
Other Asia	117.80	21.29	2.56	19.43	0.71	−1.02	7.67	58.39	7.10	1.67
Oceania	104.30	29.99	5.13	13.18	0.44	−1.02	3.22	46.60	1.26	5.49
				B. Periods 1–4 (1970I/1973–1982I/1985)						
North America	59.42	51.56	0.35	2.36	−0.11	−0.22	1.84	3.22	0.25	0.18
Latin America	40.39	27.89	1.42	3.17	−0.17	−0.48	3.07	4.72	0.41	0.36
Western Europe	33.02	7.42	0.01	18.07	−0.27	−0.17	4.20	3.24	0.40	0.12

Region	FMA	North America	Latin America	Western Europe	Eastern Europe	Sub-Saharan Africa	North Africa and Middle East	Southeast Asia	Other Asia	Oceania
Eastern Europe	33.95	6.81	-0.00	18.28	-0.35	-0.17	5.22	3.57	0.48	0.13
Sub-Saharan Africa	34.71	12.55	-0.06	6.20	-0.25	-1.03	8.58	7.23	1.08	0.41
North Africa and Middle East	48.38	9.50	-0.03	10.32	-0.24	-0.32	21.09	6.45	1.37	0.25
Southeast Asia	47.88	8.54	-0.12	2.88	-0.19	-0.49	4.82	30.18	1.39	0.86
Other Asia	45.74	9.62	-0.12	4.81	-0.25	-0.59	10.73	16.86	4.13	0.55
Oceania	37.34	13.10	-0.24	2.32	-0.22	-0.81	4.51	15.30	0.95	2.43

C. Periods 4–7 (1982/1985–1994/1997)

Region	FMA	North America	Latin America	Western Europe	Eastern Europe	Sub-Saharan Africa	North Africa and Middle East	Southeast Asia	Other Asia	Oceania
North America	66.90	56.37	1.81	4.50	0.25	-0.13	-0.34	4.14	0.05	0.26
Latin America	50.17	22.23	12.75	7.71	0.42	-0.27	-0.64	7.27	0.10	0.59
Western Europe	46.06	6.07	1.08	32.96	1.71	-0.27	-0.98	5.19	0.08	0.22
Eastern Europe	45.45	5.65	1.08	31.65	2.50	-0.30	-1.16	5.71	0.09	0.24
Sub-Saharan Africa	38.40	10.90	3.44	13.06	0.75	-1.05	-1.91	12.33	0.21	0.69
North Africa and Middle East	36.69	7.32	1.60	15.31	0.89	-0.51	1.91	9.59	0.19	0.39
Southeast Asia	66.59	7.14	1.56	6.87	0.43	-0.16	-0.96	50.37	0.33	1.00
Other Asia	49.44	8.01	1.84	10.03	0.66	-0.29	-2.10	28.50	2.04	0.77
Oceania	48.75	12.30	3.91	7.91	0.48	-0.15	-0.94	22.79	0.23	2.23

Notes: A region's FMA is the sum of the values of FMA for all countries within that region. Regional FMA growth is decomposed into the percentage contributions of each partner region using equations (12) and (13). The exporting region is reported in the rows of the table and the importing partner in the columns.

border effects with dummies for whether or not two countries lie within the same geographical region. Thus the measure of bilateral trade costs becomes $(T_{ij})^{1-\sigma} = \text{dist}_{ij}^{\hat{\theta}} \cdot \exp(\hat{\gamma}\text{bord}_{ij})\prod_k \exp(\hat{\phi}_k\text{region}_{kk})$, where $\hat{\phi}_k$ is the estimated coefficient on the dummy for whether or not countries i and j lie within region k. This specification allows for differences in trade costs on within-region transactions and between-region transactions in a general way that imposes minimal structure on the data. At the same time, we are able to analyze how the coefficient on the within-region trade dummy changes over time and relate these changes to explicit policy-based attempts at regional integration, including, for example, the North American Free Trade Agreement (NAFTA) and the European Union (EU).

The results of estimating the gravity equation including the within-region trade dummies are reported in table 3.4. As shown in the table, the within-region trade dummies are jointly statistically significant at the 10 percent level in all periods, and their level of joint statistical significance increases markedly over time. The dummies capture anything that affects the ease of trading within the region, and therefore it is not surprising that some of the estimated coefficients are negative, particularly at the beginning of the sample period. Sub-Saharan Africa is a case in point, where a recent literature has emphasized the importance of physical geography and infrastructure in explaining trade and development in Africa (see, e.g., Amjadi, Reincke, and Yeats 1996; Gallup, Sachs, and Mellinger 1998; Limao and Venables 2001). Africa has few east-west navigable rivers to facilitate water-borne trade within the continent, and there is much evidence of low levels of transport infrastructure investment that may have a particularly severe impact on within-region trade. International political conflict and patterns of specialization clearly also play a role. For example in the Middle East, within-region conflict and the importance of petroleum exports to industrialized countries outside the region generate a negative estimated within-region effect.

Over time, we observe a systematic increase in the estimated values of almost all the within-region effects. This provides evidence of the increasing regionalization of international trade that does not rely on a particular parameterization of the regional integration process. Nonetheless, one important explanation for increasing regionalization is clearly the proliferation of regional preferential trade agreements. This is particularly clear for North America. Here, at the beginning of the sample period, we find a negative within-region effect, which may reflect policies of import substitution in Mexico that particularly restricted within-region trade or the fact that the largest cities of Canada and United States (on which our measures of distance are based) are closer than the true economic centres (taking into account the whole distribution of economic activity). Nevertheless, over time, we observe a rise in the estimated within-region effect that is both

Table 3.4 Bilateral Trade Equation Estimation and Within-Region Trade Costs (country and partner dummies)

$\ln(X_{ij})$	Period						
	(1)	(2)	(3)	(4)	(5)	(6)	(7)
N	9,981	9,981	9,981	9,981	9,981	9,981	9,981
Period (years)	1970–73	1974–77	1978–81	1982–85	1986–89	1990–93	1994–97
$\ln(dist_{ij})$	−0.669	−0.69	−0.71	−0.779	−0.704	−0.688	−0.74
	(0.089)	(0.077)	(0.076)	(0.081)	(0.071)	(0.075)	(0.086)
$bord_{ij}$	0.778	0.659	0.578	0.526	0.488	0.416	0.401
	(0.145)	(0.124)	(0.119)	(0.12)	(0.112)	(0.113)	(0.118)
Within North America	−0.467	−0.277	−0.205	−0.333	−0.019	0.417	0.543
	(0.289)	(0.271)	(0.281)	(0.278)	(0.273)	(0.327)	(0.335)
Within Latin America	−0.531	−0.278	−0.168	−0.013	0.313	0.626	0.58
	(0.233)	(0.202)	(0.201)	(0.209)	(0.191)	(0.201)	(0.24)
Within Western Europe	0.565	0.642	0.732	0.657	0.811	0.876	0.802
	(0.161)	(0.14)	(0.135)	(0.142)	(0.13)	(0.142)	(0.172)
Within Eastern Europe	1.038	−0.274	3.424	4.139	4.014	2.409	1.817
	(1.452)	(1.75)	(0.305)	(0.28)	(0.261)	(0.212)	(0.256)
Within Sub-Saharan Africa	−3.913	−4.067	−4.849	−5.615	−5.2	−1.485	−1.334
	(0.586)	(0.609)	(0.609)	(0.525)	(0.449)	(0.316)	(0.322)
Within North Africa and Middle East	−2.972	−4.225	−4.903	−4.257	−4.073	−3.631	−3.381
	(0.658)	(0.595)	(0.704)	(0.664)	(0.683)	(0.804)	(0.853)
Within Southeast Asia	0.852	0.638	0.225	−0.174	−0.217	−0.232	−0.382
	(0.297)	(0.272)	(0.265)	(0.293)	(0.223)	(0.219)	(0.23)
Within Other Asia	−4.65	−0.715	−0.422	−0.574	−0.86	−0.356	−1.278
	(1.637)	(0.751)	(0.962)	(0.773)	(0.788)	(0.634)	(0.789)
Within Oceania	0.929	1.09	1.214	0.965	1.177	1.483	1.591
	(0.525)	(0.429)	(0.431)	(0.339)	(0.289)	(0.29)	(0.39)
Country dummies	yes	yes	yes	yes	yes	yes	yes
Partner dummies	yes	yes	yes	yes	yes	yes	yes
Estimation	WLS	WLS	WLS	WLS	WLS	WLS	WLS
Prob. > F(dummies)	0.077	0.011	0.005	0.004	0.000	0.000	0.000
Prob. > $F(\cdot)$	0.000	0.000	0.000	0.000	0.000	0.000	0.000
R^2	0.868	0.856	0.859	0.853	0.903	0.912	0.904
Root MSE	0.864	0.873	0.869	0.933	0.736	0.677	0.701

Notes: Huber-White Heteroscedasticity robust standard errors in parentheses; $\ln(X_{ij})$ is log bilateral exports from country i to partner j plus one; $\ln(dist_{ij})$ is log bilateral distance between countries i and j; and $bord_{ij}$ is a dummy for whether or not the two countries share a common border. All specifications include exporting-country and importing-partner fixed effects. Within North America is a dummy that takes the value of 1 if *both* trade partners lie within North America and zero otherwise. The other within-region dummies are defined analogously. Prob > F(dummies) is the p-value for a F-test of the null hypothesis that the coefficients on the regional dummies are jointly equal to zero. Prob > $F(\cdot)$ is the p-value for a F-test of the null hypothesis that all coefficients are jointly equal to zero. Since the within-region dummies exploit bilateral information, they are separately identified from the country and partner fixed effects. Observations are weighted by the product of country and partner GDP. To capture the effects of NAFTA, Mexico is included in the definition of North America. N = number of observations; Prob. = probability; $F(\cdot)$ = F-statistic; WLS = weighted least squares; MSE = mean square error.

large and statistically significant. Thus, the estimated coefficient becomes positive in the period 1990–1993 during which NAFTA was signed.

The exception is Southeast Asia where the intraregional effect diminishes sharply through time. This does not reflect diminishing intraregional trade, but rather the particularly rapid growth of trade with countries outside the region. Thus, it shows the extent to which the region's trade was becoming more externally rather than internally oriented over the period.

Other examples of the importance of trade policy in shaping regional integration include Western and Eastern Europe. In Western Europe, we again observe a systematic rise in the estimated within-region effect over time. In Eastern Europe, the value of the within-region effect follows an inverted U-shape, rising between the 1970s and 1980s consistent with the policies of the Council for Mutual Economic Cooperation (COMECON) in stimulating trade within the former Soviet bloc and declining markedly in the 1990s following the fall of the Berlin Wall and the abandonment of the COMECON system of public procurement and trading preferences.

3.5   Determinants of Export Performance

We have so far undertaken decompositions based on the identity that a country's exports are the product of its supply capacity, s_i, and FMA, M_i. We now turn to the next stage of the analysis—asking what determines supply capacity? We expect that it depends on a number of underlying country characteristics including country size, endowments, and internal geography. It will also depend, in equilibrium, on FMA, since this is one of the variables that determines the potential return to exporting. Our objective in this section is to econometrically estimate the importance of these factors. We contribute to a growing literature on the role of geography in determining the ratio of trade to income and trade performance more generally (see, e.g., Ciccone and Alcalá 2001; Frankel and Romer 1999; Leamer 1988; Radelet and Sachs 1998; Wei 2000).

3.5.1   Theory

In order to endogenize supply capacity, we have to add to the material of section 3.2 some general equilibrium structure of the economy. We do this in a very compact way by simply specifying a supply curve for exports, implying that as the quantity of exports produced in a country increases, so does their price. Using our previous analysis, the quantity of exports demanded from country i, $n_i x_i = n_i \sum_{j \neq i} x_{ij}$, is given by

$$(14) \qquad n_i x_i = \frac{s_i M_i}{p_i} = n_i (p_i)^{-\sigma} (t_i)^{1-\sigma} M_i$$

(using equations [4] and [8]). The supply relationship we specify by the function Ω is

(15) $$n_i x_i = a_i \Omega(p_i/c_i), \quad \Omega' > 0.$$

We assume that the function Ω is the same for all countries, but add country-specific parameters c_i and a_i to the relationship; c_i is a measure of comparative costs in the export sector of country i, and a_i is a measure of the size of the economy. This is a general equilibrium relationship capturing the opportunity cost of resources used in the export sector. Expanding the volume of exports produced moves the economy around the production-possibility frontier, increasing the price of exports. Thus, as the export sector expands, it draws resources out of other sectors of the economy—the import-competing and nontradeable-activities sectors. Drawing resources out of other sectors tends to bid up their prices, raising costs and hence price in the export sector.

Cross-country variation is captured by linearization of these relationships. Logarithmically differentiating equations (14) and (15) gives

(16) $$\hat{x} = -\sigma\hat{p} + (1 - \sigma)\hat{\iota} + \hat{M},$$

$$\hat{n} + \hat{x} = \hat{a} + \omega(\hat{p} - \hat{c}),$$

where ω is the price elasticity of export supply and $\wedge$ denotes a proportional deviation from some reference point. Eliminating the price term gives

(17) $$\hat{x}(\omega + \sigma) + \sigma\hat{n} = \omega[\hat{M} - \sigma\hat{c} + (1 - \sigma)\hat{\iota}] + \sigma\hat{a}.$$

The total value of exports, $V_i = n_i p_i x_i = s_i M_i$ (equation [7]), varies according to

(18) $$\hat{V} = \hat{n} + \hat{p} + \hat{x} = \hat{a} - \hat{c}\omega + [M + (1 - \sigma)\hat{\iota} - \hat{x}]\frac{(1 + \omega)}{\sigma},$$

where the second equation uses equation (16). One further step is needed, which is to specify whether export volumes vary through changes in the number of varieties, n, or through output per variety, x. In a standard monopolistic-competition model equilibrium, output per commodity is a constant, $\hat{x} = 0$; in which case, equation (18) is

(19) $$\hat{V} = \hat{a} - \hat{c}\omega + [\hat{M} + (1 - \sigma)\hat{\iota}]\frac{(1 + \omega)}{\sigma}.$$

At the other extreme, if the number of varieties that can be produced by a country is fixed, $\hat{n} = 0$, then using equations (17) in (18) gives

(20) $$\hat{V} = \frac{\{(\sigma - 1)(\hat{a} - \hat{c}\omega) + [\hat{M} + (1 - \sigma)\hat{\iota}](1 + \omega)\}}{(\sigma + \omega)}.$$

These equations form the basis of the econometric investigation, with variation in terms provided by cross-country observations. Notice that the coefficient on FMA in these equations is not generally equal to unity, reflecting the endogeneity of supply capacity. Thus if σ is large relative to ω

(or, in the second equation if $\sigma > 1$), then the coefficient on $\hat{M}$ is less than unity. High levels of FMA are associated with a less than proportional increase in exports and a lower level of supply capacity (since $V_i = s_i M_i$). This arises because increased demand for exports encounters diminishing returns in the domestic-supply response, bidding up p_i. The coefficient on $\hat{M}$ is smaller for low values of ω, this measuring a more tightly curved production-possibility frontier and lower supply elasticity.

Other terms in the equations are as would be expected. Cross-country variation in internal geography is captured by $\hat{t}$, entering with negative coefficient providing $\sigma > 1$. Domestic size, $\hat{a}$, increases the value of exports, although not necessarily proportionately. And a high-cost export sector, $\hat{c} > 0$, means that a lower volume of exports is supplied for a given price.

3.5.2   Estimation

Motivated by the theoretical analysis of the previous section (equations [19] and [20]), we estimate the following empirical specification.

$$(21) \qquad \ln(V_i) = \beta_0 + \beta_1 \ln(\text{GDP}_i) + \beta_2 \ln(\text{Pop}n_i) + \beta_3 \ln(M_i)$$
$$+ \beta_4 \ln(t_i) + \beta_5 c_i + \mu_k + \varepsilon_i$$

The dependent variable is the log of the value of exports. The log of GDP and of population are included as two separate measures of country size, and M_i is FMA as calculated in section 3.3; t_i represents the internal geography of the country and is measured empirically using the percentage of the population living within 100 kilometers of the coast or navigable rivers (see appendix for sources).

To capture the comparative costs of exporting in each country, c_i, we use a measure of institutional quality, as has been widely used in the cross-country growth literature (see, e.g., Acemoglu, Johnson, and Robinson 2001; Hall and Jones 1999; Knack and Keefer 1997). The measure is an index of the protection of property rights and risk of expropriation (see appendix), and a higher value of the index corresponds to better institutional quality.

We also include a full set of dummies for the nine geographical regions, μ_k, in order to control for unobserved heterogeneity across regions in the determinants of export performance, including other unobserved institutions, features of technology, and characteristics of regions.

Before presenting estimates of equation (21), a number of points merit discussion. First, the measure of FMA (M) included on the right-hand side as a determinant of countries' export performance has itself been constructed from the export data. It is constructed from the solution of a system of simultaneous equations for all countries' total exports and total imports, and any individual country's exports enter this system of simultaneous equations as just one out of the $2R$ observations on exports and imports. A country's FMA depends on market capacities in all *other* countries, weighted by bilateral trade costs (equation [8]). Nevertheless, to ensure that shocks to an individual country's exports are not driving our measure of FMA, we also construct for each country an alternative measure that completely excludes information on the country's own exports. In this alternative measure, M^*, we exclude one country i at a time and solve the system of equations in equations (7) to (10) for the $R-1$ other countries $j \neq i$ (excluding information on country i's exports to and imports from these other countries). This yields measures of market capacity and supplier capacity in all other countries $j \neq i$. The alternative FMA measure for country i is then constructed as the trade-cost-weighted sum of these market capacities. We repeat the analysis for all countries $i \in R$. This alternative measure provides a robustness check, and the measure turns out to be very highly correlated with the FMA measure of section 3.3.

Second, the income term, GDP_i, may itself be endogenous. We consider two approaches to this problem. First, we impose a theoretical restriction that $\beta_1 = 1$ and take as the dependent variable the export-income ratio, V_i/GDP_i. In this specification, we focus on the ability of the explanatory variables to explain variation in the share of exports in GDP. Second, we use lagged values of GDP_i for the independent variable. We estimate equation (21) using the cross-sectional variation in the data and focus on the final time period 1994–1997. Here, the corresponding lagged income variable is 1990–1993.

Third, our primary interest in this section is not consistently estimating the structural parameters of equation (21). Rather, our main concern is conditioning on the right-hand side variables and examining how much of the cross-country variation in export performance can be statistically explained by these considerations and how much remains unexplained in the regional dummies.

Estimation results are reported in table 3.5. The first column gives our base specification, using the lagged GDP variable. As expected, the coefficient on GDP is positive and highly significant, although also significantly less than unity, reflecting the fact that large economies are less open than smaller ones. This suggests that working with the ratio of exports to GDP as dependent variable would be inappropriate. The other size measure, population, is insignificant.

We find a positive and statistically significant effect of both external and internal geography in determining exports. The coefficient on $\ln(M)$ is significantly less than unity, indicating that an increase in FMA increases exports less than proportionately. This is in line with the preceding theoretical discussion as the expansion in exports raises costs and prices in the sector, thereby reducing supply capacity. This finding is also consistent with earlier work (Redding and Venables 2003; Overman, Redding, and Venables 2003), which shows that a higher level of FMA is associated with

Table 3.5   The Role of Internal Geography, External Geography, and Institutions in Determining Export Performance, 1994–1997

	(1)	(2)	(3)	(4)
Dependent variable	$\ln(V)$	$\ln(V/\text{GDP})$	$\ln(V)$	$\ln(V/\text{GDP})$
Period (years)	1994–97	1994–97	1994–97	1994–97
No. of observations	95	95	95	95
$\ln[\text{GDP}(1991–93)]$	0.734		0.730	
	(0.052)		(0.051)	
$\ln(\text{population})$	−0.038	−0.262	−0.025	−0.256
	(0.057)	(0.043)	(0.057)	(0.043)
$\ln(M)$	0.46	0.479	0.342	0.298
	(0.195)	(0.205)	(0.119)	(0.127)
Population within				
100km coast and	0.581	0.416	0.596	0.441
rivers (%)	(0.191)	(0.061)	(0.187)	(0.199)
Institutional quality	0.202	0.023	0.198	0.016
	(0.062)	(0.387)	(0.061)	(0.061)
Region effects	yes	yes	yes	yes
Estimation	OLS	OLS	OLS	OLS
	$F(13,81) = 137.600$	$F(12,82) = 7.732$	$F(13,81) = 142.200$	$F(12,82) = 7.747$
Prob $> F$	0.000	0.000	0.000	0.000
R^2	0.957	0.531	0.958	0.531

Notes: Standard errors in parentheses. Columns (1) and (2), FMA is as computed in section 3.3. Columns (3) and (4), FMA is computed omitting own country, M^*.

higher wages. The coefficient on the proportion of population within 100 kilometers of the coast or a navigable river is also significant and positive, capturing internal geography. Similar results are obtained if the proportion of population is replaced by the proportion of land area. The measure of institutional quality (risk of expropriation) has a positive and statistically significant effect on export performance, consistent with an important role for the protection of property rights in determining countries ability to export.

The second column of table 3.5 gives results for the specification with the export ratio taken as the independent variable. Coefficients on $\ln(M)$ and on internal geography are similar to those in the first column. However, the population term becomes negative and significant, and the coefficient on institutional quality becomes smaller and insignificant. The fact that smaller economies tend to export less is being captured by the negative coefficient on population and perhaps also by a positive correlation between institutional quality (now with a smaller coefficient) and per capita income.

Columns (3) and (4) repeat the exercise with the alternative measure of FMA discussed above, M^*. Signs and significance levels are unchanged using this alternative variable. The size of the coefficient on $\ln(M^*)$ is somewhat smaller than that on $\ln(M)$, although the difference is not statistically significant at conventional critical values.

3.5.3 Effects by Region

We use these econometric estimates to shed light on patterns of export performance across the nine geographical regions. To what extent are the divergent performances of these regions explained by this model, and which of the independent variables are more important in explaining the variation in performance across regions?

The expected value of exports by region k relative to the expected value for the world, $E_{i \in R(k)} \ln(V_i) - E_i \ln(V_i)$, can be expressed as a linear function of regional deviations in independent variables multiplied by their estimated coefficients. Formally, regression equation (21) implies that

(22) $\quad E_{i \in R(k)} \ln(V_i) - E_i \ln(V_i) = \alpha_k(a) + \alpha_k(M) + \alpha_k(t) + \alpha_k(c) + \mu_k,$

where μ_k is the regional dummy of equation (21), and remaining terms are the regional contributions of the independent variables.

(23) $\quad\quad\quad \alpha_k(a) \;\; = \beta_1[E_{i \in R(k)} \ln(\mathrm{GDP}_i) - E_i \ln(\mathrm{GDP}_i)]$

$$+ \beta_2[E_{i \in R(k)} \ln(\mathrm{Pop}n_i) - E_i \ln(\mathrm{Pop}n_i)],$$

$$\alpha_k(M) = \beta_3[E_{i \in R(k)} \ln(M_i) - E_i \ln(M_i)],$$

$$\alpha_k(t) \;\; = \beta_4[E_{i \in R(k)} \ln(t_i) - E_i \ln(t_i)],$$

$$\alpha_k(c) \;\; = \beta_5[E_{i \in R(k)} c_i - E_i c_i].$$

Thus, $\alpha_k(M) \equiv \beta_3[E_{i \in R(k)} \ln(M_i) - E_i \ln(M_i)]$ is region k's FMA, relative to that of the world, multiplied by the estimated coefficient on FMA. Terms $\alpha_k(t)$ and $\alpha_k(c)$ are the analogous measures for internal geography and institutions, while size effects are combined in $\alpha_k(a)$.

We illustrate results for each region in figure 3.3, where values are based on the estimates given in the first column of table 3.5. The first bar in each of the regional boxes, labeled $\alpha_k(V)$, is the region's export performance relative to the world average once size effects have been conditioned out, $\alpha_k(V) \equiv E_{i \in R(k)} \ln(V_i) - E_i \ln(V_i) - \alpha_k(a)$. Remaining bars sum to this first bar, since they divide $\alpha_k(V)$ into four components (see equation [22]). Bars two to four give the contributions of FMA (M), internal geography (t), and institutions (c), respectively. The residual, after controlling for these factors, is the regional dummy μ_k, illustrated as the final bar in each chart.

What do we learn from this decomposition? North America (including Mexico) has high trade relative to the world, given its income and population. This is explained partly by relatively good market access and partly by institutions. It is offset by relatively poor internal geography, leaving a

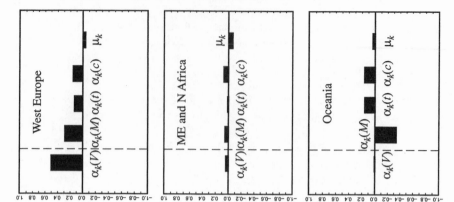

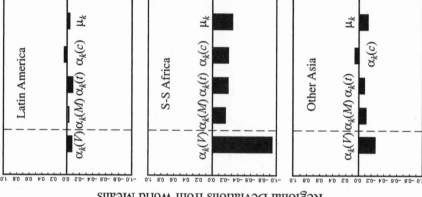

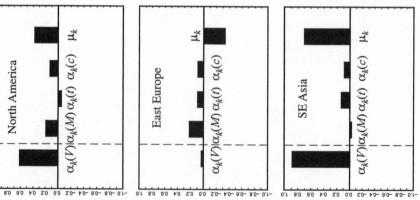

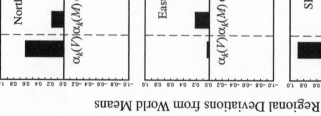

Fig. 3.3   Regional export performance, 1994–1997

Note: Contributions of foreign-market access $\alpha_k(M)$; internal geography $\alpha_k(t)$; institutions $\alpha_k(c)$; and residual μ_k.

substantial unexplained residual. Western Europe's high level of exports is accounted for by a combination of good market access, good internal geography, and good institutions, leaving virtually nothing to the residual dummy variable. For Eastern Europe, the benefits of good market access and better than average internal geography and institutions are not fully reflected in the actual level of trade, leaving a large negative regional dummy. This is consistent with the idea that the legacy of communism during the postwar period has had a long-lasting effect on Eastern Europe's exports, captured here in the regional dummy. The outcome for Oceania combines low market access with good internal geography and institutions.

Sub-Saharan African has low trade volumes given its income level, and these are accounted for by below average performance on all three measures together with some negative residual. Thus, each of $\alpha_k(M)$, $\alpha_k(t)$, $\alpha_k(c)$ and μ_k account for between 20 percent and 30 percent of sub-Saharan Africa's low level of trade after conditioning on country size, $\alpha_k(V)$. At the other extreme is the performance of Southeast Asia, with high trade levels only partly explained by good institutions and internal geography. There remains a large positive residual, in part due to the entrepôt activities of Hong Kong and Singapore and in part due to aspects of the Asian Miracle that are not captured by our approach.

3.6 Concluding Comments

The changes in countries' export performance over recent decades are symptomatic, at least, of the extent to which they have succeeded in benefiting from globalization. The real value of world exports doubled between the early 1970s and mid-1980s and doubled again from the mid-1980s to late 1990s. In the second of these periods, Latin American exports went up by just 54 percent, sub-Saharan Africa's went up by 10 percent, and those of the Middle East and North Africa fell by 16 percent.

This paper takes some steps towards understanding the determinants of cross-country variation in both the levels and growth of exports. There are several main findings. First, geography creates substantial cross-country variation in the ease of access to foreign markets, and this is an important determinant of countries' export performance. For example, once country size factors are controlled for, sub-Saharan Africa has poor export performance, about one-quarter of which is attributable to its poor foreign-market access. Furthermore, the growth of FMA varied widely across regions during the periods we studied. This accounted for some of the poor performance of regions, such as sub-Saharan Africa, not neighbored by countries with fast-growing import demand.

Second, export performance also depends on internal geography, which is measured in this paper by the proportion of the population close to the coast or navigable rivers. Looking at sub-Saharan Africa again, another one-quarter of its poor export performance is accounted for by this variable.

Finally, export performance also depends on many other domestic supply-side factors. This paper takes a small step towards analysis of these by looking at the role of institutional quality in determining exports. This, as it turns out, accounts for a further one-quarter of sub-Saharan Africa's low export levels. Perhaps the main contribution of this paper is to show how to measure and control for the external and internal geographic factors that shape performance. Our hope is that, once these are successfully controlled for, then research will be better able to identify domestic factors (some of them subject to policy control) that also determine export performance.

Appendix

Data

- Bilateral Trade: Data on bilateral trade flows are from the NBER World Trade database. Declared by U.S. GDP deflator
- GDP per capita: Data on current price (U.S.$), GDP, and on population are from the World Bank. Deflated by U.S. GDP deflator
- Geographical variables: Data on bilateral distance, existence of a common border (from the World Bank)
- Physical geography: Data on proportion of land and population close to coast or navigable rivers from Gallup, Sachs, and Mellinger (1998; the data can be downloaded from http://www.2.cid.harvard.edu/ciddata)
- Institutions: Expropriation risk from International Country Risk Guide database
- Regional groupings:
    North America—Canada, the United States, and Mexico
    Latin America and the Caribbean—Argentina, Bolivia, Brazil, Chile, Colombia, Costa Rica, Dominican Republic, Ecuador, El Salvador, Guatemala, Haiti, Honduras, Jamaica, Nicaragua, Panama, Peru, Trinidad and Tobago, Uruguay, and Venezuela
    Western Europe—Austria, Belgium (including Luxembourg), Denmark, Finland, France, Germany, Greece, Ireland, Italy, Netherlands, Norway, Portugal, Spain, Sweden, Switzerland, Turkey, and the United Kingdom
    Eastern Europe—Albania, Bulgaria, Czechoslovakia, Hungary, Poland, and Romania

Sub-Saharan Africa—Angola, Benin, Cameroon, Côte d'Ivoire, Cameroon, Ethiopia, Gabon, Ghana, Guinea, Kenya, Madagascar, Malawi, Mali, Mauritius, Mozambique, Morocco, Nigeria, Senegal, South Africa, Sudan, Tanzania, Uganda, Zaire, Zambia, and Zimbabwe

Middle East and North Africa—Algeria, Egypt, Iran, Israel, Jordan, Kuwait, Lebanon, Morocco, Oman, Saudi Arabia, Syria, Tunisia, and United Arab Emirates

Southeast Asia—Cambodia, China, Hong Kong, Indonesia, Japan, Korea, Malaysia, Papua New Guinea, Philippines, Singapore, Taiwan, and Thailand

Other Asia—Bangladesh, India, Sri Lanka, Nepal, and Pakistan

Oceania—Australia and New Zealand

Table 3A.1   **Country Sources of Export Growth and the Regional Concentration of Foreign-Market-Access Growth (%)**

Country	Period (1)	Supply Capacity (2)	FMA (3)	Exports (4)	Own Region FMA (5)	Other Region FMA (6)
	North America					
Canada	1970/73–1982/85	2.71	73.91	78.62	69.4	4.5
	1982/85–1994/97	2.46	70.61	74.81	65.3	5.3
Mexico	1970/73–1982/85	307.49	46.72	497.87	36.3	10.4
	1982/85–1994/97	56.81	65.22	159.09	48.8	16.4
The United States	1970/73–1982/85	52.56	20.65	84.06	3.3	17.3
	1982/85–1994/97	37.90	49.10	105.61	19.4	29.7
	Latin America					
Argentina	1970/73–1982/85	3.96	29.04	34.15	0.5	28.5
	1982/85–1994/97	41.04	63.79	131.01	30.3	33.5
Bolivia	1970/73–1982/85	13.40	29.65	47.02	−1.6	31.2
	1982/85–1994/97	−35.03	59.35	3.53	24.8	34.6
Brazil	1970/73–1982/85	105.77	31.49	170.58	−1.6	33.1
	1982/85–1994/97	−6.65	51.21	41.16	14.1	37.1
Chile	1970/73–1982/85	18.58	28.77	52.70	−2.0	30.8
	1982/85–1994/97	83.77	56.08	186.83	19.9	36.2
Colombia	1970/73–1982/85	23.71	40.40	73.69	3.3	37.1
	1982/85–1994/97	53.89	46.69	125.74	11.7	35.0
Costa Rica	1970/73–1982/85	4.72	45.78	52.65	5.1	40.7
	1982/85–1994/97	62.72	45.46	136.68	8.3	37.2
Dominican Republic	1970/73–1982/85	−10.00	49.76	34.78	2.7	47.1
	1982/85–1994/97	108.67	40.72	193.64	3.3	37.4
Ecuador	1970/73–1982/85	151.37	39.19	249.88	2.0	37.2
	1982/85–1994/97	−8.07	48.06	36.11	11.1	37.0
El Salvador	1970/73–1982/85	−28.01	44.20	3.81	2.2	42.0
	1982/85–1994/97	−18.40	48.24	20.97	8.6	39.6

(continued)

Table 3A.1   (continued)

Country	Period (1)	Supply Capacity (2)	FMA (3)	Exports (4)	Own Region FMA (5)	Other Region FMA (6)
Guatemala	1970/73–1982/85	–0.24	45.09	44.75	2.2	42.9
	1982/85–1994/97	–16.50	56.30	30.51	7.3	49.0
Haiti	1970/73–1982/85	180.97	48.56	317.41	2.2	46.3
	1982/85–1994/97	–81.19	43.96	–72.92	6.8	37.2
Honduras	1970/73–1982/85	6.25	44.23	53.24	2.1	42.1
	1982/85–1994/97	–36.84	46.62	–7.40	7.7	38.9
Jamaica	1970/73–1982/85	–43.36	50.44	–14.79	2.9	47.6
	1982/85–1994/97	3.69	42.64	47.90	4.4	38.3
Nicaragua	1970/73–1982/85	–51.99	44.38	–30.69	2.7	41.7
	1982/85–1994/97	–24.25	47.62	11.82	9.1	38.6
Panama	1970/73–1982/85	–14.80	42.78	21.64	1.8	41.0
	1982/85–1994/97	6.19	47.03	56.12	9.4	37.7
Peru	1970/73–1982/85	–10.25	35.59	21.69	1.2	34.4
	1982/85–1994/97	–1.93	53.90	50.92	17.7	36.2
Trinidad and	1970/73–1982/85	40.46	44.13	102.44	3.0	41.2
Tobago	1982/85–1994/97	–52.42	41.09	–32.87	4.6	36.5
Uruguay	1970/73–1982/85	52.02	15.49	75.57	–6.4	21.9
	1982/85–1994/97	–7.14	87.22	73.85	58.5	28.7
Venezuela	1970/73–1982/85	39.69	43.63	100.63	1.9	41.8
	1982/85–1994/97	–32.04	47.58	0.30	10.6	37.0
	Western Europe					
Austria	1970/73–1982/85	44.54	28.48	85.71	16.8	11.7
	1982/85–1994/97	58.77	54.54	145.37	39.8	14.7
Belgium (incl.	1970/73–1982/85	11.74	33.90	49.62	24.9	9.0
Luxembourg)	1982/85–1994/97	45.43	48.24	115.58	40.5	7.8
Denmark	1970/73–1982/85	22.67	31.32	61.09	19.6	11.7
	1982/85–1994/97	34.43	50.51	102.34	39.6	10.9
Finland	1970/73–1982/85	37.30	30.62	79.33	12.0	18.6
	1982/85–1994/97	77.39	40.70	149.60	23.6	17.1
France	1970/73–1982/85	27.92	29.60	65.79	18.0	11.6
	1982/85–1994/97	43.09	52.71	118.51	42.6	10.1
Germany	1970/73–1982/85	27.51	28.29	63.59	14.5	13.8
	1982/85–1994/97	37.36	49.64	105.55	32.3	17.3
Greece	1970/73–1982/85	65.23	40.26	131.76	15.4	24.9
	1982/85–1994/97	20.21	39.84	68.11	23.5	16.4
Ireland	1970/73–1982/85	102.15	34.20	171.28	18.6	15.6
	1982/85–1994/97	133.79	45.39	239.91	32.1	13.3
Italy	1970/73–1982/85	40.84	34.67	89.67	15.2	19.5
	1982/85–1994/97	61.49	43.50	131.74	28.5	15.0
The Netherlands	1970/73–1982/85	32.22	32.16	74.74	21.5	10.7
	1982/85–1994/97	19.07	46.99	75.02	37.5	9.5
Norway	1970/73–1982/85	93.16	31.80	154.59	15.0	16.8
	1982/85–1994/97	22.67	40.04	71.79	24.8	15.2
Portugal	1970/73–1982/85	21.12	38.31	67.52	16.1	22.2
	1982/85–1994/97	125.85	49.78	238.28	32.5	17.3

Table 3A.1   (continued)

Country	Period (1)	Supply Capacity (2)	FMA (3)	Exports (4)	Own Region FMA (5)	Other Region FMA (6)
Spain	1970/73–1982/85	100.36	35.68	171.84	15.1	20.5
	1982/85–1994/97	116.11	41.68	206.18	26.2	15.5
Sweden	1970/73–1982/85	5.65	33.87	41.43	16.0	17.9
	1982/85–1994/97	39.53	40.54	96.10	24.3	16.2
Switzerland	1970/73–1982/85	33.72	31.84	76.30	20.5	11.4
	1982/85–1994/97	43.52	51.53	117.47	41.7	9.8
Turkey	1970/73–1982/85	129.06	36.75	213.24	11.8	24.9
	1982/85–1994/97	87.06	35.69	153.82	19.2	16.5
The United	1970/73–1982/85	36.68	38.55	89.38	22.7	15.8
Kingdom	1982/85–1994/97	36.49	35.09	84.38	22.0	13.1
	Eastern Europe					
Albania	1970/73–1982/85	84.57	36.57	152.07	0.0	36.5
	1982/85–1994/97	−43.46	37.34	−22.35	1.3	36.0
Bulgaria	1970/73–1982/85	27.01	35.56	72.17	−0.7	36.3
	1982/85–1994/97	−9.33	43.17	29.81	3.0	40.2
Czechoslovakia	1970/73–1982/85	2.86	31.08	34.83	−0.5	31.6
	1982/85–1994/97	77.54	54.48	174.26	2.9	51.6
Hungary	1970/73–1982/85	−11.31	34.92	19.66	−0.6	35.5
	1982/85–1994/97	44.67	41.52	104.73	3.3	38.2
Poland	1970/73–1982/85	−0.44	31.34	30.76	−0.2	31.5
	1982/85–1994/97	57.83	49.69	136.25	1.8	47.8
Romania	1970/73–1982/85	47.75	37.74	103.52	0.1	37.6
	1982/85–1994/97	−28.69	38.34	−1.36	2.4	35.9
	Sub-Saharan Africa, North Africa, and Middle East					
Angola	1970/73–1982/85	14.67	30.48	49.62	−2.8	33.3
	1982/85–1994/97	13.81	37.95	57.01	−1.9	39.9
Benin	1970/73–1982/85	4.81	36.35	42.91	3.1	33.2
	1982/85–1994/97	−5.98	32.10	24.21	−4.9	37.0
Cameroon	1970/73–1982/85	154.00	37.41	249.03	3.7	33.7
	1982/85–1994/97	−53.45	31.61	−38.73	−5.1	36.7
Côte d'Ivoire	1970/73–1982/85	30.17	32.94	73.04	−1.5	34.5
	1982/85–1994/97	−22.83	39.04	7.30	−1.1	40.1
Ethiopia	1970/73–1982/85	−33.83	41.87	−6.12	−0.8	42.7
	1982/85–1994/97	−29.71	35.62	−4.68	−0.9	36.5
Gabon	1970/73–1982/85	169.54	35.08	264.10	0.9	34.2
	1982/85–1994/97	−16.34	34.97	12.92	−3.5	38.4
Ghana	1970/73–1982/85	−51.31	35.75	−33.90	1.5	34.2
	1982/85–1994/97	35.02	35.38	82.80	−3.3	38.6
Guinea	1970/73–1982/85	134.95	33.49	213.63	−1.9	35.4
	1982/85–1994/97	−23.31	39.84	7.25	−1.2	41.0
Kenya	1970/73–1982/85	29.93	36.42	77.24	−1.8	38.2
	1982/85–1994/97	−12.85	38.40	20.61	−0.5	38.9
Madagascar	1970/73–1982/85	−37.96	35.22	−16.11	−1.5	36.7
	1982/85–1994/97	−50.35	42.61	−29.19	0.0	42.6

(*continued*)

Table 3A.1 (continued)

Country	Period (1)	Supply Capacity (2)	FMA (3)	Exports (4)	Own Region FMA (5)	Other Region FMA (6)
Malawi	1970/73–1982/85	20.67	30.46	57.43	–3.6	34.0
	1982/85–1994/97	–18.21	40.66	15.05	0.3	40.4
Mali	1970/73–1982/85	–88.27	36.63	–83.97	0.5	36.1
	1982/85–1994/97	–12.42	38.54	21.33	–1.3	39.9
Mauritius	1970/73–1982/85	37.04	36.29	86.77	–1.5	37.7
	1982/85–1994/97	97.37	43.71	183.63	–0.5	44.2
Mozambique	1970/73–1982/85	–75.03	27.47	–68.17	–3.5	30.9
	1982/85–1994/97	–56.84	43.73	–37.96	4.1	39.6
Nigeria	1970/73–1982/85	122.31	35.22	200.60	–1.0	36.2
	1982/85–1994/97	–49.43	39.04	–29.69	–0.7	39.7
Senegal	1970/73–1982/85	–13.97	35.84	16.87	–1.3	37.1
	1982/85–1994/97	–48.02	40.77	–26.83	–0.9	41.6
South Africa	1970/73–1982/85	–6.22	34.18	25.83	–1.2	35.4
	1982/85–1994/97	33.19	44.56	92.54	–0.5	45.1
Sudan	1970/73–1982/85	–42.06	43.21	–17.02	–0.8	44.1
	1982/85–1994/97	–67.13	34.88	–55.67	–0.5	35.4
Tanzania	1970/73–1982/85	–48.49	34.51	–30.72	–2.3	36.8
	1982/85–1994/97	–29.50	39.75	–1.48	0.0	39.7
Uganda	1970/73–1982/85	–48.21	35.19	–29.98	–1.8	37.0
	1982/85–1994/97	–27.45	37.45	–0.28	–0.6	39.0
Zaire	1970/73–1982/85	–34.05	33.43	–12.00	–0.9	34.3
	1982/85–1994/97	–54.51	37.86	–36.87	–1.3	39.2
Zambia	1970/73–1982/85	–67.90	33.14	–57.26	–0.8	33.9
	1982/85–1994/97	–49.35	41.39	–28.38	1.6	39.8
Zimbabwe	1970/73–1982/85	341.18	24.27	448.27	–6.8	31.1
	1982/85–1994/97	19.76	41.05	68.92	1.7	39.3
Algeria	1970/73–1982/85	203.95	37.06	316.59	5.7	31.4
	1982/85–1994/97	–51.74	40.67	–32.12	0.4	40.3
Egypt	1970/73–1982/85	85.79	40.23	160.54	13.8	26.4
	1982/85–1994/97	–36.75	40.37	–11.21	0.4	36.2
Iran	1970/73–1982/85	131.64	48.88	244.86	18.8	30.0
	1982/85–1994/97	–50.45	37.76	–31.74	–2.9	40.7
Israel	1970/73–1982/85	30.83	59.69	108.92	34.2	25.5
	1982/85–1994/97	130.86	23.37	184.80	–7.5	30.9
Jordan	1970/73–1982/85	312.61	46.86	505.96	26.9	20.0
	1982/85–1994/97	–20.10	50.75	20.46	24.4	26.4
Kuwait	1970/73–1982/85	–5.83	72.11	62.07	44.9	27.2
	1982/85–1994/97	–60.10	22.24	–51.23	–8.8	31.0
Lebanon	1970/73–1982/85	–42.87	51.98	–13.17	27.6	24.4
	1982/85–1994/97	–41.90	35.03	–21.45	4.0	31.1
Morocco	1970/73–1982/85	8.57	38.31	50.16	6.6	31.8
	1982/85–1994/97	17.92	40.40	65.56	–1.9	42.3
Oman	1970/73–1982/85	153.43	63.84	315.21	33.8	30.0
	1982/85–1994/97	–18.49	37.80	12.32	3.0	34.8

Table 3A.1 (continued)

Country	Period (1)	Supply Capacity (2)	FMA (3)	Exports (4)	Own Region FMA (5)	Other Region FMA (6)
Saudi Arabia	1970/73–1982/85	181.50	42.94	302.39	15.1	27.8
	1982/85–1994/97	–55.62	42.06	–36.96	3.7	38.3
Syria	1970/73–1982/85	107.20	41.39	192.95	18.5	22.9
	1982/85–1994/97	8.35	42.70	54.62	9.6	33.1
Tunisia	1970/73–1982/85	134.51	38.48	224.75	7.8	30.7
	1982/85–1994/97	59.91	34.60	115.24	–2.3	36.9
United Arab	1970/73–1982/85	510.10	63.88	899.83	34.9	29.0
Emirates	1982/85–1994/97	–27.55	26.40	–8.42	–7.8	34.2
Southeast and Other Asia						
Cambodia	1970/73–1982/85	–95.59	38.73	–93.89	22.4	16.4
	1982/85–1994/97	3187.36	85.00	5981.78	69.7	15.3
China	1970/73–1982/85	149.75	47.05	267.26	31.3	15.7
	1982/85–1994/97	208.31	62.89	402.20	48.0	14.9
Hong Kong	1970/73–1982/85	127.59	47.08	234.75	29.3	17.8
	1982/85–1994/97	184.02	67.31	375.21	51.2	16.1
Indonesia	1970/73–1982/85	291.97	45.78	471.92	27.1	18.7
	1982/85–1994/97	–4.76	63.79	55.99	46.0	17.8
Japan	1970/73–1982/85	91.49	45.33	178.30	19.4	26.0
	1982/85–1994/97	10.83	70.04	88.46	44.9	25.2
Korea,	1970/73–1982/85	361.86	50.83	596.65	35.3	15.6
Republic of	1982/85–1994/97	113.44	44.47	208.37	30.4	14.1
Malaysia	1970/73–1982/85	97.90	62.23	221.05	47.0	15.3
	1982/85–1994/97	85.98	87.44	248.59	75.1	12.3
Papua New	1970/73–1982/85	83.12	40.37	157.04	20.0	20.4
Guinea	1982/85–1994/97	37.54	50.31	106.73	28.2	22.1
Philippines	1970/73–1982/85	24.96	47.43	84.24	30.2	17.2
	1982/85–1994/97	64.21	60.92	164.25	44.8	16.2
Singapore	1970/73–1982/85	201.65	45.31	338.34	27.9	17.5
	1982/85–1994/97	123.47	74.01	288.86	58.0	16.0
Taiwan	1970/73–1982/85	201.47	53.89	363.93	37.2	16.7
	1982/85–1994/97	85.18	64.30	204.26	49.5	14.8
Thailand	1970/73–1982/85	111.71	44.20	205.30	24.3	19.9
	1982/85–1994/97	230.18	60.93	431.34	43.6	17.3
Viet Nam	1970/73–1982/85	3.95	48.86	54.74	31.0	17.9
	1982/85–1994/97	844.27	70.77	1512.52	55.0	15.7
Bangladesh	1970/73–1982/85	132.16	45.29	237.32	3.7	41.6
	1982/85–1994/97	114.21	53.24	228.26	2.1	51.2
India	1970/73–1982/85	20.29	45.17	74.61	2.7	42.5
	1982/85–1994/97	89.57	48.34	181.20	1.1	47.2
Nepal	1970/73–1982/85	–2.75	45.52	41.52	4.6	40.9
	1982/85–1994/97	114.41	53.92	230.02	2.5	51.4
Pakistan	1970/73–1982/85	13.46	48.16	68.10	5.8	42.4
	1982/85–1994/97	55.26	43.67	123.07	3.6	40.1
Sri Lanka	1970/73–1982/85	7.04	44.18	54.34	3.6	40.6
	1982/85–1994/97	52.39	48.27	125.94	0.5	47.7

(*continued*)

Table 3A.1   (continued)

Country	Period (1)	Supply Capacity (2)	FMA (3)	Exports (4)	Own Region FMA (5)	Other Region FMA (6)
		Oceania				
Australia	1970/73–1982/85	9.21	37.74	50.43	0.6	37.1
	1982/85–1994/97	20.59	49.90	80.77	0.6	49.3
New Zealand	1970/73–1982/85	2.81	36.97	40.81	4.2	32.8
	1982/85–1994/97	19.38	47.66	76.29	3.8	43.9

Notes: Columns (2) through (4) of the table are based on equation (7). Column (2) is the rate of growth of supplier capacity (s); column (3) is the rate of growth of foreign-market access (FMA); and column (4) is the rate of growth of exports. The rates of growth of supplier capacity and FMA compound to the rate of growth of total exports. Columns (5) and (6) are based on equation (13). Column (5) reports the contribution of a country's own region FMA growth, while column (6) gives the corresponding contribution of other-region FMA growth.

References

Acemoglu, D., S. Johnson, and J. Robinson. 2001. The colonial origins of comparative development: An empirical investigation. *American Economic Review* 91 (5): 1369–1401.

Amjadi, A., U. Reincke, and A. Yeats. 1996. Did external barriers cause the marginalization of sub-Saharan Africa in world trade? Washington, D.C.: World Bank.

Anderson, J. 1979. A theoretical foundation for the gravity equation. *American Economic Review* 69 (1): 106–16.

Anderson, J., and E. Van Wincoop. 2003. Gravity with gravitas: A solution to the border puzzle. *American Economic Review* 93 (1): 170–92.

Ciccone, A., and F. Alcalá. 2001. Trade and productivity. Center for Economic Policy Research (CEPR) Discussion Paper no. 3095. London: CEPR.

Deardorff, A. 1998. Determinants of bilateral trade: Does gravity work in a neoclassical world? In *The regionalisation of the world economy,* ed. J. Frankel, 7–32. Chicago: University of Chicago.

Eaton, I., and S. Kortum. 2002. Technology, geography, and trade. *Econometrica* 70 (5): 1741–79.

Feenstra, R. 2001. World trade flows, 1980–97. University of California, Davis, Department of Economics. Mimeograph.

———. 2002. Border effects and the gravity equation: Consistent methods for estimation. *Scottish Journal of Political Economy* 49 (5): 491–506.

Feenstra, R., R. Lipsey, and H. Bowen. 1997. World trade flows, 1970–92, with production and tariff data. NBER Working Paper no. 5910. Cambridge, Mass.: National Bureau of Economic Research, January.

Frankel, J., and D. Romer. 1999. Does trade cause growth? *American Economic Review* 89 (3): 379–99.

Fujita, M., P. Krugman, and A. J. Venables. 1999. *The spatial economy: Cities, regions, and international trade.* Cambridge, Mass.: MIT Press.

Gallup, J., J. Sachs, and A. Mellinger. 1998. Geography and economic development. In *Proceedings of World Bank Annual Conference on Development Economics,* ed. B. Pleskovic and J. Stiglitz, 127–78. Washington, D.C.: World Bank.

Hall, R., and C. Jones. 1999. Fundamental determinants of output per worker across countries. *Quarterly Journal of Economics* 114 (1): 83–116.

Knack, S., and P. Keefer. 1997. Does social capital have an economic payoff? *Quarterly Journal of Economics* 112 (4): 1251–88.

Leamer, E. 1988. Measures of openness. In *Trade policy issues and empirical analysis,* ed. R. Baldwin, 147–200. Chicago: University of Chicago Press.

Limao, N., and A. J. Venables. 2001. Infrastructure, geographical disadvantage and transport costs. *World Bank Economic Review* 15:451–79.

Noland, M. 1997. Has Asian export performance been unique? *Journal of International Economics* 43 (1–2): 79–101.

Overman, H. G., S. Redding, and A. J. Venables. 2003. The economic geography of trade, production, and income: A survey of empirics. In *Handbook of International Trade,* ed. J. Harrigan and K. Choi. London: Basil Blackwell.

Radelet, S., and J. Sachs. 1998. Shipping costs, manufactured exports, and economic growth. Paper presented at the American Economic Association Meetings, 1 January 1998, Chicago, Harvard University.

Redding, S., and A. J. Venables. 2003. Economic geography and international inequality. *Journal of International Economics,* forthcoming.

Richardson, D. 1971. Constant market shares analysis of export growth. *Journal of International Economics* 1 (2): 227–39.

Rodriguez, F., and D. Rodrik. 2000. Trade policy and economic growth: A skeptic's guide to the cross-national evidence. In *NBER macroeconomics annual 2000,* ed. B. S. Bernanke and K. Rogoff. Cambridge, Mass.: MIT Press.

Rodrik, D., A. Subramanian, and F. Trebbi. 2002. Institutions rule: The primacy of institutions over geography and integration in economic development. NBER Working Paper no. 9305. Cambridge, Mass.: National Bureau of Economic Research, November.

Sachs, J., and A. Warner. 1995. Economic reform and the process of global integration. *Brookings Papers on Economic Activity,* Issue no. 1:1–95.

Wei, S. 2000. Natural openness and good government. NBER Working Paper no. 7765. Cambridge, Mass.: National Bureau of Economic Research, June.

Comment   Keith E. Maskus

I would like to congratulate Steve Redding and Tony Venables on providing another solid contribution that helps establish a useful empirical context for analyzing how processes of geography, trade, and growth fit together. They do this by offering a decomposition of changes in the value of exports over several time periods into changes arising from domestic supply capacity (coming from size, as a measure of endowments, internal trade costs, and an index of the quality of governance) and from foreign

Keith E. Maskus is chair of the economics department at the University of Colorado, Boulder.

market access (FMA; coming from bilateral trade costs and foreign market demand).

This approach is straightforward and appealing. It generates sensible results that reinforce our basic understanding of the sources of export growth in various regions. For example, sub-Saharan Africa (SSA) has performed worse than the world average in every factor but it is clear that weakness in institutions (protection of property rights) is particularly important in restraining supply capacity. For another, East Asia saw greatly expanded market access in the 1980s but also subsequently developed large average increases in domestic supply capacity. Finally, market access within North America is itself largely responsible for export growth within that region. The paper reminds us that both FMA and supply capacity are important, a significant message for developing countries hoping to succeed through export-led growth. Simply observing larger foreign market growth may not raise exports much without reducing domestic supply costs.

Again, I appreciate the approach for being straightforward and easy to implement if one has the data. However, I would like to raise a few questions about the inevitable simplifications that must be made in order to get the approach to work.

First, is it really the case that supply-capacity factors and FMA are so neatly separable that they can be treated without considering any interactions between them? Here is one obvious example, consistent with the globalization theme of this conference, although many others could be suggested. Suppose that a particular country finds that all its export markets increase their effective access by cutting trade barriers. Under some circumstances this might induce more inward foreign direct investment (FDI) into low-wage countries, a direct increase in supply capacity. It could also generate an indirect expansion of capacity through enhancing competition and learning spillovers. In such a case we might not be attributing enough export-growth impact to FMA.

Clearly sorting out such interrelationships would require a different kind of model structure and would not lend itself to readily available measures. However, I think more effort to entertain such interrelationships could be rewarding and perhaps could help explain the many large residuals that show up in the later regional export-growth decompositions.

Second, a related point is that while the decomposition of supply capacity growth into its determinants is quite useful, it leaves room for much more work. For example, even given the same growth in size and institutional capacity, an economy that is more open to technology flows may have greater capacity growth. Here, an important concept that goes unmeasured and unused in the paper is *technology distance,* or how costly it is to transfer and absorb advanced technology from abroad. This process depends on a number of market features, such as market competition, access to science and technology information, regulation of technology transfer, skill endowments, and so on. Consider, for example, a country with an effective telecommunications structure that permits ready access to Internet-based science. That country is likely to increase its supply capacity more rapidly in response to growth in foreign knowledge (and therefore demand) than would be a country with a weak telecommunications infrastructure.

Third, I find it surprising that the measure of trade costs, coming from the inclusion of distance and border dummies into a gravity equation of trade, does not explicitly account for trade barriers, especially tariffs. To an important degree, such trade restrictions are embedded into the general gravity equation. However, it would be useful for policy purposes to say something explicit to African policymakers about the nature of their trade costs. If the problem is simply that they are far from export markets, which is an important observation made by the authors, there is not much that can be done about that basic geography. But if distance were needlessly augmented by high trade barriers a completely different policy message would emerge.

Fourth, how readily can we make inferences about policy changes from the results presented? The authors find large market access effects in North America and attribute this to the effects of NAFTA and to earlier Mexican trade liberalization. It is conceivable, however, that NAFTA itself was an endogenous response to regional trade growth and may indeed be diverting some trade relative to an underlying export trend. This is an important question, for the implicit message in the paper is favorable to regional trade agreements. This message cannot readily be supported simply on the basis of the results here.

Fifth, I wonder about the endogeneity of some capacity measures to trade growth. The authors do a commendable job of controlling for endogeneity arising from home market growth. But consider the measure of internal trade costs, which is the percentage of the population near rivers and coasts. This measure places a heavy weight on water transport, which is questionable in light of effective road and railroad infrastructure in many nations. As for endogeneity, surely the decisions of people to locate near the coast are dependent on export growth, as the case of China exemplifies. Thus, I am not sure that this measure really is a primitive of the model.

Sixth, I like the idea of attributing supply-capacity growth to underlying determinants. However, it is hard to see how the governance measure, an index of property rights protection, actually captures rising costs as the economy specializes in export goods. The theory refers to rising marginal costs as the economy concentrates its resources in exports, which is a natural way of capturing general-equilibrium resource constraints. However, the limiting impacts of weak property rights surely operate at any level of commodity mix or unemployment and there seems little relationship to its claimed use in the paper.

A final comment, which is a bit inconsistent with the fourth point above, is to ask for more comments about the policy relevance of the results. What can we conclude about policy changes that we did not already know? Surely we want to raise FMA for poor countries, although one wonders how likely this is in the wake of the recent U.S. agricultural bill. We also want to cut internal trade barriers and improve governance that restrains trade. All of this makes sense at the aggregate level. But, to get more specific, can we conclude much from these results about specific institutional reforms to recommend? How might such reforms interrelate with barriers to trade in goods and services and to restraints on investment? I suppose I am asking for more thinking about what explains the residuals that emerge for many of the regional aggregates.

These comments are more in the nature of asking for better measures and more analysis than in criticizing the underlying model and approach. The paper provides interesting evidence on the sources of export growth for a large cross-section of countries, which in itself is a valuable exercise. The results for SSA in particular are compelling and convincing. Thus, I look forward to seeing more analysis using this model and additional perspective on the nature of institutional and geographical restraints on export growth.

4

Globalization and International Commodity Trade with Specific Reference to the West African Cocoa Producers

Christopher L. Gilbert and Panos Varangis

4.1 Introduction

Since the early 1980s, dramatic changes in export commodity markets, shocks associated with price declines, and changing views on the role of the government have ushered in widespread market-liberalization programs to agricultural commodity markets in Africa. These programs have significantly reduced government participation in marketing and pricing of export commodities. Market liberalization entails a greater reliance on markets to direct resource utilization and investment. In the context of this paper, market liberalization refers to steps taken toward opening domestic and export markets to competition and toward putting in place public and private institutions consistent with and supportive of private markets.[1]

Critics have raised several concerns about the trend toward market liberalization. These include the claim that, although liberalization may make sense for an individual exporting country, when several countries do it simultaneously, they increase exports so strongly that they drive down the prices and revenues that they receive from exporting and make themselves worse off. Critics also sometimes argue that liberalization has opened farmers up to price and income fluctuations from which they were previ-

Christopher L. Gilbert is professor in the Faculty of Economics, University of Trento, Italy. Panos Varangis is lead economist at the Agriculture and Rural Development Department, The World Bank.

This paper was prepared for the International Seminar on International Trade (ISIT), 24–25 May 2002, Stockholm. We are grateful to participants at the ISIT conference in particular, to Joshua Aizenman and Bob Baldwin for comments on the presentation of earlier material; and to Erin Bryla for research assistance.

1. Bates (1989) notes that markets adjust automatically, leaving the realignment of government institutions as the real task of structural adjustment.

ously insulated. Economic theory makes it clear that all these problems can arise in particular circumstances, so the real questions are empirical. This chapter provides some answers by exploring one case of primary-commodity liberalization in some detail: cocoa in West Africa. We show that such distributional issues are of first-order importance to the political debate about globalization.

We need to distinguish between liberalization and globalization. Liberalization is the move to market-determined prices from what was previously a regulated regime. One of the implications of liberalization is that the prices received by farmers in different producing countries move together much more closely than prior to liberalization. It also implies that markets in each producing country are more closely interconnected than previously, with the result that decisions taken in one country affect farmers in each of the other producing countries. We refer to these two aspects of liberalization as globalization. Governments decided (or agreed) to liberalize, while globalization was a consequence of these decisions and not an objective in itself.

For commodity markets, liberalization has meant reducing government involvement in marketing and in production, increasing participation of the private sector in these activities, and reducing distortions in commodity prices, especially producer prices. Measures implemented to achieve these goals vary, but often they have included the elimination of government marketing agencies, the introduction of competition in marketing, the elimination of administered prices, reduction in explicit and implicit taxes, and the privatization of government-owned assets.

Events triggering market liberalization were not independent of broader political and economic changes in most countries, and the consequences of liberalization are often linked as well. However, issues related to the approaches and effects of general and agricultural market liberalization have been discussed elsewhere and receive minimal treatment here (for full treatment, see World Bank 1994; Engberg-Pedersen et al. 1996; and Mosley, Harrington, and Toye 1991). Instead, our purpose is to discuss market liberalization in the specific context of cocoa and, particularly, to examine the impact of liberalization on the prices obtained by west African cocoa producers and the revenues they receive. We also empirically estimate supply and demand elasticities for west African producers and use these to simulate the welfare effects of liberalization on west African cocoa producers, non-African producers and world consumers of cocoa products, and the revenue loss to west African governments.

West Africa accounts for nearly two-thirds of the world's cocoa production. Before the late 1980s, west African cocoa was entirely produced and marketed under government-controlled systems. However, starting in the late 1980s and continuing into the 1990s, all four of west Africa's largest cocoa-producing countries—Cameroon, Côte d'Ivoire, Ghana, and Nigeria, together with Togo (a smaller cocoa producer)—took steps toward liberalizing their cocoa markets. Much of the aim of the reforms was to improve efficiency by reducing domestic marketing costs, provide a higher pass-through of international prices to producer prices, and increase the producer share of the free on board (f.o.b.) price. According to Akiyama et al. (2001), market liberalization in cocoa had a positive effect on producer prices, relative to both f.o.b. prices and production.

The claimed increase in production raises the question of whether or not liberalization by the west African producers, despite the relative rise in producer prices, may have led to a net loss in total welfare in these countries as the result of the likely negative impact of the production increase on the world cocoa price. To the extent that this occurred, the incidence of the benefits from liberalization will have been on cocoa consumers, most of whom are in the developed market economies. Developed country governments already have to counter the charge of hypocrisy ("incoherence," in official parlance) in that they advocate market liberalization in the Third World while maintaining regulated and subsidized domestic agricultural markets. If it is also the case that the incidence of the liberalization benefits is significantly enjoyed by developed-country consumers, it may be difficult to avoid the impression that these governments and the international agencies are guilty of pursuing self-interested policies in the developing world.

This is an instance of the well-known adding-up problem. Here, the problem arises as the welfare effects of unilateral liberalization by an individual and relatively small cocoa producer will differ from and be lower than the welfare effects of multilateral liberalization by a group of producing countries, which collectively constitute a large proportion of the world market. In the former case, it may be reasonable to take the world price as unaffected by the liberalization, while in the latter case, this assumption would be absurd. The adding-up problem has generated a large literature starting from Johnson (1953, 1958) and Bhagwati (1958) and, more recently, Krishna (1995). Schiff (1994) states that countries with market power in commodities should proceed with trade and domestic liberalization and should apply optimal export taxes to those commodities in which they have market power. Akiyama and Larson (1994) argued as a practical matter that it is not feasible to design a regional commodity-production and trade policy for cocoa-producing countries in Africa mainly because of the difficulty of equitably distributing the benefits of such a policy.

In a related literature, Evenson (2002) looks at the impact of technology on agricultural prices. He finds that there are significant costs to countries that do not adopt new technology because they suffer from low prices and lack of production growth. New technologies have led to lower prices, but countries that have adopted new technologies have benefited from expanded production. Liberalization has lowered marketing costs and margins in the same way as has technological advance, and its impact on production should therefore also be similar. Countries cannot afford to be left behind in this process.

The choice of cocoa to examine these questions is deliberate and advised.

- Along with coffee, rice, sugar, and wheat, cocoa has historically been one of the most heavily regulated commodity markets.
- In common with coffee, but unlike sugar and wheat, it is almost entirely a developing-country commodity.[2]
- Unlike coffee, regulation was predominantly at a national rather than an international level.[3]
- The liberalization process can be fairly cleanly dated in the cocoa market. The rice, sugar, and wheat markets remain less fully liberalized.

It is our belief that the concentration of production in four west African countries, all of which had heavily regulated internal markets, makes it likely that the adverse (from the point of view of the liberalizing countries) adding-up effects of liberalization will be both larger and more clear than in any other major market.

The present paper is structured as follows. Section 4.2 discusses the economics of liberalization, while section 4.3 highlights certain aspects of the world cocoa market, particularly in relation to market liberalization. In section 4.4, we look at the direct consequences of liberalization and globalization in the world cocoa market. Section 4.5 presents a world cocoa-market model, and section 4.6 indicates the beneficiaries of market liberalization based on the results of the model simulations. Section 4.7 concludes.

4.2   The Economics of Market Liberalization

The market-liberalization programs enjoined upon developing-country governments in the markets for tropical commodities had two complementary objectives. The first was to ensure that farmers would receive a higher proportion of world prices than had been the case in the preliberalization period. This often involved a reduction in (implicit or explicit) export tax rates. The second objective was to align incentives with world prices, both for farmers and more generally in the marketing chain, with the expectation that production and marketing would be more efficient. It was hoped that these incentives would increase both production and revenues in the liberalizing economies. This price-realignment process in-

---

2. There is a very small quantity of OECD cocoa production in Australia.
3. See Gilbert (1987, 1996) for a discussion regarding international commodity-market regulation in cocoa and coffee.

volved an ending of previous interannual, intra-annual, and intranational (interregional) price stabilization arrangements and paralleled the simultaneous abandonment of attempts to stabilize international prices through commodity agreements. At the same time, previously monopsonistic marketing systems were opened up to competition. See Akiyama et al. (2001) and Gilbert and ter Wengel (2001) for a summary of these developments.

Market liberalization is part of the globalization phenomenon in that producers of tropical commodities now react in a more or less uniform manner to a common world price whereas, previously, domestic and international marketing arrangements often shielded them from the world price.

The practical effects of market liberalization are often both complicated and controversial. We will accept that liberalization has indeed increased the farmers' share of the port (f.o.b.) price, because of both reduced taxation and reductions in marketing cost. Varangis and Schreiber (2001) discuss the cocoa outcomes. The balance between these two effects, the first of which is a transfer and the second a pure efficiency gain, undoubtedly varies across commodities and also across countries for the same commodity.[4]

The globalization aspects of market liberalization align domestic prices more closely with the volatile world cocoa price, and the reining back of the marketing boards and *caisses de stabilisation* (see section 4.3) reduces governments' capacities to offset this volatility. The consequence is that farmers, in general, will be more exposed to commodity-price variability. This imposes additional costs on them, both through the costs of uncertainty as well as from the direct costs of low prices (see Gilbert 2002). We make the standard assumption that developing-country farmers lack access to either credit or risk-management instruments. They are therefore obliged to self-insure through diversification.[5]

Proponents of liberalization hoped and intended that, by ensuring that farmers would get a higher share of f.o.b. prices, they would be better off. The farmers themselves note that, in practice, they have been rewarded by a higher share of a lower price. They often go on to argue that they are no better off and perhaps worse off than before liberalization. Of course, because prices are volatile, these complaints are more often heard in low-price than in high-price years. It is also possible to respond with the counterfactual argument that, because of continued productivity advances in tropical agriculture, prices would have fallen relative to the prices of manufactures in the absence of liberalization so that, even if it is true that farmers are no

4. There are also arguments, which we do not explore in this paper, that market liberalization may have resulted in a deterioration in crop quality (see Gilbert and Tollens 2003).
5. It might be suggested that even if farmers lack access to credit, they are always able to save in good times, but not in bad times (see Paxson 1993). However, the almost complete absence of rural banks in West Africa makes it difficult even to save.

better off than previously, they are at least better off than they would have been in the absence of liberalization. In our experience, it is difficult to persuade developing-country farmers that this is more than self-justifying sophistry. Furthermore, farmers believe that the fall in tropical-commodity prices has been induced in large measure by the liberalization process itself.

It is easy to see why this should be the case. Holding the world price constant, the farmers will be willing to supply more at that world-price level to the extent that market liberalization has increased the price obtained by those farmers. They can do this either by exploiting existing capital more intensively (by increased application of effort and purchased inputs) or by expanding the area under cultivation. The supply curve from the liberalizing country therefore shifts right and, so long as the supply of the liberalizing country is not negligible compared to world supply, the aggregate supply function will also shift right. This will induce a fall in the world price which will be larger to the extent that (a) a significant fraction of world production is affected in this way and (b) the demand curve is inelastic.

This is a standard instance of the old Johnson (1953, 1958) and Bhagwati (1958) adding-up problem. If one confines attention to market liberalization in a single "small" country, it is legitimate to hold the world price constant, at least as a first approximation. However, if one considers liberalization either in a major producer of the commodity or in a significant group of individually small producers, it will be important to take into account the effect on the world price. The implication is that the sum of the benefits to each of the individual liberalizers, under the assumption the world price does not change, will exceed the actual total welfare effects in the liberalizing countries, taking into account the decline in the world cocoa price. Proponents of liberalization have always admitted the principle of this argument but have proceeded on the basis that the adding-up effect is of the second order of importance. Instead, the anti-liberalizers may be interpreted as suggesting that the adding-up costs are of a comparable order to the original liberalization benefits, and indeed that they may even exceed these benefits (see figure 4.1 where supply shifts from S to S' and the world price falls from P to P').

It is straightforward to obtain a first-order approximation for the size of the adding-up effect.[6] The international price of the commodity is P; the domestic-producer price in producing country j is p_j ($j = 1, \ldots, n$); and the production in country j is $Q_j = Q^j(p_j, \sigma_j)$, where we have supposed that production depends not only on the price received by farmers in j, but also on the variability of the price as measured by the log standard deviation of domestic prices. The aggregate (world) demand for the commodity is $D(P)$. Suppose the effects of liberalization on the level of the domestic price in country j can be represented as

---

6. The estimates reported in section 4.6 are based on exact numerical solution of the model.

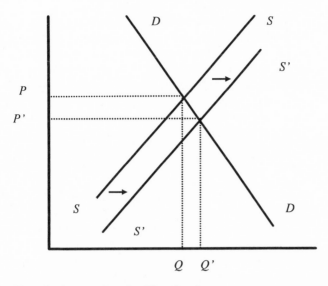

Fig. 4.1   The price impact of market liberalization

(1) $\Delta \ln p_j = \Delta \ln P + \delta_j,$

This equation states that the direct effect of liberalization is to raise the producer price in the country by the proportion δ_j, but there may also be an indirect effect through the (negative) impact of liberalization on the world price P.[7] Making the reasonable assumption that liberalization has no effect on desired inventory holdings, market clearing requires

(2) $\sum_{j=1}^{n} Q^j(p_j, \sigma_j) = D(P),$

and differentiating and approximating by finite differences,

(3) $\sum_{j=1}^{n} \frac{\partial Q^j}{\partial p_j / p_j}(\Delta \ln P + \delta_j) + \sum_{j=1}^{n} \frac{\partial Q_j}{\partial \sigma_j}\Delta\sigma_j = \frac{\partial D}{\partial P/P}\Delta \ln P.$

The supply elasticity in country j is $\varepsilon_j = \partial \ln Q_j / \partial \ln p_j$, the volatility semi-elasticity is $\theta_j = \partial \ln Q_j / \partial \sigma_j$, and the aggregate price elasticity of demand is $\eta = -\partial \ln D / \partial \ln P$, and we define the production share of country j as $\omega_j = Q_j / \Sigma_{i=1}^{n} Q_i$. Using this notation, we may approximate equation (3) to give

(4) $\Delta \ln P = -\dfrac{\sum_{i=1}^{n} \omega_i \varepsilon_i \delta_i - \sum_{i=1}^{n} \omega_i \theta_i \Delta\sigma_i}{\eta + \sum_{i=1}^{n} \omega_i \varepsilon_i}.$

7. It is possible that this volatility effect may be sufficiently large as to dominate the impact of the higher price on production. This would result in an increase in the world price (see Newbery and Stiglitz 1981, 327–29). Kanbur (1984) shows that in the case of cocoa, under plausible assumptions, the risk benefits from stabilization are lower than the transfer benefits.

Consider the simple case in which supply elasticities and volatility semi-elasticities are equal in all producing countries. Suppose further that there are m liberalizing countries (aggregate share α) each of which sees producer prices rise relative to the world price by a uniform amount of δ and price volatility rise by the uniform amount v. By implication, there are $n - m$ nonliberalizers with share $1 - \alpha$. Equation (4) simplifies to

(5) $$\Delta \ln P = -\alpha \frac{\varepsilon\delta - \theta v}{\eta + \varepsilon},$$

and the domestic price in liberalizing country j rises by

(6) $$\Delta \ln p_j = \frac{[\eta + (1 - \alpha)\varepsilon]}{\eta + \varepsilon}\delta + \frac{\alpha\theta v}{\eta + \varepsilon}.$$

Consider first the case in which production is unaffected by changes in price variability ($\theta = 0$). A unilateral liberalization by a small producer will be associated with a value of α close to zero. The impact on the world price will be negligible, and the incidence of the producer price will be entirely on the producers in the liberalizing country. However, the larger the share of the liberalizing countries and the higher the supply elasticities relative to the demand elasticity, the greater the dissipation of the effects of liberalization through decline in the world price. The limiting case is if demand is completely inelastic ($\eta = 0$), and the entire set of producers liberalize ($\alpha = 1$). In this case, $\Delta \ln p_j = 0$ ($j = 1, \ldots, n$) and $\Delta \ln P = -\delta$, implying that liberalization results in a transfer from producing-country governments to consumers with farmers unaffected. Farmers are never made worse off by liberalization, but they may not be much better off. Consumers will always be better off, and producing-country governments worse off. Depending on the welfare weight given to government, producing countries as a whole may well be worse off.

Allowing a production response to increased volatility reduces the impact of globalization on the world price, hence raising local prices ceteris paribus, but also opens the possibility that liberalization may worsen the position of farmers.

4.3   The World Cocoa Market and Cocoa-Market Liberalization

Cocoa is a tropical-tree-crop commodity. Furthermore, it is the west African crop par excellence. Côte d'Ivoire is the single largest producer and exporter of cocoa and Côte d'Ivoire, Ghana, Nigeria, and Cameroon, together, are responsible for over 60 percent of world production (see figure 4.2, which gives averages for the 1990s). In west Africa, cocoa is almost entirely a smallholder crop. All four of the major west African cocoa-producing countries had regulated marketing structures that they inherited from their colonial administrations. The major non-African cocoa ex-

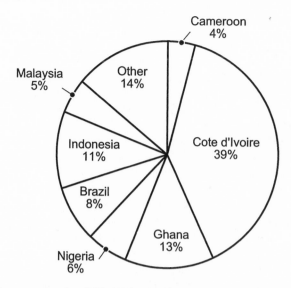

Fig. 4.2   Cocoa production 1990–1991 to 1999–2000

porters are Indonesia (the second most important exporter) followed by Malaysia and Brazil where, for different reasons, production has been declining.

The standard crop marketing structure adopted in countries with a British colonial history was of monopoly-monopsony marketing boards. In the ex-French colonies ownership of the crop remained with the private sector, but the state intervened by setting producer and export prices, by issuing export licenses, and by stabilizing prices through a *caisse de stabilisation*. In cocoa, Ghana and Nigeria operated marketing boards, while Côte d'Ivoire operated a *caisse* system. Cameroon, which combines ex-British and ex-French colonial territories, adopted a hybrid model. Marketing boards and *caisses* were never a feature of non-African cocoa-producing countries.

Marketing board and *caisse* structures were justified in terms of price stabilization (interyear and intrayear), quality assurance, and provision of services to farmers (subsidized-input purchase and extension). These systems came under significant pressure over the 1980s and 1990s, in particular from the two major donor institutions—the World Bank and the European Union (EU), which was involved as the consequence of the Stabex program established under the succession of Lomé Treaties with the ACP (Asian, Caribbean, and Pacific) group of countries.

Donor pressure is often seen as having been ideologically motivated, and there is no doubt an element of truth in this, although it is difficult to argue that the EU has always exhibited an overriding general commitment to liberalized agricultural markets. In any case, other factors were of greater importance.

- Primary-commodity prices were at historically low levels in the second half of the 1980s. The cocoa price fell more or less steadily from its 1977 peak to a low in the early 1990s, and subsequently has recovered only to a modest extent. Stabilization agencies that attempted to maintain cocoa-producer prices at levels that had been feasible in the 1970s and early 1980s consequently found themselves in financial problems. In certain countries, these were exacerbated by the fact that accumulated stabilization surpluses from earlier years had typically been "invested" in illiquid and poorly performing assets. The result was that a number of boards and *caisses* became technically insolvent.
- Marketing-board and *caisse* arrangements were viewed as nontransparent. Accounts were often late and opaque. It was difficult to distinguish taxes, which were potentially available to finance government expenditure, from marketing costs.
- The stabilization agencies became large organizations, often exercising significant political power and absorbing a substantial share of countries' cocoa-export earnings. Cocoa-marketing costs were therefore significantly higher in African producing countries than elsewhere, and there was reason to suppose that this involved a significant element of rent extraction. For example, Williams (1985) wrote of the Nigerian agricultural-marketing boards shortly before their abolition in 1986, "They have replaced the European firms at the apex of the buying system and shaped it to serve the needs of ruling parties, governments and the Northern aristocracy to expand and consolidate their networks of patronage" (13).
- Farmers have the residual claim on crop revenues. Falling world prices in conjunction with an unchanged marketing wedge exerted significant downward pressure on farm incomes.
- Stabilization also proved to be expensive for farmers. For them, stabilization often meant lower overall prices in exchange for stable prices. McIntire and Varangis (1999) evaluated the trade-off between stability and level of prices for the case of Côte d'Ivoire. They found that the benefits of stable prices did not compensate for the overall lower level of prices paid to the Ivorian cocoa farmers.

Donor institutions balked at refinancing the insolvent stabilization agencies, perhaps in part because they preferred free markets, but also because it was clear that the major beneficiaries of refinancing would be the stabilization agencies, themselves, and the political causes they espoused. Furthermore, nontransparency made it difficult to account for uses of funds provided. Farmers were seen by the donors as being poorly represented in the African political process, particularly in countries where regimes are less than fully democratic. Liberalization therefore came to be seen as a means of reducing marketing costs and raising farmers' share of the f.o.b. price.

The first African cocoa liberalization was that of Nigeria in 1986. Although the World Bank had argued that the Nigerian agricultural-marketing boards were ineffective and had sought their abolition as part of a structural adjustment program, the Nigerian government rejected that program but decided to abolish the marketing boards unilaterally. The World Bank would have preferred agricultural liberalization to be sequenced after foreign-exchange liberalization, which was not implemented at that time. There was little preparation for liberalization, and the process is regarded as having been unnecessarily chaotic (see Gilbert 1997).

Cameroon, the smallest of the major African producers, was next to move. This liberalization took place in stages starting in 1989 and concluding in 1995 (see Gilbert 1997 for details). The major impetus to liberalization was the insolvency of the stabilization agency, the Office National du Commercialisation des Produits de Base (ONCPB), which had responsibility for coffee as well as cocoa. The EU made replacement of the ONCPB by an organization with a more limited role (the Office National du Café et du Cacao; ONCC) a condition of Stabex financial support and required a sharp reduction in the price offered to farmers. The World Bank was never significantly involved with the Cameroon cocoa sector. Unlike the Nigerian liberalization, the Cameroonian reforms were never fully "owned" by the government or the Cameroonian media, which has consistently seen them as imposed by the donors. But despite the questionable ownership of reforms in Cameroon and problems in Nigeria, cocoa farmers in these two countries benefited significantly as prices paid to them rose substantially following the reforms.

Both Nigeria and Cameroon may be seen as small producers (see figure 4.1). This cannot be said of Côte d'Ivoire. Ivorian cocoa policy was administered through the Caisse de Stabilisation et du Soutien des Prix des Produits Agricoles, normally known simply as the Caistab. Prior to 1989, Ivorian cocoa prices were set at levels very similar to those in Cameroon, partly reflecting the common currency, but possibly also on the basis of common external advice. Caistab therefore experienced financial problems in the late 1980s similar to those of the Cameroonian ONCPB. However, the EU was prepared to offer greater assistance to the Ivorians. A sequence of piecemeal reforms was made through the 1990s with the objective of increasing the transparency of the process by which exporters bid for *déblocage* (i.e., permission to export). Supposedly complete liberalization came in 1999, largely as the consequence of World Bank insistence, although in practice there has been considerable back-tracking on the spirit of those commitments. As in the Cameroonian case, reform ownership remains problematic.

It is notable that the 1999 Ivorian liberalization coincided with a sharp fall in cocoa prices attributed by many farmers and also by some government officials and their advisors to the liberalization process. Our view, which coincides with that of the cocoa industry, is that this price fall was due to lack of growth in cocoa consumption and was completely unrelated to the liberalization process.[8] In any case, the fall in price led to significant civil disobedience and put pressure on the government to assist cocoa farmers. Cocoa prices recovered sharply in 2001 and 2002 as consumption rose in the context of weak production, which reflects the neglect of cocoa trees during the previous low-price years.

Ghana is the remaining major African cocoa producer. Currently (2003), it has only liberalized partially and tentatively. The Ghana Cocoa Board, generally referred to as Cocobod, historically enjoyed monopsony-monopoly power. Licenced private buyers are now permitted to operate, but they are still required to sell to Cocobod and, in principle, are required to buy from farmers at a uniform regulated price. Ghanaian farmers, however, are now obtaining a significantly higher share of the f.o.b. price than during the 1980s, reflecting a partial retreat from the interannual-stabilization objective, some reduction in cocoa taxation, and a sharp fall in the Cocobod establishment.

Ghanaian cocoa sells at a significant premium relative to cocoa from other origins, in part because of a good fat content, but most importantly because of the reliability and rigor of Cocobod quality controls. These controls depend in large measure on Cocobod's monopoly-monopsony powers. Although there is an issue of the size of the Ghanaian premium in relation to the cost of producing cocoa of this quality,[9] the Ghanaians are clearly correct to worry that liberalization could result in an erosion of this premium.

4.4   The Direct Impact of Liberalization and Globalization

The complexity and diversity of the west African cocoa-market-liberalization process makes it difficult to identify the appropriate dates for before-and-after comparisons. Liberalization is a legal act and can therefore be dated precisely—1986–1987 for Nigeria, 1989, 1991, and 1995 for Cameroon, and 1999 for Côte d'Ivoire, with Ghana still to fully liberalize. By contract, globalization is a process that is partially consequential on liberalization, as in Nigeria and Cameroon, but that may also anticipate lib-

---

8. Cocoa grindings were effectively constant in 1998–1999 (2.77 tonnes against 2.78 tonnes in 1997–1998), while production rose 4.5 percent over the same period (from 2.61 tonnes to 2.80 tonnes; ICCO 2002).

9. The major cost arises from the diversion of sub-export-quality beans to domestic processing, for which purpose they are sold at what is believed to be a significant discount to world prices.

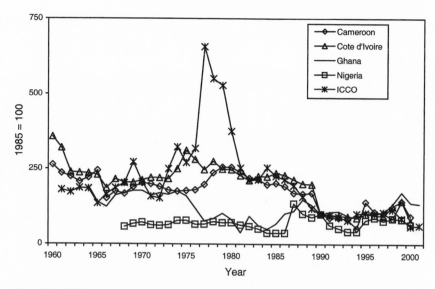

Fig. 4.3   Deflated cocoa producer prices and deflated ICCO indicator price (1985 = 100)

eralization if, as in Côte d'Ivoire and Ghana, administered prices are brought increasingly into line with the world price.

Figure 4.3 charts producer prices in the four west African countries and also the International Cocoa Organization (ICCO) indicator price, which we interpret as the world price.[10] It is apparent that these five prices have moved much more closely together since 1990 than in earlier years. This visual impression is broadly confirmed by the correlations shown in table 4.1. The nonitalic correlations above the diagonal give correlations between the proportionate price changes in the four producing countries over crop years 1968–1969 to 1985–1986 (the year prior to the Nigerian liberalization). The italicized correlations beneath the diagonal give the same correlations over crop years 1989–1990 to 1998–1999. The table also includes the correlations with changes in the ICCO indicator price lagged one year. The table shows the prices in Cameroon, Côte d'Ivoire, and Ghana (as well as Nigeria, although to a much lesser extent) moving much more closely together after 1990 than before 1986. The leading principal component of the four price-change series accounts for 43.9 percent of the price variation prior to liberalization and 69.8 percent after liberalization. All four prices also move more closely with the ICCO price in the postliberalization period.

On the basis of these figures, we conclude that the west African cocoa

10. The four producer prices are in domestic-currency units and are deflated by national consumer price indexes. The ICCO price is in U.S.$ and is deflated by the U.S. CPI (International Monetary Fund [IMF] 2001). The five prices are measured as indexes normalized at 100 in 1990. There is, however, no implication that the five 1990 prices are equal.

Table 4.1   Price Correlations 1968–1969 to 1985–1986 (above diagonal) and
1989–1990 to 1998–1999 (beneath diagonal)

1989–1990 to 1998–1999	1968–1969 to 1985–1986				
	Cameroon	Côte d'Ivoire	Ghana	Nigeria	ICCO
Cameroon		0.1183	−0.0404	0.5161	0.6345
Côte d'Ivoire	*0.4773*		0.0816	0.3703	0.6035
Ghana	*0.7011*	*0.8038*		0.2950	0.0170
Nigeria	*0.6395*	*0.4334*	*0.5061*		0.6251
ICCO	*0.8051*	*0.7820*	*0.7575*	*0.8115*	

Note: Correlations are between annual changes in the logarithms of the producer prices. The ICCO price change is lagged one year.

producers globalized, in the sense of moving to a common world-cocoa price from the start of the 1990s. The Nigerian liberalization was three years prior to this, and the institutional liberalizations in Cameroon and Côte d'Ivoire came over the course of the following decade. However, crucially, the start of the 1990s saw the move away from interannual price stabilization in both these two countries (under EU pressure) and also in Ghana. In the calculations that we report in section 4.6, we therefore regard the period up to (and including) 1985–1986 as preglobalization and the period from 1989–1990 to date as postglobalization.

The principal objective of liberalization was to raise the share of the f.o.b. price received by farmers. There are two possible approaches to the problem of measuring this impact.

- The first approach is to take time averages of the shares of the producer prices, converted into dollars, in the world price before and after liberalization. However, this exercise is complicated by the complicated nonmarket-exchange-rate regimes operated by Ghana and Nigeria over the periods of interest.
- The second uses point estimates of the shares of producer prices in f.o.b. port prices, both measured in local currency. This procedure gives a clearer comparison but necessarily introduces a degree of arbitrariness in the dates selected for the comparison; it is apparent from figure 4.1 that the extent to which the various producer prices were divorced from the world price varies considerably over time.

We adopt the second of these procedures. Table 4.2 brings together some estimates of the effects of liberalization on the farmers' share of the f.o.b. price. These figures allow comparison of the four liberalizing origins in west Africa with Brazil, Indonesia, and Malaysia, which have no history of internally regulated cocoa markets. Figures relating to liberalized markets are italicized. There is broad agreement between the Ruf and de Milly

Table 4.2   **Producer Prices as Share of F.O.B. Price (%)**

	Ruf and de Milly (1990) 1989	World Bank 1994–95	LMC 1996	Gilbert and Tollens (1999) 1998–99
Cameroon	41	*71*	*75*	*73*
Côte d'Ivoire	48	48	47	63
Ghana	52	49	56	56
Nigeria	*74*	72	*88*	*90*
Brazil	*79*	72	72	n.s.
Indonesia	*87*	78	78	*88*
Malaysia	*72*	*94*	*91*	n.s.
Average, liberalized	*78.0*	*77.4*	*80.8*	*84.0*
Average, nonliberalized	47.0	48.5	51.2	59.7
Liberalization effect	31.0	28.9	29.6	24.3

Note: Figures relating to liberalized markets are italicized. n.s. = not stated.

(1990) figures for 1989 and those taken from the World Bank, LMC International,[11] and Gilbert and Tollens (1999). This comparison highlights not only the sharp jump in the Cameroonian share after liberalization, but also the steady increase in the Ivorian share prior to the formal liberalization in the 1999–2000 season.

On the basis of these figures, we take the preliberalization shares in Cameroon and Côte d'Ivoire to be those given by Ruf and de Milly (1990) and the postliberalization shares to be equal to the 81 percent average reported by LMC for 1996. Ghana and Nigeria pose greater problems. In Ghana, which has yet to fully liberalize, we lack a postliberalization share, while for Nigeria, which liberalized before the Ruf and de Milly (1990) survey, we lack a preliberalization estimate. Furthermore, it is apparent from figure 4.1 that Ghana had already commenced raising its producer-price share prior to 1989. We take a starting value for both countries of 47 percent, the nonliberalized average from Ruf and de Milly (1990), and see the Nigerian share rising by 41 percent to the LMC figure of 88 percent, with the Ghanaian share rising by 34 percent to the LMC liberalized average of 81 percent.[12] These estimates are clearly orders of magnitude at best and should be treated as such. The impact of rises in the producers' share of the f.o.b. price on actual producer prices will depend on the impact on the world price.

These increases in the farmers' share of the world price result from two

11. The figures were received by private communication (LMC International is a commodity consulting firm).

12. The very high LMC estimate of the share of the Nigerian producer price in the f.o.b. price reflects the lack of dependence of the Nigerian government on taxes on agricultural exports. We would expect Ghana to continue to tax cocoa-export revenues even after full liberalization. Note that, because intermediation costs are largely independent of the cocoa price, the producer share, which is a residual, will be positively correlated with the price.

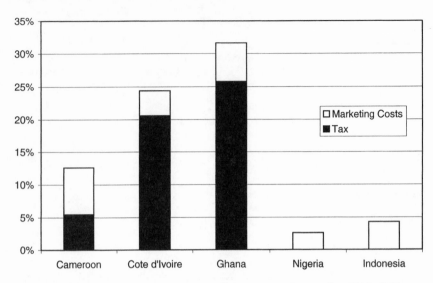

Fig. 4.4   Taxes and marketing costs as shares of the producer price, 1998–1999

separate effects. The first is cost reductions arising out of more efficient intermediation. The second is the reduction in taxation. One might, in principle, regard the administrative expenses of the stabilization agencies as
either taxation or as an intermediation-cost item—we follow the latter
approach. Figure 4.4, which is based on statistics taken from Gilbert and
Tollens (1999), shows the dramatic differences between tax levels in the two
nonliberalized countries (Côte d'Ivoire and Ghana) compared with that in
the liberalized economies. On the basis of these statistics, we estimate that
75 percent of the increase in the producers' share in the liberalization process arises from reduced taxation.

That estimate is conjectural. Reductions in intermediation costs are important in the welfare analysis we perform in section 4.6 because these may
be interpreted as efficiency gains, while reductions in taxation generate
transfers. Relatively little information is available on the scale of these benefits. Gilbert and Tollens (1999), who interviewed new and established cocoa exporters in Cameroon, estimated that intermediation costs had fallen
by 5 percent (relative to the producer price) in the three years following full
liberalization.[13]

Globalization will also have affected, and generally increased, the variability of the prices received by farmers. Figure 4.5 shows the unconditional, interannual, logarithmic standard deviations of the four (deflated)

13. They attributed these differences to the fact that newer exporters utilized less capital
and made greater use of specialized intermediaries (such as transportation companies). Despite this, Cameroonian intermediation costs remained (and remain) high.

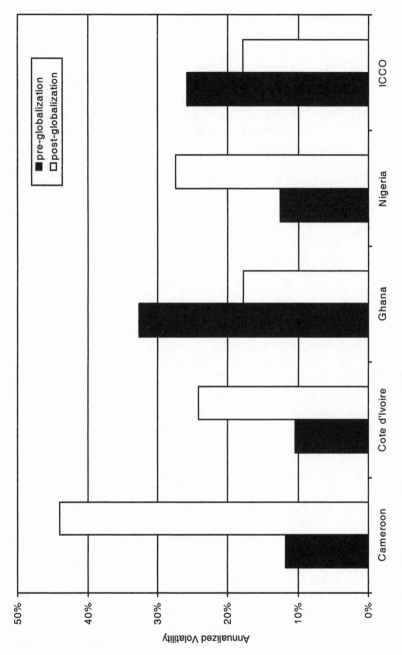

Fig. 4.5   Producer price volatility before and after globalization

producer prices before and after globalization. Farmers in Cameroon have experienced the largest increase in price variability—a 32 percent rise from 12 percent to 44 percent. Instead, Côte d'Ivoire and Nigeria have seen more modest rises, while volatility in Ghana has actually fallen. This last, paradoxical, finding is the consequence of the lack of success of Cocobod in its declared stabilization objective during the 1980s, when sharp movements in inflation movements resulted in the supposedly stabilized domestic price becoming, in real terms, more variable than the world price. Note that, except in Ghana, where the nominal producer price continues to be fixed for the entire crop-year, the figures tabulated in figure 4.4 may underestimate the extent to which the increase in variability experienced by farmers since liberalization has also increased intra-annual-price variability.

Figure 4.4 also reports the variability of the world (ICCO indicator) price over the same period. The modest decline in world-price variability implies that the rises in Cameroon, Côte d'Ivoire, and Nigeria cannot be attributable to any greater variability in the postglobalization world price.

4.5   A Model of the World Cocoa Market

Because our interest is in the four major west African producing countries that have liberalized their cocoa sectors, our strategy is to model production in these countries in detail but to embed these equations in what is otherwise a highly aggregated world model. A benefit of this approach is that we do not need to make gratuitous assumptions about other aspects of the cocoa market. A cost is that highly stylized modeling of consumption and non-African production may distort our results.

For each of the four origins ($j = 1, \ldots, 4$) we consider, we model production Q_{jt} in period t as a linear function of a quadratic time trend, current and lagged expected prices, and price volatility.

$$(7) \quad \ln Q_{jt} = \beta_{j0} + \beta_{j1}t + \beta_{j2}\frac{t^2}{100} + \beta_{j3}E_{t-1}\ln P_{jt} + \beta_{j4}E_{t-2}\ln P_{jt-1}$$
$$+ \beta_{j5}\sigma_{jt} + u_{jt}$$

The quadratic trend is required to account for the declines and subsequent rises in production in Ghana and Nigeria. It may be argued that these changes were determined, in fact, by the movements in producer prices in those countries; if this is so, these effects arise from the cumulative effects of prices over a long period and are not easily modeled in terms of simple lag distributions. In any case, part of these two declines and the subsequent reversals reflect changes in infrastructure investment, the provision of extension, and other factors that cannot be directly related to price levels.

The expected producer prices $E_{t-1}\ln P_{jt}$ and $E_{t-2}\ln P_{jt-1}$ in equation (7) are generated as the one-period predictions from estimated trend-augmented first-order autoregressions.

(8) $$\ln P_{jt} = \gamma_0 + \gamma_1 \ln P_{j,t-1} + v_{jt}$$

Equation (8) is estimated separately for each country for the preglobalization and postglobalization periods.[14] This specification supposes that farmers form price expectations rationally on the basis of the limited information set consisting of the local price history and without any need to learn the price processes.[15] In principle, one would expect only the current-period expectations $E_{t-1} \ln P_{jt}$ to explain production, but in practice the lagged expectation $E_{t-1} \ln P_{jt-1}$ is also required.

The price volatility σ_{jt} is the unconditional standard deviation of proportionate price changes in country j estimated separately for the pre- and postglobalization periods.[16] The expected sign of the coefficient β_{j5} is negative as farmers self-insure by diversifying effort away from the risky crop.

The estimated-price autoregressions (equation [8]) are given in table 4.3. The divide between the preglobalization sample I and the postglobalization sample II is taken as between the 1988–1989 and 1989–1990 crop years for Cameroon, Côte d'Ivoire, and Ghana, and between the 1986–1987 and 1987–1988 crop years for Nigeria. The trend terms are dropped from the Cameroonian and Ivorian price autoregression equations, as they are insignificant (real producer prices in these two countries dropped sharply in 1989, but not within the two samples). Chow tests give clear rejections of sample homogeneity for Cameroon and Côte d'Ivoire, but not for Ghana, where full liberalization has yet to take place, or (more surprisingly) for Nigeria.[17]

Estimates of the production equations (equation [7]) are given in table 4.4. The first set of estimates for each origin employs ordinary least squares

14. The time periods are as follows: Cameroon and Côte d'Ivoire, 1960–1961 to 1988–1989 and 1990–1991 to 1998–1999; Ghana, 1964–1965 to 1988–1989 and 1989–1990 to 1999–2000; Nigeria, 1968–1969 to 1985–1986 and 1988–1989 to 1998–1999; and the ICCO, 1962–1963 to 1988–1989 and 1989–1990 to 2000–2001.

15. We explored two alternative specifications for the price-expectations variables. The first was to allow the preliberalization expectations to be formed on the basis of actual, announced, nominal-producer prices in conjunction with a rational expectation of the rate of inflation. This specification gave a significantly inferior fit in the production equations. The second alternative was to allow price expectations to be formed on the basis of the lagged world (i.e., ICCO indicator) price in addition to the lagged domestic price. This gave qualitatively similar results for the estimated production equations to the specification employed and was marginally inferior in terms of fit for Cameroon, Côte d'Ivoire, and Ghana, and marginally superior for Nigeria.

16. An alternative would have been to use a volatility conditional on generalized autoregressive conditional heteroscedasticity (GARCH). The only price equation that showed evidence of GARCH effects and was the preliberalization equation for Cameroon.

17. The differences between the two samples are more evident in the set of estimates (not reported) based on the specification that also includes the lagged world price. These estimates show the burden of the dependence shifting from the lagged domestic price in sample I to the lagged world price in sample II.

Table 4.3   Estimated Domestic Price Equations

Dependent Variable ln $P_{j,t}$	Cameroon I	Cameroon II	Côte d'Ivoire I	Côte d'Ivoire II	Ghana I	Ghana II	Nigeria I	Nigeria II
Constant	1.8946	5.4288	2.0176	4.8712	1.9997	2.2273	1.1496	1.4281
	(2.58)	(1.58)	(0.64)	(2.56)	(1.97)	(2.11)	(1.69)	(1.11)
ln $P_{j,t-1}$	0.6404	-0.1925	0.6173	-0.0587	0.6085	0.2975	0.7843	0.5976
	(2.58)	(0.55)	(5.31)	(0.14)	(3.30)	(1.18)	(5.30)	(2.80)
Trend					-0.0088	0.0301	-0.0153	0.0073
					(0.80)	(2.26)	(2.52)	(0.38)
Sample	1960–61 1988–89	1990–91 1999–2000	1960–61 1988–89	1990–91 1999–2000	1965–65 1988–89	1989–90 2000–01	1968–69 1985–86	1987–88 1999–2000
No. of observations	29	10	29	10	25	12	18	13
R^2	0.4438	0.0371	0.5110	0.0025	0.5352	0.5667	0.8226	0.4445
SE	0.1075	0.2965	0.0900	0.1894	0.3071	0.1398	0.1127	0.2498
D.W.	2.00	2.01	1.93	1.83	2.00	1.84	1.60	1.60
Chow test	$F(2,35) = 15.32$ [0.00%]		$F(2,35) = 10.28$ [0.03%]		$F(3,31) = 0.77$ [52.22%]		$F(3,25) = 1.82$ [16.99%]	

Notes: t-statistics in parentheses. The Chow test tests for common coefficients in samples I and II (tail probabilities in square brackets). Blank cells indicate that the variable is omitted from the equation specification. SE = standard error; D.W. = Durbin Watson.

Table 4.4　Estimates of Production Equations (1969–1970 to 1999–2000)

Dependent Variable ln Q_{jt}	Cameroon		Côte d'Ivoire		Ghana		Nigeria	
	OLS	FIML	OLS	FIML	OLS	FIML	OLS	FIML
Constant	2.6155	2.7518	3.0137	2.2600	2.8578	4.9955	4.2815	4.6299
	(4.61)	(7.91)	(4.86)	(13.4)	(1.17)	(6.02)	(6.24)	(7.30)
Trend	−0.0326	−0.0361	0.0687	0.0507	−0.0667	−0.1114	−0.0907	−0.0952
	(2.21)	(2.93)	(3.81)	(3.48)	(2.16)	(4.65)	(4.35)	(4.67)
Trend²/100	0.0981	0.1110	0.0185	0.0700	0.1395	0.2204	0.1493	0.1617
	(2.87)	(4.22)	(0.44)	(2.43)	(2.35)	(4.84)	(3.62)	(4.07)
$E_{t-1} \ln P_{j,t}$	0.1833	0.1705			0.3683	0.2359	0.3406	0.3150
	(1.32)	(1.97)			(2.20)	(1.59)	(2.52)	(0.43)
$E_{t-2} \ln P_{j,t-1}$	0.2599	0.2552	0.2560	0.4258	0.3832	0.1899	0.1519	0.1108
	(1.80)	(2.92)	(2.01)	(*)	(2.36)	(*)	(1.14)	(*)
Elasticity	0.4431	0.4258	0.2560	0.4258	0.7115	0.4258	0.4925	0.4258
F(2,26)	6.91				8.68		7.27	
	[0.39%]				[0.13%]		[0.31%]	
Volatility		−0.2423		−0.2423		−0.2423		−0.2423
		(2.83)		(*)		(*)		(*)
R^2	0.3940		0.9733		0.8337		0.7602	
SE	0.0811	0.0871	0.1104	0.1144	0.1298	0.1334	0.1445	0.1404
D.W.	1.66		1.93		2.13		2.40	

Notes: t-statistics (not corrected for generated variable bias) in parentheses, (*) indicates a restricted coefficient; SE = standard error; D.W. = Durbin Watson. The F-statistic tests the joint significance of the two expected price coefficients in the OLS estimates (tail probability in square brackets). Likelihood ratio test on FIML restrictions $\chi^2(39) = 47.97$ [15.4%].

(OLS). The coefficient β_{23} in the Ivorian equation, where the unrestricted estimate was negative, was set to zero. The significance of the individual-price coefficients for the remaining three origins is not high in every case, but the joint significance of the two coefficients, examined by the standard F-test, is high. Estimated supply elasticities $\beta_{j3} + \beta_{j4}$ vary from 0.26 (Côte d'Ivoire) to 0.71 (Ghana).

These single-equation estimates suffer from two problems.

- They result in different supply elasticities for the different origins. It is plausible to argue that these differing estimated responses reflect sampling error rather than genuine differences in farmers' behavior.
- They do not permit estimation of the volatility effects (since the volatility variable for a single country is indistinguishable from a shift dummy at the sample break).

We address these two problems by reestimating the model as a system using full information maximum likelihood (FIML).[18] The system estimates allow us to impose the restriction of equal supply elasticities across all four producing countries.

$$(9) \qquad \beta_{j3} + \beta_{j4} = \beta_{13} + \beta_{14} \quad (j = 2, 3, 4)$$

It also allows us to estimate the volatility coefficients by imposing the restrictions

$$(10) \qquad \beta_{j5} = \beta_{15} \quad (j = 2, 3, 4).$$

The estimated equations using the FIML procedure are given in the second set of country columns in table 4.3. The (uniform) estimated supply elasticity is 0.43, and the volatility response is estimated as −0.24, in both cases the coefficients being significantly different from zero. A standard likelihood-ratio test establishes that coefficient restrictions in equations (9) and (10) are acceptable.[19]

Ideally, we should also estimate supply elasticities for the remainder of the world. Unfortunately, we have not been able to obtain producer-price series of sufficient length for the other major origins to estimate realistic equations. This is in part a consequence of the fact that, in a liberalized regime, domestic prices are not uniform and that there is seldom any official interest in collecting information on prices actually paid. Pursing the alternative track of specifying equations in terms of the world (ICCO indicator) price failed to generate a production elasticity that was either eco-

18. A third problem is that the standard errors in the reported OLS regressions will suffer from generated regressor bias (see Pagan 1984). We do not correct for this because we will be primarily interested in the FIML estimates.

19. The most problematic restriction is that relating to the Ivorian price elasticity β_{24}. One may have some confidence that the estimated volatility coefficient is indeed measuring a volatility effect due to the fact that volatility has declined in one the four origins (Ghana) in the period since 1989, while it has increased in the remaining three origins.

nomically or statistically significant. Since it would be unreasonable to suppose that non-African cocoa production is unresponsive to prices, we have chosen to suppose that the estimated non-African elasticity is equal to the elasticity previously reported for the major African origins.

We also require a demand-elasticity estimate. Apparent consumption of cocoa is referred to in the trade as grindings. We estimate a standard, logarithmic, partial-adjustment-demand function relating aggregate world grindings G_t to the gross domestic product (GDP) of the industrialized countries (GDP$_t$), a linear time trend, and the current-dollar world price deflated by the U.S. consumer price index (CPI; PW_t). The resulting estimates only conform moderately well with theory—there is evidence of a continuing shift in taste toward cocoa consumption at around 2 percent per annum but no evidence that this is related to income, at least as measured by GDP.[20] The estimated price elasticity is relatively small at 0.19. This may seem surprising, but it should be noted that cocoa now only makes up between 5 percent and 10 percent, by value, of a chocolate bar and even less of a chocolate-covered confectionary product. Estimation is by instrumental variables,[21] treating the current world price as endogenous. The estimated equation is (t-statistics in parentheses)

$$(11) \qquad \ln G_t = 4.1567 + .0100t + 0.4812 \ln G_{t-1}$$
$$ (3.73) \quad (3.88) \quad\quad (3.50)$$

$$+ 0.5991\Delta \ln \text{GDP}_t - 0.0961 \ln PW_t$$
$$ (1.71) \quad\quad\quad\quad\quad (3.08)$$

Sample: 1969–1970 to 1998–1999
Standard errors: 0.0266
Instrument validity: $\chi^2(7) = 3.04$ [88.1%]

In section 4.6, we use the estimated elasticity from this equation in conjunction with the supply-elasticity and volatility coefficient from the FIML estimates reported in table 4.3 to evaluate the effects of globalization of the cocoa market.

4.6 Incidence—Who Benefited?

We consider two scenarios:

- Unilateral liberalization-globalization by each country considered separately and
- Joint liberalization by all four origins.

---

20. The t-statistic on the variable ln GDP$_t$, dropped from equation, was 0.19.
21. We use as instruments the exogenous variables included in the production equations. These are the current and lagged expected producer prices in the four west African origins (only the lagged expected price for Côte d'Ivoire was dropped since the current price was incorrectly signed from the Ivorian production equation) and the quadratic trend.

Table 4.5   Parameter Values

	Cameroon	Côte d'Ivoire	Ghana	Nigeria	Weighted Average	Source
δ increase in producers' share of world price (%)	83	73	72	87	75	Table 4.2
ε production elasticity	0.45	0.45	0.45	0.45	0.45	Table 4.4
η demand elasticity	0.19	0.19	0.19	0.19	0.19	Equation (11)
ν increase in price volatility (%)	32.2	13.7	−14.8	14.8	9.0	Figure 4.4
θ volatility semi-elasticity	0.24	0.24	0.24	0.24	0.24	Table 4.4
ω share of liberalizing countries in world production (%)	5.6	30.9	11.2	6.1	53.7 (total)	1985–86 to 1989–90

Table 4.6   Impacts of Unilateral and Multilateral Liberalization (%)

	Cameroon	Côte d'Ivoire	Ghana	Nigeria	Multilateral Impact
Producer price shock	95.0	56.8	66.8	84.4	
Unilateral impact on world price	−3.7	−12.4	−4.2	−3.3	−20.0
Impact of volatility shock	0.7	1.6	−0.6	0.3	2.0
Total unilateral impact	−3.0	−10.8	−4.8	−3.0	−19.3
Net unilateral price rise	91.6	50.6	64.1	81.7	
Net multilateral price rise	59.5	36.2	39.1	51.1	

Notes: Calculated using parameter values given in table 4.5. Blank cells indicate that no effects are calculated.

As discussed in section 4.3, the actual liberalization process was less clear-cut than this and indeed is still incomplete; globalization has—to some extent—anticipated full liberalization.

Table 4.5 collects together the parameter values that we use in the incidence calculations. We do this in conjunction with equation (4) to estimate the effects of unilateral and joint (multilateral) liberalization, which are reported in table 4.6. The small-country assumption appears reasonable for Cameroon and Nigeria, where liberalization is seen as having depressed the world price by 3 percent in each case, but not for Côte d'Ivoire, where liberalization is seen as reducing the world price by 10 percent. Ghana, where liberalization would push the world price down by 5 percent, is intermediate. It is notable that Nigeria and Cameroon were the first major African cocoa producers to liberalize and that liberalization was resisted in Ghana and Côte d'Ivoire, where the spillover effects onto the world price are larger. The impact of increased volatility on the world price is seen as small but nonnegligible. Turning to the multilateral liberalization, the world price is seen as falling by 20 percent in conjunction with a weighted-average rise in African producer prices of 76 percent.

The global-welfare impact of these changes may be analyzed by reference to figure 4.6, which has the world price on its vertical axes. The first

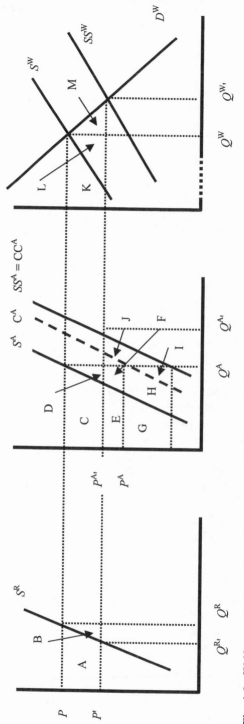

Fig. 4.6 Welfare analysis: (a), Non-African supply; (b), African supply; (c), World supply and demand

panel (a) shows the non-African supply curve S^R, while the second panel (b) displays the preliberalization African supply curve S^A, which is above the marginal cost curve C^A by the taxation wedge. The producer price is P^A. The initial world price is P but this falls to P' after liberalization.

We see liberalization as shifting the marginal-cost curve in the liberalizing economy down to CC^A through cost reductions and as eliminating the tax wedge. This shifts the postliberalization supply function to SS^A, which is coincident to the new marginal cost schedule CC^A. The producer price is shown as rising to $P^{A'}$.[22] World supply S^W is the horizontal sum of S^A and S^R ($Q^W = Q^A + Q^R$), which becomes SS^W after liberalization (see panel [c]). The world-demand curve is D^W. Production in the nonliberalizing economies falls from Q^R to $Q^{R'}$, and consumption rises from Q^W to $Q^{W'}$. Ignoring the complicating factor of price volatility, welfare changes are as follows.

Farmers in nonliberalizing economies: $-A$
Governments of liberalizing economies: $-(C + D + E + F)$
Farmers in liberalizing economies: $E + F + G + H + I + J$
Consumers: $K + L + M$

Provided we count one dollar to an African government as equivalent to one dollar to an African farmer, the net benefit to the liberalizing country is $(G + H) + (I + J) - (C + D)$. The country benefits in net terms so long as the efficiency gains $(I + J)$ exceed the transfer to foreign consumers $(C + D)$. With the same assumption and noting that $A + C = K$ and $B + D = L$, the net world benefit is $B + (G + H) + (I + J) + M$. Triangle B is the efficiency gain from substituting low-cost cocoa in the liberalizing economies for higher-cost cocoa in the rest of the world; rectangle $G + H$ is the cost reduction on the original quantity Q^A in the liberalizing economies;[23] triangles $I + J$ represent the efficiency gain from cost reduction in the liberalizing countries; and triangle M is additional consumer surplus arising from the lower world price.

We evaluate these quantities using the parameters displayed in table 4.5 and in relation to average price and production levels for the period 1985–1986 to 1989–1990 (i.e., prior to the impact of all the liberalizations except that of Nigeria). The effect of liberalization-globalization on the world price is obtained by numerical solution of the production and consumption equations through the market-clearing identity. The results of this exercise are given in table 4.7 (unilateral, country-by-country liberalization) and table 4.8 (multilateral liberalization and globalization by the four African cocoa-producing countries). Table 4.9 gives a break down of the estimated efficiency gains.

---

22. If the cost reduction is large relative to the tax reduction, $P^{A'}$ can be beneath P^A.
23. One might argue that $G + H$ is not entirely a benefit to the liberalizing economy if the resources liberated by the cost reduction do not find alternative use.

Table 4.7   **Incidence of Unilateral Liberalization Benefits (annual $US millions)**

	Relation to Figure 4.6	Cameroon	Côte d'Ivoire	Ghana	Nigeria
Benefit to farmers	$E + F + G + H + I + J - N$	130.8	486.3	221.4	126.8
Benefit to government	$-(C + D + E + F)$	-92.7	-446.5	-164.6	-89.7
Total producing country benefit	$(G + H) + (I + J) - (C + D) - N$	38.2	39.8	56.8	37.1
Benefit to other African producers	A (part)	-53.2	-89.3	-74.7	-52.3
Benefit to non-African producers	A (part)	-51.2	-180.6	-81.2	-50.8
Benefit to consumers	$K + L + M$	111.8	404.6	178.3	110.9
Total world benefit	$B + G + H + I + J + M - N$	45.5	174.6	79.1	44.9

Notes: Parameter values as in table 4.5. Area N is not identifiable on figure 4.6.

Table 4.8   **Incidence of Multilateral Liberalization and Globalization Benefits (annual $US millions)**

	Cameroon	Côte d'Ivoire	Ghana	Nigeria	Africa Total	Other Producers	Consumers	Total World
Benefit to farmers	92.3	382.8	154.8	83.5	713.4			
Benefit to government	-92.7	-446.5	-164.6	-89.7	-793.4			
Total benefit	-0.3	-63.8	-9.8	-6.1	-80.0	-315.8	730.2	334.4
Total benefit (%)	-0.2	-5.7	-2.4	-2.9	-4.1	-18.6	20.1	9.2

Notes: Parameter values as in table 4.5. Prices and quantities are averages of 1985–1986 to 1989–1990. Percentage benefit is relative to average revenues or expenditures over that period. Blank cells indicate that no effects are calculated.

Considering first the unilateral liberalization calculations (table 4.7), the major effect is a transfer of resources from government to farmers. Farmers benefit most in Côte d'Ivoire (nearly $500 million per annum), followed by Ghana (nearly $225 million per annum) and then Cameroon and Nigeria (around $125 million per annum). These benefits are in proportion to the size of the respective producing sectors. However, they are offset by governmental losses of tax revenue, which are of the same order of magnitude, so the net dollar benefits to the countries are much smaller—a little less than $40 million on an annual basis for each of Cameroon, Côte d'Ivoire, and Nigeria, and a little more than $55 million for Ghana.[24] The Ivorian benefits are relatively modest since the producer price is seen as ris-

24. If one were to take the view that one dollar to a government is worth less than one dollar to a smallholder farmer, then the producing countries would benefit more substantially.

Table 4.9   Analysis of Efficiency Gains (annual $US millions)

	Unilateral				
	Cameroon	Côte d'Ivoire	Ghana	Nigeria	Multilateral
Allocation gains					
Liberalizing producers	15.0	32.8	19.2	14.7	57.8
Other producers	0.7	6.9	1.7	0.7	15.2
Consumers	0.3	4.4	0.8	0.3	14.9
Cost reductions	30.9	148.8	54.9	29.9	264.5
Volatility costs	–1.4	–18.3	2.6	–0.8	–17.9
Total	45.5	174.6	79.1	44.9	334.4

ing by less than in the other origins (the preliberalization level was higher), and the price rise is dissipated to a greater extent through a fall in the world price. Consumers, who are predominantly in the developed economies, are seen as major beneficiaries, particularly from an Ivorian liberalization, while nonliberalizing producers lose heavily. Total world benefits are modest and in broad proportion to sectoral size—around $45 million annually from Cameroonian and Nigerian liberalizations, $80 million from Ghanaian liberalization, and $175 million from Ivorian liberalization. They are dominated by the transfer benefits both within the liberalizing economy (from the government to farmers) and from nonliberalizing producers to consumers.

Table 4.8 gives the estimated results of a multilateral liberalization. It is important to note that this does not represent the actual experience to date in that both Côte d'Ivoire and Ghana have both only partially liberalized marketing and maintain export taxes. (The price shocks we list in table 4.5 are substantially greater than those observed to date in these two countries.) The estimates given in table 4.8 therefore relate to a hypothetical full liberalization and not to the actual observed events. An analysis of the impact of the actual liberalizations would be considerably more complicated and would require a fully specified econometric model.

The estimates in table 4.8 show that although farmers would have benefited in each Cameroon, Ghana, and Nigeria, these benefits are almost exactly offset by the losses of governmental tax revenue with the result that the countries as whole would be slightly worse off. In Côte d'Ivoire, the revenue loss so substantially exceeds the benefit to farmers that the net loss is unambiguous. As in the unilateral exercise, to the extent that government cocoa revenues were spent on wasteful activities, the countries (taken as wholes) may have benefited in welfare terms even in this case. This must be a judgmental matter. Nonliberalizing countries also are seen as losing revenues, and their farmers would have been worse off. The major beneficiaries would have been consumers in the developed-market economies, who would have benefited to the order of $725 million per annum, around 20 percent of their cocoa expenditures.

The analysis of the net efficiency gains reported in table 4.9 shows that cost reductions consequential on liberalization are the major source of net benefit. We have supposed that 25 percent of the increase in the producer-price share may be attributed to cost reductions, but we acknowledge that this figure is highly conjectural. Allocational gains in the liberalizing economies are the next largest item. These arise from elimination of the tax wedge between the producer price and marginal-production costs. Allocational gains in consuming and nonliberalizing producer countries are small, reflecting low elasticities. The increased volatility arising out of globalization imposes only small costs, except in Côte d'Ivoire.

These exercises assume that liberalizing governments totally eliminate export taxes. The unilateral liberalization exercise reported in table 4.7 shows that Cameroon, Ghana, and Nigeria all benefit from increasing production and would therefore lose revenues from export taxes. In Côte d'Ivoire, the net benefit is small in relation to production, implying that revenues would be broadly unaffected by restricting production. The results of the multilateral exercise reported in table 4.8 further show that the four African producers would all benefit substantially from a coordinated restriction of production. This must be subject to the qualifications that prolonged periods of high prices may provoke new production in other countries (including countries that are not currently significant cocoa exporters) and that the conclusion will not follow if government revenues are less highly valued than farmers' incomes. However, our model, which is specified as having isoelastic demand and supply functions, is not well suited to the calculation of optimal export taxes.

4.7 Conclusions

Donor agents and the developed-country governments have exerted considerable pressure on African producers of tropical export crops to liberalize their internal marketing systems for these products. They have also pressed for the elimination or reining back of intertemporal and interregional stabilization schemes, which were seen as responsible for fiscal excess and manifest waste. The major objective of these liberalization programs has been to ensure that farmers obtain a higher share in the f.o.b. prices for which the crop is sold at the ports.

Globalization of these markets is a direct consequence of liberalization—the prices in the now liberalized markets move substantially more closely together than did the preliberalized prices so that the world price has become the effective pricing basis in the producing as well as the consuming countries. Globalization has two unsought consequences for producing countries:

- The prices received by farmers have become more volatile (except in Ghana, where the nominal price stabilization had been counter productive).
- The effects of one country's actions in the market have a much more direct impact on farmers in other producing countries than previously.

This second aspect of globalization is the cause of the adding-up problem. A cost-reducing market liberalization in a small producing country raises the share of the world price obtained by farmers and has a negligible effect on the world price itself. However, if a country with a large share of the world market liberalizes, this will shift the world-supply curve to the right and, in conjunction with highly inelastic demand, will depress the world price. Farmers will then find that they obtain a larger share of a lower price. The same is true if one considers multilateral liberalization in a large group of individually small producers.

Cocoa is produced entirely in developing countries and largely in west Africa, where a system of internal market regulation inherited from colonial governments prevailed until the late 1980s. In our view, these unintended consequences of globalization are likely to be more apparent in the cocoa market than in any other commodity market. The first African producers to liberalize their internal cocoa-marketing systems were Nigeria in 1986 and Cameroon in 1989–1995, both of which had small shares in world exports. Adding-up effects were therefore unimportant. In 1999, after a long period of pressure, the donors pushed Côte d'Ivoire, the largest producer with one-third of world production, into reluctant liberalization. Ghana, which is also a significant producer, still maintains significant controls. If both of these producers fully liberalize their markets, the impact on the world price will be significant. Our calculations indicate that the world price would fall in total by around one third of the rise in producer prices calculated on a constant world-price basis. This figure reflects the inelasticity of demand and the high market share of the African producers.

Despite the projected fall in the world cocoa price, African farmers do benefit from liberalization, so in that sense the liberalization programs achieve their intended objective. However, these benefits are largely the consequence of a transfer from governments to farmers. The net dollar benefit to the country is positive for a country that liberalizes unilaterally, but the depressing effect on the world price is such that these benefits become negative if all four African cocoa-producing countries liberalize. For this reason, consumers, most of whom live in the developed-market economies, turn out to be the major beneficiaries from lower cocoa prices. The scale of this benefit is substantial. The losers are non-African farmers and the governments (and hence the taxpayers) of the African producing countries. The overall efficiency gains to the world are dominated by cost reductions consequent on liberalization, but it is difficult to be confident about the size of these gains.

One reaction to these results would be to argue that producing countries are better advised not to liberalize their agricultural-export sectors, and there are many who have taken this position. We regard this view as ill advised. First, the policy is not obviously feasible since individual producing countries each do have an incentive to liberalize. (In cocoa, this incentive is relatively small for Côte d'Ivoire.) The result is a classic Prisoners' Dilemma in which the cooperative nonliberalization equilibrium is not sustainable. But even if the African producers were able to devise an enforcement mechanism to support the nonliberalization equilibrium, they would be unable to prevent increased production elsewhere, including from countries that are currently not major cocoa exporters. Furthermore, to the extent that liberalization does significantly reduce production costs, intermediation costs or both (and we have discussed some evidence that suggests this is the case), nonliberalizing producers will find that any competitive advantage they currently possess will be steadily eliminated.

The development agencies have tended to see liberalization as a means of redistributing resources back to farmers. We have shown, however, that the incidence of the long-run benefits of liberalization is predominantly for developed-country consumers. It is therefore essential that liberalization should be accompanied by policies that attempt to redress the unfavorable redistributive effects arising from global liberalization.

Our thesis is not about market liberalization per se, but about the global impact of multilateral liberalizations by a group of commodity-producing countries responsible for a large share of the world market. Liberalization benefits each country taken individually; but, with inelastic demand, multilateral liberalization shifts the benefits away from the producers and toward the consumers. At the country level, primary-producing developing countries will feel that they have been cheated if, collectively, they do not receive a significant share of the benefits. Political support for liberalization will depend on the distribution of the gains both within the producing countries themselves and on a global level. Governments need to apply complementary policies to accompany liberalization, and the international agencies should be prepared to advise and assist in this process.

Clearly, one case study is insufficient to allow generalizations about globalization even in the primary sector. Furthermore, we have focused on cocoa as presenting what is possibly the most extreme case of an adverse distributional impact. We hope that our analysis and results will shed light on the globalization process affecting all primary-commodity markets and provide a benchmark against which other commodity markets and countries might be compared.

References

Akiyama, T., J. Baffes, D. Larson, and P. Varangis. 2001. Market reforms: lessons from country and commodity experiences. In *Commodity market reforms: Lessons from two decades,* ed. T. Akiyama, J. Baffes, D. Larson, and P. Varangis, 5–34. Washington, D.C.: World Bank.

Akiyama, T., and D. Larson. 1994. The adding-up problem: Strategies for primary commodity exports in sub-Saharan Africa. Policy Research Paper no. 1245. Washington, D.C.: World Bank.

Bates, R. H. 1989. The reality of structural adjustment: A skeptical appraisal. In *Structural adjustment and agriculture: Theory and practice in Africa and Latin America,* ed. S. Commander, 221–227. London: Overseas Development Institute.

Bhagwati, J. 1958. Immiserizing growth: A geometrical note. *Review of Economic Studies* 25, 201–05.

Engberg-Pederson, P., P. Gibbon, P. Raikes, and L. Udshott. 1996. *Limits of adjustment in Africa: The effects of economic liberalization 1986–94.* Portsmouth, N.H.: Heinemann.

Evenson, R. E. 2002. Technology and prices in agriculture. Yale University, Department of Economics. Manuscript.

Gilbert, C. L. 1987. International commodity agreements: design and performance. *World Development* 15, 591–616.

———. 1996. International commodity agreements: an obituary notice. *World Development* 24, 1–19.

———. 1997. *Cocoa market liberalization.* London: Cocoa Association of London.

———. 2002. Commodity risk management: preliminary lessons from the International Task Force. In *Resource management in Asia Pacific developing countries,* ed. R. Garnault, 39–69. Canberra: Asia Pacific Press.

Gilbert, C. L., and E. Tollens. 1999. Effets de la libéralisation dans les sous-secteurs café-cacao au Cameroun (Effects of liberalization in the Cameroonian Cocoa-Coffee Sector). Vol. 1. Yaoundé, Cameroon: European Commission.

———. 2003. Does market liberalization jeopardize export quality? Cameroonian cocoa, 1985–2000. *Journal of African Economics.*

Gilbert, C. L., and J. ter Wengel. 2001. The production and marketing of primary commodities. In *Commodities and development at the turn of the Millennium,* 21–62. Amsterdam: Common Fund for Commodities.

International Cocoa Organization (ICCO). 2002. *Quarterly Bulletin of Cocoa Statistics, Cocoa Year 1999–2000.* 26 (3). London: ICCO.

International Monetary Fund (IMF). 2001. *International financial statistics.* Washington, D.C.: IMF.

Johnson, H. G. 1953. Equilibrium growth in an international economy. *Canadian Journal of Economics and Political Science* 19, 478–500.

———. 1958. *International trade and economic growth.* London: George Allen and Unwin.

Kanbur, S. M. R. 1984. How to analyse commodity price stabilisation: A review article. *Oxford Economic Papers* 36, 336–58.

Krishna, K. 1995. The adding-up problem: A targeting approach. NBER Working Paper no. 4999. Cambridge, Mass.: National Bureau of Economic Research, January.

McIntire, J., and P. Varangis. 1999. Reforming Côte d'Ivoire's Cocoa Marketing and Pricing System, World Bank Policy Research Working Paper no. 2081. Washington, D.C.: World Bank.

Pagan, A. R. 1984. Econometric issues in the analysis of regressions with generated regressors. *International Economic Review* 25, 221–47.

Paxson, C. 1993. Consumption and income seasonality in Thailand. *Journal of Political Economy* 101, 39–72.

Ruf, F., and H. de Milly. 1990. Comparison of cocoa production costs in seven producing countries. Paper presented at the International Cocoa Organization (ICCO) Advisory Group on the World Economy. 18–20 June, Accra, Ghana.

Schiff, M. 1994. Commodity exports and the adding-up problem in developing countries: Trade, investment, and lending policy. Policy Research Working Paper no. 1338. Washington, D.C.: World Bank.

Varangis, P., and G. Schreiber. 2001. Cocoa market reforms in West Africa. In *Commodity market reforms: Lessons from two decades,* ed. T. Akiyama, J. Baffes, D. Larson, and P. Varangis, 35–82. Washington, D.C.: World Bank.

Williams, G. 1985. Marketing with and without marketing boards: The origin of state marketing boards—Nigeria. *Review of African Political Economy* 34, 4–15.

World Bank. 1994. *Adjustment in Africa.* New York: Oxford University Press.

Comment   Joshua Aizenman

This interesting paper deals with a case study of the effects of liberalizing the cocoa market. The facts that make this study interesting are that cocoa is produced exclusively by developing countries. The demand for cocoa is relatively inelastic. The major suppliers are located in Africa. Hence, this case study provides insight into the challenges facing attempts to liberalize the production of major crops and commodities that are frequently dominated by the supply of developing countries.

The objective of the liberalization was to increase farmers' share of the crop's prices. Prior to the liberalization, most farmers obtained artificially low prices for their crops as part of the operation of schemes intended to tax exports, either for the direct benefit of the taxpayer or for the indirect benefits of the holders of the quasi rent generated by this tax.

The liberalization was initiated by countries that are minor players in the global market: Nigeria in 1986, and Cameroon in 1989–1995. The largest producer, Ivory Coast (counting for one-third of the global share), liberalized in 1999. Ghana, another large producer, still maintains controls.

By-products of the liberalization have been the following:

- The domestic price facing farmers moved closer to the international price.
- The prices facing farmers are more volatile.
- Global supply rose, thereby reducing the global prices.
- Farmers are getting a greater share of a lower global price.

Joshua Aizenman is professor of economics at the University of California, Santa Cruz, and a research associate of the National Bureau of Economic Research.

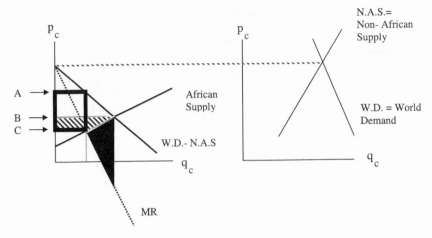

Fig. 4C.1   Optimal export tax for the African producers, and the welfare cost of liberalization

Notes: For simplicity, we assume a negligible share of domestic consumption of the major supplies of Cocoa in Africa. Right-hand side: global demand and non-African supply of cocoa. Left-hand side: the market for cocoa facing the African countries. Price A = world price before liberalization; Price C = price paid to farmers before liberalization; A – C = export tax prior to liberalization; and Price B = price paid to farmers after liberalization = world price after liberalization. The rectangle is the tax revenue lost following liberalization; the trapezoid is the farmers' gain following liberalization; and the triangle is the welfare cost of liberalization to African countries.

The paper conducts an estimation of the global market for cocoa, and a simulation in order to evaluate two scenarios: unilateral liberalization by each country separately, and joint liberalization by all four countries. The estimated effects are as follows:

- African governments in the producing countries are worse off.
- African farmers and world consumers are better off.
- The losers are non-African farmers, and the agents in Africa that benefited from the quasi rents prior to the liberalization (taxpayers, agencies, etc.).
- Multilateral liberalization would imply that the gains of the farmers in the liberalized countries would be almost exactly offset by the losses of governmental tax revenue, with the result that the countries as a whole should be slightly worse off. To the extent that government cocoa revenues were spent on wasteful activities, the countries, taken as wholes, will have benefited in welfare terms even in this case.
- The world price would fall by about one-third of the rise in producer prices. The major beneficiaries would have been the consumers in the importing OECD countries, who would have benefited on the order of 20 percent of their cocoa expenditure (about $0.7 billion per annum).

Ignoring coordination costs and rent seeking, the optimal policy for the African cocoa producers is to impose an export tax. This is a classical application of the market power enjoyed by the "cartel" of cocoa producers. As farmers are atomistic, the optimal policy requires an export tax, or the adaptation of institutions that would deliver a similar outcome. Figure 4C.1 summarizes this argument. For simplicity, it is drawn for the case where the share of domestic cocoa consumption is negligible relative to the supply of the African exporting nations. The right-hand side plots the world demand (W. D.) and the supply of the non-African producers (N. A. S.). The left-hand side focuses on the situation confronting the African exporters. The derived demand facing these exports is obtained by the horizontal subtraction W. D. – N. A. S. The marginal revenue curve corresponding to the derived demand is MR. The competitive supply of cocoa of the African countries is the upward-sloping curve. The optimal policy for the African cocoa-producing countries is to restrict the supply to the level where the marginal cost equals the marginal revenue. This can be accomplished by imposing an export tax of A – C. Such a tax will artificially depress the prices facing the farmers, to the benefit of the tax authorities. A complete liberalization will eliminate the tax revenue (given by the rectangle corresponding to the tax A – C), and will increase farmers' rents by the trapezoid. The net welfare effect is the difference between the two, as is captured by the shaded triangle. Starting from the optimal tax, the liberalization reduces welfare. The main beneficiaries are the world consumers, benefiting by about $0.7 billion dollars a year.

Secondary beneficial effects of the liberalization may include a drop in rent seeking associated with the "tax rectangle." An issue that deserves further attention is to what degree such benefits had been observed in the reforming countries. Indeed, one wonders why the African countries would not link the liberalization process with foreign aid (AIDS funds, education, etc.).

Globalization and Dirty Industries: Do Pollution Havens Matter?

Jean-Marie Grether and Jaime de Melo

5.1 Introduction

In the debate on globalization and the environment, there is concern that the erasing of national borders through reduced barriers to trade will lead to competition for investment and jobs, resulting in a worldwide degradation of environmental standards (the "race-to-the-bottom" effect) and/or in a delocalization of heavily polluting industries in countries with lower standards (the "pollution-havens" effect). Moreover, environmentalists and ecologically oriented academics argue that the political economy of decision making is stacked up against the environment. In the North, Organization for Economic Cooperation and Development (OECD) interest groups that support protectionist measures for other reasons continue to invoke the race-to-the-bottom model, relying on the perception that the regulatory gap automatically implies a race to the bottom, even though some have argued that countries may circumvent international agreements on tariffs by choosing strategic levels of domestic regulation. Because avoidance of a race to the bottom would call for the enforcement of uniform environmental standards in all countries, which cannot be created, they argue for trade restrictions until the regulatory gap is closed. In the

Jean-Marie Grether is professor of international economics at the University of Neuchâtel. Jaime de Melo is professor of political economy at the University of Geneva, research fellow at the Center for Economic Policy Research (CEPR), and professor at Centre d'Études et de Recherches sur le Développement International (CERDI).

An earlier version of this paper was presented at the CEPR, National Bureau of Economic Research (NBER), and Studieförbundet Näringsliv och Samhälle (SNS; Center for Business and Policy Studies) international seminar on international trade, Challenges to Globalization, 24–25 May 2002, Stockholm. We thank Céline Carrère for data and much appreciated support, Nicole Mathys for excellent research assistance, Robert Baldwin for many helpful suggestions, and conference participants for useful comments.

South, corruption is likely to result in poor enforcement of the regulatory framework. Finally, at the international level, environmental activists fear that the dispute settlement mechanism of the World Trade Organization (WTO) favors trade interests over environmental protection.

To sum up, the arguments raised above, as well as empirical evidence reviewed below, suggest that trade liberalization and globalization (in the form of reduced transaction costs) could lead to a global increase in environmental pollution as well as to an increase in resource depletion as natural resource–exploiting industries, from forest-logging companies to mining companies, relocate to places with less strict standards or use the threat of relocation to prevent the imposition of stricter standards. These effects are likely to be more important the further environmental policy is from the optimum and the less well-defined property rights are (as is the case for the so-called global commons). It is therefore not surprising that, even if trade liberalization and globalization more generally can lead both to an overall increase in welfare (especially if environmental policy is not too far from the optimum) and to a deterioration in environmental quality, a fundamental clash will persist between free-trade proponents and environmentalists.

This paper addresses the relation between globalization and the environment by reexamining evidence of a North-South delocalization of heavily polluting industries.[1] Section 5.2 reviews the evidence on pollution havens,[2] arguing that it is either too detailed (firm-specific or emission-specific evidence) or too fragmentary (case studies) to give a broad appreciation of the extent of delocalization over the past twenty years. The subsequent sections then turn to new evidence based on worldwide production and trade data (fifty-two countries) at a reasonable level of disaggregation (three-digit international standard industrial classification [ISIC]) and over a sufficiently long time period, 1981–1998.[3] In section 5.3, we report on the worldwide evolution of heavy polluters (the so-called dirty industries) and on the evolution of North-South revealed comparative advantage indexes. Section 5.4 then estimates a gravity trade model to examine bilateral patterns of trade in polluting products. Estimates reveal that transport costs may have acted as a brake on North-South relocation, and fail to detect a regulatory-gap effect.

    1. The causes of any detected relocation will not be identified because we are dealing with fairly aggregate data.
    2. In the public debate, the "pollution-havens" effect refers either to an output reduction of polluting industries (and an increase in imports) in developed countries or to the relocation of industries abroad via foreign direct investment in response to a reduction in import protection or a regulatory gap.
    3. The main database has been elaborated by Nicita and Olarreaga (2001). The appendix to this chapter describes data manipulation and the representativity of the sample in terms of global trade and production in polluting activities.

5.2 Pollution Havens or Pollution Halos?

We review first the evidence on trade liberalization and patterns of trade in polluting industries based on multicountry studies that try to detect evidence of North-South delocalization. We then summarize results from single-country (often firm-level) studies that use more reliable environmental variables and are also generally better able to control for unobservable heterogeneity bias. We conclude with lessons from case studies and political-economy considerations.

5.2.1 Evidence on Production and Trade in Dirty Products

Evidence from aggregate production and trade data is based on a comparison between "clean" and "dirty" industries, the classification relying invariably on U.S. data, either on expenditure abatement costs or on emissions of pollutants.[4]

Table 5.1 summarizes the results from these studies. Overall, the studies, which for the most part use the same definition of dirty industries as we do,[5] usually find mild support for the pollution-havens hypothesis.

The large number of countries and the industrial-level approach gives breadth of scope to the studies described in table 5.1, but at a cost. First, changing patterns of production and trade could be due to omitted variables and unobserved heterogeneity that cannot be easily controlled-for in large samples where aggregated data say very little about industry choices which would shed light on firms or production stages (Zarsky 1999, 66). For example, as pointed out by Mani and Wheeler (1999) in their case study of Japan, changes in local factor costs (price of energy, price of land) and changes in policies other than the stringency of environmental regulations could account for observed changes in trade patterns. Second, these studies give no evidence on investment patterns and on how these might react to changes in environmental regulation, which is at the heart of the pollution-havens debate.[6] It is therefore not totally surprising that the papers

---

4. Most work on the United States is based on pollution-abatement capital expenditures or on pollution-abatement costs (see, e.g., Levinson and Taylor 2002, table 1). It turns out that the alternative classification based on emissions (see Hettige et al. 1995) produces a similar ranking for the cleanest and dirtiest industries (five of the top six pollution industries are the same in both classifications).

5. As in this paper, polluting industries were classified on the basis of the comprehensive index of emissions per unit of output described in Hettige et al. (1995). That index includes conventional air, water, and heavy metals pollutants. As to the applicability of that index based on U.S. data to developing countries, Hettige et al. conclude that, even though pollution intensity is likely to be higher, "the pattern of sectoral rankings may be similar" (1995, 2).

6. Smarzynska and Wei (2001) cite the following extract from "A Fair Trade Bill of Rights" proposed by the Sierra Club: "In our global economy, corporations move operations freely around the world, escaping tough control laws, labor standards, and even the taxes that pay for social and environmental needs."

Table 5.1   Multicountry Studies on the Pollution Havens Hypothesis

Paper	Dependent Variable	Environmental Measure	No. of Countries	Years	Main Findings
Low and Yeats (1992)	RCAs for polluting industries	PACE	109	1965–88	RCAs increased in polluting industries for LDCs. RCAs decreased in polluting industries in DCs.
Hettige, Lucas, and Wheeler (1992)	TRI per unit of output	Toxic release based on UE EPA TRI	88	1960–88	Toxic intensity increased in DCs in 1960s (decreased in 1970s and 1980s). Toxic intensity increased in LDCs in 1970s and 1980s. Higher toxic intensity in economies closed to trade.
Tobey (1990)	Net exports (of PACE-based industries)	Ordinal index 1–7	23	1977	Net exports not determined by environmental stringency.
Grether and de Melo (1996)	RCAs for polluting industries	PACE	53	1965–90	RCAs increased in polluting industries for LDCs, stable for DCs.
Van Beers and Van den Bergh (1997)	Bilateral trade in 1992	Composite index compiled from OECD data	30	1992	Coefficient on environmental index no larger for polluting industries than on average.
Mani and Wheeler (1999)	Factor intensities, production and consumption ratios	IPPS OECD	92	1965–92	Pollution intensive output fell steadily in OECD.

Notes: DCs = developed countries; LDCs = developing countries; RCA = revealed comparative advantage; TRI = toxic release index; PACE = pollution abatement expenditures (U.S. data); and IPPS = industrial pollution projection system (Hettige et al. 1995). Composite emission index (see text).

surveyed in Dean (1992) and Zarsky (1999), by and large, fail to detect a significant correlation between the location decisions of multinationals and the environmental standards of host countries. This suggests that, after all, when one goes beyond aggregate industry data, the pollution-havens hypothesis may be a popular myth.

Recent studies respond to the criticism that the evidence so far does not address the research needs because of excessive aggregation. However, this recent evidence, summarized below, is still very partial, and heavily focused on the United States.

5.2.2   Evidence on the Location of Dirty Industries

Levinson and Taylor (2002) revisit the single-equation model of Grossman and Krueger (1993), using panel data for U.S. imports in a two-equation model in which abatement costs are a function of exogenous industry characteristics while imports are a function of abatement costs. Contrary to previous estimates, they find support for the pollution-havens hypothesis: Industries whose abatement costs increased the most saw the largest relative increase in imports from Mexico, Canada, Latin America, and the rest of the world.[7]

Drawing on environmental costs across the United States that are more comparable than the rough indexes that must be used in cross-country work, Keller and Levinson (2002) analyze inward foreign direct investment (FDI) into the United States over the period 1977–1994. They find robust evidence that relative (across states) abatement costs had moderate deterrent effects on foreign investment.

Others have analyzed outward FDI to developing countries. Eskeland and Harrison (2003) examine inward FDI in Mexico, Morocco, Venezuela, and Côte d'Ivoire at the four-digit level using U.S. abatement-cost data controlling for country-specific factors. They find weak evidence of some FDI being attracted to sectors with high levels of air pollution, but no evidence of FDI to avoid abatement costs. They also find that foreign firms are more fuel-efficient in that they use lower amounts of "dirty fuels." This evidence supports the pollution-halo hypothesis: superior technology and management, coupled with demands by "green" consumers in the OECD, lift industry standards overall.[8]

Smarzynska and Wei (2001) estimate a probit of FDI of 534 multinationals in twenty-four transition economies during the period 1989–1994 as a function of host-country characteristics. These include a transformed (to avoid outlier dominance) U.S.-based index of dirtiness of the firm at the

---

7. Ederington and Minier (2003) also revisit the Grossman and Krueger study, assuming that pollution regulation is endogenous, but determined by political-economy motives. They also find support for the pollution-havens hypothesis, this time because inefficient industries seek protection via environmental legislation.

8. The mixed evidence on the pollution-halo hypothesis is reviewed in Zarsky (1999).

four-digit level, an index of the laxity of the host country's environmental standards captured by a corruption index, and several measures of environmental standards (participation in international treaties, quality of air and water standards, observed reductions in various pollutants). In spite of this careful attempt at unveiling a pollution-haven effect, they conclude that host-country environmental standards (after controlling for other country characteristics, including corruption) had very little impact on FDI inflows.

5.2.3   Case Studies and Political-Economy Considerations

Reviewing recently available data, Wheeler (2001) shows that suspended particulate matter release (the most dangerous form of air pollution) has been declining rapidly in Brazil, China, and Mexico, fast-growing countries in the era of globalization and big recipients of FDI. Organic water pollution is also found to fall drastically as income per capita rises (poorest countries have approximately tenfold differential pollution intensity).[9] In addition to the standard explanations (pollution control is not a critical cost factor for firms; large multinationals adhere to OECD standards), Wheeler also points out that case studies show that low-income communities often penalize dangerous polluters even when formal regulation is absent or weak. Wheeler concludes that the "bottom" rises with economic growth.

This result is reinforced by recent evidence based on a political-economy approach that endogenizes corruption in the decision-making process. Assuming that governments accept bribes in formulation of their regulatory policies, Damia, Fredriksson, and List (2000) find support in panel data for thirty countries over the period 1982–1992 that the level of environmental stringency is negatively correlated with an index of corruption and positively with an index of trade openness. Given that corruption is typically higher in low-income countries, this corroborates the earlier finding mentioned above, that environmental stringency increases rapidly with income.

5.3   Shifting Patterns of Production and Comparative Advantage in Polluting Industries

Direct approaches to the measurement of pollution emission (e.g., Grossman and Krueger 1993; Dean 2002; Antweiler, Copeland, and Taylor 2001; and several of the studies mentioned above) use emission estimates at geographical sites of pollutant particles (sulfur dioxide is a fa-

---

9. These results accord with independent estimates of environmental performance constructed by Dasgupta et al. (1996) from responses to a detailed questionnaire administered to 145 countries (they find a correlation of about 0.8 between their measure of environment performance or environment policy and income per capita).

vorite) or the release of pollutants into several media (e.g., air, water, etc.). That approach has several advantages: Emissions are directly measured at each site, and it is not assumed that pollutant intensity is the same across countries. On the other hand, activity (e.g., production levels) is not measured directly. Arguably, this is a shortcoming if one is interested in the pollution-havens hypothesis. Indeed, emissions could be high for other reasons than the relocation of firms to countries with low standards (China's use of coal as an energy source is largely independent of the existence of pollution havens).

The alternative chosen here is to use an approach in which emission intensity is not measured directly. We adopt the approach in the studies summarized in table 5.1, where dirty industries are classified according to an index of emission intensity in the air, water, and heavy metals in the United States described in footnote 4. We selected the same five most polluting industries in the United States in 1987 selected by Mani and Wheeler (1999; three-digit ISIC code in parenthesis): iron and steel (371), nonferrous metals (372), industrial chemicals (351), nonmetallic mineral products (369), and pulp and paper (341).[10] According to Mani and Wheeler, compared to the five cleanest U.S. manufacturing activities—textiles, (321), nonelectric machinery (382), electric machinery (383), transport equipment (384), and instruments (385)—the dirtiest have the following characteristics: 40 percent less labor-intensive; capital-output ratio twice as high; and energy-intensity ratio three times as high.

5.3.1 Shifting Patterns of Production

We start with examination of the broad data for our sample of fifty-two countries over the period 1981–1998. The sample (years and countries) is the largest for which we could obtain production data matching trade data at the three-digit ISIC level. Compared to the earlier studies mentioned in table 5.1, this sample has production data for a larger group of countries, though at a cost because comprehensive data—only available since 1981—implies that we are missing some of the early years of environmental regulation in OECD countries in the seventies.

Because there is a close correlation between the stringency of environmental regulation and income per capita, we start with histograms of indexes of pollution intensity ranked by income per capita quintile (the data are three-year averages at the beginning and end of period). Given our sample size, each quintile has ten or eleven observations.

Figure 5.1 reveals a slight change in the middle of the distribution of production and consumption of dirty industries, as the second-richest quintile sees a reduction in production and consumption shares in favor of the

---

10. Mani and Wheeler (1999, table 1) describe the intensity of pollutant emissions in water, air, and heavy metals.

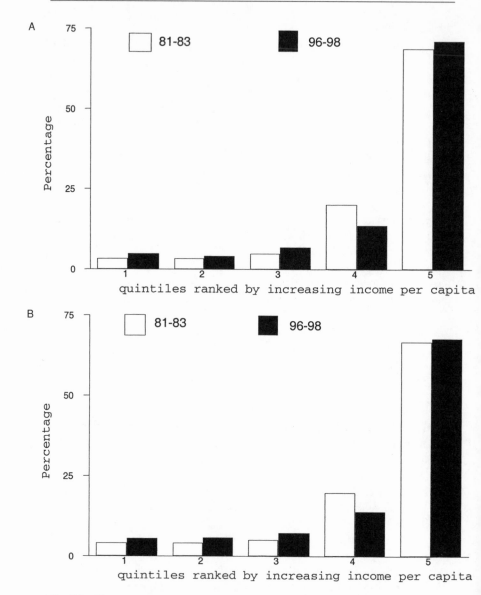

Fig. 5.1 Histograms of output and consumption shares of polluting products:
A, Output; B, Consumption

highest and lowest quintiles. Turning to export and import shares (fig. 5.2), one notices a reduction in both trade shares of the highest quintile in favor of the remaining quintiles.

These aggregate figures mask compositional shifts apparent from inspection of the histograms at the industry level (see appendix fig. 5A.1).

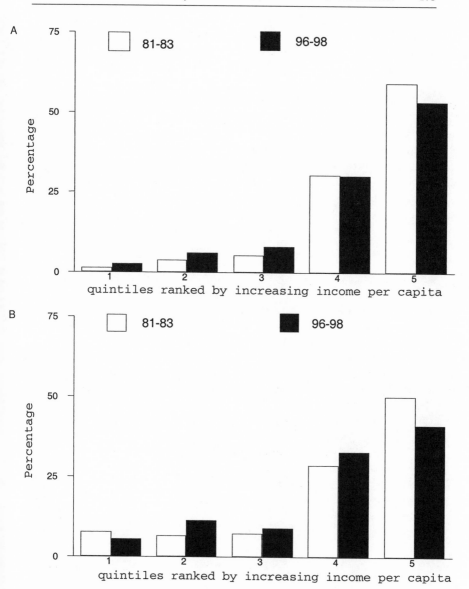

Fig. 5.2   Histograms of exports and imports shares of polluting products:
A, **Exports;** *B,* **Imports**

For the second-richest quintile, the output share is always decreasing, but changes in the export share vary a lot across sectors. For the richest quintile, the output share is decreasing except for paper and products (ISIC 341) and other nonmetallic mineral products (369), while the export share is always decreasing, except for nonferrous metals (372).

In sum, these broad figures suggest some delocalization of pollution industries to poorer economies. However, aggregate effects are weak, partly because of opposite patterns at the sector level.

5.3.2 Shifting Patterns of Revealed Comparative Advantage

We look next for further evidence of changes in trade patterns in dirty industries. We report on revealed comparative advantage (RCA) indexes computed at the beginning or at the end of the sample period; RCA indexes are not measures of comparative advantage, since they also incorporate the effects of changes in the policy environment (trade policy, regulatory environment, etc).

The RCA index for country i and product p is given by

$$\text{(1)} \qquad \text{RCA}_i^p = \frac{S_{wp}^{ip}}{S_{wa}^{ia}} = \frac{S_{ia}^{ip}}{S_{wa}^{wp}}$$

where $S_{wp}^{ip}(S_{wa}^{ia})$ is country i's share in world exports of polluting products (of all products) and $S_{ia}^{ip}(S_{wa}^{wp})$ is the share of polluting products in total exports of country i (of the world).

Countries are split into two income groups (see appendix table 5A.1) that replicate the distinction between the three poorest and two richest quintiles of the previous section: twenty-two high-income countries (1991 gross national product [GNP] per capita larger than U.S.\$7,910 according to the World Bank) and thirty low- and middle-income countries. Hereafter, the former group is designed by developed countries (DCs) or "North," and the latter by less-developed countries (LDCs) or "South."

A first glimpse at the aggregate figures (see table 5.2) confirms that LDCs' share in world trade of polluting products is on the rise. But the average annual rate of growth is lower for polluting products than for exports in general. As a result, LDCs as a whole exhibit a decreasing RCA (and an increasing revealed comparative disadvantage) in polluting products (see last columns of table 5.2).

However, inspection at the industry level (see appendix table 5A.5) re-

Table 5.2   Developing Countries' World Trade Shares (percentages except for RCA, RCD)

| | Polluting Products | | All Products | | Revealed Comparative Indexes | |
| | | | | | Advantage (RCA) | Disadvantage (RCD) |
	Exports (1)	Imports (2)	Exports (3)	Imports (4)	(1)/(3)	(2)/(4)
1981–83	9.08	18.87	9.40	15.73	0.97	1.20
1996–98	14.46	22.98	15.93	18.67	0.91	1.23
Average annual growth rate	3.15	1.32	3.58	1.15		

Note: Blank cells indicate not calculated.

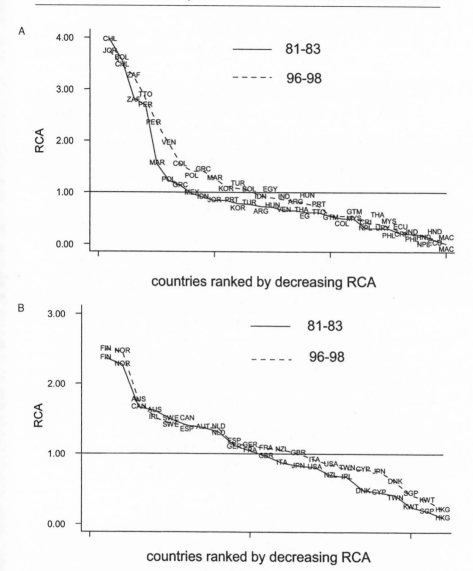

Fig. 5.3   **Revealed comparative advantage indexes in polluting products:** *A,* **Developing countries;** *B,* **Developed countries (countries ranked by decreasing RCA)**

veals that this reverse-delocalization outcome is due to the dominating effect of nonferrous metals (ISIC 372). All four of the other industries present some ingredient of delocalization, with a particularly strong increase in RCA for industrial chemicals (351). Interestingly, nonferrous metals represented more than 40 percent of LDCs exports at the beginning and less than 25 percent at the end of the period, while the pattern is exactly opposite for industrial chemicals.

To unveil cross-country variations, figure 5.3 ranks countries by decreasing order of RCAs for both income groups. In each case, the dashed line represents the end-of-period pattern, with countries ranked by decreasing order of comparative advantage so that all observations above (below) unity correspond to countries with a revealed comparative advantage (disadvantage). A shift to the right (left) implies increasing (decreasing) RCA, and a flattening of the curve, a less-pronounced pattern of specialization.

Overall, LDCs' pattern of RCAs is characterized by higher upper values of RCAs and a steeper curve than for high-income countries. Over time, both curves appear to shift right[11] and to become somewhat flatter. The increase in RCAs seems larger in LDCs, where it is concentrated in the middle of the distribution, while it basically affects the end of the distribution in the other income group. At the industry level (see appendix figure 5A.2) results for LDCs are quite similar, except for nonferrous metals, where the RCA curve shifts in.[12]

Still, the above pattern does not say anything about the changing pattern of RCAs between the North and the South, which is what the delocalization hypothesis is about. To measure this effect, we introduce a new decomposition that isolates the impact of geography on the RCA index. From equation (1), note that the RCA of country i in product p (RCA_i^p) can be decomposed into

$$(2) \qquad RCA_i^p = \sum_{j=1}^{N} RCA_{ij}^p S_{iwa}^{ija},$$

where the bilateral RCA (RCA_{ij}^p) is defined as the ratio between the share of product p in all exports of country i to country j (S_{ija}^{ijp}) and the share of product p in total world exports (S_{wa}^{wp}). This share is weighted by the share of country j in total exports of country i to the world (S_{iwa}^{ija}).

Now let the world be divided in two groups of countries: n_S in the South and n_N in the North ($n_S + n_N = N$). Then equation (2) can be rewritten as

$$(3) \qquad RCA_i^p = S_i^p + N_i^p \equiv \sum_{j=1}^{n_S} RCA_{ij}^p S_{iwa}^{ija} + \sum_{j=1}^{n_N} RCA_{ij}^p S_{iwa}^{ija},$$

where S_i^p is the South's contribution and N_i^p the North's contribution to RCA_i^p. Thus, in terms of variation between the end (1996–1998) and the beginning (1981–1983) of the sample period, one obtains

---

11. This result may seem puzzling, but the contradiction is only apparent: the weighted sum of RCAs is indeed equal to 1.0, but the weights can vary. Thus, a simultaneous increase in all RCA indexes may well happen, provided a larger weight is put on smaller values.

12. Note that the pattern illustrated by figure 5.3 reflects only a "structural" effect, i.e., the change of individual RCAs. The evolution of the aggregate RCA for LDCs as a group is also governed by a "composition" effect, namely the impact of changes in countries' shares keeping RCA indexes constant. Straightforward calculations reveal that for LDCs the composition effect (–0.19) has been stronger than the structural effect (0.13), leading to a net decrease of the aggregate RCA reported in table 5.2 (for results at the industry level, see table 5A.6).

Table 5.3   **North-South Bilateral RCAs for Polluting Products**

Sector	ΔRCA	ΔN	ΔS
Pulp and paper (341)	0.23	0.10	0.13
Industrial chemicals (351)	0.41	0.21	0.20
Nonmetallic minerals (369)	0.38	0.61	−0.22
Iron and steel (371)	0.66	0.39	0.27
Nonferrous metals (372)	−0.57	−0.79	0.22

Note: Computed from equation (4).

$$(4) \qquad \Delta\text{RCA}_i^p = \Delta S_i^p + \Delta N_i^p$$

Results from applying this decomposition to the two groups of countries are reported in table 5.3. For each polluting sector, we report the (unweighted) average of both sides of equation (4) over the LDCs' group. It appears that in all cases but one, the North's contribution to the change in LDCs' RCA is positive. This result is consistent with the pollution-havens effect. Again, the only exception is nonferrous metal, where North-South trade has negatively contributed to the RCA of the South.

In sum, the RCA-based evidence on delocalization of polluting activities toward the South is rather mixed. As a group, developing countries exhibit a surprising reverse-delocalization pattern of increasing revealed comparative disadvantage in polluting products. However, as shown above, this reflects both the pattern of one particular industry (nonferrous metals) and a composition effect: within the group of developing countries, those less prone to export polluting products have gained ground. In fact, most developing countries have actually experienced an increase in their RCA in polluting products. Moreover, after controlling for geography, it turns out that for all but for one case (nonferrous metals), North-South trade has had a positive impact on LDCs' comparative advantage in these products.

5.4   Bilateral Trade Patterns in Polluting Products

Dirty industries are typically weight-reducing industries. They are also intermediate-goods-producing industries. As a result, if they move to the South, then transport costs must be incurred if the final (consumer goods) products are still produced in the North—as would be the case, for example, in the newspaper-printing industry. Hence the reduction in transport costs and protection that has occurred with globalization may not have had much effect on the location of these industries.

Our third piece of evidence consists of checking if, indeed, polluting industries are not likely to relocate so easily because of relatively high transport costs. To check whether this may be the case, we estimate a standard bilateral trade gravity model for polluting products, and compare the coefficients with those obtained for nonpolluting manufactures.

Take the simplest justification for the gravity model. Trade is balanced (in this case at the industry level, which some would find unrealistic), and each country consumes its output, and that of other countries according to its share, S_i, in world GNP, Y^W. Then (see Rauch 1999) bilateral trade between i and j will be given by $M_{ij} = (2 Y_i Y_j)/Y^W = f(\mathbf{W}_{ij})$. The standard "generalized" gravity equation (which can be obtained from a variety of theories) can be written as $M_{ij} = f(\mathbf{W}_{ij})(\theta_{ij})^{-\sigma}$ where θ_{ij} is an index of barriers to trade between i and j. $\mathbf{W}_{ij}$ is a vector of other intervening variables that includes the bilateral exchange rate, e_{ij}, and prices, and σ is an estimate of the ease of substitution across suppliers.

In the standard estimation of the gravity model, θ_{ij} is captured either by distance between partners, or if one is careful, by relative distance to an average distance among partners in the sample, $\overline{DIST}$ (i.e., by $DT_{ij} = DIST_{ij}/\overline{DIST}$). Dummy variables that control for characteristics that are specific to bilateral trade between i and j (e.g., a common border, BOR_{ij}, landlockedness in either country, $LL_i[LL_j]$) are also introduced to capture the effects of barriers to trade.[13] Here, we go beyond the standard formulation by also including an index of the quality of infrastructure in each country in period t, $INF_{it}(INF_{jt})$, higher values of the index corresponding to better quality of infrastructure.[14] Finally, because we estimate the model in panel, we include the bilateral exchange rate, RER_{ijt}, defined so that an increase in its value implies a real depreciation of i's currency.

The above considerations lead us to estimate in panel the following model (expected signs in parenthesis):

$$(5) \quad \ln M_{ijt} = \alpha_0 + \alpha_t + \alpha_{ij} + \alpha_1 \ln Y_{it} + \alpha_2 \ln Y_{jt} + \alpha_3 \ln INF_{it}$$
$$+ \alpha_4 \ln INF_{jt} + \alpha_5 \ln RER_{ijt} + \alpha_6 BOR_{ij} + \alpha_7 LL_i$$
$$+ \alpha_8 LL_j + [\alpha_9 \ln DY_{ijt}] + \beta_1 \ln DT_{ij} + \eta_{ijt}$$

$$(\alpha_1 > 0, \alpha_2 > 0, \alpha_3 > 0, \alpha_4 > 0, \alpha_5 < 0, \alpha_6 > 0, \alpha_7 < 0, \alpha_8 < 0, \beta_1 < 0)$$

In equation (5), α_0 is an effect common to all years and pairs of countries (constant term), α_t an effect specific to year t but common to all countries (e.g., changes in the price of oil), α_{ij} an effect specific to each pair of countries but common to all years, and η_{ijt} the error term.

In a second specification we introduce the difference in GNP per capita

13. Brun et al. (2002) argue that the standard barriers-to-trade function is misspecified and propose a more general formulation that captures both variables that include country-specific characteristics and variables that capture time-dependent costs (e.g., the price of oil). Since here we are interested only in country-specific characteristics, time-dependent shocks are captured by time dummies.

14. The index is itself a weighted sum of four indexes computed each year: road density, paved roads, railway, and the number of telephone lines per capita.

$DY_{ij} = [(Y_i/N_i) - (Y_j/N_j)]$ in the equation, this additional variable presumably capturing the effects of the regulatory gap across countries. If the regulatory-gap effect is important, one would expect a positive sign for α_9.[15]

For estimation purposes, equation (5) can be rewritten as

(6) $$\ln M_{ijt} = \mathbf{X}_{ijt}\phi + \mathbf{Z}_{ij}\delta + u_{ijt} \text{ with } u_{ijt} = \mu_{ij} + v_{ijt},$$

where $\mathbf{X}(\mathbf{Z})$ represents the vector of variables that vary over time (are time invariant) and a random error-component is used because the within-transformation in a fixed-effects model removes the variables that are cross-sectional time invariant. To deal with the possibility of correlation between the explanatory variables and the specific effects, we use the instrument variable estimator proposed by Hausman and Taylor (1981). However, we also report fixed-effects estimates which correspond to the correct specification under the maintained hypothesis (columns [1] and [2] of table 5.4).

Because the null hypothesis of correlation between explanatory variables and the error term cannot be rejected, we reestimated the random-effects model treating the gross domestic product (GDP) variables as endogenous. The results are reported in columns (3) through (6) of table 5.4. Coefficient estimates are robust and, after instrumentation, the coefficient estimates are quite close in value to those obtained under the fixed-effects estimates.

First note that all coefficients have the expected signs and, as usual in gravity models with large samples, are robust to changes in specification.[16] Notably, the dummy variables for infrastructure have the expected signs and are highly significant. So is the real exchange rate variable, which captures, at least partly, some of the effects of trade liberalization that would not have already been captured in the time dummy variables (not reported here). Income variables are also, as expected, highly significant. Overall then, except for the landlocked variables, which are at times insignificant, all coefficient estimates have expected signs and plausible values.

Compare now the results between the panel estimates for all manufactures—except polluting products—(column [5]) with those for the five polluting industries (column [6]). Note first that the estimated coefficient for distance is one-third higher for the group of polluting industries compared to the rest of manufacturing.[17] Second, note that the proxy for the regulatory gap captured by the log difference of per capita GDPs is negative for

---

15. In a full-fledged model with endogenous determination of environmental policy, Antweiler, Copeland, and Taylor (2001) obtain a reduced form in which the technique effect (change in environmental policy) is captured by changes in income per capita.

16. We also experimented with other variants (not reported here) by including population variables and obtained virtually identical estimates for the included variables.

17. One could note that the coefficient estimates on infrastructure are much higher for these weight-reducing activities, which is also a plausible result signifying another brake on North-South delocalization.

Table 5.4 Gravity Equation: Panel Estimates for Polluting (POL) and Nonpolluting (NPOL) Products

Independent Variable	Fixed Effects		Random Effects I[a]		Random Effects II[b]	
	NPOL (1)	POL (2)	NPOL (3)	POL (4)	NPOL (5)	POL (6)
Coefficient in equation (5)						
α_1 $\ln(Y_{it})$	1.84**	1.60**	1.81**	1.50**	1.81**	1.50**
	(30.0)	(21.5)	(25.9)	(19.4)	(25.9)	(19.4)
α_2 $\ln(Y_{jt})$	1.23**	0.99**	1.28**	0.92**	1.27**	0.92**
	(20.3)	(13.2)	(17.5)	(10.9)	(17.5)	(10.9)
α_9 $\ln(Y_{it}/N_{it}) - \ln(Y_{jt}/N_{jt})$	−0.06**	0.003	n.a.	n.a.	−0.06**	0.007
	(2.6)	(0.1)			(3.0)	(0.3)
β_1 $\ln DIST_{ij}$	n.a.	n.a.	−0.83**	−1.12**	−0.82**	−1.12**
			(16.8)	(17.6)	(16.6)	(17.7)
α_6 BOR_{ij}	n.a.	n.a.	1.28**	1.30**	1.27**	1.30**
			(6.7)	(5.5)	(6.6)	(5.5)
α_7 LL_i	n.a.	n.a.	−0.89**	0.50	−0.92**	0.49
			(3.7)	(1.7)	(3.74)	(1.66)
α_8 LL_j	n.a.	n.a.	−0.43	−0.42	−0.42	−0.42**
			(1.78)	(1.21)	(1.74)	(1.22)
α_3 $\ln INF_{it}$	0.15*	0.003	0.37**	0.46**	0.36**	0.46**
	(2.2)	(0.04)	(5.8)	(6.4)	(5.7)	(6.43)

α_4 ($\ln \text{INF}_{ji}$)	0.38** (5.1)	0.70** (7.7)	0.37** (5.8)	0.64* (7.7)	0.39** (6.0)	0.64** (7.7)
α_5 ($\ln \text{RER}_{ijt}$)	−0.34** (15.5)	−0.46** (17.5)	−0.32** (13.4)	−0.40** (14.3)	−0.32** (13.4)	−0.40** (−14.3)
No. of observations (NT)	34,563	34,563	30,345	34,563	30,345	30,345
No. of bilateral (N)	2,371	2,371	2,300	2,371	2,300	2,300
R-squared[c]	0.54	0.46	0.49	0.52	0.52	0.47
Bilateral fixed effect	34.2** $F(2,370; 32,171)$					31.0** $F(2,299; 28,024)$
Hausman test W versus GLS Chi-2 (Kw)	265.3** Chi-2(21)	n.a.		n.a.		161.3** Chi-2(21)
Hausman test HT versus GLS Chi-2(K)		496.6** Chi-2(24)	758.9** Chi-2(24)	413.1** Chi-2(25)	614.7** Chi-2(25)	

Notes: Dependent variable = $\ln M_{ijt}$. T-student in parentheses. Time dummies and constant term not reported. n.a. = not applicable.

[a] Hausman-Taylor (HT) estimator, with endogenous variables Y_i, Y_j.

[b] HT estimator, with endogenous variables Y_i, Y_j, $(Y_i/N_i - Y_j/N_j)$.

[c] Calculated, for HT, from $1 - $ (Sum of Square Residuals)/(Total Sum of Squares) on the transformed model. Note that the impact of random specific effects are not in the R^2 but are part of residuals.

**Significant at the 99 percent level.

*Significant at the 95 percent level.

nonpolluting manufactures (as one would expect from the trade-theory literature under imperfect competition where trade flows are an increasing function of the similarity in income per capita) while it is insignificant (though positive) for polluting industries. Now, if indeed the regulatory gap can be approximated by differences in per capita GDPs across partners, the presence of pollution havens would be reflected in a significant positive coefficient for this variable.

Compositional effects for the coefficients of interest are shown in table 5.5. Nonferrous metals (and, to a lesser extent, iron and steel) stand out with low elasticity estimates for distance. If one were to take seriously cross-sector differences in magnitude, one would argue that the South-North "reverse" (in the sense of the pollution-havens hypothesis) delocalization of nonferrous metals according to comparative advantage in response to the reduction in protection would have occurred because of fewer natural barriers to trade. Of course, there are other factors as well to explain the developments in these sectors, including the heavy protection of these industries in the North.

The sectoral pattern of estimates for α_9 indicates that the regulatory gap would have had an effect on bilateral trade patterns for two sectors: nonmetallic minerals and iron and steel, and marginally for the pulp and paper industry. Again, nonferrous metals stands out, suggesting no effect of differences in the regulatory environment once other intervening factors are controlled for.

In sum, the pattern of trade elasticities to transport costs obtained here makes sense. Most heavily polluting sectors are intermediate goods, so proximity to users should enter into location decisions more heavily than

Table 5.5   Panel Estimates, by Industry

Industry	Equation (5)	
	β_1	α_9
Nonpolluting industries	−0.82**	−0.06**
All polluting industries	−1.12**	0.007
Pulp and paper (341)[a]	−1.40**	0.08*
Industrial chemicals (351)	−1.23**	0.03
Nonmetallic minerals (369)	−1.21**	0.12**
Iron and steel (371)	−1.12**	0.11**
Nonferrous metals (372)[a]	−0.95**	−0.04

[a]An estimate of −1.40 [−0.95] implies that if trade flows are normalized to 1 for a distance of 1,000 km, a doubling of distance to 2,000 km would reduce bilateral trade volume to 0.38 [0.52].

**Significant at the 99 percent level.
*Significant at the 95 percent level.

customs goods that are typically high-value, low-weight industries that can be shipped by air freight. Interestingly, after controlling for a number of factors that influence the volume of bilateral trade, we find little evidence of the presence of a regulatory gap, thus broadly supporting (indirectly) the pollution-halo hypothesis.

5.5 Conclusions

Concerns that polluting industries would "go south" was first raised in the late eighties, at a time when labor-intensive activities like the garment industries were moving south in response to falling barriers to trade worldwide. Such delocalization could be characterized as a continuous search for "low-wage havens" by apparel manufacturers in an industry that has remained labor intensive. Fears about pollution havens were already expressed at the time, notably because of the possible impact of the regulatory gap between OECD economies where polluters paying more would lead them to search for "pollution havens" analogous to low-wage havens. Later, with the globalization debate, the hypothesis gained new momentum by those who have read into globalization a breakdown of national borders, making it difficult to control location choices by multinationals.

This paper started with a review of the now-substantial evidence surrounding this debate, which can be classified in three rather distinct families. First, aggregate comparisons of output and trade trends based on a classification of pollution industries based on U.S. emissions revealed very marginal delocalization to the South. Second, firm-level estimates of FDI location choices by and large found at best marginal evidence either of location choice in the United States in response to cross-state differences in environmental regulations, or of location choices by multinational firms across developing countries in response to differences in environmental regulations. Reasons for this lack of response to the so-called regulatory gap were found in the third piece of evidence largely assembled from developing-country case studies. Taking into account political-economy determinants of multinational behavior in host countries and the internal trade-offs between leveling up emission standards (to avoid dealing with multiple technologies) and cutting abatement expenditures, overall this literature finds no evidence of havens, but rather of "halos."

Turning to new evidence, this paper drew on a large sample of countries accounting for the bulk of worldwide production and trade in polluting products over the period 1980–1998. Globally, we found that RCA in polluting products by LDCs fell as one would expect if the environment is indeed a normal good in consumption. At the same time, however, the decomposition indicates that the period witnessed a trend toward relocation of all (but one) polluting industries to the South. The exception was the reverse delocalization detected for nonferrous metals. We argued that this reverse delocalization was as one would expect, according to a comparative-advantage-driven response to trade liberalization in a sector where barriers to trade turn out to be relatively small. Finally, in the aggregate, RCA decompositions revealed no evidence of trade flows' being significantly driven by the regulatory gap, again with the exception of some positive evidence for the nonmetallic and the iron and steel sectors.

Estimates from a panel gravity model fitted to the same industries showed that, in comparison with other industries, polluting industries had higher barriers to trade in the form of larger elasticities of bilateral trade with respect to transport costs. These results confirm the intuition that most heavy polluters are both weight-reducing industries and intermediates for which proximity to users should enter location decisions more heavily than for customs goods (i.e., differentiated products) that are typically high-value products. Finally, after controlling for several factors that influence the volume of bilateral trade, we find little evidence of the presence of a regulatory gap.

In sum, the paper provided some support for the pollution-havens hypothesis, a result in line with several earlier studies reviewed here. Beyond this result, the paper contributed to the debate by identifying a new explanation for the less-than-expected delocalization that had been neither identified nor quantified in the literature: relatively high natural barriers to trade in the typical heavily polluting industries.

In concluding, one should however keep in mind two important caveats with respect to the pollution-havens debate. First, like the rest of the literature reviewed in the paper, we only examined manufactures. This implies that we did not take into account resource-extracting industries that may have successively sought pollution havens. Second, even within the narrow confines of trade-pattern quantification, a fuller evaluation of the debate on trade, globalization, and the environment would also have to examine the direct and indirect energy content of trade.

Appendix

This appendix describes the data, transformations, and sample representativity; gives sectoral tables corresponding to the aggregate results for all polluting products given in tables 5.2 and 5.4 in the text; and does the same for figures 5.1 to 5.3 in the text.

Table 5A.1   **Categories of Polluting Products**

ISIC Code	Description[a]
341	Paper and products (6)
351	Industrial chemicals (3)
369	Other nonmetallic mineral products (5)
371	Iron and steel (1)
372	Nonferrous metals (2)

Notes: Ranks in parentheses.

[a]Mani and Wheeler (1999, table 8.1). As in Mani and Wheeler, we have excluded petroleum refineries (ISIC = 353) from the sample.

Data Sources and Sample Representativity

The database is extracted from the Trade and Production Web site of the World Bank (www1.worldbank.org/wbiep/trade/data/TradeandProduction.html) and covers the period 1976–1999 for sixty-seven countries. It includes ISIC three-digit data on imports, exports and mirror exports. For the first five years and for the last year of the open-sample period, many countries reported missing values. Moreover, mirror exports are only available since 1980. Therefore, a closed sample was defined over the years 1981 to 1998, with fifty-two countries (five low-income countries, twenty-five middle-income countries, twenty-two high-income countries) reporting nonmissing values for the three-digit trade data over this period. Categories of polluting products are presented in table 5A.1, and closed-sample countries[18] are listed in table 5A.2.

Sample Representativity

Open and Closed Samples

With respect to the open sample, and using the average trade shares for 1995–1996 (the years with the maximum amount of nonmissing values), the closed sample represents about 95 percent of the open-sample trade.

Regarding the representativity of the open sample itself, this was estimated using world trade data reported by the World Bank (2001). Results are shown in table 5A.3. These figures may appear quite low. However, it should be kept in mind that world trade figures used in these calculations are, themselves, estimated. As a result, even in the original World Bank

18. Income groups were defined on the basis of 1991 GNP per capita figures. Following the World Bank cut-off levels, the sample was split into three income groups: low- (income lower than U.S.$635), middle- (between U.S.$635 and U.S.$7,910), and high- (larger than U.S.$7,910) income countries.

Table 5A.2   Countries of the Closed Sample (1981–1998)

Low-Income		Middle-Income		High-Income	
EGY	Egypt	ARG	Argentina	AUS	Australia
HND	Honduras	BOL	Bolivia	AUT	Austria
IDN	Indonesia	CHL	Chile	CAN	Canada
IND	India	COL	Colombia	CYP	Cyprus
NPL	Nepal	CRI	Costa Rica	DNK	Denmark
		ECU	Ecuador	ESP	Spain
		GRC	Greece	FIN	Finland
		GTM	Guatemala	FRA	France
		HUN	Hungary	GBR	The United Kingdom
		JOR	Jordan	GER	Germany
		KOR	Korea, Republic of	HKG	Hong Kong
		MAC	Macau	IRL	Ireland
		MAR	Morocco	ITA	Italy
		MEX	Mexico	JPN	Japan
		MYS	Malaysia	KWT	Kuwait
		PER	Peru	NLD	The Netherlands
		PHL	The Philippines	NOR	Norway
		POL	Poland	NZL	New Zealand
		PRT	Portugal	SGP	Singapore
		THA	Thailand	SWE	Sweden
		TTO	Trinidad and Tobago	TWN	Taiwan
		TUR	Turkey	USA	The United States
		URY	Uruguay		
		VEN	Venezuela		
		ZAF	South Africa		

Table 5A.3   Representativity of the Open and Closed Samples (%, using reported world totals by the World Bank)

	Open Sample		Closed Sample		Original Source[a]	
	Exports	Imports	Exports	Imports	Exports	Imports
1981	48.8	44.3	48.7	43.7	81.5	81.3
1990	58.9	59.5	57.3	57.9	86.4	86.2
1998	63.6	66.3	60.5	63.6	94.5	94.5

Sources: Sample data and World Bank (2001).
[a]Sum over the 207 countries reported in the World Bank database.

data, the sum of exports and imports over 207 countries represent less than 100 percent of world totals (see last two columns of table 5A.3).

Income Groups

Similar world totals were not available for income groups. In this case, world totals were estimated by the sum of exports or imports over all the

Table 5A.4   **Representativity of the Open and Closed Samples by Income Groups (%, 1998)**

	Open Sample		Closed Sample	
	Exports	Imports	Exports	Imports
Low-income countries	64.6	61.4	52.1	46.8
Middle-income countries	74.9	72.2	56.4	56.1
High-income countries	92.8	92.9	92.8	92.9
All	88.3	87.5	84.1	83.7

Sources: Sample data and World Bank (2001).

Notes: Using calculated world totals (sum over the 207 countries reported in the World Bank database).

Table 5A.5   **Imports-over-Exports Ratios**

	Polluting Products (1)	All Products (2)	(1)/(2)
1981	0.96	0.92	1.04
1990	1.11	1.03	1.08
1998	1.14	1.03	1.10

countries available in the World Bank source. To account for a maximum number of nonmissing reporters, these calculations, whose results appear in table 5A.4, are limited to year 1998.[19]

Generally speaking, representativity is larger for high-income countries (and of course for the open sample). However, even for low- and middle-income countries in the closed sample, the coverage of world trade is larger than 50 percent (except for low-income countries' imports).

Polluting Products

Similar calculations were not possible for polluting products, as world trade data were not available at this level of disaggregation. However, a very crude indicator of the representativity of the sample for these products is simply the ratio of imports over exports, which should be equal to 1.0 in case of complete coverage. These figures, along with their standardized value obtained by dividing them by the import/export ratio for all products in the sample, are reported in table 5A.5.

Overall, the ratio is reasonably close to 1.0, which suggests an acceptable level of representativity for polluting products. The sectoral results appear in tables 5A.6–5A.8, and in figures 5A.1 and 5A.2.

19. Accordingly, it is a more recent classification of countries by income groups (based on 1999 GNP figures) that is applied in this particular table.

Table 5A.6 **Shares of Developing Countries in World Trade**

	Polluting Products		All Products		Revealed Comparative Advantage	Revealed Comparative Disadvantage
	Exports (1)	Imports (2)	Exports (3)	Imports (4)	(1)/(3)	(2)/(4)
Paper and Products (ISIC = 341)						
1981–83	3.70	12.70	9.40	15.73	0.39	0.81
1996–98	9.55	19.92	15.93	18.67	0.60	1.07
Rate of growth	6.53	3.05	3.58	1.15		
Industrial Chemicals (ISIC =351)						
1981–83	5.11	21.55	9.40	15.73	0.54	1.37
1996–98	12.12	24.33	15.93	18.67	0.76	1.30
Rate of growth	5.92	0.82	3.58	1.15		
Other Nonmetallic Mineral Products (ISIC = 369)						
1981–83	11.42	22.33	9.40	15.73	1.22	1.42
1996–98	16.28	19.16	15.93	18.67	1.02	1.03
Rate of growth	2.39	–1.02	3.58	1.15		
Iron and Steel (ISIC = 371)						
1981–83	9.09	23.63	9.40	15.73	0.97	1.50
1996–98	18.38	26.85	15.93	18.67	1.15	1.44
Rate of growth	4.81	0.86	3.58	1.15		
Nonferrous Metals (ISIC = 372)						
1981–83	24.01	10.31	9.40	15.73	2.56	0.66
1996–98	22.91	17.88	15.93	18.67	1.44	0.96
Rate of growth	–0.31	3.73	3.58	1.15		

Table 5A.7 **Decomposition of Aggregate Change in Revealed Comparative Advantage (RCA) for Developing Countries**

ISIC Code	Total Change in RCA	Composition Effect	Structural Effect
341	0.206	–0.060	0.266
351	0.216	–0.087	0.303
369	–0.193	–0.301	0.108
371	0.186	–0.260	0.446
372	–1.118	–0.529	–0.589

Table 5A.8   **Gravity Equation: Hausman-Taylor Estimates**

Independent Variable	M_{ijt}					
	POL-HT	341	351	369	371	372
$\ln(Y_{it})$	1.50**	1.26**	1.27**	1.69**	1.82**	1.91**
	(19.4)	(12.6)	(16.39)	(15.4)	(16.5)	(17.8)
$\ln(Y_{jt})$	0.92**	0.58	1.86**	−0.58**	−0.32*	−0.16
	(10.9)	(5.0)	(21.8)	(5.0)	(2.5)	(1.3)
$\ln(Y_{it}/N_{it}) - \ln(Y_{jt}/N_{jt})$	0.007	0.08*	0.03	0.12**	0.11**	−0.04
	(0.3)	(2.0)	(1.1)	(3.5)	(2.7)	(1.1)
$\ln DIST_{ij}$	−1.12**	−1.40**	−1.23**	−1.21**	−1.12**	−0.95**
	(17.7)	(14.4)	(19.1)	(12.9)	(7.9)	(6.8)
BOR_{ij}	1.30**	1.68**	1.15**	1.70**	0.96**	0.87
	(5.5)	(4.01)	(4.6)	(4.2)	(2.8)	(1.6)
LL_i	0.49	0.52	−0.28	1.76**	2.79**	2.26**
	(1.66)	(1.0)	(0.9)	(3.4)	(4.23)	(3.3)
LL_j	−0.42**	−2.48**	−1.99**	−4.39**	−3.79**	−2.48**
	(1.22)	(3.8)	(5.4)	(6.9)	(4.25)	(3.3)
$\ln INF_{it}$	0.46**	0.48**	0.43**	0.98**	0.51**	0.55**
	(6.43)	(5.1)	(6.1)	(9.3)	(4.4)	(4.9)
$\ln INF_{jt}$	0.64**	1.19**	0.26**	2.22**	1.43**	0.15
	(7.7)	(9.9)	(3.0)	(18.6)	(9.9)	(1.2)
$\ln RER_{ijt}$	−0.40*	−0.57**	−0.35**	−0.66**	−0.71**	−0.19**
	(14.3)	(14.3)	(12.6)	(16.3)	(16.6)	(5.1)
No. of observations (*NT*)	30,345	21,831	28,087	20,907	21,122	21,591
No. of bilateral (*N*)	2,300	2,017	2,240	1,970	1,938	1,956
R^2	0.52	0.51	0.52	0.44	0.51	0.35
Hausman test HT vs. Chi-2(*K*)	614.7**	413.1**	589.6**	13.7**	97.9**	182.5**
	Chi-2(25)	Chi-2(25)	Chi-2(25)	Chi-2(25)	Chi-2(25)	Chi-2(25)

Notes: Dependent variable: M_{ijt} (imports of i from j in period t). T-student in parentheses. Time dummy variables and constant term not reported. Random effect estimates (endogenous variables: Y_i and Y_j and $[Y_i/N_i] - [Y_j/N_j]$).

**Significant at the 99 percent level.

*Significant at the 95 percent level.

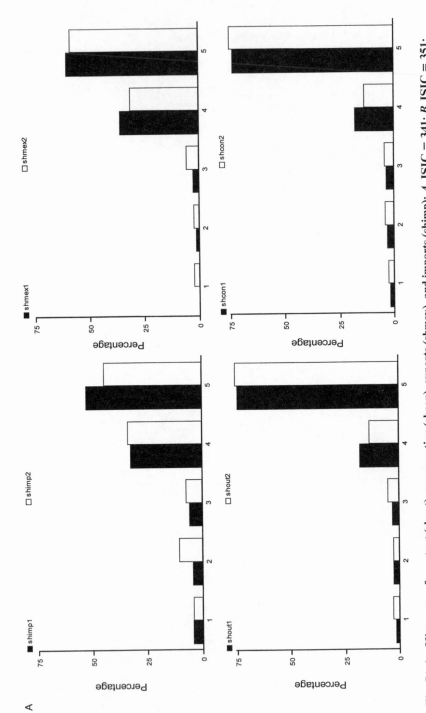

Fig. 5A.1 Histograms for output (shout), consumption (shcon), exports (shmex), and imports (shimp): *A*, ISIC = 341; *B*, ISIC = 351; *C*, ISIC = 369; *D*, ISIC = 371; *E*, ISIC = 372

Notes: 1: beginning of period; 2: end of period.

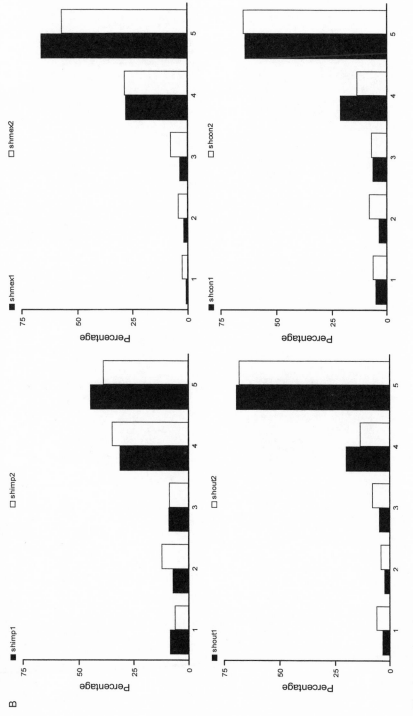

Fig. 5A.1 (cont.)

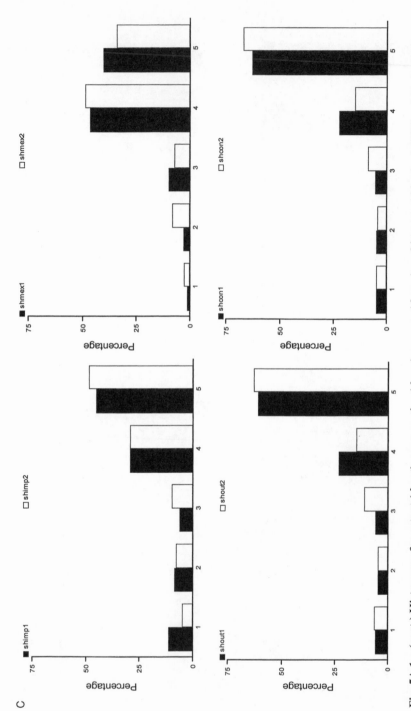

Fig. 5A.1 (cont.) Histograms for output (shout), consumption (shcon), exports (shmex), and imports (shimp): *A*, ISIC = 351; *B*, ISIC = 341; *C*, ISIC = 369; *D*, ISIC = 371; *E*, ISIC = 372

Notes: 1: beginning of period; 2: end of period.

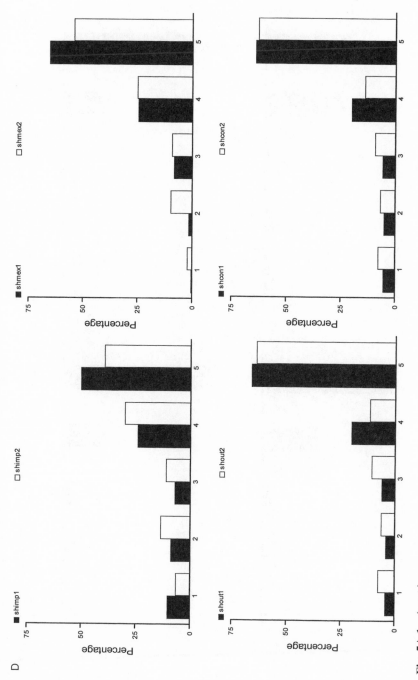

Fig. 5A.1 (cont.)

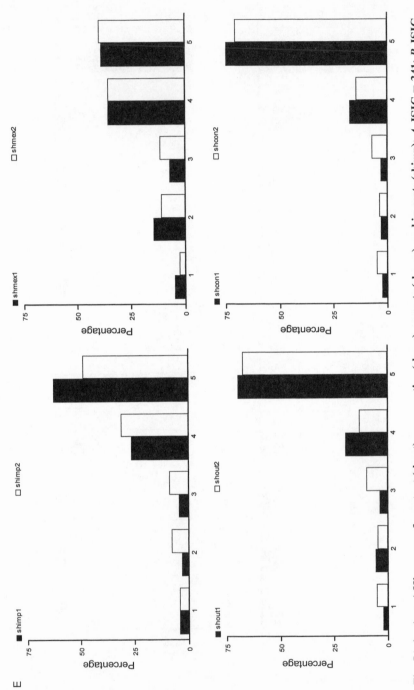

Fig. 5A.1 (cont.) Histograms for output (shout), consumption (shcon), exports (shmex), and imports (shimp): *A,* ISIC = 341; *B,* ISIC = 351; *C,* ISIC = 369; *D,* ISIC = 371; *E,* ISIC = 372

Notes: 1: beginning of period; 2: end of period.

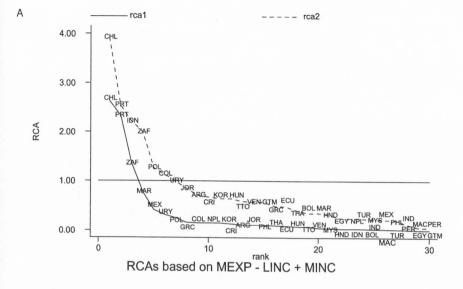

RCAs based on MEXP - LINC + MINC

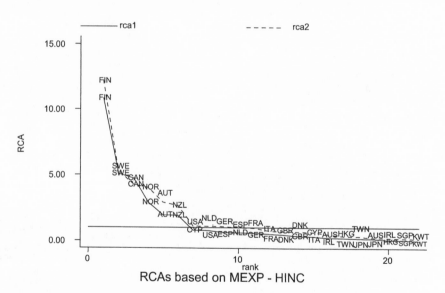

RCAs based on MEXP - HINC

Fig. 5A.2   Beginning-of-period (1) and end-of-period (2) RCAs, by country group:
A, ISIC = 341; *B*, ISIC = 351; *C*, ISIC = 369; *D*, ISIC = 371; *E*, ISIC = 372

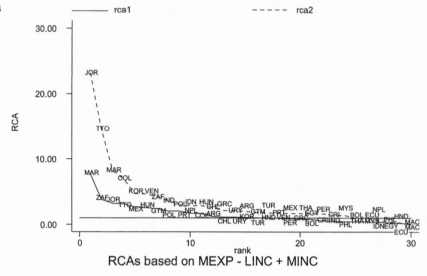

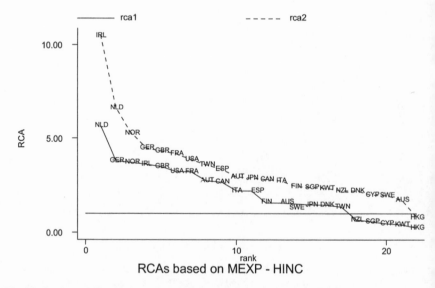

Fig. 5A.2 (cont.) **Beginning-of-period (1) and end-of-period (2) RCAs, by country group:** *A,* ISIC = 341; *B,* ISIC = 351; *C,* ISIC = 369; *D,* ISIC = 371; *E,* ISIC = 372

C

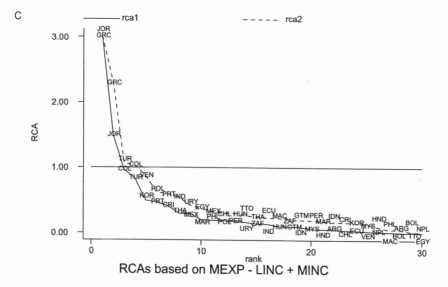

RCAs based on MEXP - LINC + MINC

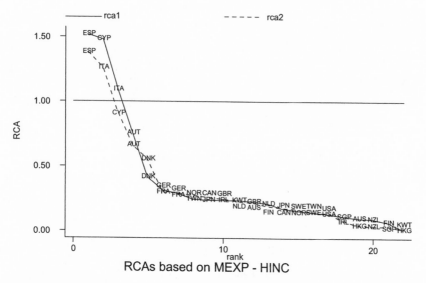

RCAs based on MEXP - HINC

Fig. 5A.2 (cont.)

D

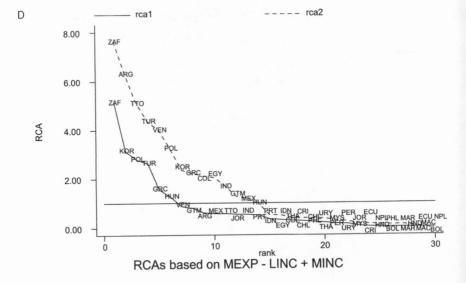

RCAs based on MEXP - LINC + MINC

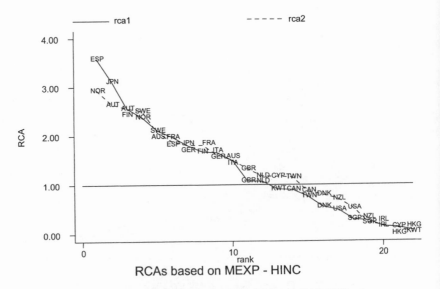

RCAs based on MEXP - HINC

Fig. 5A.2 (cont.) Beginning-of-period (1) and end-of-period (2) RCAs, by country group: *A*, **ISIC = 341;** *B*, **ISIC = 351;** *C*, **ISIC = 369;** *D*, **ISIC = 371;** *E*, **ISIC = 372**

E

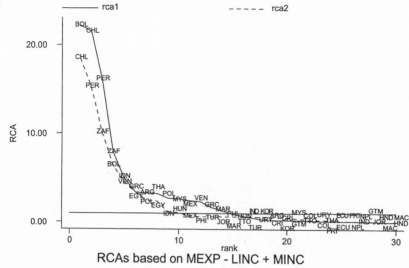

RCAs based on MEXP - LINC + MINC

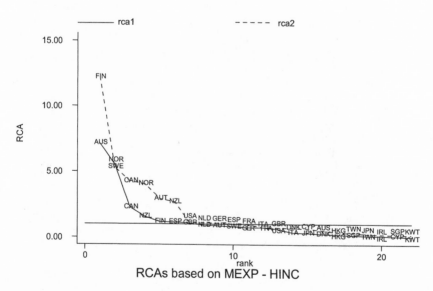

RCAs based on MEXP - HINC

Fig. 5A.2 (cont.)

References

Antweiler, A., B. Copeland, and M. S. Taylor. 2001. Is free trade good for the environment? *American Economic Review* 91 (4): 877–908.

Brun, J. F., C. Carrère, P. Guillaumont, and J. de Melo. 2002. Has distance died? Evidence from a panel gravity model. Clermont-Ferrand, France: University of Auvergne, Center of Studies and Research on International Development (CERDI). Mimeograph.

Damia, R., P. Fredriksson, and J. List. 2000. Trade liberalization, corruption, and environmental policy formation: Theory and evidence. Center for International Economic Research (CIES) Discussion Paper no. 0047. Adelaide, Australia: Adelaide University.

Dasgupta, S., A. Mody, S. Roy, and D. Wheeler. 1996. Environmental regulation and development: A cross-country empirical analysis. Policy Research Working Paper no. 1448. Washington, D.C.: World Bank.

Dean, J. 1992. Trade and the environment: A survey of the literature. In *International trade and development,* ed. P. Low, 15–28. Washington, D.C.: World Bank.

———. 2002. Does trade liberalization harm the environment? *Canadian Journal of Economics* 35 (4): 819–842.

Ederington, J., and J. Minier. 2003. Is environmental policy a secondary trade barrier? An empirical analysis. *Canadian Journal of Economics* 36 (1): 137–154.

Eskeland, G., and A. Harrison. 2002. Moving to greener pastures? Multinationals and the pollution havens hypothesis. *Journal of Development Economics* 36 (1): 1–23.

Grether, J. M., and J. de Melo. 1996. Commerce, environnement et relations Nord-Sud: Les enjeux et quelques tendances recentes (Trade, environment, and North-South relationships: The issues and some recent trends). *Revue d'Économie du Développement,* Issue no. 4:69–102.

Grossman, G. M., and A. B. Krueger. 1993. Environmental impacts of a North American Free Trade Agreement. In *The Mexico-U.S. free trade agreement,* ed. P. M., Graber, 13–56. Cambridge: MIT Press.

Hausman, A., and E. Taylor. 1981. Panel data and unobservable individual effects. *Econometrica* 49 (6): 1377–98.

Hettige, H., R. E. B. Lucas, and D. Wheeler. 1992. The toxic intensity of industrial production: Global patterns, trends, and trade policy. *American Economic Review* 82 (2): 478–481.

Hettige, H., P. Martin, M. Singh, and D. Wheeler. 1995. IPPS: The Industrial Projection System. Policy Research Working Paper no. 1431. Washington, D.C.: World Bank.

Keller, W., and A. Levinson. 2002. Pollution abatement costs and foreign direct investment inflows to the U.S. states. *Review of Economics and Statistics* 84 (4): 691–703.

Levinson, A., and S. Taylor. 2002. Trade and the environment: Unmasking the pollution haven effect. Georgetown University, Department of Economics. Mimeograph.

Low, P., and A. Yeats. 1992. Do dirty industries migrate? In *International trade and the environment,* ed. P. Low, 89–103. World Bank Discussion Paper no. 159. Washington, D.C.: World Bank.

Mani, M., and D. Wheeler. 1999. In search of pollution havens? Dirty industry in the world economy, 1960–95. In *Trade, global policy, and the environment,* ed. P. Fredriksson, 115–128. World Bank Discussion Paper no. 402. Washington, D.C.: World Bank.

Nicita, A., and M. Olarreaga. 2001. Trade and production, 1976–1999. World Bank, Trade and Production Database. Mimeograph.

Rauch, J. E. 1999. Networks versus markets in international trade. *Journal of International Economics* 48:7–35.

Smarzynska, B., and S. J. Wei. 2001. Pollution havens and foreign direct investment: Dirty secret or popular myth? NBER Working Paper no. 8465. Cambridge, Mass.: National Bureau of Economic Research, September.

Tobey, J. 1990. The effects of domestic environmental policies on patterns of world trade: An empirical test. *Kyklos* 43 (2): 191–201.

Van Beers, C., and J. Van den Bergh. 1997. An empirical multi-country analysis of the impact of environmental regulations on foreign trade flows. *Kyklos* 50 (1): 29–46.

Wheeler, D. 2001. Racing to the bottom? Foreign investment and air pollution in developing countries. *Journal of Environment and Development* 10 (3): 225–245.

World Bank. 2001. *World economic indicators.* Washington, D.C.: World Bank.

Zarsky, L. 1999. Havens, halos, and spaghetti: Untangling the evidence about foreign direct investment and the environment. In *OECD proceedings: Foreign direct investment and the environment,* 47–73. Paris: Organization for Economic Cooperation and Development.

Comment   Simon J. Evenett

Although much commentary on the consequences of the latest wave of international market integration has focused on economic matters, a vocal and important element of the policymaking community has been concerned with the environmental effects of globalization. With an eye to journalistic and policymaking audiences, environmental critics of trade, investment, and other reforms quickly coined two terms that have subsequently gained widespread currency, specifically the "pollution havens" hypothesis and the "race to the bottom" hypothesis. These seemingly plausible conjectures about how firms and governments behave in the global economy have now been subject to considerable scrutiny by researchers, as the balanced and methodical paper by Grether and de Melo ably demonstrates. It turns out that neither hypothesis is an accurate general characterization of firm or government behavior; yet certain circumstances can be identified where these hypotheses might not be at odds with observed behavior. This conclusion probably confirms what cautious observers from all camps have known all along, and serves the useful purpose of taking some of the wind out of the sails of the more partisan commentators.

In this comment I shall focus on the fourth section of Grether and de Melo's chapter, which attempts to quantify the effects of regulatory gaps on

Simon J. Evenett is a university lecturer at the Said Business School, Oxford University, and fellow of Corpus Christi College, Oxford.

international trade flows in selected nonpolluting and polluting industries. One of the goals of their analysis is to examine whether higher international transportation costs in polluting industries would—for a given regulatory gap—diminish the incentives for firms to relocate production from the industrialized economies to the developing countries. The logic, apparently, is that relocation would require shipping products from a production location in a new, developing country to customers in industrialized countries and that high international transportation costs would erode (if not entirely offset) any cost advantage of shifting production to a jurisdiction with less-stringent environmental regulations. Consistent with this thesis, Grether and de Melo found that, in a traditional gravity equation framework, the (absolute value) of the estimated distance elasticities were larger for five goods that are known to involve greater pollution during production than a composite of other goods that are thought to involve less pollution. In interpreting this finding, much turns on how convinced one is that the estimated distance parameters are really picking up international transportation costs and not some other distance-related cost of conducting international trade, such as the cost of acquiring information at potential sales opportunities. Indeed, one might ask what the evidence is that the latter costs are greater for products made in polluting industries. In this regard, it is also worth noting Grossman's (1998) skepticism about the plausibility of the magnitude of estimated distance elasticities in gravity equation studies.

In my view, the weakest aspect of Grether and de Melo's analysis concerns the construction and interpretation of the variable proxying for the regulatory gap. Grether and de Melo use bilateral differences in per capita national income to proxy for national differences in the stringency of environmental regulation, an assumption that they justify by making reference to a prediction of a theoretical model in Antweiler, Copeland, and Taylor (2001). They then go on to examine whether the estimated parameter for this proxy variable is a statistically significant determinant of bilateral trade flows. In only two of the five polluting industries (nonmetallic minerals, and iron and steel) is the estimated proxy positive and statistically significant (see the parameter estimates for α_9 in table 5.5). Moreover, these positive elasticities are remarkably small when compared to the size of the estimated elasticities of the traditional gravity variables, such as national income. Taking a unitary elasticity for national income (which is in line with the relevant parameter estimates reported in table 5.4), in the case of nonmetallic minerals the estimated elasticity on the regulatory gap term implies that a 1 percent increase in this gap would have an effect on trade flows equal to an eighth of the size of a 1 percent change in gross domestic product of either trading partner. It would seem, then, in terms of the impact on trade flows, that national differences in environmental regulation have little economically significant effect on trade flows.

Or do they? The interpretational problem arises from the fact, as Grether and de Melo note, that in many trade models differences in per capita national incomes are an independent determinant of international trade flows—that is, independent of environmental regulation. Unfortunately, the authors do not draw out the implications of this observation for the interpretation of the estimated parameters. Essentially, the estimated parameter on differences in per capita national incomes conflates the effect on trade flows created by national differences in environmental regulations with another independent determinant of trade flows. Worse, in the approach taken in this chapter, there appears to be no way to separate out these two influences. This implies that the estimated parameter for per capita income differences of -0.06 for nonpolluting manufacturing industries could include a small component that is due to regulatory gaps (say, $+0.02$). Or the latter could be large (say, $+0.7$). The point is that we just cannot tell how large the effects of the regulatory gap are. Consequently, this chapter does not accomplish one of its own objectives, namely, to estimate the effect of national differences in environmental regulation on international trade flows. It would appear, then, that another proxy for those national differences is called for if this hurdle is to be overcome in future research.

References

Antweiler, A., B. Copeland, and M. S. Taylor. 2001. Is free trade good for the environment? *American Economic Review* 91:877–908.
Grossman, Gene. 1998. Comment. In *The regionalization of the world economy,* ed. J. Frankel. Chicago: University of Chicago Press.

III

Factor Markets: Labor

6

The Role of Globalization in the Within-Industry Shift Away from Unskilled Workers in France

Vanessa Strauss-Kahn

6.1 Introduction

An important correlate of recent extensions in international trade and globalization has been the observation that in nearly all countries less-skilled labor has fared less well than skilled labor. In some cases the wages of the unskilled have fallen absolutely whereas elsewhere they have simply increased much less rapidly. Likewise, while job opportunities for the skilled have been increasing strongly, those for the unskilled have been falling, frequently resulting in high involuntary unemployment rates among them. At the same time, an important component of recent globalization has been the huge growth in vertical specialization—the completion of the different production stages of a good in different countries and the international transportation of parts and components between countries. Moreover, the trends suggest that such "dividing up of the value chain" is likely to become more important in future.

This paper asks whether these two phenomena are linked—in particular, whether vertical fragmentation has allowed firms to move unskilled-labor-intensive activities away from industrial countries and toward less-developed ones, and thus to reduce their demand for the relatively expensive unskilled workers in the former. If so, globalization of this form could explain the poor relative showing of unskilled labor in industrial countries. This in turn suggests that the internal politics of trade liberal-

Vanessa Strauss-Kahn is assistant professor of economics at INSEAD.

I would like to thank Raquel Fernandez, Kei-Mu Yi, Christopher Flinn, editors Robert Baldwin and Alan Winters, and conference participants for helpful comments on previous version of this paper. I am also grateful to Bernard Salanie and Sebastien Jean for their help in collecting the data used in this paper. The usual disclaimer applies.

ization and international investment will become more difficult and complex, as the unskilled—already a major force in industrial-country trade policy determination—become further detached from the increase in prosperity. Ultimately, such distributional consequences of globalization will need to be addressed by governments, by means of complementary policies or even by modifying the nature or extent of openness.

Strauss-Kahn (2002) sets forth theoretically the potential role of trade (via international vertical specialization) in explaining an increase in the within-industry share of unskilled labor. The present paper aims at assessing empirically the magnitude of this vertical specialization effect. I first show that international vertical specialization occurred in France over the past two decades and then estimate its contribution to the observed within-industry shift away from unskilled workers. Following Krugman's (1995) argument, I focus on employment rather than wages because of the particularly inflexible aspects of the French labor market (e.g., strong unions and a high minimum wage). This choice will be discussed more extensively in section 6.4. To determine the extent of international vertical specialization, I build an index that measures the value of imported inputs embodied in goods produced, using primarily data from input-output tables. The labor data used in the regression analysis distinguish workers per occupation within industry. All data come from the French National Institute of Statistics and Economic Studies (INSEE).[1] I find that international vertical specialization rose significantly over the period, from 9 percent in 1977 to 14 percent in 1993. A more limited index, restricted to inputs purchased from the same aggregated sector as the good being produced, shows an increase from 5 percent to 7.5 percent for the same period. I then show that international vertical specialization has contributed from 11 percent to 15 percent of the decline in the share of unskilled workers in manufacturing employment over the 1977–1985 period and for 25 percent of the decline in the 1985–1993 period.

France features several relevant characteristics that make it a particularly good case study. It has a large and diverse trading area because of (among other factors) preferential trade agreements with Eastern European countries and former colonies. Moreover, free markets in France have dramatically increased over the past three decades, as the European Union (EU) has been enlarged from six to fifteen member states and the free movement of goods, persons, services, and capital among members has been progressively established. Because labor costs differ across member countries, this market

1. Sebastien Jean has kindly provided the labor data used in this paper. The industry occupational decomposition is derived from an annual industry survey managed by the INSEE. The distinction between skilled and unskilled workers depends on occupation rather than education. Occupations have been divided into two groups that are roughly equivalent to the U.S. white-collar/blue-collar decomposition. For further information on these data, see Cortes and Jean (1997).

integration has probably increased international vertical specialization between France and its partners. In addition, the high French unemployment rate affects unskilled workers more than their skilled counterparts. The skilled-unskilled unemployment rate differential in France widened in the 1980s, rising from 2.4 percentage points in 1981 to 7.6 percentage points in 1994.[2] This increase in the unemployment rate of unskilled workers has been accompanied by a decrease in the share of the unskilled in total employment, as labor demand has shifted away from unskilled workers. Accordingly, many French citizens perceive international vertical specialization as one of the main causes of unskilled unemployment. To my knowledge, the accuracy of this belief has yet to be tested in any empirical work.

This paper is related to two strands of literature: one on vertical specialization and the other on the impact of trade on income distribution. Campa and Goldberg (1997) study vertical specialization in Japan, the United Kingdom, Canada, and the United States; Hummels, Ishii, and Yi (2001) consider the French case among other countries in the Organization for Economic Cooperation and Development (OECD). While both papers focus on the magnitude and evolution of vertical specialization, they neglect the effect of vertical specialization on the labor market. I also use a different index of vertical specialization and a higher level of industrial disaggregation than Hummels, Ishii, and Yi. In the large literature on trade and income distribution, my work is closest to Feenstra and Hanson (1996, 1997), which estimate the impact of outsourcing (vertical specialization) for the United States. They find that outsourcing made a significant contribution in explaining the observed increase in the relative wages of skilled workers during the 1980s.

The remainder of the paper is in five parts. Section 6.2 explains my measure of vertical specialization and the data used to construct it. It also presents results on vertical specialization levels and trends. In section 6.3, I examine the accuracy of the index by carrying out two different variance decompositions. Section 6.4 presents evidence on the within-industries shift away from unskilled labor. In section 6.5, I estimate the impact of vertical specialization on employment inequality through a regression analysis. Section 6.6 concludes.

6.2   The Index of Vertical Specialization

In order to assess the degree of vertical specialization across industries and its evolution over time, I build and study an index denoted by V. The

---

2. The unemployment rate for males with low education (i.e., levels 0, 1, and 2, up to lower secondary education) rose from 5.4 percent in 1981 to 13.5 percent in 1994. The unemployment rate for males with high education (levels up to tertiary education) increased from 3.0 percent in 1981 to 5.9 percent in 1994. The gap for female unemployment rate per education level is even larger. Data are from the OECD.

index is computed at the industry level and measures the share of imported inputs embodied in production. I primarily use input-output tables that include sector-level data on inputs. Data for outputs, value-added, imports, and consumption are derived from national account tables. All data come from INSEE and encompass 100 sectors, among which 50 are of interest for this paper.[3] The database covers the 1977–1993 period. Input-output tables provide the value of inputs used in production and distinguish between the different sources of supplies (i.e., the industries in which the inputs have been produced). However, these tables do not distinguish between domestically produced and imported inputs. In order to obtain an estimate of the value of imported input from industry j used in producing the output of industry i, I multiply the total value of inputs from industry j used in producing the output of industry i, namely, q_{ji}, by the ratio of the value of imported goods from industry j to the value of the domestic use of goods from industry j, namely, m_j, where domestic use includes use as final goods, intermediate goods, and capital goods. Dividing this estimate of imported inputs from industry j by the value of total production in industry i, and summing this ratio for all the n industries with imported inputs into industry i, yields the vertical specialization index for industry i, namely, V_i.

$$(1) \qquad V_i = \sum_{j=1}^{n} \frac{m_j q_{ji}}{p_i}$$

The fact that the import penetration ratio mixes final goods, intermediate goods, and capital goods limits the precision of the index. It is indeed likely that the share of imported inputs in total consumption of intermediate inputs differs from the share of imported final goods in total consumption of final goods. One might expect the first ratio to be lower than the second due to quality/adequacy issues of international trade in intermediate goods. If such is the case, the index of international vertical specialization is overstated. However, because changes in variables are considered in the regression analysis, this issue is not a significant concern. More importantly, it is likely that imports in intermediate goods do not vary across industries in the same proportion as imports in final goods over the period considered. The manner in which this issue will bias the index, however, is unclear. Given this limitation, the import penetration ratio is used as the best available approximation of the share of intermediate-goods imports in intermediate-goods consumption.

This index V seems to capture adequately any changes in production

3. The 100 sectors are divided in six industries: agriculture, business, manufactures, mining, services, and transportation. Agriculture, mining, and manufactures account for 90 percent of traded goods and are the sectors covered in this study. Index V has been computed for the services, transportation, and business sectors, however, and indicates low levels of vertical specialization (under 5 percent in 1996).

structure toward more or less international vertical specialization (i.e., if V increases then an industry becomes more vertically specialized). However, in order to measure the impact of vertical specialization on unskilled labor shares, I also calculate a modified version of the original index. The modified index only measures inputs purchased from the same aggregated sector as the good being produced. This provides information on the relative extent of international intermediate-goods specialization within the same industry. As most of the decline in unskilled labor shares occurred within industries (see section 6.4), the modified index captures such an intra-industry movement. The rationale of using the so-called limited index may be illustrated as follows. If (to use a common example) the French automobile industry imports more steel, this will not affect French workers in the automobile industry but rather those in the steel industry. In contrast, if the French automobile industry imports more automobile parts, then automobile workers will be affected—especially if the parts were formerly made by the same company (or, at least, were purchased in France). The limited index of vertical specialization, Vl, is constructed the same way as V, with the input subscripts i and j belonging to the same aggregated sectors (i.e., three-digit industry j belongs to two-digit industry i.)

In constructing the Vl index, I would ideally like to have firm-specific data on the production process that included the amount of imported inputs in total production, among which are parts and components and also contracts done by others. Such data would be more precise than the data used here and would provide information on stages of production that are located abroad. For example, many French-contracted goods involve domestic design, marketing, and headquarter activities but are produced abroad and then directly exported to their final destinations. Hence such goods do not appear in the French input-output tables. This type of outsourcing, which tends to separate production and nonproduction activities internationally, has dramatically increased over the past few decades. Among the multitude of European- and U.S.-branded goods made abroad, a typical example is Nike,[4] which employs 2,500 persons for marketing and headquarter activities in the United States and about 75,000 persons for production activities in Asia. Firm-specific data are collected for the United States in the *Annual Survey of Manufactures.*[5] Unfortunately, equivalent data do not exist for France. The unavailability of "contracts done by others" data tends to reduce the level of international vertical specialization and therefore to underestimate its impact on the changes in the share of unskilled workers. Nevertheless, I believe that Vl, using available data, captures a significant part of the vertical specialization trend. One should,

4. Mentioned in Feenstra and Hanson (1996).
5. The *Annual Survey of Manufactures* provides information, at a high level of disaggregation, on such outsourcing as (a) parts and components, (b) resales, and (c) contracts done by others.

Table 6.1   Index V and Limited Index Vl of International Vertical Specialization: Overall and Selected Results

	1977	1993	% Growth
Index V			
Overall	0.092	0.138	50.0
Apparel and other fabricated textile products	0.080	0.181	126.3
Synthetic fibers	0.164	0.323	96.9
Miscellaneous plastic products	0.155	0.303	95.5
Textile industries	0.097	0.188	93.8
Aircraft	0.129	0.239	85.3
Motor vehicles	0.084	0.154	83.3
Nonelectrical industrial machinery	0.093	0.169	81.7
Industrial chemicals	0.117	0.196	67.5
Farm machinery and equipment	0.083	0.137	65.1
Electronic computing equipment	0.081	0.123	51.9
Primary steel industries	0.143	0.216	51.0
Metalworking machinery	0.067	0.098	46.3
Wood product	0.093	0.074	−20.4
Iron mining	0.085	0.030	−64.7
Limited Index Vl			
Overall	0.049	0.073	49.0
Miscellaneous plastic products	0.012	0.037	208.3
Apparel and other fabricated textile products	0.072	0.164	127.8
Textile industries	0.059	0.127	115.3
Synthetic fibers	0.136	0.279	105.2
Motor vehicles	0.039	0.079	102.6
Aircraft	0.107	0.212	98.1
Industrial chemicals	0.085	0.168	97.7
Electronic computing equipment	0.042	0.079	88.1
Farm machinery and equipment	0.028	0.047	67.9
Nonelectrical industrial machinery	0.049	0.080	63.3
Metalworking machinery	0.015	0.024	60.0
Primary steel industries	0.139	0.208	49.6
Wood product	0.084	0.059	−29.8
Iron mining	0.016	0.004	−75.0

however, keep in mind that Vl represents the lower bound of the potential magnitude of international vertical specialization.

Table 6.1 presents overall estimates of the level of international vertical specialization as measured by V and Vl, as well as sectoral results for selected industries. It also shows growth rates in the indexes for the 1977–1993 period. Overall, V increases from 9 percent to 14 percent, which represents more than a 50 percent growth over the period. Campa and Goldberg (1997) computed a similar measure of vertical specialization for the 1974–1993 period for the United States and other countries. They found that V rose from 4 to 8 percent in the United States, from 16 to 20 percent in Canada, and from 13 to 22 percent in the United Kingdom. Japan, in contrast, experienced decreasing vertical specialization, with V falling from 8 to 4 percent. My growth rate estimates for France are roughly similar (although somewhat lower) than Campa and Goldberg's estimates for the United Kingdom when their longer-coverage period is taken into account. This similarity may be explained by the fact that the two countries have several common features (European countries, part of the EU, size, etc.). Moreover, Campa and Goldberg use more aggregated data (about twenty sectors) than in this paper and do not include the agricultural sector in their calculation, which tends to increase the index's value.[6] Hummels, Rapoport, and Yi (1998) and Hummels, Ishii, and Yi (2001) consider the value of imported inputs embodied in goods that are exported. Their measure, although more limited than mine, gives a useful estimate of vertical specialization in goods sold abroad. However, my index measures the shift in labor demand whether the final good is exported or consumed domestically. Their index shows a rise in vertical specialization in France from 18 percent in 1972 to 24 percent in 1990. Two factors inflate their index compared to mine. First, Hummels and colleagues take into account the imported inputs embodied in domestic inputs purchased. Second, sectors featuring the highest share of imported inputs are relatively more export-oriented (the correlation between the levels of vertical specialization and the level of export orientation is 0.45).[7] This observation supports the idea of undertaking vertical specialization for cost-advantage reasons, since export-oriented sectors must be competitive in international markets.

In examining V by sector, two broad relationships emerge.[8] First, the level of vertical specialization varies widely across sectors. Although certain industries experience a rapid increase, V declines in a number of industries (e.g., iron mining or wood products). Second, the sectors most affected by international vertical specialization in France (in level as well as in trend) tend to be the same than in other countries. In France, among the industries that experience the greatest rise (for a significant level of V) are chemicals and allied products (drugs and medicines, industrial chemicals, soaps and cosmetics, and synthetic fibers); electronic computing equipment; nonelectrical industrial machinery; textiles (apparel and other fabricated textile products, footwear industries, leather and leather products, and textile industries); transportation equipment (aircraft, motor vehicles, and ship and boat building); and rubber and plastics products. These findings are consistent with those of Hummels, Rapoport, and Yi (1998), Hummels, Ishii, and Yi (2001), and Campa and Goldberg (1997) for other industrial countries.

6. Omitting the agricultural sector, the French vertical specialization rises from 10 percent in 1977 to 16 percent in 1993, with a growth of 67 percent.

7. Author's calculation.

8. Table 6.2 reports the index for selected representative sectors. Results for all sectors are available upon request.

Results obtained with the restricted measure of international vertical specialization are also reported in table 6.1. Overall, Vl increases from 5 percent in 1977 to 7.5 percent in 1993, a 49 percent growth over the period. As would be expected, Vl is lower than V across all sectors. Certain sectors, however, exhibit significantly high limited vertical specialization index *and* growth in limited vertical specialization. Such sectors belong to the chemicals and allied products industries, transportation equipment industries, machinery industries, and textile industries. In these sectors it is apparently relatively easy to "divide up the value chain" and import inputs from abroad.

Distinguishing international vertical specialization by regional source of imported inputs provides interesting results. In disaggregating these imports into OECD versus non-OECD import sources I find that the levels and growth rates of the overall V and Vl can be mainly imputed to OECD imports.[9] In fact, 79 percent of international vertical specialization is attributed to OECD countries in 1977, and 85 percent in 1993. Breaking the results down by subperiods reveals that vertical specialization involving OECD countries accounts for 100 percent of the growth in vertical specialization for 1977–1985, but only 80 percent for 1985–1993. The importance of vertical specialization involving OECD countries reflects the French pattern of trade.[10] However, results on trends are more significant. While import growth rates declined during the 1977–1993 period—from 64 percent for the 1977–1985 period to 42 percent for the 1985–1993 period—international vertical specialization growth rates increased over the period. Import growth rates from OECD countries show a similar declining trend as total import growth rates. Growth rates in vertical specialization involving OECD countries reached 27 percent in the two subperiods. More importantly, whereas imports from non-OECD countries grew by 58 percent from 1977 to 1985, vertical specialization involving nonmember countries did not increase. However, for 1985–1993, imports from non-OECD countries grew by 54 percent, with V and Vl increasing by 16 percent and 21 percent, respectively. This suggests that, in the second period, imports from non-OECD countries became more oriented toward sectors that vertically specialize. Sectoral decomposition of the international vertical specialization index shows a dramatic growth in V and Vl from non-OECD countries in electronic computing equipment, office and computing machinery, and all the textiles industries. It is plausible that some issues specific to trade in intermediate inputs, such as quality or adequacy of products along the pro-

9. The OECD data used in this paper cover only those countries that were members prior to 1994 (i.e., the data exclude the Czech Republic, Hungary, Mexico, Poland, and South Korea).

10. About 84 percent of French imports came from OECD countries during 1977–1993, with this share being stable over the period.

duction chain, became less important over time as communication (and thereby monitoring) was eased. Further research on patterns of trade and vertical specialization according to source countries would be of great interest. However, such research is beyond the scope of this paper, which focuses more specifically on the broad impact of international vertical specialization on French employment shares of unskilled and skilled workers.[11]

6.3   Is the Index a Good Measure of International Vertical Specialization?

The index of international vertical specialization aims at capturing changes caused by the relocation of different stages of production across countries. International vertical specialization is hence expected to occur at the industry level and to increase international trade. Thus, it is important to verify (a) that the index captures the change in intensity of a sector's vertical specialization (and not the variation in sector composition of total production) and (b) that it reflects a variation in the share of imported inputs in production for a given level of inputs (and not a variation in the use of inputs independently of the supply's source).

A rise in V or VI could be due simply to an increase in production shares of highly vertically specializing sectors relative to production of other sectors. I check for this possibility by decomposing the variance of V and VI. The change in these indexes for the 1977–1993 period is decomposed into the variation in intensity of a sector's vertical specialization (the *within* component) and the variation in sector share of total production (the *between* component):

$$\Delta V = \Delta \sum_{i=1}^{n} \theta_i V_i = \sum_{i=1}^{n} \overline{\theta}_i \Delta V_i + \sum_{i=1}^{n} \overline{V}_i \Delta \theta_i,$$

where θ_i is industry i's share of total manufacturing production at time t. (Henceforth, a bar over a variable denotes the mean value over the considered period.)

Overall results of this variance decomposition are summarized in table 6.2.[12] The between-and-within sector decomposition of the rise in vertical specialization is indicated for the entire period 1977–1993 as well as for the subperiods 1977–1985 and 1985–1993. The column labeled "Total" reports the annual percentage-point increase in vertical specialization. A comparison of the rates between periods shows an acceleration over time. In terms of V (VI), the rise in vertical specialization occurred at a rate of 0.20 (0.10)

---

11. Note that the importance of vertical specialization with OECD countries does not affect its potential impact on unskilled and skilled labor shares. Within the OECD, differences in labor costs could lead France to relocate its unskilled-intensive activities to lower-wage countries (e.g., southern European countries).

12. Detailed results across sectors are available upon request.

Table 6.2   Industry/Sector Decomposition of the Rise in International
             Vertical Specialization

	Between	Within	Total	Within/Total
V				
1977–1985	0.00	0.20	0.20	101%
1985–1993	0.01	0.30	0.31	97%
1977–1993	0.01	0.27	0.27	98%
VI				
1977–1985	0.00	0.09	0.10	98%
1985–1993	−0.01	0.18	0.17	105%
1977–1993	0.00	0.14	0.14	101%

Sources: National Institute of Statistics and Economic Studies (1977–1992, 1977–1996, 1993–1996) and author's calculations.

Notes: The "Total" columns report the sum of the within and the between components. Due to rounding, total numbers vary slightly across tables.

percentage points per year during the 1977–1985 period and increased to 0.31 (0.17) percentage points per year during the 1985–1993 period.

The within component dominates in both periods, accounting for 0.20 (0.09) of the 0.20 (0.10) percentage point per annum increase in vertical specialization for V (VI) in the 1977–1985 period and for all the acceleration between the two periods. Over all sectors, the within component of the variance decomposition accounts for almost 98 percent (101 percent) of the total variation in vertical specialization indexes for 1977–1993. The increase in V and VI is thus due mainly to an increase in the individual sector's vertical specialization intensity.

I also want to determine if the observed vertical specialization is internationally oriented. The growth in V and VI could actually be caused either by an increase in the use of inputs from all sources or by a shift from domestically produced inputs to imported inputs. Obviously, vertical specialization affects the domestic labor market only if it occurs internationally, substituting foreign for French labor. For this purpose, I decompose the variance of the index of vertical specialization by industry into the variation in the use of production inputs, independently of the supply's sources (the within component) and the variation in share of imported input in production for a given level of inputs (the between component):

$$(3) \qquad \Delta V_i = \sum_{j=1}^{n} \overline{m_j} \Delta\left(\frac{q_{ji}}{p_i}\right) + \sum_{j=1}^{n} \overline{\left(\frac{q_{ji}}{p_i}\right)} \Delta m_j,$$

where V_i is the level of vertical specialization in sector i, m_j is the import penetration ratio of industry j, q_{ji} is the value of inputs from industry j used in the production of industry i, p_i is the value of total production in industry i, and n is the number of industries considered.

Table 6.3   **Source Decomposition of the Rise in International Vertical**
                    Specialization: Domestic versus Foreign

	Between	Within	Total	Between/Total
V				
1977–1985	0.23	−0.02	0.21	112%
1985–1993	0.31	−0.01	0.30	103%
1977–1993	0.30	−0.02	0.27	108%
VI				
1977–1985	0.11	−0.01	0.09	114%
1985–1993	0.19	−0.01	0.18	103%
1977–1993	0.16	−0.01	0.14	108%

Sources: See table 6.2.
Notes: See table 6.2.

Overall results of this decomposition are presented in table 6.3.[13] The
between component, which corresponds to a rise in foreign outsourcing,
accounts for all the increase in vertical specialization in each period, and
thus, for all the acceleration. As measured by $V(VI)$, it increases from 0.23
(0.11) percentage points per year during the 1977–1985 period to 0.31
(0.19) percentage points per year during the 1985–1993 period. The within
component, which captures the annual rate of change in outsourcing from
all sources, is negative and stable over the entire period.

The variance decompositions indicate that vertical specialization occurs
within-industry and internationally. While results from the second decomposition are in accordance with the findings of Thesmar and Thoenig
(2002), the fact that we do not observe any decrease in the use of inputs from
all sources (the within component) is somewhat surprising. However, sectoral results show that this feature varies widely across industries. In most
machinery, textile, and transportation industries, the within component accounts for a significant share of vertical specialization (i.e., these industries
outsource more of their inputs independently of the supply source). For example, the within component represents 20 percent of total change in the
footwear industry and 30 percent in the motor vehicles industry. In contrast,
most agriculture and mining industries show a negative within component,
suggesting that these industries have become increasingly self-sufficient over
time. Technological progress could explain part of this latter development,
as new machines and techniques may allow firms to produce goods that
would have been outsourced otherwise. Excluding the agriculture and mining sectors changes the overall decomposition results. The between component now accounts for only 93 percent of the total change. In any case, these
results suggest that most of the vertical specialization occurs internationally
as imports substitute for inputs outsourced from other domestic firms.

13. Sector results are available upon request.

6.4   The Within-Industry Shift Away from Unskilled Workers

An analysis of the declining intraindustry share of skilled to unskilled workers or of the widening wage gap between skilled and unskilled workers requires explaining both supply and demand factors. However, there is evidence that changes in the relative supply of skilled to unskilled labor did not play a major role. In most industrialized countries, the share of skilled workers in the labor force rose over the period being studied. For example, the ratio of low- to high-educated workers in the French population decreased from 6.6 in 1981 to 2.7 in 1994; for the United Kingdom, the decline is from 3.6 in 1984 to 1.3 in 1994.[14] One would expect this change in relative supply to be reflected by a decline in the relative wage of skilled workers and an increase in the ratio of skilled to unskilled workers across industries. Hence, the observed increase in wage premia for skilled workers seems to refute the hypothesis of predominant supply-side effects on wage inequality. Moreover, although the supply of unskilled workers fell relative to the supply of skilled workers, evidence on the employment/population ratio for these two groups indicates a relative decline for unskilled workers. For example, in France the difference in the employment-population ratio for highly skilled versus less skilled workers increased by more than 11 percentage points over the 1981–1994 period.[15] Therefore, in analyzing these changes, I focus on the demand side of the labor market.

In this paper, I focus on the employment shares of skilled versus unskilled workers. Although it could be argued that one should focus on the change in the relative wages (earnings) of these two groups, I believe that changes in employment shares is the more appropriate variable to analyze in considering the French case. Over the past three decades the French earnings dispersion between skilled and unskilled workers did not significantly rise, whereas France's employment share of skilled workers increased dramatically. This behavior of relative wages is common to most continental European countries and differs greatly from the U.K. and U.S. experience. Data from the OECD *Employment Outlook* (1996, 1997) show the trends: earnings dispersion (as measured by the ratio of the upper earnings limit of the 9th decile of workers to the 1st decile) shows a significant increase in the United States and the United Kingdom over the 1970–1995 period, while it is stable for France and for most continental European countries.[16] Moreover, employment-share differentials between more-educated and less-educated workers rose by 95 percent for the 1981–1994 period in France yet increased by only 28 percent in the United States and 48 percent in the United Kingdom for equivalent periods. This suggests significant factor-price rigidities in the French labor market and the strong

14. A low level of education corresponds to levels up to lower secondary education. A high level of education corresponds to levels up to tertiary education.
15. All data in this paragraph are from the OECD *Employment Outlook* (1997).
16. This feature is robust to the choice of deciles.

role of institutions and regulations. In fact, strong unions and a high minimum wage have probably compressed wage dispersion in continental Europe and have induced instead an increasing employment-share differential. Hence, following Krugman (1995), I believe that in Europe the effects of trade are manifested mainly in changes in industry employment shares of less-educated (unskilled) versus more-educated (skilled) workers.

If firms vertically specialize to take advantage of labor-cost differentials across countries, the skilled-unskilled relative demand for labor should change within industries. In relatively high-skill countries (such as France), the share of unskilled workers within industries should decrease as firms outsource their unskilled-intensive stages of production. In fact, vertical specialization, as well as skill-biased technological change, shift the skill composition of labor demand within industries. In contrast, trade in final goods shifts the skill composition of labor demand between industries: from unskilled-intensive to skilled-intensive industries. A variance decomposition analysis of the aggregate shift away from unskilled labor indicates which of these effects has been dominant in France during the past two decades. Following Berman, Bound, and Griliches (1994), the change in the aggregate share of unskilled workers in total employment is decomposed into the change in the allocation of employment across industries (the between component) and the change in the allocation of employment within industries (the within component):

$$(4) \qquad \Delta E = \sum_{i=j}^{n} \overline{E}_i \Delta s_i + \sum_{i=l}^{n} \overline{s}_i \Delta E_i,$$

where s_i is the employment share of industry i at the national level. The E term denotes the aggregate share of unskilled workers, that is,

$$E = \sum_{i=l}^{n} E_i s_i,$$

where E_i is the share of unskilled workers in industry i.

Table 6.4 reports the within-and-between components of the change in

Table 6.4   **Industry/Sector Decomposition of the Decline in the Share of Unskilled Workers**

	Between	Within	Total	Within/Total
All sectors				
1977–1985	−0.24	−0.40	−0.65	63%
1985–1993	−0.21	−0.48	−0.69	70%
1977–1993	−0.23	−0.44	−0.67	65%
Manufacturing sectors				
1977–1985	−0.08	−0.49	−0.57	86%
1985–1993	−0.06	−0.43	−0.50	88%
1977–1993	−0.08	−0.46	−0.53	86%

Sources: Author calculation; Cortes and Jean (1997) database.

the aggregate share of unskilled workers for the entire economy and for the manufacturing sector. Over all sectors, the shift away from unskilled labor occurs at a rate of 0.65 percentage points per year for 1977–1985 and accelerates to 0.69 percentage points per year for 1985–1993. The annual rate of decrease is lower when only the manufacturing sector is considered (0.53 percentage points per year over the entire period) and shows a deceleration between the two periods.

The within component strongly dominates in each period. In the manufacturing sector, for example, it accounts for 0.46 percentage points of the 0.53 percentage points per annum decrease. The within-industry shift away from unskilled workers accounts for 86 percent of the fall in demand for this type of worker in total manufacturing employment.

To explain the change in the employment shares of unskilled and skilled workers, one must therefore focus on factors that affect the within-industry employment structure. As mentioned earlier, vertical specialization and skill-biased technological progress are the most likely explanatory factors.[17]

6.5 Estimation of the Impact of Vertical Specialization on the Labor Market

The contribution of vertical specialization to the observed decrease in the within-industry share of unskilled workers is assessed through a regression analysis. An appropriate way to do so is to estimate a cost function. Following Berman, Bound, and Griliches (1994) and Feenstra and Hanson (1996, 1997), I estimate a cost-share equation of a translog function. This specification allows using the within-industry share of unskilled workers as a dependent variable in a regression that estimates the parameters of the cost function. Related studies in the literature use instead the level change in the share of less-skilled workers in industry wage bill. While it is theoretically a more appropriate regressand, as it results directly from the short-run cost-minimization problem of firms which face a translog production technology, I believe that using level change in the share of less-skilled workers in industry employment is appropriate for France. As already discussed in the previous section, relative wages of unskilled to skilled workers in continental European countries such as France have been relatively stable over the period and thus the main impact of vertical specialization has been on changing the employment share of unskilled workers within industries. Brown and Christensen (1981) also show that, with such a specification, level data can be used for quasi-fixed factors. This allows me to use quantity data for the quasi-fixed factor (i.e., capital)

17. In the rest of the paper, the limited measure of international vertical specialization is used in all the calculations, although it will be referred to as vertical specialization.

instead of price data, which are rarely available. Thus, the specification for estimating the change in the share of unskilled labor in industry i over the time period t, namely, δE_{it}, is

$$(5) \qquad \delta E_{it} = \beta_0 + \beta_1 \delta \ln\left(\frac{W_{uit}}{W_{sit}}\right) + \beta_2 \delta \ln\left(\frac{K_{it}}{Y_{it}}\right) + \beta_3 \delta \ln Y_{it}$$
$$+ \beta_4 \delta V_{it} + \beta_5 PD_t + \varepsilon_{it}.$$

Here, for each period t, E_i is the share of unskilled workers in industry i, W_{ui}/W_{si} represents the relative wages of skilled to unskilled labor in industry i, K_i is industry i's level of capital utilization, Y_i is industry i's level of gross output, V_i is industry i's level of vertical specialization, and PD is a period dummy.

The sign of the coefficient on the (logarithmic) relative wage, β_1, is ambiguous and depends on the elasticity of substitution between skilled and unskilled labor. The coefficient on the (logarithmic) share of capital in production, β_2, should be negative owing to the substitutability between capital and unskilled labor. Similarly, the coefficient on the (logarithmic) level of output, β_3, is expected to be negative. The output regressor controls for industry scale, and I expect firms to take the opportunity of increased production to decrease their shares of unskilled labor. Such an outcome is likely in a rigid labor market such as the French one, where layoffs are cumbersome and costly. The coefficient on the (logarithmic) index of international vertical specialization, β_4, should have a negative sign because French and foreign unskilled labor are supposedly substitutes, and vertical specialization should take place to exploit lower unskilled labor cost abroad. The measure β_0, of cross-industry changes (including technological progress and institutional change), is expected to be negative. Finally, $\beta_0 + \varepsilon_i$ represents industry-specific changes.

Following Berman, Bound, and Griliches (1994), I assume that, although there might be some industry-specific mixes of skill types, the relative price of labor does not vary across industries. Then, to avoid endogeneity problems, I omit relative wages from equation (5). This omission should affect only the constant term. Thus, the estimated regression is

$$(6) \qquad \delta E_{it} = \beta_0 + \beta_1 \delta \ln\left(\frac{K_{it}}{Y_{it}}\right) + \beta_2 \delta \ln Y_{it} + \beta_4 PD_t + \varepsilon_{it}.$$

Endogeneity problems may arise when estimating equation (6), since changes in the dependent variable and changes in capital utilization may be correlated. There are, indeed, factors (such as computer innovations), that could simultaneously affect the share of unskilled workers in total employment and the level of capital. Consequently, the independent variable K_{it} and the unexplained change in the share of unskilled labor (captured in

ε_i) could be correlated. This is a serious issue because the correlation might significantly bias the slope estimates. Two different approaches are considered to address this problem.

For the capital variable, I use both net capital stock and electricity consumption as proxies. Net capital stock data, provided by INSEE, are constructed according to the rule of perpetual inventories. This method provides estimated data on net capital stock which are measured with error. More importantly, French data on net capital stock are not available at high levels of industrial disaggregation—a restriction that limits the estimation possibilities.[18] I therefore use electricity consumption as a proxy for capital at the three-digit industry level. This strategy was first used by Griliches and Jorgenson (1967) and thereafter by (among others) Costello (1993) and Burnside, Eichenbaum, and Rebelo (1995). All these authors argue that electricity consumption is a good measure of capital utilization, and Anxo and Sterner (1994) offer convincing proof in a paper devoted to the issue. Regression analysis performed with both measures of capital at the two-digit industry level confirms that the choice of the proxy used for capital does not significantly affect the results.

Assessing endogeneity therefore implies considering both capital stock and electricity consumption as measures of capital. Following Berman, Bound, and Griliches (1994) I assume that, when net capital stock is used, the endogeneity bias should not be significant because investments in capital and change in the share of unskilled workers should not have the same timing, since new investments last several years. I also instrumentalize electricity consumption by its lagged values to verify that it is not an endogenous variable. Past electricity consumption is, a priori, a good instrument since it is not affected by current innovation and since it is correlated (at more than 30 percent) with current electricity consumption. Estimations (not reported here but available upon request) show that the effect of changes in electricity consumption on changes in the unskilled share in employment is robust with respect to the instrumentation. A Hausman test confirms that electricity consumption is nonendogenous.

Determining the appropriate data to be used for Y is also a concern. Two potential candidates are value-added and gross output. Berman, Bound, and Griliches (1994) use value-added, since labor and capital are the only independent variables in their specification. Feenstra and Hanson (1996, 1997) include a measure of outsourcing as regressor but also equate Y to value-added.[19] Equation (6) introduces data on material inputs other than

18. Data on net capital stock exist at the two-digit standard industrial classification (SIC) level, whereas data on all other variables are available at the three-digit SIC level. The French nomenclature differs slightly from the American; the SIC terminology is used for simplicity.
19. Berman, Bound, and Griliches (1994), as well as Feenstra and Hanson (1996, 1997), equate Y to value-added. However, because of the unavailability of certain price deflators, these authors use shipment in their empirical estimates. Consequently, using value-added and gross output interchangeably when performing the regression analysis does not seem to be an issue of major concern.

capital and labor (recall that vertical specialization is the share of imported inputs in production). Hence gross output would seem to be a more appropriate measure for Y. However, results are robust to the use of value-added.[20]

It is necessary to control for the output level in equation (6). Wald tests performed on equation (6) strongly confirm that omitting Y would misspecify the model, as the null hypothesis of an insignificant Y is systematically rejected at the 1 percent significance level. The output level controls for industry scale. Such control is especially important owing to the French labor market's inflexibility. Firms willing to alter their shares of unskilled to skilled labor encounter difficulties in laying off workers because of strong unions and protective labor laws. Hence, changes in the share of unskilled labor in employment often occur as firms increase production.

Endogeneity of output is also considered as a potential issue. I therefore perform an instrumental-variables estimation using the lagged value of Y as the instrumental variable. (Table 6.7 reports results for standard and instrumental-variables estimation over the 1982–1987 and 1987–1992 periods combined.) The coefficient for output varies across specification; however (and more importantly), the international vertical specialization coefficient is not greatly affected by the change in specification.

Finally, I consider the possibility of multicollinearity. The tests for correlation between output and vertical specialization and for correlation between output and capital utilization do not show any evidence of multicollinearity (the correlations are always under 0.7 and include some extremely low levels, depending on the considered data).

Data are weighted by the industry's average share in total manufacturing employment over each period. A weighted least-squares estimation is conducted, which considerably reduces the industry-specific heteroskedasticity. The weights have been chosen so that, over each period, summing up the dependent variables gives the total within-industry change. I estimate the slope parameters by running equation (6) over the 1977–1985 and 1985–1993 periods combined. Variables are in annual changes averaged over the corresponding period.[21] Both OECD and non-OECD measures of international vertical specialization are considered. Robustness is checked by extending the time period to three subperiods: 1977–1982, 1982–1987, and 1987–1992. Further exploitation of the time-series properties of the data could give misleading results, since the long-run change relationship may not be isolated from business-cycle effects.[22]

Table 6.5 gives the annual rates of change in the (logarithmic) variables for the three-digit industry sample. As reported in section 6.4, we observe

---

20. All the estimations were conducted using value-added. Results are not reported in this paper but are available upon request.

21. For example, averaged over the 1977–1985 period for the 1977–1985 change.

22. Results are available upon request.

Table 6.5   Mean Rate of Change of Variables

	1977–1985	1985–1993
δ Eu	–0.485	–0.435
δ ln($Kelc/Y$)	2.345	1.905
δ ln(Y)	0.954	1.060
δ V	0.094	0.185
δ Voecd	0.102	0.146
δ Vnoecd	–0.008	0.039

Sources: Author calculations; Cortes and Jean (1997) database for labor data; and National Institute of Statistical Economic Studies (1977–1992, 1977–1996, 1993–1996) for data on output capital, and vertical specialization.

Notes: Data are weighted by the industry share of unskilled employment in total manufacturing employment. The sample consists of 50 three-digit industries. Variables are defined as follows: δEu = 100 · annual change in unskilled workers' share of total employment; δ ln($Kelc/Y$) = 100 · annual change in ln([electricity consumption]/[real output]); δ ln(Y) = 100 · annual change in ln(real output); and δV = 100 · annual change in vertical specialization.

an annual within-industry decrease in the share of unskilled workers in total employment, with a deceleration in the second period. This share decreases at a rate of 0.49 annual percentage points in the first period and of 0.44 annual percentage points in the second period. The annual growth rate of production rises over time, and production becomes more capital-intensive in both periods regardless of the measure chosen to proxy capital. However, while the growth rate of net capital stock used in production rises over the two periods (results obtained at the two-digit industry level), the electricity used in production increases at a decreasing rate. Most notably, vertical specialization increases over both periods with an acceleration over time. The growth rate of vertical specialization is 0.094 percent per year for 1977–1985 and 0.185 percent per year for 1985–1993. Finally, the table shows that the growth rate in vertical specialization involving non-OECD countries is actually slightly negative in the first period and is lower than growth in vertical specialization from OECD countries in both periods.

The regression results for equation (6) are presented in tables 6.6 and 6.7. In table 6.6, the subperiods 1977–1985 and 1985–1993 are combined; in table 6.7, the subperiods 1982–1987 and 1987–1992 are combined. Estimations are made using net capital stock at the two-digit Standard Industrial Classification (SIC) level and using electricity consumption at the three-digit SIC level. Specification (1) in table 6.6 reports unweighted estimates based on the two-digit industry sample, while specification (2) reports unweighted estimation using the three-digit industry sample. Specifications (3) and (4) provide the corresponding weighted estimates. In specifications (4), (4'), and (4''), results are reported for all countries combined, OECD countries, and non-OECD countries, respectively. In table 6.7, the instru-

Table 6.6   **Regression Results: 1977–1993**

	Specification					
	(1)	(2)	(3)	(4)	(4')	(4")
$\delta \ln(K/Y)$	0.008	−0.014	−0.028	0.002	0.001	0.004
	(0.034)	(0.015)	(0.030)	(0.015)	(0.016)	(0.015)
$\delta \ln(Y)$	−0.063***	−0.032***	−0.126***	−0.082***	−0.079***	−0.081***
	(0.025)	(0.012)	(0.029)	(0.02)	(0.02)	(0.021)
δV	−0.511**	−0.703***	−0.857***	−0.584***		
	(0.282)	(0.225)	(0.331)	(0.180)		
δVoecd					−0.690***	
					(0.196)	
δVnoecd						−1.175**
						(0.552)
Constant	−0.348***	−0.301***	−0.291***	−0.357***	−0.342***	−0.428***
	(0.073)	(0.067)	(0.064)	(0.065)	(0.065)	(0.054)
1985–1993	−0.052	−0.093	0.138*	0.114	0.091	0.126*
	(0.095)	(0.084)	(0.090)	0.091	0.093	0.093
Adjusted R^2	0.123	0.091	0.453	0.438	0.423	0.415
Contribution V						
1977–1985			15%	11%	15%	0%
1985–1993	.		26%	25%	23%	10%
N	44	100	44	100	100	100

Sources: See table 6.5.

Notes: The dependent variable is the annual change in ratio of unskilled employment to total employment. Regressions are weighted by the average share of industry employment in total manufacturing employment. Numbers in parentheses are the estimated White standard errors, which are robust to cross-sectional heteroskedasticity and correlation. N = number of observations.

***Significant at the 1 percent level.

**Significant at the 5 percent level.

*Significant at the 10 percent level.

mental-variables estimations are presented. Specifications (5), (5'), and (5") provide estimates of the variables for all countries combined, OECD countries, and non-OECD countries using current output value for Y, whereas specifications (6), (6'), and (6") utilize lagged values of output as the instrumental variable for Y.[23]

In all specifications, the coefficient of international vertical specialization, which ranges between −0.408 and −0.857, is statistically and economically significant. The decomposition by country source of imports shows similar features. Results on capital utilization are ambiguous. In most (but not all) cases, coefficients have the expected negative sign, which reflects

23. A likelihood ratio test and a Wald test are used to test the hypothesis of groupwise heteroskedasticity. A Breush-Pagan Lagrange multiplier test is used to test the hypothesis of cross-sectional correlation.

Table 6.7   Regression Results: 1982–1992

	Specification					
	(5)	(5′)	(5″)	(6)	(6′)	(6″)
δ ln(K/Y)	−0.010	−0.011	−0.006	−0.027	−0.028	−0.017
	(0.016)	(0.016)	(0.016)	(0.022)	(0.023)	(0.022)
δ ln(Y)	−0.069***	−0.067***	−0.070***	−0.147***	−0.145***	−0.135***
	(0.019)	(0.020)	(0.019)	(0.0391)	(0.039)	(0.040)
δV	−0.408***			−0.465***		
	(0.144)			(0.157)		
δVoecd		−0.513***			−0.481***	
		(0.206)			(0.190)	
δVnoecd			−1.178***			−1.219***
			(0.399)			(0.491)
Constant	−0.378***	−0.382***	−0.401***	−0.271***	−0.274***	−0.362***
	(0.079)	(0.080)	(0.076)	(0.109)	(0.107)	(0.110)
1987–1992	0.209***	0.199***	0.222***	0.307***	0.294***	0.303***
	(0.081)	(0.081)	(0.081)	(0.102)	(0.103)	(0.098)
Adjusted R^2	0.313	0.310	0.317	0.196	0.183	0.207
Contribution V						
1982–1987	13%	12%	10%	15%	14%	0%
1987–1992	20%	18%	18%	23%	20%	10%
N	100	100	100	100	100	100

Sources: See table 6.5.
Notes: See table 6.6.
***Significant at the 1 percent level.
**Significant at the 5 percent level.
*Significant at the 10 percent level.

the substitutability between unskilled labor and capital. However, the capital coefficients are all statistically insignificant and make only a small contribution in explaining the decline in the share of unskilled workers in employment. The observed deceleration in the annual rate of change in the share of unskilled workers in employment is mirrored by the positive coefficient on the time dummy. This is especially significant in specifications (5) and (6) and can be explained by the large deceleration in the annual decrease in the share of unskilled employment that occurred between the two periods: from −0.515 during 1982–1987 to −0.415 during 1987–1992.

Tables 6.6 and 6.7 also report the contributions of the increase in vertical specialization to the decline in the share of unskilled workers in manufacturing employment. These are calculated by multiplying the slope coefficients by the annual rate of change in the corresponding variable and dividing them by the annual rate of change in the share of unskilled workers. For example, consider specification (4)'s vertical specialization coefficient of −0.584 in table 6.6. In the first period, the annual growth rate in vertical specialization at the three-digit industry level is 0.094. Dividing the product of these two numbers by the annual rate of change in the share of unskilled labor of –0.485 for this period (see table 6.5) yields a figure of 11 percent for the contribution of vertical specialization to the annual decrease in the share of unskilled workers in manufacturing employment for the 1977–1985 period. The contribution of vertical specialization is always positive for all countries and for OECD countries alone and varies between 11 percent and 26 percent over the two periods. Moreover, contributions do not significantly vary with either the sample size or the choice made to proxy capital utilization (see specifications [3] and [4]). In specification (4), which is the preferred specification due to its high level of disaggregation, vertical specialization contributes 11 percent of the annual decline in the share of unskilled workers in manufacturing employment for 1977–1985 and 25 percent for 1985–1993. The observed acceleration in vertical specialization corresponds to an increase in its contribution to the decline in the share of unskilled workers. The persistently low level of non-OECD vertical specialization is reflected by a negligible contribution during 1977–1985, but this contribution reaches 10 percent during 1985–1993 as non-OECD vertical specialization takes off.

The results described here are consistent with those found by Feenstra and Hanson (1996, 1997). These authors find that vertical specialization contributes from 11 percent to 15.2 percent of the decline in the share of production workers in the wage bill over the 1979–1990 period. They obtained these results using a limited measure of outsourcing (within the same two-digit industries) that is similar to mine. I believe that our results are in line; data discrepancy and country specificity explain the limited differences. The decrease in the share of unskilled workers in manufacturing employment that is not explained by changes in measured factors is presumably caused by skill-biased technological change and/or some institutional factors.

6.6   Conclusion

Vertical specialization rose dramatically in France over the 1977–1993 period. To the extent that this increase is due to a decline in trade costs, one expects globalization to affect the relative wages and employment shares of skilled and unskilled workers—by shifting relative labor demand across countries. In the case of France, which is typical of continental European countries, the relative wages of skilled to unskilled labor have been comparatively stable for various institutional reasons over the period examined. Consequently, globalization has manifested itself mainly in the form of a significant decline in the within-industry share of unskilled workers.

Regression analysis indicates that vertical specialization has contributed appreciably to the observed decline in the within-industry share of unskilled workers in French manufacturing employment. It accounts for

11 to 15 percent of the within-industry shift away from unskilled workers toward skilled workers over the 1977–1985 period and to about 25 percent over the 1985–1993 period. Although such figures are not negligible, most of the increase in inequality has other causes, among which skilled-biased technological progress presumably is the most important contributing element. It is striking, consequently, to observe that, whereas globalization often incites strong criticism, it is rare to hear that technological progress should be limited because of its effect on income distribution. In fact, policies should be encouraged that aim at supporting (via training or relocation subsidies) those unskilled workers who suffer from the effects of international integration. However, policies in line with the view of anti-globalization groups, which would aim at reducing trade and thereby vertical specialization, are economically inappropriate, as international trade has been widely shown to increase average welfare.

References

Anxo, D., and T. Sterner. 1994. Using electricity data to measure capital utilization. *Energy Economics* 16 (1): 63–74.

Berman, E., J. Bound, and Z. Griliches. 1994. Change in the demand for skilled labor within U.S. manufacturing: Evidence from the *Annual Survey of Manufactures. Quarterly Journal of Economics* 109 (May): 367–98.

Brown, R., and L. Christensen. 1981. Estimating elasticities of substitution in a model of partial static equilibrium: An application to U.S. agriculture, 1947 to 1974. In *Modeling and measuring natural resource substitution,* ed. E. Berndt and B. Fiel, 209–29. Cambridge: MIT Press.

Burnside, C., M. Eichenbaum, and S. Rebelo. 1995. Capital utilization and returns to scale. In *NBER macroeconomics annual 1995,* ed. B. S. Bernanke and J. J. Rotemberg, 67–110. Cambridge: MIT Press.

Campa, J., and L. Goldberg. 1997. The evolving external orientation of manufacturing: Evidence from four countries. *Economic Policy Review* 3 (2): 53–81.

Cortes, O., and S. Jean. 1997. Quel est l'impact du commerce extérieur sur la productivité et l'emploi? (What is the impact of international trade on productivity and employment?) Centre d'Etudes Prospectives et Informations Internationales (CEPII) Working Paper no. 97-108. Paris: CEPII.

Costello, D. 1993. A cross-country comparison of productivity growth. *Journal of Political Economy* 101 (April): 207–22.

Feenstra, R., and G. Hanson. 1996. Foreign investment, outsourcing, and relative wages. In *The political economy of trade policy: Essays in honor of Jagdish Bhagwati,* ed. R. C. Feenstra, G. M. Grossman, and D. Irwin, 89–127. Cambridge: MIT Press.

———. 1997. Foreign direct investment and relative wages: Evidence from Mexico's *maquiladoras. Journal of International Economics* 42 (May): 371–94.

Griliches, Z., and D. Jorgenson. 1967. The explanation of productivity change. *Review of Economic Studies* 34 (99): 249–80.

Hummels, D., J. Ishii, and K. Yi. 2001. The nature and growth of vertical specialization in world trade. *Journal of International Economics* (June): 75–96.

Hummels, D., D. Rapoport, and K. Yi. 1998. Vertical specialization and the changing nature of world trade. *Federal Reserve Bank of New York Economic Policy Review* 4 (June): 79–99.
Krugman, P. 1995. Growing world trade: Causes and consequences. *Brookings Papers on Economic Activity,* Issue no. 1:327–77.
National Institute of Statistics and Economic Studies (INSEE). 1977–1992. Input-
output tables. Paris: National Account.
———. 1977–1996. Trade data 1977–1996. Paris: International Trade Office.
———. 1993–1996. Input-output tables. Paris: National Account.
Organization for Economic Cooperation and Development (OECD). 1996. *Employment outlook.* Paris: OECD.
———. 1997. *Employment outlook.* Paris: OECD.
Strauss-Kahn, V. 2002. Firms' location decision across asymmetric countries
and employment inequality. INSEAD Working Paper no. 60/eps. Fontainebleau,
France: INSEAD.
Thesmar, D., and M. Thoenig. 2002. Outsourcing, product market entry, and the
rise in job uncertainty. Paper presented at the CEPR European Research Work-
shop in International Trade, 14–17 June, Munich.

Comment   Mari Kangasniemi

Increasing worker inequality (between skilled and unskilled workers) in
developed countries has been a topic of heated debate during the last
decade. The main reasons for increasing inequality that have been suggested in the earlier literature are globalization, especially trade liberalization, and technological change. Vanessa Strauss-Kahn's paper studies the
effects of a specific form of globalization: international vertical specialization. This phenomenon also represents one facet of technical change.
Given the political weight that these considerations carry, as well as the
academic dispute over globalization and inequality, it is important to study
their relevance empirically, and this paper is an excellent contribution to
such a discussion.

Strauss-Kahn's work on constructing the measures of vertical specialization deserves special recognition. The justification for the chosen measure and discussion of the robustness of the index as a measure of vertical
specialization are in general thorough and detailed. The problems arising
from the fact that the import penetration rate is based on both final goods
and inputs are also discussed to a sufficient extent.

An issue of major importance in the context of inequality is the institutional setup of the labor market. Strong unions and labor laws are briefly
mentioned in Strauss-Kahn's analysis, but I think institutions enter the
equation more strongly than that. Both the justification for using changes

Mari Kangasniemi was a research fellow in the economics department at the University of
Sussex at the time of writing.

in employment as a measure of changing inequality and the details of the empirical approach chosen would require confirmation that no crucial *changes* in the institutional setup have occurred over the period studied.

As Strauss-Kahn points out, the argument that has often been presented in the inequality debate is that the same underlying phenomenon (e.g., trade or technological change) has different implications in countries with competitive labor markets (United States, United Kingdom) and countries that have more centralized, regulated wage-settings systems (most of continental Europe). In the United States and the United Kingdom the increase in wage inequality has been very pronounced, whereas in continental Europe, more attention has been paid to relative unemployment rates, which is also what the author does in her introduction. It is not clear-cut, however, whether the difference in unemployment rates is solely the result of a major shift in technology and thus in the demand for unskilled labor. Unemployment rates and differences therein are heavily dependent on the institutional setup of the labor market. For example, changes in the nature of employment contracts from permanent to temporary, or changes in minimum wages or replacement ratios, are likely to have more impact on the unemployment rates of unskilled than of skilled workers. Nickell and Bell (1996) also point out that relative, rather than absolute, changes in unemployment rates are the relevant indicator of asymmetric changes in demand for skilled and unskilled workers.

The author's justification for concentrating on employment and not wages is, correctly, the fact that wages in France are relatively rigid. She points out that changes in wages do not support the hypothesis of supply-side effects on inequality. However, in the presence of wage rigidity or institutionally determined wage rates, changes in labor supply may not necessarily have implications for wages either. Although demand shocks are indeed the most likely reason for the increase in inequality, the issue of labor supply is complicated because effective labor supply also depends on institutions (like unemployment benefits). Thus it does not necessarily equal the share of skilled or unskilled workers in the population, which is the measure mentioned in the paper.

The institutional background is also of major importance when justifying the empirical model chosen. At least the author should justify why institutional factors need *not* be controlled for in the estimations, as they can have considerable impact on the relative employment for aforementioned reasons. It is not completely clear to me why (at the industry level) factor prices (or at least the price of labor) would be completely exogenous, although from an individual firm's point of view this may be the case. Similarly, the assumption of a fixed relative price of skill across industries is highly restrictive. The definition of *skill* used is typically broad, and in reality I think it is quite plausible that some industries require very specific skills, the supply of which may be relatively small or inelastic, and thus that industry-specific relative wages will differ. In terms of results this might have considerable implications, and as pointed out in the paper, the issue of endogeneity would have to be dealt with if relative wages were used as an explanatory variable. Also, attributing all the change in relative employment not explained by vertical specialization to technical change and some undefined institutional changes is a crude simplification. There is no reason to assume that institutional changes cannot be observed (and thus controlled for or at least noted); and, on the other hand, "technical change" is here interpreted in a very broad manner. An interesting issue to discuss, also related to the institutional setup, is the extent to which the results can be generalized and the analysis can be used in the context of other countries.

I find the decision to ignore the temporal aspect by averaging over periods slightly troubling, although it is obviously a standard method in this field of literature. Also, the time periods that the changes are averaged over are relatively short. More experimentation with different methods could be done to see if this produces different results. Industry-specific technical change is mentioned, but actual panel specification (with a firm-specific effect in the *change* of employment) is not used. Using the data as a panel in addition to the current approach (either as an annual one with corrections for the business cycle, or with averages of the periods used in the current specification) would also provide an opportunity to take into account the industry-specific change in relative employment. If this effect is correlated with vertical specialization, which is possible as both of them relate to technological change, the panel dimension could be used to obtain unbiased estimates of the coefficient of interest.

Reference

Nickell, Stephen, and Brian Bell. 1996. The collapse in demand for unskilled and unemployment across Europe. *Oxford Review of Economic Policy* 11 (1): 40–62.

7

The Brain Drain: Curse or Boon?
A Survey of the Literature

Simon Commander, Mari Kangasniemi,
and L. Alan Winters

7.1 Introduction

The term "brain drain" appears to have gained wide usage in the late 1960s when growth in the migration of skilled personnel from developing to developed countries accelerated.[1] The developed countries, by attracting scarce skilled labor, were widely held to be pursuing policies that were costly to developing countries, both in the short and longer run. The costs were not only in terms of output and employment, but also—depending on the way in which education was financed—through additional fiscal costs associated with public subsidies to education. A variety of policy proposals, mostly centered around taxation, were floated, although none were ultimately implemented. Part of this may be attributed to likely difficulties with implementation—measurement problems (including temporary migration and migration linked to education enrolment in developed countries) and ambiguities with respect to the welfare consequences.

Many of the same issues and debates have undergone a recent revival.

This paper has been prepared for the Center for Economic Policy Research (CEPR), the National Bureau of Economic Research (NBER), and the Studies förbundet Näringsliv och Samhälle International Seminar on International Trade, 24–25 May, 2002, Stockholm. The research is supported by the U.K. Department for International Development. We thank Jagdish Bhagwati, Gnanaraj Chellaraj, Jim de Melo and other participants of ISIT for comments on an earlier version.

Simon Commander is a visiting senior research fellow in the economics department and director of the Centre for New and Emerging Markets (CNEM) at the London Business School and adviser in the Office of Chief Economist at the European Bank for Reconstruction and Development (EBRD). Mari Kangasniemi is a research fellow in the economics department at the University of Sussex. L. Alan Winters is professor of economics at the University of Sussex. He is a research fellow of the Centre for Economic Policy Research (CEPR) and a senior visiting fellow of the Centre for Economic Performance at the London School of Economics.

1. Note, however, that labor mobility was actually at its peak pre-1914.

This can be attributed to a number of factors. In the first place, it is commonly believed that the emigration of skilled labor from developing countries has again accelerated over the last decade, not least in association with the growth-of-information and knowledge-intensive activities. Second, the developed economies have actively and openly set out to poach talent, using a range of incentives and institutional mechanisms for attracting skilled labor. In particular, the use of temporary skilled-migrant visas whether in the United States or, more recently, in Western Europe, has been striking.

Possible explanations for why poaching has increased are various. They include skill shortages resulting from rapid skill-biased technical change as well as educational failures. Gaining access to international competence—heterogeneity—may be another factor, while access to technical or market knowledge may be another. The first explanation generally is taken as bringing in substitutes to local human capital, although this need not necessarily be the case. The importing firm would gain through lowering wage costs, dampening any domestic-wage pressure, or both. The other explanations, however, may be consistent with complementarity (at least in static or short-run terms). By widening the talent pool, poaching may result in the selection of the best candidates and hence impart a positive productivity effect.

At the same time, there has been growing recognition not only of the global benefits of greater mobility, but also that the emigration of skilled labor may not be negative for the sending country. In the first place, emigration of talent may provide a positive signal that motivates others in the sending country to acquire more education, thereby raising human capital and possibly promoting growth. Second, emigrants may, in due course, return or, through networks and resource repatriation (such as through remittances), provide essential inputs to new businesses and activities in the sending country. Third, emigration may actively promote a more effective flow of knowledge and information. Fourth, the changing nature of mobility—in part due to major advances in communications technology—may be limiting the extent to which skills are actually lost. A network industry, like software, is possibly a case in point.

This paper has several objectives. First it attempts to take stock of our knowledge concerning the scale, composition, and direction of migration from developing to developed countries in the recent period. Second, it places that mobility in the context of the existing literature, and, third, it attempts to indicate ways in which, at both an analytical and empirical level, progress can be made in better understanding the phenomenon and, in particular, the appropriate policy implications.

The paper is organized as follows. Section 7.2 provides a brief empirical survey of our knowledge concerning the scale, distribution, and composition of skilled labor flows. Section 7.3 surveys a class of models developed in the 1970s that focused primarily on the implications of emigration for labor markets in the sending countries. Section 7.4 surveys the subsequent class of dynamic models in particular, those that endogenize human-capital decisions. We extend the analysis to take account of possible screening by developed countries. Section 7.5 then examines the empirical evidence for screening, while section 7.6 looks at the relevance of return flows, remittances, and diasporas—factors that may offset some of the negative effects associated with skilled migration. Section 7.7 then turns to examining the relevance of economic geography models for understanding the brain drain and not least the reasons for why agglomeration occurs. Section 7.8 then moves on to look in a little bit more detail at two sectors— software and health—that have features that may be helpful in under-standing sectoral differences. Section 7.9 concludes.

7.2   The Facts

Quantification of the movement of skilled individuals across coun-tries—let alone the exact measurement of any associated brain drain— remains very patchy. National authorities have maintained very limited databases on migration with highly inconsistent skill or education cate-gories.[2] There is a lack of data on the attributes of the individual migrants and the changing nature of migration—which is away from permanent, point-to-point migration—has itself complicated matters. Furthermore, the link between education and migration has changed over time. For ex-ample, a significant component of skilled migration is now accounted for by students that stay on after completion of degrees.

7.2.1   Skilled Migration in The Recent Period

Carrington and Detragiache (1998) provide a benchmark for skilled mi-gration in 1990. They compiled the U.S. census and the Organization for Economic Cooperation and Development (OECD) migration statistics for that year and then compared the immigrant stocks to the size of the educated population in the sending country using Barro and Lee's (1996) education data for 1993. Their study has several shortcomings: In addition to possible deficiencies of the basic data they use,[3] their figures fail to take into account skilled migration to the Middle East, which for countries like India actually accounts for a large proportion of the total migration. Also, the immigration to the United States in their study includes all types of migration, not only employment based, which is what is usually understood by brain drain.

Despite their shortcomings, the Carrington and Detragiache estimates are probably the best available estimates of brain drain. We use them to

2. The United Nations (UN) recommends defining a migrant in terms of residence by time, short term being less than a year, and long term more than twelve months, but actual defini-tions vary widely, as do those for skill or education levels.

3. Many countries are not included because the lack of data and the number of educated migrants to OECD countries is estimated on the basis of the education level of migrants to the United States. The estimates of educated population by Barro and Lee are partly based on historical-enrollment data, and it is not clear whether the migrants are included in these esti-mates or not.

study the relationships between population, the gross domestic product (GDP), and migration. Table 7.1 provides information on population, on expenditure on tertiary education, and a measure of the intensity of migration (i.e., the share of a country's labor force having tertiary education that has migrated). The share presented in the table is based on the assumption that the Barro and Lee estimates do not include the migrants. What emerges is that there are a significant number of small countries—principally in the Caribbean, Central America, and Africa—with very high skilled-migration rates. Figure 7.1 plots the migration rates against the country's population while excluding some clear outliers. There is a negative correlation between the migration rates and total population. The excluded outliers confirm this observation. For large countries like India and China, which dominate in terms of absolute numbers, skilled migration does not amount to a significant share of their educated workforces. Indeed, only 1.1 and 1.4 percent of India and China's skilled labor forces, respectively, had moved to the United States in 1990, although additional evidence suggests that these migrants come from the top end of the skill distribution. For very small countries, the migration rate is of a significant magnitude. These patterns are replicated if the reference is extended to the OECD. In Ghana, for example, over a quarter of the educated labor force lived in OECD countries in 1990, the share rises to over 60 percent for the Gambia, and approaches 80 percent for Jamaica.

Similar exercises comparing skilled-migration rates and GDP per capita also yield negative correlations. Countries where the fraction of highly educated workers and general productivity (GDP per capita) is already low also tend to lose relatively more skilled workers. Of course, this raises some difficult issues of interpretation. For instance, if the productivity of skilled labor in these countries is low because of factors—such as lack of managerial talent (Rauch 1991) and inability to achieve economies of scale that are hard, if not impossible to correct—then the emigration of skilled labor may indeed be the best outcome. We return to these questions below.

What has happened since 1990? The general consensus appears to be that skilled migration has accelerated, yet the data are limited mainly to census and labor-force surveys. Salt (1997) has arrived at some estimates for high skilled-migrant flows to selected OECD countries from a number of developing and transition countries. He draws a number of (weak) inferences to the effect that the stocks of highly skilled foreign workers in OECD countries have increased since 1990. Certainly, the flows of the highly skilled have been increasing at a higher rate than those of less-skilled migrants. With respect to the European Union as a whole, labor-force-survey data show that highly skilled migrants (International Standard of Classification of Occupations [ISCO] categories 1–3)[4] in 1997 accounted

---

4. The ISCO categories 1, 2, and 3 include managers, professionals, and associate professionals.

Table 7.1   **Population, Migration, and Education Expenditure**

	Population (in millions)	Migration Rate	Total Expenditure on Tertiary Education, Per Student (international $)
Fiji	0.79	21.3	n.a.
Guyana	0.85	77.3	n.a.
Mauritius	1.16	7.2	5,080.9
The Gambia	1.22	59.1	3,842.6
Trinidad and Tobago	1.29	57.2	n.a.
Lesotho	2.06	2.9	18,452.6
Jamaica	2.58	67.3	n.a.
Panama	2.76	19.5	2,006.1
Congo	2.78	0.5	n.a.
Uruguay	3.29	3.7	2,047.2
Central African Republic	3.48	1.7	n.a.
Costa Rica	3.53	7	n.a.
Togo	4.46	1.3	6,572.2
Papua New Guinea	4.60	2.2	n.a.
Nicaragua	4.79	18.7	n.a.
Sierra Leone	4.85	24.1	n.a.
Paraguay	5.22	1.9	n.a.
Benin	5.95	0.4	2,141.0
El Salvador	6.06	26.1	312.0
Honduras	6.16	15.7	1,623.9
Bolivia	7.95	4.2	1,176.0
Rwanda	8.11	2.2	n.a.
Dominican Republic	8.25	14.2	1,567.4
Senegal	9.04	1.6	n.a.
Tunisia	9.34	1.6	3,764.8
Zambia	9.67	5	2,574.2
Malawi	10.53	2	9,066.7
Mali	10.60	0.9	2,573.4
Guatemala	10.80	13.5	1,074.4
Zimbabwe	11.69	4.6	8,783.9
Ecuador	12.18	3.8	1,114.3
Cameroon	14.30	3.2	n.a.
Chile	14.82	3.3	1,670.2
Syria	15.28	3.1	n.a.
Mozambique	16.95	8.6	n.a.
Ghana	18.46	15.1	n.a.
Sri Lanka	18.78	3.7	2,476.9
Uganda	20.90	15.4	n.a.
Malaysia	22.18	4.4	4,901.7
Venezuela	23.24	1.6	n.a.
Peru	24.80	3	680.5
Sudan	28.35	1.7	n.a.
Kenya	29.29	9.9	n.a.
Algeria	29.92	0.7	n.a.
Argentina	36.13	1.9	2,325.0
Colombia	40.80	5.6	2,173.6

(*continued*)

Table 7.1   (continued)

	Population (in millions)	Migration Rate	Total Expenditure on Tertiary Education, Per Student (international $)
South Africa	41.40	2.6	n.a.
Korea	46.43	5.7	881.0
Thailand	61.20	1.2	1,618.3
Egypt	61.40	2.5	n.a.
Iran	61.95	14.7	398.6
Turkey	63.45	1.4	3,365.2
The Philippines	75.17	6.6	560.1
Mexico	95.85	10.3	3,459.9
Bangladesh	125.63	0.6	n.a.
Pakistan	131.58	2.4	448.3
Brazil	165.87	0.6	n.a.
Indonesia	203.68	1.4	387.2
India	979.67	1.1	2,014.4
China	1,238.60	1.4	1,943.4

Sources: Carrington and Detragiache (1998) and World Bank (2001).
Note: n.a. = not available.

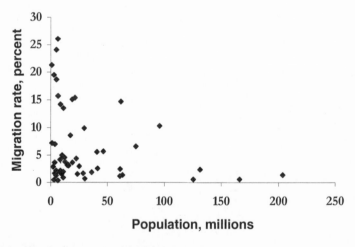

Fig. 7.1 Population versus migration rate
Source: Carrington and Detragiache (1998).

for around 38 percent of the total migration inflow into employment, but that inflow represented only a minute fraction of the total employment stock—no larger than 0.5 percent (Auriol and Sexton 2002).

Available evidence also points to significant variation in the sectoral incidence of skilled migration. In the 1960s and 1970s, much of the concern about a brain drain revolved around the emigration of doctors, nurses, and teachers from developing countries. Both sectors are characterized by large externalities and developing countries, by definition, remain under-provided in such services, particularly in rural areas. The possible welfare implications of emigration are evident. In the health sector, the likely neg-ative effects arise from the direct impact on the population's health status with associated consequences for the productivity and welfare of the pop-ulation. Furthermore, the health sector has properties that require a bal-anced mix of skills (doctors, nurses, midwives, etc.) and technology to be effective.[5] As such, loss of part of the skill chain may lead to substantial and adverse ripple effects.

In the recent period, it appears that substantial emigration of health workers has continued. For example, in the United Kingdom, the General Medical Council's data show that the number of newly registered doctors who have obtained their qualifications overseas has remained high throughout the 1990s. The share of non–European Union doctors among new registrants has remained stable at around 40 percent. The leading country in terms of the numbers of registered doctors is India. Chanda (2001) has estimated that there are at least 60,000 doctors of Indian origin in the United Kingdom, which amounts to around 12 percent of the total stock of doctors in India and 30 percent of registered doctors in the United Kingdom.[6] However, skilled emigration has become far more diversified in terms of sectoral characteristics. Indeed, much of the recent discussion has followed from the movement of skilled information and communications technology (ICT)–sector workers from developing countries.

Although there has apparently been greater sectoral diversity, it is likely that migration has become significantly less diversified in terms of migrant characteristics, as educational-cum-skill thresholds have risen and evi-dence of screening by developed countries become more apparent. This screening feature looks to be a relatively recent innovation and—as we shall see in section 7.4—has strong implications for the sending countries. We now turn to reviewing the analytical frameworks developed for under-standing the brain drain.

7.3 Early Models of Brain Drain

7.3.1 Static Analysis

The welfare implications of brain drain in static models crucially depend on the assumptions made about wage setting.[7] Some of the earliest work—

---

5. Services are, moreover, not very mobile although some recent developments in telemed-icine have made them slightly less dependent on the location of the health workers.

6. According to the Medical Council of India there were 503,900 registered medical prac-titioners in India (India, Central Bureau of Health Intelligence 1999) in 1998, and the Gen-eral Medical Council in the United Kingdom has a total of 193,000 doctors on their register with 5,700 overseas doctors on limited registration (General Medical Council 2000).

7. Alan Deardorff's excellent comment on this chapter offers further details of some of these models drawing explicitly on international-trade theory.

particularly Grubel and Scott (1966)—was set in the context of perfectly competitive markets. With all markets clearing, wages set equal to marginal product, and no externalities, there was evidently no welfare impact on those left behind as long as domestic wage did not rise as a result of shift in labor supply.[8] This would be the case with, for example, factor-price equalization through international trade. Thus, the policy conclusion of Grubel and Scott was inevitably laissez passer. Introducing distortions (as with a gap between social- and private-marginal product, a public subsidy for education, or both) would naturally undermine these conclusions and result in a welfare loss for those who did not emigrate. Indeed, much of the subsequent literature that emerged in the 1970s was organized around precisely these two types of departures from a perfectly competitive setting.

Bhagwati and Hamada (1974) worked with a general-equilibrium framework. It was used principally to model the sending or home-country labor market and to pin down the welfare implications of skilled emigration for those who were left behind and, ultimately, for the sending country. Two sets of distortions were introduced; the first distortion to the wage setting, the second, to the financing of education. Then the implications for employment were traced through. The model, which was subsequently widely employed, can be boiled down to a fairly simple set of blocs.

The economy produces two outputs (M_1 and M_2) with standard neoclassical production functions, $M_1 = F_1(L_1)$; $M_2 = F_2(L_2)$ where L_1 is the amount of skilled labor employed in production of M_1, and L_2 is the amount of unskilled labor involved in production of M_2. The two types of labor are exclusively allocated to their respective sectors. The commodity-price ratio is exogenously fixed, $p_1/p_2 = \pi$, and M_2 is the numeraire. The real wage for skilled workers, w_1, is determined by unions and includes an element of international emulation whereby skilled wages are partly related to skilled wages abroad. Minimum unskilled wages, w_2, are fixed by association with the skilled wage, or "leap frogging"—a rise in skilled wage leading to an increase in the unskilled wage. In addition, the supply side reflects the incentive for education to be acquired so long as the expected wage for educated (skilled) labor exceeds the uneducated (unskilled) wage. A fixed educational cost, k, is introduced. Unemployment enters the initial equilibrium. There is also an exogenous flow of educated emigrants, Z_1, so that the labor-market-balance equations read $L_1 + U_1 + Z_1 = N_1$; $L_2 + U_2 = N_2$; $N_1 + N_2 = N$.

In this model, the international integration of the skilled labor market can affect both sectors' wages through emulation and leap-frogging, as well as expected wages through the actual foreign wage *and* probability of emi-

---

8. Johnson (1967), however, points out that the effect actually depends on how much capital the emigrants take with them. If capital is internationally mobile this argument does not hold.

gration. Insofar as the latter affects education decisions (and education in turn carries a fixed cost), the channels by which skilled emigration can have an impact on the sending-country's labor market and on welfare, more generally, are clear.

With respect to unemployment, emigration may act directly to lower skilled unemployment, but it also exerts two other effects. First, it can raise the expected wage by lowering unemployment (and hence may have a supply-side effect), and this can be amplified if the emigration wage enters the expected wage. The net result depends on the elasticity of demand for skilled labor, which determines whether the skilled-labor-wage bill increases or not. If the elasticity is lower than unity, an x percent increase in skilled wages will increase the wage bill and thus be associated with a less than x percent fall in employment. Therefore, the expected wage will have increased, and the supply of skilled workers will tend to rise as a result. To the extent that the acquisition of skills through education is subsidised, this will similarly raise the cost to the sending country.

Second, if the skilled wage increases because of emigration, this may also spill over into other sectors and hence have an impact on unemployment in those other sectors. Wage leap-frogging—letting unskilled wages follow skilled wages—would simply tend to extend unemployment to the unskilled and amplify the welfare-reducing consequences of skilled-labor migration. With respect to national income, a rise in the skilled wage tends to reduce national income because of the decline in the employment of skilled labor without any offsetting effect from the unskilled sector (in the case of no associated effect on unskilled wages), while the cost of education will also tend to increase. However, with the assumption of wage leap-frogging, the implications for national income are not so clear cut. Furthermore, to the extent that emigration raises the wage of the emigrant, this implies that emigrants were receiving less than their marginal product. This surplus— as measured over the group—would be lost to the sending country in the event of emigration. The size of the loss depends on the extent to which such workers are replaceable.

Bhagwati and Hamada (1974, 1975) extended their early work by introducing a number of refinements to labor markets in the sending countries. For example, if emigration induced a ladder effect that better matched the remaining skilled workers to skilled, rather than unskilled, jobs (which reduces unskilled unemployment—a variant of Harris and Todaro 1970)— then the effects of emigration could indeed be positive. By contrast, while emigration of skilled workers, such as doctors, might reduce labor-market slack, it could also reduce the flow of doctors from urban to rural areas and limit any positive diffusion effect. There is some confirming evidence. From 1996 to 1998 the number of doctors working in rural primary-health centres in India actually decreased by 9 percent and the total number of doctors and specialists in rural areas also fell by 4 percent. Over the same period, the number of registered medical practitioners rose by 24 percent (Government of India 1998, 2000). Finally, to the extent that the external labor market is more efficient at screening workers, the result would be the loss of the most efficient to the sending country.[9]

A number of dynamic models, particularly Rodriguez (1975), had similar points of departure including, inter alia, a Harris-Todaro labor market and sticky wages. In this setup, flexible wages implied the complete independence of all steady state-factor returns from the cost of migration or the foreign wage. For sticky wages, the long-run rate of unemployment would also be independent, but, in the short run, any increase in the migration cost would raise unemployment. In the Rodriguez case, this was only for unskilled labor. Other differences with respect to Bhagwati and Hamada (1974) include, education not receiving a public subsidy, so that—with some restrictions—the educational decision depends exclusively on the monetary rate of return.

In short, these early classes of models treat the demand side for emigrants as exogenous and have a range of assumptions regarding education costs, with a public subsidy to education commonly assumed. At their heart lies the respective specifications of the sending-country's labor market. Under assumptions of wage rigidity, it was generally found that emigration would tend to lower sending-country employment with the distribution over sectors being contingent on relative wage setting and ex ante employment levels.

What was lacking, however, was any systematic matching of these results to data or, indeed, any disaggregation beyond the skilled and unskilled categories. Sectoral properties were ignored, and there was no attempt to take the analysis to the level of the firm. Moreover, while the stylization was always in terms of sending- and recipient-countries characterized by a difference in income levels, there was no attention to heterogeneity between sending countries. For example, the literature clearly signals the importance of ex ante employment and skill levels. Thus, a thick labor market for skills with employment slack in the sending country could generate a very different set of welfare implications from a small, tight skilled-labor market. This points to the likely importance of size, not least at the level of the country. As we shall see, country size indeed appears to be an important factor in understanding the impact of skilled migration.

Another assumption characteristic of this literature was the dichotomy between those who emigrate and those who stay. Yet, technological change—not least the advent of modern communications—has had some radical implications for the ways in which work can be done across space. Indeed, the recent growth in software activity has been striking for its high network content, linking firms and individuals in developing and devel-

9. See also Arrow (1973) and Spence (1974).

oped countries without necessarily inducing spatial migration (section 7.8 contains more discussion of this point).

This early literature was also notable for containing explicit policy conclusions. The possibilities to tax brain drain and for an optimal tax scheme for migrants were extensively explored (see, e.g., Bhagwati 1976a; Bhagwati and Partington 1976; Bhagwati and Wilson 1989). Bhagwati and Hamada (1974) proposed a tax on emigrants, with that tax levied by the receiving (developed-country) party and transmitted in one form or other to the sending (developing) country. In terms of the impact on the incomes of those that did not emigrate, two channels could be identified. There is a direct revenue effect, which would depend on the elasticity of emigration with respect to taxation. The second set of indirect effects would affect employment through the impact on expected and actual wages. To the extent that this elasticity of emigration with respect to the tax was less than unity, the income of those left behind would improve. However, other work in this area (such as McCulloch and Yellen 1975) was more ambiguous in its findings. Not only could total labor earnings fall under plausible assumptions, but a tax would likely raise the relative wage of nonmigrating skilled workers at the expense of unskilled workers (and hence have distributional implications), while also affecting the relative size of modern and traditional sectors.

The practical aspects of taxing nonresident citizens are also problematic. In some countries (e.g., the United States, Mexico, and the Philippines) taxation is indeed based on citizenship. Enforcing a tax on nonresidents has, however, proved difficult, and extensive assistance from the receiving countries would be required for successful implementation of the Bhagwati tax (Pomp 1989). The idea has been resurrected recently by Desai, Kapur, and McHale (2002a,b), but they also recognize the difficulties and end up suggesting a new research agenda, rather than presenting concrete conclusions about what form the tax should take.

7.3.2 Empirical Foundations

What empirical relevance do the early models have? Estimates of relative wages across countries with appropriate controls are scarce. Nevertheless, all the available (and generally biased) estimates of relative-wage differentials signal substantial wage gaps for most categories of skilled workers when comparing developing with developed countries over time. For example, for the software sector, Arora et al. (2001) have compared salaries of professionals in India and the United States. The numbers are for starting salaries in large establishments, but they do not control for characteristics like experience or education. What emerges from this biased comparison is that salaries in the United States for some occupational categories are at least ten times higher than in India, while salaries, generally, in the United States are several multiples those in India.

Indeed, other evidence confirms that skilled workers systematically earn less (adjusted for purchasing power) in developing than in developed countries. A recent study of new immigrants to the United States, for example, finds that the average immigrant realized major earnings gains over their last job abroad. Men experienced a 68 percent increase in earnings, and women a 62 percent increase. New immigrants who came primarily for work reasons experienced by far the largest increases in earnings (Jasso et al. 2000). The reasons for such persistent wage differentials are interesting, not least because skilled-wage differentials in favor of developed countries contradict the predictions of much modern growth theory.[10]

It is hardly surprising news that there is a substantial income differential across countries that motivates emigration. What of the impact on the sending countries' labor market? In particular, can we find evidence of widespread emulation effects? Data concerning occupational wages of professionals in developing countries is scarce. Using Indian data, Arora et al. (2001) and Kumar (2000) have found that one of the major problems perceived by Indian ICT firms is a shortage of skilled labor. Furthermore, the late 1990s boom in the Indian software sector has clearly been associated with increased demand for engineers, and there is evidence of this forcing up skilled wages.

We lack quality data on the two sectors—software and health—that we are particularly interested in, but the limited and anecdotal evidence that we do have suggests large-order differences in wages between their last employment in a developing country and their employment in a developed country. Part of this can, of course, be attributed to differences in physical capital per worker, but much can be attributed to technology, access to high-quality capital, network externalities, and so on.

Finally, there is the central question as to whether or not human capital formation has an impact on performance. The recent empirical-growth literature has, for example, generally found that increases in educational attainment have not had any significant, positive impact on growth.[11] Part of this may be attributable to imprecisions in the measurement of education. In addition, there is evidence that suggests that the relatively low gains from the match between education and jobs posted in many developing countries may be at the heart of the problem. This points to possible mismatch between acquired skills and the quality of jobs on offer.

7.3.3   Cost of Education and Its Financing

The characteristics of the education system are of major importance for the potential costs and benefits in these traditional models of brain drain,

10. On the assumption that human capital is immobile, this should imply that both skilled wages and the skill premium should be higher in developing than in developed countries (Easterly and Levine 2001).

11. For an overview of this literature see, Easterly and Levine (2001), also Pritchett (2001).

as well as for the possibility of a beneficial brain drain to which we turn later in section 7.4.

A cost to developing countries that has been widely highlighted concerns lost educational investment. Indeed, in most developing countries at least some part of the cost of education is borne by the government, partly because the social return from education is higher than the private one. However, in the last decade, there has been an increase in the provision of private-educational services in many developing countries where the cost is largely, if not exclusively, borne privately. However, even when this is the case, any additional social returns to education, as well as public investment in primary and secondary education, are lost when an individual emigrates.

Estimating the exact cost of education is a very difficult task and the result depends on the approach that is taken in allocating fixed costs across outputs. There are some available cost estimates. For example, the total cost of a medical degree in India has been estimated to be eight times the annual GDP per capita (Jayaram 1995), and, for an engineering degree, it is four times the annual GDP per capita (Salim 1996). World Bank and the United Nations Educational, Scientific, and Cultural Organization (UNESCO) data (reported previously in table 7.1) show that average government expenditure per student on tertiary education varies a lot, but mostly lies in the range of 1,000–3,000 (international) dollars. In both China and India the expenditure is around 2,000 dollars per student.

Yet simply assuming that the education costs in developing countries are largely publicly financed misses some important innovations in educational-services supply and financing that have occurred in the 1990s. These may in turn have been positively influenced by the emigration of the skilled. For example, in India, private institutions have begun training specialists for the software industry. According to Arora et al. (2001), while the supply of engineering graduates from the main public-educational institutions is relatively inelastic in the short run, the supply of software professionals has increased substantially due to private training, which dampens the wage effect of the demand-side changes.

In China, there are also a number of private institutions. It has been estimated that there has been a strong expansion of private education since the 1980s. According to the official figures in 1998, there were 1,274 private tertiary institutions, the majority of which prepare students for national exams rather than confer degrees. However, an estimated 4 million students study in private tertiary institutions, which are not recognized by the Ministry of Education (Dahlman and Aubert 2001).

Of course, such innovations have had little or no impact in sectors where certification and regulation have been far tighter. Both healthcare and teaching are cases in point. Indeed, it is still broadly correct to assume that the bulk of doctors, nurses, and teachers in developing countries receive substantial public subsidy toward their training. Although the question of new methods of financing higher education has been raised strongly, in most developing countries, students' own contributions to the costs of higher education are still small (Johnstone, Arora, and Experton 1998; Tilak 1997; Jayaram 1995).

7.4 Endogenous Growth and the Beneficial Brain Drain

7.4.1 Analytics

Recent literature has located the brain drain in explicitly dynamic models and has, on the whole, come up with significantly more optimistic results than the earlier work discussed in section 7.3. The central proposition is that if the possibility of emigration encourages more skill creation than skill loss, sending (or home) countries might increase their stocks of skills as opportunities to move or work abroad open up. If, in addition, this accumulation of skills has beneficial effects beyond the strictly private gains anticipated by those who acquire the skills, the whole economy can benefit. Examples of such benefits include enhanced intergenerational transmission of skills and education (Vidal 1998) and spillovers between skilled workers (Mountford 1997).

There are two critical features of these models. The first is the nature of the social benefit resulting from higher skills, for which several approaches are evident. In the simplest form, Stark, Helmenstein, and Prskawetz (1997, 1998) merely assume that increasing the average skill level of the sending economy is desirable. Mountford (1997) postulates a production externality whereby the productivity of current labor depends positively on the share of the population who had education in the previous period. Beine, Docquier, and Rapaport (2001a) formalize this by allowing the average skill of one generation to pass directly to the next, who can then build on it by taking education. In all these cases, emigration has a negative direct effect by draining skilled labor from the sending economy—the drain effect—but a potentially beneficial effect in encouraging human-capital formation—the brain effect.

Vidal (1998) assumes an intergenerational transfer whereby the higher the human-capital level of one generation, the more effective is the human-capital formation of the next generation. This too would seem to be a force for divergence because skilled emigration would appear to make future human-capital acquisition cheaper in the receiving country and dearer in the home country. But, in fact, Vidal prevents this by assuming that, for the purposes of the spillover, migrants' human capital remains at home. This makes no sense for permanent migration—the traditional and main concern of the brain-drain literature—but it may be plausible for temporary migration, an area of more recent interest. In particular, if we are interested in modeling an ability to sell labor services at higher prices abroad while effectively maintaining domicile at home, then it may be reasonable to assume that intergenerational spillovers are likely to be at home. In this case, work opportunities abroad may exert a positive impact on developing countries' ability to accumulate human capital.[12]

The second critical issue for the beneficial brain drain is the mechanism that generates an increased incentive to acquire education but leaves some skilled workers back at home. All the current literature starts with wages for given levels of skills and ability being higher abroad than at home. From there, the predominant approach—taken by Mountford (1997); Stark, Helmenstein, and Prskawetz (1998); Vidal (1998), and Beine, Docquier, and Rapaport (2001a)—has been to assume that there is uncertainty about the ability to migrate, so that, of the N amount who acquire education, only $\pi N(\pi < 1)$ actually emigrate. If π were unity, a permanent brain drain could not be beneficial since all the incremental education would be lost. A further critical assumption is that the probability of migration is fixed and exogenously given for any individual would-be migrant. This implicitly arises because foreign firms cannot screen migrants to distinguish the able from the less able, and it is this market failure that makes it possible for the brain drain to be beneficial.

We can illustrate the importance of this assumption, using a highly simplified model that nonetheless captures Mountford's (1997) important insight. Following Beine, Docquier, and Rapaport (2001a), assume that ability is uniformly distributed between *Amin* and *Amax* and that education yields private returns that increase with ability, as in the line in figure 7.2, "with educ." With a given private cost of education, indicated by the horizontal line, people with ability between A^* and *Amax* find it profitable to take education. At point A^*, the private cost of education equals expected returns. Now, allow for the possibility of migration for educated people. If an individual can migrate, his or her private returns increase to the line "with educ. and migrn." With a probability of migration $0 < \pi < 1$, the expected returns to education lie between the domestic and emigration rates of return (around "E (with educ. and migrn.)") and individuals between A^{**} and *Amax* will take education. Of these, however, a proportion, π, will emigrate, leaving the domestic economy with $(1 - \pi)(Amax - A^{**})$ educated people, which may or may not exceed $(Amax - A^*)$. Adding social returns to education is conceptually simple, for they have no immediate effect on private decisions. For simplicity, let social benefits be proportional to the stock of educated remaining at home, that is, $\delta(Amax - A^*)$ with no migration, and $\delta(1 - \pi)(Amax - A^{**})$ with migration.

---

12. Such temporary movement of workers is the subject of negotiations under the World Trade Organization (WTO), at least so far as services provision is concerned (see Winters et al. 2002).

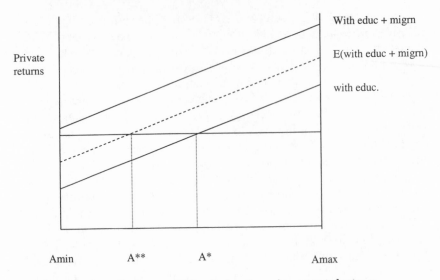

Fig. 7.2   Mountford—the possibility of migration raises expected returns to education

The possibility of migration raises expected welfare for anyone who takes education. Hence there is an increase in aggregate private income, although, of course, some individuals who do not manage to emigrate will regret their education decisions ex post. The uneducated see no direct change in private returns, and welfare and consequently gross private income rises when migration is permitted. What happens to aggregate welfare, of course, also depends on the social benefits of education.

Fundamental to this story is that every educated individual has probability π of emigrating—hence all of them experience increased expected returns, so that, in our linear example, line "E (with educ. and migrn.)" lies uniformly above "with educ." But now suppose that the country or organization of immigration can screen migrants perfectly for ability. They admit immigrants, but only from the top echelons, so that if, say, they want M people from our target country, they get the top M lying between A_M and $Amax$ in figure 7.3. If this is known, the incentives for individuals with ability below A_M are unchanged. The private returns to education follow the thick line in figure 7.3; $(Amax - A^*)$ are the educated, of whom $(A_M - A^*)$ remain. The increment to total private income is larger than if the migrants had been randomly selected because the same number of migrants makes gains, but no one makes ex post education decisions that they regret. However, there is a loss of social welfare of δM, as M educated people are lost and the social welfare was proportion δ of the number of educated individuals.

Clearly, perfect screening is implausible, but even with imperfect screen-

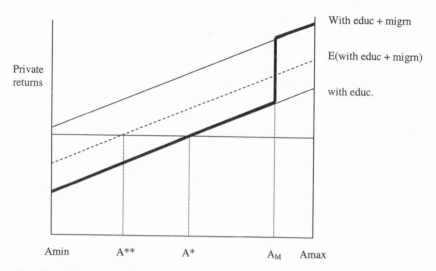

Fig. 7.3   Mountford with perfect screening

Note: The incentives for the marginal student do not change because they will never be chosen for migration.

ing all that would happen is that the vertical section of the thick private-returns line would become sloped. But as long as it meets "with educ." above A^*, offering migration would affect no one's education decisions. Thus, a necessary criterion for a beneficial brain drain to have any chance of applying is that the marginal person in education has a positive probability of emigrating.

Of course, actual decisions about education are taken with respect to subjective probabilities of migration, not with ex post observed probabilities. Thus, if individuals are overly optimistic about their prospects, marginal candidates may believe they face improved expected returns even when they do not. In line with most long-run modeling, however, we discount everlasting errors of this sort and presume that eventually subjective probabilities converge to actual ones.

The importance of effective screening is also evident in Stark, Helmenstein, and Prskawetz (1997), who distinguish between education and innate ability. For them, the increased incentive to acquire education among less-able workers is that, while foreign firms can recognize educational qualifications, they cannot, at first, distinguish high- from low-ability workers. As a result, for a period, they offer all migrants with a given level of education the same wage (the mean level averaged over ability for that level of education), with the consequence that less-able workers are overpaid. Over time, foreign firms may discern workers' true ability and offer more appropriate wages, at which time the benefits of emigration erode and, at least with finite probability, the workers return home. Even if they have acquired no skills or networks abroad, they are better educated than they would have been in the absence of migration. In this case, it is precisely the imperfections in screening—how quickly and with what probability foreign firms discern true ability—that create the incentives to acquire education.

A possible development of the screening model is that the sending or home country has some unexploited capacity for education in the sense that the returns to education are primarily determined by the demand for skilled workers rather than the ability of the population. In this case, even a perfectly screened emigration would generate net benefits. Suppose that as the workers between A_M and $Amax$ migrated, they left openings for newly educated workers to take jobs with precisely the same returns. The net effect on the home economy would be to have the same number of educated workers as without migration and, hence, the same spillovers but with M fewer uneducated workers. This would raise average incomes slightly (and average skill levels, which in some models is important). In addition, the migrants would record positive private gains.

It is also worth mentioning that the positive effects of brain drain for the sending country could also arise from a different mechanism that is related to the terms of trade as opposed to education. As Davis and Weinstein (2002) point out in their work, a technologically superior country, like the United States, is likely to experience inflow of all factors of production, including skilled and unskilled labor. This will eventually lead to deterioration of its terms of trade and consequential gains for the labor-sending country.

7.4.2 Empirical Extensions

An important step forward in the literature on the beneficial brain drain is due to Beine, Docquier, and Rapaport (2001a,b), who aim to test the model empirically using cross-sectional data. Their first attempt was hamstrung by data difficulties (e.g., having to use gross migration to proxy the brain drain), but it demonstrates that the probability of emigration does appear to boost human-capital formation in poor countries and that the stock of human capital does appear to influence growth positively.[13] These are both necessary conditions for the beneficial brain drain.

Beine, Docquier, and Rapaport (2001b) advance these results in several ways. They use Carrington and Detragiache's (1998) data set, which covers more countries, as well as a fuller set of additional explanatory variables in the equations for migration, human capital, and growth. The new estimates reinforce the earlier results except that the marginal effect of migration on human-capital formation appears to apply equally to all countries, rather than more strongly in the poorer countries, as the theory would pre-

---

13. This latter finding is, of course, rather different from the results of much of the empirical-growth literature, see Pritchett (2001).

dict. They also go on to use their estimates to decompose the effects of migration into a "brain" effect—human-capital accumulation—and a "drain" effect—losses due to actual emigration. They identify several countries that would benefit from a decline in 1990 stocks of skilled emigration (i.e., reducing the outflow and receiving some nationals back). These countries typically have high rates of emigration coupled with relatively ineffective education and training systems. Some would even benefit from a complete ban on skilled migration. Interestingly, however, the loss of growth due to emigration appears to be rather small, of the order of 0.05 percent per annum. The obverse of these results is that countries would typically gain from higher emigration if they currently have low rates of emigration and low levels of human capital (i.e., where the costs of further emigration are relatively low and the benefits in terms of incentives relatively high). There are limited numbers of countries in this class, but they include the larger developing countries, such as Brazil, China, and India.

These results are promising. The basic finding that a beneficial brain drain is possible seems quite robust. Their subsequent translation into policy recommendations toward skilled emigration, however, is fragile and cannot be viewed as anything other than illustrative, at present. It depends on point estimates from only one functional specification. Given that theory offers so little information on how precisely to model the relationship between the variables concerned, a great deal more testing of functional forms and more attention paid to estimation and data errors will be needed.

7.5 Screening: Empirical Evidence

The discussion in section 7.4 pointed to the possible importance of screening. In addition, we have already indicated that there appear to be strong sectoral dimensions to skilled migration. What evidence—if any— is there that these features have become more important in the recent period? Certainly, a closer look at targeted visa programs established in the last decade, as well as information on the job and location choices of developing-country students who have received some part of their education in a developed country (in this case the United States), may be instructive.

The clearest example of screening is the visa program implemented by the United States since the late 1980s and known as the H1-B visa. This program admits professional and specialized workers for up to six years on the basis of employer's declaration that U.S. workers are not available at the prevailing wage. However, although initially temporary, if an H1-B visa holder can find an employer to sponsor their certification, he or she can eventually become an immigrant. Over the 1990s, the quota for H1-B visas has increased steadily and is currently at around 195,000 per year. Table 7.2 gives the relative shares of selected major-source countries of

Table 7.2   Total Issue of U.S. H-1 Visas and Sending Country Shares, 1989–1999

	1989	1990	1991	1992	1993	1994	1995	1996	1997	1998	1999
India	4.4	4.6	6.9	10.7	18.0	22.9	26.3	32.0	39.3	44.0	47.2
China	1.7	1.0	1.9	1.7	2.4	2.5	3.2	3.9	4.0	4.2	5.0
The Philippines	12.4	12.4	12.2	14.6	18.0	17.8	17.0	7.7	3.3	3.0	2.6
Mexico	6.0	6.4	5.4	4.8	3.1	2.3	2.5	3.2	3.5	2.5	2.1
Russia	4.6	6.3	6.6	3.2	4.5	2.5	2.0	2.1	1.7	1.5	1.4
Total LDCs	29.2	30.8	33.1	35.1	46.0	48.1	50.9	48.8	51.8	55.4	58.2
The United Kingdom	13.6	12.2	14.8	13.0	9.5	8.6	8.1	9.3	8.6	6.9	5.7
Japan	7.5	6.5	8.7	5.4	5.1	4.5	3.5	4.0	3.6	3.1	2.9
France	4.7	3.9	4.1	3.3	2.1	2.0	2.1	2.4	2.3	2.3	2.3
Germany	3.7	2.8	3.2	2.9	2.4	2.2	2.5	2.5	2.6	2.5	2.1
Australia	1.8	1.4	1.9	1.9	2.0	2.1	1.8	1.9	1.8	1.8	1.4
Total developed countries	31.4	26.8	32.6	26.5	21.1	19.5	17.9	20.2	19.0	16.7	14.3
Others	39.4	42.4	34.3	38.4	32.9	32.4	31.2	31.1	29.3	27.9	27.4
Total no. of visas	48,820	58,673	59,325	51,667	42,206	49,284	59,093	60,072	80,608	91,378	116,695

Source: U.S. Immigration and Naturalization Service (1997, 1999, 2000).

H-1[14] visa issuances. It is not possible to extract the exact share of all individual developing countries in total issuances from this data, but it is obvious from the total share of developing countries that their importance as source countries has been growing steadily. In 1999, at least 58 percent of H-1 visas were granted to individuals from developing countries, and this figure has risen since the early 1990s.

The new Immigration and Naturalization Service Nonimmigrant Information System[15] has detailed records on admissions of nonimmigrants into the United States since 1996. These numbers are much larger than the actual visa issuances because each entry of a visa holder is recorded, rather than the number of individuals with permission to enter the United States. These data also show that since 1996 the share of H-1 admissions of nationals from developing countries has increased from 53 percent in 1996 to 74 percent in 1999. The ratio of admissions to issuances (which in general is much higher for nationals of developed countries) has also increased for some developing countries. For example, for China the ratio was 1.88 in 1996 and 1.97 in 1999, and for Russia the ratio has increased from 1.75 to 2.16 during the same period. This may indicate a change in the nature of immigration.

However, what is particularly striking is the rapid growth in that period of H1-B visa holders coming from just one developing country, India. Since 1995, Indians have accounted for over 40 percent of all H1-B visas. Needless to say, these migrants have accounted for a minute share of the total receiving- and sending-labor forces, but a nontrivial share of their respective sectors, particularly at the sending end. A very rough estimate suggests that the stock of Indian H1-B visa holders at the end of the 1990s may have accounted for around 30 percent of the India-based software labor force.[16] Other advanced economies—particularly in the European Union—have also begun to operate visa programmes designed to attract skilled workers for the ICT sector.[17]

The growth of the H1-B visa category has a great deal to do with the overall growth of the ICT sector and the software industry, in particular. A recent estimate has put the new immigrant share of ICT workers at around a sixth.[18] But it would be misleading to view this as simply the long-run

14. The H-1 visas include H-1A and H-1B visas, H-1A being the visa type issued to registered nurses. The number of H-1A visas has been very small after 1995.

15. The numbers of admissions from the system are reported in the Immigration and Naturalization Service (INS) *Statistical Yearbook*; 1997 records were not published because of reengineering of data entry and database management components.

16. This estimate is based on the sum of H-1B visa issuances in 1997–1999 and an estimate of total professional employment in software sector in India, presented by Rajetva Ratna Shaath from the Ministry of Information Technology 23 October, 2001 (available at http://www.nasscom.org/events/india_eu_it_summit/shah_srr.ppt).

17. See OECD (2002).

18. Of course, this includes new immigrants from other developed countries (see Guellec and Cervantes 2001).

movement of skilled labor away from developing countries. Indeed, it is precisely in this period that ICT sectors—including software—have grown in India and China. Particularly in the former case, this has been associated with the advent of tightly networked communities of firms and individuals that have spanned continents and have been enabled by advances in communications technology. Saxenian (2001) has argued that these new networks of highly mobile professionals, and linked firms operating over a range of spatial locations violate a more simplistic view of knowledge and asset transfer. However, such networks, although enabled by advances in communications, may still be associated with divisions of labor that may not necessarily work to the advantage of the developing country or firm.

Turning now to the education channel, over the 1990s, there has been strong growth in the numbers of students from developing countries pursuing education in developed countries. The proportion of students who were foreign in the OECD countries rose by 4.6 percent between 1995 and 1998 (OECD 2002), with as much as half of these being from developing countries.[19] For example, by 1998–1999 just over 10 percent of all international students enrolled in U.S. higher education were from China, and a further 8 percent were from India. At a doctoral level, between 80–90 percent of these students were enrolled in science and engineering faculties.[20] Clearly, a significant share of such students has tended to stay on, but the proportion that do return home is unclear. Guochu and Wenjun (2001) hazard the view that roughly one-third of Chinese students return home upon completion of their studies, but for those Chinese who have studied in the United States the rate of return has been lower at under 15 percent. One survey found that only 19 percent of the 160,000 Chinese students who studied in the United States between 1978 and 1998 had returned home.[21]

Other examples of return migration exist. Following a large outflow of students from Taiwan to the United States in the 1960s to the 1970s, returnees increased dramatically in the 1980s and have indeed played a central role in subsequently developing that country's ICT sector. This is partly reflected in a National Science Foundation study of doctoral students' work intentions covering the period 1988–1996. Of those surveyed, between 80–85 percent of Indian and Chinese doctoral students intended to try and stay in the United States. This figure falls to under 50 percent for Taiwanese students (see table 7.3). The share of Chinese and Indian doctoral students with firm plans to stay was around 50 percent and for the Taiwanese under 30 percent. Clearly, there are several factors at work here. One is the ability to secure employment in the United States; another is the

19. See the OECD Education Database; different countries have slightly varying definitions of foreigners, and thus exact numbers cannot be given.
20. See OECD (2002).
21. Cited in Saxenian (2001).

Table 7.3   **Number and Percent of Foreign Science and Engineering Doctoral Recipients with Plans to Stay in the United States, by Selected Countries and Regions, 1988–96**

		Foreign S&E Doctoral Recipients			
Region and Country	Total	With Plans to Stay	Percent	With Firm Plans to Stay	Percent
Asia	43,171	28,280	65.5	16,964	39.3
China	16,550	14,145	85.5	7,935	47.9
India	7,843	6,200	79.1	4,290	54.7
Korea	8,851	3,197	36.1	2,005	22.7
Taiwan	9,927	4,738	47.7	2,734	27.5
Europe	8,760	4,898	55.9	3,521	40.2
France	653	275	42.1	181	27.7
Germany	1,283	714	55.7	520	40.5
Greece	1,343	710	52.9	494	36.8
Italy	658	288	43.8	198	30.1
United Kingdom	1,132	784	69.3	595	52.6
Other Western European Countries	1,725	870	50.4	655	38.0
Scandinavian countries	612	276	45.1	195	31.9
Eastern Europe	1,354	981	72.5	683	50.4
North America	3,513	1,739	49.5	1,294	36.8
Canada	2,387	1,322	55.4	1,027	43.0
Mexico	1,126	417	37.0	267	23.7
Total: Selected countries	55,444	34,917	63.0	21,779	39.3

Source: Saxenian (2001).

average income level in the developing country as well as the ability to absorb returnees.[22]

The relationship between screening, talent, and relative earnings still poses major empirical challenges. However, it is interesting that, in a relatively small sample of members of the U.S. National Academy of Sciences and National Academy of Engineering, foreign-born scientists have tended to earn significantly more on average than native ones (Guellec and Cervantes 2001). This might suggest that they represent the higher end of the ability scale (if we assume that abilities have the same distribution in all countries), that they have the incentive to put more effort into their work, or both. Of course, selection in abilities can occur through selection in the initial emigration decision, screening by employers in the receiving country, or selection occurring through return migration. Whatever the channel, if screening is efficient, the result will be that the developing country

22. Bratsberg (1995) has studied the determinants of the return rate of students from different countries in the United States. Returns to education in the source country are inversely related to the rate of staying in the United States, as might be expected.

loses some access to its best talent, the portion of which depends in part on the sector. To the extent that the best talent leaves, there may be nontrivial implications for the developing country's ability to implement technological progress and move activities up the value chain.

7.6   Remittances, Diasporas, and Return Flows

It has long been recognized—but not explicitly modeled in this literature—that any adverse consequences of skilled emigration might be partly or wholly offset by remittances and return migration. Return migrants could come back with enhanced skills.

As usual, the data limitations are severe. Concerning remittances, aside from considerable imprecision in the aggregate numbers, it is not possible to separate out the volume of remittances coming from migrants of different skill groups.[23] Such information that is available confirms that remittances vary systematically with respect to income, conditions in the sending country, planned duration of stay, and household attributes.[24] It is likely that remittances from highly skilled migrants follow a very different pattern from those of low-skilled migrants.

As to return migration, a positive channel would occur when migrants return with experience, financial resources, links to networks, and skills from a stay abroad that are then productively deployed at home. Of course, these effects are not fixed but interrelated with each other, as well as with remittances, incentives to remit, and desires to save, and depend on the planned duration of migration, which in turn depends on migration and visa policies as much as individual intentions. In general, individuals can decide to return if the migrant prefers consumption in the sending or home country, if prices are lower there or if human capital acquired in the receiving country is more valuable in the sending country (Dustmann 1996).

There is some evidence that return migrants tend to choose self-employment or entrepreneurial activity because their savings diminish credit constraints. For example, Dustmann and Kirchkamp (2001) have studied returning Turkish migrants and their choice of activity and migration duration as a simultaneous decision. They find that most returnees choose self-employment or nonemployment and that highly educated individuals are more likely to be active after return. Ilahi (1999) has studied occupational choices on return and finds that the level of savings is positively correlated with the choice of self-employment on return. Similarly, McCormick and Wahba (2001) use survey data to investigate links between savings, overseas work experience, and choice of activity after re-

---

23. Remittances are discussed in detail and existing research reviewed in Puri and Ritzema (2000).
24. For example, Straubhaar (1986) for a study of remittances to Turkey.

turn. They find that duration of stay overseas along with savings increases the probability of becoming an entrepreneur for literate return migrants, which would suggest that skills obtained overseas have are useful on return. Positive effects from return migration obviously in turn depend on a variety of factors, including government policy in the sending or home country (see Castles 2000; Dustmann 1996).

Another important aspect of return migration is the possibility that it is a result of screening of the migrants. Borjas and Bratsberg (1996) have studied the outmigration decisions of foreign-born people in the United States, and conclude that return migration accentuates the type of selection that generated the immigrant flow. In other words, if emigrants represent the high end of the skill distribution in the source country, the returnees are the least skilled of the emigrants. Cohen and Haberfeld (2001) also find that Israeli immigrants returning from the United States are likely to be negatively selected from those Israelis who emigrated in the first place. Reagan and Olsen (2000), on the other hand, do not find any skill bias in return migration in their study on the National Longitudinal Survey, when skill is measured with Armed Forces Qualifying Test.

In sum, studies of return migration suggest that those who return may be those that have performed relatively poorly when abroad; the best migrants tend to stay. Of course, these observations do not necessarily hold true for all different migrant groups or countries. Furthermore, other related research suggests that aspects that do not require return migration of skilled individuals can be of major importance. Such channels for beneficial effects are exports and business and network links related to diaspora populations. There is evidence that such diaspora can have very beneficial effect on exports (Rauch 1999; Rauch and Trinidade 2002). Similarly, foreign direct investment and venture capital—particularly in the recent period—have often been related to ethnic networks. An example of this is the Hsinchu Science park in Taipei, where a large fraction of companies have been started by returnees from the United States (Luo and Wang 2001). There is some evidence of these types of networks effects being quite powerful in the Indian software industry.

7.7 Economic-Geography Models

We now turn to the recent economic geography literature (Krugman 1991; Fujita, Krugman, and Venables 1999) that brings together in a formal way two of the key elements of the brain drain story—labor mobility and a tendency for uneven development (core-periphery outcomes). The unique contribution of this literature has been to show that uneven outcomes are possible even when countries have identical starting points and when there are no direct spillovers between mobile workers or market failures in the labor market. Rather, their unevenness stems from the pecuniary externalities implicit in the interactions between imperfectly competitive firms. The appendix attempts a relabelling exercise to see how far geography can help us to understand high-skilled migration. Here we summarize the main points.

Economic-geography models show how economies of scale and transaction costs can combine to determine the level of industrial concentration. The former are necessary for concentration to emerge at all, whereas the latter curtail concentration because they increase the benefits of locating production close to demand. The simplest geography model formalizes the notion of cumulative causation in the industrial sector. Imagine an initial expansion of industry in one country. This draws industrial labor into the country from elsewhere, and this labor increases the country's demand for industrial output. This, in turn, is met by local producers because, being local, they avoid the transportation costs (and tariffs) faced by overseas producers. Thus, higher sales stimulate output which in turn stimulates labor demand, and so on. The constraint on this process in Krugman (1991) is the existence of an agricultural sector that cannot move and as a consequence generates demand for industrial goods that cannot be concentrated. In extreme versions of the model, with two identical countries, two sorts of outcome are possible: the complete concentration of industry or an equal split between the two countries. At very high transportation costs, perfect diversification rules, whereas, at low costs, perfect concentration does. In-between there is a range where both equilibria are stable. Precisely where this lies depends in part on the relative sizes of demand from mobile and immobile workers. If demand from the latter is large, agglomeration may not be possible, and certainly will not occur until trade costs have fallen very substantially. When economies of scale are not too strong and there are many countries in the world, the model generalizes to create several agglomerations, as indeed are observed.

If we think of industry as being the high-technology sector and agriculture as the rest of the economy, we have a potential model of the brain drain as industrial (high-skill) labor migrates in the process of concentration. Moreover, if we add in some further frictions to the model—such as congestion costs—in which industry agglomerates and there is an unwillingness by some high-technology workers to move, outcomes between the two extremes are possible.

Reinterpreted geography models suggest three significant conclusions. First, the pressure for a brain drain may vary as the parameters of the world economy change. In particular, the pressure for the agglomeration of industry, and thus of the factors of production used in industry, depends on the costs of international trade of final goods. If the latter are very high, production is constrained to locate close to demand, and, provided the latter starts off relatively dispersed over space, agglomeration never gets underway. As trade costs fall, for either policy reasons (lower barriers) or with technological advance, agglomeration may become more feasible and so pressure for a brain drain may emerge. Such developments *could* lie behind the apparent recent revival in skilled-labor mobility in certain sectors.

Second, geography models suggest that uneven development—and hence brain drain pressure—is a natural and inevitable phase of global development, even if countries start off from identical positions. Third, the simplest geography models suggest that a brain drain will be detrimental to those left behind in the brain-exporting (sending or home) country even in the absence of the labor-market failures (including in the absence of direct spillovers between skilled workers) that we have discussed so far. That is, the advantages of agglomeration stem from the fact that proximity economizes on transactions and transportation costs, making real wages higher in the core and lower in the periphery than they would be under more even development. This effect could be additive to any of the direct spillovers discussed so far.

The previously presented geography models offer a return to an earlier vintage of brain-drain models (albeit in more sophisticated form), because they admit none of the more recently identified developments that could generate a beneficial brain drain. They have no mechanism for stimulating return migration, have no network or diaspora effects, and, because they take the world's stock of skilled labor as given, are unable to consider the education-incentives version of the brain drain.

If, however, there *are* positive direct spillovers between skilled workers, agglomeration will increase average productivity and world aggregate output. This raises the possibility that even workers in the brain-exporting country gain from the brain drain because world output increases. At least in simple models, however, one can show that, as transportation costs fall from infinity, the workers in the nonindustrial country are worse off when agglomeration first starts. They start to gain only as transportation costs fall far enough that they can more cheaply buy the goods from the concentration of industry in the other country (see Baldwin and Forslid 2000).

A strength of the economic-geography approach is its general equilibrium nature, which endows it with a strong internal consistency. On the other hand, this makes it a poor predictor of sectoral effects. There is clearly a general equilibrium dimension to the brain drain. In particular, very small economies just may not be able to generate the density of demand necessary to make the application of high levels of skill profitable. However, there are equally clear differences between sectors regarding the extent of and incentives for agglomeration. These cannot be due to the demand linkages that are central to Krugman's geography model, for these are completely general across all industrial sectors. The alternative pecuniary externality found in the geography literature—(that is, input-output linkages when intermediate demand relocates with firms [Fujita, Krugman, and Venables 1999])—could conceivably offer an explanation, but it entails no labor mobility.

We conclude, therefore, that, while geography provides useful insights into the general position of nations in the brain drain cycle, it cannot be the complete story behind the movements that we observe in areas such as health and ICT. For these, direct and sector-specific spillovers must also be at work too.

7.8   Sectoral Dimensions

The available evidence points to skilled migration having strong sectoral properties. At the same time, technology itself has had an impact on the structure of demand and the spatial distributions of skilled labor. Two examples stand out: health and software. Both have been subject to skilled emigration but with different durations and dynamics at both the sending and receiving ends.

Skilled migration of health-care workers appears to be the starkest and most persistent form of brain drain (our future research will try to quantify these costs carefully). Health care is generally underprovided in developing countries, and provision also tends to be skewed towards urban and relatively privileged consumers. As highly regulated activity, there are long lags on the supply side of healthcare, while educational financing tends to have a strong public component in most developing countries. Furthermore, health care work generally has a strong team component; doctors have complementary inputs from nurses and ancillary staff. Advances in medical technology have, if anything, accentuated the team component. As such, loss of some part of this chain may have large, knock-on effects. Among other things, this suggests that relatively narrow interventions that might seek to raise some part of the chain's incentives for staying (or penalize them for leaving) will have limited efficacy. Indeed, the organization of the industry suggests sector-wide solutions. On the demand side, it appears to be largely public health care systems in the developed economies that are the main sources of demand, thereby raising the public-policy dimension directly.

The growth of a highly mobile software sector is of more recent origin. Furthermore, the sector has a far smaller public-sector involvement. Clearly, an important factor behind its growth has been the falling cost of communications. Thus, the use of satellites (VSATs) has become central to the growth of software firms in India by enabling firms in that country to work effectively with partners or clients in developed countries. In addition, there are clear educational thresholds. It is no accident that software sectors in developing countries have mostly emerged in countries with ex ante, thick, skilled-labor markets. The sector has everywhere then been characterized by agglomeration, which can be attributed to gains from knowledge sharing, teamwork, and demand-and-supply (backward-and-forward) linkages. This also appears to be associated with positive spillovers, including learning by doing, and hence positive productivity effects.

One possible channel for productivity gain is likely to be the reduction in skill-technology mismatch in the developing country.[25] Increased investment in human capital will raise skill levels in turn allowing firms to match workers to new-generation technologies more easily. Certainly, anecdotal evidence from the software sector shows workers in developing countries working with very similar technologies as their counterparts in the advanced economies. Over time, this should reduce the productivity and wage gap.[26] This, in turn, will lower income differences across countries. By contrast, within-country inequality in incomes may well rise, as returns to the skilled increase relative to the unskilled returns.

This potentially very positive picture does, however, need qualification. Available evidence suggests that the most highly skilled personnel have moved (with screening) to firms located in advanced economies (i.e., the Silicon Valley). This may be less on account of outright technology differences than on account of differences in the ability to network, in the business environment, and so on. One possible outcome would be that the skills available to developing-country firms then result in them choosing to work lower down the value chain, for example, by concentrating more on outsourced coding than conceptualizing.[27] Yet even this is far from clear. Movement of skilled workers across borders has often been temporary, and—at least in India—there is widespread evidence of high integration in activity between firms in the developing- and developed-country agglomerations.

What are the welfare implications for the sending or home country in this type of arrangement? Clearly, the sending country gains from the matching of domestic skilled workers to relatively high-productivity jobs, particularly if—as indicated in section 7.4—there is an associated and positive shock to the supply of skills. However, it loses the top end of the skill distribution and with it, embodied education costs (although there is increasing evidence of greater private-education finance). That loss will be potentially qualified by such movers retaining or developing business links at home and by any associated networking effects. It also partly depends on the labor market and the presence or absence of slack. With ex ante slack, emigration may lead to better matching at home. Absent such slack, emigration would directly affect relative wages and, ultimately, the factor mix.

25. We noted previously that such factors might explain part of the wage gap across countries for skilled labor.
26. Thereby counteracting some of the factors analysed in Acemoglu and Zilibotti (2001).
27. See Desai (2000).

Faced with the high turnover associated with poaching, firms may simply make production and technology decisions that match to skill levels with lower poaching probabilities. Note also that high poaching probabilities will exacerbate the problem of firms' refusing to internalize training costs.

What might be the longer-run implications? On the assumption that developed-country firms continue to poach talent, a key question relates to the incentive properties that screening-cum-cherry-picking imparts for others. As the analysis in section 7.4 shows, if the human-capital-acquisition incentives could then be absent or minimal, the long-run effect may be adverse for the sending country. Equivalently, it may affect the way in which talent is distributed. To the extent that the education taken abroad is privately financed (against some public-financing component for those that get recruited later), there will be a fiscal saving. However, there are also likely to be negative externalities from the loss of the best students that may ultimately have an impact on the quality of instruction and graduates. Certainly, these questions require further investigation and more formal treatment—tasks that we reserve for later.

Finally, we should signal that the size of a country (and hence the size of its skill pool) is likely to matter. Small developing countries will find it difficult to retain skills; they lack the mass for agglomeration and other scale effects to set in. This makes them particularly prone to skills poaching.

7.9 Conclusion

In this paper, we have surveyed the literature and some of the evidence on the brain drain. A body of early work concentrated on modeling the sending countries' labor markets in the presence of a range of distortions, particularly of the labor market in the sending country. The gist of this analysis was that skilled migration lowered welfare for the population remaining behind in the sending country, but this was highly sensitive to assumptions regarding wage setting and ex ante employment levels. (There was never any case that the migrants themselves did not gain.) In the main, migration exacerbated the efficiency losses caused by the various distortions—for example, the subsidy to public education or the underemployment of skilled or other labor arising from distorted wage setting. This literature led to calls for the prevention or taxation of skilled migration from developing countries, although, as history shows no concrete action ever resulted.

Later more truly dynamic models of the brain drain focused on the motivation for human-capital accumulation and noted how these were affected by the introduction of a nontrivial probability of emigration. Thus although migration drained talent out of a country, in this class of model, it also encouraged the creation of skills, and the latter effect could be the dominant one. The mechanisms through which this occurred relied on information failures—most commonly the assumption that, after taking education, developing-country residents had an equal, exogenous, and less-than-unity probability of migrating. Implicit in the first condition is the assumption that the receiving country cannot screen potential migrants effectively; it merely chooses randomly among the educated cohort of the developing country. But, in fact, it appears that recipients screen immigrants quite actively—for example, via recruitment effort, the offer of temporary visas during which workers reveal themselves, and via their local education establishments. In this case, however, the beneficial brain drain can evaporate, for if the recipients can choose only the most able among developing-country residents, the incentives for the marginal student to acquire education will not be affected since they will have no possibility of emigrating. This disappointing outcome may be moderated if screening is imperfect or if there is some ex ante underemployment of skilled labor in the sending country. In the latter case, the employment ratchet effect resulting from screened emigration could eliminate the social losses while still permitting the strong positive private gains for the migrants themselves.

A third stream of some relevance is the literature on economic geography. This has not (so far) been concerned directly with brain-drain issues, but its models can be massaged to offer an alternative view of skilled migration. Doing so provides a number of insights into the factors behind agglomeration—including that in skills—and some likely implications for developing countries. From these extensions, it appears that the brain drain is likely to be a temporary phenomenon, arising only as the transactions costs for talent-intensive activity decline through falling communications costs, and the situation will possibly reverse itself as they decline even further. While it occurs, however, the brain drain will have negative welfare implications for the "periphery" (the brain-exporting home countries) as, inter alia, its mobile labor emigrates to the "core." This is likely to be especially true of very small countries, which are unable to achieve the mass required to exploit talented labor efficiently. The economic-geography explanation of the brain drain is explicitly general equilibrium, which is a conceptual and also empirical strength for these very small economies. However, among economies large enough to support agglomerations in principle, it is a potential weakness because it precludes explaining the different experiences of different high-technology sectors.

Indeed, casual observation suggests that, in the 1990s, multiple sites for agglomeration, including those in the periphery, have developed. For example, there is clear evidence of agglomeration in the software industry in India, as in the United States. This might point to some evolving division of labor and associated distribution of skills across space. As such, this may indeed be where the main welfare implications of a particular type of skilled migration lie, and this in turn implies closer attention to the properties of specific sectors and skills.

Overall, our conclusion has to be that, while there is clearly a possibility that the brain drain is beneficial to the residents left behind in the home countries, there are reasons—some of them of recent origin—to be suspicious of that conclusion. It is not even certain that there is an overall global-welfare gain from the brain drain, although given the apparently large private benefits of the migrants themselves and their higher productivity in their new locations, it seems highly likely. Like all good academic surveys, we conclude that much more research is needed to pin down the relevant magnitudes. These are likely to vary by sector, and so this work will need to be at a detailed level.

Appendix
Reinterpreting the Economic Geography Model

The standard geography model postulates a simple, costlessly traded, competitive-numeraire sector, agriculture (A), distributed uniformly and immobile across space. In addition, it has a differentiated manufacturing sector (M), which is costly to trade and which uses industrial labor (L). The latter is internationally mobile but fixed in global supply. Krugman assumes that labor relocates to eliminate real-wage differences, and, although it does so only gradually, he is ultimately concerned only with the final outcomes. Assuming two identical countries, the latter comprise two possibilities—a diversified symmetric equilibrium, in which labor earns the same real wage in both locations, and a concentrated one, in which manufacturing clusters in one country and its workers earn more than they could in the other country even if a few manufacturing firms were to set up there. Which of these equilibria arises depends on, inter alia, the importance of manufacturing in demand (and hence in production and income generation), the costs of transportation, fixed costs, and the degree of product differentiation in manufacturing (the last two of which determine the extent of economies of scale). It also depends on history. One of the fundamental insights of this literature is that there is an area of the parameter space in which both sorts of equilibria exist and are stable, so that which one prevails depends on which prevailed as the economy entered that area. In the concentrated equilibrium, agriculturists also have higher real incomes in the industrialized country than they would under symmetry because, although agricultural nominal wages are fixed and equal across locations, the price of manufactures is lower in the industrialized country. The opposite applies to agriculturists in the deindustrialised country. It is important to note that this clustering depends on pecuniary externalities not technological spillovers.

If we reinterpret A as the base economy (including agriculture and immobile, basic manufacturing and services), M as foot-loose activities including the skill intensive, and L as foot-loose and skilled labor, we would appear to have a potential model of a brain drain. It explains the existence of a brain drain, as well as its consequences, and does so without recourse to the technological spillovers between skilled workers usually assumed in brain drain models.

There are, however, a number of reservations to be noted. It is not clear why foot-loose goods should be subject to trading costs while basic ones are not, and, although the model can be adapted to allow the latter to have such costs (Fujita, Krugman, and Venables 1999), doing so seems quite likely to make the concentrated (i.e., brain drain) equilibrium infeasible. Similarly if the high-skilled part of the economy is small, most demand is generated by the basic sector that is assumed to be immobile, and concentration is less likely. Additionally, the division between basic and foot-loose parts of the economy is problematic. If the latter is drawn narrowly in order to capture the high-skill element of the brain drain, it may be too small to generate agglomeration, while it is not obvious that the basic part of the economy will be free from tendencies to agglomerate. Agriculture may be "nailed down," but basic manufacturing and services are not, and, as Fujita, Krugman, and Venables (1999) show, agglomeration is feasible even without migration through backward- and forward-linkages among industrial firms. If, on the other hand, the foot-loose sector is large, the mobile labor flows will not be particularly highly skilled, and hence we start to lose the brain component of the brain drain story.

In sum, the economic-geography framework is too rarefied to be applied directly. Nonetheless, it offers a number of insights that may be of use in thinking about the brain drain. The critical parameter in exploring possible outcomes is the cost of trading M, which is now the skill-intensive sector. At very high costs, production must be located near consumption, and the world economy has a symmetric, diversified equilibrium. As trade costs fall, the concentrated equilibrium becomes feasible, at first, and then, at lower costs, unique. In the simple model, concentration remains the unique outcome right down to zero trade costs, but in more complex variants with diminishing returns (e.g., if A also has trade costs or if there are additional locationally fixed factors), the concentrated equilibrium gives way to the symmetric one at positive levels of trade costs (possibly again with a range in which both types are feasible).[28] If countries were initially perfectly identical, the model cannot predict which will end up with the concentration, but it is easy to see that tiny advantages for one country (technological, size, or historical) would make it the preferred location and leave it with all

---

28. When the trade costs of M are zero, location ceases to matter, so any other location equilibrium would be equally feasible.

the M industry. Thus, if the world were characterized by improving communications for skill-intensive sectors, we could see a tendency for a brain drain from less- to more-favored countries to emerge and then eventually to reverse.

Of course, these are parables and possibilities rather than predictions. At present we have no feeling for what the critical values of trade costs are or where actual costs lie in the world. In addition, the models really need to be extended before they can be fitted to the real world. In particular, migration is unlikely to denude one country of skilled labor completely. One can avoid this in a number of modeling ways, but prominent among them would be to recognize that not everyone wants to move. Second, it is desirable to recognize the possibility of direct externalities in the agglomeration of skilled labor. Fortunately, extensions exist in both these dimensions. Third, the lags assumed in migratory flows are not consistent with fixed global supplies of skilled labor. Relaxing the last constraint is necessary for examining the training-incentive version of the beneficial brain drain, and it awaits attention.

Ludema and Wooton (1997) add preferences over location to the standard geography model. Not surprisingly, doing so makes the symmetric, diversified, equilibria more likely (feasible and unique for a larger range of trade costs) and allows the concentrated equilibrium to stop short of 100 percent concentration of M. This is clearly more realistic than the extremes we saw previously and increases the legitimacy of considering whether a brain drain can occur even in the absence of spillovers between skilled workers.

Externalities between skilled labor have not, to our knowledge, been explicitly added into the standard economic-geography model, but Baldwin and Forslid (2000) take a step in the right direction. In keeping with our interpretation of manufacturing as the skill-intensive sector, they postulate that each manufacturing enterprise needs a unit of capital, which is produced with skilled labor using a technology that involves positive learning-by-doing externalities.[29] This combines geography with endogenous growth and thus comes closer to the traditional approach to the brain drain. It makes concentrated equilibria more likely but raises the possibility that a concentrated equilibrium is beneficial even for the deindustrialized country. The static losses (from geography) may be offset by the increase in the global growth rate resulting from the concentration of skilled workers in one place. For this to happen, one needs the technological spillovers to be (largely) national—if they were perfectly international, skilled workers would have equal productivity in capital goods wherever they were lo-

---

29. This capital lasts only one period, so it as if each manufacturing firm needs an extra input of skilled labor, but that input declines through time according to how much has been used for that purpose previously.

cated—and trade costs to be relatively low. Interestingly, in this model, the level of trade costs at which the growth effects offset the static losses is lower than that at which concentration occurs and hurts the deindustrialized country. That is, as trade costs fall, the deindustrializing country first experiences falls in welfare from losing its skilled labor and only subsequently benefits from the higher world-growth rate.

References

Acemoglu, Daron, and Fabrizio Zilibotti. 2001. Productivity differences. *Quarterly Journal of Economics* 115 (3): 563–606.

Arora, Ashish, Vallampadugai S. Arunachalam, Jai Asundi, and Ronald Fernandez. 2001. The Indian software services industry. *Research Policy* 30 (8): 1276–87.

Arrow, Kenneth J. 1973. Higher education as a filter. *Journal of Public Economics* 2 (3): 193–216.

Auriol, Laudeline, and Jerry Sexton. 2002. Human resources in science and technology: Measurement issues and international mobility. In *International mobility of highly skilled,* OECD, 13–28. Paris: OECD.

Baldwin, Richard E., and Rikard Forslid. 2000. The core-periphery model and endogenous growth: Stabilising and de-stabilising integration. *Economica* 67 (267): 307–24.

Barro, Robert, and Jong-Wha Lee. 1996. International measures of schooling years and schooling quality. *American Economic Review* 86 (2): 218–23.

Beine, Michael, Frederic Docquier, and Hillel Rapoport. 2001a. Brain drain and economic growth: Theory and evidence. *Journal of Development Economics* 64 (1): 275–89.

————. 2001b. Brain drain and growth in LDCs: Winners and losers. Paper presented at the European Economic Association Congress, 29 August–1 September, Lausanne, Switzerland.

Bhagwati, Jagdish N., ed. 1976. The brain drain and taxation, theory and empirical analysis. Amsterdam: North Holland.

Bhagwati, Jagdish N., and Koichi Hamada. 1974. The brain drain, international integration of markets for professionals and unemployment: A theoretical analysis. *Journal of Development Economics* 1 (1): 19–42.

Bhagwati, Jagdish N., and Martin Partington, eds. 1976. Taxing the brain drain, a proposal. Amsterdam: North Holland.

Bhagwati, Jagdish N., and John Douglas Wilson, eds. 1989. *Income taxation and international mobility.* Cambridge, Mass.: MIT Press.

Borjas, George J., and Bernt Bratsberg. 1996. Who leaves? The outmigration of the foreign-born. *Review of Economics and Statistics* 78 (1): 165–76.

Bratsberg, Bernt. 1995. The incidence of non-return among foreign students in the United States. *Economics of Education Review* 14 (4): 373–84.

Castles, Stephen. 2000. The impacts of emigration on countries of origin. In *Local dynamics in an era of globalisation,* ed. Shahid Yusuf, Weiping Wu, and Simon Evenett, 45–56. Washington, D.C.: World Bank.

Carrington, William J., and Enrica Detragiache. 1998. How big is the brain drain? International Monetary Fund (IMF) Working Paper no. 201. Washington, D.C.: IMF.

Chanda, Rupa. 2001. Trade in health services. Commission for Macroeconomics and Health Working Paper no. WG4:5. Geneva: World Health Organization; ICRIER Working Paper no. 63. New Delhi: Indian Council for Research on International Economic Relations.

Cohen, Yinon and Yitchak Haberfeld. 2001. Self-selection and return migration: Israeli-born Jews returning home from the United States during the 1980s. *Population Studies* 55 (1): 79–91.

Dahlman, Carl J., and Jean-Eric Aubert. 2001. China and the knowledge economy. Seizing the 21st century. World Bank Institute (WBI) Development Studies. Washington, D.C.: World Bank.

Davis, Donald R., and David E. Weinstein. 2002. Technological superiority and the losses from migration. NBER Working Paper no. 8971. Cambridge, Mass.: National Bureau of Economic Research, May.

Desai, Ashok. 2000. The peril and the promise. Broader implications of the Indian presence in information technologies. Center for Research on Economic Development and Policy Reform. Working Paper no. 70. Stanford, Cal.: Stanford University.

Desai, Mihir A., Devesh Kapur, and John McHale. 2002a. The fiscal impact of high skilled emigration: Flows of Indians to the U.S. Harvard University. Working Paper.

———. 2002b. Sharing the spoils: Taxing international human capital flows. Weatherhead Center for International Affairs. Working Paper no. 02-06. Boston: Harvard University.

Dustmann, Christian. 1996. Return migration: The European experience. *Economic Policy: A European Forum* 0 (22): 213–42.

Dustmann, Christian, and Oliver Kirchkamp. 2001. The optimal migration duration and activity choice after re-migration. Institute for the Study of Labor (IZA) Discussion Paper no. 266. Bonn, Germany: IZA.

Easterly, William, and Ross Levine. 2001. It's not factor accumulation: Stylised facts and growth models. *The World Bank Economic Review* 15 (2): 177–219.

Fujita, Masahisa, Paul Krugman, and Anthony J. Venables. 1999. *The spatial economy: Cities, regions and international trade.* Cambridge, Mass.: MIT Press.

General Medical Council. 2000. *Changing times, changing culture: A review of the work of the GMC since 1995.* London: General Medical Council.

Government of India. 1998. *Health information of India (1995–96).* New Delhi: Government of India.

———. 2000. *Health information of India (1997–98).* New Delhi: Government of India.

Grubel, Herbert, and Anthony Scott. 1966. The international flow of human capital. *American Economic Review* 56 (1/2): 268–74.

Guellec, Dominique, and Mario Cervantes. 2001. International mobility of highly skilled workers: From statistical analysis to policy formulation. In *International mobility of highly skilled,* OECD, 71–98. Paris: OECD.

Guochu, Zhang, and Li Wenjun. 2001. International mobility of China's resources in science and technology. In *International mobility of highly skilled,* OECD, 189–200. Paris: OECD.

Hamada, Koichi, and Jagdish N. Bhagwati. 1975. Domestic distortions, imperfect information and the brain drain. *Journal of Development Economics* 2 (3): 265–79.

Harris, John R., and Michael P. Todaro. 1970. Migration, unemployment, and development: A two-sector analysis. *American Economic Review* 60 (1): 126–42.

Ilahi, Nadeem. 1999. Return migration and occupational change. *Review of Development Economics* 3 (2): 170–86.

Jasso, Guillermina, Douglas S. Massey, Mark R. Rosenzweig, and James P. Smith.

2000. The new immigrant survey pilot study: Overview and new findings about U.S. legal immigrants at admission. *Demography* 37 (1): 127–38.

Jayaram, N. 1995. Political economy of medical education in India. *Higher Education Policy* 8 (2):

Johnson, Harry G. 1967. Some economic aspects of the brain drain. *Pakistan Development Review* 7 (3): 379–411.

Johnstone, D. Bruce, Alka Arora, and William Experton. 1998. *The financing and management of higher education: A status report on worldwide reforms.* Washington, D.C.: World Bank.

Krugman, Paul. 1991. Increasing returns and economic geography. *Journal of Political Economy* 99 (3): 483–99.

Kumar, Nagesh. 2000. Small information technology services, employment, and entrepreneurship development: Some explorations into Indian experience. *Indian Journal of Labor Economics* 43 (4): 935–48.

Ludema, Rodney D., and Ian Wooton. 1997. Regional integration, trade, and migration: Are demand linkages relevant in Europe? Center for Economic Policy Research (CEPR) Discussion Paper no. 1656. Paris: CEPR.

Luo, Y-L., and W-J. Wang. 2001. High-skill migration and Chinese Taipei's industrial development. In *International mobility of highly skilled,* OECD, 253–70. Paris: OECD.

McCormick, Barry, and Jackline Wahba. 2001. Overseas work experience, savings and entrepreneurship amongst return migrants to LDCs. *Scottish Journal of Political Economy* 48 (2): 164–78.

McCulloch, Rachel, and Janet L. Yellen. 1975. Consequences of a tax on the brain drain for unemployment and income inequality in less developed countries. *Journal of Development Economics* 2 (3): 249–64.

Mountford, Andrew. 1997. Can a brain drain be good for growth in the source economy? *Journal of Development Economics* 53 (2): 287–303.

Organization for Economic Cooperation and Development (OECD). 2002. *International mobility of the highly skilled.* Paris: OECD.

Pomp, Richard D. 1989. The experience of the Philippines in taxing its nonresident citizens. In *Income taxation and international mobility,* ed. Jagdish N. Bhagwati and John Douglas Wilson, 43–82. Cambridge, Mass.: MIT Press.

Pritchett, Lant. 2001. Where has all the education gone? *World Bank Economic Review* 15 (3): 367–91.

Puri, Shivani, and Tineke Ritzema. 2000. Migrant worker remittances, microfinance and the informal economy: Prospects and issues. Working Paper no. 21. Geneva: International Labour Office, Social Finance Unit.

Rauch, James E. 1991. Reconciling the pattern of migration with the pattern of trade. *American Economic Review* 81 (4): 775–96.

Rauch, James E. 1999. Networks vs. markets in international trade. *Journal of International Economics* 48 (1): 7–35.

Rauch, James E., and Vitor Trindade. 2002. Ethnic Chinese networks in international trade. *Review of Economic Studies* 84 (1): 116–130.

Reagan, Patricia B., and Randall J. Olsen. 2000. You can go home again: Evidence from longitudinal data. *Demography* 37 (3): 339–50.

Rodriguez, Carlos. 1975. Brain drain and economic growth: A dynamic model. *Journal of Development Economics* 2 (3): 223–48.

Salim, A. Abdul. 1996. Institutional cost of higher education—A case study of Kerala. *Manpower Journal* 32 (1): 1–14.

Salt, John. 1997. International movements of the highly skilled. International Migration Unit Occasional Paper no. 3. Paris: OECD.

Saxenian, AnnaLee. 2001. The Silicon Valley connection: Transnational networks and regional development in Taiwan, China and India. *Industry and Innovation* 9 (2).

Spence, A. Michael. 1974. *Market signalling.* Cambridge, Mass.: Harvard University Press.

Stark, Oded, Christian Helmenstein, and Alexia Prskawetz. 1997. A brain gain with a brain drain. *Economics Letters* 55 (3): 227–34.

————. 1998. Human capital depletion, human capital formation, and migration: A blessing or a curse? *Economics Letters* 60 (3): 363–67.

Straubhaar, Thomas. 1986. The determinants of workers' remittances: The case of Turkey. *Weltwirtschaft liches Archiv* 122 (4): 728–40.

Tilak, Jandhyala B. G. 1997. The dilemma of reforms in financing higher education in India. *Higher Education Policy* 10 (1): 7–21.

U.S. Immigration and Naturalization Service. 1997. *Statistical yearbook of the Immigration and Naturalization Service 1996.* Washington, D.C.: GPO.

————. 1999. *Statistical yearbook of the Immigration and Naturalization Service 1998.* Washington, D.C.: GPO.

————. 2000. *Statistical yearbook of the Immigration and Naturalization Service 1999.* Washington, D.C.: GPO.

Vidal, Jean-Pierre. 1998. The effect of emigration on human capital formation. *Journal of Population Economics* 11 (4): 589–600.

Winters, L. Alan, Terrie L. Walmsley, Zhen Kun Wang, and Roman Grynberg. 2002. *Negotiating the liberalisation of the temporary movement of natural persons.* London: Commonwealth Secretariat.

World Bank. 2001. *World development indicators.* Washington, D.C.: World Bank.

Comment   Alan V. Deardorff

I learned a lot from this paper, which does an excellent job of providing an overview of the literature on the brain drain from less developed countries. Indeed, the paper by Commander, Kangasniemi, and Winters does a better job than you might know from the presentation here, because Alan did not have time to cover all of it. I encourage all of you to read the paper, especially the sections that he was not able to get to. You will find it valuable.

I do not myself know much of this literature, and so I have to assume that the paper is complete in its coverage. I was struck, however, by the absence from the paper of a couple of things, things that I presume are also absent from the brain-drain literature.

First, I did not find in the paper, at least explicitly, two of the more obvious models that one might expect to be used to analyze a brain drain. I did not see, first, any use of the simplest supply-and-demand analysis of a labor market, even though I would have thought that to be the place to start in understanding a change in labor supply. No doubt this is implicit in the paper, and perhaps explicit in some of the papers reviewed, for I found it nec-

Alan V. Deardorff is the John W. Sweetland Professor of International Economics and professor of public policy at the Gerald R. Ford School of Public Policy, University of Michigan.

essary to keep such a model in my mind in order to understand many of the conceptual points that the paper made. Second, I saw no explicit reference to the Heckscher-Ohlin (HO) trade model, even though this too seems an obvious place to start for understanding a change in a labor endowment in general equilibrium. I will therefore devote my comment to relating some of the points of the paper to what these two sorts of model can help us with.

One thing that these models provide is a reminder of some of the market effects that a brain drain might be expected to have, and that also seemed to be neglected in the paper. The first, and presumably most important, is the effect of a brain drain on the local wage rate in the country of emigration. The second is the effect on world prices of traded goods, and thus on the terms of trade of that country. I will touch on both of these in turn.

Effect on the LDC Wage

To start then, consider figure 7C.1, which shows the simple supply and demand for skilled labor in a country, yielding in equilibrium the skilled wage, w_s. A brain drain is the departure from that market of a portion of the supply, shown as ΔM, which migrates abroad presumably in expectation of a higher wage. The effect is to shift the supply curve to the left, as shown, raising the equilibrium wage. The standard welfare analysis of this change includes a gain to the remaining domestic workers of area a, but also a loss to everyone else in the country, whose concerns enter the market through the demand curve, as the larger area $a + b$. Thus, while the brain

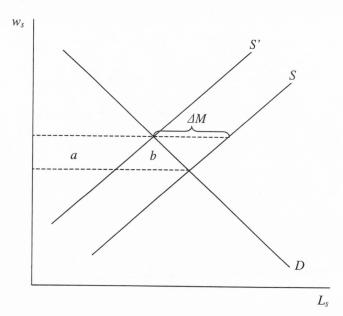

Fig. 7C.1   Brain drain in a competitive labor market

drain in this case benefits the skilled workers who stay behind, the country as a whole loses.

All of this depends, of course, on the wage's being able to rise. The paper's first dip into the theory of the brain drain refers to Grubel and Scott (1966). This paper is not listed in the papers references, but it apparently disagrees with this result, perhaps for a reason I will get to below. Commander, Kangasniemi, and Winters then turn with somewhat more detail to an analysis by Bhagwati and Hamada (1974), who explicitly depart from this by assuming that the wage is set not by a market but by a labor union. If the union holds the wage fixed at above the market-equilibrium level, then the story is the different one shown in figure 7C.2. Here, the wage remains fixed at $\overline{w}_s$, and although the brain drain again shifts the supply curve to the left, the effect now is simply to reduce unemployment, presumably generating no cost and only a benefit. This was only a starting point for Bhagwati and Hamada, however, who went on to allow, among other things, for the union to raise its wage demand so as to "emulate" the higher wage earned by the migrants. Thus, even while denying that the labor market clears, they included something like the market effect of raising the wage. I suspect that other stories could also be told to account for unemployment while also giving some scope for this market effect. I therefore view the simple message of figure 7C.1 as still worth retaining, even though LDCs do typically have lots of unemployment.

Another variation on the theme arises, however, if we imbed the labor

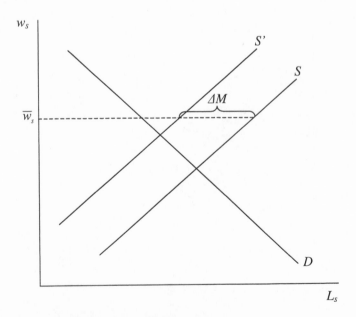

Fig. 7C.2   Brain drain with a fixed union wage

market in a HO general equilibrium. Here, with given world prices and diversification, the factor-price-equalization (FPE) theorem implies a demand for labor that is not downward sloping throughout, but rather has a flat portion as shown in figure 7C.3. The limits of this flat are the bounds of the diversification cone, signifying that as long as the country remains diversified, then the withdrawal of labor due to the brain drain will not raise the equilibrium wage.

I suspect that this was the story told by Grubel and Scott (1966), but it clearly depends on much more than just perfect competition, with labor being paid its marginal product. It depends also on the remaining labor's being reallocated across sectors so as to keep that marginal product constant in the face of the increased scarcity of skilled labor, something that is of course possible under the assumptions of the standard HO model with diversification. Unfortunately, it is also true under those assumptions that skilled labor would be earning the same wage abroad as it is at home, so that the simple economic motivation for the brain drain is lost. If instead we relax those assumptions enough to get a higher wage for skilled labor abroad than at home, perhaps by introducing an international difference in technologies, the implication of a flat portion in the labor demand curve may be lost as well. Thus again I find the simple analysis of figure 7C.1 to be worth retaining.

The Commander, Kangasniemi, and Winters paper also discusses, in some detail, a model of heterogeneous labor supply in which a brain drain

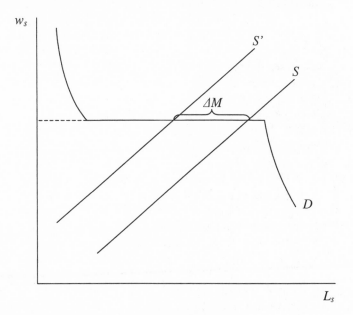

Fig. 7C.3   Brain drain with factor price equalization

may induce additional workers in the LDC to acquire skill. This then has further dynamic implications for the country that are favorable in the context of an endogenous growth model, leading to the idea of a "beneficial brain drain." In fact, one need not depart far from the picture of figure 7C.1 to get much of what that model suggests. First, the upward sloping labor supply curve in figure 7C.1 can easily represent heterogeneous workers, with more and more workers acquiring skill and thus supplying skilled labor as the wage rises. Thus the fact of heterogeneous labor does not interfere with the implication of the labor market that the departure of some skilled workers will raise the wage. Commander, Kangasniemi, and Winters do not acknowledge that effect, either because they neglect the labor market or, more likely, because they assume that wages are fixed by one of the mechanisms above. But if in fact those mechanisms are absent or do not fully prevent wages from changing, then an increase in the wage is what we should expect. This is especially true in the case the authors stress, that of a brain drain with "selection" where only the most able workers are invited abroad. In their analysis of this case, this selection removes the incentive for other workers to acquire skill. However, without those lost workers, the market for skilled labor will not clear, the skilled wage will rise, and this rise in the wage will itself motivate more workers to become skilled. So their result of zero additional skill acquisition depends again on the implicit assumption that wages are somehow constant.

If wages rise, we do get more workers acquiring skill, but the welfare effects of this have several components. These include the gains to the workers and the losses to labor demanders noted in figure 7C.1, and in addition they may include the more dynamic benefits of skill acquisition that appear in the growth model. Without the complexity of a growth model, however, we can see the possibilities by simply adding an externality to the labor market so far considered. In figure 7C.4, suppose that every unit of skilled labor generates an externality E, measured up from the origin on the vertical axis. In general this externality could be negative, reflecting instead a cost of publicly subsidizing education, but I assume it here to be a benefit. This benefit could attach, as Commander, Kangasniemi, and Winters discuss, to the presence of skilled labor within the country, in which case its total value is E times the amount of labor actually employed. Or it could attach to the total amount of labor that has been trained, in which case it also includes E times the amount of labor that has left the country down the brain drain. The additional effect of the brain drain due to the externality is therefore either for the total externality to fall from $c + d$ to c, or for it to rise form $c + d$ to $c + d + e$. A beneficial brain drain is therefore possible, but only if the externality is generated by the departing workers as well as remaining ones, and then only if this benefit exceeds the net loss of area b already identified above.

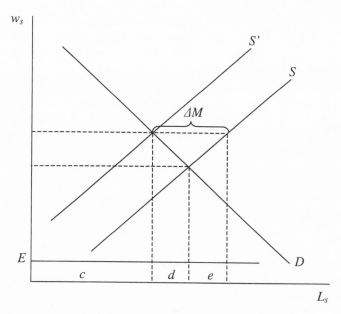

Fig. 7C.4   Brain drain with positive externality from employment

Effect on the LDC Terms of Trade

All of this ignores another effect that a brain drain might have, especially if it involves a significant amount of skilled labor moving internationally: an effect on the terms of trade. This too is an effect that would not occur under the apparent assumptions of Grubel and Scott (1966), in the traditional HO trade model with FPE. In that model, countries need not be small in order for labor migration (or any movement of factors, for that matter) to leave world prices unchanged, so long as the movement is not large enough to move any country out of the diversification cone. Instead, outputs will expand and contract à la Rybczynski in both the country of emigration and the country of immigration by equal and opposite amounts, leaving world outputs unchanged. There will therefore be no need for world prices to change, since neither supply nor demand of any good has altered.

However, as already noted, in this world of FPE there would have been no incentive for labor to move in the first place, and we certainly would not observe the substantial differentials in wages of skilled labor between developed and developing countries that the authors document. To generate such differentials, we need to assume a different model, perhaps the HO model with specialization and/or multiple cones, or perhaps a model with different technologies in the two countries. A two-cone, two-factor, common-technology model will do the job, but in a rather unsatisfactory manner since it can only provide the incentive for skilled labor to move from where it is abundant to where it is scarce—hardly the drain of brains from LDCs that we are concerned with.

A third factor could avoid this undesirable feature, but instead I will follow a very recent paper by Davis and Weinstein (2002), who note that it is not just one kind of labor, or even labor alone, that currently seems to move into the United States. Instead, there seem to be incentives for all three of the obvious factors of production—unskilled labor, skilled labor, and capital—to migrate into the United States. This is consistent, they argue, only with some sort of difference in technology that makes all three factors more productive in the United States than abroad. And they go on to argue that, when a country attracts inflows of all three factors, then one should expect its terms of trade to turn against it. Indeed, they calculate, based on rather rough-and-ready estimates of parameters, that the presence of foreign-originating factors in the United States has, through terms-of-trade deterioration, cost the United States an amount that is comparable to the gains from recent trade liberalizations.

Their argument applies in reverse to countries other than the United States, including the developing countries and the brain drain. Specifically, assuming that factors are indeed more productive in the United States than in the developing world, then the outflow of skilled labor from the latter to the former will change U.S. outputs more than it changes LDC outputs, causing a net increase in world supply of goods the United States exports. This will force down the world price of U.S. exports and, conversely, raise the world price of LDC exports. Thus, once we allow for terms-of-trade effects, we do in the end find a case for a brain drain being beneficial.

References

Bhagwati, Jagdeesh N., and Koichi Hamada. 1974. The brain drain, international integration of markets for professionals, and unemployment: A theoretical analysis. *Journal of Development Economics* 1 (1): 19–42.

Davis, Donald R., and David E. Weinstein. 2002. Technological superiority and the losses from migration. NBER Working Paper no. 8971. Cambridge, Mass.: National Bureau of Economic Research, May.

Grubel, H., and A. Scott. 1966. The international flow of human capital. *American Economic Review* 56 (1/2): 268–74.

8

The Effects of Multinational Production on Wages and Working Conditions in Developing Countries

Drusilla K. Brown, Alan V. Deardorff, and Robert M. Stern

8.1 Introduction

This paper is designed to assess the empirical evidence on the effects of multinational production on wages and working conditions in developing countries. It is motivated by the controversies that have emerged, especially in the past decade or so, concerning whether or not multinational firms in developing countries are exploiting their workers with "sweatshop" conditions—that is, paying low wages and subjecting them to coercive, abusive, unhealthy, and unsafe conditions in the workplace. Thus, in section 8.2, we address these controversies in the context of the efforts and programs of social activist groups and universities and colleges involved in the anti-sweatshop campaign in the United States and the related issues of the social accountability of multinational firms and the role of such international institutions as the International Labor Organization (ILO) and World Trade Organization (WTO) in dealing with labor standards and trade. We then turn more broadly in section 8.3 to a conceptual treatment of the effects of foreign direct investment (FDI) on wages in host countries and the effects of outsourcing and subcontracting by multinational firms. Thereafter, the empirical evidence on multinational-firm wages in developing countries is reviewed in section 8.4 together with evidence on the relationship between FDI and labor rights. Conclusions are presented in section 8.5.

Drusilla K. Brown is associate professor of economics at Tufts University. Alan V. Deardorff is the John W. Sweetland Professor of International Economics and professor of public policy at the Gerald R. Ford School of Public Policy, University of Michigan. Robert M. Stern is professor emeritus of economics and public policy at the University of Michigan.

8.2   Political Economy Issues

As mentioned, our paper has been motivated by the controversies as to whether or not multinational firms are exploiting and mistreating their workers by employing them under sweatshop conditions. What this means is exploiting the workers by paying low wages and subjecting them to violations of certain universal social norms or standards governing their employment. In this connection, Moran (2002) has stressed the importance of distinguishing low-wage, relatively unskilled-labor-intensive industries, such as apparel and footwear, from industries that employ more highly skilled workers and produce relatively more skill-intensive products, such as electronics and automotive products. Many social activists and activist organizations that are critical of multinational wages and working conditions in developing countries do not make this distinction. Rather, much of the criticism by social activists, in the United States especially, has been directed at multinational operations in the apparel and footwear industries that are allegedly producing under sweatshop conditions.[1] Accordingly, we next consider the salient anti-sweatshop issues.

8.2.1   The Anti-Sweatshop Campaign in the United States

Elliott and Freeman (2001, 15–16) note that

> Sweatshops have characterized apparel production since industrial revolution days, and so too have campaigns to improve labor conditions in the industry. . . . many of the issues are the same, but a major difference between anti-sweatshop campaigns at the turn of the 21st century and those at the turn of the 20th century is that sweatshops then were largely local whereas today they are found mostly in poor developing countries. This means that U.S.-based activists cannot lobby the U.S. government to improve labor standards. Instead they must target U.S.-based corporations who operate or source in developing countries or pressure the world trading community to demand changes in less developed countries.[2]

1. Graham (2000, 101–102) has noted that products originating in the footwear, apparel, toy-making, and sporting goods industries, combined, accounted for less than 10 percent of world merchandise exports in 1997. He then states that "if indeed sweatshop conditions are concentrated in these industries, they do not represent the greater part of globalized economic activity." It would be more meaningful, however, to consider how important the exports of these goods are for developing countries, rather than for the world as a whole. Graham's source, WTO (1999), does not report trade by level of development. But its geographic data are suggestive: WTO (2001) reports textile exports, as a percent of manufactured exports, to be only 2.3 percent for Latin America, 3.6 percent for Africa, and 6.9 percent for Asia, excluding Australia, Japan, and New Zealand.

2. Robert Baldwin has pointed out to us that the unfavorable perception of FDI and industrialization, in general, may be related historically to the change from a household to a factory system of production. Thus, one does not usually think of a family engaged in household production as working under sweatshop conditions. It is mainly when workers are assembled to produce in factories that it is believed that they may be subjected to sweatshop conditions, even though their wages may be higher and children may have more access to education and better medical care.

Elliott and Freeman (2001, 48–49 and appendix exhibit A) provide a timeline of U.S. anti-sweatshop activities from 1990 to spring 2000[3] and a list of transnational labor-rights activist organizations. As they note, during this period, multinationals such as Levi Strauss, Gap, Phillips-VanHeusen, and others were singled out for condoning undesirable labor practices. And Wal-Mart, a major retailer, was cited as selling clothing made by child labor in Bangladesh and Honduras (Elliott and Freeman 2001, 16–17). Many of the firms involved in producing or sourcing abroad have responded to the criticisms by adopting codes of conduct that are designed presumably to guide their operations.[4] In 1996, the Clinton Administration established the Apparel Industry Partnership (AIP) to address sweatshop issues globally by bringing together apparel firms, unions, and nongovernment organizations (NGOs) by means of a code of conduct and a monitoring system that were introduced in April 1997 and that would be applicable to the firms involved. Subsequently, in November 1998, the AIP established the Fair Labor Association (FLA) to implement and monitor the code. Some groups, in particular the Union of Needletrades, Industrial, and Textile Employees (UNITE), were critical of the AIP/FLA program, complaining as Elliott and Freeman (2001, 17) note that "the code failed to require payment of a living wage; had weak language with respect to union rights in nondemocratic countries; and had a weak monitoring and verification system." Nonetheless, by fall 2000, 140 colleges and universities had become affiliated with the FLA, and, as of the end of 2001, the number had grown to 192.[5]

It was during this period that student activism on sweatshops took hold at a number of American campuses. A group called Students Against Sweatshops was established at Duke University in August 1997. With assistance from UNITE, the United Students Against Sweatshops (USAS) was established on a national basis in summer 1998. In expressing their dissatisfaction with the FLA, the student members of the USAS orchestrated sit-ins during 1999 at a number of prominent universities and colleges. On October 19, 1999, the USAS announced the creation of the Worker Rights Consortium (WRC) and urged institutions to withdraw from the FLA and join the WRC, which purportedly had a stronger code of conduct, a focus on worker complaints and worker-rights education, and a requirement for disclosure of the name and location of factories producing licensed apparel. As of June 2000, fifty institutions had become affiliated with the WRC. The number had grown to ninety-two as of December 13, 2001, and forty-nine of these institutions continued to remain affiliated with the FLA.[6]

---

3. See also Varley (1998, 12–13).
4. We have more to say on this matter in the following discussion.
5. The list of colleges and universities affiliated with the FLA can be found at http://www.fairlabor.org/htm/affiliates/university.html.
6. The list of institutions affiliated with the WRC can be found at http://www.workersrights.org/as.asp.

Elliott and Freeman (2001, 18) note that a number of additional organizations were created that formulated codes of conduct and mechanisms for monitoring adherence to the codes. These organizations include such U.S. groups as Social Accountability International, which administers its SA8000 code on a global and multi-industry basis; the Collegiate Licensing Company (CLC); the Worldwide Responsible Apparel Production (WRAP); and Verité, which monitors human rights especially. There is also the European-based Ethical Trade Initiative, and there are NGOs based in developing countries. There are a number of private monitoring groups, including Price WaterhouseCoopers (PWC) and Ernst and Young. In addition, many American academic institutions have established codes of conduct,[7] although they depend for the most part on the monitoring to be carried out by the FLA or WRC.[8] It is of interest therefore to compare the main features of the FLA and WRC.

8.2.2   Comparison of the Fair Labor Association (FLA) and Worker Rights Consortium (WRC)

As noted above, the FLA was established in 1998 as an outgrowth of the AIP sponsored by the Clinton Administration. Its focus is on improving working conditions in the global apparel industry.[9] In considering the relative merits of membership in the FLA and WRC, the University of Michigan Advisory Committee on Labor Standards and Human Rights (2000, 30–33) noted, for example, the following positive features of the FLA: (a) The FLA membership includes most of the largest apparel producers, is well funded, may be cost effective in avoiding the proliferation of codes of conduct and monitoring, and may provide economies of scale in coordinating its membership and carrying out monitoring; and (b) The FLA focuses on the apparel industry as a whole, and its charter gives universities the option to pursue more flexible strategies if so desired. Some of the concerns expressed about the FLA were that it might be dominated by corporate interests that would favor a weak code of conduct on such issues as health and safety, women's rights, compensation, and hours and overtime, and that it would be reluctant to provide public disclosure of factory locations.

With regard to the WRC, the Michigan Advisory Committee Report (2000, 29–31) cited the following attractive features:[10] (a) emphasis on disclosure, transparency, and public information on conditions in apparel fac-

---

7. See, for example, the University of Michigan code of conduct in University of Michigan Advisory Committee on Labor Standards and Human Rights (2000, 7–8).

8. It is noteworthy that the University of Chicago decided against joining either organization. According to the *University of Chicago Magazine* (2000), they opted to rely on Barnes & Noble, which operates the university bookstore locations, to require that all merchandise sold complies with FLA standards.

9. The code of conduct of the FLA can be found at http://www.fairlabor.org.

10. The code of conduct of the WRC can be found at http://www.workersrights.org.

tories; (b) emphasis on the investigation of complaints as a means of focusing attention on factories where problems are reported rather than relying on monitoring per se; (c) commitment to involve workers and their representatives in the development and implementation of WRC policies; (d) insistence on including a living-wage standard in the WRC code of conduct to focus the attention of universities and licensees on wage issues; (e) concentration on university-licensed apparel rather than on the entire apparel industry as a means of enhancing the leverage of universities; and (f) independence from the FLA and other groups as a means of providing a check on the quality and reliability of other monitoring efforts. Some concerns expressed about the WRC were: (a) its adversarial approach towards licensees, with the consequence that licensees may view the WRC with suspicion, make them hesitant in self-reporting their activities, undermine the credibility and legitimacy of the WRC investigation of reported complaints, and disrupt university-business relationships with licensee partners; (b) the WRC objective of educating workers and encouraging them to act on their own rights may compromise the impartial and independent investigation of worker complaints; (c) there may be an overreliance on complaint investigation insofar as it presumes that workers are aware of their rights and willing to take risks in filing complaints; and (d) that the independence and credibility of the WRC may be compromised because of the presence on its governing board of UNITE or other U.S. unions with a documented history of trade protectionism and discouragement of apparel-job creation in developing countries.[11]

From the perspective of many American colleges and universities, it should be evident from the foregoing discussion that there are some important differences between the FLA and WRC in terms of their objectives and mode of operation. Two issues that stand out are deserving of further comment: the living wage and the conditions of work, including the right of association and collective bargaining.

8.2.3 The Living Wage

The FLA code (available at http://www.fairlabor.org) defining wages and benefits is

Wages and Benefits. Employers recognize that wages are essential to meeting employees' basic needs. Employers shall pay employees, as a floor, at least the minimum wage required by local law or the prevailing

11. In this regard, it is of interest to note the statement in the *University of Chicago Magazine* (2000): "It is the WRC's apparent intention to move beyond a monitoring function to an advocacy role—supporting particular social, political, and environmental positions—that troubles the University administration and faculty. . . . As . . . outlined by the faculty in the 1967 Kalven Committee Report on the University's Role in Political and Social Action: 'A university . . . is a community but only for the limited, albeit great, purposes of teaching and research. It is not a club, it is not a trade association, it is not a lobby.'"

industry wage, whichever is higher, and shall provide legally mandated benefits.

The WRC code (available at http://www.workersrights.org) relating to wages and benefits is

1. Wages and Benefits: Licensees recognize that wages are essential to meeting employees' basic needs. Licensees shall pay employees, as a floor, wages and benefits which comply with all applicable laws and regulations, and which provide for essential needs and establish a dignified living wage for workers and their families. [A living wage is a "take home" or "net" wage, earned during a country's legal maximum work week, but not more than 48 hours. A living wage provides the basic needs (housing, energy, nutrition, clothing, health care, education, potable water, childcare, transportation and savings) of an average family unit of employees in the garment manufacturing employment sector of the country.]

It is evident that the WRC concept of what constitutes a living wage is much more explicit than the FLA basic-needs criterion of the payment of the minimum wage or prevailing industry wage, whichever is higher. As noted by Elliott and Freeman (2001, 50), the WRC is apparently willing to postpone the implementation of its living-wage standard pending the completion of further research. This is essentially similar to the position of the FLA, which called for a wage study that was carried out by the U.S. Department of Labor (2000) and a request for a follow-up on this study with possible annual updates.[12] In any event, the question at issue is how to define and measure what constitutes a living wage or basic needs and how this relates to the wages that workers are actually receiving.

The information on wages that we will present in section 8.4 suggests that there is pervasive evidence that workers employed in multinational firms and subcontracting in developing countries are being paid wages that are on average higher than compared to alternative domestic employment. Of course, these wages are low in absolute terms in comparison with wages of workers in developed countries. Granting this, many observers have argued that workers' wages in developing countries may not be sufficient to satisfy basic needs—hence, the pressure for higher wages.

In this connection, for example, a group of students from the Columbia University School of International and Public Affairs carried out a study in 1999 for the National Labor Committee to calculate a living wage for maquila workers in El Salvador (see Connor et al. 1999). They found that most maquila workers earned the legal monthly minimum wage of 1,260 colones, which was estimated to be barely sufficient to meet basic food requirements. According to the formula used, it was estimated that maquila

12. See http://www.fairlabor.org/html/faqs.html.

workers in El Salvador required a living wage of 4,556 colones to cover the basic needs of a family of 4.3 people living on one wage and allowing for 12.5 percent to be saved for the future. It was recommended that the process for setting wages according to a living-wage formula be standardized and that multinational firms should adopt industry-wide standards for paying a living wage.

Moran (2002, chap. 4, 10–12) has pointed out the extraordinary complexities involved in calculating a living wage.

1) There is a need to determine the nutritional standards, types of housing, expenditure categories, savings, and provisions for contingencies to be included in the living-wage formula and to make allowance for intercountry differences in purchasing power parity and macroeconomic conditions.

2) Estimates of family size as a basis for wage adequacy may be arbitrary and discriminatory since average family size may vary, and there may be differences among wage earners depending on their age, gender, and family relationships.

Using South Asia as an example, Srinivasan (2001) also questions the relevance of attempting to calculate and administer a living wage. He notes the following.

1) In South Asia, over half of the labor force is self-employed and the proportion of regularly employed wage-paid workers is small;

2) Workers employed by multinationals are generally well paid, unionized, have legal protection of their rights, and receive mandated benefits, so that payment of a living wage to these workers may be redundant;

3) Focusing on paying a living wage to workers employed by multinationals diverts attention from the far more serious and relevant problem of poverty and from the need to promote rapid economic growth to help eradicate poverty; and

4) The goal of the living-wage proponents would be better served if they would lobby to eliminate barriers in developed countries on imports of labor-intensive manufactures and on other trade barriers more generally, and to relax immigration restrictions on unskilled workers. By the same token, efforts should be made in developing countries themselves to eliminate bureaucratic corruption, remove barriers to trade, and dismantle domestic policies that are inimical to the poor.

While living-wage proponents may grant many of the foregoing objections, they commonly argue nonetheless that multinationals can well afford to pay higher wages to workers in developing countries because those wages are typically but a tiny fraction of the selling price of the product. In this connection, some examples noted in Moran (2002, chap. 4, 15–16) are of interest: In 2000, the piece rate plus benefits of jeans produced in Nicaragua was $0.66 compared to the U.S. retail sales price of $21.99; in

2000, the unit labor cost, inclusive of benefits, for a ladies' jacket made in Hong Kong was $0.84 compared to the U.S. retail price of $99; in 2001, the unit wage was $0.40 for a sport shoe produced in Indonesia that sold for $100 in the United States; and, in 2001, Nike reported that the labor cost of Nike shoes was $2.43 compared to a retail price of $65.

What are we to make of these comparisons? One can argue that the comparisons are inappropriate because they do not take into account the costs of further processing, transportation, advertising, and distribution. There is also a presumption that the multinational firms may be capturing oligopoly rents because of brand preferences, private labels, and name recognition that they have established. While it is conceivable that some of the largest multinationals may be capturing oligopoly rents, it is unclear how pervasive this is, especially for firms competing at the retail level. But suppose for the sake of argument that some multinationals are mandated or may opt to divert some of their profits to pay higher wages to their workers in developing countries. It is by no means clear exactly how this would be done and what would prevent the companies from shifting their operations to locations with already higher wages and higher productivity.

The difficulty of paying higher wages would be even more pronounced if subcontracting firms were obliged to do so. Thus, as Moran notes (2002, 16) in the examples cited above, the local wage-bill range is 20 percent of the pretax profit for the firm producing footwear in Indonesia, 46 percent for the jeans production in Nicaragua, and 250 percent for the Nike shoes. Since subcontracting firms are generally independently owned, mandating higher wages for them in these circumstances would almost surely motivate them to search out less-costly production locations.

The view that mandating higher wages for workers in developing countries can be accomplished with minimum disruption to employment within and between countries has been colored by the research of Card and Krueger (1995) which finds that increases in the minimum wage in the United States in the early 1990s did not reduce teenage employment. In our judgment, contrary to Card and Krueger, there is reason to believe that labor-intensive manufacturing in developing countries is relatively sensitive to changes in wage levels. This is particularly true for the production of apparel and footwear, which are prototype "footloose" industries. This is borne out, for example, by the experiences of Japan and the Asian Tigers—Hong Kong, Singapore, South Korea, and Taiwan—insofar as increased labor costs in these countries in the course of their economic expansion from the 1960s onward resulted in a shift of the location of labor-intensive industries to China and Southeast Asia and to some extent to South Asia. Also worth mentioning are the experiences of Mauritius and Madagascar, noted by Moran (2002, chap. 4, 9), that suggest that labor-intensive producers were sensitive to changes in relative wage levels in deciding where to expand or contract employment and change the location of production.[13] More recently, there have been news reports about maquiladora factories closing down in Mexico and moving to Asia or Eastern Europe and about garment and shoe-manufacturing orders being lost in Indonesia to competitors in China and Vietnam, where wages are lower and quality and delivery schedules more reliable.[14]

A common response to this argument—that mandating a living wage will cause employers to change locations—is to say that the living wage should be mandated in all countries, not just a few, so that there is no place for employers to go, but this misses the point. Wages vary across countries due to differences in labor productivity, which typically rises with the level of development. However the living wage may be defined, it will be above the productivity-based market wages in some countries and below that in others. If employers are required to pay the living wage, they will tend to move to countries where the living wage is justified by productivity.[15]

We conclude therefore that efforts to define and measure the living wage are fraught with insuperable difficulties,[16] and that it is likely that the imposition of a living wage that exceeds existing market-determined wage levels will result in employment shifts in developing countries that would be detrimental to economic efficiency and welfare.[17]

13. See also Helene Cooper's article "Fruit of the Loom: Can African Nations Use Duty-Free Deal to Revamp Economy?" (*Wall Street Journal,* January 2, 2001) for a journalistic account of the experiences of the two countries.

14. See the articles of Ginger Thompson (*New York Times,* June 29, 2002) and Timothy Mapes (*Wall Street Journal,* August 14, 2002).

15. In an econometric study of the effects of labor costs on foreign direct investment (FDI), while controlling for labor productivity, Kucera (2001, 28) has noted that "coefficients of the wage share [of value added] variable are more and significantly negative for LDCs" and that "a 10 percent increase in wage share would be associated with a 6.6 to 8.5 percent decline in FDI inflows in LDCs, compared with a 4.3 to 5.8 percent decline for all countries."

16. The most comprehensive effort to define and measure the living wage is to be found in U.S. Department of Labor (2000, vi): their conclusion is that "for the countries considered, there appears to be little conclusive evidence on the extent to which wages and non-wage benefits in the footwear and apparel [industries] meet workers' basic needs."

17. Neumark (2002) has studied the effects of living-wage ordinances that have been adopted in many cities across the United States. These ordinances typically mandate a minimum-wage floor that is often considerably higher than the traditional minimum wages set by state and federal legislation. Among the most significant findings are the following: (a) Living wage ordinances have sizable positive effects on the wages of low-wage workers; (b) employment is reduced among the affected workers; (c) a detectable number of families may be lifted above the poverty line, even allowing for employment reductions; and (d) unionized municipal workers especially may gain from narrow living-wage laws covering city contractors. Thus, while there is some evidence that living wages may provide some assistance to the working poor, Neumark notes that such ordinances may not be the best policy for helping the urban poor and that a range of other issues needs to be addressed, including budget implications, the incidence of the measures, effects on taxes and local development, the provision of city services, productivity, compliance and enforcement, and equity and overall economic welfare. See also the variety of comments on Harvard's living-wage debate in *Harvard Magazine* (2001).

8.2.4   The Right of Association and Collective Bargaining

The pertinent FLA code (available at http://www.fairlabor.org) is

Freedom of Association and Collective Bargaining. Employers shall recognize and respect the right of employees to freedom of association and collective bargaining.

The pertinent WRC code (available at http://www.workersrights.org) is

9. *Freedom of Association and Collective Bargaining:* Licensees shall recognize and respect the right of employees to freedom of association and collective bargaining. No employee shall be subject to harassment, intimidation or retaliation in their efforts to freely associate or bargain collectively. Licensees shall not cooperate with governmental agencies and other organizations that use the power of the State to prevent workers from organizing a union of their choice. Licensees shall allow union organizers free access to employees. Licensees shall recognize the union of the employees' choice.

The right of association and collective bargaining is arguably the most contentious of issues in countries with low-wage labor and specialization in labor-intensive industries like apparel and footwear. As Moran (2002, chap. 3, 14) finds, the problems include (a) the representation of workers and anti-union discrimination; (b) the right to strike; and (c) the threat to close plants that form unions.

Many employers have initiated worker-management associations designed to foster good relations with employees, and, according to Moran (2002, chap. 3, 15), there is evidence for examples of relatively high wages and good treatment of workers in the Philippines, the Dominican Republic, and Costa Rica. By the same token, there have been allegations and evidence offered of cases of discrimination against workers seeking to organize unions in a number of countries.[18] This has been a problem especially when there already exists a government-sponsored or government-favored union or when unions are prohibited by the government. Moreover, workers have been dismissed in some cases for participating in strikes, and replacement workers have been hired. Furthermore, the threat to close plants that form unions has been alleged to occur at times.

There are divergent views on the issues of the right of association and collective bargaining. Thus, it can be argued that encouragement of unions and collective bargaining may enhance the efficiency of labor markets and increase the productivity of workers, especially when there are monop-

---

18. A recent example is a strike by about 800 workers making collegiate apparel for Nike in the Korean-owned factory, Kukdong International Mexico, located in Atlixco, Mexico, after some of their fellow workers had been fired in connection with their involvement in labor-rights disputes. For more information, see Verité (2001).

sonistic employers.[19] There may also be significant political and social spillover effects as democratic institutions and social harmony are strengthened. Furthermore, it may be the case that governments are weak and that there is nobody to protect the workers but the workers themselves. On the other hand, as noted in the previous discussion of the living wage, it may be the case in many low-income countries that labor unions are already concentrated in the formal manufacturing sector, and there may be substantial numbers of workers employed in public enterprises. As a consequence, the fostering of unions could be harmful to workers and families in the informal sectors and in the rural or agricultural sectors who would have to absorb the workers displaced from these organized sectors. This is where much of the labor force is self-employed, often doing "home work" on a piece-rate basis, and the numbers of regularly employed wage-paid workers may be limited.[20]

The point just made should not be construed as condoning the suppression of unions and worker rights. Rather, the issue is whether or not the right of association and collective bargaining should be considered to be the prime objective, as emphasized by the WRC, to enhance the welfare of workers in low-income countries. That is, account needs to be taken of the wages and benefits that workers are actually receiving together with the treatment that they are being accorded in the workplace. Thus, as Moran (2002) in particular has stressed, there is considerable evidence suggesting that market forces combined with judicious government policies can provide the basis for enhancing worker welfare in poor countries. There may well be cases in which workers are mistreated in terms of not receiving their rightful wages or are subjected to poor working conditions.[21] In these instances, corrective measures should be taken by government in conformity with domestic law.

8.2.5   The Academic Consortium on International Trade (ACIT) and Scholars Against Sweatshop Labor (SASL) Initiatives

We have had occasion in the preceding discussion to review the issues that are pertinent to the anti-sweatshop campaign, which focused attention on the wages and working conditions in multinational firm operations in the apparel and footwear industries in low-income countries. Much of this campaign is being played out in the efforts of organizations like the

---

19. See, for example, Freeman (1993).

20. In this connection, Srinivasan (1998, 239) has remarked that "where the freedom to form unions has been exercised to a considerable extent, namely in the organized manufacturing and public sectors in poor countries, labor unions have been seen promoting the interests of a small section of the labor force at the expense of many. . . . it should be recognized . . . that unionized labor often constitutes a small labor aristocracy in poor countries."

21. For documentation, see, for example, Business for Social Responsibility (BSR) Education Fund, Investor Responsibility Research Center (2000) and Verité (2000).

WRC and the FLA to provide codes of conduct and monitoring of firms engaged in the production and marketing of apparel and related items bearing university and college logos.

As mentioned above, the strategy of the WRC and associated student groups has been one of confrontation with university and college administrations in the form of protests and sit-ins that were resolved in most cases by agreeing to membership in the WRC. At the same time, the FLA has been active in its efforts to engage and induce universities and colleges to become FLA members. As noted above, the FLA had 192 members at the end of 2001. The WRC had 92 members, and 49 of them were also members of the FLA.

Following the failure of the WTO Ministerial Meeting in Seattle in December 1999, Jagdish Bhagwati of Columbia University and Robert M. Stern of the University of Michigan convened a group of academic international-trade economists and lawyers that met in January 2000 at the Georgetown University Law Center. The objective of the meeting was an effort to review what had happened in Seattle and the role that academic trade specialists might play in bringing their expertise to bear on the important issues of trade policy and engaging the attention of policy makers and the public. After the Georgetown meeting, it was decided to establish the ACIT with the foregoing objectives in mind. An ACIT Steering Committee was established and comprised of Robert E. Baldwin, University of Wisconsin; Jagdish Bhagwati, Columbia University; Alan V. Deardorff, University of Michigan; Arvind Panagariya, University of Maryland; T. N. Srinivasan, Yale University; and Robert M. Stern, University of Michigan, as Head of the Steering Committee. An ACIT website (http://www.Fordschool.umich/edu/rsie/acit) was created as a repository for academic papers, reports, policy statements, and news articles dealing with trade policy and related issues.

One of the most contentious issues at the Seattle Ministerial Meeting was that of trade and labor standards. This is a topic that most of the members of the ACIT Steering Committee had addressed individually and jointly in their published theoretical and policy-oriented writings. These writings explored the analytical complexities, political economy, empirical evidence, and the policies of national governments and international organizations involving trade and labor standards. The ACIT group concluded that much of the social activism in the United States regarding labor standards was motivated by protectionist considerations, especially on the part of organized labor. The interests of low-income developing countries were seen therefore to be especially at risk, particularly if efforts were made to mandate higher labor standards, including higher wages, by means of trade sanctions or other pressures on low-income countries.

It was with these concerns in mind that the ACIT Steering Committee decided to address the decisions taken by university and college administrators to design codes of conduct on their own, to become affiliated especially with the WRC to deal with issues of sweatshop labor, or both. The ACIT Steering Committee prepared a letter that was sent in September 2000 to around 600 university and college presidents, stating that the actions taken or to be taken on sweatshop issues at many institutions were possibly not well informed and therefore were ill advised. This letter is available on the ACIT website and in Broad (2002, 222–23). It was first circulated to academic trade specialists and other members of the academic community, and 352 (primarily) economists and other academics indicated that they wished to be signatories of the letter. The list of signatories is available on the ACIT website.

It is noteworthy that only a small number of university presidents or administrators acknowledged receipt of the letter. These included Columbia; Duke; the University of California, Berkeley; Harvard; and some smaller institutions. But what is perhaps more significant is that the ACIT letter received considerable press and media coverage, much of which can be found on the ACIT website.

It stands to reason that some members of the academic community would take issue with the position expressed in the ACIT letter. Thus, a group calling itself Scholars Against Sweatshop Labor (SASL) was formed, and they prepared a letter that was endorsed by 434 signatories (73 percent economists) and thereafter sent in October 2001 to more than 1,600 university and college presidents. The SASL letter is reproduced on the SASL website (http://www.umass.edu/per/sasl/) and in Broad (2002, 224–27). The list of signatories is also included on the SASL website. There are several points in the SASL letter that are worthy of comment.

- Are colleges and universities making decisions about codes of conduct without adequate consultation? The SASL assertion is that "colleges and universities that have adopted codes of conduct have generally done so after careful consultation with appropriate faculty and/or outsider experts." Our Evaluation is as follows: The SASL ignores the fact that the adoption of a code of conduct at many institutions was in response to campus sit-ins and protests and that there was not a broad representation of alternative views, faculty expertise, and campus-wide student involvement.
- Regarding worldwide consultation and monitoring the SASL assertion is that the three organizations (WRC, FLA, and Social Accountability International) bring different strengths to the task of establishing and monitoring effective labor standards worldwide. Ongoing cooperation and competition between these groups should also raise the general performance standard for all three." Our evaluation is that, as we have noted in our earlier discussion, the primary focus of the WRC on workers rights, collective bargaining, a living wage, the influ-

ence of protectionist labor unions, and the adversarial approach to the business community may serve to limit the effectiveness of the WRC.
- Regarding wages, labor costs, and employment opportunities in the global garment industry, the SASL asserts that "while caution is clearly needed in setting minimum decent standards for workplace conditions, workers rights, and wage levels, there is still no reason to assume that a country or region that sets reasonable standards must experience job losses." Our Evaluation follows: The fact remains that workers in low-income developing countries are generally being paid wages that are higher than in alternative employment. Mandatory increased wages and more-stringent labor standards may improve the position of some workers in the affected industries, but it is almost certain to disadvantage other workers not covered by the mandated changes and may induce firms to seek out lower cost production locations.

In our judgment, many of the points raised in the ACIT letter remain valid and have apparently been accepted in the SASL statement. We remain critical, however, of the SASL statement on the grounds that it (a) glosses over the ways in which the anti-sweatshop campaign led by student activists has intimidated the administrations of many academic institutions; (b) apparently accepts the objectives and operation of the WRC; and (c) downplays the possibly detrimental effects of labor-market interventions in low-income countries. The question remains then as to what the most effective ways may be to address the issues of multinational wages and working conditions in developing countries. One way we will now consider is the provision of voluntary codes of conduct designed to promote the social accountability of multinationals.

8.2.6   Social Accountability of Multinational Firms

Having just reviewed the issues involved in the anti-sweatshop campaign and the efforts of activist organizations and academic institutions in the United States to address these issues, we now focus on the options that multinational firms may choose to pursue on matters of social accountability. In this connection, it might be argued, with externalities aside, that in a competitive environment, all that matters to a firm is profit maximization and, to society, the resultant optimal allocation of resources and increased consumer welfare. In this context, competitive firms need not concern themselves with their social accountability, although questions might arise about the distribution of income. But when there are market failures, including the possible exercise of market power by imperfectly competitive firms, there will be grounds for intervention at the firm or industry level that is designed to achieve the social optimum.

Market failures aside, it appears to us that the thrust of the anti-sweatshop campaign and other anti-globalization activities represents an effort primarily to alter the distribution of income between rich and poor countries. Under the circumstances, if there is a desire to reduce international income and related inequalities, the optimal policy is to provide direct income transfers and technical assistance from the rich to the poor countries. Furthermore, maintaining and extending open markets for the imports from developing countries will be similarly beneficial. It will be suboptimal therefore, in terms of resource misallocation, if multinational firms are mandated or pressured by interest groups to effect income transfers in the guise of higher wages to workers in developing countries. More seriously, there is the real possibility that such measures will transfer income not from rich countries to poor countries, but only from workers in poor countries to workers in rich countries.

If the preceding reasoning is accepted, it might be argued that the anti-sweatshop campaign aimed at multinationals is misdirected.[22] The evidence to be presented in section 8.4 generally bears this out. Nonetheless, multinational firms have come under increased scrutiny by activist organizations for their alleged violations of social norms especially in low-wage, labor-intensive industries. It is essential therefore for multinational firms to devise modes of response to allegations of the mistreatment of workers so as to ward off consumer reactions that may be detrimental to their sales and profitability. This is especially the case for firms whose image in the eyes of consumers is derived from a recognized brand name or private label.

As already mentioned, it has become commonplace especially for large multinationals to devise codes of conduct. Thus, as noted in Moran (2002, chap. 5, 5), the Organization for Economic Cooperation and Development (OECD) had 246 corporate codes in its inventory in the year 2000 covering a variety of industries.[23] This included (Moran 2002, chap. 5, 7) thirty-seven firms in the textile and apparel industry, twenty-five of which were U.S. firms, but what should be noted is that a written code of conduct in itself may not be sufficient. What is needed to complement such codes is a monitoring or certification system that is designed to assure code compliance. This is of course what the FLA is intended to do for the apparel industry, and what both it and the WRC intended for university and college suppliers. As we have noted earlier, there are several additional NGOs that have been established to carry out monitoring and certification, and there are a number of private monitoring groups as well.

Moran (2002, chap. 5, 9) notes that the "movement toward meeting the

22. This has led Graham (2000) to entitle his book *Fighting the Wrong Enemy: Antiglobal Activists and Multinational Enterprises.*
23. See also Varley (1998, 505–94) for the texts of a subset of 46 (out of a total of 121) codes of conduct collected for a variety of multinational firms. The Investor Responsibility Research Center (IRRC) has posted profiles of these 46 firms and 8 others on its website (http://www.irrc.org). We should mention as well UN Secretary General Kofi Annan's Global Compact, which has been signed onto and endorsed by many multinational firms and a number of labor unions and NGOs.

prerequisites for credibility and legitimacy [in monitoring and certifica-tion] has not been smooth." Some of the issues that have proven trouble-some include circumscribing the availability of information on plant loca-tions on confidentiality grounds; the use of business and auditing firms to conduct inspections; public disclosure of alleged code violations and efforts at remediation; and comprehensiveness of scheduling of monitor-ing and follow up.[24] It is no doubt too much to expect that a system of mon-itoring and compliance will be perfect. Nonetheless, as Moran (2002, chap. 5, 12) has concluded, "there has . . . been considerable movement, albeit contentious movement, toward meeting the conditions needed to create a credible 'voluntary' system for certifying plants that comply with good worker standards and identifying plants that do not."

If this judgment is correct, it suggests that many multinational firms have found it in their interests to devote resources as a kind of insurance against the possibility of unfavorable publicity regarding their operations that could prove damaging to them in the eyes of consumers and thereby reduce their sales and profitability.[25] By the same token and apart from the issues of code monitoring and compliance, it should be recognized, as Moran (2002) has stressed in his study *Beyond Sweatshops,* that the im-provement of wages and working conditions is an ongoing process as economies evolve, which brings about endogenous changes in the structure and composition of output and conditions of employment, including a movement towards more technologically advanced industries. For this to happen, as already mentioned, it is necessary for governments to adopt do-mestic policies that will enhance economic efficiency and welfare and thereby provide the basis for improvements in workers' skills and the con-ditions of work.

8.2.7 The Role of the International Labor Organization (ILO) and the World Trade Organization (WTO)

We have focused thus far on the efforts and issues involving the design of codes of conduct, monitoring, and compliance applicable to multina-

---

24. See Varley (1998, especially chapters 11 and 12) for discussions entitled "Corporations Grapple with Codes of Conduct" and "The Compliance Conundrum."

25. Bhagwati (2001) makes the case more strongly in arguing that "the truly, indeed the only, compelling reason for corporations to assume social responsibility is that it is the right thing to do. For, in so doing, they will *accelerate* the social good that their economic activities promote, and for which there is now much evidence." Ruggie (2002), who served as an advi-sor to UN Secretary General Kofi Annan in helping to develop the Global Compact, notes that the Global Compact is based on a learning approach to induce corporate change rather than a regulatory arrangement involving a legally binding code of conduct with explicit per-formance criteria and independent monitoring of company compliance. Ruggie notes further that the Global Compact comprises a network form of organization that comprises the UN, business, labor, and civil-society organizations. The hope is that the Global Compact will as-sist companies in internalizing the relevant principles of social policy embodied in the Global Compact and thereby induce the companies to shape their business practices accordingly. Whether or not this objective can be attained, Ruggie concludes, will depend on the viability of the interorganizational networks being developed.

tional-firm operations in these countries. These various issues have also been addressed at the multilateral level, and there has been a continuing debate on both whether or not and how to deal with trade and labor standards in the ILO and WTO.

The crux of the argument is that the ILO is an international organization that was established around eighty years ago for the purpose of improving labor conditions in its member countries. The ILO mandate is carried out by specifying conventions covering a variety of labor issues and conditions of work to which member countries agree to adhere. These conventions include the so-called core labor standards, which cover forced labor, freedom of association, the right of collective bargaining, equal pay for men and women, discrimination in the workplace, the minimum age of employment, and ban on the most egregious types of child labor. These core and other labor standards have been incorporated in various forms into most of the codes of conduct of NGOs, colleges and universities, and multinational firms. The modus operandi of the ILO is to monitor member-country compliance with the various conventions, call attention to departures from the conventions, and provide technical and financial assistance for developing countries to help them upgrade their labor standards. The ILO thus functions as a clearinghouse to provide information on labor issues and as a facilitator to improve labor conditions. It carries out its mandate without either the use or threat of sanctions against noncomplying member countries.

The WTO is an international organization whose main purpose is to design and implement rules governing the conduct of international trade among its member countries. In contrast to the ILO, the WTO does have sanctioning authority that permits member countries to impose trade restrictions in cases in which trading partners are found via the WTO dispute-settlement process to be in violation of particular WTO rules. The trade sanctions can remain in place until such time as the violation is corrected by a change in policy. As tariffs have been increasingly reduced in periodic multilateral trade negotiations, there have been efforts to probe more deeply into the domestic nontariff regulatory policies of member countries that may impede trade. It is in this context that proposals have been made to link labor standards and trade on the grounds that countries with allegedly low labor standards may have an unfair advantage in their trade that is detrimental to their trading partners. In Brown, Deardorff, and Stern (forthcoming), we have explored the pros and cons of linking trade and labor standards in the WTO. In the final analysis, such linkage may be subject to capture by protectionist interests in the developed countries and be detrimental therefore to the trade and welfare of developing countries. This would be avoided by allowing labor standards to continue to be the responsibility of the ILO.

This concern about protectionist influence relates as well to the anti-sweatshop campaign discussed earlier, especially in view of the support that UNITE and other organizations with a protectionist orientation have provided to activist organizations such as the WRC. Of course, there are many activist organizations that are motivated by concerns over human rights and international inequalities in the distribution of income. In our view, while these concerns are commendable, they are for the most part misdirected against the operations of multinational firms. There is a real danger therefore that well-intentioned efforts to raise the wages and working conditions of workers in developing countries may work to the detriment of these workers and their families.

8.3 Conceptual Considerations

The preceding discussion was designed to focus on sweatshop and related issues as specific examples of interest to many concerned about the impact of multinational firms on wages and working conditions in developing countries. With this in mind, we now turn our attention more broadly to a review of what economic theory has to say about the effects of FDI and multinational firms on wages and working conditions in host countries. We begin with a brief discussion of the motivations for FDI and multinational-firm activity. One lesson shown is that multinationals exist for a variety of reasons and perform a variety of functions, and so we cannot identify them with any single activity whose effects we should explore. Rather, we need to consider them in several roles, each of which may have different implications for wages and working conditions.

We look broadly at four such roles. The first is as a conveyer of additional capital to the host country, either as an addition of the world's capital stock or in place of capital that would otherwise be in the source country. For this purpose, we address the question in the context of the general-equilibrium models with perfect competition that are familiar in international-trade theory. Second, we consider the possibility that FDI carries with it, instead of or in addition to capital, technologies that may be superior to those previously available and that may also spill over to domestic workers, firms, or both in the host country. Again, FDI as a source of improved technology can be analyzed in the context of perfectly competitive general-equilibrium trade models. Third, we acknowledge that, even with unchanged capital and technology, multinational production may involve different sets of production activities than simpler national firms, and we look at how the choice of activities may matter for labor markets. This may happen, for example, within multinationals that use their parent-firm location to provide headquarters support for activities in subsidiaries abroad, or more generally it may involve production processes that are fragmented across countries, perhaps even done in different unaffiliated firms through subcontracting. Fourth and finally, we note that, because of their size, multinationals may have the power to set prices, wages, or both to a degree that perfectly competitive firms could not. We examine several ways that their price-setting behavior could matter for wages, including monopsony pricing of labor, efficiency wages, and rent sharing.

Throughout this section, for convenience, we focus only on wages, rather than explicitly considering the full package of wages, other compensation, and the hours and working conditions that firms ask of and provide to their workers. In practice, of course, all of these are determined together, either in the competitive interactions of firms and workers, or in negotiation between them. In general, therefore, when we say that an event such as FDI raises or lowers wages, one should think here of the whole package of wages and working conditions as improving or worsening to an extent that is determined by these interactions.[26]

8.3.1   Motivations for Foreign Direct Investment

Foreign direct investment consists of the acquisition of physical capital in a host country, usually in the form of a production facility or a retail establishment owned at least in part by a parent firm in the home, or source, country.[27] When done among developed countries, FDI often takes the form of acquisition of an existing facility, but most FDI into developing countries is "greenfield" investment—that is, newly constructed establishments—which therefore add to the physical capital of the host country.[28] Strictly speaking, such capital need not be financed from the home country, and it therefore need not in any sense be a movement of capital from the home country to the host country, although in practice it is often interpreted that way. However, for our purpose, of examining the effects of FDI on the host country, this distinction is not important. What matters is primarily the fact and the nature of the capital addition in the host country.

Also, FDI often carries with it a technology that may not have been previously available in the host country. That, as well as the additional possibility that such technology may spread to workers and firms outside the foreign-owned establishment, is something we will consider in a later subsection. To start, we will focus only on the role played in the host country by the additional capital.

To some extent, that role may depend on the motivation for the FDI it-

---

26. Lim (2001, 41) notes that "higher wages are usually correlated with better labor standards."

27. It should be noted that FDI may span a variety of industries, including extractive, manufacturing, and service industries. The literature tends to focus especially on FDI in manufacturing, but our discussion is intended to encompass FDI covering the range of different industries. According to Kucera (2001, 17), "as of 1997, 50.1 percent of FDI flows into LDCs went to manufacturing (down from 66.8 percent in 1988), compared to 41.3 percent to services . . . and 4.6 percent to the primary sector." The remaining FDI was "unspecified."

28. See Graham (2000, 85). Kucera (2001, 4) notes that "for less developed countries, the value of M&As (mergers and acquisitions) in relation to total FDI inflows increased from about 15 to 30 percent from 1993 to 1999."

self. Broadly speaking, there are two types of FDI: the type intended to serve the host-country market and the type intended to produce for export.[29] Obviously, there exists some FDI that serves both purposes, but if so, one purpose is usually dominant and the other incidental. The distinction can be important because the firms that engage in FDI usually have alternative means available for achieving either of these objectives, and their choice of FDI is an indication of market conditions that favor FDI over these other means.[30]

In the case of serving the host-country market, the alternatives are to export the product from the home country or, especially in the case of services, to franchise or otherwise license its production by a local firm in the host country. Since the firm's competitive advantage originated with production in its home country, the choice of FDI instead of these alternatives indicates that there must be extra costs associated with them. For exports, these extra costs include transport costs, tariffs, and other trade barriers; for licensing, they include costs of controlling quality or protecting technology. In both cases, FDI is likely to be a higher-cost method of producing the product than the alternative, chosen only because these other costs are even higher. This second-best nature of FDI in such cases may undermine the benefits that one would otherwise expect from freely functioning markets. For example, "tariff-jumping" FDI may involve production that is so inefficient that it lowers the welfare of the host country. Likewise, concerns about control of technology may induce firms to use only outmoded machines for serving a host-country market.

In the case of FDI for export, the alternatives are, first, not to involve the host country at all, producing either at home or in a third country, and second, again, the possibility of licensing production to a host-country firm. Here there is no reason to produce in the host country at all unless it can be done for lower cost (or higher quality), so the presumption is that the host country offers an advantage in the form of cheaper inputs, higher-quality inputs, or both, such as labor or some natural resource. The decision to own the facility rather than to license it could, again, reflect distrust of local firms that outweighs the cost advantage that local firms presumably have due to their familiarity with host-country conditions. However, it may be more likely, since the local market is now less important, that the firm can achieve cost or quality advantages itself by using its own personnel. The result here is a presumption that FDI for export will reduce the cost of providing the product to the home or to the world market, and we would expect this cost reduction to be beneficial, at least from a global perspective.

---

29. These types of FDI are also frequently referred to, respectively, as "horizontal" and "vertical" FDI, as noted in Kucera (2001, 4–5).
30. The points made here and in the next two paragraphs draw on Moran (2002).

What is it that allows a multinational to achieve such a cost reduction that a local firm, unaffiliated with the multinational, could not? The answer may only be that the multinational has better access to capital, which is why we start by considering the effects of capital flows on wages. Or the multinational may have a technology that is not available in the developing country, or even outside the multinational itself, as we examine second. But a third possibility is that the multinational produces an input in one country, perhaps the source-country location of the parent firm, that contributes to the productivity of other activities that it performs in the host country. One or both of these activities may also have the nature of a public good, expanding productivity of multiple affiliates in multiple countries, but that is not essential for our concern here with effects on host-country labor markets. What is important is that the multinational provides the motivation for locating a fragment of its production activity in the source country, an activity that without the multinational would not be viable. This fragmentation is the third source of cost reduction that we will examine.

8.3.2 Effects of International Capital Flows

The simplest story one can tell about FDI is in a one-sector model. Suppose that all countries produce the same good, using inputs of capital and labor in a neoclassical, constant-returns-to-scale, production function: $X = F(K, L)$, where X is output and K and L are factor inputs of capital and labor respectively. FDI from abroad then increases a host country's capital stock and raises its output. With competitive-factor markets paying factors the value of their marginal products, the increased capital stock will raise the marginal product of labor and thus its wage. There is no possibility here of FDI hurting the host country's labor, and if the amount of FDI is large enough to matter at all, it will surely help it. Of course, the flip side of this is in the source country where, if the FDI entails a drop in the capital stock there, the opposite occurs. But that is not our concern here.

One need not go far to find a different theoretical answer, however. In standard Heckscher-Ohlin (HO) trade theory, with two sectors producing two goods in each of two countries, the factor-price-equalization (FPE) theorem tells us that an increase in the capital stock of a country will leave both factor prices unchanged in either of two circumstances.[31] First, if the host country is small so that any change in its outputs will not affect world prices, then an increase in its capital stock, whatever its source, will leave its factor prices unchanged as long as the country continues to produce both goods. And second, even if the host country is large, if the increase in its capital stock matches an equal decline in the capital of another country

---

31. It is this implication of the FPE theorem that causes Leamer and Levinsohn (1995) to rename it the factor-price-insensitivity theorem.

(as it would if FDI actually moves capital from place to place) and then if that other country also produces both goods both before and after the change, the factor prices will again stay the same.

Considering the obvious importance of international trade in the world today, one might think that this two-sector HO model easily ought to be preferred over the one-sector model and that we should forget about FDI affecting wages. But the case just considered is actually very special, and there are many other possibilities within the general HO framework that do not yield this result.

First, the simple specific-factors model with mobile labor and two kinds of immobile capital (which can be thought of as a three-factor, two-good case of the general HO model) has the property that an increase in either capital stock raises the wage even in a small country. Second, with specialization, the HO model behaves much more like the one-sector model, with each country producing a single, albeit different, good. Third, without complete specialization but with multiple cones of diversification,[32] a movement of capital from a capital-abundant to a labor-abundant cone will cause prices of goods to change in a way that causes internationally unequal factor prices to move closer together. In this last case, far different on its surface from the one-sector model, FDI again causes the wage to rise in the host country and to fall in the source country, with opposite changes in returns to capital.

Perhaps the richest variant of the HO model for use in describing developing countries is a two-factor (capital and labor) model with many cones of diversification. In this model, FDI that raises the capital stock of an initially poor, small country sufficiently will cause it to grow from cone to cone, with the wage remaining constant as it advances within a cone, but then rising as it moves up to the next cone. This sort of progress, which has been explored theoretically by Krueger (1977) and Deardorff (2000) and has been documented empirically by Moran (2002), may offer the best hope for developing countries to escape poverty if they can accumulate capital (or skill, although this is outside these simple models) either on their own or with the help of FDI.

So far we have considered models with only two factors, capital and labor. Equally important is the distinction between skilled and unskilled labor, but to address this along with capital flows requires allowing for three

32. This refers to the property of HO models with more goods than factors that equilibria can involve FPE for groups of countries whose factor endowments lie within a cone-shaped subset of factor space. If there is only one such cone, then all countries either completely specialize (and are thus outside the cone) or share common factor prices. If there are multiple cones, then countries whose factor endowments are within the same cone (and thus are in that sense similar in their factor endowments) diversify and share a common set of factor prices, but they have different factor prices than countries in another cone. A popular model of trade between developed and developing countries has two such cones, with capital-abundant developed countries in one and capital-scarce developing countries in the other.

factors of production. This opens up more possibilities than we can consider here, and we therefore look only at a single case, but it is one that seems particularly appropriate for today's world.

The model is another variant of the HO model, introduced by Feenstra and Hanson (1996). They assumed a continuum of goods, each produced with capital and a fixed-coefficient aggregate of skilled and unskilled labor. The skill and unskilled intensities varied along the continuum, while the shares of capital versus aggregate labor did not. In their equilibrium, factor endowments differed between their two countries, North and South, sufficiently that factor prices were unequal, and each country produced a different range of goods—i.e., they were in different cones. In particular, Feenstra and Hanson (1996) assumed that the return to capital was higher in South than in North, and that the ratio of the skilled wage to the unskilled wage was also higher in South than in North.[33]

Feenstra and Hanson (1996) used this model to derive a result that is very relevant here. When capital moves from North to South, it expands the range of goods that can be produced in South and contracts that range in North. The goods whose production location moves are the least skill-intensive industries that were previously produced in North, which then become the most skill-intensive now produced in South. As a result, the average skill intensity of production rises in both countries. This also raises the relative demand for skilled labor in both, causing the skilled wage to rise in both places and the unskilled wage to fall. This is the first sign we get, in theory, of FDI causing a fall in any wage in the host country. It does so because, rather than moving into producing the goods that use the cheapest factor in that less-developed country (i.e., unskilled labor), FDI instead expands production of relatively skill-intensive products there. As we will see in our look at the empirical evidence, this is exactly what a great deal of FDI into developing countries actually does. Why does it do this? In the Feenstra and Hanson (1996) model, it happens because production of the least skill-intensive goods is already, in the initial equilibrium, being done exclusively in the South. In those industries, there is nothing to move. So, if capital is going to move to South at all, in order to take advantage of the higher return to capital there, it must produce something else, and therefore the more skill-intensive goods are all that are available.

This is an interesting result that strikes us as important, and we will return to it frequently later in the paper. However, there is a qualification that Feenstra and Hanson do not mention. Theirs is a two-country model with both countries of significant size. We are often concerned not with a massive flow of capital from the developed to the developing world, but rather

---

33. This is nicely consistent with having both wages realistically lower in South than in North, although FH also allowed international differences in technology that could lead to this result.

Table 8.1   Effect of FDI as Capital Flow on Host-Country Wage

Model (sectors × factors)	Small Country[a]	Two-Country Model[b]
One-sector (1 × 2)	+	+
HO (2 × 2) diversified	0	0
HO (2 × 2) specialized	+	+
Specific factors (2 × 3)	+	+
HO (3+ × 2) two-cone, diversified	0	+
Feenstra-Hanson (∞ × 3) two-cone, diversified		
Skilled labor	+	+
Unskilled labor	+	−

[a]The small country is defined by facing world prices that are fixed independently of what it produces.

[b]In the two-country model, FDI here takes the form of an increase in the capital stock of the host country and an equal decrease in the capital stock of the other country.

with flows into particular developing countries that might better be viewed as small. What effects would FDI have into a small country that is embedded in what is otherwise the Feenstra and Hanson (1996) framework? The answer is that it would not affect relative wages in the small country at all.

The reason is essentially that a small developing country in the Feenstra and Hanson (1996) framework is within the cone of diversification of the South, and its factor prices are constrained by those of the South as well. This is not to say that factor prices will be equalized. The small country will be able to specialize completely in the only one of the continuum of goods that fully employs its skilled and unskilled labor, and thus the FPE theorem does not apply. However, to keep producers from shifting to any other good in the continuum within the cone, the ratio of the skilled wage to the unskilled wage must remain the same as in all of the other countries of the larger South.[34] As a result, as FDI expands the capital stock of the small country, and the wages of both skilled and unskilled labor rise in the same proportion, while the return to capital falls.

All of the theoretical results discussed so far are collected in table 8.1, which shows the direction of change in the real wage of labor in the host country due to capital-inflow FDI. Each of the models considered is identified by the number of sectors and factors that it assumes. Also indicated is whether the host country is diversified or specialized into production of a single good and whether or not, where relevant, the world equilibrium

34. This can be seen in the FH model by differentiating the (log of the) cost function with respect to the index of the good, z, in the FH notation. This derivative depends on the factor prices only through the ratio of the two wages, q_i/w_i. If a small country had a wage ratio differing from that of the larger South at the z that can fully employ its two kinds of labor, then its cost function would cut South's from above or below, and firms would seek to produce only goods of higher or lower z. Labor markets would not both clear.

has two cones of diversification. Results are reported for both the case of a small country, which takes prices as given from a much larger world economy of the sort indicated, and for a two-country model. In the latter case, the FDI is assumed to take the form of an increase in the capital stock in the host country together with an equal decline in the capital of the source country.

The results, clearly, are somewhat varied in that there are several cases where wages do not change and even one where a particular wage—that of unskilled labor—falls. However, most of the cases show labor earning a higher wage as a result of an inflow of FDI, and we regard this as the normal case, in the absence of knowledge that circumstances are otherwise.[35]

8.3.3   Effects of Technology Flows

It is arguably the case that multinationals who engage in FDI possess technologies that others do not, particularly other firms in their host countries. They must, after all, have some sort of advantage in order to overcome the disadvantage of operating in an unfamiliar environment. And if this is the case, then FDI is not fully captured by the simple inflow of capital considered above. Indeed, some FDI may actually involve no addition to a host country's capital stock at all if the capital already exists and is simply acquired by the multinational through merger or acquisition. In that case, FDI may consist purely of the introduction of an improved technology into the host country.

This is not necessarily technology transfer, if the secrets of the technology remain with the acquiring firm and its source-country personnel. But the technology will still be applied to factors in the host country, and it will increase the output that they produce, even if the advantage would be lost if the firm pulled out. Thus we can model this as an improvement in technology and ask its effects. If technology transfer does take place, willingly on the part of the firm or otherwise, then these effects will be just that much larger and longer lasting.

Graham (2000, appendix A) argues that an improvement in technology must raise wages. After all, he says, technology raises productivity, and workers are paid their marginal product, which will be larger as a result of the improved technology. However, this ignores the interaction of supply and demand. A competitive industry with an improved technology will expand output and employment until the value of labor's marginal product equals its wage, but this could happen in several ways: by a fall in the price of the good, as output expands relative to demand; by a fall in the marginal product of labor, as employment expands relative to other factors such as

---

35. It is not inevitable that even some labor must gain. For example, in a one-sector model with three factors—labor, capital, and land—if capital is a complement for land and a substitute for labor, a rise in the capital stock could reduce the wage of all labor.

capital; and by a rise in the wage, as workers are induced to leave other industries or to give up leisure. Only the third of these mechanisms entails an increase in the wage, and it will not happen at all in some contexts, such as that of FPE. Thus there really is no assurance that an improvement in technology due to FDI will raise the host country wage at all. It will depend on the circumstances, just as did the effect of a capital inflow above.

Consider first a single multinational firm that brings an improved technology into a host country. Will it pay a higher wage than what prevails in the local market? It may, for any of several reasons that we will discuss below, but the increased marginal product of labor is not one of those reasons. If the marginal-revenue product of labor is initially higher than the prevailing wage, then the firm will expand its use of labor to the point where this would not be true for an additional unit of labor. But even then it has no reason, on account of the technology alone, to pay more than the market wage. This argument applies as well to larger numbers of firms as long as they do not alter the technology of all firms operating in the sector—a case we consider next. Of course, with more firms expanding employment, the effect on the market wage itself may become significant with the wage rising as labor is pulled up its supply curve, but if this happens, it is due to the expanded demand for labor and is independent of whether or not its cause was an improvement in technology.

Suppose next that FDI brings to a host country an improved technology for a whole sector of the economy, either because multinationals themselves take over the whole sector or because spillovers of the technology raise productivity in local firms as well. Like the previous case of an increased capital stock, several possibilities arise depending on country size and patterns of specialization. In the simplest case of a one-sector economy, the effect of technology depends on its factor bias. Hicks neutral improvement will raise all factor prices in the same proportion, while improvement that is biased toward use of one factor or another will raise one factor price more than another and may even cause one factor price to fall. Thus it is possible, if the new technology is biased strongly enough away from using labor, for it to reduce the wage, although this seems an unlikely outcome.

With multiple sectors, on the other hand, as has been discussed at length in the "trade and wages" literature, the effects of a technological improvement on wages depend on the relative factor intensity of the sector in which it occurs.[36] In a small, two-sector, diversified economy, for example, improvement in the capital-intensive sector will lower the wage, while improvement in the labor-intensive sector will raise it. With more sectors and multiple cones, it is again the factor intensity of the sector in which technological change takes place that matters for factor prices, although here

36. See Krugman (2000) and the references cited therein.

Table 8.2   Effect of FDI as Technology Flow on Host-Country Wage

Model (sectors × factors)	Nature of Technology Change	Effect on Wage
One-sector (1 × 2)	Neutral	+
	Labor using	+
	Labor saving	+ or −
HO (2 × 2) diversified	In labor-intensive sector	+
	In capital-intensive sector	−
HO (3+ × 2) two-cone, diversified	In labor-intensive sector of cone	+
	In capital-intensive sector of cone	−

it is factor intensity relative to other sectors in the same cone, not relative to all sectors. All of these theoretical results are summarized in table 8.2.

8.3.4   Fragmentation

So far, we have treated multinationals as providing capital, technology, or both to developing countries and then using it within the same industries that already exist, either there or in the source countries. In fact, an increasing amount of multinational-firm activity involves changes in the organization of production so that portions of a previously integrated activity can be done elsewhere. This phenomenon, which has gone under many different names, we will here call "fragmentation." It may take the form of a source-country firm building a subsidiary abroad to perform some of the functions that it once did at home, such as making particular parts for its product or completing particular steps in its production process. Or it may take the form of subcontracting such activities to local firms in the host country and providing those firms with detailed specifications and even fragments of its technology. In both cases, this activity may be included in what is often called "outsourcing." And in both cases too, it may or may not be accompanied by an increase in the host-country capital stock or by an improvement in technology. What is distinctive about fragmentation is that a portion of the activity that was previously done in the source country now becomes possible to do in the host country instead. Fragmentation may not require any expansion of the multinational firm's direct operations, and it therefore may not be recorded as FDI, but it is nonetheless the existence of the multinational firm that makes it possible.

By the same token, it is often the potential for fragmentation that makes a multinational firm possible, or at least provides the economies that make multinational firms more efficient than national ones. It is not unusual for some fragments of a firm's activities to serve the needs of multiple other fragments, creating a form of economies of scale. For example, research and development need only be done once for all of the subsidiaries of a multinational firm. Indeed, it is this feature of many multinationals that

Markusen (1984) and Helpman (1984) used as the basis for their seminal models of multinationals.[37] For our purposes here, it is what a multinational does and not so much why it does it that is important. Once a fragment of production is located in a host country, it matters little for that country's labor market whether the multinational is there because of multiplant economies or for some other reason.

Fragmentation is both motivated and constrained by the same things that matter for international trade in general. A fragment of a production process will be moved abroad only if it can be done there more cheaply, which means that fragmentation is responsive to the same determinants of comparative advantage as any other trade. In particular, it is likely to occur only if factor prices differ across countries. Even then, it will not occur if the extra costs that are associated with fragmentation outweigh the gain from lower cost of the activity itself. These extra costs may include transportation, communication, and other costs needed to coordinate the activity with what is still being done in the home country.

Both the causes and the effects of fragmentation in general-equilibrium models have been examined by Deardorff (2001a,b), among others. There is some tendency for fragmentation, like trade more generally, to cause internationally unequal factor prices to move closer together. However, no general conclusion in this regard seems to be possible, and the effects of any particular instance of fragmentation may do this or its opposite, depending on the factor intensities of the fragments.

Thus, to take a not implausible example similar to the movement of capital studied by Feenstra and Hanson (1996), suppose that an industry has previously functioned entirely within a developed country where the relative wage of skilled labor is relatively low due to its abundance. Now it becomes possible to split off a portion of that production process, one that is less skill-intensive than the industry as a whole. In the absence of factor-price equalization, this fragment of production will cost less in the developing country to which it will now move if the cost savings more than cover any increased cost of transportation, communication, and so forth. How it will affect factor prices there, however, depends on the extent to which the host country is unskilled-labor intensive. If that feature of production is more skill-intensive than the average of existing production there—as it may well be, since all activities in the developing country are less skill intensive that those at home—then it will put upward pressure on the relative wage of skilled labor in the developing country. Since this relative wage was already higher than in the developed country, this particular example of fragmentation may be moving the two countries' factor prices further

---

37. See also references cited in Carr, Markusen, and Maskus (2001) for more extensive modeling of multinational firms based on this assumption.

apart.[38] Of course, this is just one example, and fragmentation could equally well cause an even less skill-intensive fragment to be outsourced, in which case the effect on factor prices would be the reverse. The lesson is only that anything can happen, depending on factor intensities of fragments relative to factor endowments of the country, and there seems to be no reason to expect any one pattern of these factor intensities more than any other.

8.3.5   Imperfect Competition

We have assumed so far that firms engaged in FDI are perfectly competitive in all markets. Since these are multinational firms, large almost by definition, many would undoubtedly question this assumption. In fact, we believe that the assumption is not that bad in many cases, since even large, multinational firms face considerable competition, both from others like themselves and from smaller actual and potential entrants. But it is surely worth asking whether market power can cause a firm engaging in FDI to pay wages higher or lower than we would expect from perfect competitors.

Imperfect competition can take many forms, of course, and there probably exist market structures that will yield just about any theoretical result that one wants to get. We won't play that game, but we will merely assume that the firms we consider have some market power. That is, they face market prices that depend on the quantities they buy or sell, and we ask how this matters. Formally, our firms are now monopolists or monopsonists, or perhaps monopolistic competitors without our considering effects on entry.

The most obvious place for market power to matter for wages is in the labor market itself. Suppose that FDI creates a monopsonist buyer of labor in the host country. If it faces an upward-sloping supply curve of labor, such a firm will employ less labor and pay lower wages than it would under perfect competition since it recognizes that the wage needed to elicit an additional unit of labor must be paid to all employees. Does this mean that such FDI actually lowers wages? Probably not, since the labor-supply curve reflects whatever residual options the workers have, such as subsistence farming, and, without the FDI, the wage from these other sources would be no better and perhaps even lower. However, it is not difficult to construct a scenario in which monopsonist FDI lowers wages. Suppose that, prior to the FDI, labor was employed by a competitive local industry with a more primitive and therefore low-productivity technology than the multinational's. If the FDI, due to its superior technology, displaces those

---

38. What happens to factor prices in the other country depends on the factor intensities of the industry before and after fragmentation occurs, relative to factor endowments there. See Deardorff (2001a).

local firms and if the resulting monopsonist multinational, because of its market power, pays less than the workers' (now higher) marginal product, then wages might go down. This is only a possibility, of course; wages might just as well rise. It depends on the parameters of the problem.

Monopsony in labor markets is possible, and historically it may even have been quite common. But today's multinationals often tend to be attracted especially to urban areas where they must compete in labor markets with many other firms, and so monopsony today is arguably less of a concern.

More obviously, many multinationals appear to have market power in output markets. One thinks immediately of prominent brands like Nike and McDonalds, but they are hardly alone. In fact, a great deal of production by and for multinationals is of inputs that are produced by many competing firms, so we would not regard market power in output markets as the norm, but it surely exists.

Suppose, then, that FDI is undertaken by a multinational firm that is a monopoly as a seller of its product, either to the world market or to the local, host-country market. How will this firm's behavior differ from that of a perfect competitor? The answer, of course, is that it will produce a smaller quantity and charge a higher price than a perfect competitor, meaning that its price will be above its marginal cost of production. On the surface, this says nothing about the wages this firm will pay, and, in fact, since we have now assumed no market power in the labor market, it will simply pay the market wage.

What is notable, however, is that, unlike a perfect competitor, this firm does not pay a wage that is equal to the value of its labor's marginal product. Instead, its wage is equal to its marginal-revenue product, taking into account that the output of an additional worker would have to be sold on the product market by charging a lower price on all inframarginal units. Put simply, because the monopolist charges a monopoly price for its product, the value of what a worker produces at the margin (valued at the monopoly price) is higher than the wage. Of course, there are many reasons why the market price of a Nike shoe is much higher than the cost of the labor that produces it, including payments to many other inputs in both production and distribution, but the fact that the shoe is sold for a monopoly price contributes to this. This does not mean that Nike's market power in the shoe market has permitted it to pay a lower wage to labor: It has not. But it does contribute to the perception that Nike could afford to pay its workers more, and indeed it could, if it were somehow willing or compelled to accept a smaller monopoly profit.

Under the heading of imperfect competition, we should also consider the possibility that labor markets may depart from the perfectly competitive norm on the supply side, rather than (or as well as) on the demand side. That is, labor markets may be unionized or might have the potential for being unionized if multinational firms were not present. Here is perhaps the clearest case we can see for FDI and multinational firms to reduce wages, since any market power that workers may be able to acquire by organizing is bound to be diminished if the firms that they bargain with have the option, as multinationals, of producing elsewhere. Unions are in fact notoriously weak in developing countries, and they were already weak, in most cases, before the arrival of multinational firms. But as these countries' incomes rise, it is plausible that unions would gain in strength, and that they would gain faster, other things equal, if multinational firms were not present. Other things would not be equal, however, and, without FDI, the growth of income that permits the growth of unions might not occur.

The presence of unions matters in another way, however, when it is combined with product-market power by the employers. Bargaining over wages will result in workers sharing a part of the firm's monopoly profits, as discussed and documented by Katz and Summers (1989).[39] If a multinational has greater profit than a domestic employer, then it may well pay higher wages for this reason, offsetting the effects of its greater bargaining power.

8.3.6 Payment of Above-Market Wages

Except for this last-mentioned possibility of bilateral monopoly involving a multinational and a union, the theories we have considered so far do not allow for or explain a phenomenon that we will see below to be quite common: That multinational firms pay higher wages than do local, host-country firms. To a partial extent, this phenomenon is an artifact of the data. If multinational firms draw on different parts of the labor market than average local firms, then they may pay higher wages just because, on average, they require different sorts of workers in terms of education, skill, or location. However, the evidence below will show that multinationals continue to pay higher wages than local firms even after accounting for these effects as well as several others. Standard competitive models and even most familiar models of imperfect competition do not explain this, and nor does the suggestion, often made, that workers are somehow more productive in multinational firms. As we have seen in looking at the role of technology, this does not provide a valid theoretical reason for firms to pay higher wages than are needed to attract their workers.

Relatively standard explanations for this behavior do exist, however, in the macroeconomic literature on efficiency wages that was developed to explain both downward wage rigidity and unemployment. There are several versions of this theory, summarized, for example, in Yellen (1984), and all of them provide reasons why workers will become more productive or efficient as a result of being paid more. That is, in efficiency-wage theory, the high wage is not the result of higher productivity, but its cause.

39. See also Budd, Konings, and Slaughter (2002) and references cited therein.

The simplest and apparently oldest version of efficiency-wage theory applies best to developing countries, where market wages may be insufficient to sustain workers' health. Firms may therefore pay higher than the market wage in order to improve the health of their workers and thus their productivity. Other versions of the theory depend on somewhat more complex modeling of interactions between firms and workers. They can be summarized by saying that firms pay higher-than-market wages in order to (a) reduce shirking (or elicit greater effort); (b) reduce turnover and the costs of retraining; (c) attract and retain the most able and productive workers from a heterogeneous workforce; and (d) improve worker morale in a context where social pressures can make workers more productive.

An alternative explanation for payment of above-market wages is possible in precisely the context that anti-globalization protest is serving to create. In the preceding section, we discussed the anti-sweatshop campaign and other public pressures that have been brought to bear on multinationals for allegedly mistreating their workers. This pressure may well be creating a reluctance on the part of at least the most visible multinationals to be seen providing wages and working conditions that could become a source of embarrassment and lost sales, even when these are at levels generally prevailing in local markets. In response to that pressure, they may pay above-equilibrium wages even when they do not expect this to improve the productivity of their workers. It is unlikely that much of the empirical evidence for high wages by multinationals could be due to this, since the data mostly predate the anti-globalization movement. However, it is plausible that multinationals may currently be responding to that pressure, and that future studies of wages paid by multinationals will reflect that.

In all of these stories, it is clear that the workers who receive the above-market wages are better off than those who do not (although, in the case of efficiency wages, this gain may be partially offset by any extra effort that they provide in return). Additionally, if FDI expands employment in firms that pay above-market wages, a larger number of workers will enjoy these benefits. However, it is not necessarily clear that all members of the country's labor force are, on average, better off. The efficiency-wage models, in particular, were developed in part to help explain unemployment. Indeed it is likely that above-market wages, whatever their cause, will be accompanied by increased unemployment of workers who are waiting and hoping to get these desirable jobs.

Years ago, Harris and Todaro (1970) proposed a model in which a given above-equilibrium wage was paid in the urban sector of an economy, inducing migration from the rural sector and urban unemployment to the point that the expected wage of these migrants equaled the lower rural wage. This expected wage included not only the high wage of employed workers, weighted by the probability of employment, but also the zero wage of the unemployed weighted by the probability of not finding a job.

This same model could be applied within an urban sector where certain firms pay higher than market wages for any of the reasons we have discussed. They too will attract a larger pool of workers than they can employ, workers who will accept either unemployment or lower-than-market wages in return for the chance of eventually getting one of these high-paid jobs. In equilibrium, workers as a group, both employed and unemployed, are not better off than those who continue to work elsewhere in the economy for the market wage. Of course, there is the additional unhappy consequence of greater inequality among workers, some of whom have these high-paying jobs and others of whom do not.

In this framework, the market offers potential workers the same expected wage that they can earn somewhere else, far from the high-wage sector. Therefore, simply adding more firms that pay above-market wages may not change that equilibrium expected wage. Instead, although the market looks very different from the usual competitive model, the underlying forces that will change economy-wide average wages will be the same forces of supply and demand that we have discussed earlier.

In the case of efficiency wages, the firms get something in return for their higher wages that they could not necessarily get elsewhere—higher productivity from their employees—and that, together with the low market wage to which the wage premium is added, is what attracts them to produce in these countries in the first place. But when above-market wages are being paid for other reasons, such as pressures from NGOs, enforcement of minimum-wage laws, or even fear of government sanctions, the benefit of avoiding public censure may be obtained as well by producing somewhere else rather than by paying higher wages in poor countries. Whatever may be the level of wages and working conditions that will satisfy a critical public, firms may choose to produce in countries where that level is already the equilibrium due to workers' higher productivity. If so, then an additional effect of the pressure to pay higher wages will be a loss of employment in low-wage countries.

Leamer (1999) has provided an account of wage differentials that differs somewhat from the efficiency-wage story, although it too rests on the degree of effort exerted by workers. His model has the advantage of being amenable to general-equilibrium analysis. In his model, "effort" determines total factor productivity in a two-sector, two-factor context that is otherwise like that of the HO model. Since the return to effort is, in effect, higher in the more capital-intensive sector, equilibrium has that sector paying higher wages and requiring greater effort from its workers than the labor-intensive sector. This model has a long list of striking implications, only one of which need concern us here.

In Leamer's effort model, an increase in a country's capital stock, which could (but need not) be due to FDI, has remarkably different implications in closed and open economies. In a closed economy, increased capital lowers the relative price of the capital-intensive good. This lowers the return to effort and leads to a reduction in effort levels in both sectors. In a small, open economy, on the other hand, increased capital may, in one type of equilibrium, leave factor prices and effort levels unchanged, through a variant of FPE. But, in another type of equilibrium, it may lead instead to new production of capital-intensive goods, thus creating higher-effort, higher-wage jobs.

All of the cases we have considered in this theoretical overview—capital flow, technology flow, and fragmentation—have failed to yield unambiguous conclusions about the effects of FDI and multinational firms on equilibrium wages in host countries. Even when we examined reasons for multinationals to pay above-equilibrium wages, there was no assurance that they would do so. There seems to be a presumption, at least in the case of capital flows, that FDI will raise at least some wages, but even this is not certain, and it becomes even less so when we recognize other forms of multinational activity, such as fragmentation. It is therefore an empirical question whether the actual operations of multinationals have raised or lowered wages in developing countries. It is to that empirical question that we now turn.

8.4   Effects on Wages and Working Conditions: What are the Facts?

In keeping with the broad conceptual focus in the preceding section, we turn now to a review of the empirical evidence on wages and working conditions associated with multinationals.[40] We first consider the effects on wages and thereafter the relationship between FDI and labor rights broadly conceived.

8.4.1   Foreign Ownership and Wages

The published evidence on the effects of foreign ownership on wages in developing countries is based on ad hoc observations and surveys as well as a number of studies using econometric methods.

Lim (2001, 39–40) provides a useful summary of some evidence that foreign-owned and subcontracting firms in manufacturing industries tend to pay higher wages than domestic firms.[41]

---

40. In his conference comment, André Sapir suggested that we should have focused more narrowly on the production, trade, wages, and working conditions in the apparel industry and on the respective roles of multinational firms and subcontractors. While Sapir's suggestion is well taken, the approach that we took was designed to provide a broader context for the conceptual and empirical issues involved.

41. See also Nicholas D. Kristof and Sheryl WuDunn's article "Two Cheers for Sweatshops" (*The New York Times Magazine,* 24 September 2000). Much of the available information evidently refers to wages in manufacturing. It would be useful accordingly to obtain information on wages paid by foreign-owned and subcontracting industries in extractive industries such as mining and in service industries in different developing countries.

- Affiliates of U.S. multinational enterprises pay a wage premium that ranges from 40 percent in high-income countries to 100 percent, or double the local average, in low-income countries[42] (Graham 2000).
- Workers in foreign-owned and subcontracting apparel and footwear factories in Vietnam rank in the top 20 percent of the population by household expenditure (Glewwe 2000).
- In Nike subcontractor factories in June–July 2000, annual wages were $670 compared with an average minimum wage of $134. In Indonesia, annual wages were $720 compared with an average annual minimum of $241 (Lim 2000).
- In Bangladesh, legal minimum wages in export-processing zones are 40 percent higher than the national minimum for unskilled workers, 15 percent higher for semiskilled workers, and 50 percent higher for skilled workers (Panos 1999).
- In Mexico, firms with between 40 and 80 percent of their total sales going to exports paid wages that were, at the low end, 11 percent higher than the wages of non-export-oriented firms; for companies with export sales above 80 percent, wages were between 58 and 67 percent higher (Lukacs 2000).
- In Shanghai, a survey of 48 U.S.-based companies found that respondents paid an average hourly wage of $5.25, excluding benefits and bonuses, or about $10,900 per year. At a jointly owned GM factory in Shanghai, workers earned $4.59 an hour, including benefits; this is about three times higher than wages for comparable work at a non-U.S. factory in Shanghai (Lukacs 2000).

According to a report on Nike contract factories in Vietnam and Indonesia by students from the Amos Tuck School at Dartmouth College (Calzini et al. 1997, 2),

- For factory workers living on their own, Nike contract-factory wages allow workers to generate discretionary income in excess of basic expenditures such as food, housing, and transportation.
- For workers living in extended-family households, Nike contract-factory wages are used to augment total household income to raise overall living standards.
- Nike contract-factory workers consistently earn wages at or above government-mandated minimum wage levels.
- Given the employment opportunities available, Nike contract factories offer an economically attractive alternative for entry-level workers. Nike contract-factory jobs provide workers with a consistent

---

42. It may be further noted, according to OECD (2001, figure 8) that compensation per employee of firms under foreign control in the OECD countries was substantially higher than the average for national firms.

stream of income in contrast to common alternatives, such as farming or shopkeeping. There are significantly more applicants than factory positions available.

- In Indonesia, noncash benefits provided help to offset recurring expenses for food, housing, and transportation.
- In Vietnam, overtime wages are perceived by workers to be an attractive means to supplement base-income levels.

Moran (2002, chap. 1, 2) provides extensive evidence on wages and related benefits of FDI and foreign-originated subcontracting in low-skill and low-wage sectors in developing countries as follows.

- The ILO (1998) finds, based on worker surveys, that wages paid in export-processing zones (EPZs) are higher than in the villages from which workers are typically recruited.
- The U.S. Department of Labor (2000) finds that footwear and apparel manufacturers in selected countries pay higher wages and offer better working conditions than those available in agriculture.
- The International Youth Foundation (IYF; 2000) surveyed three footwear and two apparel factories in Thailand and found that 72 percent regarded their wages as "fair" and that 60 percent were able to accumulate savings.
- Bhattacharya (1998) reports that garment workers in Bangladesh earn 25 percent more than the country's average per capita income.
- Razafindrakoto and Roubaud (1995, 226) find that EPZ workers in Madagascar earned 15 to 20 percent more than the average worker in the rest of the economy, even after controlling for education level, extent of professional experience, and tenure in employment.
- Workers in the Philippine EPZ reported themselves to be better off after finding employment in the EPZ during the 1990s. As reported by the World Bank (1999, appendix C), 47 percent of workers earned enough to have some savings, as compared to 9 percent before employment in the zone. In addition, employees received social security, medical care, paid vacation, sick leave, maternity leave, and other employee benefits.

Let us next consider some econometric-based evidence on the wage effects of multinationals. The earliest evidence grew out of a literature examining the role of FDI in transmitting technology internationally. The impact of FDI on wages was used as an indication that technological know-how raises labor productivity. For example, Aitken, Harrison, and Lipsey (1996) explored the impact of foreign ownership in Mexico, Venezuela, and the United States. They found that the presence of foreign ownership significantly raises wages within the plant in all three countries, but the impact spills over into locally owned plants only in the United States.

For all three countries, manufacturing-survey data were analyzed. In the case of Mexico, 2,113 plants were surveyed concerning factor usage, sales, equity ownership, and input and output prices. Data were also available on industry and location. For Venezuela, data were available on foreign ownership, assets, employment, input costs, and location for all plants employing more than 50 workers. The log of the industry-region average wage was regressed on the proportion of employment in foreign-owned firms within the industry region and on a measure of the capital stock, royalty payments, and average output and input prices. Aitken, Harrison, and Lipsey (1996) found that a 10 percent increase in the share of foreign investment in regional-industry employment raised wages on the order of 2.5 percent in Mexico and Venezuela. However, when the analysis was restricted to domestic-owned firms, the foreign-investment variable was insignificant.

The empirical analysis was then performed at the plant level, incorporating information on plant size and age. As with the industry-level analysis, the extent of foreign ownership raised wages of both skilled and unskilled workers, with the impact on skilled workers about 50 percent higher than for unskilled workers. However, as will be seen in the case for Indonesia, about one-third of the wage premium paid by foreign-owned firms was accounted for by larger plant size.

In order to identify the source of the FDI wage premium, Aitken, Harrison, and Lipsey (1996) analyzed a cross-section of firms for Venezuela and the United States in 1987 and Mexico in 1990. They took as a point of departure that foreign-owned firms in all three countries paid about 30 percent more than domestic firms for both skilled and unskilled labor. Controlling for industrial sector, they first found that this accounted for a significant portion of the FDI wage premium. That is, foreign firms tended to locate in higher-paying sectors of the economy. For the United States, industry effects accounted for about half of the premium. In Mexico, the figure was two-thirds, and, for Venezuela, the figure was one-third. They then considered location. In the case of the United States, foreign-owned firms actually tended to locate in low-wage regions. As a consequence, controlling for region made the FDI wage premium larger. However, foreign affiliates were located in high-wage regions of Venezuela and Mexico. Nevertheless, even after controlling for region, foreign-owned firms paid more than domestic firms. Finally, Aitken, Harrison, and Lipsey (1996) controlled for plant size and capital intensity. Foreign-owned firms tended to operate larger facilities, giving rise to economies of scale that may raise wages. However, as with location and industry, the foreign-ownership variable retained some explanatory power. Unfortunately, Aitken, Harrison, and Lipsey (1996) did not report regression results in which they controlled simultaneously for industry, location, plant size, and capital intensity. As a consequence, it is not possible to tell whether foreign ownership serves as a proxy for the omitted variables in each equation. Nevertheless, the Aitken, Harrison, and Lipsey (1996) results support the view that foreign-owned firms pay premium wages.

Further supporting evidence is found by Feenstra and Hanson (1997) in their study of the impact of foreign-owned capital on the skilled-labor wage premium in Mexico for the period 1975–1988. They found, in particular, that foreign capital impacts the demand for skilled labor disproportionately. Foreign direct investment constitutes a significant and growing portion of the capital stock in Mexico. In 1987, FDI accounted for 13.7 percent of total fixed investment in Mexico, a level sufficient to affect the demand for labor. A surge in investment in the border region occurred following liberalization measures enacted by Mexico between 1982 and 1985. Rules prohibiting majority foreign ownership were relaxed, and the average tariffs were lowered from 23.5 to 11.8 percent. In the immediate aftermath, the share of FDI in total investment in Mexico rose nearly sixfold. At the same time, the wages of skilled and unskilled workers began to diverge after nearly twenty years of convergence.

In order to test whether or not FDI in the maquiladoras contributed to the growing wage disparity in Mexico during the 1980s, Feenstra and Hanson analyzed labor-market census data for nine 2-digit International Standard Industrial Classification (ISIC) categories in thirty-two states for the three periods 1975–1980, 1980–1985, and 1985–1988. The nonproduction wage bill as a fraction of the total wage bill was regressed on a measure of alternative wages for skilled and unskilled workers, on the state's domestic capital stock, and on the ratio of maquiladoras in a state to the number of domestic-owned establishments. They found that the fraction of establishments that are foreign-owned significantly raised the relative return to skilled labor. Between 1985 and 1988, FDI accounted for 52.4 percent of the increase in the wage share of nonproduction workers in the border region.

Although Feenstra and Hanson's results are informative, they focus primarily on the impact that foreign ownership has on the demand for labor in local factor markets, thereby providing little evidence on the specific labor practices of multinational firms. The evidence presented above supports the view that multinational firms are improving the lives of at least some workers by raising overall labor demand. However, in order to respond to some of the challenges raised by the issue of sweatshop labor, we might also want to know whether foreign-owned firms play a positive role by altering industry characteristics or by paying above-market wages.

To this end, Lipsey and Sjöholm (2001) analyzed the wages paid by foreign-owned plants in Indonesia.[43] They were specifically interested in

---

43. Hill (1990) and Manning (1998) also find that foreign firms pay higher wages than domestic firms in Indonesia.

whether or not foreign-owned firms pay more for local workers than do domestic firms and, if so, why. Can the difference be attributed to plant characteristics, worker characteristics, or industry characteristics? Furthermore, do the labor practices of multinationals affect the wages paid by local firms? Lipsey and Sjöholm analyzed survey evidence for all plants in Indonesia that had more than twenty employees. In 1996, 19,911 plant managers responded to the survey, providing data on value-added, energy inputs, location, and labor characteristics for blue-collar and white-collar workers.

Lipsey and Sjöholm used the plant-level data to estimate a standard-wage equation. The log of the average plant-level wage was regressed on average education level (as measured by proportion of workers with primary, junior, senior, and university education), plant characteristics including size, proportion of workers that are female, energy inputs, other inputs, and binary variables for foreign ownership, government ownership, sector, and location.

Three separate wage equations were estimated. First, Lipsey and Sjöholm controlled only for ownership and education level. They found that foreign-owned firms paid 33 percent more for blue-collar workers and 70 percent more for white-collar workers than did locally owned firms. So the next question was, what is it about foreign-owned firms that produces the premium? When the region- and sector-dummy variables were added to the regression equation, the premium fell to 25 percent for blue-collar workers and 50 percent more for white-collar workers. Finally, controlling for plant size, energy inputs per worker, other inputs per worker, and the proportion of female employees, the foreign-ownership premium fell to 12 percent for blue-collar and 22 percent for white-collar workers. So, about one-third of the foreign-ownership premium for labor of a specific quality was accounted for by region and industry, one-third by inputs and plant size, leaving one-third of the premium unexplained. Thus, foreign-owned firms are raising wages for blue-collar and white-collar workers above and beyond the impact of increased productivity associated with more inputs per worker and a more efficient scale of production.

Lipsey and Sjöholm suggested several reasons why foreign-owned firms might pay a higher wage for the same quality of labor and in the same industrial setting. One possibility, of course, is that they are responding to social pressure to combat desperately poor working conditions. However, foreign-owned firms may have less knowledge of the local market, want to invest in the skills of their employees, or fear the loss of competitive advantage to locally owned firms. Alternatively, workers may prefer domestic-owned firms, requiring foreign firms to pay a premium.

Lipsey and Sjöholm also considered whether the presence of FDI raises the wages in domestic-owned plants. They regressed the log of wages in domestic-owned plants on worker, plant, and industry characteristics but also included a variable indicating the proportion of industry value-added produced in foreign-owned plants. In contrast to the results obtained by Aitken, Harrison, and Lipsey (1996) in the case of Mexico and Venezuela, the presence of foreign-owned firms in an industry significantly affected the wages paid by domestically owned firms in Indonesia. This was the case whether industries were defined at the 2-, 3-, or 5-digit level.

Given these findings that foreign-owned firms pay higher wages even after controlling for scale, worker quality, industry, age of facility, inputs, and industry and regional characteristics, one might wonder whether firms are motivated by humanitarian concerns or public pressure. Similarly, foreign-owned firms could be more likely to conform with laws regulating minimum wages, overtime pay, and benefits. However, if humanitarian concern or public and legal pressure are the motivating factors, we might expect that the impact would be most pronounced for the most poorly paid workers. However, this is not the case. That is, the largest bonus for working with foreign capital apparently accrues to skilled, white-collar workers in the form of higher wages. Thus, while foreign capital may raise wages on average, it may also tend to worsen the distribution of income between skilled and unskilled workers.

Alternatively, it has been suggested (as discussed above) that foreign firms pay premium wages for unobservable characteristics such as intelligence, flexibility, or discipline. Employees who reveal these capabilities after they are hired are likely to be retained with higher-than-average compensation.

However, it is important to note first that there is considerable evidence that the FDI wage premium is a consequence of total-factor and labor-productivity gains associated with foreign ownership. In this connection, a positive correlation between productivity gains and foreign ownership was found by Aitken and Harrison (1994) for Venezuela; Haddad and Harrison (1993) for Morocco; Harrison (1996) for Côte d'Ivoire; and Luttmer and Oks (1993) for Mexico.

Furthermore, Budd and Slaughter (2000) and Budd, Konings, and Slaughter (2002) present evidence that multinationals share profits with local and foreign workers. They find, in particular, that affiliate wages are positively correlated with parent profits. They argue that such profit sharing is profit maximizing in a model in which both workers and firms are risk averse. Profit sharing will also emerge if wages are set in a bargaining framework in which the firm's ability to pay depends positively on profitability.

8.4.2   Foreign Direct Investment and Labor Rights

In addition to the controversy about the effects of multinationals on wages, it is often argued that they are attracted to markets where worker rights are poorly protected. That is, multinationals are alleged to seek out havens that are safe from union activism, and there is no shortage of governments willing to accommodate the interests of foreign capital. The allegation stems, in part, from the view that foreign firms have lower labor costs in locations with weak labor protections. Indeed, several studies find that FDI is attracted to regions with low labor cost after controlling for productivity.

Studies of the role of labor costs in foreign-investment decisions provide ambiguous evidence, with some studies finding a positive correlation and others a negative correlation. (See, for example, Schneider and Frey (1985); Jun and Singh (1997); Wheeler and Moody (1992); Billington (1999); Cooke and Noble (1998); and Head, Ries, and Swenson (1999). However, these studies all suffer from the weakness that they do not control for labor productivity. As a consequence, studies that find a positive correlation between wages and FDI, without controlling for productivity, suffer from the weakness that wages are probably a proxy for productivity rather than labor costs.

In contrast, Culem (1988), in an analysis of bilateral FDI flows among a selection of industrialized countries between 1969 and 1982, found that FDI was significantly adversely affected by high labor costs once output per worker was introduced as an explanatory variable. Similarly, Friedman, Gerlowski, and Silberman (1992) found that the allocation of FDI across individual states in the United States between 1977 and 1988 was significantly affected by the relative labor costs of individual states, after controlling for state-level labor productivity.

However, in a recent survey of managers of transnational corporations reported by Hatem (1997), several other factors were considerably more important than labor cost when selecting a site for FDI. Market size, political and social stability, labor quality, the legal and regulatory environment, and infrastructure were all rated as more important than the cost of labor. Labor rights that promote political stability and enhance labor quality may in fact make a particular location attractive to foreign investors.

For this reason, it is useful to separate the role that worker rights play in raising labor costs relative to labor productivity from those that improve the efficient functioning of a production facility. For example, Head, Ries, and Swenson (1999) found that the unionization rate in a U.S. state lowered the inflow of Japanese investment. Cooke and Noble (1998) found similar adverse effects of unionization in developing countries. However, Friedman, Gerlowski, and Silberman (1992) found that Japanese firms were more likely to locate a plant in a U.S. state with a high-unionization rate after controlling for wages and productivity. Thus, it seems that, as long as the union does not raise wages above worker productivity, Japanese firms appear to believe that unions play a positive role in the plant.

Of course, worker rights are not limited to collective bargaining. The empirical evidence on worker rights more broadly defined is unambiguous.

No matter how worker rights are defined, foreign investors do *not* appear to be attracted to countries with poorly protected worker rights. Similarly, political and social stability have a positive impact on the choices of foreign investors.

Cooke and Noble (1998) found that U.S. outward FDI was positively correlated with the number of ILO conventions ratified. The OECD (2000) found that FDI was positively correlated with the right to establish free unions, the right to strike, the right to collective bargaining, and protection of union members. Rodrik (1996) found that U.S. outward FDI between 1982 and 1989 was positively correlated with a Freedom House democracy index but was deterred by a high index of child labor. This was the case even though countries with a high-democracy index and a low child-labor index had higher labor costs.

The work on FDI and worker rights has been criticized on two counts. Martin and Maskus (2001), in particular, note the problems with relying on ILO conventions ratified and the Freedom House indicators of democracy. Furthermore, the studies listed above did not control for other determinants of FDI. Kucera (2001) has attempted to improve on the existing literature on worker rights and labor costs by using multiple definitions of each type of worker rights.

Following Rodrik, Kucera first regressed the log of wages per employee on value added per employee in manufacturing, GDP per capita, manufacturing share of GDP, the urbanization rate, multiple measures of freedom of association and collective bargaining, child labor, and gender inequality. Data were for the period 1992–1997 in a sample of 127 countries, including 27 "high-income economies" and 100 LDCs. First, like Rodrik (1999), Kucera found that wages were positively correlated with all of the measures of political freedom. Surprisingly, the unionization rate had an insignificant negative impact on wages. However, other measures of free-association and collective-bargaining rights had a positive impact on wages. These measures may be more meaningful since they are based on observed rights violations. The evidence on child labor and wages was quite curious. First, wages were positively correlated with labor-force-participation rates for ten- to fourteen-year-olds. The coefficient on the secondary nonenrollment rate was also positive. Kucera noted that it is difficult to interpret such results. Finally, in countries where the female proportion of the labor force was higher than average, wages were lower than average. However, this effect was not generally statistically significant.

Kucera then turned to estimate the impact of worker rights on FDI. Each country's share of world FDI inflows was regressed on wages relative to value-added in manufacturing, population, per capita GDP, international trade's share of GDP, exchange-rate growth, urbanization, literacy, and the measures of worker rights. He found several very interesting results for the cross-section of all countries as well as for the LDCs separately.

1. Foreign direct investment is attracted to countries with a higher civil-liberties index even though labor costs are higher. An increase in the civil-liberties index of one unit (on a 10-point scale), controlling for wages, is associated with an 18.5 percent increase in FDI flows. When the negative impact of increased wages in democracies is factored in, a one-unit increase in the civil-liberties index raises FDI inflows by 14.3 percent. So even though democracies pay higher wages for a given level of worker productivity, they still provide an attractive location for foreign investors.

2. Unionization rates are positively correlated with FDI, controlling for wages relative to labor productivity in equations that also include regional dummies.

3. Foreign direct investment is higher in countries with fewer episodes in which rights to free association and collective bargaining are repressed.

4. Foreign direct investment is negatively correlated with labor-force participation rates for ten- to fifteen-year-olds. Otherwise results are mixed and not statistically significant.

5. Measures of gender discrimination are not statistically significant.

In short, there is no solid evidence that countries with poorly protected worker rights attract FDI. If anything, investors apparently prefer locations in which workers and the public more generally function in a stable political and social environment in which civil liberties are well established and enforced.[44] This evidence is also consistent with FDI causing improvements in worker rights and working conditions. As we noted in our theoretical discussion earlier in this chapter, the same forces that may lead multinational firms to pay higher wages are likely, in equilibrium, to improve working conditions as well.

8.5 Conclusions

The popular press is rife with anecdotes about foreign workers who labor for multinational firms for low wages and for excruciatingly long hours under horrific conditions in low-income countries to produce goods for Western consumers. This negative impression that multinationals are exploiting and mistreating their workers is reinforced by calculations that la-

---

44. A caveat to this conclusion is that it is based in large measure on cross-sectional regression analysis and may therefore not apply directly to individual countries such as mainland China, which is a major recipient of FDI even though it may lack the worker protection and civil liberties found in many other developing countries. However, in a separate communication based on the regression residuals in his analysis, Kucera has informed us that "all in all, the results suggest that China does not receive so much FDI because of its weak FACB [freedom of association and collective bargaining] rights." It should also be mentioned that most empirical studies do not clearly distinguish FDI for export purposes and FDI to serve the host-country market. Further, most studies treat manufacturing in the aggregate and thus lack the sectoral detail of interest, especially for the relatively labor-intensive industries such as apparel and footwear that are the focus of the anti-sweatshop activists.

bor costs are typically a tiny fraction of the retail-selling price of the goods being produced and that the multinationals therefore can and should pay higher wages to their workers.

It is true that, as a theoretical matter, multinationals can have an array of positive and negative impacts on host-country workers. However, as an empirical matter, some anecdotal evidence notwithstanding, there is virtually no careful and systematic evidence demonstrating that, as a generality, multinational firms adversely affect their workers, provide incentives to worsen working conditions, pay lower wages than in alternative employment, or repress worker rights. In fact, there is a very large body of empirical evidence indicating that the opposite is the case. Foreign ownership raises wages both by raising labor productivity and by expanding the scale of production and, in the process, improves the conditions of work. Furthermore, there appears to be some evidence that foreign-owned firms make use of aspects of labor organizations and democratic institutions that improve the efficiency characteristics of their factory operations.

It is undoubtedly the case that public pressure can and ought to be brought to bear on some multinational firms and their suppliers who are abusing social norms to the detriment of their workers. But great care needs to be exercised since, generally, measures that are punitive or provide firms an incentive to alter the location of production are unwarranted and may adversely affect the very workers they are intended to benefit.

References

Aitken, Brian, and Ann Harrison. 1994. Do domestic firms benefit from foreign direct investment: Evidence from panel data. Policy Research Working Paper no. 1248. Washington, D.C.: World Bank.

Aitken, Brian, Ann Harrison, and Robert E. Lipsey. 1996. Wages and foreign ownership: A comparative study of Mexico, Venezuela, and the United States. *Journal of International Economics* 40 (3–4): 345–71.

Bhagwati, Jagdish. 2001. Corporate conduct. *World Link* (March/April). http://www.worldlink.co.uk/stories/storyreader/625.

Bhattacharya, Debapriya. 1998. *Export processing zones in Bangladesh: Economic impact and social issues.* Working Paper no. 80. Geneva: International Labor Office.

Billington, Nicholas. 1999. The location of foreign direct investment: An empirical analysis. *Applied Economics* 31 (1): 65–76.

Broad, Robin, ed. 2002. *Global backlash: Citizen initiatives for a just world economy.* New York: Rowman and Littlefield Publishers, Inc.

Brown, Drusilla K., Alan V. Deardorff, and Robert M. Stern. Forthcoming. Pros and cons of linking trade and labor standards. In *The political economy of policy reform,* ed. Douglas R. Nelson.

Budd, John W., Jozef Konings, and Matthew J. Slaughter. 2002. International rent sharing in multinational firms. NBER Working Paper no. 8809. Cambridge, Mass.: National Bureau of Economic Research, February.

Budd, John W., and Matthew J. Slaughter. 2000. Are profits shared across borders? Evidence on international rent sharing. NBER Working Paper no. 8014. Cambridge, Mass.: National Bureau of Economic Research, November.

Business for Social Responsibility (BSR) Education Fund, Investor Responsibility Research Center (IRRC), and Dara O'Rourke. 2000. *Independent university initiative: Final report.* http://hacs.harvard.edu/~pslm/hsas/iui.pdf.

Calzini, Derek, Jake Odden, Jean Tsai, Shawna Huffman, and Steve Tran. 1997. Survey of Vietnamese and Indonesian domestic expenditure levels, Nike Inc. *Field Studies in International Business* Dartmouth College, The Amos Tuck School, Hanover, New Hampshire. Manuscript.

Card, David, and Alan Krueger. 1995. *Myth and measurement: The new economics of the minimum wage.* Princeton: Princeton University Press.

Carr, David L., James R. Markusen, and Keith E. Maskus. 2001. Estimating the knowledge-capital model of the multinational enterprise. *American Economic Review* 91 (3): 693–708.

Connor, Melissa, Tara Gruzen, Larry Sacks, Jude Sunderland, and Darcy Tromanhauser. 1999. The case for corporate responsibility: Paying a living wage to maquila workers in El Salvador. Study for the National Labor Committee, Program in Economic and Political Development. Columbia University, School of International and Public Affairs. Manuscript, May.

Cooke, William, and Deborah Noble. 1998. Industrial relations systems and U.S. foreign direct investment abroad. *British Journal of Industrial Relations* 36 (4): 581–609.

Culum, Claudy G. 1988. The locational determinants of direct investments among industrialized countries. *European Economic Review* 32 (4): 885–904.

Deardorff, Alan V. 2000. Patterns of trade and growth across cones. *De Economist* 148 (June): 141–66.

———. 2001a. Fragmentation across cones. In *Fragmentation: New production patterns in the world economy,* ed. Sven W. Arndt and Henry Kierzkowski, 35–51. Oxford: Oxford University Press.

———. 2001b. Fragmentation in simple trade models. *North American Journal of Economics and Finance* 12 (2): 121–37.

Elliott, Kimberly Ann, and Richard B. Freeman. 2001. White hats or Don Quixotes? Human rights vigilantes in the global economy. NBER Working Paper no. 8102. Cambridge, Mass.: National Bureau of Economic Research, January.

Feenstra, Robert C., and Gordon H. Hanson. 1996. Foreign investment, outsourcing, and relative wages. In *The political economy of trade policy: Essays in honor of Jagdish Bhagwati,* ed. Robert C. Feenstra, Gene M. Grossman, and Douglas A. Irwin, 89–127. Cambridge, Mass.: MIT Press.

———. 1997. Foreign direct investment and relative wages: Evidence from Mexico's maquiladoras. *Journal of International Economics* 42 (3–4): 371–93.

Freeman, Richard B. 1993. Labor market institutions and policies: Help or hindrance to economic development? In *Proceedings of the World Bank Annual Conference on Development Economics 1993,* ed. World Bank, 117–44. Washington, D.C.: World Bank.

Friedman, J., D. Gerlowski, and J. Silberman. 1992. What attracts foreign multinational corporations? Evidence from branch plant location in the United States. *Journal of Regional Science* 32 (2): 403–18.

Glewwe, Paul. 2000. Are foreign-owned businesses in Vietnam really sweatshops?

University of Minnesota Extension Service Newsletter 701 (Summer). http://www.extension.umn.edu/newsletters/ageconomist/components/ag237-701a.html.

Graham, Edward M. 2000. *Fighting the wrong enemy: Antiglobal activists and multinational enterprises.* Washington, D.C.: Institute for International Economics.

Haddad, Mona, and Ann Harrison. 1993. Are there positive spillovers from direct foreign investment? Evidence from panel data for Morocco. *Journal of Development Economics* 42 (1): 51–74.

Harris, John R., and Michael P. Todaro. 1970. Migration, unemployment and development: A two-sector analysis. *American Economic Review* 60 (1): 126–42.

Harrison, Ann. 1996. Foreign investment in three developing countries: Determinants and consequences. In *Industrial evolution in developing countries: Micro patterns of turnover, productivity and market structure,* ed. M. Roberts and J. Tybout, 163–87. New York: Oxford University Press.

Harvard Magazine. 2001. Ways and means: Harvard's wage debate. *Harvard Magazine* 104 (2). http://www.harvardmagazine.com/on-line/110182.html.

Hatem, Fabrice. 1997. *International investment: Towards the year 2001.* New York: United Nations.

Head, C. Keith, John Ries, and Deborah Swenson. 1999. Attracting foreign manufacturing: Investment promotion and agglomeration. *Regional Science and Urban Economics* 29:197–218.

Helpman, Elhanan. 1984. A simple theory of international trade with multinational corporations. *Journal of Political Economy* 92 (3): 451–71.

Hill, Hal. 1990. Indonesia's industrial transformation part II. *Bulletin of Indonesian Economic Studies* 26 (3): 75–109.

International Labor Organization (ILO). 1998. *Labor and social issues relating to export processing zones.* Geneva: ILO.

International Youth Foundation (IYF). 2002. *Needs assessment for workers and communities.* Baltimore, Md.: Global Alliance for Workers and Communities. http://www.theglobalalliance.org/assessment.cfm/6/31/47.

Jun, Kwang, and Harinder Singh. 1997. The determinants of foreign direct investment: New empirical evidence. *Transnational Corporations* 5 (2): 67–105.

Katz, Lawrence F., and Lawrence H. Summers. 1989. Industry rents: Evidence and implications. *Brookings Papers on Economic Activity,* 209–75. Washington, D.C.: Brookings Institution.

Krueger, Anne O. 1977. Growth, distortions, and patterns of trade among countries. *Princeton Studies in International Finance* no. 40. Princeton, N.J.: Princeton University.

Krugman, Paul R. 2000. Technology, trade, and factor prices. *Journal of International Economics* 50:51–71.

Kucera, David. 2001. The effects of core worker's rights on labour costs and foreign direct investment: Evaluating the "conventional wisdom." Decent Work Research Programme Discussion Paper no. 130. Geneva: International Labor Organization.

Leamer, Edward E. 1999. Effort, wages and the international division of labor. *Journal of Political Economy* 107:1127–62.

Leamer, Edward E., and James Levinsohn. 1995. International trade theory: The evidence. In *Handbook of international economics.* Vol. 3, ed. Gene M. Grossman and Kenneth Rogoff. Amsterdam: North Holland.

Lim, Linda Y. C. 2000. My factory visits in Southeast Asia and UM code and monitoring, September 6. http://www.fordschool.umich.edu/rsie/acit/Documents/LimNotes00.pdf.

————. 2001. *The globalization debate: Issues and challenges.* Geneva: International Labour Organization.

Lipsey, Robert E., and Fredrik Sjöholm. 2001. Foreign direct investment and wages in Indonesian manufacturing. NBER Working Paper no. 8299. Cambridge, Mass.: National Bureau of Economic Research, May.

Lukacs, Aaron. 2000. *WTO report card III: Globalization and developing countries.* Trade Briefing Paper. Washington, D.C.: Center for Trade Policy Studies, Cato Institute.

Luttmer, Erzo, and Daniel Oks. 1993. *Productivity in Mexican industries.* Washington, D.C.: World Bank.

Manning, Chris. 1998. *Indonesian labour in transition: An East Asian success story?* Cambridge: Cambridge University Press.

Markusen, James R. 1984. Multinationals, multiplant economies, and the gains from trade. *Journal of International Economics* 16:205–26.

Martin, Will, and Keith Maskus. 2001. The economics of core labor standards: Implications for global trade policy. *Review of International Economics* 9:317–28.

Moran, Theodore. 2002. *Beyond sweatshops: Foreign direct investment in developing countries.* Washington, D.C.: Brookings Institution.

Neumark, David. 2002. *How living wage laws affect low-wage workers and low-income families.* San Francisco: Public Policy Institute of California.

Organization for Economic Cooperation and Development (OECD). 2000. *International trade and core labour standards.* Paris: OECD.

————. 2001. *Manufacturing sector.* Vol. 1 of *Measuring globalization: The role of multinationals in OECD economies.* Paris: OECD.

Panos. 1999. *Globalization and employment: New opportunities, real threats.* Panos Briefing no. 33. London: Panos, May. http://www.panos.org.uk/resources/reportdetails.asp?id=1015.

Razafindrakoto, Mireille, and Francois Roubaud. 1995. Les entreprises Franches a Madagascar: economie d'enclave ou promesse d'une novelle prosperité? Mouvel exclavage ou opportunité pour le developpement du pays? (French enterprises in Madagascar: Economic enclave or promise of a new prosperity? New exploitation or opportunity for economic development?) *Economie de Madagascar 2.*

Rodrik, Dani. 1996. Labor standards in international trade: Do they matter and what do we do about them? In *Emerging agenda for global trade: High stakes for developing countries,* ed. Robert Lawrence, Dani Rodrik, and John Whalley, 35–79. Washington, D.C.: Overseas Development Council.

————. 1999. Democracies pay higher wages. *Quarterly Journal of Economics* 114 (3): 707–38.

Ruggie, John Gerard. 2002. The theory and practice of learning networks: Corporate social responsibility and the global compact. *Journal of Corporate Citizenship* 5 (Spring): 27–36.

Schneider, Friedrich, and Bruno Frey. 1985. Economics and political determinants of foreign direct investment. *World Development* 13 (2): 161–75.

Srinivasan, T. N. 1998. Trade and human rights. In *Constituent interests and U.S. trade policies,* ed. Alan V. Deardorff and Robert M. Stern, 225–53. Ann Arbor: University of Michigan Press.

————. 2001. Living wage in poor countries. Yale University, Department of Economics. Manuscript.

U.S. Department of Labor, Bureau of International Labor Affairs. 2000. *Wages, benefits, poverty line, and meeting workers' needs in the apparel and footwear industries of selected countries.* Washington, D.C.: GPO.

University of Chicago Magazine. 2000. Student Activists Raise Signs Over Sweatshops. *University of Chicago Magazine* 92 (5). http://magazine/uchicago.edu/0006/campus-news/report-sweatshops.htm.

University of Michigan. 2000. *The final report of the advisory committee on labor standards and human rights* Ann Arbor, Mich.: University of Michigan, May. http://www.umich.edu/~newsinfo/BG/humright.html.

Varley, Pamela, ed. 1998. *The sweatshop quandary: Corporate responsibility on the global frontier.* Washington, D.C.: Investor Responsibility Research Center.

Verité. 2000. *Pilot project for licensing labor code implementation.* Final Report. Amherst, Mass.: Verité, October.

Verité. 2001. *Comprehensive factory evaluation report on Kukdong International Mexico, S.A. de C.V.* 5–7 February, Atlixco, Puebla, Mexico. http://ur.rutgers/edu/news/ACLA/veritereporte3901.htm.

Wheeler, David, and Ashoka Mody. 1992. International investment location decisions: The case of U.S. firms. *Journal of International Economics* 33:57–76.

World Bank. 1999. *The Philippines: The case of economic zones.* Washington, D.C.: World Bank.

World Trade Organization (WTO). 1999. *International trade statistics 1998.* Geneva: WTO.

———. 2001. *International trade statistics 2000.* Geneva: WTO.

Yellen, Janet L. 1984. Efficiency wage models of unemployment. *American Economic Review Papers and Proceedings* 74:200–05

Comment   André Sapir

In the introduction to their paper, Brown, Deardorff, and Stern (BDS) state that its objective is to assess the empirical evidence on the effects of multinational production on wages and working conditions in developing countries. They also indicate that the paper is motivated by recent controversies in the United States as to whether multinational firms in developing countries are exploiting their workers by employing them under "sweatshop" conditions.

Quite logically, therefore, the paper is divided into two parts. The first (section 8.2) focuses largely on the anti-sweatshop campaign in the United States. The second examines the theoretical (section 8.3) and empirical (section 8.4) effects of foreign direct investment (FDI) on wages and working conditions in host developing countries.

A major problem with the paper is the lack of coherence between the subjects covered in its two parts. Sweatshop, the topic of the first part, is in fact hardly related to foreign direct investment, the topic of the second part.

Originally, the term "sweatshop" referred to a type of industrial relation.

André Sapir is professor of economics at the European Centre for Advanced Research in Economics and Statistics (ECARES) at the Free University of Brussels.

It denoted a system of subcontracting wherein the work is let out to contractors operating in small shops. Later on, it came to be associated with the working conditions that often characterize such shops. For instance, in the United States, the General Accounting Office defines a sweatshop as "an employer that violates more than one federal or state law governing minimum wage and overtime, child labor, industrial homework, occupational safety and health, workers' compensation or industry regulation."

In the recent U.S. debate, the term "sweatshop" encompasses both notions. It usually refers to multinational operations in the apparel and footwear industries involving large numbers of contractors alleged to violate certain labor regulations. Elliott and Freeman (2001) give a number of examples of multinational operations in the apparel and footwear industries with large numbers of contractors: JC Penney, the U.S. retailer, contracts with over 2,000 suppliers in more than eighty countries for the production of infant and children's apparel; Nordstrom, a sportswear company, has over 50,000 contractors and subcontractors; Wal-Mart, another retailer, contracts with over 1,000 companies in China alone; and Disney licenses products in over 30,000 factories around the world. The important point is that these contractors (which may be sweatshops) are not generally owned by the U.S. (or any other foreign) companies that contract them and, therefore, fall outside the realm of foreign direct investment, as commonly defined.

I now turn to a discussion of the two main sections of the paper.

Section 8.2 begins with a description of the anti-sweatshop campaign in the United States. The description largely focuses on the efforts by student activist groups aimed at the adoption, by colleges and universities, of codes of conduct imposing certain labor practices on manufacturers of college apparel. The paper explains how student activism led to the establishment of two rival groupings among college and university professors: the Academic Consortium on International Trade (ACIT), which regards activism in favor of labor standards as misguided or manipulated by protectionist interests, and the Scholars Against Sweatshop Labor (SASL), which views this brand of social activism with clear sympathy. The discussion here is more partisan than analytical, which is perhaps not surprising given that two of the three authors are on the steering committee of one of the two academic groupings (the ACIT).

Having discussed the pros and cons of the anti-sweatshop campaign, BDS turn their attention to the options that "multinational firms may choose to pursue on matters of their social accountability." These multinational corporations (MNCs) are those firms that contract with suppliers in developing countries, and are accused of operating under sweatshop conditions. Based on the view that the anti-sweatshop campaign aimed at multinationals is misdirected and on "[t]he evidence to be presented in section 8.4," the authors brush off the option that MNCs should meet their social accountability by seeking to improve the labor conditions of their contractors. Rather than attempting to change the conditions of producers in the developing countries, they suggest instead that MNCs concentrate their efforts on measures that impact more directly on the *perception* of the problem by consumers in the developed countries. The idea is simply for MNCs to defend themselves "against the possibility of unfavorable publicity regarding their operations that could prove damaging to them in the eyes of consumers and thereby reduce their sales and profitability."

The option favored by BDS hinges crucially on the evidence presented in section 8.4. Unfortunately, this evidence is all but compelling.

Section 8.4 is divided into two parts. The first examines the effects of foreign ownership on wages based on descriptive surveys and econometric studies. The surveys tend to indicate that workers in foreign-owned and subcontracting apparel and footwear plants in various developing countries earn wages at or above minimum-wage levels. This may well be the case, but the critical reader will remain unimpressed by evidence such as "a report on Nike contract factories in Vietnam and Indonesia by students from The Amos Tuck School at Dartmouth." The authors also report econometric-based evidence from three studies: Aitken, Harrison, and Lipsey (1996), which explores the impact of foreign ownership in Mexico, Venezuela, and the United States; Feenstra and Hanson (1997), which studies the impact of foreign-owned capital on the skilled-labor wage premium in Mexico; and Lipsey and Sjöholm (2001), which analyzes the wages paid by foreign-owned plants in Indonesia. Clearly none of these studies is directly relevant for the issue of sweatshops since they focus neither on the right sectors (namely, apparel and footwear) nor on the right type of firms (namely contractors instead of foreign-owned plants). The second part suffers from the same type of problem. It examines the link between foreign direct investment and labor rights, and concludes that "there is no solid evidence that countries with poorly protected worker rights attract FDI." This may well be correct, but once again the more relevant issue for the sweatshop debate is whether contractors (not owned by foreign companies and therefore falling outside the category of FDI) respect worker rights.

In the end, the reader is left with little "scientific" evidence for judging the merits or weaknesses of the anti-sweatshop campaign. If academic economists want to refute the anecdotes of the popular press and social activists, they will have to do better than rely on scant or inappropriate evidence.

References

Aitken, Brian, Ann Harrison, and Robert E. Lipsey. 1996. Wages and foreign ownership: A comparative study of Mexico, Venezuela, and the United States. *Journal of International Economics* 40 (3–4): 345–71.

Elliott, Kimberly Ann, and Richard B. Freeman. 2001. White hats or human rights vigilantes in the global economy. NBER Working Paper no. 8102. Cambridge, Mass.: National Bureau of Economic Research, January.

Feenstra, Robert C., and Gordon H. Hanson. 1996. Foreign investment, outsourcing, and relative wages. In *The political economy of trade policy: Essays in honor of Jagdish Bhagwati,* ed. R. C. Feenstra, G. M. Grossman, and D. A. Irwin, 89–127. Cambridge: MIT Press.

Lipsey, Robert E., and Fredrick Sjöholm. 2001. Foreign direct investment and wages in Indonesian manufacturing. NBER Working Paper no. 8299. Cambridge, Mass.: National Bureau of Economic Research, May.

IV

Factor Markets: Capital

9

Home- and Host-Country Effects of Foreign Direct Investment

Robert E. Lipsey

9.1 Introduction

Protests against "globalization" involve a wide spectrum of discontents with modern life and market economies. They include the growth of international trade and specialization, and the disruptions of traditional or established economic practices they entail. They include also the actions of intergovernmental agencies, such as the International Trade Organization (ITO), International Monetary Fund (IMF), the World Bank, and the regional development banks. And it is rare that multinational firms are not mentioned, as the presumed leaders and chief beneficiaries of globalization.

There are also more specific accusations against multinationals. Many evils are alleged. They depress wages and employment at home by moving production abroad. They depress wages in their host countries by exploiting helpless workers. They stifle host-country growth by displacing local firms and obstructing their technological progress. Anyone who believes that these fears are a new phenomenon should read the chapter on "The Reactions to Foreign Investment" in Wilkins (1989, chap. 16), where the author describes how "in the mid-1880s and into the 1890s, a passionate, hitherto unmatched fury mounted against foreign investment in the United States" (566).

Robert E. Lipsey is professor emeritus of economics at Queens College and the Graduate Center, City University of New York, and a research associate and director of the New York office of the National Bureau of Economic Research (NBER).

I am indebted to Li Xu for help in searching for, assembling, and reviewing the many papers discussed here. Robert E. Baldwin, of the University of Wisconsin; Andrew Bernard, of Yale University; Vanessa Strauss-Kahn, of INSEAD; and Birgitta Swedenborg, of the Center for Business and Policy Studies, Stockholm, made helpful comments on earlier versions of this paper.

To the extent that opposition to globalization stems from different values that view as bad traditional economic goods such as higher consumption or the growth of production and exchange, I do not attempt to deal with them. Many of the other accusations are framed in vague terms. I attempt to appraise them by classifying the effects of multinational operations under several homogeneous headings and reviewing what research has concluded with respect to each topic. On home-country effects, I summarize the findings on home-country exports and home-country factor demand. On host-country effects, I discuss wages, productivity, exports, the introduction of new industries, and the rate of economic growth.

There are two concepts of foreign direct investment (FDI) and two matching ways of measuring it. One is that FDI is a particular form of the flow of capital across international boundaries. It gives rise to a particular form of international assets for the home countries, specifically, the value of holdings in entities, typically corporations, controlled by a home-country resident or in which a home-country resident holds a certain share of the voting rights. The other concept of direct investment is that it is a set of economic activities or operations carried out in a host country by firms controlled or partly controlled by firms in some other (home) country. These activities are, for example, production, employment, sales, the purchase and use of intermediate goods and fixed capital, and the carrying out of research.

The former of these two concepts is the one reflected in balance-of-payments accounts. The measures of it, flows and stocks of direct investment, are the only virtually ubiquitous quantitative indicators of FDI. However, if the effects of FDI stem from the activity of the foreign-owned firms in their host countries, the balance-of-payments measures have many defects for any examination of these impacts. The activity is frequently not in the same industry as the stock, or not in the same host country, or has not originated from the same home country (Lipsey 2003; United Nations 2001). For this reason, wherever possible, I emphasize studies based on activity, such as production or employment, rather than those based on balance-of-payments stocks and flows.

9.2   What Happens When a Foreign Direct Investment Is Made?

Much of the earlier economics literature on FDI, but not the business literature, treated it as a part of the general theory of international capital movements, based on differences among countries in the abundance and cost of capital. If country A makes a direct investment in country B, there is an addition to the physical capital of country B, and new production capacity is created there. The investing firm in A will have chosen to use some of its capital in B instead of in A. If the output is tradable, some production that now takes place in country B may replace production that formerly took place in country A. The investing firm may have reduced its production in its home country, A, possibly by shutting down or selling a plant, and opened up a new plant abroad to serve the same market.

A different possibility is that when a firm in country A makes a direct investment in country B, the stock of physical capital and the level of production are unchanged in both countries. Country A owners and managers in industry X, using the skills they have acquired in home production, buy out country B owners with lower skills in that industry and operate the industry X plants in country B more efficiently than before. Country B owners use their capital, released by the buyout, in other industries. They might, for instance, lend it to other owners and managers in country B, skilled in industry Y, to enable them to buy out less competent owners in that industry in country A. No net movement of physical or financial capital is necessarily implied, although it could take place.

This latter picture belongs to what Markusen (1997) and Markusen and Maskus (2001) have called the "knowledge-capital model" of the multinational enterprise. It is related also to what Caves (1996, chap. 1) refers to as the dependence of multinational enterprises on "proprietary assets," or "firm-specific" assets. And it also fits with Romer's distinction (1993a,b) between the roles in economic development of what he calls "ideas" in contrast to "objects." Caves (1996) traces the decline of the view that multinationals are principally arbitrageurs of financial or physical capital to Hymer (1960) and to Kindleberger (1969), who adopted many of Hymer's ideas. Dunning (1970, 321) summarized their view as being that "the modern multi-national company is primarily a vehicle for the transfer of entrepreneurial talent rather than financial resources."

The capital-flow story depends on the advantages of countries as locations for production, and changes in such advantages. The entrepreneurship story, on the other hand, hinges on characteristics of firms and their managers, rather than those of countries. Capital flows imply changes in the industrial composition of production and employment in home and host countries. In industries producing tradables, they imply shifts in the composition of exports and imports. Entrepreneurship explanations contain implications for the ownership of production, but not necessarily for the location of production.

It is desirable to distinguish the location choices within firms from the location choices for industries in the aggregate. If, for example, because of a decline in communication costs, or an increase in the severity of currency fluctuations, firms in all countries decided to diversify their production locations, each firm in each country might shift production from home to foreign locations through FDI. However, there might be no change in the geographical location of production as a whole, because in each country, the outward shift of home-country firms' production might be balanced by the inward shift of foreign firms' production. Or there could be a general shift of production toward markets in each industry.

If there is a geographical relocation of production, the force behind it might be a change in factor prices, such as a rise in the home-country price of labor, or a rise in the home-country price of a natural resource. In that case, we would expect a shift in the production of labor-intensive or resource-intensive goods away from the home country, both within firms and in the aggregate. That might be reflected in a decline in firm and home-country exports, but it might also be the case that it was the decline of home-country exports, or the expectation of such a decline, that precipitated the production shift. It is difficult to distinguish between trade shifts produced by exogenous production-location decisions and location shifts produced by exogenous shifts, or potential shifts in trade. The difficulty of that distinction has haunted most analyses of home-country impacts.

There is some indication that the exchange of ownership has become a larger part of FDI flows over time and particularly during the 1990s. One piece of evidence is that the value of mergers and acquisitions has risen relative to the value of FDI flows and relative to world output (United Nations [UN] 2000, chap. 4). Most of this merger and acquisition activity has taken place among the developed countries. The rising trend seems to reflect an increase in mergers and acquisitions in general, rather than one mainly in international, or cross-border, ones: the international share appears to have been relatively constant since the late 1980s (UN 107). Much of this activity has taken the form of exchanges of stock, where relatively little net capital flow is involved.

There are important policy issues behind the strong interest in effects of the internationalization of production. Should countries promote or discourage the internationalization of their home-country firms, or should policy be neutral? Should countries encourage the entrance of foreign producers, or discourage it, or leave the decisions to market forces? Some of the early studies of U.S. direct investment abroad were motivated by the belief that features of the U.S. taxation of corporations were important inducements to foreign investment. That question may not have been settled, but the spread of the practice of internationalization from firms based in the United States to those from many other countries suggests that there were forces beyond any distortionary U.S. tax policies that were driving these trends.

9.3   Home-Country Effects of Outward Foreign Direct Investment

9.3.1   Outward Foreign Direct Investment and Home-Country Exports

Since the United States was the dominant outward direct investor in the period after World War II, much of the debate about the home-country consequences of FDI took place first there. The debate over the possible substitution of U.S. firms' foreign production for U.S. exports was most intense during the time of worries about the balance of payments during the

1960s. Curiously, earlier studies of U.S. foreign investment, such as Lewis (1938) and Madden, Nadler, and Sauvain (1937), did not take up the export substitution issue, despite the high unemployment levels of the 1930s. In the 1960s, there was a campaign against outward investment, largely fueled by fears about effects on U.S. exports and, presumably, domestic employment, that was supported by labor unions and culminated in the unsuccessful attempt to pass the Burke-Hartke bill.

The controversies of this period spawned a series of studies relating outward FDI to home-country exports. There are a number of different questions that can be asked, and they have not always been clearly distinguished, although the implications of the answers to them differ considerably. One set of questions is about the relationships within the individual investing firm. One is about the relation, for an individual parent firm, between its production in a host country and its exports to that country. A second is about the relation of a firm's production in a country to its exports to the world, taking account of the possibility that affiliate exports to other countries might affect parent markets there. A third is about the relation between a firm's production in all foreign countries and its exports to the world, taking account of all interrelationships between production abroad and exports. All of these are issues of firm strategy: how a firm chooses to serve markets around the world. There are no necessary inferences to be drawn about effects on the firm's home country as a whole, without knowledge about how other firms in the home country or other countries respond or react to the same stimuli.

A second set of questions is about the relation of the aggregate of decisions by a country's firms about production abroad to home-country exports in the same industry or in the aggregate, or to a home-country or industry employment or employment of different types of labor. These aggregate decisions incorporate the reactions of one firm in a country to the actions of other firms.

A third set of questions is about the relation between the decisions on the location of production made by firms from all countries on the worldwide pattern of production, trade, and employment, or on any particular countries' position. One reason these questions are rarely asked is that little is known about the outward FDI activities of about half or more of the world's direct investors, because most countries do not inquire into what their firms do outside their countries' borders.

The basic problem with studies of these questions has always been the close connection between the factors that determine a firm's exports and those that determine its foreign direct investment. A country's most competent and successful firms tend to export and to invest in production abroad, and the same is generally true of the most successful industries. All the research indicates an awareness of the problem, and the studies attempt to deal with it, usually in ways found unsatisfactory by critics.

The most common type of study was of the first question described above. Exports by a firm or an aggregate of firms in an industry to a foreign market were related to the firm's investment or production or employment in that market. The interrelations between exports and investment could be dealt with by assumption, as in the case of the Reddaway reports, that in the absence of a British-owned plant in a market, the alternative was a foreign-owned plant of the same size in the same industry (Reddaway et al. 1967, Reddaway, Potter, and Taylor 1968). That assumption essentially guaranteed a positive, or complementary, relationship between a firm's exports and its foreign production. In the other direction, Bergsten, Horst, and Moran (1978, 98) described the assumptions in Frank and Freeman (1975), and some in Hufbauer and Adler (1968), as assuming ". . . that foreign investment can only displace U.S. exports." Their own analysis of the first set of questions, based on U.S. aggregate data, cautiously summarized, pointed to mainly complementary relationships (Bergsten, Horst, and Moran 1978, 93–96). The studies by Lipsey and Weiss (1981, 1984), the first of exports, by industry, to individual destinations, and the second of total exports by individual U.S. firms, concluded that exports and production abroad by U.S. firms were, for the most part, complementary. A study using a later U.S. census of direct investment abroad found more mixed results for effects on total U.S. exports, mostly no relation, but where there was a significant relation, more frequently positive than negative (Blomström, Lipsey, and Kuchycky 1988).

Two of the few studies based on access to the confidential individual firm data collected by the U.S. Department of Commerce were Brainard (1997) and Brainard and Riker (1997). The focus of the Brainard and Riker study was on employment, rather than exports, but it is relevant here because employment issues lie behind much of the interest in exports. A feature of these studies, in contrast to many earlier ones of the United States and Sweden, is a more standard definition of complementarity and substitution, relating employment changes to wage changes in various locations. The limitation of this definition of complementarity is that it excludes home-country responses to variables other than the price of labor. These might include income growth, trade restrictions, policies toward direct investment, or changes in nonlabor costs of producing outside the home country. Brainard and Riker concluded that while there is some competition between a manufacturing firm's employment at home and that abroad, the degree of substitution is low. Mostly, competition takes place among workers in affiliates in different developing countries. Brainard (1997), testing the importance of factor price differences as an explanation for the location of foreign operations, dismisses it in favor of explanations based on the advantages of proximity to markets, among other factors. She suggests that "the overall complementarity between trade and affiliate sales" is attributable to the fact that both "are increasing in market size and intellectual property advantages . . ." (539).

A study along similar lines for Swedish firms based on individual firm data, Braconier and Ekholm (2000), produced different results. There was evidence of "a substitutionary relationship between parent employment in Sweden and affiliate employment in other high-income locations" but no "evidence of a relationship in either direction between parent firm employment and affiliate employment in low-income locations" (459).

Concerns in Sweden about home-country effects of FDI led to a series of studies by Swedenborg (1973, 1979, 1982, 1985, 2001), and by Swedenborg, Johansson-Grahn, and Kinnwall (1988). An important and innovative feature of Swedenborg (1979) was the use of two-stage least squares to attempt to deal with the endogeneity of exports and the mutual determination with investment. That procedure was carried into her later work as well. The latest of her papers (Swedenborg 2001), in addition, takes advantage of the longitudinal aspect of the Swedish data to examine the effects on firm exports of changes in a firm's foreign production over time. She concludes that "the enormous growth of foreign production by Swedish firms in the thirty-year period, 1965–94 has not, in itself, had a negative effect on parent-company exports" (121). These studies examine parent-company exports to individual countries as well as total parent exports. Blomström, Lipsey, and Kuchycky (1988, 268–69), using total Swedish exports and changes in them, rather than parent exports as the dependent variables, found mainly positive relationships with production abroad and its growth.

As data on Japanese multinationals have become available for research in recent years, similar calculations have been carried out, with both parent exports (Lipsey, Ramstetter, and Blomström 2003) and Japanese industry exports (Lipsey and Ramstetter 2003) as dependent variables. In the minority of industries where any relationship between exports and overseas production can be discerned, the relation was positive, as in the United States and Sweden. The relationships for the three countries are compared and summarized in Lipsey, Ramstetter, and Blomström (2000).

With the rise in unemployment levels in Europe and the increase in outward FDI by European firms, the possible connection between the two has become a popular subject for study in Europe. In a study of bilateral trade and direct investment relationships for France, Fontagné and Pajot (2002) found complementarity between investment flows and net exports both for countries as a whole and for individual industries, and concluded that much of the complementarity between countries came from spillovers among industries. Studies by Chédor and Mucchielli (1998) and by Chédor, Mucchielli, and Soubaya (2002), the latter based on panel data for individual French firms and the former concerned with effects of developed countries' direct investment in developing countries, both produced conclusions that investment and home-country exports were complementary.

A recent survey of Australian firms' investment overseas concluded that "outward direct investment by Australian firms is mainly tapping into new growth and market opportunities for firms, rather than substituting for, or displacing, operations in Australia" (Australia Productivity Commission 2002, 24). The questions about effects on employment and production in Australia both produced more than 70 percent "no change" answers, but of those who reported changes increases were more common than decreases. The question on effects on exports from Australia also yielded a majority of "no change," but of those who reported an effect, the overwhelming majority reported an increase (25).

There have been many studies for other countries, mostly examining the relation of firms' or industries' foreign production to firm or industry exports. While there are some examples of negative associations, they are not frequent, and positive associations are more common. What is noticeable in a review of past studies, but is not commented on so often, is the frequency of results indicating no association in either direction. The elements of gravity equations are consistently significant in the expected direction, while the influence of FDI production is spotty and varies among host countries, industries, and types of parent-company exports. Bergsten, Horst, and Moran (1978) refer to the relationship as "haphazard" (97) and to "the presence of complementary and substitutional relations" (98). Lipsey and Weiss (1984) found mostly complementarity, but in half the industries there were no significant relationships at all. Blomström, Lipsey, and Kulchycky (1988, 275) reported that "[t]he predominant relationship between production in a country by affiliates of Swedish and U.S. firms and exports to that country from Sweden and the United States is something between neutrality and complementarity." Swedenborg, in her latest paper, concludes that ". . . the net effect of foreign production is probably close to zero" (2001, 117).

One way of interpreting these findings is that there are no universal relationships between production abroad by a firm or a country's firms and exports by the investing firms, their industries, and the country as a whole. There are circumstances in which foreign production tends to add to exports and circumstances in which it tends to reduce exports. The effect may depend on whether the foreign operations' relation to home operations is "horizontal" or "vertical," a distinction stressed by Markusen and Maskus (2001). It may also depend on the extent to which the foreign operations are in goods production or in service activities, are in developed or developing countries, or are in industries with plant-level or firm-level economies of scale.

It seems plausible that horizontal FDI should tend to substitute for parent exports, at least in manufacturing, if not in services, and that vertical FDI might tend to add to parent exports. But there is not much evidence for this conjecture. It is difficult to classify actual foreign operations into these theoretically neat categories. A firm's foreign operations usually include some activities similar to those of the parent, but the industry identifications in most data do not distinguish among segments of an industry. The foreign operation may omit some parent activities, because they are performed for the affiliate by the parent. And the foreign operation may include some activities that are not performed by the parent, because they are provided by the home country's infrastructure or by a network of outside suppliers that does not exist in the host country. This distinction between horizontal and vertical FDI is more useful for thinking about multinational behavior or constructing models of it than for empirical research.

A problem with most studies of effects of FDI on home-country exports is that the terms "substitution" and "complementarity" are not clearly defined. That is partly because no policy measures are specified as determining the changes in investment or production. It is rare to find a clear counterfactual to which the existing situation is being compared.

The problem is illustrated by the example of a host-country tariff on imports that leads to both a reduction or cessation of imports and the establishment of host-country production owned by the former exporters. Higher local production is accompanied by reduced exports, an apparent case of substitution. The implied counterfactual is the original level of exports. In fact, the alternative to the establishment or expansion of host-country production may have been no exports and no sales by the parent firm or its country. That counterfactual would lead to the conclusion that the production and trade were either not related or were complementary, instead of the apparent substitution that appears in the data.

A possible interpretation of these studies is that foreign production by a firm or industry has very little influence on exports from the parent firm or its home country. Mainly, trade is determined by other factors, such as countries' changing comparative advantages in production. Direct investment is mainly about the ownership of production, not its location. What moves from country to country when a direct investment takes place is not primarily physical capital or production capacity, but rather intellectual capital, or techniques of production, unobserved and unmeasured. There may be movements of physical or financial capital accompanying the intellectual capital, but there need not be, and they are not the essence of the investment.

9.3.2   Foreign Direct Investment and Home-Country Factor Demand

Even if direct investment did not affect the location of total production and had no effect on a home country's exports, it could influence home-country factor demand and factor prices through changes in the allocation of types of production within the firm. For example, multinationals based in rich countries might allocate their more labor-intensive production to their affiliates in poor countries, while concentrating their more capital-intensive or skill-intensive operations at home. Large differences in capital intensity between U.S. (home) operations and affiliates in developing countries were noted in Lipsey, Kravis, and Roldan (1982), but the response of capital intensity to labor costs was tested only among affiliates. If multinationals tended to allocate their production in this way, larger affiliate output relative to parent output should be associated with lower labor intensity and higher skill intensity in home production. In a study based on 1982 data, that relationship for labor intensity, measured by numbers of workers per unit of output, was found fairly consistently among industries in Kravis and Lipsey (1988), and less consistently for skill intensity, as measured by hourly wages. A similar calculation based on 1988 data (Lipsey 1995) found the same negative relation between affiliate net sales and parent employment, given the level of parent output. When affiliate activity was divided between manufacturing and nonmanufacturing operations, it was the manufacturing operations that accounted for the negative relation to parent employment; higher net sales by nonmanufacturing affiliates were associated with higher parent employment, given the level of parent output. In a later study covering the United States and Sweden, Blomström, Fors, and Lipsey (1997) found that larger production in developing countries by a U.S. firm was associated with lower labor intensity at home. In a further analysis of these data, Lipsey (2002) found that the effects on parent factor use across all types of countries were concentrated in the machinery and transport-equipment industries. There were positive effects on parent employment per unit of output in the machinery sectors and negative effects in transport equipment.

Swedish firms tended to use more labor per unit of output at home if they produced more abroad. That might be because production abroad required supervisory and other auxiliary employment at home. Or it might be that only the existence of foreign production enabled firms in a small market such as Sweden to develop and support extensive headquarters and research services. One explanation offered for the difference between Swedish and U.S. firms was that the Swedish investments in developing countries were concentrated in import substitution activities, and the affiliates exported little of their output, much less than U.S. affiliates. The Swedish affiliates could not, therefore, be woven into a worldwide division of labor that took account of factor price differences.

A later paper added Japanese firms to these comparisons (Lipsey, Ramstetter, and Blomström 2000). As in Swedish firms, higher levels of foreign output, given the level of home output, led to higher employment at home per unit of home output, presumably for supervision. It was suggested that Japanese firms could not easily shed redundant home-country workers even if they had wished to do so.

No explicit home-country production functions were fitted in these studies. Therefore, the variable for affiliate output incorporated the influence of any home-country firm characteristics that were associated with the size of affiliate production. Furthermore, most of these results are from cross-sections. A different approach is taken by Slaughter (2000), examining what he refers to as "MNE [multinational enterprise] transfer," the shift, in percentage terms, of activities from parents to their foreign affiliates. He asks whether such "transfer" causes "skill upgrading," increases in the share of nonproduction worker wages in industry total wage bills, in the corresponding domestic U.S. industries.

Slaughter fits translog cost functions to data on the share of nonproduction worker wages in the total wage bills of thirty-two U.S. manufacturing industries, taking account of relative wage rates for production and nonproduction workers, capital-labor ratios, and output. Various measures of MNE transfer are added to these equations. All the transfer measures are based on ratios of affiliate activity in U.S. MNEs to total activity in the United States in the industries of the affiliates. The expectation of an effect on total industry skill levels is based on the fact that the parents of the affiliates account for most of their respective industries.

While higher investment in plant and equipment and higher industry output both led to skill upgrading, increases in affiliate activity in host countries had no significant impact. Slaughter (2000, 467) concludes that his finding "is inconsistent with models of MNEs in which affiliate activities substitute for parent unskilled-labor-intensive activities." That conclusion is reached despite the fact that there are no data for parent, rather than industry, skill levels, and that the MNE transfer measure is not specific to transfers to low-wage countries.

A different conclusion is reached by Head and Ries (2002) for the foreign operations of Japanese firms. Their calculations on an industry basis, similar to those of Slaughter (2000) for the United States, match his findings. The ratio of affiliate employment to the total of home and affiliate employment in an industry does not significantly affect the share of nonproduction worker wages in the total wage bill in the home country. However, once they move to a firm-level analysis, they do find that a higher affiliate employment share in the multinational firm produces a higher nonproduction worker wage share in the parent firm. That positive effect is associated with affiliate employment in low-wage countries; more employment in the United States appears to have the opposite effect. Thus, overseas production in low-wage countries seems to raise the parent firm's demand for skilled workers at home relative to the demand for unskilled workers.

The contrast between industry- and firm-level results suggests the possibility that substitution among types of activities may take place not only between home and foreign operations of a firm, but also between parent firms and nonmultinational firms in the same industry at home. That is a subject that has received very little attention, but deserves investigation.

9.3.3   Home-Country Exports and Home-Country Multinationals' Exports

The idea that firms have comparative advantages separate from those of their home countries has been illustrated by several episodes. One is the contrast between the export shares of the United States and of U.S.-based multinational firms. During the period from 1966 to 1987, the U.S. share of world exports of manufactured goods fell from 17 percent to about 11 percent, a decline of a third. Over that same period, U.S.-based multinational firms' share of these exports, from the parent companies and their overseas affiliates combined, was quite stable, ending up in 1987 about where it began in 1966. The way this stability was achieved was that, as the world share of exports by the parent firms fell, the share of the overseas affiliates of these companies, exporting from their host countries, grew. The U.S. multinationals retained their shares of world exports, while the United States as a country was losing a large part of its share, because the multinationals' share depended on their firm-specific advantages, and the multinationals could exploit their firm-specific advantages by producing in other countries (Lipsey 1995, 12–13).

The divergence between home countries and home-country firms was not confined to the United States. For example, as Japanese export shares fell after the currency revaluations in 1985, Japanese affiliate export shares increased enough to approximately offset the decline in the country's share. Swedish shares in world manufactured exports fell by almost a third between 1965 and 1990, but Swedish multinationals' shares of world exports remained stable, or even increased a little (Lipsey 1995, 14–15).

For all these countries' multinationals, foreign production was apparently not only a way of exploiting their firm-specific assets in foreign markets, but also a way of protecting these market shares against unfavorable home-country developments. These might be exchange rate appreciations, increases in home-country wage levels, increases in taxes, or other changes that reduced the geographical advantages of their home countries as locations for production.

9.4   Host-Country Effects of Inward Foreign Direct Investment

9.4.1   Host-Country Wages

There are several ways in which the entrance or existence of foreign firms might affect wages in the host countries where they operate. One is if these firms offer higher wages than are paid by domestic firms. That possibility raises the question, dealt with in the next subsection, of whether they do pay higher wages. Even if they did pay higher wages, there might be no overall impact on wage levels if the higher wages simply reflected the selection by foreign firms among workers, plants, or locations. They might select superior workers who would command high wages from any employer, or acquire higher-wage plants or firms, or concentrate their activities in high-wage industries or regions of a country. Thus, the second question is whether the payment of higher wages by foreign-owned firms results in higher wages in domestically owned firms, or "wage spillovers." The third question which I think is the most important from a policy point of view, is whether the activities of foreign-owned firms cause wages in general to be higher, on average, where they operate. That could be the result of the combination of higher wages in the foreign-owned plants and wage spillovers to domestically owned plants, but it could result from higher wages paid by foreign-owned firms even if there were no wage spillovers, or there were negative spillovers, to domestically owned plants. It could also occur without any wage differential between foreign-owned and domestically owned operations if labor markets were sufficiently competitive and the rise in demand for labor from foreign-owned operations forced all firms to raise their wage levels equally.

The measurement of wage levels is in some ways simpler than the measurement of productivity levels, taken up in section 9.4.2. It has its own problems, however. Most of the data are calculated as compensation/number of workers. Very few take account of hours of work, probably most important outside manufacturing but a possible source of mismeasurement in all industries. Probably more important is that there are few sources of data that contain information on the characteristics of workers, so that is impossible in most cases to distinguish between differences in wage rates for identical workers and differences in labor quality.

Wage Comparisons

It is rare to find a study of FDI and wages in any host country that does not find that foreign-owned firms pay higher wages, on average, than at least privately owned local firms. That is the case not only in developing countries, where most of the research has taken place, but also in developed, high-wage countries. To some extent, the differential can be explained by the industry composition of FDI, weighted toward relatively high-wage industry sectors. However, the differential exists within industries, in most industries in most countries.

There are two broad types of questions that can be asked about this phenomenon. One is about how labor markets operate in these host countries, particularly whether foreign firms pay higher prices for labor, in the sense of paying higher wages for workers of the same quality. The other is about how inward FDI affects labor markets, whether or not the effects can be accounted for by firm size, industry, capital intensity, research and development (R&D) intensity, or other characteristics associated with foreign firms, that could belong to domestic firms as well as to foreign firms.

Why would a foreign-owned firm pay a higher price than a domestic firm for labor of a given quality? It presumably could pay more than a domestically owned firm of the same size if its superior technology produced higher marginal labor productivity, but the expected response would be to expand output rather than to raise wages. Several reasons have been suggested. One is that it may be forced to do so by host-country regulations or home-country pressures. The Findlay model assumes that foreign firms pay a higher wage for labor of the same quality "for purposes of good public relations" (1978, 9). It might be that workers prefer locally owned firms, and must be compensated to overcome this preference. A third possibility is that foreign-owned firms pay a premium to reduce worker turnover, because they have brought some proprietary technology and wish to reduce the speed with which it leaks out to domestic rivals as employees change jobs. A fourth is that foreign firms, because of their limited understanding of local labor markets, pay higher wages to attract better workers, while more knowledgeable local firms can identify and attract better workers without paying them higher wages.

Studies attempting to measure the pure effect of foreignness are akin to successive distillations to remove impurities. The impurities in this case are explanations for differentials that are not necessarily intrinsic to foreignness, although they may be associated with it in practice. What may be more relevant to judging the optimum policies toward inward direct investment are studies with not quite as many controls. A state or a region or a country that wishes to estimate the effect of allowing inward FDI where it had been prohibited, or reducing obstacles to it, may not care why the foreign firm will pay higher wages. It is not relevant whether it is because the firm is foreign, because it is large, or because it brings more capital-intensive or skill-intensive production methods or better access to world markets. A domestic firm with the same attributes might have the same impact, but there may not be any such domestic firm, or if there is one, it may not be willing to make this particular investment.

If foreign firms are found to pay higher wages than local firms, for whatever reason, there are still several questions to be asked about the impact. If foreign firms hired high-wage workers away from local firms, or acquired local firms with skilled labor forces, we might find that foreign ownership was associated with higher wages in the foreign-owned firms and lower wages in domestic firms, but no difference in average industry wage levels. If foreign firms paid more, but did not differentially poach the best workers from local firms, one should find a larger presence of foreign ownership associated with higher wages in the industry, but not in locally owned firms in the industry. Or finally, we might find examples of "spillover," where higher foreign presence was associated with higher wages in domestically owned establishments.

Data on wage differences come in several different forms. Some are simple comparisons of average wages, or average wages by industry, where wage differences reflect any effects of firm or plant characteristics, such as size or capital intensity, and of worker characteristics, such as age and education. Others adjust for differences in plant characteristics, asking whether foreign-owned plants pay wages different from those in otherwise identical domestically owned plants. A third type, less common, adjusts for differences in worker characteristics, asking whether foreign-owned plants pay different wages from those in domestically owned plants for identical workers. And a fourth type, still more rare, adjusts for both plant and worker characteristics, asking whether foreign-owned plants pay different wages from those in identical domestically owned plants for identical workers.

Observations of higher wages in foreign-owned firms in developing countries go back a long time, although the earliest ones were not the result of careful statistical studies. An early study of American firms in Colombia concluded that "Colombian labor, whenever it is paid a stipulated wage, is better remunerated and granted more sanitary living quarters by foreigners than by natives, but the foreigners probably exact more systematic and strenuous effort" (Rippy 1931, 190). Another partial explanation for the higher wages was that "the American companies are eager to attract the most efficient labor" (Rippy, 191).

A study by Blomström (1983) of Mexican manufacturing industries in 1970 found that foreign-owned firms paid wages about 25 percent above those in domestically owned firms in manufacturing as a whole. Foreign firms' wage levels were also higher in each of four major groups of manufacturing industries, by 25 to 30 percent, except in capital goods industries, where the difference was much smaller (18–19).

Many of the recent studies of wages in foreign plants in developing countries have been based on manufacturing-sector data on individual establishments collected in national surveys and assembled by the World Bank. A number of them were carried out by Ann Harrison, in collaboration with several others, and wage data for three of these studies are summarized in Harrison (1996). There were statistically significant differences between wages in foreign-owned and domestically owned plants in three out of twelve industries in Côte d'Ivoire, twelve out of eighteen in Morocco, and eight out of nine in Venezuela. Ratios of foreign to domestic plant wages, where the differences were significant, ranged from 1.1 to 1.9 in Côte d'Ivoire, 1.3 to 2.6 in Morocco, and 1.2 to 2.0 in Venezuela. These are simple differences without adjustment for plant or worker characteristics. One problem with cross-sectional analyses of wage differences is the unknown role of unmeasured aspects of plant heterogeneity. For Venezuela, that problem could be dealt with by examining wages in individual plants over time. While the relationship between wages and foreign ownership of a plant was weaker, and the differential smaller than in aggregated data, foreign ownership of a plant, controlling for plant size, industry, and capital intensity, resulted in wages higher by 16–18 percent (Aitken, Harrison, and Lipsey 1996, 368).

A paper on Morocco by Haddad and Harrison (1993) found that wages were 70 percent higher, on average, in foreign firms (58). The difference partly reflected the greater size of the foreign-owned firms; in weighted means, calculated to eliminate the size effect, the difference was reduced to 30 percent. The weighted average mean real wages were significantly higher in foreign-owned firms in sixteen out of eighteen individual industries. All the industries in which the wage differences were statistically significant showed higher wages in the foreign-owned plants. Something of an oddity, which casts some suspicion on the productivity measures discussed later, is that these higher wages in foreign-owned plants were accompanied by lower output per worker, at least in the weighted averages, and lower total factor productivity.

Several studies of Indonesia, such as Hill (1990) and Manning (1998), found that foreign firms paid higher wages than domestic firms. A recent paper using establishment data for Indonesia (Lipsey and Sjöholm 2003) found that in 1996, foreign-owned firms paid about 50 percent higher wages than private domestically owned firms in manufacturing as a whole, for both blue-collar and white-collar workers. When account was taken of the education levels of the workers, and of the industry and location of plants, foreign ownership was associated with wages about 25 percent higher for blue-collar workers and 50 percent higher for white-collar workers. Much of the differential was associated with the larger size of foreign-owned plants and greater inputs of energy and other intermediate product. The authors concluded that there was strong evidence that foreign firms "paid a higher price for labor than domestically-owned plants" (13). They paid a higher price, by a large margin, for workers of a given educational level (something most studies do not have information on, because business censuses rarely include labor-force characteristics). Even with the effects of plant and worker characteristics removed, blue-collar workers in foreign-owned plants earned about 12 percent more than in domestic plants and white-collar workers about 20 percent more (Lipsey and Sjöholm).

In four East Asian countries for which Ramstetter (1999, table 2) reported wages in foreign and domestic plants or firms, averaged over fourteen- to twenty-three-year periods, wages were higher in the foreign-owned ones, although in Singapore and Taiwan the differences were not significant.

Similar questions can be asked about wages in foreign-owned plants in developed countries. The increasing availability of individual firm and establishment microdata sets has encouraged such studies. In the United States, the linking of Economic Census establishment data with Bureau of

Economic Analysis (BEA) surveys of inward FDI was a catalyst. Using the BEA-Census data for 1987, the first such match, Lipsey (1994) found that workers in foreign-owned establishments earned 10–12 percent more than those in domestically owned establishments in the same two-digit standard industrial classification (SIC) industries and states. They earned 6–7 percent more in manufacturing and 12–15 percent more in other industries. Howenstine and Zeile (1994), using access to more-detailed information by industry and location not available outside the Department of Commerce, found similar differentials in manufacturing, all of which they could explain by differences in establishment size. Using individual manufacturing-plant data, Doms and Jensen (1998) found that even controlling for four-digit industry, state, plant size, and plant age, foreign-owned plants paid higher wages. They attributed the higher wage in foreign plants to the fact that they were parts of multinational firms, a theory they felt was confirmed by the fact that the highest wages of all were paid by domestic plants that were parts of U.S. multinational firms. One question about this comparison is whether foreign subsidiaries in the United States were comparable to the establishments of U.S. multinationals, since the latter could include firm headquarters operations, a high-paid category probably not part of the U.S. operations of foreign multinationals.

A recent paper used both the 1987 and 1992 BEA-Census matches for establishments, combined into state by detailed industry cells for foreign-owned and domestically owned establishments (Feliciano and Lipsey 1999). Foreign-owned establishments in the United States paid higher wages than domestically owned ones in all industries taken together, by 23 percent in 1987 and 15 percent in 1992 (table 2). Once average establishment size, education levels in the state and industry, state unionization levels, and percent female in the state labor force were accounted for, and industry dummies were included, there was no significant difference in manufacturing. However, foreign-owned establishments paid higher wages in nonmanufacturing, by 8.5 to 9.5 percent (tables 3A and 3B).

While the United States has been the subject of the largest number of studies, there have been some for other developed countries as well. An early study of American direct investment in Australia (Brash 1966) concluded, from a survey, that "it . . . appears beyond a doubt that even within each industry American-affiliated firms on average pay higher total incomes to their employees than do firms without American connections" (129). Globerman, Ries, and Vertinsky (1994) reported higher wages in foreign-owned plants in Canada.

In recent years, establishment microdata have become available for the United Kingdom, and these have been used for wage and other comparisons. Griffith and Simpson (2001) report that foreign-owned establishments in the United Kingdom paid higher wages than domestically owned establishments for both operatives and administrative and technical employees, in both 1980 and 1995. The margin was larger for the lower-skill employees, and widened considerably over the period. An earlier paper (Griffith 1999) compared wages in foreign-owned plants of companies based in France, Germany, Japan, and the United States with those in domestically owned plants. It found no significant differences for 1980, except in U.S.-owned plants, but higher wages in foreign-owned plants in 1992, by margins ranging from 8 to 25 percent (Griffith, 428). In the motor vehicle and engines industry, examined in more detail in the article, there were only small margins for operatives, 2 to 4 percent, but foreign-owned plants paid around 25 percent more to administrative, technical, and clerical workers (431).

A set of "survivors," establishments present in the U.K. Annual Census of Production (or ARD) throughout the period 1973–1993, was assembled by Oulton (2001). He reports that foreign-owned establishments paid average wages for operatives that were above the average for U.K.-owned establishments by 17 percent for non-U.S. establishments and 26 percent for U.S.-owned establishments. The margins for administrative, technical, and clerical (ATC) employees were 12 and 24 percent. The plants differed in other respects as well: foreign-owned plants, and especially U.S.-owned plants, were characterized by higher capital per worker, much higher intermediate input per worker, and higher proportions of ATC employees (129). Although there is no evidence on worker quality, Oulton attributes the wage differential to higher human capital per worker in the foreign plants, because "companies do not pay higher wages out of the goodness of their hearts" (130). A set of regressions including industry dummy variables indicates that industry composition accounts for little of the differential. Within industries, U.S.-owned establishments paid 14 to 15 percent more than domestic establishments, and other foreign establishments paid 10 percent more to operatives and 8 percent more to ATC workers (132).

Using a large sample of U.K. firms from 1991 to 1996, Girma, Greenaway, and Wakelin (2001) reported an overall wage differential of 14 percent in favor of workers in foreign-owned firms, and a differential of almost 10 percent when industry and scale of operations are taken into account. In addition, wage growth was higher by 0.4 percent per year in the foreign-owned firms (tables 1 and 2). They summarized their reading of earlier literature as showing "considerable evidence to support a wage differential in favour of foreign owned firms" (121).

Driffield and Girma (2003) reported that foreign-owned establishments in the U.K. electronics industry in 1980 to 1992 paid wages higher by 7.6 and 6.0 percent for skilled and unskilled workers, respectively, and also employed a higher proportion of skilled workers (14).

Since there is always a problem of the effect of unknown firm characteristics on these comparisons, a tempting solution is to observe firms that are acquired by foreign owners. That solution is rare because of the lack of accessible data, but Conyon et al. (1999) were able to construct panels of firms in the United Kingdom taken over by domestic and foreign acquirers and matching data for over 600 firms that did not change ownership. At the time of acquisition, the firms acquired by foreigners paid wages about the same as those of firms acquired by domestic owners. However, in the first, second, and third years after acquisition, firms acquired by foreigners raised their wages faster than did firms acquired by domestic owners (table 5). Controlling for fixed firm and industry effects and aggregate time shocks, the authors found that wages rose by 3.4 percent in firms acquired by foreigners and fell by 2.1 percent in firms acquired by domestic owners. Controlling also for firm size and industry wages hardly changed the results. Adding productivity change as a control variable eliminated the differential in favor of foreign firms (p. 9 and table 6), but if one is interested in measuring wage differentials rather than explaining them, productivity change is not an appropriate control.

The evidence seems to me overwhelming that foreign-owned firms in all kinds of economies pay higher wages than domestically owned firms. It is harder to say whether they also pay a higher price for labor—that is, a higher wage for workers of a given quality—although one of the few studies that incorporates quality measures finds that they do. Much of the differential, all of it in some studies, can be associated with the larger size of the foreign-owned operations. However, higher capital intensity and higher inputs of intermediate products, leading to higher productivity, are also important. If regions or countries encouraging inward investment are interested in encouraging high-wage plants, foreign investors seem to meet that desire.

Wage Spillovers

Whether or not foreign-owned firms in a country pay higher wages than domestic firms, their presence might still affect the level of wages in domestically owned plants. Such effects are referred to as wage spillovers to domestically owned plants. They would not take place in the world envisioned in the Findlay (1978, 8) model. There, "[t]he economy is considered able to draw on a reservoir of labor in a 'peasant hinterland' as in the famous model of Arthur Lewis (1954) and also on a substantial 'industrial reserve army' of urban unemployed." However, domestic firm wage effects from inward investment could take place in any world where the supply curve for labor was not horizontal.

Calculations of wage spillovers in two developing countries, Mexico and Venezuela, are included in Aitken, Harrison, and Lipsey (1996). Impacts of shares of employment in foreign-owned plants in an industry and region on wages in domestically owned establishments were measured. In Mexico, wages in domestically owned plants appeared to be lower where foreign ownership was high, but the coefficients were not statistically significant.

However, in Venezuela, there seemed to be a significant negative influence of foreign presence on wages in domestically owned plants. To some extent, this result could reflect a reallocation of the labor force to foreign plants, through the "poaching" of better workers or the acquisition of higher-paying plants by foreigners. However, if this had been the whole story, there would not have been, as there was, a positive effect of higher foreign ownership on total industry wages.

Lipsey and Sjöholm (2003, 26–27) made a variety of calculations of spillovers from foreign presence to wages in domestically owned establishments in Indonesia, calculating foreign presence at various levels of industry and geographical detail. In every variant, there were significant spillovers to domestically owned establishments. The coefficients on foreign shares in wage equations were larger than the observed wage differentials, suggesting some impact through increases in the demand for labor. The coefficients were generally higher for white-collar than for blue-collar workers.

In their study of South Carolina counties described below, Figlio and Blonigen (2000) did not have the data needed for testing for spillovers from inward investment. However, they concluded that the effect of the investment on aggregate wage levels was so large that it could not have been confined to the foreign plants themselves, and must have involved some spillovers to domestically owned plants (352, n 12).

In Feliciano and Lipsey (1999), the existence of two years of data permitted the authors to examine the effects of changes in the extent of foreign ownership in the United States in a state by industry cell on wages in domestically owned establishments. In manufacturing, there were no significant effects (table 4a). In nonmanufacturing industries, there were large and statistically significant effects on domestic firm wages, although the significance became marginal when state by industry education levels were added.

Girma, Greenaway, and Wakelin (2001) test for wage spillovers to domestic firms in their U.K. company data set for the 1991–1996 period and find no overall spillover effect on wage levels and a small negative effect on wage growth (128). The only firm characteristic that appears to influence the extent of wage spillovers is the gap in productivity between a firm and the firm in the industry at the 90th percentile in productivity. The larger the productivity gap, the smaller the wage spillover. The only industry characteristic that affects wage spillovers is the degree of import penetration. The higher it is, the larger the wage spillover.

Some of the literature on wage spillovers from foreign-owned to domestically owned firms has recently been reviewed by Görg and Greenaway (2001). They summarize the results of panel data studies as showing mostly negative spillovers and cross-section studies as showing positive spillovers. There is no overlap in the countries studied, but the authors are skeptical about all findings from cross-section studies on the ground that they cannot take account of unknown firm characteristics. My own judgment is that there are enough indications of positive wage spillovers, even in panel data studies, to preclude any conclusion that they are typically negative. What is needed most is more consideration of the different circumstances and policies of countries, industries, and firms that promote or obstruct spillovers.

Effects on Average Wages

Whether or not wages are higher in foreign-owned plants than in domestically owned plants, and whether or not, where there are higher wages, they spill over to domestically owned plants, a higher degree of foreign ownership could affect the average level of wages in a country or industry. It might do so either by raising the demand for labor or through the higher wages paid by the foreign plants themselves.

Aitken, Harrison, and Lipsey (1996, 352) reported that, even though there were no spillovers or negative spillovers to domestically owned plants in Mexico and Venezuela, there was a significant effect of foreign ownership shares in raising average industry wages. The effect was larger for skilled workers than for unskilled, and larger in Venezuela than in Mexico.

Feenstra and Hanson (1997), defining skilled workers simply as nonproduction workers, found that a higher level of *maquiladora* activity in a Mexican industry within a state led to a higher share of total wages' going to skilled workers. They interpreted this increase in the nonproduction wage share as implying a rise in the demand for skilled labor relative to unskilled labor resulting from the growth in *maquiladora* production by foreign, mainly U.S., firms. The increase in the wage share of nonproduction workers could be a combination of relative wage increases for them or relative increases in their numbers. However, there is some evidence of particularly large relative wage growth for nonproduction workers in the border region, where most of the *maquiladoras* are located, in the periods after investment rules were liberalized.

The effect of changes in foreign ownership from 1987 to 1992 on average wages in state by industry cells in the United States were found to be insignificant in manufacturing by Feliciano and Lipsey (1999, tables 5a and 5b). However, outside the manufacturing sector, increases in foreign ownership were associated with increases in average wages.

One avenue of relative wage increases that might be associated with increases in foreign ownership is skill upgrading, shifting the demand for labor in an industry toward higher skill. Blonigen and Slaughter (2001), measuring skill upgrading by the share of skilled wages in the total wage bill, find no evidence of such an effect from increases in foreign presence in U.S. manufacturing industries, a result that matches Feliciano and Lipsey (1999). They find some negative effect from Japanese investment in U.S.

manufacturing, but other studies have shown that Japanese investments are not typical.

In a more local study, Figlio and Blonigen (2000) reported that, in South Carolina, the addition of foreign-owned manufacturing plants was associated with increases in real wages for all workers in the same industry and county. The gain was much larger than that from the addition of new, domestically owned plants.

I would summarize the sparse evidence on overall wage levels as pointing to positive effects of FDI activity. When there are no spillovers, the effect might be wholly from the higher wages offered by the foreign firms, or it might reflect the impact of foreign firms on the aggregate demand for labor. When there are positive spillovers, they add to the impact of the foreign firms. Even when there are negative spillovers, they do not seem to be large enough to offset the positive effect of the foreign firms' high wages or the effects of increased demand for labor.

9.4.2 Host-Country Productivity

The issues that arise with respect to measuring effects on wages in host countries are also involved in judging effects on productivity. The impact on the host countries in this respect presumably stems mainly from the superior efficiency of the foreign-owned operations. The first question, then, is whether foreign-owned firms or establishments are more efficient. If they are, the second question is whether their superior productivity spills over to locally owned firms in their industries, or their industries within their regions, or related industries. Locally owned firms might increase their efficiency by copying the operations of the foreign-owned firms, or be forced by competition from foreign-owned firms to raise their efficiency to survive. On the negative side, it is conceivable that foreign-owned operations are more efficient only because foreigners have taken over the more-efficient local firms, leaving the less efficient in local ownership. Or by taking markets from local firms, foreign-owned firms might force the locally owned firms into less-efficient scales of production. The third and broadest question is whether, as a result of the operations of foreign-owned firms, there are improvements in aggregate industry efficiency. Those could arise from spillovers, but they could come simply from the higher efficiency of foreign firms, even if the higher efficiency is confined to the foreign firms. There could also be increases in aggregate productivity without any visible productivity differentials between foreign-owned and domestically owned firms, if the industry were sufficiently competitive that the entry of foreign-owned firms forced their domestically owned competitors to match them quickly to survive. These possibilities point to the importance of examining not only firms that remain in an industry over the period of observation, but also firms that enter or exit, because they may account for many of the changes in productivity for an industry or country.

The choices in defining efficiency range from value added per unit of labor input (the simplest) to value-added per unit of labor and capital input and value of output per unit of labor, capital, and intermediate product input. Some studies fit production functions that also incorporate scale economies. The result is to ignore any host-country benefit from the acquisition of physical capital, or from any advance in technology that consists of the adoption of more capital-intensive methods of production or larger scale production.

Most theoretical discussions of the possible role of inward investment refer to the transmission of superior technology. The examination of productivity is an attempt to measure technology gaps and changes in technology. That is a narrow view of multinationals' technology advantages, which may consist more of their knowledge of world markets or methods of coordinating production over many countries. Almost all the measurement is confined to manufacturing, a large part of multinational activity, but far from the whole of it.

Many of the problems in studying productivity involve the measurement of capital input. Most sources of establishment data either do not report capital stocks, or report nominal values. These are likely to bear a small resemblance to market values, especially in countries that have undergone major inflation. Where even nominal capital values are missing, they are often calculated from past expenditures using the perpetual-inventory method. Such calculations, if done properly, should be based not on general deflators but on capital-goods price indexes—scarce and subject to serious doubts even in the best of statistical systems. The complications suggest caution in drawing conclusions and the advisability of comparing total factor productivity measures with labor productivity and wages to see whether the relations among them are logical.

Productivity Comparisons

Comparisons of productivity between foreign-owned and domestically owned firms have been far more common than comparisons of wage levels. Much of the productivity literature has been directed at the question of whether there were spillovers to domestic firms, but that question itself implies the expectation that foreign firms are more efficient. The comparisons themselves range from simple overall productivity comparisons to attempts to explain differences between foreign and domestic firms. The explanatory variables, aside from nationality of ownership, include capital intensity, skill intensity, and the scale of operations. These comparisons ask, in effect, whether foreign firms that differ from domestic firms differ because they operate on different production functions or because they operate at different points on the same functions.

Most of the productivity comparisons have been for the manufacturing sectors in developing countries. Blomström and Wolff (1994), examining

Mexican manufacturing data for 1970, found both value-added and gross output per employee to have been more than twice as high in multinational corporation– (MNC) owned plants overall as in private domestic plants, and higher in each of 20 individual manufacturing industries (266). Since capital intensities in MNC plants were also much higher, the total factor productivity (TFP) margins were smaller. They were about a third overall, and three industries showed higher TFP in the domestic plants (267, 268). Okamoto and Sjöholm (1999), examining Indonesian manufacturing microdata from 1990 to 1995, reported higher foreign shares of gross output than of employment in almost every industry, implying that labor productivity was higher in the foreign-owned plants. Sjöholm (1999) examined Indonesian establishment data for 1980 and 1991, calculating differences in "technology" between foreign-owned and domestically owned establishments. Technology differences were measured as the coefficients on foreign-ownership dummies in equations relating value-added per worker in 1980 and 1991 to scale, 1980 investment expenditure per worker as a proxy for capital intensity, and dummy variables for 1991 observations and foreign ownership. The estimated technology differences were found to be in favor of the foreign-owned establishments in twenty-six out of twenty-eight industries. Kokko, Zejan, and Tansini (2001) reported that in Uruguay in 1988, productivity, as measured by value-added per worker, was about twice as high on average in foreign firms as in domestic firms. Haddad and Harrison (1993) found, for Morocco in 1985–1989, that output per worker was higher, and deviations from best-practice frontiers were smaller in foreign-owned firms than in domestically owned firms in twelve out of eighteen industries, and in all eight of the industries in which the differences were statistically significant.

Kathuria (2000) studied Indian firms in twenty-six manufacturing industries over the fourteen years from 1975–1976 to 1988–1989, in a "pre-liberalization period when Indian industry was highly regulated in terms of industrial and technology policy" (346). The main productivity measurement used was a firm's distance from its industry's technological frontier. In thirteen of the twenty-six industries, a foreign firm was the technological leader, and in fifteen industries, foreign firms were, on average, more efficient. An unusual feature of the data is that because employment was not reported, it was estimated from compensation, assuming that local and foreign firms pay the same wages. That assumption, if we can judge from the wage studies, almost certainly overstates employment in foreign firms and understates their productivity.

Chuang and Lin (1999) report that among a random sample of manufacturing firms in Taiwan in 1991, foreign-owned firms had considerably higher labor productivity than domestically owned firms, but only very slightly higher TFP. The foreign-owned firms were much larger and much more capital intensive. For Malaysia, in 1992–1996, Oguchi et al. (2002)

found that in manufacturing as a whole, foreign and domestic firms operated with about equal efficiency. However, foreign-owned firms were more efficient in twenty-three out of twenty-nine 3-digit industries, including both nonelectrical and electrical machinery. In the electronic components 5-digit industry, an extremely important one for Malaysia as an exporter, foreign-owned firms were more than 3.5 times as efficient as domestically owned firms.

Comparing foreign-owned with domestically owned firms or plants in five East Asian countries over fifteen- to twenty-year periods, Ramstetter (1999) reported that value-added per employee was higher in the foreign-owned plants in all the countries. However, Malaysian data confined to large firms showed higher productivity in the local firms in the later part of the period. Foreign-owned Turkish plants in 1993–1995 had higher productivity than domestically owned plants even when various elements of the production function are taken account of (Erdilek 2002).

There have been fewer examinations of the productivity of foreign-owned and domestically owned firms within developed countries. Notable studies of the United States include Howenstine and Zeile (1994), and Doms and Jensen (1998), mentioned earlier. Howenstine and Zeile, using the combined BEA and Census establishment data for manufacturing, found that foreign-owned plants had higher labor productivity than domestically owned ones. They attributed the difference largely to "the tendency for foreign-owned establishments to be concentrated in industries in which productivity is high" and the within-industry differences to "plant size, capital intensity, and employee skill level—rather than foreign ownership per se." Doms and Jensen concluded that foreign-owned plants were superior to U.S.-owned plants of nonmultinational firms, even large firms, in both labor productivity and TFP, but that they were behind plants owned by U.S. multinationals. Thus they find multinationality of the firm to be strongly associated with productivity levels, beyond the association with size and other plant characteristics. A similar hierarchy characterized the ranking with respect to the "number of technologies" used in each type of plant (246–250).

Comparisons within the United Kingdom go back for many years, at least to Dunning (1958) and Dunning and Rowan (1970). Some recent studies, such as Griffith and Simpson (2001), Conyon et al. (1999), and Girma, Greenaway, and Wakelin (2001), are based on individual establishment data from the ARD. Dunning (1958) compared output per man-year in a sample of U.S. affiliates with that in the average U.K. firm (including the affiliates) in ten industrial groups in 1950 and 1954. He found that the U.S. affiliates' productivity was higher in every one (table 16). Dunning and Rowan (1970) applied a number of different tests of efficiency to U.S.- and U.K.-owned firms in the United Kingdom. Although each test seemed subject to one bias or another, the preponderance of evidence pointed to greater efficiency in the U.S.-owned firms. Davies and Lyons (1991) reported that gross value-added per worker in foreign-owned manufacturing enterprises in the United Kingdom was, on average, almost 50 percent higher than that of domestically owned enterprises in 1987. No more than half the difference was due to the industrial composition of the foreign-owned firms, but some might be due to "differentials in labour skills, capital input, vertical integration, or monopoly power" (593). The differentials within the United Kingdom in 1977 were significantly related to the international productivity differentials, by industry, between the United States and the United Kingdom in 1976. Girma, Greenaway, and Wakelin (2001) found in their data set for 1991–1996 that among firms with no change in ownership, productivity in foreign-owned firms in the United Kingdom was about 10 percent above that for domestically owned firms and TFP about 5 percent higher. Labor and TFP growth rates in foreign-owned plants were higher by about 1.5 percent per year. Conyon et al. (1999) found that acquisitions of U.K. firms by foreigners led to increases in their profitability. A study by Harris and Robinson (2002) of the selection of establishments for foreign acquisition, also based on the ARD, confirmed the suspicion that foreign firms selected relatively high-productivity plants to acquire. Each group of plants was compared to a reference group of plants belonging to U.K. multiplant firms that did not sell any plants to foreign firms during 1982–1992. Plants that were foreign-owned during the whole period were more productive than those in the control group. Plants that were sold by U.K. firms to foreign firms in 1982–1986 or 1987–1992 were still more productive, as were plants sold by one U.K. firm to another. Thus, plant turnover in general seemed to involve relatively productive plants.

The evidence on productivity, whatever the measure, is close to unanimous on the higher productivity of foreign-owned plants in both developed and developing countries. Some of that higher productivity, but not all in most comparisons, can be attributed to higher capital intensity or larger scale of production in the foreign-owned plants.

Productivity and Knowledge Spillovers to Domestic Firms

Theories of the effect of direct investment on host countries have generally taken it for granted that foreign-owned firms possessed superior technology and that some of that technological knowledge spills over to the host-country economy. Findlay (1978) hypothesized that "the rate of change of technical efficiency in the backward region is an increasing function of the relative extent to which the activities of foreign firms with their superior technology pervade the local economy" (5). He also combined with that assumption the idea that the larger the gap in technology, the faster the transmission, provided that "the disparity must not be too wide for the thesis to hold" (2). Wang and Blomström (1992) added, as explanations for the speed of transmission, the characteristics of the host-country environment and host-country firms. The transmission of technology would be accelerated by a more competitive business environment and greater investment in learning and imitation by competing host-country firms (153).

Most studies of productivity spillovers from foreign investment assume that they occur mainly in the industry in which the foreign firm operates. Blomström and Kokko (1998) refer to the literature on backward linkages as examples of spillovers outside those industries, to supplying industries. These arise partly from efforts by multinational firms to improve the quality of the intermediate products they buy locally, sometimes under duress. However, they may arise without explicit help, from the competition among local firms to become the suppliers to the multinationals. The only statistical examination of this issue they report is from an unpublished paper on Venezuela by Aitken and Harrison (1991), which reported negative effects of FDI in an industry on productivity in upstream industries. The reason offered was that foreign firms shift the demand for intermediate inputs from domestic to foreign producers, reducing the scale of output, and therefore productivity, in domestic production. The paper did, however, report positive effects of FDI on downstream industries. These calculations do not appear in the later, published, version of the paper. On the whole, the interindustry effects of foreign participation have received a great deal of speculation, but little statistical testing. However, a recent examination of the existence of spillovers in Lithuanian manufacturing industries from 1996 to 2000 (Smarzynska 2002) concluded that there were positive spillovers through backward linkages. The evidence for productivity gains by supplying firms was stronger for foreign affiliates in the same region as the supplier, and was larger for foreign affiliates serving the host-country market than for those serving export markets.

Among studies of spillovers within industries, one for Venezuela by Aitken and Harrison (1999, 616) found that "increases in foreign equity participation are correlated with increases in productivity" for small plants, but that increases in foreign ownership in an industry negatively affected productivity in domestically owned plants in the same industry. The positive effects within the foreign plants exceeded the negative effects, but only slightly. The positive relationships found by others, they argued, were due to the tendency of foreign firms to invest in high-productivity sectors and firms (616, 617). The authors report similar findings for Indonesia, except that there the positive effects are larger than in Venezuela and the negative effects smaller (617).

Using data from the Mexican Industrial Census for 1970, Blomström (1983) and Blomström and Persson (1983) found that the labor productivity in domestically owned plants was positively related to the extent of foreign presence in the industry. That was true even when differences in capital intensity and in the quality of labor employed were accounted for. In a study based on the same Mexican census, Kokko (1994) confirmed the existence of productivity spillovers to locally owned firms and found some evidence that high capital intensity in an industry and a high level of technology might inhibit spillovers. A stronger conclusion was that the combination of large technology gaps between foreign and domestic firms and large foreign market shares, which the author describes as "enclave" situations, discourages spillovers. Blomström and Wolff (1994), on the basis of Mexican census data, concluded that higher foreign shares in an industry in 1970 led to higher rates of productivity growth in locally owned firms over the next five years. Local firm productivity growth was higher in industries in which the local firms' productivity levels were initially closer to those of the foreign-owned firms (270). Higher foreign shares in an industry were also associated with faster convergence of Mexican-industry productivity toward U.S.-industry productivity levels, again more strongly in industries in which the initial gap was smaller (275).

Kathuria (2000), in a study of spillovers to Indian manufacturing firms, found that a division of the manufacturing sectors into "scientific" and "nonscientific" subgroups showed positive spillovers in the scientific sectors, but none in the nonscientific ones. One conclusion was that "spillovers are not found to be automatic consequences of foreign firms' presence, but they depend to a large extent on the efforts of local firms to invest in learning or R&D activities so as to decodify the spilled knowledge" (364). He thus supports the theoretical model proposed by Wang and Blomström (1992). Buckley, Clegg, and Wang (2002) studied several types of spillovers in China in a study based on the Third Industrial Census of China, for 1995, early in the Chinese FDI boom. Higher foreign presence in an industry resulted in higher labor productivity in domestically owned firms, holding constant capital intensity, R&D intensity, and labor quality.

A pioneering attempt to measure impacts on domestic firms in developed countries was Caves (1974), on Canada and Australia. He found some evidence that higher shares in an industry for foreign subsidiaries were weakly, and negatively, related to the profitability of Canadian firms, a possible indication that foreign firms raised the level of competition and reduced the excess profits that had been earned by their local rivals. However, he was not certain that the relation was not due entirely to differences in the attainment of economies of scale. In Australian manufacturing, he found that "higher subsidiary shares do apparently coincide with higher productivity levels in competing domestic firms" (190). However no such relationship could be found between changes in foreign shares and changes in the productivity of domestic firms, a fact that reduced his confidence in the significance of the finding for levels (190–191). A later study by Globerman (1979), for a sample of manufacturing industries in 1972, concluded that differences across Canadian industries in labor productivity "derive, in part, from spillover efficiency benefits associated with foreign direct investment" (53).

Haskel, Pereira, and Slaughter (2002) use British panel data to relate changes in TFP of domestically owned British establishments to changes in foreign presence, measured by shares in employment, in the establishment's industry, region, or industry in the region. Significant evidence is found for positive spillovers within industries. Positive spillovers are found to come from U.S. and French presence, but Japanese presence produces negative spillovers. The authors conclude that, of the aggregate increase of 11 percent in British TFP from 1972 to 1992, 5 percent could be ascribed to spillovers from foreign-owned plants (17). Girma, Greenaway, and Wakelin (2001) find no significant effect of foreign presence, measured by shares of employment or output, on the labor productivity or TFP of U.K. firms in general during 1991–1996. However, the higher the skill level of the industry, and the greater the degree of foreign competition in the industry, the larger the productivity spillover. And the larger the individual firm's distance from the productivity leader in its industry (the firm at the 90th percentile in TFP), the smaller the spillover (129). Thus they point to the importance of firm and industry characteristics in determining the extent of spillovers, as well as, possibly, trade policy, as represented by import penetration levels. Examining changes in productivity in domestically owned U.K. firms between 1989 and 1992, Driffield (2001) finds no spillovers related to the amount of sales by foreign-owned firms or their R&D stock. However, the growth of labor productivity among foreign-owned firms in the previous period, from 1986 to 1989, did lead to productivity growth among domestically owned firms in the same industry. He concluded that "the foreign productivity advantage was responsible for an average increase in domestic productivity of 0.75 per cent a year" (113). Girma and Wakelin (2000), also using U.K. microdata for manufacturing establishments, found evidence of positive spillovers to domestic firms in the same region as the foreign firms, but some evidence of negative spillovers outside the regions. They also concluded that low technology gaps between domestic and foreign firms and location in more technologically advanced regions promoted spillovers.

In a study of labor-productivity spillovers in Italian manufacturing in 1988, Imbriani and Reganati (1997) found that, across all industries, foreign shares in employment were positively associated with revenue per worker in domestically owned firms. When industries were divided according to the size of the technology gap between foreign-owned and domestically owned firms, there was a positive effect of foreign presence in the sectors with small gaps, much larger than that for all industries together. However, there was a negative effect on domestic firms, smaller, but statistically significant, in industries where the technology gap was large.

Blomström and Kokko (1998, 24) end a review of productivity spillovers to host countries by concluding that "such effects exist and . . . they may be substantial both within and between industries, but there is no strong evidence on their exact nature and magnitude." Furthermore, "the positive effects of FDI are likely to increase with the level of local capability and competition." Blomström, Kokko, and Globerman (2001), in a later review of this literature, summarize the "limited evidence" for developed countries as pointing to a dependence of productivity spillovers on the absorptive capacity of domestically owned firms. They conclude that small productivity gaps encourage spillovers, while large gaps inhibit them. They report similar findings among developing countries, and they attribute the more mixed results on spillovers in studies of such countries to the greater frequency of wide technology gaps between foreign and local firms (42–43). They also report that spillovers are encouraged by vertical linkages between MNCs and local firms, a characteristic that would also depend partly on local firm capabilities.

Görg and Greenaway (2001) summarize the results of the productivity studies with respect to spillovers from foreign-owned to domestically owned firms by saying that "only limited evidence in support of positive spillovers has been reported. Most work fails to find positive spillovers, with some even reporting negative spillovers, at the aggregate level" (23). In contrast, Görg and Strobl (2000) take spillovers for granted in their study of firm survival in Ireland, and find that foreign presence reduces exit by domestically owned firms, at least in high-tech industries, an effect they attribute to spillovers. Görg and Strobl (2002) find also that foreign presence encourages entry by domestically owned firms. Görg and Greenaway (2001) are inclined to attribute the variety of findings on spillovers mainly to the difference between cross-section and panel data studies. However, there is evidence that differences among firms in their capabilities, differences among industries in their characteristics, and differences among countries in both capabilities and policies may be important explanations for this diversity of results. A more formal "meta-analysis" of spillover findings from twenty-one studies by Görg and Strobl (2001), using the t-statistic in spillover equations as the dependent variable, concluded that the use of cross-section data was a strong positive influence. Of the eight studies that used panel data, four found significant negative spillovers, confirming the importance of the distinction between panel data and cross-section results.

Since quite a few studies report that spillovers are discouraged by very large gaps between foreign and domestic firms, by restrictive trade regimes, or by other institutional factors, the composition of the sample of countries covered by the small collection of panel data may be important. Of the four developing countries with panel data included by Görg and Strobl (2001)—Colombia, India, Morocco, and Venezuela—none are listed as "outward-oriented" during the period covered by the panel data in World Bank (1987). India is called "strongly inward-oriented" and Colombia "moderately inward-oriented," and Morocco and Venezuela are not rated. Of forty-two countries ranked by Wheeler and Mody (1992), Venezuela is ranked in the next-to-lowest category with respect to openness. In World Economic Forum (2002), Colombia, India, and Venezuela are in the lower half of developing countries with respect to "Technology" and "Growth Competitiveness." Perhaps these are not of a random sample of developing countries and are not the most likely ones in which to find spillovers.

The studies of productivity comparisons between foreign-owned and domestically owned firms and establishments have generally found that foreign-owned entities had higher productivity. Almost all the studies showed that some of the higher labor productivity in the foreign-owned entities could be explained by their greater capital intensity, their larger size, and their greater use of purchased inputs. The same variables, except for the capital intensity (and sometimes the purchased inputs), accounted for the differences in TFP. Even after these factors are removed from the comparison, it is frequently, but not always, found that there is a residual productivity advantage for the foreign-owned firms. There is more logic to removing the influence of these other factors in comparisons within developed countries than in comparisons within developing countries. In developed countries it can more easily be assumed that there are domestic firms capable of producing with the same capital intensity and managing plants of the same size. In developing countries, there may be a better case for suggesting that the technological impact of the foreign firms is broader than what is measured by their TFP. It also involves their knowledge of how to produce on a large scale and market the output, how to use capital-intensive techniques, and how to combine local inputs with purchased inputs from the multinational itself or other suppliers. If that is the case, one should study differences and look for spillovers not only in TFP but also in plant size, capital intensity, and use of other inputs.

An unusual study of spillovers to the host country that was focused directly on spillovers of knowledge, and did not depend on TFP measures at all, was Branstetter's (2000) examination of patent citations. The higher the level of Japanese affiliates sales in the United States, lagged two years, the larger the number of U.S. citations to Japanese patents in U.S.-firm patent applications. A recent paper by Singh (2002), analyzing citations in U.S. patent filings, finds evidence of knowledge flows from local firms to multinationals' foreign affiliates and from the affiliates to local firms, and summarizes other studies based on patent citations. This line of research is a promising addition to studies of knowledge diffusion, bypassing the problems of productivity measurement.

Another suggestion that common measures of technology-transfer miss the point was made in an analysis of the impact of inward FDI on China

(Chen, Chang, and Zhang 1995). It refers to "FDI's less than satisfactory contribution in high technology transfer to China" (700), which it explains by the high proportion of FDI coming from Hong Kong and Taiwan. The impact of such investment was that it brought "the modern concept of management and marketing" (700). That is a contribution that would be missed by standard measures of TFP.

Productivity-spillover studies typically assume that the effect on domestic firms should be linearly or log-linearly dependent on the foreign share of an industry. It is not obvious that this should be the case, particularly as the foreign share goes to high levels. Spillover is not obviously maximized at a foreign share of 100 percent. One way this problem is recognized is in Kokko (1996), where industries with foreign shares above 50 percent are dropped, being categorized as "enclave industries."

A broader problem is that there is little basis for assuming any particular form of the relationship. Some mechanisms might suggest a linear relation to the foreign participation share, but others might suggest a strong effect from foreign entry, but little effect from changes in share.

One of the few studies to examine productivity growth in general, rather than only spillovers to domestic firms was a cross-country, cross-industry study covering nine Organization for Economic Cooperation and Development (OECD) countries from 1979 to 1991, by Baldwin, Braconier, and Forslid (1999). They examined labor productivity growth in seven broad industry aggregates. Although the title of the paper refers to spillovers, no distinction was made between productivity in foreign-owned firms and that in domestically owned ones. This does not match the usual definition of spillovers, in which that distinction is important, but the results are of interest because they measure the total impact on an industry, a topic rarely studied. The authors reported that higher FDI penetration levels led to more rapid growth in industry labor productivity.

Another of these rare attempts to measure effects on industries as a whole, rather than only on domestically owned firms, was an unpublished paper by Nadiri (1992). He used U.S.-owned affiliates' stocks of plant and equipment, rather than financial flows, as the measure of foreign investment in the manufacturing sectors of four developed host countries: France, Germany, Japan, and the United Kingdom. United States–owned affiliates' capital reduced the cost and price of output, and increased output and TFP. The increase in output raised the demand for labor and materials, but the higher U.S. FDI capital reduced the demand for labor and materials per unit of output.

As mentioned earlier, a serious problem with TFP measures, especially in developing countries, is the weakness of the data on capital stocks. Another problem with productivity comparisons and productivity-spillover measures is that it is extremely rare to find any measure of output other than value-added, or even any comparison with alternative measures. The assumption underlying the measurement of output by value-added, which is an input measure, is that the firm or establishment is operating in a competitive environment. If a firm paid wages that exceeded worker productivity, for example, output would not be exaggerated because profits would be correspondingly reduced, and value-added would still represent output. However, if a firm operated in a protected market because it was government owned or because it sold to the government, or because it sold to its parent, or because competition was limited in other ways, its value-added output measure would be inflated. Similarly, a firm earning monopoly profits would appear to be highly productive even if wages were not inflated, because value-added would be inflated. Thus, for example, if the entry or growth of foreign-owned firms broke up a local-firm monopoly, the decline in local-firm monopoly profits would appear in the data disguised as a decline in their productivity resulting from foreign entry.

While the technological superiority of foreign firms seems clear, as is expected on theoretical grounds, the evidence on spillovers is mixed. No universal relationships are evident. However, there is substantial evidence from several countries that inward FDI has been most beneficial to the productivity of local firms where the local firms are not extremely far behind the multinationals' affiliates.

9.4.3   Exports and the Introduction of New Industries

One of the main contributions of inward direct investment in some cases has been to introduce new industries to a country or drastically change the composition of production. Lipsey (2000) describes the large role of U.S. affiliates in the electronics industry in East Asia, especially in the early development of the industry. The earliest data available show U.S. affiliates accounting for three-quarters of exports in some cases, with the share declining over time. Labor-intensive industries, such as food, textiles, and apparel, declined, while the share of chemical and machinery industries in exports rose to more than half (163). Some of the country studies in Dobson and Chia (1997) are summarized as showing that "[f]oreign firms . . . saw a way to integrate these countries into worldwide networks of production. . . . Foreign firms supplied the technology and the links to other parts of the production networks that completed the set of resources necessary for the growth of these industries" (163).

In a set of country- and industry-specific case studies collected in Rhee and Belot (1990), the authors refer in their summary to "the critical role of transnational corporations (TNCs) in the transfer of technical, marketing, managerial know-how to developing countries—a role more important than the transfer of financial resources associated with DFI [direct foreign investment] by TNCs" (viii). The development of plywood manufacturing and export in Indonesia in the 1980s was started by firms from Korea and Taiwan. They had developed their skills when these countries replaced

Japan in plywood manufacturing and transferred "technical, marketing, and managerial know-how through joint ventures" after the home countries lost their comparative advantage as their wages rose (Rhee and Belot 1990, 22–29). A military-uniform exporter from Zambia grew from a joint venture with a German firm that originally was aimed at the domestic market but could draw on export experience from the German parent when selling locally became impractical (33–34). In Côte d'Ivoire, a joint venture with a French company, experienced in marketing and technically skilled, brought the country into the semiprocessed-cocoa market (39–40). The ingredients for expansion of Jamaican exports of garments to the United States were provided by a joint venture with a Korean company that supplied "effective management, effective training in advanced technology, efficiency of operations, and marketing skills and channels" (42). Not all the catalysts described in the report involved FDI, but quite a few of them did, and the contribution they made seemed to have little to do with supplying capital and much to do with technology and marketing knowledge. Buckley, Clegg, and Wang (2002) found, for Chinese manufacturing industries in 1995, that a higher foreign share of capital in an industry increased the development of new and high-tech products by domestically owned firms, as well as their export intensities.

Since export data are available in much more detail than production data in many countries, the development of new industries or subindustries or of new varieties of products may be evident most clearly in the growth of exports. Blomström (1990) describes the role of multinationals in shifting production in developing countries toward tradable goods and, among tradables, away from import substitution and toward export markets. The role of access to parent networks in promoting exports by U.S. affiliates in Asia is assessed in Lipsey (1998).

Ireland was an unusual example for Western Europe, in that it went from being extremely hostile to inward investment until the late 1950s, to welcoming and even favoring it by tax and other policies. One could not have predicted the current comparative advantage of Ireland from its comparative advantage before inward investment was liberalized, which was that of an agricultural country. The entrance of foreign firms, together with Ireland's joining the European Union, transformed the economy into one where foreign firms, exporting over 70 percent of their output, accounted for two-thirds of manufacturing net output and almost half of manufacturing employment. In relatively high-tech industries, the foreign firms were geared almost entirely to export markets (Ruane and Görg 1999, 51–53).

Most of the studies of the effects of FDI on host-country exports examine the behavior of the affiliates themselves, generally finding that they are more export oriented than domestically owned firms. Sousa, Greenaway, and Wakelin (2000) investigated whether the presence and activities of foreign-owned firms affected the exporting of domestically owned firms in the United Kingdom. Using a database of U.K.-owned manufacturing firms from 1992 to 1996, they found that foreign firms' R&D in the United Kingdom, their exporting, and their importance in U.K. production in an industry were all significantly related to the probability that a domestic firm in that industry would be an exporter. There were also some indications that foreign firms' activities raised the export propensities of domestically owned firms. The only comparable study the authors cite is Aitken, Hanson, and Harrison (1997), for manufacturing establishments in Mexico in 1986–1990. That study found that higher production by foreign-owned firms in a sector, as well as greater export activity by those firms, increased the likelihood that domestic firms would export.

A study of China's aggregate trade and FDI relationships with individual partner countries (Liu, Wang, and Wei 2001) found, in causality tests, that China's imports from a country tended to precede inward FDI from that country, and that inward FDI then preceded exports to the investing country. The initial effect of inward FDI from a country on China's exports to the source country was negative, but all the subsequent lagged terms were positive and much larger, so that the net effect of inward FDI was an increase in Chinese exports to the investing country.

The positive influence of inward FDI on host-country exports seems well established, whatever the mechanism. And the few studies of spillovers of exporting from affiliates to domestic firms point in the same direction.

9.4.4   Host-Country Growth

One of the main reasons for examining productivity spillovers from foreign-owned to domestically owned firms is to understand the contribution of inward FDI to host-country economic growth. If the higher productivity of the foreign firms was at the expense of lower productivity in domestic firms, there might be no implications for aggregate output or growth. There could be growth effects without spillovers, just from the operations of the foreign firms themselves, but that possibility is rarely explored, except by implication in studies of the impact of the entrance or growth of foreign firms on the output or growth of a country.

An optimistic appraisal of the impact of inward FDI was that of Romer (1993a), who suggested that, for a developing country trying to keep up with or gain on more advanced countries, the main obstacle was the gap in knowledge or ideas rather than in physical capital. Much of that capital was the human or organizational capital of multinational firms. For more rapid growth, "one of the most important and easily implemented policies is to give foreign firms an incentive to close the idea gap, to let them make a profit by doing so . . . by creating an economic environment that offers an adequate reward to multinational corporations when they bring ideas from the rest of the world and put them to use with domestic resources" (548).

One way in which the influence of FDI on host-country growth has been studied is through comprehensive cross-country studies in which the rate of growth of real gross domestic product (GDP) or GDP per capita is related to the stock or inflow of FDI. In general, the results of these studies indicate that the size of inward FDI stocks or flows, relative to GDP, is not related in any consistent way to rates of growth. However, most studies find that among some subsets of the world's countries, FDI, or FDI in combination with some other factors, is positively related to growth. Blomström, Lipsey, and Zejan (1994) did find that, among developing countries, from 1960 to 1985, ratios of FDI inflow to GDP in a five-year period were positively related to growth in the subsequent five-year period. However, when the developing countries were divided between higher- and lower-income countries, FDI promoted growth only in the higher-income countries. Borensztein, De Gregorio, and Lee (1998) found, among sixty-nine developing countries from 1970 to 1989, that FDI inflows, by themselves, only marginally affected growth; but that FDI interacted with the level of education of a country's labor force was a significant positive influence. That relationship was confirmed for FDI inflows in five-year periods and growth in subsequent periods in Lipsey (2000).

An explanation for the variety of results was offered by Bhagwati (1978), who suggested that the growth effects of inward FDI could be favorable or unfavorable, depending on the incentives offered by host-country trade policies. The efficiency of FDI in promoting growth would be increased by an export-promotion policy and decreased by an import-substitution policy. A test of this hypothesis by Balasubramanayam, Salisu, and Sapsford (1996) persuaded the authors that in ten to eighteen export-promotion-policy developing countries, higher inward FDI flows were associated with faster growth. No effect was found in the remaining developing countries, presumably following import-substitution trade policies. This idea that the effect of inward FDI on growth is enhanced by liberal trade and investment policies in host countries is emphasized in Moran (2002, chap. 9).

A panel data study of aggregate country effects, without industry distinctions (de Mello 1999), found that FDI inflows raised growth in both developed and developing countries. In developed countries, FDI inflows raised TFP growth, but not fixed investment, while in developing countries it raised fixed investment, but not TFP growth. An earlier survey of eleven studies by de Mello (1997) found a majority reporting positive effects of FDI inflows on growth, and stronger effects associated with greater openness or export-promotion policies and with a higher level of development. The influence on technological change, and particularly domestic factor productivity, was in the same direction, but observed in fewer studies, again varying with the same set of country characteristics.

An alternative explanation for the variety of experience with FDI is offered by Alfaro et al. (2002). They find, in a regression analysis for the period 1975–1995 as a whole, and using various measures of financial development, that the existence and extent of local financial markets is an important determinant of the extent to which FDI affects growth. That idea, which they trace back to Goldsmith (1969), among others, is here based on the proposition that in the absence or weakness of local financial markets, local firms are unable to take advantage of the various kinds of knowledge that they gain from the presence of foreign firms.

A recent study including developed and developing countries by Carkovic and Levine (2000) finds no significant effect of FDI inflows over the whole period 1960–1995, and only irregularly significant effects in five-year periods. They find that none of the variables found in other studies consistently determine the effect of FDI on growth, although some are significant in some combinations of conditioning variables.

In a narrower group of countries (twenty-five Central and Eastern European and former Soviet transition countries), Campos and Kinoshita (2002, 22) find that FDI "is a crucially important explanatory variable for growth," and that the finding survives "correcting for reverse causality, endogeneity, and omitted variable bias." They allege that FDI represents more of a pure transfer of technology in these transition countries than in most developing countries, because these countries were industrialized and had relatively well-educated labor forces.

As with the studies of wage and productivity spillovers, but more so because most of those studies narrowly focus on manufacturing, the studies of the effects of FDI inflow on national economic growth are inconclusive. Almost all find positive effects in some periods, or among some groups of countries, in some specifications, but one cannot say from these studies that there are universal effects. There are circumstances, periods, and countries where FDI seems to have little relation to growth, and others where there seems to be a positive relation.

9.5 Conclusions

Among the early fears about the effects of the growth of multinationals on their home countries, the worry that they would cause exports from the home country and aggregate employment to fall has mostly dissipated. There is probably no universal relationship between outward investment and home-country exports, and to the extent that any relationship is present, outward FDI is more often found to promote exports than to compete with them.

There are some indications that multinational operations have led to a shift toward more capital-intensive and skill-intensive production in the United States, as labor-intensive—and particularly unskilled-labor-intensive—production has been allocated to affiliates in developing countries. The alternative to this shift may have been a shift to nonaffiliated firms in those countries. However, even that reallocation does not appear to have occurred in Sweden or Japan, so it cannot be considered a universal consequence of multinational operations.

One function that outward FDI seems to have played for home countries' firms is that of preserving export markets for the firms even when home-country economic changes such as exchange rate movements, increases in costs, or other events threaten home-country firms' competitiveness. Examples of this defensive role of foreign affiliates can be found for the United States, Japan, and Sweden.

Within host countries, it has been abundantly shown that foreign-owned firms pay higher wages than domestically owned firms. Some, but not all, of the higher wage levels can be associated with characteristics of the affiliates, such as their size and capital intensity. Where it can be measured, higher quality of labor also accounts for some, but again not all, of the difference. Beyond that, there is some evidence that foreign-owned firms pay a higher price for labor, in the sense of paying more for a worker of given quality, but there are not many studies that include data on worker characteristics.

Evidence on wage spillovers (i.e., effects of foreign entry or participation in an industry or region, or industry within a region) on the wages paid by domestically owned firms, is sparse, and not conclusive as to direction. However, there is more evidence that, whatever the extent and direction of spillovers to domestically owned plants, the effect of foreign firms' presence is to raise the average level of wages. The effect may come simply from higher wages in the foreign-owned operations, even without any effect on locally owned ones. It might come from positive spillovers to locally owned plants or from the effects of the increased demand for labor, even if there is no difference in wage levels between foreign-owned and domestically owned plants.

Many wage studies, if they are based on individual firm or establishment data, include controls for plant size and, where possible, for capital intensity and other plant characteristics. They attempt in this way to learn whether wage levels reflect these characteristics other than foreignness itself, since wage levels are, for example, almost always positively associated with establishment or firm size. From a policymaker's point of view, this distillation of the effects of pure foreignness may not be relevant. An expansion of foreign presence may be desirable because foreign firms bring larger-scale, more capital-intensive, or more technically advanced methods of production. It does not matter that an identical domestic firm would produce the same results, because there may not be any such firms, or they may not find it profitable to make these same investments.

Even if foreign entry and larger foreign shares of production almost always raise wage levels, there are some host-country losers from their participation. Small or inefficient local firms may be forced to contract or leave the industry altogether. That may be viewed as a healthy redeployment of capital, but it is an explanation for some host-country opposition to foreign multinationals.

Productivity comparisons between foreign-owned and domestically owned firms or establishments almost always find that the foreign-owned firms have higher productivity levels. As with the wage comparisons, some of the differences can be associated with the larger size of foreign-owned plants or other plant characteristics.

Evidence on spillovers of superior foreign productivity to domestically owned firms is mixed. Some observers conclude that there is substantial evidence for positive spillovers and others see the evidence as inconclusive. Even where no spillovers are found to all domestic firms as a group, they are often found for subsets of domestic firms, particularly those not too far behind the foreign firms technologically, or those in higher-technology industries. The mixed story for spillovers, combined with the strong evidence for superior productivity in foreign-owned firms, suggests that overall productivity is improved by the presence of foreign-owned operations.

In many of these productivity studies there has been a substantial effort to calculate TFP comparisons, rather than labor productivity comparisons, and to remove the influence of firm or establishment size. An effort is made, in effect, to learn whether foreign and domestic firms are on different production functions. It is not always clear why it is so important to measure the effect of foreignness alone, untainted by differences in capital intensity and size. Much of the growth of presently developed countries came from increases in the scale of production and in its capital intensity. The contribution of foreign firms may come partly by introducing larger-scale or more capital-intensive methods of production, or differences in technology may be inextricably tied to differences in scale and capital intensity.

One frequent effect of foreign entry is the introduction of new industries or products to the host-country economy and the tighter linking of the host country to the world trading system. The contribution of the foreign-owned firms is mainly of knowledge, particularly knowledge of demand in the world market, and knowledge about how the host country can find a place in the worldwide allocation of intermediate steps in the path of production that can be geographically separated. By the development of new (to the host country) products, inward direct investment is associated with faster economic growth, although attempts to find a consistent relation between the extent of FDI inflows and national economic growth do not produce strong and consistent relationships.

One issue that is missing from the discussion of effects of FDI—a strange omission from a literature dominated by economists—is the impact on consumers. There could be effects on home-country consumers from imports of cheaper goods produced by foreign affiliates. There could be effects on host-country consumers from more efficient production of goods and services sold locally and from the weakening of local-producer monopoly positions. There have been analyses in the trade literature of consumer gains from imports, but studies of host countries ignore the relation of consumer prices to the presence or activities of foreign affiliates.

A proven association of FDI with more trade and faster economic growth would not necessarily please critics of multinationals. Trade links reduce the freedom of action of a country's government domestically, if not that of its people. Fast growth involves disruptions and the destruction of the value of old techniques of production and old skills. Those who value stability over economic progress will not be convinced of the worth of the gifts brought by foreign involvement. That is especially true if the gains are captured by small elements of the population or if no effort is made to soften the impact of the inevitable losses.

References

Aitken, Brian J., Gordon H. Hanson, and Ann E. Harrison. 1997. Spillovers, foreign investment, and export behavior. *Journal of International Economics* 43 (1–2): 103–32.

Aitken, Brian J., and Ann Harrison. 1991. Are there spillovers from foreign direct investment? Evidence from panel data for Venezuela. MIT, Economics Department, and World Bank. November (processed).

———. 1999. Do domestic firms benefit from direct foreign investment? Evidence from Venezuela. *American Economic Review* 89 (3): 605–18.

Aitken, Brian J., Ann E. Harrison, and Robert E. Lipsey. 1996. Wages and foreign ownership: A comparative study of Mexico, Venezuela, and the United States. *Journal of International Economics* 40 (3–4): 345–71.

Alfaro, Laura, Areendam Chanda, Sebnem Kalemli-Ozcan, and Selin Sayek. 2002. FDI and economic growth: The role of local financial markets. Harvard Business School, North Carolina State University, University of Houston, and International Monetary Fund. April (Processed).

Australia Productivity Commission. 2002. *Offshore investment by Australian firms: Survey evidence.* Commission research paper. Canberra: AusInfo.

Balasubramanyam, V. N., M. Salisu, and David Sapsford. 1996. Foreign direct investment and growth in EP and IS countries. *Economic Journal* 106 (434): 92–105.

Baldwin, Richard E., Henrik Braconier, and Rikard Forslid. 1999. Multinationals, endogenous growth and technological spillovers: Theory and evidence. Center for Economic Policy Research (CEPR) Discussion Paper no. 2155. London: CEPR.

Bergsten, C. Fred, Thomas Horst, and Theodore H. Moran. 1978. *American multinationals and American interests.* Washington, D.C.: Brookings Institution.

Bhagwati, Jagdish N. 1978. *Anatomy and consequences of exchange control regimes. Special conference series on foreign trade regimes and economic development,* vol. 11. Cambridge, Mass.: Ballinger.

Blomström, Magnus. 1983. *Foreign investment and spillovers.* London: Routledge.

————. 1990. *Transnational corporations and manufacturing exports from developing countries.* New York: United Nations.

Blomström, Magnus, Gunnar Fors, and Robert E. Lipsey. 1997. Foreign direct investment and employment: Home country experience in the United States and Sweden. *Economic Journal* 107 (445): 1787–97.

Blomström, Magnus, and Ari Kokko. 1998. Multinational corporations and spillovers. *Journal of Economic Surveys* 12 (2): 247–77.

Blomström, Magnus, Ari Kokko, and Steven Globerman. 2001. The determinants of host country spillovers from foreign direct investment: A review and synthesis of the literature. In *Inward investment, technological change, and growth,* ed. Nigel Pain, 34–65. Basingstoke, U.K.: Palgrave.

Blomström, Magnus, Robert E. Lipsey, and Ksenia Kulchycky. 1988. U.S. and Swedish direct investment and exports. In *Trade policy issues and empirical analysis,* ed. Robert E. Baldwin, 259–97. Chicago: University of Chicago Press.

Blomström, Magnus, Robert E. Lipsey, and Mario Zejan. 1994. What explains the growth of developing countries? In *Convergence of productivity: Cross-national studies and historical evidence,* ed. William J. Baumol, Richard R. Nelson, and Edward N. Wolff, 243–59. New York: Oxford University Press.

Blomström, Magnus, and Håkan Persson. 1983. Foreign investment and spillover efficiency in an underdeveloped economy: Evidence from the Mexican manufacturing industry. *World Development* 11 (6): 493–501.

Blomström, Magnus, and Edward N. Wolff. 1994. Multinational corporations and productivity convergence in Mexico. In *Convergence of productivity: Cross-national studies and historical evidence,* ed. William Baumol, Richard R. Nelson, and Edward N. Wolff, 263–84. Oxford: Oxford University Press.

Blonigen, Bruce A., and Matthew J. Slaughter. 2001. Foreign-affiliate activity and U.S. skill upgrading. *Review of Economics and Statistics* 83 (2): 362–76.

Borensztein, Eduardo, Jose De Gregorio, and Jong-Wha Lee. 1998. How does foreign direct investment affect economic growth? *Journal of International Economics* 45 (1): 115–35.

Braconier, Henrik, and Karolina Ekholm. 2000. Swedish multinationals and competition from high- and low-wage locations. *Review of International Economics* 8 (3) 448–61.

Brainard, S. Lael. 1997. An empirical assessment of the proximity-concentration trade-off between multinational sales and trade. *American Economic Review* 87 (4): 520–44.

Brainard, S. Lael, and David A. Riker. 1997. Are U.S. multinationals exporting U.S. jobs? NBER Working Paper no. 5958. Cambridge, Mass.: National Bureau of Economic Research, March.

Branstetter, Lee. 2000. Is foreign direct investment a channel of knowledge spillovers? Evidence from Japan's FDI in the United States. NBER Working Paper no. 8015. Cambridge, Mass.: National Bureau of Economic Research, November.

Brash, Donald T. 1966. *American investment in Australian industry.* Cambridge: Harvard University Press.

Buckley, Peter J., Jeremy Clegg, and Chengqi Wang. 2002. The impact of inward FDI on the performance of Chinese manufacturing firms. *Journal of International Business Studies* 33 (4): 637–55.

Campos, Nauro F., and Yuko Kinoshita. 2002. Foreign direct investment as technology transferred: Some panel evidence from the transition economies. *The Manchester School* 70 (3): 398–419.

Carkovic, Maria, and Ross Levine. 2002. Does foreign direct investment accelerate economic growth? University of Minnesota, Department of Finance. Working Paper, June.

Caves, Richard E. 1974. Multinational firms, competition, and productivity in host-country markets. *Economica* 41 (162): 176–93.

———. 1996. *Multinational enterprise and economic analysis,* 2nd ed. Cambridge: Cambridge University Press.

Chédor, Séverine, and Jean-Louis Mucchielli. 1998. Implantation à l'étranger et performance à l'exportation: Une analyse empirique sur les implantations des firmes francaises dans les pays emergents (Implantation abroad and export performance: An empirical analysis of the implantation of French firms in emerging countries). *Revue Économique* 49 (3): 617–28.

Chédor, Séverine, Jean-Louis Mucchielli, and Isabel Soubaya. 2002. Intra-firm trade and foreign direct investment: An empirical analysis of French firms. In *Multinational firms and impacts on employment, trade, and technology,* ed. Robert E. Lipsey and Jean-Louis Mucchielli, 84–100. London: Routledge.

Chen, Chung, Lawrence Chang, and Yimin Zhang. 1995. The role of foreign direct investment in China's post-1978 economic development. *World Development* 23 (4): 691–703.

Chuang, Yih-Chyi, and Chi-Mei Lin. 1999. Foreign direct investment, R&D, and spillover efficiency: Evidence from Taiwan's manufacturing firms. *Journal of Development Studies* 35 (4): 117–34.

Conyon, Martin, Sourafel Girma, Steve Thompson, and Peter Wright. 1999. The impact of foreign acquisition on wages and productivity in the U.K. Centre for Research on Globalisation and Labour Markets Research Paper no. 99/8. Nottingham, U.K.: University of Nottingham.

Davies, Stephen W., and Bruce R. Lyons. 1991. Characterising relative performance: The productivity advantage of foreign-owned firms in the U.K. *Oxford Economic Papers* 43 (4): 584–95.

De Mello, Luiz R., Jr. 1997. Foreign direct investment in developing countries and growth: A selective survey. *Journal of Development Studies* 34 (1): 1–34.

———. 1999. Foreign direct investment–led growth: Evidence from time series and panel data. *Oxford Economic Papers* 51:133–51.

Dobson, Wendy, and Chia Siow Yue, eds. 1997. *Multinationals and East Asian integration.* Ottawa, Canada: International Development Research Centre.

Doms, Mark E., and J. Bradford Jensen. 1998. Comparing wages, skills, and productivity between domestically and foreign-owned manufacturing establishments in the United States. In *Geography and ownership as bases for economic accounting,* ed. Robert E. Baldwin, Robert E. Lipsey, and J. David Richardson, 235–58. Vol. 59 of *Studies in income and wealth.* Chicago: University of Chicago Press.

Driffield, Nigel. 2001. The impact on domestic productivity of inward investment in the U.K. *The Manchester School* 69 (1): 103–19.

Driffield, Nigel, and Sourafel Girma. 2003. Regional foreign direct investment and wage spillovers: Plant-level evidence from the electronics industry. *Oxford Bulletin of Economics and Statistics* 65:453–474.

Dunning, John H. 1958. *American investment in British manufacturing industry.* London: George Allen & Unwin.

———. 1970. The effects of United States direct investment on British technology. In *Studies in international investment,* ed. John H. Dunning, 345–400. London: George Allen & Unwin.

Erdilek, Asim. 2002. Productivity and spillover effects of foreign direct investment in Turkish manufacturing: A plant-level panel data analysis. Case Western Reserve University, Department of Economics. (Processed).

Feenstra, Robert C., and Gordon H. Hanson. 1997. Foreign direct investment and relative wages: Evidence from Mexico's maquiladoras. *Journal of International Economics* 42 (3–4): 371–94.

Feliciano, Zadia, and Robert E. Lipsey. 1999. Foreign ownership and wages in the United States, 1987–1992. NBER Working Paper no. 6923. Cambridge, Mass.: National Bureau of Economic Research, January.

Figlio, David N., and Bruce A. Blonigen. 2000. The effects of foreign direct investment on local communities. *Journal of Urban Economics* 48 (2): 338–63.

Findlay, Ronald. 1978. Relative backwardness, direct foreign investment, and the transfer of technology: A simple dynamic model. *Quarterly Journal of Economics* 92 (1): 1–16.

Fontagné, Lionel, and Michaël Pajot. 2002. Relationships between trade and FDI flows within two panels of U.S. and French industries. In *Multinational firms and impacts on employment, trade, and technology*, ed. Robert E. Lipsey and Jean-Louis Mucchielli, 43–83. London: Routledge.

Frank, Robert F., and Richard T. Freeman. 1975. Multinational corporations and domestic employment. Cornell University, Department of Economics. (Processed).

Girma, Sourafel, David Greenaway, and Katherine Wakelin. 2001. Who benefits from foreign direct investment in the U.K.? *Scottish Journal of Political Economy* 48 (2): 119–33.

Girma, Sourafel, and Katherine Wakelin. 2000. Are there regional spillovers from FDI in the U.K.? Centre for Research on Globalisation and Labour Markets Research Paper no. 2000/16. Nottingham, U.K.: University of Nottingham.

Globerman, Steven. 1979. Foreign direct investment and "spillover" efficiency benefits in Canadian manufacturing industries. *Canadian Journal of Economics* 12 (1): 42–56.

Globerman, Steven, John Ries, and Ilan Vertinsky. 1994. The economic performance of foreign affiliates in Canada. *Canadian Journal of Economics* 27 (1): 143–56.

Goldsmith, Raymond W. 1969. *Financial structure and development*. New Haven: Yale University Press.

Görg, Holger, and David Greenaway. 2001. Foreign direct investment and intra-industry spillovers: A review of the literature. Globalisation and Labour Markets Programme Research Paper no. 2001/37. Nottingham, U.K.: Leverhulme Centre for Research on Globalisation and Economic Policy.

Görg, Holger, and Eric Strobl. 2000. Multinational companies, technology spillovers, and firm survival: Evidence from Irish manufacturing. Centre for Research on Globalisation and Labour Markets Research Paper no. 2000/12. Nottingham, U.K.: University of Nottingham.

———. 2001.Multinational companies and productivity spillovers: A meta-analysis. *Economic Journal* 111 (475): F723–F739.

———. 2002. Multinational companies and indigenous development: An empirical analysis. *European Economic Review* 46 (7): 1305–22.

Griffith, Rachel. 1999. Using the ARD establishment-level data to look at foreign ownership and productivity in the United Kingdom. *Economic Journal* 109 (456): 416–42.

Griffith, Rachel, and Helen Simpson. 2001. Characteristics of foreign-owned firms in British manufacturing. Institute for Fiscal Studies Working Paper no. 01/10. London: Institute for Fiscal Studies.

Haddad, Mona, and Ann Harrison. 1993. Are there positive spillovers from direct foreign investment? *Journal of Development Economics* 42 (1): 51–74.

Harris, Richard, and Catherine Robinson. 2002. The effect of foreign acquisitions on total factor productivity: Plant-level evidence from U.K. manufacturing, 1987–1992. *Review of Economics and Statistics* 84 (3): 562–68.

Harrison, Ann. 1996. Determinants and effects of direct foreign investment in Côte d'Ivoire, Morocco, and Venezuela. In *Industrial evolution in developing countries,* ed. Mark J. Roberts and James R. Tybout, 163–86. New York: Oxford University Press.

Haskel, Jonathan E., Sonia C. Pereira, and Matthew J. Slaughter. 2002. Does inward foreign direct investment boost the productivity of domestic firms? NBER Working Paper no. 8724. Cambridge, Mass.: National Bureau of Economic Research, January.

Head, Keith, and John Ries. 2002. Offshore production and skill upgrading by Japanese manufacturing firms. *Journal of International Economics* 58 (1): 81–105.

Hill, Hal. 1990. Indonesia's industrial transformation, part II. *Bulletin of Indonesian Economic Studies* 26:75–109.

Howenstine, Ned G., and William J. Zeile. 1994. Characteristics of foreign-owned U.S. manufacturing establishments. *Survey of Current Business* 74 (1): 34–59.

Hufbauer, Gary C., and F. M. Adler. 1968. Overseas manufacturing investment and the balance of payments. Tax Policy Research Study no. 1. Washington, D.C.: Department of the Treasury.

Hymer, Stephen H. 1960. The international operations of national firms: A study of direct foreign investment. Ph.D. Diss. MIT, Department of Economics.

Imbriani, C., and F. Reganati. 1997. Spillovers internazionale di efficienza nel settore manifatturiero Italiano (International productivity spillovers in the Italian manufacturing sector). *Economia Internazionale* 50 (4): 583–95.

Kathuria, Vinish. 2000. Productivity spillovers from technology transfer to Indian manufacturing firms. *Journal of International Development* 12 (3): 343–69.

Kindleberger, Charles P. 1969. *American business abroad: Six lectures on direct investment.* New Haven, Conn.: Yale University Press.

Kokko, Ari. 1994. Technology, market characteristics, and spillovers. *Journal of Development Economics* 43 (2): 279–93.

———. 1996. Productivity spillovers from competition between local firms and foreign affiliates. *Journal of International Development* 8 (4): 517–30.

Kokko, Ari, Mario Zejan, and Ruben Tansini. 2001. Trade regimes and spillover effects of FDI: Evidence from Uruguay. *Weltwirtschaftliches Archiv* 137 (1): 124–49.

Kravis, Irving B., and Robert E. Lipsey. 1988. The effects of multinational firms' foreign operations on their domestic employment. NBER Working Paper no. 2760. Cambridge, Mass.: National Bureau of Economic Research, December.

Lewis, Arthur. 1954. Economic development with unlimited supplies of labour. *Manchester School* 22 (2): 139–91.

Lewis, Cleona. 1938. *America's stake in international investments.* Washington, D.C.: Brookings Institution.

Lipsey, Robert E. 1994. Foreign-owned firms and U.S. wages. NBER Working Paper no. 4927. Cambridge, Mass.: National Bureau of Economic Research, November.

———. 1995. Outward direct investment and the U.S. economy. In *The effects of taxation on multinational corporations,* ed. Martin Feldstein, James R. Hines Jr., and R. Glenn Hubbard, 7–41. Chicago: University of Chicago Press.

————. 1998. Trade and production networks of U.S. MNEs and exports by their Asian affiliates. In *Globalization, trade, and foreign direct investment*, ed. John H. Dunning, 204–16. Oxford: Elsevier Science, Ltd.

————. 2000. Affiliates of U.S. and Japanese multinationals in East Asian production and trade. In *The role of foreign direct investment in East Asian development and trade*, ed. Takatoshi Ito and Anne O. Krueger, 147–90. Vol. 9 of *NBER East Asian Seminar on Economics*. Chicago: University of Chicago Press.

————. 2002. Foreign production by U.S. firms and parent firm employment. In *Multinational firms and impacts on employment, trade, and technology: New perspectives for a new century*, ed. Robert E. Lipsey and Jean-Louis Mucchielli, 3–23. London: Routledge.

————. 2003. Foreign direct investment and the operations of multinational firms: Concepts, history, and data. In *Handbook of international trade*, ed. E. Kwan Choi and James Harrigan, 287–319. London: Blackwell.

Lipsey, Robert E., Irving B. Kravis, and Romualdo A. Roldan. 1982. Do multinational firms adapt factor proportions to relative factor prices? In *Trade and employment in developing countries: 2. Factor supply and substitution*, ed. Anne O. Krueger, 215–55. Chicago: University of Chicago Press.

Lipsey, Robert E., and Eric Ramstetter. 2003. Japanese exports, MNC affiliates, and rivalry for export markets. *Journal of the Japanese and International Economies* 17 (2): 101–17.

Lipsey, Robert E., Eric Ramstetter, and Magnus Blomström. 1999. Parent exports and affiliate activity in Japanese multinational companies, 1986, 1989, 1992. In *Analytical research based on data from the survey of overseas business activities, survey research on harmonizing globalization based on the 1997 survey of overseas business activities*, 93–146. Tokyo: Institute for International Trade and Investment.

————. 2000. Outward FDI and parent exports and employment: Japan, the United States, and Sweden. *Global Economic Quarterly* 1 (4): 285–302.

Lipsey, Robert E., and Fredrik Sjöholm. 2003. Foreign direct investment, education, and wages in Indonesian manufacturing. *Journal of Development Economics,* forthcoming.

Lipsey, Robert E., and Merle Yahr Weiss. 1981. Foreign production and exports in manufacturing industries. *Review of Economics and Statistics* 63 (4): 488–94.

————. 1984. Foreign production and exports of individual firms. *Review of Economics and Statistics* 66 (2): 304–08.

Liu, Xiaming, Chengang Wang, and Yingqi Wei. 2001. Causal links between foreign direct investment and trade in China. *China Economic Review* 12 (2–3): 190–202.

Madden, John T., Marcus Nadler, and Harry C. Sauvain. 1937. *America's experience as a creditor nation.* New York: Prentice Hall.

Manning, Chris. 1998. *Indonesian labour in transition: An East Asian success story?* Cambridge: Cambridge University Press.

Markusen, James R. 1997. Trade versus investment liberalization. NBER Working Paper no. 6231. Cambridge, Mass.: National Bureau of Economic Research, October.

Markusen, James R., and Keith E. Maskus. 2001. General-equilibrium approaches to the multinational firm: A review of theory and evidence. NBER Working Paper no. 8334. Cambridge, Mass.: National Bureau of Economic Research, June.

Moran, Theodore H. 2002. *Beyond sweatshops: Foreign direct investment and globalization in developing countries.* Washington, D.C.: Brookings.

Nadiri. 1992. U.S. direct investment and the production structure of the manufacturing sector in France, Germany, Japan, and the U.K. New York University. Manuscript.

Oguchi, Noriyoshi, Nor Aini Mohd Amdzah, Zainon Bakar, Ravzah Zainal Abidin, and Mazlina Shafii. 2002. Productivity of foreign and domestic firms in the Malaysian manufacturing industry. *Asian Economic Journal* 16 (3): 215–28.

Okamoto, Yumiko, and Fredrik Sjöholm. 1999. FDI and the dynamics of productivity: Microeconomic evidence. Working Paper Series in Economics and Finance no. 348. Stockholm, Sweden: Stockholm School of Economics, December.

Oulton, Nicholas. 2001. Why do foreign-owned firms in the U.K. have higher labour productivity? In *Inward investment, technological change, and growth*, ed. Nigel Pain, 122–61. New York: Palgrave.

Pain, Nigel, ed. 2001. *Inward investment, technological change, and growth.* New York: Palgrave.

Ramstetter, Eric D. 1999. Comparisons of foreign multinationals and local firms in Asian manufacturing over time. *Asian Economic Journal* 13 (2): 163–203.

Reddaway, W. B., in collaboration with J. O. N. Perkins, S. J. Potter, and C. T. Taylor. 1967. *Effects of U.K. direct investment overseas: An interim report.* Cambridge University, Department of Applied Economics. Occasional Paper no. 12.

Reddaway, W. B., S. J. Potter, and C. T. Taylor. 1968. *Effects of U.K. direct investment overseas: Final report.* Cambridge University, Department of Applied Economics. Occasional Paper no. 15.

Rhee, Yung Whee, and Therese Belot. 1990. Export catalysts in low-income countries. World Bank Discussion Paper no. 72. Washington, D.C.: World Bank.

Rippy, J. Fred. 1931. *The capitalists and Colombia.* New York: Vanguard Press.

Romer, Paul M. 1993a. Idea gaps and object gaps in economic development. *Journal of Monetary Economics* 32 (3): 543–73.

————. 1993b. Two strategies for economic development: Using ideas and producing ideas. In *Proceedings of the World Bank annual conference on development economics, 1992,* ed. Lawrence H. Summers and Shekhar Shah, 63–91. Washington, D.C.: World Bank.

Ruane, Frances, and Holger Görg. 1999. Irish FDI policy and investment from the EU. In *Innovation, investment, and the diffusion of technology in Europe,* ed. Ray Barrell and Nigel Pain, 44–67. Cambridge: Cambridge University Press.

Singh, Jasjit. 2002. Knowledge diffusion and the role of multinational subsidiaries: Evidence using patent citation data. Boston: Harvard Business School, October. (Processed).

Sjöholm, Fredrik. 1999. Technology gap, competition, and spillovers from foreign direct investment: Evidence from establishment data. *Journal of Development Studies* 36 (1): 53–73.

Slaughter, Matthew J. 2000. Production transfer within multinational enterprises and American wages. *Journal of International Economics* 50 (2): 449–72.

Smarzynska, Beata K. 2002. Does foreign investment increase the productivity of domestic firms? In search of spillovers through backward linkages. Washington, D.C.: World Bank. (Processed).

Sousa, Nuno, David Greenaway, and Katherine Wakelin. 2000. Multinationals and export spillovers. Centre for Research on Globalisation and Labour Markets. Research Paper no. 2000/14. London: University of Mottingham, School of Economics.

Swedenborg, Birgitta. 1973. *Den Svenska industrins investeringar i utlandet* (Swedish industries' investment in foreign countries). Stockholm: Industriens Utredningsinstitut.

———. 1979. *The multinational operations of Swedish firms: An analysis of determinants and effects.* Stockholm: Industriens Utredningsinstitut.

———. 1982. *Svensk Industri I Utlandet. En Analys av Drivkrafter och Effekter.* Stockholm: Industriens Utredningsinstitut.

———. 1985. Sweden. In *Multinational enterprises, economic structure, and international competitiveness,* ed. John Dunning, 217–48. London: Wiley.

———. 2001. Determinants and effects of multinational growth: The Swedish case revisited. In *Topics in empirical international economics,* ed. Magnus Blomström and Linda S. Goldberg, 99–131. Chicago: University of Chicago Press.

Swedenborg, Birgitta, Goran Johansson-Grahn, and Mats Kinnwall. 1988. *Den Svenska industrins utlandsinvesteringar, 1960–1986* (Swedish industries' foreign investment, 1960–1986). Stockholm: Industriens Utredningsinstitut.

United Nations. 2000. *World investment report, 2000: Cross-border mergers and acquisitions and development.* Geneva: United Nations Conference on Trade and Development (UNCTAD).

———. 2001. *Measures of the transnationalization of economic activity.* Geneva: United Nations Conference on Trade and Development (UNCTAD).

Wang, J. Y., and Magnus Blomström. 1992. Foreign investment and technology transfer: A simple model. *European Economic Review* 36 (1): 137–55.

Wheeler, David, and Ashoka Mody. 1992. International investment location decisions: The case of U.S. firms. *Journal of International Economics* 33 (1–2): 57–76.

Wilkins, Mira. 1989. *The history of foreign investment in the United States to 1914.* Cambridge: Harvard University Press.

World Bank. 1987. Trade policy and industrialization. *World development report, 1987,* 78–94. New York: Oxford University Press.

World Economic Forum. 2002. *Global competitiveness report, 2001–2002.* Geneva: World Economic Forum.

Comment   Vanessa Strauss Kahn

Robert Lipsey's paper surveys the existing literature on foreign direct investment (FDI) in an attempt to elucidate the effects of multinational activity on the home and host countries. Based on a comprehensive review of mostly empirical papers, the paper summarizes the effects of FDI on exports and factor demand in the home country and on wages, productivity, and growth in the host country.

Robert Lipsey's expertise in the field of FDI and his extensive knowledge of the literature show in the paper. I find myself almost wholly in agreement with the author, also partly, perhaps, because he so graciously took account of comments I had made on the first draft of this paper. Hence, my comments are few and mainly consist on suggestions for further developments.

First, I think that further distinctions could be made between cost-

Vanessa Strauss-Kahn is assistant professor of economics at INSEAD.

oriented FDI and FDI that aims at accessing a market. While I would agree with Lipsey that such a distinction is not always straightforward, some FDI activities clearly aim at reducing production costs by locating plants abroad.[1] In such cases, most of the local production is exported to the multinational enterprise's (MNE's) parent in the home country or to a third country for final consumption. Distinguishing the type of FDI is important because the effects of FDI on the home and the host countries may differ accordingly. If the internationalization of production follows countries' comparative advantage, MNEs will tend to relocate plants of production in which the home country is relatively less efficient to foreign countries. Such relocation of production may not have negative effects on average wages and employment levels in the home country. However, it may have important distributional effects among home-country workers, because changes in labor demand likely affect wages and employment of the less-skilled workers more than their skilled counterparts.

I also believe that the paper should further distinguish FDI effects on developed and developing countries. For instance, most studies concluded that foreign-owned firms pay higher wages than their domestically owned counterparts. Reducing worker turnover and attracting better workers are worldwide explanations of such features. However, compensating for home-biased preferences seems to be a consideration more specifically adapted to inward FDI in a developed country. In developing countries other explanations (e.g., closing wage gaps between the multinational entities) may lead to this wage differential. Similarly, there is strong evidence that foreign-owned plants have higher productivity than domestically owned ones. The higher efficiency of foreign-owned firms in developing countries is predictable, as foreign-owned plants are likely to use more capital and/or more advanced production and managerial organization techniques. Two main reasons induce the higher productivity of foreign-owned plants in developed countries. First, there may be a selection bias as firms investing in multinational activities could likely be the most productive in the first place. Second, most FDI occurred through ownership consolidation, which usually leads to higher efficiency through firms' restructuring. Empirical studies aiming at estimating the productivity of foreign-owned firms relative to their domestically owned counterparts should hence control for efficiency gains from national firms' consolidation. As mentioned by Lipsey, one study by Harris and Robinson (2002) goes in that direction. It concludes that plant turnover seems to involve relatively more productive plants. I would encourage further research on that issue.

More importantly, I believe that future empirical studies on multinational activity and its effects on home and host countries should make use of micro-level data. For example, most empirical studies focusing on the

---

1. For example, Intel's decision to develop FDI in Costa Rica in 1996–1997.

effects of outward FDI on the home country concluded that exports and production abroad were, for the most part, complementary. Such a result is surprising, as standard theory of MNEs would assume both substitution and complementarity effects (see, e.g., Rob and Vettas 2003). Most studies, however, analyze the relationship between FDI and one of the following home-country variables: country exports, industry exports, or, in the best cases, firms' exports. While these results are important, they do not exclude the possibility that substitution arises when one looks at more disaggregated data levels. For example, if an MNE exports intermediate goods to its foreign assembly line, it induces complementarity between exports and foreign production at the industry or the firm level. However, at the product level (i.e., the final good), foreign production substitutes for exports. Notably, Blonigen (2001) uses product-level data and finds substantial evidence for both substitution and complementarity between foreign production and exports.

Studying micro-level data could also improve the current knowledge on the effect of FDI on wages and employment. If the labor mix (skilled to unskilled workers) were similar across products, using disaggregated data would not add significance to firm-level or industry-level data. However, if the labor mix varies across products with, say, a higher employment share of skilled workers in the production of parts and components than in assembly line, then increased FDI may have a significant impact on wage dispersion. Feenstra and Hanson (1999) use detailed data on imported inputs to assess the effect of outsourcing on the relative wage of skilled to unskilled workers. They find that outsourcing explains at least 15 percent of the U.S. wage-premium increase (this number may reach 40 percent in certain specifications). Although their research does not focus on FDI per se, as it also encompasses arm's-length production, I believe that their analysis sheds light on the effects of FDI on wage dispersion. Similarly, and as mentioned in the paper, Head and Ries (2002) find that affiliate employment does not affect the share of unskilled workers' wage in the total wage bill in the home country when they use industry-level data. In contrast, when they use firm-level data, they find that there is substitution between home and foreign activities of the firms toward a lower share of unskilled workers' wage in the total wage bill in the home country.

Should countries promote or discourage FDI, or leave it to market forces? As Lipsey put it in the introduction of the paper, these are important policy issues. They might be even more so for developing countries in search of a high positive-growth path. While most of the literature has been not conclusive as to the direction of wage and productivity spillovers, there is strong evidence that FDI raises the average level of wages in the host country and that foreign-owned firms have higher productivity levels than domestically owned ones. Are these features convincing enough to support costly FDI promotion policies (e.g., tax rebates or reduced tariffs on imports)? I believe that further research should focus on identifying the necessary conditions for successful FDI. While there seems to be no clear-cut answer for this question, one could attempt to define industries in which technological spillovers are positive, and identify countries' characteristics that help enhance such spillovers (education is a likely candidate). Among such sector-specific studies I believe that the issue of spillovers to suppliers has received too little attention. Apart from two unpublished papers by Aitken and Harrison (1991) and Smarzynska (2002), this area of research indeed lacks evidence. Finally, it could be interesting to obtain some empirical evidence on the potential effect of inward FDI on host-country industrial agglomeration. More specifically, one could wonder whether the establishment of foreign-owned firms in a country leads to industrial clusters, by attracting upstream and downstream activities in that location.

References

Aitken, B., and A. Harrison. 1991. Are there spillovers from foreign direct investment? Evidence from panel data for Venezuela. Processed, MIT and the World Bank, November.

Bloningen, B. 2001. In search of substitution between foreign production and exports. *Journal of International Economics* 53:81–104.

Feenstra, R., and G. Hanson. 1999. The impact of outsourcing and high-technology capital on wages: Estimates for the United States, 1979–1990. *Quarterly Journal of Economics* 114 (3): 907–940.

Harris, R., and C. Robinson. 2002. The effect of foreign acquisitions on total factor productivity: Plant-level evidence from U.K. manufacturing, 1987–1992. *Review of Economics and Statistics* 84:562–568.

Head, K., and J. Ries. 2002. Offshore production and skill upgrading by Japanese manufacturing firms. *Journal of International Economics* 58:81–103.

Rob, R., and N. Vettas. 2003. Foreign direct investment and exports with growing demand. *Review of Economics Studies,* forthcoming.

Smarzynska, B. 2002. Does foreign investment increase the productivity of domestic firms? In search of spillovers through backward linkages. World Bank Research Working Paper no. 2923. Washington, D.C.: World Bank.

10

Competition for Multinational Investment in Developing Countries: Human Capital, Infrastructure, and Market Size

David L. Carr, James R. Markusen,
and Keith E. Maskus

10.1 Introduction

Globalization is a complex process about which little can be said confidently without sustained and systematic empirical investigation into its sources, channels, and effects. Unfortunately, both avid critics and supporters of globalization processes tend to argue on the basis of anecdotes, which are always available to support a particular case. One of the more significant complaints about multinational enterprises is that, when locating in developing countries, they look for countries with weak labor rights. Such conditions presumably permit firms to exploit local workers by paying them less than some notion of a fair wage. Given the breadth and complexity of the world economy, claims of this kind can be misleading and may support faulty policy prescriptions. Thus, economists look for systematic evidence in large data sets and use statistical techniques to identify underlying regularities amidst the noise.

The purpose of this paper is to give a broad outline and discussion of what knowledge we may claim with a reasonable degree of confidence about the patterns and determinants of foreign direct investment (FDI) flows to developing countries. We restrict the analysis to long-term direct investment and do not consider more volatile short-term capital move-

David L. Carr is an assistant professor of economics at the American University, Washington, D.C. James R. Markusen is professor of economics at the University of Colorado, Boulder, and a research associate of the National Bureau of Economic Research. Keith E. Maskus is chair of the economics department at the University of Colorado, Boulder.

Prepared for the Center for Economic Policy Research (CEPR) and National Bureau of Economic Research (NBER) Conference, International Seminar on International Trade (ISIT) Challenges to Globalization, 24–25 May 2002. We are grateful to Robert Baldwin, Anthony Venables, Alan Winters, and other participants at the conference for comments.

ments. A basic task is to shed light on characteristics of developing countries that attract foreign investors. When analyzed through the filters of general-equilibrium theory and extensive econometric analysis, is the "sweatshop" view, in which multinational enterprises (MNEs) are primarily attracted to countries with low-wage labor, the decisive model?

We begin with a review of recent theory in section 10.2, examining Markusen's "knowledge-capital" model that allows for both horizontal and vertical motives for foreign investment. This analysis suggests channels through which FDI should be related to host-country characteristics. We then present some summary statistics about which countries attract inward investment in section 10.3. In section 10.4, we set out an econometric specification and provide estimates of this general-equilibrium model using data on outward investment from the United States to a large sample of countries from 1986 to 1997. Compared to our earlier work (Carr, Markusen, and Maskus 2001; Markusen and Maskus 2001), the new feature of the current paper is to introduce a measure of infrastructure quality into the econometric estimation. Both the summary statistics and econometric estimates we present indicate that manufacturing FDI flows to countries with relatively large markets, a relatively high endowment of labor skills, laws and legal institutions that are friendly to investment, and sound economic infrastructure.

Thus, our results do not support the sweatshop view of what features attract MNEs. Rather, the estimates support the view obtained from basic statistics that MNEs avoid the poorest countries in the world. Indeed, the evidence suggests that increases in the differences in skill endowments between the United States and its investment partners tends to reduce local affiliate activity significantly, as found earlier in Markusen and Maskus (2002) and Blonigen, Davies, and Head (2003). However, we emphasize that the data exercise in this paper considers only FDI in aggregate manufactures, rather than FDI in labor-intensive goods.

Overall, it is in the nature of what MNEs produce that makes cheap labor not a strong attraction for production in developing countries. Our conclusion is that developing countries stand to gain little in terms of increasing FDI by artificially suppressing wages—for example, by limiting rights of workers to organize and bargain collectively.[1] That strategy is likely to reduce productivity and investment, as noted by Martin and Maskus (2001). If attracting FDI in manufacturing is a development policy, it is more sensible to increase the human capital stock and improve the economic infrastructure. The conclusion that the quality of infrastructure matters positively for attracting FDI has been demonstrated in informal analyses by Wheeler and Mody (1992) for the Organization for Economic

---

1. Maskus (1997) and Organization for Economic Cooperation and Development (OECD; 1996) discuss such policies in a number of countries.

Cooperation and Development (OECD) economies and by Cheng and Kwan (2000) for China. Interestingly, however, infrastructure seems to play relatively little role in location decisions in sub-Saharan Africa, although it is important in other developing regions (Asiedu 2002).

10.2   A Theoretical Framework

While there are many motives for direct investment, one simple taxonomy is between the horizontal (also known as market seeking) and the vertical (also called resource seeking) investments. Horizontal investments refer to multinational activities abroad that produce roughly the same goods and services as the firm produces at home. Vertical investments refer to MNEs geographically fragmenting the production process, locating each stage where the factors used intensively in that stage are cheap.

Intuition would suggest that horizontal investments are made generally to serve local markets and are therefore attracted to large markets (the proverbial carrot) that are characterized by high trade costs that deter exporting to those markets (the stick). If MNEs tend to produce relatively sophisticated goods and services for high-income consumers, then horizontal investments will tend to be directed to other relatively advanced countries. Thus, a rough hypothesis is that horizontal investments tend to occur between high-income countries and with the output sold locally rather than exported.

Vertical investments seek favorable costs for different stages of production. One reasonable generalization is that the assembly and testing stages are less skilled-labor and capital intensive than are design and component production. Thus, firms will seek countries with low-wage and scarce labor skills for assembly and testing operations. Assuming that most of the output ultimately is to be sold in high-income countries, it follows that a large portion of the output from vertical investments should be traded internationally rather than sold domestically. Thus, we might conjecture that vertical investments tend to flow from high-income to low-income countries, with a high proportion of the output exported from the host country.

These generalizations are not perfect. There is rarely activity consisting of pure horizontal investment insofar as parent firms supply knowledge-based assets, services to and often components as well to subsidiaries. The relationship between trade versus domestic sales and vertical versus horizontal investments is imperfect as well. Many U.S. firms make what we would generally think of as horizontal investments in the European Union (EU) to serve the EU market, but production might be centered in a particular location, say Ireland. Since Ireland is a small part of EU consumption, the proportion of output exported from Ireland will be high.

Markusen's (2002) knowledge-capital model makes a number of assumptions about technologies that permit different types of firms to arise endogenously as a function of the characteristics of two countries. First, he assumes the existence of firm-level scale economies, a property that he refers to as "jointness." It is assumed that knowledge-based assets are at least partially joint or public inputs across plants, giving rise to firm-level scale economies. Second, he assumes that the creation of knowledge-based assets can be geographically fragmented from output production at a fairly low cost, a process called "fragmentation." Third, he assumes that knowledge-based assets are skilled-labor intensive relative to production, but also generally claims that production is skilled-labor intensive relative to the rest of the economy. This assumption is referred to as "skilled-labor intensity."

Jointness is the key assumption that gives rise to horizontal multinationals. Firm-level scale economies encourage multiplant firms to exploit firm-level economies. If there are plant-level scale economies as well, however, it is not trivially true that firms will always choose foreign-branch plants. Foreign production will be chosen when the foreign market is large and trade costs are moderate to high relative to plant-level scale economies.

Fragmentation and skilled-labor intensity encourage the vertical dispersion of activities, locating stages of production where the factors each stage uses intensively are relatively cheap. Accordingly, skilled-labor-intensive headquarters activities and component production may be located in the high-income parent country, and less-skilled-labor-intensive production may be located in a developing country, with a large proportion of the output shipped back to the parent country.

One interesting general-equilibrium result follows from Markusen's assumption that branch-plant production (in particular, the fixed costs of setting up a branch plant) is more skilled-labor intensive than the rest of the economy. This results in an inverted U-shaped relationship for affiliate production in a developing country as a function of its skilled-labor scarcity. Vertical production in which an assembly plant is located in the developing country, for example, is most attractive for a firm when the developing country is moderately skilled-labor scarce. Resulting factor-price differences give the firm an incentive to locate its headquarters in the skilled-labor-abundant country and the assembly plant in the developing country. But as the developing country becomes very skilled-labor scarce, the price of skilled labor makes the fixed costs of the branch plant prohibitively expensive, and the firm has an incentive to keep the assembly plant at home.[2] Put a different way, the MNE needs a minimum number of skilled managers and technicians in the developing country, in which skills may

---

2. Note that such a shortage could be relieved by permitting a temporary inflow of skilled labor, perhaps within the firm from the headquarters to the plant location. The model assumes that factors are immobile across borders (which is fairly consistent with reality in many countries), thereby ruling out this possibility. The observation underscores the importance of the current global debate about the gains and losses from temporary increases in skilled-labor migration.

command a high relative price. In fact, at a sufficient degree of skilled-labor scarcity, the MNE will not invest even if unskilled labor is virtually free.

These results have some parallels in findings by Feenstra and Hanson (1996, 1997). In their model, there is a continuum of activities needed to produce a final good and these activities can be ordered by their skilled-labor intensity. Investment liberalization then leads to the shift of some less-skilled activities to developing countries. This outcome is similar to location of certain final production activities, such as assembly, in the Markusen model. Although Feenstra and Hanson do not explicitly address the question of how much activity is shifted depending on the skilled-labor scarcity of the developing country, our sense is that they would get a similar result that this output transfer would diminish as the developing country gets extremely skilled-labor scarce.

There are thus several versions of theory that predict that the price of unskilled labor is not a decisive factor in attracting inward foreign investment. The need for skilled managers and technicians means that inward investment diminishes as the potential host country gets sufficiently skilled-labor scarce.

In addition, labor-force composition in a developing country is likely correlated with other economic variables that are important to MNEs. These include physical, legal, and institutional infrastructure, in particular. Multinational firms need access to the services of roads, ports, reliable electricity, telecommunications systems, and the like. They also need a sound, transparent, and fair legal system, including an efficient customs service. Most of these variables are endogenously chosen by countries over the long run, and our intuition is that they are likely to be highly correlated with per capita income and the skill composition of the labor force. To the extent that they derive from the same primitive characteristics that determine the labor force, the bottom line is that these infrastructure requirements reinforce the view that the poorest countries will not attract much inward investment.

10.3 Some Stylized Facts

Table 10.1 presents some statistics on inward-direct-investment stocks relative to income. Specifically, the numbers are shares of inward world-FDI stocks divided by shares of world gross domestic product (GDP). Countries are grouped according to the United Nations (UN) definition in the *World Investment Report*. The "least developed countries" comprise a group of forty-eight of the poorest nations. These countries are also included in the group "developing countries," and so the latter group's figures would be larger if the least developed countries were taken out. However, this adjustment would be modest since both total FDI stocks and total GDP levels of the least developed countries are quite small. These statistics

Table 10.1   Share of Inward World FDI Stock Divided by Share of World GDP

	Developed Countries	Developing Countries	Least Developed Countries
1980	0.96	1.10	0.37
1985	0.91	1.36	0.51
1990	0.97	1.22	0.51
1995	0.92	1.40	0.72
1998	0.88	1.46	0.54

Sources: United Nations Conference on Trade and Development (UNCTAD; 2000) and Zhang and Markusen (1999).
Note: "Least developed countries" is a UN definition that consists of forty-eight countries.

reveal that there is a lot of two-way investment among the developed countries, with their share in inward investment close to their share of income. Developing countries are net recipients of inward investment, and their share of inward investment relative to their share of income has grown by 33 percent over the eighteen-year period.

The point of table 10.1, for our purposes, is the relatively low ratios for the least developed countries. These countries attract little inward investment in spite of very low wages for unskilled labor. The developing countries as a whole get about 2.5 times as much investment relative to income as do the poorest countries. We suspect that the unattractiveness of the least developed countries is a combination of poor labor skills, poor physical infrastructure, and generally poor government and legal institutions. It should be noted that the FDI-GDP ratios rose for the least developed countries over the period as well, but this trend largely reflects a declining share of world GDP generated in those nations.

Table 10.2, taken from Zhang and Markusen (1999) presents data that separate effects on inward FDI flows due to market size from effects due to per capita income. Developing countries are grouped according to per capita GDP, and then each group is decomposed into relatively large and small countries in terms of total GDP. Here we see a high correlation between GDP per capita and FDI per capita. Again, FDI in the poorest countries is remarkably small. However, within any income group, we also see that the larger countries get considerably more inward investment per capita than do the smaller countries.

We infer from this finding that investment in developing countries is not aimed solely at export production: The size of the local market matters, suggesting that a significant proportion of local output is intended for local sale. With plant-level scale economies and output produced for local sale, investment will be higher in larger economies, which is what we see in the data. If all output were destined for export markets, we should not ob-

Table 10.2   **Inward FDI Flows and Their Links with GDP Per Capita and National Incomes of Developing Countries in 1993**

Country Groups	Average FDI Per Capita
By GDP Per Capita (U.S.$)	
> 5,000	226.89
2,500–5,000	45.30
1,200–2,500	33.02
600–1,200	10.06
300–600	6.56
< 300	0.63
By Country Size in GDP (U.S.$ millions)	
>55,000	242.20
< 49,000	53.83
> 31,000	45.73
< 17,000	32.30
> 10,000	33.43
< 9,600	30.60
> 10,000	10.86
< 9,300	2.59
> 4,800	6.91
< 3,700	3.68
> 2,000	0.34
< 1,500	2.47

Sources: Table taken from Zhang and Markusen (1999). Original data for FDI as well as data for GDP and population are from International Monetary Fund (IMF; 1995a, b).

serve this relationship in the data even with significant plant-level scale economies.

10.4   Data and Estimation

We define variables in order to capture the influences suggested by theory, although we are constrained to measures for which we can obtain a panel of data. An unfortunate irony for present purposes is that much of the data on costs and infrastructure are generally not available for the poorest countries, while the lack of investment into those countries is one thing that we would like to explain.

The variables used in the estimation are as follows, in which *j* is employed as the general reference to the host country. Note that the United States is always the parent country, a problem that we will discuss further.

RSALES: Real affiliate sales of U.S. affiliates in country *j*

RSALESL: Real affiliate sales of U.S. affiliates in country *j* to the local market in *j*

RSALESE: Real affiliate sales of U.S. affiliates in country j to all export
             markets
GDPUS: Real GDP in the United States (there is significant time-
             series variation in U.S. GDP, which is important for esti-
             mation)
GDPJ: Real GDP in country j
SKJ: The share of the labor force in country j that is skilled
SKDIFF: The share of skilled labor in the United States minus that
             in country j ($SKUS - SKJ$)
INVCJ: An index of costs and barriers to investing in country j
TCJ: An index of costs and barriers to exporting into country j
INFRAJ: An index of overall infrastructure quality for country j
DISTANCE: The distance between the United States and country j

The basic estimating equation is given by

$$RSALES = \alpha + \beta_0 GDPUS + \beta_1 GDPJ + \beta_2 SKDIFF + \beta_3 SKDIFF$$

$$\cdot GDPJ + \beta_4 INVCJ + \beta_5 TCJ + \beta_6 INFRAJ + \beta_7 DISTANCE.$$

The theory underlying this formulation is discussed in Markusen (2002) and in Carr, Markusen, and Maskus (2001). Of particular interest here is the interaction term between skill differences and real GDP in the recipient country. This term is designed to capture the nonlinear relationship in the theoretical model between endowment differences and affiliate activity. This relationship varies depending on the size of the host country as discussed above. Thus, GDPJ and SKDIFF appear in two variables. Our hypotheses relate to the combination of the two effects, so consider the derivatives.

(1)
$$\frac{\partial RSALES}{\partial GDPJ} = \beta_1 + \beta_3 \cdot SKDIFF$$

(2)
$$\frac{\partial RSALES}{\partial SKJ} = -\beta_2 - \beta_3 \cdot GDPJ$$

The coefficient β_1 on GDPJ is expected to be positive, as is the coefficient β_0 on GDPUS. In the underlying two-country model, both variables capture relevant market sizes.

Recall that SKDIFF is the skilled-labor share in the United States minus the skilled-labor share in the host country. Because in most cases the United States is relatively skill abundant in comparison with its partner, this difference becomes *larger* the more skilled-labor scarce is the host. Considering such cases, the derivative in equation (2) reflects both the direct impact of an increase in host skill endowment (meaning a convergence toward the U.S. level) and the indirect impact through the interaction of skills with GDP. There is some theoretical ambiguity about the anticipated sign here, as analyzed by Markusen. A purely vertical model would predict that the derivative in equation (2) is negative. Because outward investment is unskilled-labor seeking in this case, a convergence in skills would reduce affiliate activity. However, a purely horizontal model would predict that equation (2) is positive because outward investment seeks countries that are similar to the United States and because a convergence in skills would raise activity. The hybrid knowledge-capital model predicts some nonmonotonicity, with a rise in SKJ (a fall in SKDIFF for almost all observations) decreasing outward affiliate sales for relatively similar countries but increasing outward affiliate sales when the host is already very skilled-labor scarce. The theory cannot predict where the turning point is.

The coefficient on the interactive term β_3 is involved in two partial derivatives: the change in RSALES with respect to GDPJ and the change in RSALES with respect to SKDIFF. Coefficient β_3 is thus the cross-partial derivative between GDPJ and SKDIFF. If we conjecture that the effect of an increase in host-country size is larger the more similar it is to the United States in skilled-labor abundance, then we expect β_3 to be negative. If we conjecture that an increase in SKJ (generally a decrease in SKDIFF) has a more positive (or less negative) effect the larger country j is, then we again expect β_3 to be negative. Both of these conjectures clearly fit a horizontal model, but there is some ambiguity in the hybrid knowledge-capital model, as noted earlier.

To summarize, the model does not support predictions about the signs of individual coefficients β_2 and β_3. As we shall see shortly, the coefficient β_2 and β_3 generally have different signs in the regressions and, so it is important to compute equations (1) and (2) in order to ask whether or not U.S. investment is skilled-labor seeking, rather than considering only the sign of β_2.

The hypotheses for the coefficients on INVCJ and INFRAJ are clear, for each measures certain aspects of the costs of establishment and operation. The sign on INVCJ should be negative, and the sign on INFRAJ should be positive. The sign of the coefficient on TCJ is less clear. For horizontal investments, the sign should be positive as higher inward-trade costs induce a shift from exporting to producing in the host country. But for vertical investments in which the output is exported, the sign should be zero or negative, the latter occurring if the MNE needs to ship substantial amounts of component to the host-country plant, for example.

We also have hypotheses about the how regression results ought to differ for local sales versus export sales. Local sales should be more responsive to the host-country market size and should also be more skilled-labor seeking than export sales. Local sales should respond more positively to host-country trade costs. We hypothesize that export sales likely respond more negatively to investment costs and more positively to infrastructure, since firms have alternative locations to choose from in selecting a plant location

Table 10.3   **Countries Included in the Regression Analysis**

Developed Countries	Developing Countries
Australia	Argentina
Austria	Brazil
Belgium	Chile
Canada	China
Denmark	Colombia
Finland	Costa Rica
France	Egypt
Germany	Hong Kong
Greece	India
Ireland	Indonesia
Israel	The Republic of Korea
Italy	Malaysia
Japan	Mexico
The Netherlands	The Philippines
New Zealand	Singapore
Norway	South Africa
Portugal	Turkey
Spain	Venezuela
Sweden	
Switzerland	
The United Kingdom	
The United States	
(parent country only)	

for export production. Countries in which production is located for local sale by definition have no close competitors.

Data for the estimation form a panel of cross-country observations over the period 1986–1997. There are thirty-nine host countries for which we have at least nine years of complete data over this twelve-year interval, eighteen of which we classify as developing countries. Countries are listed in table 10.3. We take real sales volume of nonbank manufacturing affiliates in each country to indicate production activity. The U.S. Department of Commerce provides annual data on sales of foreign affiliates of American parent firms and on sales of U.S. affiliates of foreign parent firms. In this paper, we are only interested in outward investments, and so, unfortunately, the United States is the parent country in every observation. Theory suggests that this limits the analysis since the United States is always the larger of the two countries in any bilateral observation.

Annual sales values abroad are converted into millions of 1990 U.S. dollars using an exchange-rate-adjusted local-wholesale-price index, with exchange rates and price indexes taken from the *International Financial Statistics* (IFS) of the IMF. Real affiliate sales (RSALES) are broken down into two components, local sales (RSALESL) and export sales (RSALESE). We should emphasize that we do not have observations for developing countries in which there is no U.S. affiliate activity. Since these are generally the world's poorest countries, this creates some bias in the estimation, a problem which will be discussed.

Real GDP is measured in billions of 1990 U.S. dollars for each country. For this purpose, annual real GDP figures in local currencies were converted into dollars using the market exchange rate. These data are also from the IFS.

Skilled-labor abundance is defined as the sum of occupational categories 0/1 (professional, technical, and kindred workers) and 2 (administrative workers) in employment in each country, divided by total employment. These figures are compiled from annual surveys reported in the *Yearbook of Labor Statistics* published by the International Labor Organization (ILO).[3] In cases where some annual figures were missing, the skilled-labor ratios were taken to equal the period averages for each country. The variable SKDIFF is the relative skill endowment of the parent country less that of the affiliate country (e.g., the variable is *positive* if the host country is skilled-labor scarce). As noted, this variable is typically positive.

The cost of investing in the affiliate country is a simple average of several indexes of perceived impediments to investment, reported in the *World Competitiveness Report* (WCR) of the World Economic Forum. The investment-barriers index includes (a) restrictions on the ability to acquire control in a domestic company; (b) limitations on the ability to employ foreign skilled labor; (c) restraints on negotiating joint ventures; (d) strict controls on hiring and firing practices; (e) market dominance by a small number of enterprises; (f) an absence of fair administration of justice; (g) difficulties in acquiring local bank credit; (h) restrictions on access to local- and foreign-capital markets; and (i) inadequate protection of intellectual property. The resulting indexes thus include some direct investment barriers and indirect measures of "good government" and are computed on a scale from 0 to 100, with a higher number indicating higher investment costs.

A trade-cost index is taken from the same source and is defined as a measure of national protectionism, or efforts to prevent importation of competitive products. It also runs from 0 to 100, with 100 being the highest trade costs. All of these indexes are based on extensive surveys of multinational enterprises. It should be noted that both the investment-cost and trade-cost indexes are ordinal and qualitative in nature and are without "natural units." Thus, regression coefficients represent the partial effects of a change in the average perceived costs of investing and trading.

Finally, we use an index of overall infrastructure quality, also taken from the WCR. We employ two measures of infrastructure. First, we take an index from the 1999 WCR that ranks countries based on the following ques-

---

3. These surveys are now available on the web at http://www.ilo.org.

tion: "The infrastructure of your country is far superior to that in other countries." This index ranges from 0 (strongly disagree) to 70 (strongly agree). There is only one observation on this variable for each country, and its value is used in every yearly observation for a given country. Consequently, there is no time variation in this measure of infrastructure, labeled INFRAJ1. A second measure does permit time variation by computing the simple averages of responses given to questions about the quality of six types of infrastructure: roads, railroads, ports, air transport, telecommunications, and power supply. Unfortunately these data go back to 1986 for only the industrialized countries and larger middle-income economies. Other countries enter the WCR database at different years during the sample. Thus, a number of imputations were made to this second measure, called INFRAJ2, to construct a full panel.[4]

We also incorporate a measure of distance, which is simply the number of kilometers of each country's capital city from Washington, D.C. It is unclear whether this variable captures elements of trade costs or of investment costs, since both should rise with distance.

For estimation we consider two samples. One uses the full sample of host countries, consisting of 452 observations. The means of the variables in this sample are shown in the top panel of table 10.4. A second sample uses only the developing countries and consists of 207 observations. Means of these variables are shown in the bottom panel of table 10.4. Most of the differences in the two samples are intuitively sensible. In the full sample average, host-country GDP, labor skills, and infrastructure are higher or more highly ranked, and investment and trade costs are lower relative to the developing-countries-only sample. One interesting feature of the data is that the share of affiliate output that is exported is slightly higher in the full sample. This is likely due in part to the influence of small, high-income countries such as Canada, Ireland, and the Nordic countries, in which foreign affiliates export a large proportion of their output to regional trading partners. Put another way, however, it is important to note the importance of local sales for foreign affiliates in the developing countries, where 64 percent of output is sold locally. This does not fit the popular image of developing-country affiliates as export-oriented assembly plants.

It is worth noting that the infrastructure variables do not on average seem to indicate significant differences between developing countries and the full sample. Using both INFRAJ1 and INFRAJ2, the mean observation in developing countries is 85 percent of that in the full sample.

Table 10.5 provides sample correlations. It is notable that real local sales are positively correlated with infrastructure quality in the large sample but are not correlated with infrastructure in the developing countries. Export

4. Details are available on request.

Table 10.4   **Basic Data on U.S. Outward Affiliate Sales and Other Variables**

Variable	Mean of Variable	Qualifying Feature
	All Countries (452 observations)	
RSALES	16,315.32	$millions. Proportion exported = 0.40
RSALESL	9,787.59	$millions
RSALESE	6,532.74	$millions
GDPJ	371.05	$billions
SKJ	0.18	Proportion of the labor force that is skilled
SKDIFF	0.11	Differences in skilled labor proportion
INVCJ	38.89	Range: 0–100; 100 = highest costs
TCJ	34.61	Range: 0–100; 100 = highest costs
INFRAJ1	45.07	Range: 0–70; 70 = best infrastructure
INFRAJ2	63.42	Range: 0–100; 100 = best infrastructure
DIST	8,555	Kilometers
	Developing Countries (207 observations)	
RSALES	5,785.49	$millions. Proportion exported = 0.36
RSALESL	3,672.97	$millions
RSALESE	2,111.07	$millions
GDPJ	161.94	$billions
SKJ	0.12	Proportion of the labor force that is skilled
SKDIFF	0.18	Differences in skilled labor proportion
INVCJ	45.26	Range: 0–100; 100 = highest costs
TCJ	39.85	Range: 0–100; 100 = highest costs
INFRAJ1	37.65	Range: 0–70; 70 = best infrastructure
INFRAJ2	54.00	Range: 0–100; 100 = best infrastructure
DIST	9,836	Kilometers

sales are positively associated with infrastructure, however. Another intriguing result is that export sales and distance are negatively correlated in the full sample but have no correlation in the developing-country sample.

There is a high degree of correlation among some of the independent variables. A larger recipient market (GDPJ) is slightly negative correlated with skill differences, as the larger countries tend to have skill ratios nearer those of the United States. Note that in the smaller sample this correlation becomes positive, indicating that smaller developing countries are more skilled-labor scarce in the data. An important distinction in the data is that, in the full sample, the correlations between GDPJ and investment costs and trade costs are essentially zero, while they are strongly positive in the developing countries. Skilled-labor scarce countries (a larger positive value of SKDIFF) have higher investment and trade costs and worse infrastructure, although these correlations are somewhat smaller in the developing-country sample than in the full sample. Note finally that investment costs and trade costs are strongly and negatively correlated with infrastructure quality.

Table 10.5   Correlations among Key Variables

	RSALES	RSALESL	RSALESE	GDPJ	SKDIFF	SKDIFF · GDPJ	INVCJ	TCJ	INFRAJ1	INFRAJ2	DIST
All Countries											
RSALES	1.00										
RSALESL	0.98	1.00									
RSALESE	0.96	0.89	1.00								
GDPJ	0.55	0.62	0.42	1.00							
SKDIFF	-0.41	-0.37	-0.44	-0.10	1.00						
SKDIFF · GDPJ	0.15	0.22	0.03	0.85	0.26	1.00					
INVCJ	-0.32	-0.25	-0.40	-0.05	0.62	0.16	1.00				
TCJ	-0.16	-0.09	-0.25	0.08	0.42	0.25	0.71	1.00			
INFRAJ1	0.34	0.30	0.37	0.26	-0.50	0.09	-0.55	-0.30	1.00		
INFRAJ2	0.31	0.26	0.36	0.18	-0.57	0.00	-0.68	-0.42	0.73	1.00	
DISTANCE	-0.37	-0.35	-0.37	-0.09	0.37	0.10	0.10	0.27	0.09	0.02	1.00
Developing Countries											
RSALES	1.00										
RSALESL	0.92	1.00									
RSALESE	0.79	0.48	1.00								
GDPJ	0.35	0.47	0.05	1.00							
SKDIFF	-0.48	-0.40	-0.45	0.15	1.00						
SKDIFF · GDPJ	0.06	0.12	-0.06	0.90	0.45	1.00					
INVCJ	-0.11	0.08	-0.37	0.41	0.39	0.40	1.00				
TCJ	-0.10	0.04	-0.28	0.44	0.40	0.43	0.75	1.00			
INFRAJ1	0.13	-0.08	0.41	-0.23	-0.39	-0.26	-0.59	-0.35	1.00		
INFRAJ2	0.16	0.01	0.34	-0.19	-0.40	-0.26	-0.54	-0.35	0.81	1.00	
DISTANCE	-0.21	-0.34	0.07	-0.04	0.26	0.08	-0.17	0.24	0.50	0.35	1.00

10.5   Estimation Strategy and Results

Our task is to estimate the general-equilibrium determinants of real affiliate sales in a panel of countries over the period 1986–1997. These data may be expected both to display cross-sectional heteroskedasticity and serial correlation within each country. Accordingly, we adopt two estimation techniques. First is weighted least squares (WLS), in which we posit that error variances depend on real GDP in the host countries and compute robust standard errors. Second is a generalized least squares (GLS) approach that permits heteroskedastic error variances and country-specific AR(1) coefficients.[5] An even more general specification would permit contemporaneous, non-zero covariances across panels, but there are insufficient degrees of freedom to implement it. As Beck and Katz (1995) demonstrate with Monte Carlo techniques, the latter approach would understate the true standard errors, while the method taken here generates less efficient but consistent estimates (Greene 2000). The GLS estimates report Newey-West standard errors robust to heteroskedasticity and first-order autocorrelation.

We do not include country effects. Most variation in the key variables of interest (size, skill differences, and especially investment costs, trade costs, and infrastructure quality) is cross-sectional rather than longitudinal. This variation is central to our analysis but would be obscured by country-specific dummies, rendering it virtually impossible to identify the impacts of those influences on sales. Instead, we control for the variables posited by the theory, with appropriately conservative standard errors. Note that the inclusion of first-order autocorrelation corrections by country poses a stiff test for estimating the coefficients of policy variables, the values of which change little over time.

Tables 10.6 through 10.8 depict regression results for the full sample for total sales (RSALES), local sales (RSALESL), and export sales (RSALESE) respectively, in which each model is estimated using each of the two infrastructure variables in turn. Considering table 10.5, both the WLS and GLS coefficients on GDPUS are positive and strongly significant, as anticipated. Use of GLS reduces the magnitudes of these coefficients, although they are robust to use of the different infrastructure measures. Investment costs significantly discourage inward investment using either method, but GLS dramatically cuts the size of the estimated impact. A similar result emerges for trade costs, which strongly encourage affiliate sales using WLS but have far smaller coefficients that fail to achieve significance at the 10 percent level using GLS.

The first and third columns indicate that high-quality infrastructure strongly encourages inward investment, using INFRAJ1. However, this

5. We also estimated a specification with an AR(1) coefficient common to all panels, but this case was rejected in favor of the more flexible approach.

Table 10.6   RSALES Regression Results for Full Sample

	Coefficients			
	WLS	WLS	GLS	GLS
GDPUS	7.06	6.38	3.47	3.53
	(4.56/0.000)	(4.08/0.000)	(8.87/0.000)	(10.17/0.000)
GDPJ	76.59	77.60	57.61	50.34
	(28.50/0.000)	(28.51/0.000)	(16.00/0.000)	(13.40/0.000)
SKDIFF	100,223.00	92,804.00	46,184.00	24,641.00
	(7.77/0.000)	(7.07/0.000)	(8.14/0.000)	(4.77/0.000)
SKD · GDPJ	−472.76	−472.57	−333.45	−267.44
	(−22.77/0.000)	(−22.34/0.000)	(−13.88/0.000)	(−12.05/0.000)
INVCJ	−619.75	−636.33	−39.46	−70.02
	(−5.91/0.000)	(−5.70/0.000)	(−2.28/0.023)	(−4.19/0.000)
TCJ	414.25	405.31	14.73	12.82
	(6.72/0.000)	(6.47/0.000)	(1.37/0.172)	(1.32/0.186)
INFRAJ1	259.29		172.17	
	(4.72/0.000)		(7.49/0.000)	
INFRAJ2		123.41		10.02
		(2.56/0.011)		(1.01/0.313)
DISTANCE	−1.77	−1.61	−0.89	−0.82
	(−9.14/0.000)	(−8.33/0.000)	(−8.17/0.000)	(−9.57/0.000)
Intercept	−34,104.00	−26,317.00	−18,421.00	−9,148.00
	(−3.01/0.003)	(−2.24/0.026)	(−7.21/0.000)	(−4.04/0.000)
Adjusted R^2	0.83	0.83		
Log likelihood			−4,084.59	−4,077.53
No. of observations	452	452	452	452

Notes: The WLS has host-country-GDP-weighted OLS with robust standard errors; GLS has heteroskedasticity and panel-specific AR(1) corrections with robust standard errors. *T*-statistics followed by *p*-values are in parentheses.

variable is defined only for the year 1998, and its values are assigned to all earlier years for each country. Thus, it takes on the nature of any variable that would be stable over the period and correlated with the perceived quality of infrastructure at the end of the period. Turning to INFRAJ2 in columns (2) and (4), when infrastructure is permitted to vary within the panel, its influence becomes smaller, although still significant using WLS and insignificant using GLS. It is likely that this weakness in the estimation stems from collinearity between infrastructure and the cost variables. Note that the inclusion of INFRAJ2 raises the size and significance of the coefficient on investment costs in the GLS approach. Judging from the log-likelihood statistics in the GLS equations, the models with INFRAJ2 fit the data slightly better than those with INFRAJ1.

Similar results pertain in the regressions on local sales in table 10.7. Investment costs negatively affect local sales in the WLS case, and the coefficients are highly significant. Again, these magnitudes fall considerably us-

Table 10.7   **RSALESL Regression Results for Full Sample**

	Coefficients			
	WLS	WLS	GLS	GLS
GDPUS	4.42	4.11	1.83	1.85
	(4.87/0.000)	(4.51/0.000)	(9.89/0.000)	(10.42/0.000)
GDPJ	48.20	48.65	35.63	35.99
	(30.56/0.000)	(30.63/0.000)	(14.75/0.000)	(15.55/0.000)
SKDIFF	53,054.00	49,129.00	14,735.00	9,964.00
	(7.01/0.000)	(6.41/0.000)	(5.04/0.000)	(3.51/0.000)
SKD · GDPJ	−281.61	−281.24	−170.11	−162.85
	(−23.10/0.000)	(−22.78/0.000)	(−12.82/0.000)	(−13.33/0.000)
INVCJ	−293.17	−307.72	−12.22	−26.21
	(−4.76/0.000)	(−4.73/0.000)	(−1.16/0.244)	(−2.56/0.011)
TCJ	270.03	266.03	4.70	3.53
	(7.46/0.000)	(7.28/0.000)	(0.74/0.458)	(0.60/0.552)
INFRAJ1	114.65		34.03	
	(3.56/0.000)		(3.13/0.002)	
INFRAJ2		46.39		−5.06
		(1.65/0.100)		(−0.85/0.40)
DISTANCE	−0.96	−0.88	−0.11	−0.08
	(−8.40/0.000)	(−7.79/0.000)	(−2.25/0.025)	(−1.85/0.064)
Intercept	−24,541.00	−20,240.00	−11,913.00	−9,208.00
	(−3.69/0.000)	(−2.95/0.000)	(−8.95/0.000)	(−7.44/0.000)
Adjusted R^2	0.84	0.85		
Log likelihood			−3,792.89	−3,782.76
No. of observations	452	452	452	452

Notes: See table 10.6.

ing GLS, although the estimate in column (4) is significant. Trade costs have a strongly positive impact using WLS, but the positive coefficients with GLS are imprecisely estimated. The first measure of infrastructure quality is positively associated with local sales, but the second measure is insignificant using GLS. Results for export sales in table 10.8 are qualitatively similar to those for local sales.

Turning to GDPJ and SKJ (a component of SKDIFF), it is not meaningful to give an economic interpretation to the direct coefficients as these factors appear in two places among the independent variables.[6] It is also inappropriate to make comparisons across the regressions in tables 10.6 through 10.8 because the dependent variables have different means. Thus, we take partial derivatives and compute elasticities in table 10.9 for each estimation method, evaluating the elasticities at the mean of each respective independent variable. Elasticities that derive from significant regression coefficients are listed in boldface.

---

6. In the tables, SKD · GDPJ refers to the product of SKDIFF and GDPJ.

Table 10.8   RSALESE Regression Results for Full Sample

	Coefficients			
	WLS	WLS	GLS	GLS
GDPUS	2.63	2.27	0.85	0.72
	(3.47/0.000)	(2.95/0.003)	(5.52/0.000)	(4.93/0.000)
GDPJ	28.42	28.98	19.42	18.29
	(21.59/0.000)	(21.67/0.000)	(14.31/0.000)	(13.11/0.000)
SKDIFF	47,283.00	43,780.00	14,402.00	11,426.00
	(7.49/0.000)	(6.79/0.000)	(5.85/0.000)	(5.52/0.000)
SKD · GDPJ	−191.28	−191.47	−111.96	−98.48
	(−18.81/0.000)	(−18.43/0.000)	(−11.39/0.000)	(−10.48/0.000)
INVCJ	−328.18	−330.29	−12.97	−11.88
	(−6.39/0.000)	(−6.03/0.000)	(−2.26/0.024)	(−1.96/0.049)
TCJ	144.44	139.50	5.25	3.83
	(4.78/0.000)	(4.53/0.000)	(1.51/0.130)	(1.17/0.241)
INFRAJ1	144.71		23.14	
	(5.38/0.000)		(1.69/0.091)	
INFRAJ2		76.97		3.70
		(3.25/0.000)		(0.91/0.36)
DISTANCE	−0.82	−0.73	−0.15	−0.08
	(−8.59/0.000)	(−7.70/0.000)	(−3.08/0.002)	(−1.99/0.047)
Intercept	−8,512.00	−6,015.00	−5,245.00	−4,215.00
	(−1.71/0.087)	(−1.04/0.299)	(−5.17/0.000)	(−4.70/0.000)
Adjusted R^2	0.76	0.75		
Log likelihood			−3,636.68	−3,625.70
No. of observations	452	452	452	452

Notes: See table 10.6.

Because the relationships between our dependent variables and GDPJ and SKJ are nonlinear, we have computed elasticities at two different points in the sample for each variable. Recall that SKDIFF is *positive* when the host-country is skilled-labor scarce relative to the United States, which is true for the bulk of the observations in the sample. At the (positive) mean value of SKDIFF, affiliate sales have a modest income elasticity of 0.56 (WLS) or 0.48 (GLS). For skilled-labor-abundant countries (SKDIFF = 0), the income elasticity is much larger. In both cases, local sales are more income elastic than export sales, which is what we would expect. There are virtually no differences between these estimates arising from the use of differing infrastructure measures.

The elasticity of affiliate sales with respect to the host-country skilled-labor endowment (SKJ) is positive at mean host-country GDP, estimated at 0.83 (WLS) or 0.86 (GLS). This means that outward investment is skilled-labor seeking. However, for smaller countries (note that these are not necessarily the developing countries) captured by estimating the elasticity at one-half the mean market size, local sales are less responsive to a

Table 10.9   **Elasticities of U.S. Outward-Affiliate Sales, Full Sample**

	Estimated with INFRAJ1				Estimated with INFRAJ2			
	At Average SKDIFF		At SKDIFF = 0		At Average SKDIFF		At SKDIFF = 0	
	WLS	GLS	WLS	GLS	WLS	GLS	WLS	GLS
With respect to GDPJ								
RSALES	**0.56**	**0.48**	**1.74**	**1.31**	**0.58**	**0.48**	**1.76**	**1.14**
RSALESL	**0.65**	**0.64**	**1.82**	**1.35**	**0.67**	**0.69**	**1.84**	**1.36**
RSALESE	**0.42**	**0.40**	**1.61**	**1.10**	**0.45**	**0.42**	**1.65**	**1.04**

	Estimated with INFRAJ1				Estimated with INFRAJ2			
	At Average GDPJ		At 0.5 Average GDPJ		At Average GDPJ		At 0.5 Average GDPJ	
	WLS	GLS	WLS	GLS	WLS	GLS	WLS	GLS
With respect to SKJ								
RSALES	**0.83**	**0.86**	−0.14	0.17	**0.91**	**0.82**	−0.06	0.28
RSALESL	**0.95**	**0.89**	−0.01	0.31	**1.02**	**0.93**	0.06	0.37
RSALESE	**0.44**	**0.75**	−0.22	0.18	**0.75**	**0.69**	−0.23	0.19
With respect to INVCJ								
RSALES	**−1.48**	−0.09			**−1.52**	**−0.17**		
RSALESL	**−1.16**	−0.05			**−1.23**	**−0.10**		
RSALESE	**−1.95**	−0.08			**−1.97**	**−0.07**		
With respect to TCJ								
RSALES	**0.88**	0.03			**0.86**	0.03		
RSALESL	**0.95**	0.02			**0.94**	0.01		
RSALESE	**0.77**	0.03			**0.74**	0.02		
With respect to INFRA								
RSALES	**0.72**	**0.48**			**0.48**	0.03		
RSALESL	**0.53**	**0.16**			**0.30**	0.02		
RSALESE	**1.00**	**0.16**			**0.75**	0.03		

Note: Parameters coming from statistically significant coefficients are in boldface.

rise in skills. Employing WLS, these elasticities are negative. For GLS, at one-third the average market size, the elasticities of RSALES and RSALESE with respect to SKJ turn negative, while that for RSALESL changes signs at one-fifth the average GDPJ. This finding suggests that affiliate production is unskilled-labor seeking in small host countries. This may be particularly true in cases where the export motive is more important for smaller nations and where production for export is more sensitive to labor costs than production for local sale. Note from the computations that export sales are less skilled-labor seeking (and more unskilled-labor seeking) than local sales.

The remaining sets of elasticities have the hypothesized signs, although they are not always significantly different from zero. There are large differ-

Table 10.10   RSALES Regression Results for Developing-Country Sample

	Coefficients			
	WLS	WLS	GLS	GLS
GDPUS	5.67	5.31	2.58	2.72
	(5.31/0.000)	(4.99/0.000)	(6.40/0.000)	(7.14/0.000)
GDPJ	81.74	80.73	71.54	73.11
	(9.74/0.000)	(9.50/0.000)	(7.82/0.000)	(8.46/0.000)
SKDIFF	−14,043.00	−24,789.00	12,640.00	10,407.00
	(−1.02/0.310)	(−1.88/0.062)	(1.61/0.108)	(1.29/0.198)
SKD · GDPJ	−317.22	−310.29	−283.48	−294.06
	(−7.86/0.000)	(−7.62/0.000)	(−7.03/0.000)	(−7.67/0.000)
INVCJ	−58.97	−83.51	−22.55	−28.16
	(−0.80/0.427)	(−1.12/0.264)	(−2.13/0.033)	(−2.45/0.014)
TCJ	5.97	−12.85	4.21	5.94
	(0.13/0.894)	(−0.29/0.773)	(0.64/0.520)	(0.85/0.396)
INFRAJ1	112.50		26.02	
	(2.14/0.034)		(0.55/0.582)	
INFRAJ2		3.96		−6.80
		(0.15/0.884)		(−0.83/0.405)
DISTANCE	−0.24	−0.04	−0.13	−0.13
	(−1.57/0.118)	(−0.31/0.759)	(−1.39/0.165)	(−1.51/0.305)
Intercept	−28,256.00	−20,379.00	−14,751.00	−13,561.00
	(−3.46/0.001)	(−2.67/0.008)	(−5.37/0.000)	(−6.52/0.000)
Adjusted R^2	0.72	0.71		
Log likelihood			−1,697.59	−1,701.37
No. of observations	207	207	207	207

Notes: See table 10.6.

ences in these parameters between the WLS and GLS estimates, with the latter being much smaller and sometimes not significantly different from zero. Again, the difference reflects the fact that the AR(1) corrections tend to remove much of the time-series variation from these policy variables. Export sales are more (negatively) sensitive to investment barriers than are local sales. The trade cost elasticities are positive for WLS but essentially zero for GLS. Total sales are positively responsive to the first infrastructure measure, as are local and export sales. The infrastructure measure that varies over time, INFRAJ2, has positive elasticities using WLS, with export sales being most sensitive to its quality. However, in GLS, this measure has no discernible impacts on any of the sales flows.

Regression estimates for the sample of developing countries are shown in tables 10.10 through 10.12.[7] Overall, the equations fit this sample to a de-

---

7. We ran the same regressions for the sample of developed countries as well. In all important respects for our purposes, the results were both qualitatively and quantitatively similar to the findings for the full sample of countries. One interesting difference was that increases in investment costs seemed to have greater deterrent impacts on inward FDI in developed

Table 10.11   **RSALESL Regression Results for Developing-Country Sample**

	Coefficients			
	WLS	WLS	GLS	GLS
GDPUS	3.06	2.93	2.05	2.12
	(5.75/0.000)	(5.53/0.000)	(10.23/0.000)	(11.12/0.000)
GDPJ	81.76	81.48	49.48	49.64
	(19.55/0.000)	(19.33/0.000)	(6.37/0.000)	(6.56/0.000)
SKDIFF	22,331.00	17,975.00	11,158.00	7,563.00
	(3.26/0.001)	(2.74/0.001)	(2.01/0.045)	(1.57/0.117)
SKD · GDPJ	−336.41	−334.27	−200.69	−201.15
	(−16.74/0.000)	(−16.55/0.000)	(−6.01/0.000)	(−6.12/0.000)
INVCJ	−36.90	−47.23	−18.30	−21.08
	(−1.00/0.319)	(−1.28/0.203)	(−2.39/0.017)	(−2.82/0.005)
TCJ	2.15	−5.59	3.15	3.59
	(0.10/0.923)	(−0.25/0.800)	(0.75/0.451)	(0.88/0.382)
INFRAJ1	42.11		18.97	
	(1.61/0.110)		(0.92/0.355)	
INFRAJ2		−1.49		−1.55
		(−0.11/0.912)		(−0.32/0.748)
DISTANCE	−0.30	−0.22	−0.17	−0.13
	(−3.90/0.000)	(−3.25/0.001)	(−3.29/0.001)	(−3.91/0.000)
Intercept	−18,491.00	−15,297.00	−10,929.00	−10,182.00
	(−4.55/0.000)	(−4.04/0.000)	(−7.35/0.000)	(−7.95/0.000)
Adjusted R^2	0.85	0.85		
Log likelihood			−1,612.15	−1,612.31
No. of observations	207	207	207	207

Notes: See table 10.6.

gree similar to the full sample for total affiliate sales and local affiliate sales, but the export sales equation performs less well. The coefficients on GD-PUS are highly significant and similar to their counterparts for the full sample, although generally somewhat smaller in magnitude, suggesting that demand in the U.S. market is a slightly less important determinant of affiliate activity in developing nations. In contrast, the coefficients on local GDP are somewhat larger in the total-sales and local-sales regressions for developing countries, indicating that size of the local market is at least as important in developing countries for attracting FDI as it is overall. These coefficients in export sales are negative and insignificant in the WLS cases for developing countries. Conceivably, this result indicates that export production has little relationship to the economic size of the host country. For example, Singapore and Hong Kong are small economies but large ex-

countries than in the overall sample. However, our overall conclusions were unchanged by considering this sample alone.

Table 10.12   RSALESE Regression Results for Developing-Country Sample

	Coefficients			
	WLS	WLS	GLS	GLS
GDPUS	2.61	2.39	0.23	0.37
	(4.25/0.000)	(3.90/0.000)	(1.57/0.117)	(2.46/0.014)
GDPJ	−0.34	−1.06	13.90	12.96
	(−0.07/0.944)	(−0.22/0.829)	(7.72/0.000)	(6.81/0.000)
SKDIFF	−36,983.00	−43,201.00	3,446.00	2,459.00
	(−4.68/0.000)	(−5.69/0.000)	(1.56/0.120)	(0.98/0.328)
SKD · GDPJ	20.70	25.43	−50.09	−48.67
	(0.89/0.373)	(1.09/0.279)	(−4.89/0.000)	(−4.88/0.000)
INVCJ	−23.27	−37.28	−2.64	−3.84
	(−0.55/0.585)	(−0.87/0.386)	(−0.86/0.388)	(−1.01/0.314)
TCJ	4.66	−6.29	1.62	2.49
	(0.18/0.86)	(−0.25/0.806)	(0.83/0.407)	(1.20/0.230)
INFRAJ1	69.47		−16.97	
	(2.30/0.023)		(−1.06/0.290)	
INFRAJ2		5.38		1.98
		(0.35/0.730)		(0.70/0.486)
DISTANCE	0.06	0.18	−0.02	−0.03
	(0.66/0.510)	(2.27/0.025)	(−0.69/0.491)	(−0.93/0.51)
Intercept	−9,623.00	−5,002.00	−1,258.00	−2,170.00
	(−2.05/0.041)	(−1.14/0.256)	(−1.41/0.158)	(−3.04/0.002)
Adjusted R^2	0.50	0.49		
Log likelihood			−1,467.92	−1,481.54
No. of observations	207	207	207	207

Notes: See table 10.6.

porters. However, the finding seems anomalous given the strongly positive coefficients registered in the GLS cases.

Regression coefficients on the policy variables in the developing-country sample are estimated less precisely than in the full sample, presumably, in part because of the smaller number of observations. In the GLS equations, local investment costs tend to have negative and significant impacts on affiliate activity, particularly for total and local sales. The effects of trade costs are imprecisely estimated and cannot be confidently signed in any of the specifications. Considering the WLS equations, the impacts of INFRAJ1 (the unchanging measure of infrastructure quality) are uniformly positive for each type of affiliate sales, but the coefficient magnitudes are generally lower than in the full sample.[8] However, the quality of infrastructure, as measured here, has no detectable impact on affiliate sales in the developing-country sample using the GLS approach. In our

8. Again, we caution that comparisons of coefficient sizes across samples can be misleading because the means of the dependent variables differ.

Table 10.13   **Elasticities of U.S. Outward Affiliate Sales, Developing-Country Sample**

	Estimated with INFRAJ1				Estimated with INFRAJ2			
	At Average SKDIFF		At SKDIFF = 0		At Average SKDIFF		At SKDIFF = 0	
	WLS	GLS	WLS	GLS	WLS	GLS	WLS	GLS
With respect to GDPJ								
RSALES	0.71	0.59	2.29	2.00	0.71	0.58	2.26	2.05
RSALESL	0.96	0.61	3.60	2.18	0.97	0.61	3.59	2.19
RSALESE	0.26	0.38	−0.03	1.07	0.27	0.33	−0.08	0.99

	Estimated with INFRAJ1				Estimated with INFRAJ2			
	At Average GDPJ		At 0.5 Average GDPJ		At Average GDPJ		At 0.5 Average GDPJ	
	WLS	GLS	WLS	GLS	WLS	GLS	WLS	GLS
With respect to SKJ								
RSALES	1.36	0.69	0.82	0.21	1.56	0.77	1.04	0.28
RSALESL	1.05	0.70	0.16	0.17	1.18	0.82	0.30	0.29
RSALESE	1.91	0.27	2.00	0.03	2.22	0.30	2.34	0.08
With respect to INVCJ								
RSALES	−0.46	−0.18			−0.65	−0.22		
RSALESL	−0.45	−0.23			−0.58	−0.26		
RSALESE	−0.50	−0.06			−0.80	−0.08		
With respect to TCJ								
RSALES	0.04	0.03			−0.09	0.04		
RSALESL	0.02	0.03			−0.06	0.04		
RSALESE	0.09	0.03			−0.12	0.05		
With respect to INFRA								
RSALES	0.74	0.17			0.04	−0.04		
RSALESL	0.44	0.20			−0.02	−0.02		
RSALESE	1.25	0.31			0.14	0.04		

Note: Parameters coming from statistically significant coefficients are in boldface.

view, this weakness likely reflects three factors. First, we have few least developed countries in the sample, for which both FDI and infrastructure quality would be low. Second, our measure of infrastructure may not capture its effects on investment adequately. Finally, the AR(1) corrections in the GLS approach essentially remove the trend increases in infrastructure quality, which seems to leave little variation across the developing-country sample.

The coefficients on SKDIFF vary across estimation techniques and across types of affiliate sales in tables 10.10 through 10.12. However, the full marginal impacts of a change in skill endowments depend on both the SKDIFF and SKDIFF · GDPJ coefficients, evaluated at various sample points. Thus, in table 10.13, we calculate relevant elasticities in a manner parallel with table 10.9, again noting in boldface those parameters coming from statistically significant coefficients. Comparing results in tables 10.9 and 10.13, it seems that total sales and local sales are more elastic with respect to income increases in the developing economies than in the overall sample. This is especially true for relatively high-skilled host countries, such as Singapore, where local production is highly income elastic. Export production is somewhat less sensitive to an increase in local market size in developing countries.

Interestingly, all of the elasticities with respect to increases in skill endowments are positive and significant in the developing-country sample. Thus, affiliate production is clearly skilled-labor seeking within this sample of largely middle-income nations. Contrary to the results for the full sample, affiliate production for export is more skilled-labor seeking than production for local sale, at least using the WLS coefficients. However, this result does not survive the use of GLS and must be left open for further research. Finally, it seems that the investment-cost variable has a negative impact on local sales (using GLS) and that infrastructure quality has a positive impact on all sales flows (using WLS). Production for export is more sensitive to infrastructure quality than are domestic and total production. Again, however, these results are sensitive to the definition of infrastructure and the estimation technique. The trade-cost variable has a very small numerical magnitude, and it is never statistically significant.

10.6   Summary and Conclusions

As is often observed, there is a strong tendency for those concerned about the effects of globalization to see MNEs as primarily drawn to low-wage labor-abundant countries. It is easy to find anecdotes to support this view. The purpose of this paper is to see whether or not this characterization holds up in a relatively comprehensive data set.

A casual look at data in the *World Investment Report* makes it clear that the poorest countries of the world receive very little investment. It is not clear whether this is due to poor labor skills, poor infrastructure, or bad governance. Thus, we construct a data set of U.S. outward-affiliate activities and try to explain the cross-country variation by a set of host-country characteristics including size, labor-force composition, investment barriers, trade costs, and physical infrastructure. We use a full sample of all host countries and a subsample using only developing countries. Unfortunately, the data exclude all of the world's poorest countries, and, since these get almost no inward investment, we are losing many of the observations that we would most like to explain.

The general conclusion is that U.S. outward investment seeks large, skilled-labor-abundant countries. In the full sample, outward investment seems to be unskilled-labor seeking for small markets, a conclusion that holds up in the developing-country subsample, which includes mainly less skilled-labor-abundant countries.[9]

The preponderance of results suggests that increases in investment costs or investment barriers discourage inward investment and affiliate activity. Higher trade costs seem to encourage investment, but this result is weak, especially in the developing-country sample. Finally, higher-quality infrastructure seems to encourage investment and affiliate sales in most of our specifications. This result is in evidence sufficiently enough that it would be worthwhile to develop a more comprehensive infrastructure index and to incorporate many more countries into the analysis.

Turning to production for local sales versus exports, the data reveal the unexpected result that the share of production sold locally is in fact a bit lower in the full sample than in the developing-country sample. The characterization that MNE enter developing countries primarily to produce for export is another view that is not supported by the analysis in this paper. Overall, we reach the following conclusions from comparing the local-sales and export-sales regressions.

First, affiliates in developing countries are not more export oriented than affiliates in the full sample of countries; local market sales are over 60 percent of the total in developing countries. Second, affiliate production is more income elastic the more similar the host country is to the United States in labor-force composition. Third, production for local sale is more income elastic than production for export sale. Fourth, production activities for both local sales and exports are generally skilled-labor seeking, but which type of flow is more skilled-labor seeking differs between the full sample and the developing-country sample. It is interesting that activity in the developing countries appears to be more responsive to an increase in local skill endowments than in the full sample, at least according to the WLS regressions. Fifth, production for export sale is more sensitive to investment costs and infrastructure quality than is production for local sale. However, these last two results are not robust to estimation technique. Note that our regressions perform worst in explaining production for export sales in developing countries, indicating that missing explanatory variables likely are important.

All of these results fit reasonably well with both formal theories of the MNE and informal conjectures about the role of infrastructure. These results and the related theory do not lend support to view that MNEs exploit and impoverish developing countries. Indeed, the theories to which the empirical results lend support suggest that inward investments are of substantial benefit to host countries, both in terms of overall income and in terms of promoting labor-skills upgrading. Finally, we note again the absence of data on the poorest of the developing countries. It would be use-

9. See also Brainard (1997), Brainard and Riker (1997), and Yeaple (2003).

ful to extend this research to include determinants of activity in those nations.

References

Asiedu, Elizabeth. 2002. On the determinants of foreign direct investment to developing countries: Is Africa different? *World Development* 30 (1): 107–19.
Beck, Nathaniel, and Jonathan N. Katz. 1995. What to do (and what not to do) with time-series cross-section data. *American Political Science Review* 89 (3): 634–47.
Blonigen, Bruce A., Ronald B. Davies, and Keith Head. 2003. Estimating the knowledge-capital model of the multinational enterprise: Comment. *American Economic Review* 93 (3): 980–94.
Brainard, S. Lael. 1997. An empirical assessment of the proximity-concentration tradeoff between multinational sales and trade. *American Economic Review* 87 (4): 520–44.
Brainard, S. Lael, and David A. Riker. 1997. Are U.S. multinationals exporting U.S. jobs? NBER Working Paper no. 5958. Cambridge, Mass.: National Bureau of Economic Research, March.
Carr, David L., James R. Markusen, and Keith E. Maskus. 2001. Estimating the knowledge-capital model of the multinational enterprise. *American Economic Review* 91 (3): 693–708.
Cheng, Leonard K., and Yum K. Kwan. 2000. What are the determinants of the location of foreign direct investment? The Chinese experience. *Journal of International Economics* 51 (2): 379–400.
Feenstra, Robert C., and Gordon H. Hanson. 1996. Globalization, outsourcing, and wage inequality. *American Economic Review* 86 (2): 240–45.
———. 1997. Foreign direct investment and relative wages: Evidence from Mexico's maquiladoras. *Journal of International Economics* 42:371–93.
Greene, William H. 2000. *Econometric analysis.* 4th ed. New York: Prentice Hall.
International Monetary Fund (IMF). 1995a. *Balance of payments statistics yearbook 1995.* Washington, D.C.: IMF.
———. 1995b. *International financial statistics yearbook 1995.* Washington, D.C.: IMF.
Markusen, James R. 2002. *Multinational firms and the theory of international trade.* Cambridge, Mass.: MIT Press.
Markusen, James R., and Keith E. Maskus. 2001. Multinational firms: Reconciling theory and evidence. In *Topics in empirical international economics: A festschrift in honor of Robert E. Lipsey,* ed. Magnus Blomstrom and Linda Goldberg, 71–95. Chicago: University of Chicago Press.
———. 2002. Discriminating among alternative theories of the multinational enterprise. *Review of International Economics* 10 (4): 694–707.
Martin, William J., and Keith E. Maskus. 2001. The economics of core labor standards: Implications for global trade policy. *Review of International Economics* 9 (2): 317–28.
Maskus, Keith E. 1997. Should core labor standards be imposed through international trade policy? Policy Research Working Paper no. 1817. Washington, D.C.: World Bank.
Organization for Economic Cooperation and Development (OECD). 1996. *Trade,*

employment and labor standards: A study of core workers' rights and international trade. Paris: OECD.

United Nations Conference on Trade and Development (UNCTAD). 2000. *World investment report 2000.* Geneva: UNCTAD.

Wheeler, David, and Ashoka Mody. 1992. International investment location decisions: The case of U.S. firms. *Journal of International Economics* 33 (1/2): 57–76.

Yeaple, Stephen Ross. 2003. The role of skill endowments in the patterns of U.S. outward foreign direct investment. *Review of Economics and Statistics,* forthcoming.

Zhang, Kevin Honglin, and James R. Markusen. 1999. Vertical multinational and host country characteristics. *Journal of Development Economics* 59 (2): 233–52.

Comment   Anthony J. Venables

The paper examines the factors that are important in attracting multinational investment to a country. This is an important issue because, as the authors point out, the charge is often made that the presence of footloose multinationals creates an incentive for countries to engage in a "race to the bottom," particularly in labor standards. However, might it not be possible that in other dimensions there is a "race to the top"? Multinationals may be attracted by good institutions, good business environments, and high-quality infrastructure. To establish the incentives that countries face we need to know what it is that attracts multinational activity, and this is precisely the goal of this paper.

The authors use data on the activities of U.S.-based multinationals to investigate the importance of a number of different factors. They start by reviewing theory, and noting that different forces are important for different sorts of FDI. The usual distinction is between horizontal (or market-serving) investment, and vertical (or production-cost-saving) investment. The authors outline the way in which these can be nested in a single model, although even then the effects are complex. Affiliate activities may be unskilled labor intensive relative to the United States, but quite skilled labor intensive relative to the endowments of many developing countries. There may then be an inverse U-shaped relationship between affiliate presence and potential host countries' skilled-labor abundance.

The econometric model developed by the authors is applied to a panel of data on sales of U.S. multinationals' affiliates located in thirty-nine host countries (unfortunately, the data set does not extend to the lowest-income countries). Affiliate activity is a function of host-country size, endowment of skilled labor, barriers to investment and to trade, infrastructure quality,

Anthony J. Venables is the Yu Kuo-Hwa Professor of International Economics at the London School of Economics.

and distance from the United States. Robust results are found on the importance of market size (positive), investment costs (negative), trade costs (positive), and distance (negative). Good infrastructure also tends to raise investment, although results are not robust over all specifications.

Insights on how the type of investment that multinationals undertake varies with the characteristics of host countries is derived by interacting measures of skill with measures of market size. The authors find that having a highly skilled labor force promotes multinational activity in large countries. However, in small countries the presence of highly skilled labor is much less important. Looking just at the extent to which multinationals export products from the host country, *low* skill intensity becomes a positive force. This suggests, then, the coexistence in the data of two types of investment. Rather skill-intensive horizontal activity goes to large and skill-abundant countries, with less skill-intensive vertical activity being more important for smaller economies.

On the critical side, a number of comments can be made about the authors' econometric specification. It is surprising that they use a linear, not log-linear, specification. It is natural to think of many of the relationships as ratios (sales relative to GDP, rather than the absolute level of sales), particularly since there is a huge range of country sizes (from Singapore to China) in the data. Their linear specification means, for example, that a 1-point increase in the index of investment costs is associated with the same absolute dollar change in multinational activity in China as in New Zealand. A proportional relationship would seem more plausible.

It would have been interesting to see estimates of the impact of various measures of production costs. The authors use an endowment quantity measure (the share of the labor force that is skilled) rather than a price measure, no doubt based on general-equilibrium reasoning. However, use of a labor-cost measure instead of (or as well as) the endowment measure would be interesting, and not subject to serious endogeneity concerns.

Finally, it would have been good if some of the trade-offs implied by the estimates had been drawn out more explicitly. If a country is more remote, how much better does its infrastructure have to be to attract the same level of multinational activity? If wages go up, does this deter investment, and how much of an improvement in the business environment can offset it? Answering these questions would establish the trade-offs that countries face in shaping policy to attract investment, and the incentives they have for engaging in races to the bottom or to the top.

The Cross-Border Mergers and Acquisitions Wave of the Late 1990s

Simon J. Evenett

11.1 Introduction

As nations' markets continue to become more closely integrated through the process commonly referred to as globalization, a concern has arisen both popularly and among policy makers about the consequences for the degree of competition between firms. Critics of globalization often charge that it extends the reach of abusive oligopolies and monopolies,[1] and policymakers in developing countries worry whether or not increased openness to trade and foreign-direct-investment flows makes them more vulnerable to "exploita-

Simon J. Evenett is a university lecturer at the Said Business School, Oxford University, and fellow of Corpus Christi College, Oxford.

I am grateful to Benno Ferrarini for his tenacious efforts to obtain data for this paper. Thanks also to seminar participants at INSEAD for some tough questions and constructive suggestions. Joshua Aizenman, Robert Baldwin, Jean Dermine, Rod Falvey, Rachel McCulloch, Matt Slaughter, Daniel Traca, Tony Venables, Xavier Vives, and Alan Winters provided many much appreciated pointers and suggestions. This paper was presented at both meetings of the International Seminar on International Trade, jointly organized by the Centre for Economic Policy Research and the National Bureau of Economic Research.

1. See, for example, the following remarks by Mr. Martin Khor, Director of the Third World Network, to the opening session of the UN"s Millennium Forum on 22 May 2000.

Our age is also defined by the process of globalisation. There are different approaches to this phenomenon. Some say it is inevitable and basically good, you just have to adjust to it and learn to reap the benefits. Others worry about the costs and advocate some safety nets to catch the losers as they fall. In truth, the essence of globalisation is the push by big companies and financial institutions to have more power, to grow bigger through taking over others, and make more profits. They have lobbied their governments, of the rich countries, to break down the national barriers that prevent them from totally free access to markets across the world, especially in the developing countries.

The text of this speech can be downloaded from http://www.twnside.org.sg/title/mk7.htm.

tion" by multinational firms.[2] Such policymakers wonder if they have—or can ever have—the national tools to tackle private anticompetitive practices.[3]

There is also a vibrant debate about the potential for international accords on competition law and enforcement. Policymakers worldwide are engaged in discussions about the desirability and viability of a multilateral framework on competition policy under the auspices of the World Trade Organization (WTO).[4] Proponents of such a framework have called for disciplines on so-called hard-core cartels, so-called core principles for competition law and enforcement, modalities for voluntary cooperation, and for the progressive strengthening of competition-policy-related institu-

2. See, for example, the following statement in a November 1998 submission by the Government of India to the World Trade Organization's Working Group on the Interaction Between Trade and Competition Policy.

In contributions of intergovernmental organizations, a dominant theme along with the issue of mergers and acquisitions is the issue of contestability of markets. Although not clearly defined, an impression is created that every aspect of domestic government policy, economic and social—would, in one way or the other, affect fair trade and the contestability of markets. In a more concrete sense this debate on contestability of markets has been witnessed during the so-called Structural Impediments Initiative in the US-Japan context. With developing countries, the dangers of the doctrine of contestability of markets eroding their ability to take domestic social and economic action are even greater. Moreover, in the name of contestability, an increase in market access for MNCs [multinational corporations] may be sought by suggesting that all sectors of WTO, in one way or another, be put to the test of contestability. This may have implications for services, intellectual property rights, subsidies and a host of other areas, not to mention investment. It will, therefore, be necessary to define it clearly and narrowly in relation to specific issues and disciplines that we wish to address in the WTO regime. Some issues to be addressed would be market allocation, refusal to deal (boycott), price fixing, collusive dealing, and differential pricing (all of which are vertical RBPs [restrictive business practices]). All of these practices distort or restrict trade and affect the international contestability of markets. This action is particularly called for as developing country markets and their commercial entities are more vulnerable to the effects of such RBPs and at their receiving end. Experiences with RBPs encountered by developing country firms in developed country markets illustrate how RBPs by the large MNCs put these firms at a competitive disadvantage. Instances of other so-called privately led restrictive business practices such as debarring Indian participation in the Dutch Flower Auction or the Basle Jewellery and Watch Fair are also relevant.

This text was taken from paragraph two of WTO document number WT/WGTCP/W/111, which can be downloaded from the WTO's website (http://www.wto.org). See also the examples described in Mehta and Nanda (2003).

3. A recent study of the experience in implementing competition law in seven developing countries offered the following remark about the ability of these countries' antitrust enforcers to address international mergers and acquisitions and anticompetitive practices.

Whether countries have special provisions for extra-territorial jurisdiction or apply the "effects" doctrine is not important when they have no means to enforce their decisions. Often the companies involved are beyond the reach of the competition agencies, which also causes problems in obtaining the information necessary to make a decision. (Consumer Union Trust Society [CUTS] 2003, 75)

4. For an excellent overview of the discussions within the WTO's Working Group on the Interaction Between Trade and Competition Policy, see that Working Group's Annual Report for 2002 (WTO 2002).

tions in developing countries.[5] Others argue for the development of best practices for competition law and enforcement in fora such as the International Competition Network and the Organisation for Economic Cooperation and Development (OECD).[6] And, others have called on industrialized economies to tackle the alleged anticompetitive practices of their multinational firms in developing economies. This proposal would involve antitrust enforcement officials expanding their traditional concern about harm done within their jurisdiction to harm done abroad. It is argued that such an approach would reduce the outlays on antitrust enforcement by developing economies.[7]

In principle, integrating national markets both reduces and enhances the opportunities and viability of anticompetitive conduct by private firms. On the one hand, as countries open up their domestic markets to foreign competition by reducing their tariffs and other trade-distorting policies, domestic incumbents that have been protected from international competition by these trade barriers are now more likely to be forced to abandon their price-raising and anticompetitive practices.[8] Moreover, the increased opportunities for international mergers and acquisitions can bring cost-reducing efficiencies that may be passed on to customers, be they private consumers, firms, or governments. On the other hand, globalization also presents new opportunities for firms to form hard-core cartels[9] with international reach and other various anticompetitive arrangements. Thus, whether globalization promotes or reduces competitive behavior, on balance, is largely an empirical rather than theoretical issue.

In this chapter, I first describe in considerable detail the nature of the wave of cross-border mergers and acquisitions (M&A) that occurred during the period of rapid globalization in the 1990s and then focus on one particular service sector, namely banking, to investigate if there is evidence

---

5. The European Commission is one of the leading proponents of such a framework. Its proposals can be downloaded from the WTO's website (http://www.wto.org). The Commission has further clarified its proposals in discussions at the WTO's Working Group (see WTO 2002). The doubts of critics and skeptics are also reported in WTO (2002). For an analysis of the implications of such a framework for the design and implementation of national competition law, for industrial policy and development policy options, and for the resource costs faced by developing countries, see Evenett (2003a).

6. For several proposals on best practices in the merger-enforcement area, see the contributions to Rowley (2002). More generally, discussions on best practices in competition law and enforcement are undertaken often in the OECD's Competition Committee. Many of the relevant documents can be found at http://www.oecd.org/EN/document/0,,EN-document-768-nodirectorate-no-22-20233-768,00.html. A number of interesting and informative documents on best practices in merger review can be found on the website of the mergers working group of the International Competition network (http://www.internationalcompetitionnetwork.org/wg1.html).

7. See Hoekman and Mavroidis (2002).

8. For a classic statement of this perspective, see Bhagwati (1968).

9. For evidence on private international cartels see Evenett (2003a), Levenstein and Suslow (2001), and OECD (2003).

that cross-border M&A in this industry resulted in greater spreads between the interest rates paid by borrowers and those rates paid to depositors. Of course, there are limits to what can be learned from a single sector study, but hopefully this analysis will contribute to the factual record and to the literature on consolidation in the banking sector, as well as shedding light on the importance of a number of factors that should be considered when coming to a view on the welfare consequences of the latest wave of cross-border mergers and acquisitions.

My analysis yields several findings. First, the recent cross-border M&A wave is in real terms at least five times larger than its predecessor in the 1980s. Even after correcting for the rising price of financial assets,[10] in this latest wave of cross-border M&A is much much larger. Second, although the latest wave involved firms from more countries than in the 1980s, the overwhelming bulk of such M&A still took place among the members of the OECD. Third, despite its greater scale in real terms, the latest wave of cross-border M&A represents purchases of only a small fraction of the publicly traded corporate assets in industrial economies, especially in the Group of Seven (G7) leading industrial economies. Foreigners are, therefore, not taking over large tranches of national economies through cross-border M&A. Fourth, the preponderance of cross-border M&A in the late 1990s were in service sectors, many of which are pretty much immune to import competition.

Fifth, in one important service sector—banking—estimating the effects of cross-border mergers and acquisitions requires paying careful attention to sample composition. Furthermore, controlling for changes in regulatory regimes and other changes in market structure in banking are important. Of the thirteen OECD nations' banking sectors considered here, eight are members of the European Union (EU). The determinants of the latters' banking spreads during the 1990s are found to be much different from those in non-EU economies. In the banking sectors of EU member states, domestic M&A and strategic alliances are found to have no net effect on bank spreads. Cross-border mergers and acquisitions are found to depress spreads, suggesting that substantial efficiencies resulted from such consolidation. In contrast, the evidence suggests that cross-border strategic alliances result in higher spreads—a finding that is consistent with the view that some such alliances have been formed to forestall further market integration and to preserve the independence of banks in Europe.

The parameters in the non-EU sample are less precisely estimated, reflecting in large part a smaller number of observations. Only cross-border strategic alliances are found to influence bank spreads in a statistically significant manner—in this case depressing them (which is the opposite of my finding in the EU sample). Nevertheless, taken together, this chapter's re-

---

10. As proxied for by national stock-market indexes, see following discussion.

sults for the banking section imply that it is hazardous to make sweeping generalizations about the net effect of cross-border transactions, especially as the latter can have both procompetitive and anticompetitive effects.

Sixth, the estimated parameters are used to forecast the net effect of all of these domestic and cross-border interfirm agreements on bank spreads in each of the thirteen countries considered in my EU and non-EU samples. In each EU member state, the combined effect of cross-border interfirm agreements on interest-rate spreads is an order of magnitude larger than for domestic interfirm agreements. Moreover, the overall beneficial effect of cross-border M&A in banking[11] in the EU has, in all of the eight EU members considered here, been completely reversed by the harm done by cross-border strategic alliances. This implies that the combined effect of the latter may not be as benign or as inconsequential as they first appear.[12] Moreover, as the number of cross-border strategic alliances in banking in the EU appears to have increased considerably after the cross-border M&A spurt began, my findings are consistent with the explanation that banks eventually took rearguard actions to increase their market power after the spread-reducing effects of efficiency-enhancing cross-border mergers and acquisitions were felt. If this view is correct, then regulators in the banking sector and competition policy officials should not focus solely on the potential consequences of mergers and acquisitions and should keep a beady eye on perhaps more innocent-looking public announcements of strategic alliances.

This paper is organized as follows. The next section describes the recent wave of cross-border mergers and acquisitions. The third section focuses on the consolidation in the banking systems in thirteen industrialized economies, establishing the factual record first and then conducting econometric analyses. The final section contains some concluding remarks.

11.2   The Cross-Border Mergers and Acquisitions Wave of the Late 1990s

11.2.1   Preliminaries

Before turning to the factual record, it may be helpful to clarify the terms used in this chapter. An important distinction is between foreign direct investment (FDI) and cross-border mergers and acquisitions. As the principal source of data on cross-border M&A used here is the United Nations Conference on Trade and Development's (UNCTAD's) annual *World In-*

---

11. This is not to say that every cross-border merger or acquisition in the banking sector generates enough efficiencies that bank customers benefit.

12. This is not say that every cross-border strategic alliance detrimentally affects the welfare of bank customers.

vestment Report, I reproduce below UNCTAD's description of the difference between cross-border M&A and FDI.

> A firm can undertake FDI in a host country in either one of two ways: greenfield investment in a new facility or acquiring or merging with an existing local firm. The local firm may be privately or state owned: privatisations involving foreign investors count as cross border M&As, which entails a change in the control of the merged or acquired firm. In a cross border merger, the assets and operation of the two firms belonging to two different countries are combined to establish a new legal entity. In a cross border acquisition, the control of assets and operations is transferred from a local to a foreign company, the former becoming an affiliate of the latter. (UNCTAD 2000, 99)

Although this quotation clarifies the distinction between investments in *new* productive entities and investments in *existing* entities it would be incorrect to infer that, in practice, the reported value of cross-border M&A transactions is always less than the reported amount of FDI. In fact, measured cross-border M&A received by a nation is taken to be the sum of (a) foreign investments in existing domestic firms that result in equity stakes greater than 10 percent, (b) foreign investments in existing domestic firms that result in equity stakes less than 10 percent, and (c) foreign investments in existing domestic firms that are paid for using capital or funds raised in the nation of the acquiring firm. In contrast, the reported amount of FDI received by a nation includes (a) and (c), plus the value of overseas investments paid for by reinvested earnings of foreign firms already resident in the nation. Consequently, as UNCTAD (1996) notes,

> It is, therefore, possible to witness a large increase in M&As that is not fully reflected in FDI flows . . . [and] . . . movements in FDI flows can take place independently of movements in M&A. In practice, however, there is a close relationship between movements in M&As and FDI flows. (UNCTAD 1996, box I.1).

To underscore the differences between measured cross-border M&A and FDI into industrial countries, table 11.1 reports the ratio of the former to the latter in thirteen OECD nations during 1995 to 1999. In some countries (Australia, France, Japan, and Spain), the ratio is far from 1—suggesting that recorded cross-border M&A and FDI differ markedly.

In collecting data on cross-border M&A, the source used by UNCTAD attempts, whenever possible, to establish the location of the "ultimate" corporate owner of a given firm, not an "intermediate" owner that may also be owned by another firm. This is done by examining newspaper announcements of actual and proposed transactions complemented by the use of databases that identify which firms own other firms. By locating the headquarters of an ultimate corporate owner, one can assign a nationality to the owner. This, of course, sidesteps the fact that a publicly traded com-

Table 11.1   **Ratio of Inward M&A Flows to Inward FDI Flows for 13 OECD Economies**

Economy	1995	1996	1997	1998	1999	Mean ratio
Spain	20.40	22.22	63.91	48.05	56.14	42.14
France	31.81	61.82	76.59	57.25	59.02	57.30
Sweden	65.39	76.19	30.35	56.71	99.42	65.61
The Netherlands	29.52	23.51	131.73	46.44	113.95	69.03
Belgium and Luxembourg	18.62	63.82	78.65	30.41	153.98	69.10
The United States	90.58	80.60	77.46	112.47	84.57	89.14
Canada	124.95	112.48	72.36	75.71	99.07	96.92
Switzerland	166.08	143.18	53.42	71.25	120.54	110.89
Germany	62.34	181.44	106.84	90.00	156.36	119.39
Italy	84.72	77.95	90.86	146.17	225.24	124.99
The United Kingdom	182.24	127.98	119.50	143.10	152.59	145.08
Australia	140.27	213.79	191.33	232.26	192.77	194.09
Japan	1387.18	859.50	96.34	126.00	124.46	518.70
Weighted mean (across economies)	84.60	87.16	86.75	96.89	102.75	
Coefficient of variation	4.32	2.51	0.47	0.58	0.48	

Source: UNCTAD (2000, appendixes).

pany may have shareholders or stockholders who are resident in more than one country—a wrinkle that is easy (and important) to state but is difficult to address adequately.

11.2.2   Factual Record

Turning now to the data, using 1987 constant dollars, table 11.2 and figure 11.1 report the extent of cross-border mergers and acquisitions activity from 1987 to 2000, the peak year of the latest boom.[13] (In 2001, reports suggest that cross-border M&A fell 40 percent in nominal terms.) As figure 11.1 makes clear, the recent wave of cross-border M&A accelerated after 1996 and reached a peak of $828 billion in 2000 (which is equivalent to $1.1 trillion dollars in year 2000 dollars). The previous wave of cross-border M&A, which took place from 1987 to 1990, reached a peak of $135 billion in 1990—less than one-fifth of the peak in the latest wave. Furthermore, developing economies played next to no role in the 1980s wave and a modest role in the most recent wave.[14] Perhaps for this reason, it might be more accurate to call the latest wave an international wave, rather than a global wave, of cross-border M&A.

For further perspective on the growth of cross-border M&A in the

13. For two descriptions of the factual record that include more discussion than is presented here of mergers and acquisitions in selected sectors, see Kang and Johansson (2000) and OECD (2001). For a recent account and analysis of foreign mergers and acquisitions in the United States, see Feliciano and Lipsey (2002).

14. Having said that, see Mody and Negishi (2000) for an account of the growing role of cross-border M&A in overseas investments in the East Asia in the late 1990s.

Table 11.2   Total Cross-Border Mergers and Acquisitions 1987–2000, Constant 1987 U.S.$ billions

Class of Economies	Year													
	1987	1988	1989	1990	1991	1992	1993	1994	1995	1996	1997	1998	1999	2000
All	74.51	111.81	130.76	135.00	69.84	66.95	68.50	102.65	147.44	175.89	232.06	400.02	567.59	828.43
Developed countries	71.87	109.67	126.47	128.40	67.18	62.86	59.79	94.16	137.27	153.61	207.08	384.81	523.48	792.38
Developing countries	2.61	2.11	3.72	6.31	2.65	4.08	8.61	8.21	10.10	21.79	24.77	14.45	42.75	30.52

Source: UNCTAD (various years).

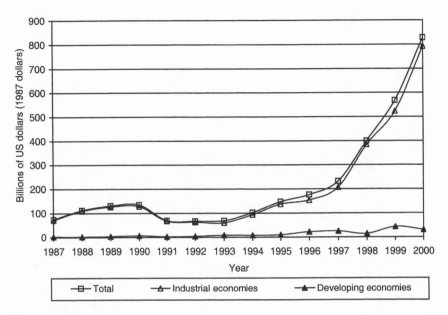

Fig. 11.1   The latest wave of cross-border M&A (1997–2000) is much larger than its predecessor (1987–1990)

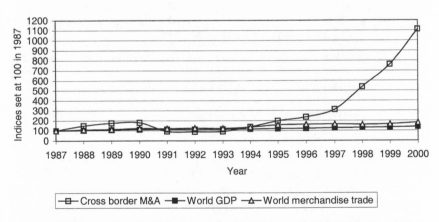

Fig. 11.2   The real increase in cross-border M&A throughout the 1990s dwarfs that of world trade and GDP

1990s, see figure 11.2. This shows that the real growth of cross-border M&A dwarfs that of world GDP and of world merchandise trade, the latter of which almost doubled in real terms in the 1990s. In figure 11.2, I deflated current values of total cross-border M&A by the same gross domestic product (GDP) deflator that I used to compute real world GDP—a procedure which can be objected to on the grounds that stock markets

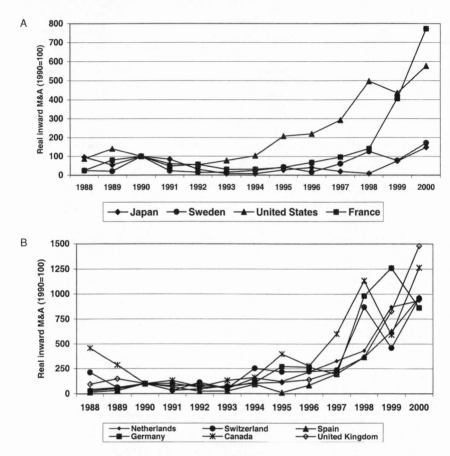

Fig. 11.3   Comparing inward M&A across booms: *A,* Economies with relatively moderate increases; *B,* Economies with large increases

soared in the 1990s, raising the possibility that the price of financial capital has grown more quickly than the GDP deflator. To examine this matter further, I deflated country-by-country values of nominal inward cross-border M&A by the changes in the value of each country's major stock-market index,[15] and normalized the amount of cross-border M&A received in 1990 at 100. (The year 1990 was the peak of the wave of cross-border M&A that started in the late 1980s.) Figure 11.3 reports this new calculation of the real value of cross-border M&A received by the ten industrialized economies throughout the 1990s. In all but two economies, real inward M&A is much lower in 1990 than in 2000, confirming that, for the

15. For nine of the ten industrialized economies, choosing the major stock-market index was straightforward. For the United States, however, one could choose either the Standard & Poor's (S&P) 500 index or the Dow Jones Industrial Index. I chose the latter index, but note that both indexes rose by similar percentages throughout the 1990s.

Table 11.3   **Total Value of Annual Cross-Border M&A Deals as a Percentage of Stock-Market Capitalization**

Economy	1980s Wave				1990s Wave			
	1988	1989	1990	Mean	1997	1996	1999	Mean
Luxembourg	0.01	0.00	5.08	1.70	10.30	0.10	20.48	10.29
Sweden	0.19	1.55	4.58	2.11	1.22	3.98	15.99	7.06
Belgium	1.35	1.08	6.83	3.08	4.34	2.79	13.51	6.88
Norway	1.67	2.38	2.56	2.20	4.00	2.10	13.66	6.59
New Zealand	10.03	5.00	41.92	18.98	4.41	9.28	5.64	6.44
Austria	2.85	0.14	1.65	1.55	6.32	10.41	1.15	5.96
The Netherlands	1.04	2.51	1.24	1.60	4.06	3.21	5.61	4.30
Australia	3.17	3.34	2.34	2.95	5.00	4.48	2.80	4.10
The United Kingdom	2.58	3.21	3.43	**3.07**	1.99	3.84	4.52	**3.45**
Denmark	0.72	0.56	1.27	0.85	0.60	3.85	4.38	2.94
Canada	3.61	3.57	2.37	**3.19**	1.50	3.02	2.99	**2.50**
France	1.23	0.91	2.60	**1.58**	2.63	1.70	1.62	**1.98**
Germany	0.52	1.18	1.75	**1.15**	1.44	1.74	2.76	**1.98**
Finland	0.27	0.75	0.22	0.41	1.00	3.09	0.90	1.67
Spain	0.79	1.30	3.44	1.84	1.40	1.42	1.35	1.39
The United States	2.29	1.96	1.79	**2.01**	0.72	1.56	1.51	**1.26**
Italy	2.29	1.77	1.46	**1.84**	0.98	0.79	1.54	**1.10**
Switzerland	1.67	0.57	2.85	1.70	0.62	0.78	0.59	0.66
Portugal	0.15	7.23	2.31	3.23	0.22	0.68	0.32	0.41
Japan	0.00	0.04	0.01	**0.01**	0.14	0.16	0.36	**0.22**
Greece	0.51	0.00	0.76	0.42	0.29	0.03	0.09	0.14

Note: Countries in bold are members of the Group of Seven Industrialized Nations (G7).

major markets in the world economy, the latest cross-border M&A wave was on a much larger scale than its predecessor in the 1980s.

Having said that, the growth of cross-border M&A is from a relatively small base and, when the level of cross-border M&A that a nation received in the late 1990s is compared to its stock market's capitalization, the amount of assets acquired by foreign firms tends to be quite small (see table 11.3). Only the smaller—and relatively more open—industrial economies saw the total value of foreign mergers and acquisitions exceed 5 percent of their total stock-market capitalizations. For the G7 leading industrial economies, the inflows of cross-border M&A are even smaller relative to the size of their stock markets. The image of aggressive foreign executives snapping up large shares of productive domestic assets conjured up during the contentious merger of Vodafone and Mannesmann AG in 2000, for example, finds little support in the data.

Figures 11.4 and 11.5 provide further indications of the broader participation in the latest wave of cross-border M&A, compared to its predecessor in the 1980s. The latter was essentially an American and British affair, with some French firms making acquisitions towards the end of the boom

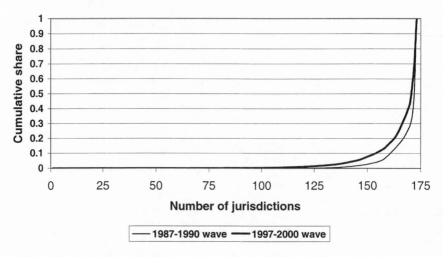

Fig. 11.4   Cumulative distribution of cross-border M&A in 1987–1990 and
1997–2000

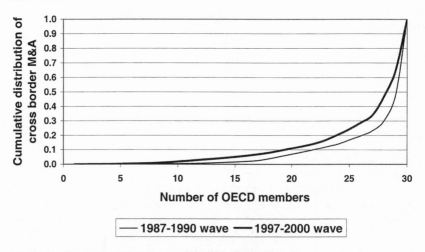

Fig. 11.5   The latest M&A wave involved more OECD nations

(principally in 1990). In contrast, the current wave involved considerable
transactions by German, French, Spanish, and Nordic firms that joined the
long standing Anglo-American interest in cross-border M&A. Figure 11.5
compares the cumulative distribution of cross-border M&A across OECD
nations in both waves, confirming the less skewed nature of the latest wave.

Another critical feature of the latest cross-border M&A wave is the important role played by so-called megadeals, those transactions whose value
exceeded one billion U.S. dollars. The number of such deals nearly quadrupled from 1996 to 2000 (see fig. 11.6), and the (constant dollar) value
of such transactions more than quadrupled (see fig. 11.7). In appendix
table 11A.1, I have listed the megadeals that were announced in 2000.

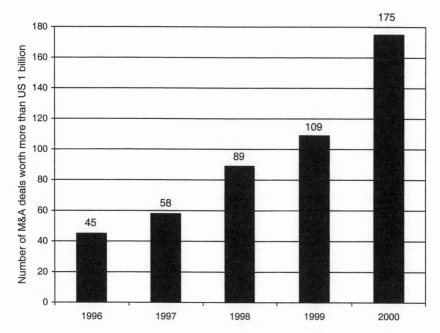

Fig. 11.6   The growing number of billion-dollar-plus M&A deals

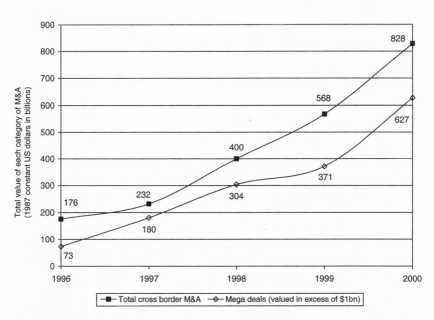

Fig. 11.7   Mega deals drove the latest wave of cross-border M&A

Table 11.4   Sectoral Composition of Cross-Border M&A

Sector/Industry	Share of Total Cross-Border M&A	
	1987–1990	1997–2000
Primary	5.04	1.43
Agriculture, hunting, forestry, and fishing	0.72	0.38
Mining, quarrying and petroleum	4.32	1.04
Manufacturing	62.24	35.11
Food, beverages, and tobacco	8.16	4.28
Textiles, clothing, and leather	0.95	0.41
Wood and wood products	3.93	1.72
Publishing, printing, and reproduction of recorded media	5.89	1.11
Coke, petroleum, and nuclear fuel	9.38	5.33
Chemicals and chemical products	12.17	6.70
Rubber and plastic products	2.03	0.48
Nonmetallic mineral products	2.30	1.39
Metal and metal products	2.86	1.67
Machinery and equipment	1.75	1.69
Electrical and electronic equipment	8.14	5.44
Precision instruments	2.20	1.21
Motor vehicles and other transport equipment	1.94	3.60
Other manufacturing	0.53	0.11
Tertiary	32.72	63.46
Electric, gas, and water	0.36	5.44
Construction	0.46	0.38
Trade	8.08	5.07
Hotels and restaurants	3.77	0.82
Transport, storage, and communications	1.84	21.94
Finance	11.03	16.19
Business services	4.39	9.44
Public administration and defence	0.00	0.08
Education	0.00	0.02
Health and social services	0.17	0.20
Community, social- and personal-service activities	2.62	3.87
Other services	0.01	0.01
Unknown	0.00	0.00

It is evident that the majority of such deals involved the service sector, notably the financial and telecommunications sectors. Few manufacturing firms can be found on this list, a point I shall return to below.

An examination of the sectoral breakdown of cross-border M&A during the 1980s and 1990s waves is revealing too (see table 11.4 and fig. 11.8). One striking finding is the relatively smaller importance of manufacturing cross-border M&A in the late 1990s, accounting for only 35.1 percent of the total value of such transactions. In the previous wave, such transactions accounted for 62.2 percent of the total. What is more, just

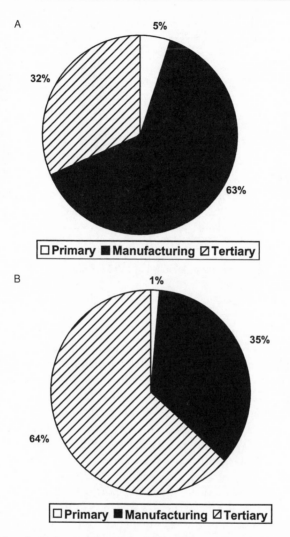

Fig. 11.8   Manufacturing dominated the 1987–1990 wave but services dominated the 1997–2000 wave: *A,* **1987–1990;** *B,* **1997–2000**

three service sectors (transport, storage, and communications; finance; and business services) account for just under one-half of total cross-border M&A in the late 1990s.

11.2.3   Policy Regimes Facing Cross-Border Mergers and Acquisitions

Much has been made in the literature and in the reports of international organizations[16] of the falling barriers to greenfield FDI during the 1990s.

16. See, for example, World Bank (2000) and the annual *World Investment Reports* published by UNCTAD (various years).

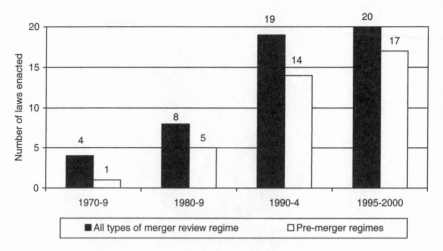

Fig. 11.9   The spread of merger-review laws 1970–2000

The UNCTAD goes so far as to tally up, on an annual basis, the number of economies that have relaxed or tightened their FDI regimes.[17] However, in industrialized economies (and in some developing economies too), cross-border mergers and acquisitions are typically influenced by two different policy regimes: merger-review policies (which are described in some detail below) and sectoral regulations. The latter can involve reviews of M&A deals (both domestic and cross-border) that occur within a given sector. Regulators in financial services, banking, telecommunications, and air transportation have been active in the 1990s reviewing proposals to merge or acquire firms. What is more, some jurisdictions allow for M&As in some sectors to be reviewed both by the relevant sectoral regulator and by the national competition-enforcement agency.[18] This raises the question of the extent to which observed levels of cross-border M&A are affected by the potential for multiple official reviews within the same jurisdiction.

In contrast to policies toward greenfield FDI, it is quite possible that, as a general proposition, policies toward M&As have become more stringent throughout the 1990s. For starters, the number of jurisdictions with merger-review regimes rose sharply in the 1990s (see fig. 11.9).[19] According

17. See UNCTAD's (various years) annual *World Investment Reports* for details.
18. For examples, see the case studies in Evenett, Lehmann, and Steil (2000).
19. Figure 11.9 reports not only the total number of merger review laws enacted since 1970, but also the total number of such laws requiring notification of proposed mergers and acquisitions before deals are completed. Among legal practitioners and scholars, the latter type of merger-review regime is, by and large, regarded as the most stringent form of merger-review law (see ICPAC 2000 for a statement of what might be called conventional legal wisdom in this regard). See, also, Evenett (2002), which confirms that, of the three main types of merger-review laws, those requiring mandatory prenotification curtail cross-border M&A the most. In the light of these remarks, it is noteworthy that a growing proportion of the merger-review

to White and Case (2001), a publication of an international law firm that conducts an annual survey of merger enforcement around the world, sixty-five economies had merger review laws in 2000 (plus the European Commission's supranational merger-enforcement regime). Thirty of these merger-review laws have been enacted since 1990. It is also noteworthy that merger-review laws are a relatively new phenomenon in some industrial economies; in other words, the spread in the last twenty years is not just a phenomenon found in developing countries. For instance, the European Commission's merger regulation only came into force in 1990, Italy's merger-review regime was enacted in 1990, Denmark's and the Netherlands' in 1997, and France's antitrust authority only celebrated its fifteenth birthday in 2002. Finally, these remarks suggest that, when studying cross-border flows associated with corporate investments abroad, it is important to locate which policy regime or regimes has the greatest bearing on the flows being examined. In many cases, measures of (or proxies for) the strength of the policy regime towards greenfield investments may provide a misleading guide to the strength of the merger-review regime or of the sectoral regulatory regime.

11.2.4   Commentary and Related Literature

The observed change in the sectoral composition of cross-border M&A reflects a number of factors. First, lower trade barriers and more intense competition in world markets for manufactures are likely to reduce the incentive to engage in cross-border M&A in order to accumulate market power or to jump tariffs. Indeed, any increments in market power are likely to result in greater supplies from competitors located at home and abroad. This suggests the following hypothesis: In those industries where international competition is fiercest, M&A is more likely to be motivated by cost-cutting rationales. Second, the increase in service-sector M&A reflects deregulation, privatization, and the relaxation on restrictions on foreign ownership in many industrial economies. Although such reforms began in the 1980s in a few industrial economies (notably Britain, New Zealand, and the United States), in many other countries they were not implemented on a wider scale until the 1990s. This is not to say that all the major service sectors are deregulated, but rather that the pace of deregulation picked up in the 1990s and that this presented opportunities for foreign investors. In many continental-European economies, the pace gathered in response to the Single Market Programme and the liberalization initiatives that ensued.

Although the corporate-finance literature on the causes and financial

---

laws enacted in the 1980s and 1990s are of the mandatory prenotification type (see fig. 11.9). This is further evidence in favor of the proposition that the *worldwide* policy regime toward M&A has become stricter over time. (It may well be the case that the policy regimes towards M&A in individual countries have been relaxed throughout the 1990s.)

effects of mergers and acquisitions is quite voluminous, there are relatively few papers on the determinants and consequences of *cross-border M&A*[20] and on *economic analyses* of the policy regimes governing such cross-border transactions.[21] Black (2000a,b) describes a number of political and economic factors that, in his opinion, account for the recent surge in cross-border M&A. He points to the "breakdown of the old antitakeover coalition" (Black 2000a, 10). Unions have weakened, and managers own more stock options, which ties their remuneration more closely to corporate performance—which, he claims, reduces the incentive to defend against the takeover of a poorly performing firm. Lower inflation and a surging stock market, it is argued, have reduced the costs of financing M&A (although this explanation surely applies to domestic M&A as well as to cross-border M&A). Finally, Black notes that there is now less opposition to concentrations of wealth and that integrating national markets have encouraged firms to aspire to activities on a worldwide scale. Pryor's (2001) focus, in contrast, is on documenting the consequences for the United States of the recent boom in domestic and cross-border M&A. He argues that such transactions have increased the concentration of manufacturing industries in the 1990s and, in his opinion, can be expected to continue to do so in the future.

An econometric approach was taken in Evenett (2002, 2003b). Employing a gravity-equation approach in both studies, Evenett estimated the contribution of different factors to the value of the American outward M&A that forty-nine foreign economies received in 1999, including the effect of national merger-review regimes. In both studies, several nation-specific factors are found to be important determinants of cross-border M&A, including the recipient nation's gross domestic product, the distance from the United States, the recipient nation's corporate-tax rate and average tariff rate, and whether or not the recipient nation was once a British colony (and is, therefore, more likely to use English as the language of business and to share a common law system with the United States). Evenett (2003b) also found that the presence of merger-review laws tends to cut in half the amount of American M&A received. This constitutes a substantial barrier to the international trade in corporate assets and is especially important given that the 1990s saw more and more developing economies adopt merger-review laws—in particular, those developing nations that hoped to join the EU at some point in the future.

Evenett (2002) also found that the combined effect of merger enforcement by national authorities in the EU and by the European Commission curtailed American overseas M&A by the same percentage[22] as compa-

20. This paucity of studies on cross-border M&A is to be contrasted with the voluminous literature on FDI, which the earlier discussion suggests is a distinct but related phenomenon.
21. There are a number of legal analyses of the policy regimes influencing cross-border mergers and acquisitions.
22. In this case, fifty percent.

rable non-European merger enforcement agencies. This finding may be of interest in the light of the sharp transatlantic dispute over the proposed merger between General Electric and Honeywell in 2001, in which accusations were made that the European merger authorities discriminated against proposed American mergers.[23]

The economic impact of cross-border M&A depends on a number of considerations that make it unlikely that sweeping claims can be made with any confidence about the desirability (or otherwise) of such international trade in corporate assets. By reducing the number of firms that supply a market, cross-border M&As may enhance the market power of the surviving firms. However, such changes in ownership may also result in the combined entity attaining greater economies of scale and scope, which, in turn, may benefit consumers in the form of lower prices, a wider range of services offered, or higher-quality goods and services. One mechanism often-mentioned is that foreign firms transfer so-called cutting-edge technologies and better managerial practices to domestic firms that they have merged with or acquired—suggesting that the beneficial effects of mergers and acquisitions could be greater in the cross-border case compared to a domestic transaction. However, there are no guarantees that these pro-competitive aspects of cross-border M&As will necessarily completely offset any anticompetitive effects of such transactions.[24]

The strength of each of these considerations is likely to vary from industry to industry. For example, as noted above, those sectors that face aggressive import competition are ceterius paribus less likely to see cross-border M&A result in higher prices. In sectors such as banking, where firms increasingly offer a wide range of financial products to customers, gains are likely to occur when mergers take place among financial institutions that sell complementary products. Another sector, telecommunications, has seen rapid technological progress in the 1990s, and cross-border M&As are often mentioned as one of the conduits by which such innovations are diffused across national borders—along with the managerial practices that are needed to make good the profitable opportunities created by these technological improvements. In terms of general findings, there-

---

23. Note that this finding in Evenett (2002) does not speak to the issue as to whether *EC* merger enforcement procedures tends to discriminate more against transactions involving American firms than transactions involving non-American firms.

24. One important—and contentious—issue is to what extent ownership changes are needed to secure the procompetitive benefits of mergers and acquisitions. Direct contracting and collaborative (or so-called strategic) alliances may provide the means by which a domestic firm can market a foreign firm's range of products, or by which a domestic firm can expand its output (potentially reaping economies of scale) by producing goods under contract for a foreign firm. This raises the possibility that all the resource-allocation benefits of cross-border M&As can be obtained by signing interfirm agreements that do not involve reducing the number of suppliers. However, the point need not to be taken too far because transactions-costs arguments often point to the need for cross-holding of equity to attenuate incentive problems. Furthermore, members of an interfirm alliance or contracting, that starts off with procompetitive effects, may well soon figure out how to turn their collaboration to price-raising ends.

fore, a sector-by-sector evaluation of the effects of cross-border M&A is probably the most one can ever realistically expect, and, in the next section, I attempt such an evaluation of the recent consolidation in the banking system in thirteen OECD nations.

A final point, whose implications tend to be thought through in many other international economic policy matters but which has, until now, received less attention in discussions of international-antitrust matters, is that cross-border M&A may well have economic effects that spill across national borders, and that national antitrust or competition authorities tend to focus only on the effects within their own jurisdictions. Therefore, no government entity exists to aggregate the effects of a proposed transaction across all the affected national markets.[25] This may lead to situations where a transaction is vetoed in some jurisdictions (where the economic consequences are thought to be adverse), even though there is a positive effect *on net* across all the affected markets.

Essentially, the *absence of any compensation mechanism* between states implies that multiple national vetoes can lead to suboptimal enforcement of cross-border mergers and acquisitions. In recent years, a leading antitrust American official has given attention to the issue of multiple national vetoes (see Muris 2001), but the importance of the lack of any compensation mechanism for resource misallocation has yet to receive much attention in legal and economic discourse on merger reviews. Indeed, the absence of such a mechanism is one of the key characteristics that differentiates the international effects of the national antitrust enforcement from trade-policy negotiations. In the latter, it has long been understood that any losses to a nation in one sector are compensated for by concessions in other sectors by trading partners. Without suggesting that cross-sectoral trade-offs are the optimal means to conduct multijurisdictional merger reviews, there is probably some value in thinking through the implications of compensation mechanisms across merger cases that prevent a proposed merger or acquisition, whose worldwide total effects are welfare improving, from being blocked by a single jurisdiction in which it is thought that the transaction's effects are adverse.[26]

11.3   Consolidation of the Banking Systems in Thirteen Industrial Nations

I now turn to an econometric evaluation of the effects of cross-border mergers and acquisitions in the banking systems of thirteen industrial economies. When conducting such evaluations, the importance of controlling for changes in regulatory structure, for sample composition, and for

25. Within the EU, for example, the European Commission could play such an aggregating role. This is not to say that it does play such a role!

26. For more discussion on the potential for resource misallocation in multijurisdictional merger review, see Evenett (2003c) and Neven and Roller (2001).

other determinants of market structure in the banking sector—such as domestic M&As, domestic entry and exit of banking, and the formation of joint ventures and strategic alliances between banks—will become evident. But, first, I review the facts on banking consolidation as presented in tables 11.5 and 11.6, which were assembled from a detailed report on bank consolidation during the 1990s that was published by the Bank of International Settlements (BIS 2001). This report referred to consolidation in thirteen OECD nations, namely, Australia, Belgium, Canada, France, Germany, Italy, Japan, the Netherlands, Spain, Sweden, Switzerland, the United Kingdom, and the United States.

During the 1990s, these thirteen OECD economies experienced 3,563 mergers and acquisitions that involved a domestic bank and another domestic bank. This domestic consolidation dwarfed in number (and in value) the amount of cross-border M&A in banks (which totaled 338 transactions worth, in current dollars, approximately $73 billion; see table 11.5). What is more, many banks engaged in joint ventures and in strategic alliances during this period, particularly in the United States, Japan, and Canada (table 11.6). In short, cross-border M&A was not the only factor influencing the concentration and the market structure of these nations' banking systems.

Research on banking mergers points to a number of rationales for this observed consolidation. Carow and Kane (2002), for example, point to the following potential benefits to firms of such mergers and acquisitions: cost-based economies of scale, brand-based economies of scale, revenue-based economies of scale, safety-net-based economies of scale, revenue-based economies of scope, X-inefficiency, market power, and managerial-agency costs (Carow and Kane 2001, table 1). Dermine (1999), whose analysis Carow and Kane developed, noted that the following attractions to bank M&As have been asserted in the literature: first, size can bring "defense based economies of scale," that is, "achieving size . . . that acts as a defensive measure against takeovers" (Dermine 1999, 16), and, second, the long-standing "quiet life" hypothesis. Moreover, strategic alliances also can generate cost efficiencies to the extent that alliance partners can reduce any duplication in distribution networks.

My interest here is in the market power and efficiency-related aspects of bank mergers and acquisitions. In particular, I focus on the effects on one important observable variable, the interest-rate spread, which is the difference between the interest rates paid by borrowers and those paid to depositors. Part of that spread will be determined by the costs associated with collecting deposits, but also by the costs associated with locating and screening potential borrowers. Another determinant of the spread is market power, and this depends on the number of options available to both depositors and the borrowers. If potential depositors have few choices as to where to place their savings, then incumbent banks can offer lower deposit

Table 11.5　Mergers and Acquisitions in the Banking Sector in 13 OECD Nations during the 1990s

Type of Transaction	Characteristics	1990	1991	1992	1993	1994	1995	1996	1997	1998	1999	Total
		Deals Classified by Country and Sector of Selling Firm										
Within border/Within industry	Number	139	244	318	390	433	435	395	425	417	367	3,563
	Total value	16.77	27.74	23.65	26.68	31.02	122.35	38.92	172.04	257.25	241.11	957.53
	Mean value	0.18	0.22	0.14	0.10	0.10	0.43	0.15	0.53	0.78	0.98	0.39
Within border/Cross industry	Number	37	39	40	45	59	58	53	71	62	79	543
	Total value	10.66	3.00	0.92	1.44	1.54	4.79	1.65	4.21	99.53	8.27	136.03
	Mean value	0.48	1.36	0.05	0.06	0.06	0.17	0.06	0.11	2.21	0.16	0.44
Cross-border/Within industry	Number	14	18	14	19	24	30	21	30	36	29	235
	Total value	2.34	0.56	0.23	1.16	1.85	8.51	3.17	5.70	13.48	13.79	50.80
	Mean value	0.39	0.07	0.08	0.17	0.15	0.47	0.29	0.34	0.75	0.77	0.43
Cross-border/Cross industry	Number	9	10	9	7	9	9	11	8	18	13	103
	Total value	1.27	0.23	1.85	0.42	0.15	0.59	2.63	5.12	2.77	7.10	22.14
	Mean value	0.32	0.05	0.26	0.11	0.03	0.10	0.44	0.64	0.21	0.65	0.32
		Deals Classified by Country and Sector of Acquiring Firm										
Within border/Within industry	Number	139	244	318	390	433	435	395	425	417	367	3,563
	Total value	16.77	27.74	23.65	26.68	31.02	122.35	38.92	172.04	257.25	241.11	957.53
	Mean value	0.18	0.22	0.14	0.10	0.10	0.43	0.15	0.53	0.78	0.98	0.39
Within border/Cross industry	Number	13	25	22	35	36	52	60	49	45	72	409
	Total value	0.25	1.13	0.52	4.49	0.77	2.09	5.06	20.34	5.67	9.71	50.02
	Mean value	0.04	0.16	0.09	0.20	0.04	0.09	0.16	0.60	0.20	0.19	2.20
Cross-border/Within industry	Number	22	20	19	22	25	44	34	42	51	50	329
	Total value	2.83	0.37	0.99	1.28	1.65	10.25	5.12	10.70	15.50	20.26	68.95
	Mean value	0.28	0.06	0.20	0.14	0.15	0.38	0.30	0.51	0.60	0.61	0.42
Cross-border/Cross industry	Number	6	8	7	7	9	21	15	17	15	17	122
	Total value	0.18	0.19	0.27	0.13	0.75	0.65	1.06	1.22	0.85	3.59	8.89
	Mean value	0.06	0.05	0.14	0.04	0.75	0.13	0.21	0.17	0.09	0.33	0.18

Note: Total value and mean value are in U.S.$ billions. These magnitudes are in current dollars.

Table 11.6   Joint Ventures and Strategic Alliances in the Banking Sector in 13 OECD Nations during the 1990s

Economy	Characteristics	1990	1991	1992	1993	1994	1995	1996	1997	1998	1999	Total
The United States	Within border	22	25	36	48	85	134	67	160	318	241	1,136
	Cross border	25	32	12	11	24	33	28	42	75	57	339
	Total	47	57	48	59	109	167	95	202	393	298	1,475
Canada	Within border	5	5	0	1	3	7	3	11	21	28	84
	Cross border	3	5	1	4	3	5	6	9	29	16	81
	Total	8	10	1	5	6	12	9	20	50	44	165
Japan	Within border	4	2	5	4	5	4	1	4	20	47	96
	Cross border	7	9	2	5	4	6	4	17	64	65	183
	Total	11	11	7	9	9	10	5	21	84	112	279
Australia	Within border	0	3	3	5	12	21	5	11	33	52	145
	Cross border	2	1	2	4	7	18	9	12	21	42	118
	Total	2	4	5	9	19	39	14	23	54	94	263
Belgium	Within border	0	0	0	0	1	1	1	1	1	1	6
	Cross border	1	1	2	1	3	1	1	0	2	3	15
	Total	1	1	2	1	4	2	2	1	3	4	21
France	Within border	2	2	4	1	4	3	2	4	1	4	27
	Cross border	9	3	7	4	3	5	3	6	12	11	63
	Total	11	5	11	5	7	8	5	10	13	15	90
Germany	Within border	2	4	4	8	2	3	0	5	8	4	40
	Cross border	3	7	1	6	5	6	2	4	16	6	56
	Total	5	11	5	14	7	9	2	9	24	10	96
Italy	Within border	1	2	13	2	2	2	0	1	1	3	27
	Cross border	4	2	9	4	2	4	1	10	8	8	52
	Total	5	4	22	6	4	6	1	11	9	11	79

(continued)

Table 11.6 (continued)

Economy	Characteristics	1990	1991	1992	1993	1994	1995	1996	1997	1998	1999	Total
The Netherlands	Within border	0	2	2	2	1	3	1	1	1	2	15
	Cross border	1	4	2	1	1	2	1	1	7	6	26
	Total	1	6	4	3	2	5	2	2	8	8	41
Spain	Within border	0	0	2	2	2	0	0	0	1	2	9
	Cross border	4	8	5	2	5	2	2	2	5	5	40
	Total	4	8	7	4	7	2	2	2	6	7	49
Sweden	Within border	2	0	0	0	0	0	1	0	0	0	3
	Cross border	1	2	0	0	1	0	1	0	4	4	13
	Total	3	2	0	0	1	0	2	0	4	4	16
Switzerland	Within border	1	1	1	1	5	3	0	0	0	4	16
	Cross border	2	1	0	0	3	0	0	2	3	3	14
	Total	3	2	1	1	8	3	0	2	3	7	30
The United Kingdom	Within border	7	13	3	8	11	39	11	25	29	47	193
	Cross border	11	15	7	5	17	24	15	16	38	60	208
	Total	18	28	10	13	28	63	26	41	67	107	401

rates which ceterius paribus raises spreads. Likewise, if potential borrowers have few alternatives to seeking funds from the incumbent banks, then the interest rate paid by the former will be higher, thus raising spreads.

In the absence of efficiencies, bank M&As can be expected to raise spreads as the number of banking options facing depositors and borrowers declines. Only if there is sufficient rivalry between banks after a merger takes place will any efficiencies created by the merger be passed on to consumers in the form of lower spreads.[27] It is an empirical question whether market power or efficiencies dominates. To date, the empirical literature on bank mergers is mixed on the relative importance of these two factors (see the discussions in Berger et al. 2000; Calomiris and Karceski 2000; Vives 2001).

To estimate the effects on interest-rate spreads of the changes in the national banking sectors documented in tables 11.5 and 11.6, I assembled from BIS (2001) and the World Bank's *World Development Indicators* (WDI) an unbalanced panel comprising the thirteen nations in the BIS study. The unbalanced nature of the panel resulted from the fact that in some countries the five firm-concentration ratios in the banking sectors were not reported in the BIS study for every year from 1990 to 1999. The BIS study provided annual data on the number of banks in each country, the number and types of strategic alliances, and the number and types of M&A.

The dependent variable for this study—the interest-rate spread—was taken from the WDI CD-ROM. This source defines the interest spread as "the interest rate charged by banks on loans to prime customers minus the interest paid to by commercial or similar banks for demand, time, or savings deposits" (WDI CD-ROM).[28]

The mean value of this spread for each economy is reported in table 11.7, which sorts the economies according to the annual average number of cross-border mergers and acquisitions. The highest mean spread (6.35 percent) is in Germany and the lowest spread is in Canada (1.34 percent). Data on three macroeconomic series—GDPs, GDP-price deflators, and stock-market capitalization—used to form control variables (which are described later) was also assembled from the WDI. Both GDP growth and the inflation rate are intended to proxy for the stage of the business cycle, whereas the size of a nation's stock market is supposed to proxy for the extent to which financial markets can act as an alternative source of finance for borrowers and as an alternative destination for personal savings.

The objective of the econometric strategy is to discern—after stripping

---

27. For a more sophisticated overview of the causes and consequences of market power in banking, see Vives (2001, section 3).

28. Some seminar participants have questioned the accuracy of the WDI data on bank spreads. I checked other available series on bank spreads—specifically, those from the International Monetary Fund and the comprehensive DATASTREAM financial database—and found that these confirmed the data on spreads reported in the WDI.

Table 11.7   Summary Statistics for the Unbalanced Panel Data Set

Economy	Years in Unbalanced Panel	Five-Firm Concentration Ratio	Number of Banks	Mean Value of Annual Observations							Interest-Rate Spread (%)
				Strategic Alliances		M&A					
				Within Border	Cross Border		Within Border	Cross Border			
Canada	1990–1999	70.9	61.0	8.4	8.1		9.8	0.4			1.34
Japan	1990–1998	30.6	161.1	5.4	13.1		6.1	0.4			2.59
Sweden	1990–1998	80.2	196.3	0.3	1.0		5.0	0.6			5.85
The Netherlands	1990–1999	77.8	172.4	1.5	2.6		3.2	1.2			5.03
Italy	1992–1999	32.3	280.9	3.0	5.8		23.6	1.5			5.62
Spain	1990–1997	45.8	317.4	0.8	3.8		6.4	1.9			3.16
Belgium	1990–1998	58.9	321.0	0.8	2.2		2.4	2.1			5.14
Australia	1991–1998	71.8	40.1	11.6	9.3		7.8	2.4			4.19
Germany	1990–1998	17.4	3969.7	4.0	5.6		16.6	2.8			6.15
Switzerland	1990–1997	53.5	418.4	2.1	2.1		9.1	3.1			2.21
France	1990–1997	66.2	1520.5	2.8	5.0		16.1	3.9			4.33
The United Kingdom	1990, 1995–1998	44.3	466.8	26.0	23.3		22.5	6.0			2.79
The United States	1990–1999	18.3	12392.1	113.6	33.9		283.6	7.5			2.73

out the variation created by the business cycle and any competition for funds created by the stock market and by the impact of regulatory changes—whether or not interest-rate spreads in the 1990s have been influenced by the formation of the numerous strategic alliances and the consummation of bank M&As. Of special interest is whether or not cross-border M&A and cross-border strategic alliances have different effects from their domestic counterparts. So that my econometric estimates are not determined entirely by the boom years of cross-border M&A (1997–2000), the data set used covers as much of the 1990s as the data sources employed here would allow.

I proceed from a parsimonious specification to richer ones. The first specification purges the variation in bank spreads of variation associated with a set of macroeconomic controls and includes country-specific fixed effects. The estimation equation is

(1)
$$\ln\!\left(\frac{1 + L_{it}}{1 + D_{it}}\right) = a_i + \overline{b}\,\ln(\mathbf{M}_{it}) + \varepsilon_{it},$$

where

$$\ln(\mathbf{M}_{it}) = b_1 \ln\!\left(\frac{GDP_{it}}{GDP_{i(t-1)}}\right) + b_2 \ln\!\left(\frac{P_{it}}{P_{i(t-1)}}\right) + b_3 \ln(S\mathbf{M}_{it}) + b_4 \ln(t) + \dots$$

and

$i = 1,\dots, N,\ N = 13;$
$t = 1990,\dots, 1999;$
a_i is a country-specific fixed effect for economy i;
L_{it} is the prime rate paid to borrowers from banks in economy i in year t;
D_{it} is the interest paid to depositors in banks in economy i in year t;
GDP_{it} is the GDP of economy i in year t;
P_{it} is the GDP deflator in economy i in year t; and
SM_{it} is the total stock-market capitalization of economy i in year t as a percentage of GDP_{it}.

The vector $\mathbf{M}_{it}$ includes the four macroeconomic controls previously outlined plus the (six) two-way interaction between these four controls. The parameter estimates, obtained by confronting specification (1) with the data from my unbalanced panel of thirteen economies, account for 6.43 percent of the within variation, see table 11.8. The estimation procedure used weighted least squares to take account of any country-specific (or groupwise) heteroskedacity.[29]

---

29. Specifically, the weight applied to each country's data in a second-stage regression is the absolute value of the estimate of the standard deviation of the residuals that were recovered from an unweighted first-stage regression using ordinary least squares.

Table 11.8   Estimating the Determinants of Bank Spreads in all 13 OECD Nations from 1990 to 1999

	Specifications													
	(1)		(2)		(3)		(4)		(5)		(6)		(7)	
Independent Variable	Parameter Estimate	t-ratio	Parameter Estimate	t-ratio	Parameter Estimate	t-ratio	Parameter Estimate	t-ratio	Parameter Estimate	t-ratio	Parameter Estimate	t-ratio	Parameter Estimate	t-ratio
Macroeconomic controls	Included		Included		Included		Included		Included		Included		Included	
Five-firm concentration ratio			0.0070	**2.8769**	0.0088	**3.2230**								
Five-firm concentration of the variation associated with the following independent variables ratio after being purged							0.0088	**3.2230**	0.0085	**3.0664**	0.0098	**4.1962**	0.0072	**2.4183**
Total number of strategic alliances					0.0028	**1.9024**	0.0026	**1.8099**	0.0030	**2.0314**				
Total number of mergers and acquisitions					-0.0011	-1.0396	-0.0006	-0.5964	-0.0010	-0.9484				
Strategic alliances														
Domestic											0.0045	**2.0285**	0.0041	**1.8390**
Cross border											0.0020	0.7445	0.0002	0.0902
Mergers and acquisitions														
Domestic											0.0030	**1.7634**	0.0039	**2.0781**
Cross border											-0.0028	-1.8473	-0.0012	-0.7583
Total number of banks									-0.0067	-1.5067	-0.0049	-1.1542	-0.0054	-1.1480
Controls for regulatory changes	Not included		Not included		Not included		Not included		Not included		Not included		Included	
Within R^2	0.0643		0.0609		0.0780		0.0780		0.0881		0.1144		0.2597	
No. of observations	97		97		97		97		97		97		97	

Note: Boldface indicates a parameter estimate that is statistically different from zero on a one-tail test.

Specifications (2) and (3) in table 11.8 include parsimonious controls for changes in market structure. Specification (2) includes the logarithm of the five firm-concentration ratio as an independent variable. Specification (3) goes further and introduces as two additional distinct independent variables the logarithms of (1 plus) the number of annual strategic alliances and (1 plus) the number of annual M&As consummated since 1990. Both specifications yield the traditional finding that increases in the concentration ratio raises interest-rate spreads. Specification (3) provides the first evidence that strategic alliances appear to raise interest-rate spreads, whereas M&As tend to have no statistically significant effect on them.

One objection to specification (3) is that the observed concentration ratio in a given year may well, in turn, be influenced by the number of strategic alliances and mergers and acquisitions that have occurred in the past or are taking place currently. Consequently, in addition to allowing for time-invariant country-specific determinants of concentration, I also purged the variation of the five firm-concentration ratio of the observed levels of strategic alliances and M&As.[30] This purged concentration ratio was used in specification (4) instead of the actual concentration ratio in specification (3). The upshot: precious little changes.[31]

Another objection to specifications (1) through (4) is that they do not take into account the entry and exit of domestic banks that is independent of M&A. Specification (5) includes as an independent variable the logarithm of the number of banks in an economy. With this additional explanatory variable, the effect of the concentration ratio on interest-rate spreads still has the correct sign and the parameter estimate on the strategic-alliance variable remains little changed. Entry of banks is found to depress spreads, but not in a statistically significant manner.

As the BIS data source enables me to differentiate between domestic and cross-border strategic alliances and between domestic and cross-border M&A, I entered them as separate independent variables in specification (6). Interestingly, domestic M&A and domestic strategic alliances are found to raise spreads, with the estimated parameter on the former 50 per-

30. Specifically, in specification (4), I regressed the concentration ratio on country-specific dummies and the logarithm of 1 plus the total number of strategic alliances and the total number of mergers and acquisitions. Following standard procedures, the estimate of the purged concentration ratio is the estimated residual of the regression described above in this footnote.

31. Note that in specifications (4) through (7) I purged the concentration ratio of country-specific fixed effects plus each of the M&A and strategic-alliance variables included in a given specification. Moreover, in specifications (5) through (7), I also purged the concentration ratio of the logarithm of the number of banks. In specification (7), I also purged the concentration ration of the explanatory power of the dummies picking up changes in bank regulatory regimes. In each specification, the goal of this purging procedure is to identify that component of the concentration ratio that cannot be attributed to the changes in national market structures in the banking sector, to national regulatory changes, or to other national characteristics that do not vary over the years of data in the sample (1990–1999).

cent larger than on the latter. In contrast, cross-border M&A does appear to reduce spreads. However, in specification (6) these findings do not survive the inclusion of controls for regulatory changes in the thirteen OECD nations during the 1990s.[32] Specification (7) includes these controls, and the parameter on the cross-border M&A variable loses its significance. Nonetheless, the estimated parameters do suggest that domestic consolidation and strategic alliances in the banking system have raised spreads whereas their cross-border counterparts do not.

The next step was to examine whether these qualitative findings held up to changes in sample composition. First, I eliminated each country one at a time from the sample and reestimated the parameters. The new parameter estimates varied little from the previous. Second, I eliminated the North American economies (Canada and the United States) from the sample, again with little effect. Third, I eliminated Japan and Australia from the sample and found not much changed. This seemingly robust set of regression findings was overturned when I split the thirteen nation sample into a sample comprising of EU members and a sample comprising the rest. Arguably, the former's banking sectors have been affected by the implementation of two European Banking Directives (and other measures to enhance the integration of European markets). Such considerations may result in banking consolidation in Europe that has different effects than in other parts of the industrialized world. Tables 11.9 and 11.10, which report the parameters estimated in table 11.8 for the eight-nation EU sample and the five-nation non-EU sample, respectively, confirm that differences do exist between these samples.

In the EU sample, cross-border strategic alliances are found to increase spreads. Perhaps such alliances in Europe were formed to frustrate entry and segment markets, rather than to enhance economies of scale and scope. Interestingly, where EU banks have gone beyond such alliances and have actually merged with banks located in another EU member, the evidence suggests that spreads do fall (see specification (7), table 11.9). In contrast, domestic interbank alliances in EU member states appear to have no effects on bank spreads—suggesting that any economies reaped are probably offset by a diminution in competition.

The performance of the specifications in the non-EU sample is rather mixed. For sure, with the inclusion of the regulatory controls (in specification (7), table 11.10), over half of the variation in the dependent variable is explained. However, few of the market structure variables—such as the purged concentration ratio—are found to have had a statistically significant effect on interest-rate spreads. This may reflect the fact that the degrees of freedom in the sample are quite small (less than 30). Even so,

32. Table 11A.2 lists the major banking-sector-related changed identified in annex II.3 of BIS (2001).

Table 11.9   Estimating the Determinants of Bank Spreads in 8 EU Nations from 1990 to 1999

								Specifications					
	(1)	(2)		(3)		(4)		(5)		(6)		(7)	
Independent Variable		Parameter Estimate	t-ratio	Parameter Estimate	t-ratio	Parameter Estimate	t-ratio	Parameter Estimate	t-ratio	Parameter Estimate	t-ratio	Parameter Estimate	t-ratio
Macroeconomic controls	Included	Included		Included		Included		Included		Included		Included	
Five-firm concentration ratio		0.0050	1.4113	0.0106	**2.6792**								
Five-firm concentration ratio after being purged of the variation associated with the following independent variables						0.0106	**2.6792**	0.0108	**2.8411**	0.0087	**2.3710**	0.0057	**1.3474**
Total number of strategic alliances				0.0049	1.4210	0.0044	1.3188	0.0046	1.3871				
Total number of mergers and acquisitions				0.0002	0.0760	0.0010	0.4133	0.0005	0.1727				
Strategic alliances													
Domestic										0.0065	1.6049	0.0012	0.2677
Cross border										0.0018	0.3823	0.0132	**2.3059**
Mergers and acquisitions													
Domestic										0.0039	1.2051	-0.0008	-0.2424
Cross border										-0.0077	**-2.0304**	-0.0056	**-1.7620**
Total number of banks								-0.0115	-1.1340	-0.0125	-1.2596	-0.0159	**-1.8156**
Controls for regulatory changes	Not included	Not included		Not included		Not included		Not included		Not included		Included	
Within R^2	0.1943	0.1903		0.2361		0.2361		0.2973		0.4403		0.4796	
No. of observations	65	65		65		65		65		65		65	

Note: Boldface indicates a parameter estimate that is statistically different from zero on a one-tail test.

Table 11.10   Estimating the Determinants of Bank Spreads in 5 Non-EU Nations from 1990 to 1999

Specifications

Independent Variable	(1)	(2) Parameter Estimate	t-ratio	(3) Parameter Estimate	t-ratio	(4) Parameter Estimate	t-ratio	(5) Parameter Estimate	t-ratio	(6) Parameter Estimate	t-ratio	(7) Parameter Estimate	t-ratio
Macroeconomic controls	Included	Included		Included		Included		Included		Included		Included	
Five-firm concentration ratio		0.0002	0.0313	0.0036	0.4322								
Five-firm concentration ratio after being purged of the variation associated with the following independent variables						0.0036	0.4322	0.0040	0.4394	0.0042	0.4248	0.0066	0.9658
Total number of strategic alliances				−0.0024	−1.0534	−0.0023	−1.0408	−0.0025	−1.0602				
Total number of mergers and acquisitions				−0.0003	−0.1793	−0.0903	−0.1632	−0.0004	−0.2014				
Strategic alliances													
Domestic										0.0005	0.1141	0.0018	0.4205
Cross border										−0.0069	−1.2936	**−0.0092**	**−2.0054**
Mergers and acquisitions													
Domestic										0.0010	0.1666	0.0027	0.4390
Cross border										−0.0004	−0.1628	−0.0011	−0.4429
Total number of banks								0.0006	0.0464	0.0085	0.5437	0.0082	0.5488
Controls for regulatory changes	Not included	Not included		Not included		Not included		Not included		Not included		Included	
Within R^2	0.1633	0.1611		0.2896		0.2896		0.3357		0.3214		0.5322	
Number of observations	45	45		45		45		45		45		45	

Note: Boldface indicates a parameter estimate that is statistically different from zero on a one-tail test.

outside the EU, cross-border strategic alliances were found to depress interest-rate spreads, suggesting that such corporate agreements generate efficiencies.

The parameter estimates from specification (7) in both tables 11.9 and 11.10 can be used to quantify the total effect of the observed domestic and cross-border consolidation in the banking sectors that occurred in the 1990s, as well as the total effect of the formation of strategic alliances. Table 11.11 reports country-by-country the point estimates of the total effect on interest-rate spreads of the domestic and cross-border banking changes observed throughout the 1990s. In every non-EU country considered here, the combined effect of the domestic banking changes was to raise spreads, but this was offset by the beneficial effects created by cross-border strategic alliances and M&A. In each EU economy, the net effect of domestic banking changes on spreads is almost zero and is dominated by the spread-increasing effects of cross-border strategic alliances. Indeed, had those cross-border strategic alliances not occurred in the 1990s, bank spreads (as measured by the dependent variable) in each EU country considered here would have been at least two whole percentage points lower in 1999. In contrast, in the five non-EU economies, cross-border strategic alliances and mergers have helped reduce spreads by between 1.3 and 3.0 percentage points.

These findings suggest that interbank agreements and consolidation in the 1990s had important effects on interest rates and, therefore, on the welfare of lenders or borrowers. What is doubtful, however, is that sweeping statements about the effects of cross-border interbank agreements can be made with any confidence. Indeed, the emphasis in much commentary on globalization regarding the role of cross-border M&A is somewhat misplaced at least in banking, since it appears that the consequences of cross-border strategic alliances are a more important part of the story.

11.4 Concluding Remarks

The cross-border mergers and acquisitions wave of the 1990s was on a different scale than its predecessor in the late 1990s: It included more firms from more countries; saw a greater number of transactions, many of which were megadeals; and was dominated by service-sector transactions. In fact, three sectors (namely, transportation and communication, finance, and business services) accounted for just under half of the value of all M&A from 1997 to 2000. An evaluation of this recent cross-border mergers and acquisitions wave is, thus, in large part an evaluation of its effects on these three sectors. What is more, in each case there are good reasons for suspecting that cross-border M&A was not the only major change in their market structures in the 1990s. The telecommunications sector saw much deregulation and technological advances, as did business services. In

Table 11.11 Contribution of Within Border and Cross-Border Transactions to Changing Spreads throughout the 1990s

| Economy | Within-Border Transactions 1990–1999 | | | | | Cross-Border Transactions 1990–1999 | | | | | Combined Effect of Within-and Cross-Border Transactions on Interest-Rate Spreads (%) |
| | Number | | Point Estimate of Effect on Interest-Rate Spreads (%) | | | Number | | Point Estimate of Effect on Interest-Rate Spreads (%) | | | |
	Strategic Alliances	M&A	Strategic Alliances	M&A	Combined Effect	Strategic Alliances	M&A	Strategic Alliances	M&A	Combined Effect	
Members of the European Union											
Belgium	5	21	0.215	-0.247	-0.032	15	21	3.728	-1.716	1.948	1.915
Sweden	3	47	0.166	-0.309	-0.143	13	7	3.545	-1.158	2.346	2.200
The Netherlands	15	32	0.333	-0.279	0.053	26	12	4.447	-1.426	2.957	3.012
Spain	9	68	0.277	-0.338	-0.062	40	21	5.024	-1.716	3.222	3.157
France	27	150	0.401	-0.401	-0.002	63	50	5.643	-2.178	3.343	3.341
Germany	40	186	0.447	-0.418	0.027	56	32	5.482	-1.939	3.437	3.465
Italy	27	212	0.401	-0.428	-0.029	52	16	5.381	-1.574	3.722	3.692
The United Kingdom	193	200	0.634	-0.423	0.208	208	44	7.306	-2.109	5.043	5.262
Economies That Are Not Members of the European Union											
Japan	96	102	0.827	1.259	2.096	183	6	-4.684	-0.214	-4.888	-2.894
Australia	145	75	0.901	1.176	2.088	118	22	-4.302	-0.344	-4.631	-2.640
The United States	1,136	2,836	1.275	2.170	3.472	339	75	-5.221	-0.475	-5.672	-2.397
Canada	84	98	0.803	1.248	2.061	81	4	-3.973	-0.177	-4.143	-2.167
Switzerland	15	79	0.500	1.190	1.696	14	28	-2.461	-0.370	-2.821	-1.173

banking, whose consolidation was studied in more detail in this chapter, strategic alliances and domestic M&As were consummated in large numbers in the 1990s. Correcting for these other developments was found to be important when accurately gauging the effect of cross-border mergers and acquisitions in the banking sector.

My empirical analysis of thirteen OECD economies' banking sectors points to a discernable impact of openness to foreign banking activities on bank spreads. In eight EU economies, the beneficial consequences of cross-border M&As was more than offset by the deleterious impact of cross-border strategic alliances. In contrast, the net effect of openness to foreign banking activities has been to benefit customers in non-European industrialized economies.

This chapter speaks to a number of themes discussed throughout this book. First, by documenting the factual record on cross-border mergers and acquisitions, a better sense of the scale of this phenomenon emerged. Facts replace assertions. For sure, cross-border mergers and acquisitions in the late 1990s were greater than in the late 1980s. However, the former still only represent a small fraction of the stock-market capitalizations of all but the smallest industrialized economies. Indeed, in almost every industrial country, foreigners are hardly snapping up domestic assets at a rate that some might find alarming.

The second important finding of this chapter relates to the concern that changes in the global economy in recent years have sought to reinforce the market power of corporations. The sectoral study of banking presented here points to the importance of correctly identifying all of the changes in a given sector's structure and its regulations before drawing any inferences about the effects of consolidation on customers. In the EU banking sector, the evidence suggests that cross-border M&As have actually benefited bank customers rather than harming them. In contrast, cross-border strategic alliances have probably hurt customers in the EU, suggesting that not all cross-border corporate acts have the same effects. More nuance is clearly needed in policy debates so that cross-border interfirm measures are not automatically branded as bad or anticonsumer.

Appendix

Table 11A.1   Megamergers and Acquisitions in 2000

Rank	Value of Cross-Border Transaction ($ billions)	Acquiring Company		Acquired Company		Headquarters Location	
		Name	Industry	Name	Industry	Acquiring Firm	Acquired Firm
1	202.8	Vodafone AirTouch PLC	Radiotelephone communications	Mannesmann AG	Radiotelephone communications	The United Kingdom	Germany
2	46.0	France Telecom SA	Telephone communications, except radiotelephone	Orange PLC (Mannesmann AG)	Telephone communications, except radiotelephone	France	The United Kingdom
3	40.4	Vivendi SA	Water supply	Seagram Cc Ltd.	Motion picture and videotape production	France	Canada
4	27.2	BP Amoco PLC	Petroleum refining	ARCO	Petroleum refining	The United Kingdom	The United States
5	25.1	Unilever PLC	Creamery butter	Bestfoods	Dried fruits, vegetables, and soup mixes	The United Kingdom	The United States
6	19.4	Zurich Allied AG	Life insurance	Allied Zurich PLC	Life insurance	Switzerland	The United Kingdom
7	16.5	UBS AG	Banks, non-U.S. chartered	PaineWebber Group Inc.	Security brokers, dealers and flotation companies	Switzerland	The United States

8	Vodafone AirTouch PLC	Radiotelephone communications	Airtel SA	Radiotelephone communications	The United Kingdom	Spain	14.4
9	Credit Suisse First Boston	Security brokers, dealers and flotation companies	Donaldson Lufkin & Jenrette	Commodity contracts, brokers, and dealers	The United States	The United States	13.5
10	Cap Gemini SA	Business consulting services, nec	Ernst & Young Consulting Bus.	Business consulting services, nec	France	The United States	11.8
11	HSBC Holdings PLC	Banks, non-U.S. chartered	Credit Commercial de France	Banks, non-U.S. chartered	The United Kingdom	France	11.1
12	NTL Inc.	Cable and other pay television services	CWC Consumer Co.	Telephone communications, except radiotelephone	The United States	The United Kingdom	11.0
13	Telefonica SA	Telephone communications, except radiotelephone	Telecom municacoes de Sao Paulo	Telephone communications, except radiotelephone	Spain	Brazil	10.2
14	BellSouth GmbH (KPN, BellSouth)	Telephone communications, except radiotelephone	E-Plus Mobilfunk GmbH (Otelo)	Radiotelephone communications	The Netherlands	Germany	9.4
15	America Online Inc.	Prepackaged software	AOL Europe, AOL Australia	Information retrieval services	The United States	Germany	8.3
16	Chase Manhattan Corp., N.Y.	National commercial banks	Robert Fleming Holdings Ltd.	Security brokers, dealers, and flotation companies	The United States	The United Kingdom	7.7
17	ING Groep NV	Life insurance	Aetna Financial Services & International Bus.	Security and commodity services, nec	The Netherlands	The United States	7.6

(*continued*)

Table 11A.1 (continued)

Rank	Value of Cross-Border Transaction ($ billions)	Acquiring Company		Acquired Company		Headquarters Location	
		Name	Industry	Name	Industry	Acquiring Firm	Acquired Firm
18	7.1	British American Tobacco PLC	Cigarettes	Imasco Ltd.	Eating places	The United Kingdom	Canada
19	7.1	Alcatel SA	Telephone and telegraph apparatus	Newbridge Networks Corp.	Telephone and telegraph apparatus	France	Canada
20	7.1	Nortel Networks Corp.	Telephone and telegraph apparatus	Afeon Websystems Inc.	Electronic components, nec	Canada	The United States
21	6.7	DaimlerChrysler Aerospace AG	Aircraft parts and equipment	Aerospatiale Matra	Aircraft	Germany	France
22	6.3	RWE AG	Electric and other services combined	Thames Water PLC	Water supply	Germany	The United Kingdom
23	6.2	Terra Networks (Telefonica SA)	Information-retrieval services	Lycos Inc.	Information-retrieval services	Spain	The United States
24	6.0	ING Groep NV	Life insurance	ReliaStar Financial Corp.	Life insurance	The Netherlands	The United States
25	5.7	NTT Communications Corp.	Telephone communications, except radiotelephone	Verio Inc.	Data-processing services	Japan	The United States
26	5.4	PowerGen PLC	Electric services	LG&E Energy Corp.	Electric services	The United Kingdom	The United States

27	5.3	CLT-UFA (Cie Luxembourgeoise)	Radio broadcasting stations	Luxembourg	Pearson Television (Pearson)	Television broadcasting stations	The United Kingdom
28	5.2	Leconport Estates	Investors, nec	Multinational	MEPC PLC	Land subdividers and developers, except cemeteries	The United Kingdom
29	5.0	British Telecommunications	Telephone communications, except radiotelephone	The United Kingdom	AT&T Worldwide Assets, Ops	Telephone communications, except radiotelephone	The United States
30	5.0	WPP Group PLC	Advertising agencies	The United Kingdom	Young & Rubicam Inc.	Advertising agencies	The United States
31	4.9	Stora Enso Oyj	Paper mills	Finland	Consolidated Papers Inc.	Paperboard mills	The United States
32	4.9	Tiscali SpA	Telephone communications, except radiotelephone	Italy	World Online International NV	Information-retrieval services	The Netherlands
33	4.8	Nordbanken Holding AB	Offices of holding companies, nec	Sweden	Media Oy	Banks, non-U.S. chartered	Finland
34	4.8	Alcan Aluminum Ltd.	Aluminum foundries	Canada	Alusuisse Lonza Group Ltd.	Packaging paper & plastics film, coated & laminated	Switzerland
35	4.6	Telefonica SA	Telephone communications, except radiotelephone	Spain	Endemol Entertainment NV	Motion-picture and videotape production	The Netherlands
36	4.4	MeritaNordbanken	Banks, non-U.S. chartered	Finland	Unidanmark A/S	Banks, non-U.S. chartered	Denmark

(continued)

Table 11A.1 (continued)

Rank	Value of Cross-Border Transaction ($ billions)	Acquiring Company		Acquired Company		Headquarters Location	
		Name	Industry	Name	Industry	Acquiring Firm	Acquired Firm
37	4.4	Tyco International Ltd.	General industrial machinery and equipment	Mallinckrodt Inc.	In-vitro and in-vivo diagnostic substances	Bermuda	The United States
38	4.3	France Telecom SA	Telephone communications, except radiotelephone	Global One Cc	Telephone communications, except radiotelephone	France	The United States
39	4.3	Same Group PLC	Computer related services, nec	LHS Group Inc.	Computer-programming services	The United Kingdom	The United States
40	4.3	Investor Group	Investors, nec	TPSA	Radiotelephone communications	France	Poland
41	4.2	National Grid Group PLC	Electric services	New England Electric System	Electric services	The United Kingdom	The United States
42	4.0	Alliance Capital Management	Investment advice	Sanford C. Bornstein & Co. Inc.	Investment advice	The United States	The United States
43	3.9	BASF AG	Industrial organic chemicals, nec	American Cyanamid Agricultural Product	Pesticides & agricultural chemicals, nec	Germany	The United States
44	3.7	NTL Inc.	Cable and other pay television services	Cablecom Holding AG	Cable and other pay television services	The United States	Switzerland

Rank	Value	Acquirer	Industry	Target	Industry	Country	Country
45	3.6	France Telecom SA	Telephone communications, except radiotelephone	MobilCom AG	Telephone communications, except radiotelephone	France	Germany
46	3.6	Koninkljke Ahold NV	Grocery stores	U.S. Foodservice Inc.	Groceries, general line	The Netherlands	The United States
47	3.6	NTT Mobile Communications Network Inc.	Telephone communications, except radiotelephone	KPN Mobile (KPN Telecom NV)	Telephone communications, except radiotelephone	Japan	The Netherlands
48	3.6	Corning Inc.	Telephone and telegraph apparatus	Pirelli SpA-Optical Components	Drawing & insulating of nonferrous wire	The United States	Italy
49	3.5	AXA	Life insurance	Sun Life and Provincial	Life insurance	France	The United Kingdom
50	3.5	Interbrew SA	Malt beverages	Bass PLC-Brewing Operations	Malt beverages	Belgium	The United Kingdom
51	3.4	WPD Holdings U.K.	Electric services	Hyder PLC	Engineering services	The United Kingdom	The United Kingdom
52	3.4	Rodamco North America NV	Real-estate investment trusts	Urban Shopping Centers Inc.	Real-estate investment trusts	The Netherlands	The United States
53	3.3	Nortel Networks Corp.	Telephone and telegraph apparatus	Xros Inc.	Telephone and telegraph apparatus	Canada	The United States
54	3.3	Nortel Networks Corp.	Telephone and telegraph apparatus	Qtera Corp.	Telephone and telegraph apparatus	Canada	The United States
55	2.9	Hellenic Bottling Cc SA	Bottled & canned soft drinks and carbonated waters	Coca-Cola Beverages PLC	Bottled & canned soft drinks and carbonated waters	Greece	The United Kingdom

(continued)

Table 11A.1 (continued)

	Value of Cross-Border Transaction	Acquiring Company			Acquired Company		Headquarters Location	
Rank	($ billions)	Name	Industry		Name	Industry	Acquiring Firm	Acquired Firm
56	2.8	Cemex	Cement, hydraulic		Southdown Inc.	Cement, hydraulic	Mexico	The United States
57	2.8	Global Crossing Ltd.	Telephone communications, except radiotelephone		IPC Communications (Citicorp)	Information retrieval services	Bermuda	The United States
58	2.8	Investor Group	Investors, nec		Deutsche Telekom AG-North	Telephone communications, except radiotelephone	The United States	Germany
59	2.8	MeritaNordbanken	Banks, non-U.S. chartered		Christiania Bank	Banks, non-U.S. chartered	Finland	Norway
60	2.8	Havas Advertising SA	Advertising agencies		Snyder Communications Inc.	Business services, nec	France	The United States
61	2.7	Preussag AG	Travel agencies		Thomson Travel Group PLC	Tour operators	Germany	The United Kingdom
62	2.7	Norske Skogindustrier AS	Pulp mills		Fletcher Challenge Paper	Pulp mills	Norway	New Zealand
63	2.7	Ford Motor Co.	Motor vehicles and passenger-car bodies		Land Rover (BMW)	Motor vehicles & passenger-car bodies	The United States	The United Kingdom
64	2.6	Flextronics International Ltd.	Printed circuit boards		DII Group	Electronic components, nec	Singapore	The United States

65	General Sekiyu (Esso Eastern)	Petroleum refining	Tonen Corp. (Exxon Mobil)	Petroleum refining	Japan	The United States
66	2.5 Hanson PLC	Men's footwear, except athletic	Pioneer International Ltd.	Ready-mixed concrete	The United Kingdom	Australia
67	2.5 Dexia Belgium	Security brokers, dealers and flotation companies	Finland Security Assurance Holdings	Surety insurance	Belgium	The United States
68	2.5 Pearson PLC	Books: publishing, or publishing & printing	National Computer Systems Inc.	Computer-peripheral equipment, nec	The United Kingdom	The United States
69	2.5 Tyco International Ltd.	General industrial machinery and equipment	Lucent Tech Inc.-Power System Unit	Electronic components, nec	Bermuda	The United States
70	2.5 Carrefour SA	Grocery stores	Gruppo GS SpA (Schemaventuno)	Variety stores	France	Italy
71	2.5 Bayer AG	Medicinal-chemicals and botanical products, radiotelephone	Lyondell Chemical-Polyfs Bus.	Petroleum-refining production	Germany	The United States
72	2.4 Telefonica SA	Telephone communications, except radiotelephone	Telesudeste Celular	Telephone communications, except radiotelephone	Spain	Brazil
73	2.4 General Motors Corp.	Motor vehicles and passenger-car bodies	Fiat Auto SpA (Fiat SpA)	Motor vehicles & passenger-car bodies	The United States	Italy

2.6

(continued)

Table 11A.1 (continued)

Rank	Value of Cross-Border Transaction ($ billions)	Acquiring Company		Acquired Company		Headquarters Location	
		Name	Industry	Name	Industry	Acquiring Firm	Acquired Firm
74	2.3	Atos SA	Computer-programming services	Origin (Philips Electronics NV)	Prepackaged Software	France	The Netherlands
75	2.3	T-Online International AG	Information-retrieval services	Club Internet (Lagardere Group)	Information-retrieval services	Germany	France
76	2.3	General Electric Capital Corp.	Personal-credit institutions	Toho Mutual Life	Life insurance	The United States	Japan
77	2.3	Unilever NV	Creamery butter	Slim Fast Foods Cc	Food preparations, nec	The Netherlands	The United States
78	2.2	Investor Group	Investors, nec	EPON NV (EDON, NUON)	Electric services	Belgium	The Netherlands
79	2.2	Investor Group	Investors, nec	ETSA Utilities, ETSA Power	Electric services	Hong Kong, China	Australia
80	2.2	Telefonica Internacional SA	Telephone communications, except radiotelephone	CEI Citicorp Equity Holdings	Offices of holding companies, nec	Spain	Argentina
81	2.2	Salomon Smith Barney Holdings	Security brokers, dealers and flotation companies	Schroders-Worldwide Investment	Security brokers, dealers and flotation companies	The United States	The United Kingdom

82	CDC Asset Management Europe	Management-investment offices, open end	France	NVEST LP	Investment offices, nec	The United States
83	Investor Group	Investors, nec	The United Kingdom	Mark IV Industries Inc.	Rubber and plastics hose and belting	The United States
84	Thomson-CSF	Guided-missile and space-vehicle parts, nec	France	Racal Electronics PLC	Electronic computers	The United Kingdom
85	BT Hawthorn Ltd.	Telephone communications, except radiotelephone	The United Kingdom	Esat Telecom Group PLC	Communications services, nec	Ireland
86	Cisco Systems Inc.	Computer-peripheral equipment, nec	The United States	Pirelli-Fibre Optic Operations	Optical instruments and lenses	Italy
87	Metsa-Seria Oy	Paper mills	Finland	MoDo Paper AB	Paper mills	Sweden
88	Rio Tinto Ltd.	Iron ores	The United Kingdom	North Ltd.	Gold ores	Australia
89	Siemens Corp. (Siemens AG)	Communications equipment, nec	The United States	Shared Medical Systems Corp.	Computer-facilities-management services	The United States
90	Cie de Saint-Gobain SA	Abrasive products	France	Meyer International PLC	Lumber, plywood, millwork and wood panels	The United Kingdom
91	Finalrealm	Food preparations, nec	France	United Biscuits (Holdings) PLC	Frozen specialties, nec	The United Kingdom
92	Rexam PLC	Sanitary-paper products	The United Kingdom	American National Can Group	Metal cans	The United States

(continued)

Table 11A.1 (continued)

Rank	Value of Cross-Border Transaction ($ billions)	Acquiring Company		Acquired Company		Headquarters Location	
		Name	Industry	Name	Industry	Acquiring Firm	Acquired Firm
93	2.0	Worms et Cie	Life insurance	Ado Wiggins Appleton PLC	Paper mills	France	The United Kingdom
94	2.0	AXA	Life insurance	Nippon Dantai Life Insurance	Life insurance	France	Japan
95	1.9	Allianz AG	Life insurance	PIMCO Advisors Holdings LP	Investment advice	Germany	The United States
96	1.9	DaimlerChrysler AG	Motor vehicles and passenger-car bodies	Mitsubishi Motors Corp.	Motor vehicles & passenger car bodies	Germany	Japan
97	1.9	Nodal Networks Corp.	Telephone and tele-graph apparatus	CoreTek Inc.	Telephone and tele-graph apparatus	Canada	The United States
98	1.9	Telenor AS	Telephone commu-nications, except radiotelephone	Sonofon	Telephone commu-nications, except radiotelephone	Norway	Denmark
99	1.9	Nortel Networks Corp.	Telephone and tele-graph apparatus	Clarify Inc.	Prepackaged software	Canada	The United States
100	1.8	Suez Lyonnaise des Eaux SA	Water supply	United Water Resources Inc.	Water supply	France	The United States
101	1.8	British Telecommu-nications PLC	Communications services, nec	Telfort	Radiotelephone communications	The United Kingdom	The Netherlands

102	1.8	NTT DoCoMo Inc.	Telephone communications, except radiotelephone	Hutchison 3G U.K. Holdings Ltd.	Telephone communications, except radiotelephone	Japan	The United Kingdom
103	1.8	Netcom AB	Communications services, nec	Societe Europeenne de Commun	Telephone communications, except radiotelephone	Sweden	Luxembourg
104	1.8	Alcatel SA	Telephone and telegraph apparatus	Genesys Telecommun Labs	Prepackaged Software	France	The United States
105	1.8	Koninklijke Numico NV	Dry, condensed & evaporated dairy products radiotelephone	Rexall Sundown Inc.	Pharmaceutical-preparations production	The Netherlands	The United States
106	1.8	Amvescap PLC	Investment advice	Trimark Financial Corp.	Security brokers, dealers and flotation companies	The United Kingdom	Canada
107	1.7	Clariant AG	Alkalies and chlorine	BTP PLC	Industrial inorganic chemicals, nec	Switzerland	The United Kingdom
108	1.7	Investor Group	Investors, nec	Shoppers Drug Mart (Imasco Ltd.)	Drug stores and proprietary stores	The United States	Canada
109	1.7	Publicis SA	Advertising agencies	Saatchi & Saatchi PLC	Advertising agencies	France	The United Kingdom
110	1.7	Elan Corp. PLC	Pharmaceutical preparations	Dura Pharmaceuticals Inc.	Pharmaceutical preparations	Ireland	The United States
111	1.7	Skandinaviska Enskilda Banken	Banks, non-U.S. chartered	Bank fur Gemeinwirtschaft AG	Banks, non-U.S. chartered	Sweden	Germany

(continued)

Table 11A.1 (continued)

Rank	Value of Cross-Border Transaction ($ billions)	Acquiring Company		Acquired Company		Headquarters Location	
		Name	Industry	Name	Industry	Acquiring Firm	Acquired Firm
112	1.7	BAE SYSTEMS North America	Aircraft engines and engine parts	Lockheed Martin-Aerospace	Search, detection, and navigation equipment	The United States	The United States
113	1.7	AES Corp.	Electric services	CA La Electricidad de Caracas	Electric services	The United States	Venezuela
114	1.6	Nationwide Mutual Insurance Co.	Fire, marine, and casualty insurance	Gartmore Investment Management	Investment offices, nec	The United States	The United Kingdom
115	1.6	EM TV & Merchandising AG	Motion-picture and videotape distribution	SLEC Holdings Ltd.	Offices of holding companies, nec	Germany	The United Kingdom
116	1.6	Fortis (NQ NV)	Life insurance	Banque Generale du Luxembourg	Banks, non-U.S. chartered	The Netherlands	Luxembourg
117	1.6	Volkswagen AG	Motor vehicles and passenger-car bodies	Scania AB (Investor AB)	Truck and bus bodies	Germany	Sweden
118	1.6	BP Amoco PLC	Petroleum refining	Vastar Resources Inc.	Crude petroleum and natural gas	The United Kingdom	The United States
119	1.6	US Foodservice Inc.	Groceries, general line	PYA/Monarch Inc.	Groceries, general line	The United States	The United States
120	1.6	Spirent PLC	Electronic components, nec	Hekimian Labs Inc.	Electrical apparatus and equip	The United Kingdom	The United States

121	1.6	Banco Santander Central Hispan	National commercial banks	Cia de Seguros Mundial	Life insurance	Spain	Portugal
122	1.5	Banco Santander Central Hispan	National commercial banks	Grupo Financiero Serfin SA de	Banks, non-U.S. chartered	Spain	Mexico
123	1.5	Volvo AB	Motor vehicles and passenger-car bodies	Renault VI/Mack (Renault SA)	Industrial trucks, tractors, trailers and stackers	Sweden	France
124	1.5	British Sky Broadcasting Group	Cable and other pay television services	KirchPayTV GmbH (Kirch Gruppe)	Cable and other pay television services	The United Kingdom	Germany
125	1.5	Saudi Telecommunications Cc	Telephone communications, except radiotelephone	FLAG Telecom Holdings Ltd.	Telegraph and other message communications	Saudi Arabia	Bermuda
126	1.5	Adecco SA	Employment agencies	Olsten Corp.	Help supply services	Switzerland	The United States
127	1.5	Old Mutual PLC	Life insurance	United Asset Management Corp.	Investment advice	South Africa	The United States
128	1.5	Cadbury Schweppes PLC	Candy and other confectionery products	Snapple Beverage Group Inc.	Bottled & canned soft drinks and carbonated waters	The United Kingdom	The United States
129	1.4	Foster's Brewing Group Ltd.	Malt beverages	Beringer Wine Estates Holdings	Wines, brandy, and brandy spirits	Australia	The United States
130	1.4	Citizens Financial Group, R1	Savings institutions, not federally chartered	UST Corp. Boston, MA	State banks, member-fed reserve	The United States	The United States
131	1.4	Corning Inc.	Telephone and telegraph apparatus	Siemens AG-Optical Fiber, Cable	Drawing and insulating of nonferrous wire	The United States	Germany

(*continued*)

Table 11A.1 (continued)

Rank	Value of Cross-Border Transaction ($ billions)	Acquiring Company			Acquired Company			Headquarters Location	
		Name	Industry		Name	Industry		Acquiring Firm	Acquired Firm
132	1.4	Littauer Technologies Cc Ltd.	Computer-related services, nec		AsiaNet (Linkage On-Line)	Information-retrieval services		The Republic of Korea	Hong Kong, China
133	1.4	Investor Group	Investors, nec		Powercor Australia (PacifCorp)	Electric services		Hong Kong, China	Australia
134	1.4	Smurfit-Stone Container Corp.	Paperboard mills		St. Laurent Paperboard Inc.	Paperboard mills		The United States	Canada
135	1.4	BNP Paribas SA	Banks, non-U.S. chartered		Cie Benelux Paribas SA	Misc business credit		France	Belgium
136	1.4	Koninklijke PTT Nederland NV	Telephone communications, except radiotelephone		Hutchison 3G UK Holdings Ltd.	Telephone communications, except radiotelephone		The Netherlands	The United Kingdom
137	1.3	Dimension Data Holdings PLC	Prepackaged software		Comparex-Eur Networking Ops	Computer-programming services		South Africa	Germany
138	1.3	Standard Chartered PLC	Investment advice		ANZ Grindlays Bank Ltd.	Banks, non-U.S. chartered		The United Kingdom	Australia
139	1.3	Standard Chartered PLC	Investment advice		Chase Manhattan-HK Banking	Banks, non-U.S. chartered		The United Kingdom	Hong Kong, China

140	1.3	Telia AB	Telephone communications, except radiotelephone	NetCom ASA	Investors, nec	Sweden	Norway
141	1.3	AES Corp.	Electric services	Gener SA	Electric services	The United States	Chile
142	1.3	BT Bumi Modern	Crude petroleum and natural gas, radiotelephone	Gallo Oil Ltd.	Crude petroleum and natural gas production	Indonesia	The United States
143	1.3	Vivendi SA	Water supply	Elektrim Telekomunikacja Sp	Telephone communications, except radiotelephone	France	Poland
144	1.3	Singapore Power Pte Ltd.	Electric services	GPU PowerNet Pty Ltd.	Combination utilities, nec	Singapore	Australia
145	1.3	Eni SpA	Crude petroleum and natural gas	British Borneo Oil & Gas PLC	Crude petroleum and natural gas	Italy	The United Kingdom
146	1.3	Intel Corp.	Semiconductors and related devices	Giga A/S (NKT Holding)	Electronic components, nec	The United States	Denmark
147	1.2	Telia AB	Telephone communications, except radiotelephone	NetCom ASA	Investors, nec	Sweden	Norway
148	1.2	Infosources SA	Information-retrieval services	Belgacom Skynet SA	Information-retrieval services	France	Belgium
149	1.2	Assa Abloy AB	Hardware, nec	Williams PLC-Yale Locks	Hardware, nec	Sweden	The United Kingdom
150	1.2	Reliant Energy	Electric services	Energieproduktie-bedrijf UNA NV	Electric services	The United States	The Netherlands

(continued)

Table 11A.1 (continued)

Rank	Value of Cross-Border Transaction ($ billions)	Acquiring Company			Acquired Company		Headquarters Location	
		Name	Industry		Name	Industry	Acquiring Firm	Acquired Firm
151	1.2	Unicredito Italiano	Banks, non-U.S. chartered		Pioneer Group Inc.	Investment advice	Italy	The United States
152	1.2	Heidelberger Zement AG	Cement, hydraulic		Cimenteries CBR (Heidelberger)	Cement, hydraulic	Germany	Belgium
153	1.2	Investor Group	Investors, nec		Fairchild Aerospace Corp.	Aircraft	Germany	The United States
154	1.2	GN Store Nord A/S	Radio & TV broadcasting and communications equipment		Photonetics SA	Measuring & controlling devices	Denmark	France
155	1.2	Morgan Stanley Real Estate	Real-estate-investment trusts		Fonspa-Non-Performing Loans	Personal-credit institutions	The United States	Italy
156	1.2	K-L Holdings Inc. (KKR)	Investors, nec		Laporte-Non Speciality Organic	Inorganic pigments	The United States	The United Kingdom
157	1.1	Investor Group	Investors, nec		Long Term Credit Bank of Japan	Banks, non-U.S. chartered	The United States	Japan
158	1.1	Danzas Holding AG	Arrangement of transportation of freight and cargo		Air Express International Corp.	Arrangement of transportation of freight and cargo	Switzerland	The United States
159	1.1	Allianz AG	Life insurance		PIMCO Advisors LP	Investment advice	Germany	The United States

160	1.1	Deutsche Telekom AG	Radiotelephone communications	Polska Telefonia Cyfrowa Sp	Communications services, nec	Germany	Poland
161	1.1	Billiton PLC	Miscellaneous metal ores, nec	Rio Algom Ltd.	Uranium-radium vanadium ores	The United Kingdom	Canada
162	1.1	Danone Group	Fluid milk	McKesson Water Products Cc	Bottled & canned soft drinks and carbonated waters	France	The United States
163	1.1	Thomson Corp.	Newspapers: publishing or publishing and printing	Primark Corp.	Computer-related services, nec	Canada	The United States
164	1.1	Thames Water PLC	Water supply	E' town Corp.	Water supply	The United Kingdom	The United States
165	1.1	Falck Holding A/S	Detective, guard, and armored-car services	Group 4 Securitas (Intl) BV	Detective, guard, and armored-car services	Denmark	The Netherlands
166	1.1	Diamond Technology Partners	Management-consulting services	Cluster Consulting	Business consulting services, nec	The United States	Spain
167	1.1	United Pan-Europe Comm NV	Communications services, nec	Eneco C&T	Cable and other pay television services	The Netherlands	The Netherlands
168	1.1	General Motors Corp.	Motor vehicles and passenger-car bodies	Fuji Heavy Industries Ltd.	Motor vehicles and passenger-car bodies	The United States	Japan
169	1.1	Bipop-Carire	Banks, non-U.S. chartered	Entrium Direct Bankers AG	Information-retrieval services	Italy	Germany

(continued)

Table 11A.1 (continued)

	Value of Cross-Border Transaction	Acquiring Company		Acquired Company		Headquarters Location	
Rank	($ billions)	Name	Industry	Name	Industry	Acquiring Firm	Acquired Firm
170	1.0	Koninklijke Philips Electronic	Household audio and video equipment	MedQuist Inc.	Data-processing services	The Netherlands	The United States
171	1.0	Amdocs Ltd.	Computer-programming services	Solect Techology Group	Prepackaged software	The United Kingdom	Canada
172	1.0	Wengen Acquisition PLC	Investors, nec	Wassail PLC	Motor-vehicle parts and accessories	The United States	The United Kingdom
173	1.0	Investor Group	Investors, nec	Cia Energetica de Pernambuco	Electric services	Spain	Brazil
174	1.0	Kyocera Corp.	Semiconductors and related devices	QUALCOMM-Land-Based Wirele	Radiotelephone communications	Japan	The United States
175	1.0	Banco Santander Central Hispan	National commercial banks	Banco Bozano Simonsen SA	Banks, non-U.S. chartered	Spain	Spain Brazil

Table 11A.2   **Major Regulatory Changes Affecting the Banking Sectors of the Thirteen OECD Nations Considered in This Paper**

OECD Nation	Year	Short Description of Regulatory Change
The United States	1994	Implementation of the Reigle Neal Interstate Act
	1999	Implementation of the Gramm-Leach-Billey Act
Canada	1992	Phasing out of banking-reserve requirements
	1999	Relaxation of rules allowing establishment of foreign banks
Australia	1992	Relaxation of rules allowing establishment of foreign banks
	1997	End of the so-called Six Pillars policy
France	1993	Privatization of some banks
	1995	Implementation of a deposit-insurance directive
Germany	1992	Implementation of second European Banking Directive
Italy	1993	Implementation of second European Banking Directive
	1994	Privatization of some banks
The United Kingdom	1998	Financial Services Authority takes on some bank regulatory powers

Source: BIS (2001, annex II.3).

Note: This table is not supposed to summarize all of the regulatory changes in the thirteen OECD nations during the years 1990 to 1999. Rather, using BIS (2001), it identifies that major regulatory changes that affected a nation's banking sector during the years that it was in the unbalanced panel. Therefore, if a nation was in the unbalanced panel from 1990 to 1993, changes in the regulatory regime for banks after 1993 would not be reported.

References

Bank of International Settlements (BIS). 2001. *Report on consolidation in the financial sector.* Basel, Switzerland: BIS.

Berger, Allen N., Robert DeYoung, Hensa Genay, and Gregory F. Udell. 2000. Globalization of financial institutions: Evidence from cross-border banking performance. In *Brookings-Wharton Papers on Financial Services: 2000,* ed. Robert E. Litan and Anthony M. Snatomero, 23–158. Washington, D.C.: Brookings Institution.

Bhagwati, Jagdish N. 1968. *The theory and practice of commercial policy.* Princeton, N.J.: Princeton University Press.

Black, Bernard S. 2000a. Is this the first international merger wave? *M&A Lawyer* (July/August): 20–26.

———. 2000b. The first international merger wave (and the fifth and last U.S. wave). *University of Miami Law Review* 54:799–818.

Calomiris, Charles W., and Jason Karceski. 2000. Is the bank merger wave of the 1990s efficient? Lessons from nine case studies. In *Mergers and productivity,* ed. Steven N. Kaplan, 93–178. Cambridge, Mass.: National Bureau of Economic Research.

Carow, Kenneth A., and Edward J. Kane. 2002. Event-study evidence on the value of relaxing longstanding regulatory restraints on banks, 1970–2000. *Quarterly Journal of Economics and Finance* 43 (summer): 649–71.

Consumer Union Trust Society (CUTS). 2003. *Pulling up our socks: A study of competition regimes of seven developing countries of Africa and Asia.* Jaipur, India: CUTS.

Dermine, Jean. 1999. The economics of bank mergers in the European Union, a review of the public policy issues. INSEAD, Finance Department. Mimeograph.

Evenett, Simon J. 2002. How much have merger review laws reduced cross border mergers and acquisitions? In *International merger control: Prescriptions for convergence,* ed. William K. Rowley. London: International Bar Association.

———. 2003a. *A study on issues relating to a possible multilateral framework on competition policy.* Report commissioned by the Secretariat of the World Trade Organization (WTO), no. WT/WGTCP/W/228, May 2003. Geneva, Switzerland: WTO.

———. 2003b. Do all networks facilitate international commerce? U.S. law firms and the international market for corporate control. NBER Working Paper no. 9663. Cambridge, Mass.: National Bureau of Economic Research, May.

———. 2003c. What future for regional competition policy in Latin America? In *Bridges for Development: Policies and Institutions for Trade and Integration,* ed. Robert Devlin and Antoni Estevad Cordal, 229–55. Washington, D.C.: The InterAmerican Development Bank, forthcoming.

Evenett, Simon J., Alexander Lehmann, and Benn Steil, eds. 2000. *Antitrust goes global: What future for transatlantic cooperation?* Washington, D.C.: The Brookings Institution Press.

Feliciano, Zadia, and Robert E. Lipsey. 2002. Foreign entry in U.S. manufacturing by takeovers and the creation of new firms. The City University of New York (CUNY), Queens College and the Graduate Center. Mimeograph.

Hoekman, Bernard M., and Petros C. Mavroidis. 2003. Economic development, competition policy and the WTO. *Journal of World Trade* 37 (1): 1–27.

International Competition Policy Advisory Committee (ICPAC). 2000. *Final report.* Washington, D.C.: GPO.

Kang, Nam-Hoon, and Sara Johansson. 2000. Cross-border mergers and acquisitions: Their role in industrial globalisation. Science, Technology, and Industry (STI) Working Paper no. 2000/1. Paris: Organization for Economic Cooperation and Development (OECD).

Levenstein, Margaret C., and Valerie Y. Suslow. 2001. Private international cartels and the effect on developing countries. Background Paper to the *World development report 2001.* Washington, D.C.: World Bank.

Mehta, Pradeep, and Nitya Nanda. 2003. Competition issues with international dimensions: How do developing countries deal with them? Consumer Union Trust Society (CUTS) Centre on Competition, Investment and Economic Regulation, Jaipur, India. Mimeograph.

Mody, Ashoka, and Shoko Negishi. 2000. Cross-border mergers and acquisitions in East Asia: Trends and implications. *Finance and Development* 38 (1): 6–9.

Muris, Timothy J. 2001. Merger enforcement in a world of multiple arbiters. Paper presented at the Brookings Roundtable on Trade and Investment Policy. December 21, 2001, Washington, D.C.

Neven, Damien, and Lans Henrik Roller. 2000. The allocation of jurisdiction in international antitrust. *European Economic Review* 44 (5): 845–55.

Organization for Economic Cooperation and Development (OECD). 2001. *New patterns of industrial globalisation: Cross-border mergers and acquisitions and strategic alliances.* Paris: OECD.

———. 2003. *Second report by the Competition Committee on Effective Action Against Hard Core Cartels.* Paris: OECD.

Pryor, Frederic M. 2001. Dimensions of the worldwide merger boom. *Journal of Economic Issues,* forthcoming.

Rowley, William K., ed. 2002. *International merger control: Prescriptions for convergence.* London: International Bar Association (IBA).

United Nations Conference on Trade and Development (UNCTAD). Various Years. *World investment report.* Geneva: UNCTAD.

Vives, Xavier. 2001. Competition in the changing world of banking. *Oxford Review of Economic Policy* 17 (4): 535–47.

White & Case. 2001. *Survey of worldwide antitrust merger notification requirements.* Washington, D.C.: White & Case.

World Bank. 2000. *The world development report 1999/2000, entering the 21st century: The changing development landscape.* Washington, D.C.: World Bank.

World Trade Organization (WTO). 2002. *Report (2002) of the working group on the interaction between trade and competition policy to the general council.* WTO document no. WT/WGTCP/6. Washington, D.C.: WTO, December.

Comment   Rod Falvey

The success of multilateral trade negotiations in reducing barriers to trade and investment flows, and the extensive programs of deregulation and privatization that have taken place in many countries, have opened up their domestic markets to greater competition from foreign firms. In traded-goods markets this competition can come through increased flows of products across borders. For nontraded goods it comes from the establishment of foreign-owned suppliers, through greenfield FDI or cross-border mergers and acquisitions (CBMA).

This chapter investigates the CBMA wave of the late 1990s. Section 11.2 describes this wave in some detail. This material provides us with a useful picture of the characteristics and magnitudes of the CBMA wave of the 1990s, both in absolute terms and relative to the smaller wave that occurred in the previous decade. Two points stand out: the relative importance of "mega deals" (those involving assets over $1 billion), and the concentration in a small number of service sectors, which are "pretty much immune to import competition."

I have two comments on this part of the paper, both concerned with the role and measurement of regulatory policies. The author observes that, in contrast to the general liberalization of policies toward greenfield FDI, national policies toward mergers and acquisitions (both within and across borders) may have become more stringent throughout the 1990s. The specific point made is that there has been an increase in the number of jurisdictions (including both developed and developing countries) with merger review requirements. Although the two are not inconsistent, this claim does sit rather awkwardly with the evidence on the magnitude of this merger wave, and appears to deserve further investigation. Controls for regulatory changes are included in the econometric analysis in section

Rod Falvey is the Leverhulme Professor of International Economics at the University of Nottingham.

11.3, and appear to have significant effects, but it is not clear whether this evidence indicates that regulators have become less lenient.

The author also comments that CBMAs may have economic effects that spill across national boundaries and that will not be taken into account by regulators. Thus, a CBMA may be vetoed in some jurisdictions even though its net global effects are positive. Of course, the same can be true of within-border MAs, whose economic effects can also extend across international boundaries. One might be concerned that a merger toward monopoly is more likely to be approved by national regulators in cases where exports are significant. Mergers and acquisitions can generate terms-of-trade effects which are gains for some jurisdictions, but which net out at the global level. The case for international cooperation may be stronger than is claimed.

Section 11.3 then undertakes an econometric investigation of whether CBMAs in the banking sector have resulted in greater or smaller interest rate spreads in thirteen OECD countries. This analysis raises a number of interesting issues.

First, the underlying argument is that the output of banks is financial intermediation, and that the interest rate spread is the "price" of such intermediation. Unless the diversity of spreads across nations (as shown in table 11.7) can be argued to reflect differences in other charges (e.g., fixed fees and transactions charges) for financial intermediation across jurisdictions, this seems to provide strong evidence that these national markets are far from internationally integrated.

Second, the summary statistics in table 11.7 (particularly those relating to the number of banks and the five-firm concentration ratios) suggest that it is very unlikely that all banks are offering the same range of financial intermediation services. This heterogeneity may help to explain the limited explanatory power of the model.

Third, both the summary data in tables 11.5 and 11.6 and the econometric results suggest that (a) mergers and acquisitions and (b) joint ventures and strategic alliances (JVSAs) perform rather different roles in the banking sector. While within-border mergers and acquisitions are far more common than CBMAs, for nine of the countries cross-border JVSAs are the more common. It would be useful to know more about the similarities and differences between these linkages, particularly since the econometric results indicate that JVSAs tend to raise the interest rate spread. Are JVSAs allowing banking firms to circumvent regulatory controls? In particular, can firms substitute some form of JVSA, where they suspect a merger or acquisition would not be approved?

Fourth, the author notes that mergers and acquisitions have two potentially opposing influences on the interest rate spread in general: they reduce the number of competitors (the "market power" effect) and (may) increase average efficiency. That CBMAs will reduce the number of competitors seems relatively straightforward for traded goods, but is less clear cut for nontraded goods and services, where the CBMA could signal the entry of an efficient foreign competitor. In common with the rest of the empirical literature, the econometric analysis uses a number of variables to explain the interest rate spread. Unfortunately, the links between these variables and the two effects are not always clear cut. Perhaps a simple Cournot model might clarify the issues. Let s denote the interest rate spread, and suppose the demand for financial intermediation can be represented by a simple linear function $d = D - s$. There are n banks, and bank j has constant unit cost c_j. Then the equilibrium spread is $s^e = (D + n\bar{c})/(n + 1)$, where $\bar{c} = (\sum_{j=1}^{n} c_j/n)$ is the average unit cost. The macroeconomic controls would then work through D. In general, we would expect mergers and acquisitions to reduce both n and $\bar{c}$. The former would raise the equilibrium spread, but the latter would reduce it. Since the regression equations control for the number of firms, the merger and acquisition variables should be capturing the effect on "average efficiency." The evidence suggests that CBMAs into the European Union (EU) have increased average efficiency. There is no evidence that the corresponding CBMAs outside the EU have changed average efficiency at all. One can also use this model to solve for the five-firm concentration ratio, which turns out to be

$$\frac{5}{n}\left[1 + \frac{(n + 1)(\bar{c} - \bar{c}_s)}{D - \bar{c}}\right],$$

where $\bar{c}_s$ is the average unit cost of the five largest (i.e., most efficient) firms. The value of this variable will also be affected by mergers and acquisitions but not in any straightforward fashion.

Finally, although this point should be fairly obvious, when the author uses the estimated parameters to quantify the effects of mergers and acquisitions and of strategic alliances on interest rate spreads, readers should recall that some of these calculations are based on parameters estimated with very limited precision.

V

Macroeconomics

12

Financial Opening: Evidence and Policy Options

Joshua Aizenman

12.1 Introduction

This paper has two goals. First, it evaluates the empirical evidence of increasing the chances of financial crises induced by opening up developing countries to short-term capital inflows. Second, it appraises the various proposals made for mitigating the severity of financial crises. We argue that there is solid evidence that financial opening increases the chance of financial crises. There is more tenuous evidence that financial opening contributes positively to long-run growth. Hence, there may be a complex trade-off between the adverse intermediate run and the beneficial long-run effects of financial opening. These findings impose the challenge to policy makers of how to supplement financial opening with policies that would improve this intertemporal trade-off. The literature abounds with proposals aimed at reducing the costs of financial crises, yet there has been limited progress in designing credible reforms to deal with these challenges.

To put this issue in a broader context, the debate about financial opening is a reincarnation of the earlier immiserizing-growth literature that identified conditions under which growth may be welfare reducing in the presence of preexisting distortions.[1] While financial opening increases welfare when the only distortion is restricting intertemporal trade across countries, financial opening may be welfare reducing in the presence of

Joshua Aizenman is professor of economics at the University of California, Santa Cruz, and a research associate of the National Bureau of Economic Research.

Prepared for the NBER Center for Economic Policy Research (CEPR) Challenges to Globalization conference, 24–25 May, 2002, Stockholm, organized by Robert Baldwin and Alan Winters. I would like to thank Bob Baldwin, Simon Evenett, Blake Lebaron, Bob Stern, and the participants at the conference meetings for very useful comments. Any errors are mine.

1. See Johnson (1967), Bhagwati (1968), and Brecher and Diaz-Alejandro (1977).

other distortions. An important example of such a distortion is moral hazard, which frequently acts as an implicit subsidy to borrowing and investment.[2] Moral hazard arises when investors believe they will be bailed out of bad investment by the taxpayer. This bailing out may be carried out by the treasury, the central bank, or by international agencies (e.g., the International Monetary Fund [the IMF], World Bank, etc.). In these circumstances, the taxpayer subsidizes the investment.

A frequent rationale for the bailing out is the "too big to fail" doctrine—the fear that allowing large borrowers to go under will trigger a systemic crisis (this fear is referred to as the "systemic risk"). See Dooley and Shin (2000) and Bongini, Claessens, and Ferri (2001) for empirical validations of the moral-hazard interpretation in the context of the recent crisis in the Far East. It can be shown that the moral-hazard argument applies even in the absence of any bail out and in circumstances where the investment is debt financed, and the riskiness of investment is private information. This result follows from the nature of the limited-liability system, which implies that the value of the firm behaves as an option, thus leading to excessive risk taking (see Aizenman 2003).

In financial autarky, the pool of domestic savings confines the cost of the moral-hazard distortion. Financial opening implies that the scale of investment will be determined by the access to global saving. In autarky, if the domestic real interest rate exceeded the global one, the resultant inflow of capital would magnify the existing distortion, thereby reducing welfare. This situation is illustrated in figure 12.1, where S depicts domestic saving, and I is the domestic investment in the absence of moral hazard. Moral hazard would shift the effective investment to I'. In these circumstances, the welfare cost of moral hazard is given by the black triangle in panel A (where the benchmark for evaluating welfare in panel A is financial autarky in the absence of moral hazard). If the global interest rate is r^*, financial opening in the presence of moral hazard reduces welfare by the shaded triangle (where the benchmark for evaluating welfare in panel B is the welfare with open financial markets in the absence of moral hazard). If the supply of domestic saving is relatively inelastic, whereas the demand for investment is relatively elastic, financial opening will tend to reduce welfare. A similar argument applies to other distortions.

The more recent literature dealing with welfare effects of financial opening added to the earlier studies by modeling the process of financial intermediation. A key difference between the earlier literature and the ones dealing with financial intermediation is the switch in focus from the commercial to the financial aspects of opening up. This matters, as the adjustment of financial markets to news and policies is much faster than that of

2. See McKinnon and Pill (1996); Corsetti, Pesenti, and Roubini (1999); Dooley (2000); and Hellmann, Murdock, and Stiglitz (2000).

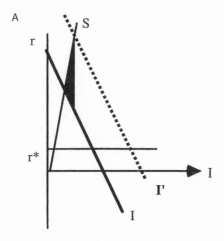

Financial   autarky

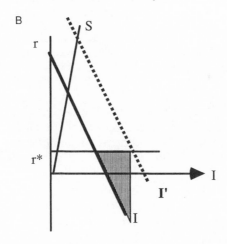

Financial   integration

Fig. 12.1   Financial opening, moral hazard, and welfare: *A,* **Financial autarky;** *B,* **Financial integration**

commercial flows of goods and services. A by-product of this switch is the focus of the new literature on conditions leading to the instantaneous reversal in the flow of financial assets, which generates financial crises.

This recent literature has led to a spirited debate concerning the wisdom of unrestricted capital mobility between the Organization for Economic

Table 12.1   The Welfare Effects of Financial Opening—Theory

The Welfare Effect of Financial Opening	Explanation
Potentially large benefits	Financial opening may lead to large benefits stemming from better risk pooling, information collection, and maturity transformation, thereby providing deeper liquidity (Greenwood and Jovanovic 1990; Obstfeld 1994; Acemoglu and Zilibotti 1998).
Positive but small benefits from financial opening	Second-order magnitude gains from international diversification of output risk (Cole and Obstfeld 1991).
Ambiguous welfare effects	If production does involve learning by doing, opening capital markets does not necessarily improve welfare for the nation or for the world as a whole (Kohn and Marion 1992). Overborrowing due to moral hazard and euphoric expectations, leading to crises (McKinnon and Pill 1996; Corsetti, Pesenti, and Roubini 1999); overborrowing due to congestion externalities, where atomistic agents do not internalize the full effects of marginal borrowing on future welfare (Aizenman 1989); and overborrowing due to free-rider problems in economies short of international collateral, a condition generated by imperfections of the domestic capital market (Caballero and Krishnamurthy 2001). Emerging markets are more prone to financial crashes. This will be the case when financial market capitalization depends on the expectations of agents regarding aggregate investment in their economy. This gives rise to potential coordination failures, which may be exacerbated for low-income countries by financial globalization (Martin and Rey 2001).

Cooperation and Development (OECD) and emerging markets. Various studies have identified circumstances in which unlimited capital mobility may be suboptimal (see table 12.1 for a summary of some of these studies). Notwithstanding the aforementioned debate, the strongest argument for financial opening is the pragmatic one. Like it or not, greater trade integration erodes the effectiveness of restrictions on capital mobility. Hence, for successful emerging markets that engage in trade integration, financial opening is not a question of if, but of when and how. Consequently, the pragmatic approach to the problem should recognize that there is no quick fix to the exposure to financial crises induced by financial opening. Instead, the challenge is to reduce the depth and the frequency of the crises. The core of the problem is that we deal with incomplete financial markets, exposing the creditors to sovereign risk and moral hazard.[3] As there are fundamental reasons for the incompletion of these markets, one doubts whether or not a smart fix exists that will prevent future crises. Instead, the hope is that new policies and improved coordination will reduce the severity of financial crises, thereby improving the odds of a positive long-run welfare effect of financial opening.

Section 12.2 starts with the review of the empirical evidence. Section

3. For a review of the literature on sovereign risk, see Eaton and Fernandez (1995).

12.3 reviews the various proposals attempting to reform the global financial system. Section 12.4 provides an appraisal of the various proposals made for preventing financial crises. Specifically, it argues that a version of the Lucas critique may limit the welfare gain of these proposals. Of course, this is not an argument against adopting reforms. It suggests, however, that a better understanding of the structural characteristics leading to exposure and crises is the key for designing a successful restructuring of the capital market. A reform that would not deal with these structural factors runs the risk of leading to disappointing welfare gains, at best, and to crises in the worst case. Some of the reforms may fall short of success due to coordination failure: They may be effective only if they would be adopted comprehensively by all the relevant financial centers. Finally, some of the proposals may be too optimistic, ignoring the time inconsistency and political-economy considerations that would challenge the practicality of the best-intended reforms, as well as presuming the ability to verify unambiguously the quality of macroeconomic adjustment.

12.2   Financial Opening and Financial Crises: The Evidence

The recent research has two common themes: It validated empirically the assertion "Good-bye financial repression, hello financial crash" (Diaz-Alejandro 1985), yet it also found tenuous evidence that financial liberalization tends to increase growth over time. Both observations suggest an intertemporal trade-off. In the short run, the fragility induced by financial opening leads frequently to crises, but if these crises would force the country to deal with its structural deficiencies, financial opening may induce a higher growth rate in the long run. The empirical literature relies frequently on cross-country methodology. Thus, it provides us with little guidance in evaluating the net-welfare effects of financial opening. For example, it remains hard to gauge if Korea would have been better off by refraining from financial opening in the early 1990s, or if Chile would have benefited by retaining financial repression in the 1980s and 1990s.[4] The an-

---

4. Obviously, the 1997 financial crisis had an adverse impact on Korea's welfare. One may argue, however, that it prevented a much deeper and longer calamity, akin to Japan's recession in the last ten years. Arguably, had Korea continued with financial repression, a Japanese type of a correction would have hit Korea later. Korea's development path resembles that of Japan—its domestic banks accumulated over time large nonperforming loans. These loans were the heritage of the earlier development strategy in which large corporations had selective access to preferential lines of credit. According to this argument, the crisis of 1997 prevented a larger buildup of these loans, saving Korea from a much deeper correction. Obviously, it is hard to provide a sound test of this argument. See Haggard (2000) for further discussion on the interaction between the public and the private sector in Korea and other countries in the Far East. Similar ambiguities apply to Chile, which has been the best performing Latin American country in recent years and is credited with a sound banking system. Yet, Chile experienced a massive banking crisis in the 1980s following earlier financial opening. Arguably, one may credit the superior recent performance of Chile to the painful earlier reforms that were triggered by the crises of the early 1980s.

swers to these questions depend crucially on the time horizon of the analysis as well as on the evaluation of what is the relevant counterfactual; both are issues to which there are no satisfactory answers.[5]

We illustrate the empirical literature by reviewing selectively several examples. Kaminsky and Reinhart (1999) found that problems in the banking sector typically precede a currency crisis and that a currency crisis deepens the banking crisis, activating a vicious spiral. Importantly, they also found that financial liberalization often precedes banking crises. Similar results were replicated in several papers using different methodologies. Glick and Hutchison (1999) investigated a sample of ninety countries during 1975 to 1997, covering 90 banking crises, 202 currency crises, and 37 twin crises. They found that banking and twin crises have occurred mainly in developing countries, and their number increased in the 1990s. Twin crises are mainly concentrated in financially liberalized emerging-market economies. These findings support the conjecture that openness of emerging markets to international capital flows, combined with a liberalized financial structure, makes them particularly vulnerable to twin crises. *The costs of these crises are substantial.* Currency crisis, on average, leads to a cost of 8 percent of precrisis gross domestic product (GDP). Simultaneous currency and banking crises reduce the precrisis GDP by 18 percent (World Bank 1998; Caprio and Honohan 1999).

Demirgüç-Kunt and Detragiache (1998) studied the empirical relationship between banking crises and financial liberalization in fifty-three countries during 1980 to 1995. They found that banking crises are more likely to occur in liberalized financial systems. The impact of financial liberalization on the fragility of banks is weaker, however, when the institutional environment is strong. (Relevant institutional characteristics are respect for the rule of law, a low level of corruption, and good contract enforcement.) They found that banks' franchise values decline after financial liberalization. Hence, the intensification of the moral hazard associated with lower franchise values may be one of the sources of increased banking-sector fragility. Financial liberalization is followed by improved financial development, while banking crises tend to slow it down. In countries that liberalize from a position of financial repression, financial development improves even if a banking crisis takes place. Their results support the view that financial liberalization should be approached cautiously where the institutions necessary to ensure law and contract enforcement and effective prudential regulation and supervision are not fully developed, even if macroeconomic stabilization has been achieved.

A useful survey of financial liberalization is Williamson and Mahar

---

5. A welfare evaluation of these issues may depend on the degree to which there are political economy trade-offs between a large crisis versus a series of smaller crises; a large crisis may be needed to overcome entrenched opposing interest groups, yet it may lead to larger welfare costs.

(1998), who focused on thirty-four countries that undertook financial liberalization between 1973 to 1996. Overall, they found a mixed record of financial liberalization—the gains are there, but the liberalization carries the risk of leading to financial crisis. Financial liberalization has yielded greater financial depth, and increased efficiency in the allocation of investment, yet it has not brought a boost in saving. The drawbacks in the liberalization process are the danger that the liberalization will lead to a financial crisis. For the majority of countries, capital-account liberalization increases its probability. The challenge is to design a liberalization program that does not bring a financial crisis in its wake. The main recommendations emerging from their study are akin to Hellman, Murdock, and Stiglitz (2000); start with macroeconomic stabilization and improve bank supervision while delaying capital-account convertibility until the end of the process. In the transition, mild financial repression, in the form of a ceiling on deposit interest rates, may be advantageous. This follows from the observation that exceedingly high interest rates encourage risk taking by borrowers—that is, moral hazard induced by self-selection. Banks in stress may wish to gamble for resurrection by lending to such borrowers, which is ultimately at a cost to the taxpayer. Williamson and Mahar conclude that maintaining high spreads may be needed in a transition until banks are able to work off the legacy of bad debt inherited from the period of financial repression. In such an environment, free entry of foreign banks may be a mixed blessing. The efficiency gains should be balanced against the threat of the gamble for resurrection by older domestic banks that are losing their franchise value. Imposing higher capital requirements increases the cost of a gamble-for-resurrection strategy. In these circumstances, deposit-rate controls may complement capital requirements.

The overall effect of financial opening on growth remains debatable. Levine (1997) found a positive association, whereas Rodrik (1998) failed to depict any positive effects of financial opening on investment, growth, and inflation. While Levine's interpretation attaches the direction of causality from financial deepening to growth, the old dictum that correlations do not indicate causality remains valid. More recently, Beck, Levine, and Loayza (2000) evaluated the empirical links between the level of financial intermediary development and economic growth, total factor productivity (TFP) growth, physical-capital accumulation, and private-savings rates. The main findings are that financial intermediaries exert a large, positive impact on total-factor-productivity growth, which feeds through to overall GDP growth. Yet, the long-run links between financial intermediary development and both physical-capital growth and private-savings rates are tenuous. Bekaert, Harvey, and Lundblad (2001) found that equity-market liberalizations, on average, lead to a one percent increase in annual real economic growth over a five-year period. The investment-GDP ratio increases postliberalization, with the investment partially financed by foreign capital, which inducing worsened trade balances. The liberalization effect is enhanced by a large secondary-school enrollment, a small government sector, and an Anglo-Saxon legal system.[6]

Rodrik's earlier methodology has been revisited by Arteta, Eichengreen, and Wyplosz (2001). While they found indications of a positive association between capital-account liberalization and growth, the effects vary with time, with how capital account liberalization is measured, and with how the relationship is estimated. The evidence that the effects of capital-account liberalization are stronger in high-income countries is fragile. There is some evidence that the positive growth effects of liberalization are stronger in countries with strong institutions. Capital-account liberalization appears to have positive effects on growth only in countries that have already opened more generally, hence sequencing matters. But there are significant prerequisites for opening, including a reduction of trade barriers and an ability to eliminate macroeconomic imbalances. These conclusions are akin to Edwards (2001a) who reported that, after controlling for other variables (including aggregate investment), countries with a more open capital account have outperformed countries that have restricted capital mobility. There is also evidence that an open capital account affects growth positively only after a country has achieved a certain degree of economic development. This provides support to the view that there is an optimal sequencing for capital account liberalization.

12.3 Proposals for Preventing Financial Crises Induced by Financial Opening

This section provides a brief summary of the various proposals.[7] These reforms can be classified along several dimensions. First, proposals differ in the weight given to reforming the incentives facing creditors, debtors, or to the interaction between the two groups. Second, proposals differ in the weight given to ex ante risk reduction, versus ex post orderly management and resolution of actual crises. Third, proposals differ in the depth of the reform. Some deal with upgrading regulations within the existing institutional environment, whereas others suggest bolder steps, envisioning the creation of new institutions. Table 12.2 summarizes the main proposals.

One line of reform focuses on the possibility that, by subsidizing sovereign borrowing, the involvement of institutions may exacerbate the problem, inducing moral hazard. For example, the belief that the IMF, World Bank, and banking-deposit-insurances schemes will bail out creditors generates overborrowing and ends with more frequent and deeper crises at the

---

6. As is frequently the case with empirical studies relying on marcrodata, endogeneity and reverse causality remain a valid concern in interpreting some of these results.

7. Several recent monographs overviewed comprehensively the various proposals; see Eichengreen (1999), Rogoff (1999), Frankel and Roubini (2003), and Feldstein (2003).

Table 12.2   Overview of Proposals

Proposition Author	Emphasis	Key Features
Meltzer Committee Report	Ex ante steps to reduce the moral hazard induced by institutional bailouts	The IMF would provide unconditional short-term credit only to countries that are preapproved (ex ante conditionality). The credit is at penalty rate. They recommend to restrain the IMF's ability to allocate credit using ex post conditionality and to prevent the IMF from supporting countries that follow loose fiscal and monetary discipline.
Basle Committee	Ex ante risk management by creditors	The adjustment of the minimum-capital standards to the risk exposure of banks, including an adjustment for sovereign risk. This is done in order to mitigate moral hazard induced by deposit insurance, which is due to the "too big to fail" systemic-risk doctrine.
Eichengreen (1999)	Ex ante risk management by debtors	Argues for Chilean-style capital-inflow taxes as the only effective solution to the dangers of an open capital account when risk management is inadequate, supervision and regulation are not effective, and there is a culture of explicit guarantees.
Sachs (1995) and Miller and Zhang (2000)	Ex post crisis resolution	Adopting international bankruptcy-style procedures akin to those applied to corporate debt. The proposed procedure provides better coordination among competing creditors, as well as a short-run relief to the debtor from the induced credit crunch, enabling the continuation of export and production. This would be done as part of a controlled restructuring, and may include issuing new senior debt.
Portes (2000)		The addition of collective-action clauses to loan agreements and the establishment of standing-bondholders committees are needed for a market-based solution to be feasible.

(continued)

Table 12.2 (continued)

Proposition Author	Emphasis	Key Features
Krueger (2001)		She proposes international workout mechanism: a framework offering a debtor country legal protection from creditors that stand in the way of a necessary restructuring in exchange for an obligation of the debtor to negotiate with its creditors in good faith and to put in place policies that would prevent a similar problem from arising in the future.
Buiter and Sibert (1999)	Crisis mitigation and resolution	They propose attaching to all foreign-currency liabilities the option entitling the borrowers to extend the debt for a specified period at a mandatory penalty rate.
Soros (1998)	Ex ante insurance against default	They propose insurance by a global authority, akin to a global FDIC. Borrowers would pay the premium. International monitors (like the IMF or the BIS) would set borrowing ceilings and no bailouts would be enforced on noninsured loans.
Jeanne (2003)		He proposes a crisis-insurance fund that bails out countries conditional on the payment of the risk premium and on making the needed fiscal adjustments.
Rogoff (1999)	Ex ante steps to reduce crises incidence	Shifting financing from debt to equity is proposed. This would be facilitated by mitigating the factors contributing to the bias towards debt [like a deposit insurance that subsidizes bank intermediation, underdeveloped equity markets in emerging markets, etc.).
Kaminsky, Lizondo, and Reinhar (1998)		They propose a warning system for crises that takes into account a broad variety of indicators.

taxpayers' expense. A profound reform of the IMF, as suggested by the Meltzer committee (Meltzer 1998), would restrict the IMF's role to helping countries meeting ex ante conditionality (see also Jeanne 2003). Another radical approach calls for the formation of a global lender of last resort (see Soros 1998), an approach that would institutionalize a global type of the Federal Deposit Insurance Corporation (FDIC) arrangement. All these proposals share the concern of minimizing ex post bailouts that were not preapproved at the lending stage.

A less aggressive approach to provide greater stability is the imposition of reserve requirements on lenders, borrowers, or both, as well as the possibility of capital-adequacy requirements that are linked to the bank's portfolio risk. The Basle committee (as well as Greenspan 1998) advocates this approach. The rationale for the reserve requirements is provided by the presence of various externalities. On the lender's side, the anticipation of bailouts is introducing an externality, where marginal lending has adverse impacts on the taxpayer. On the borrower's side, as long as partial defaults are costly, marginal borrowing affects all agents by increasing the probability of a costly default that would have an impact on all (see Aizenman and Turnovsky 2002). Alternatively, emerging markets may enact similar policies aimed at curbing short-term financial flows, akin to the Chilean system in the 1990s (see Eichengreen 1999).[8]

A different tack of reforms has focused on the ex post resolution of crises. One approach advocates institutionalizing ex ante the possibility of credit relief in bad times. This may be accomplished by attaching to all foreign-currency liabilities the option that entitles the borrowers to extend the debt for a specified period at a mandatory penalty rate (see Buiter and Sibert 1999). In order to facilitate the coordination among large numbers of diffused lenders, various proposals advocate deeper institutional changes. The adoption of a modified version of domestic bankruptcy procedure has been frequently advocated (see Sachs 1995; Miller and Zhang 2000; Kreuger 2001). Specifically, such an international workout mechanism would aim at minimizing the cost of protracted negotiations. It would allow the debtor the continuation of export and production with minimal disturbances. It would also serve to coordinate among the diffused creditors, thereby allowing smoother and faster resolution of the standoff between the involved parties.

---

8. See De Gregorio, Edwards, and Valdes (2000) for a mixed review of Chile's experience with controls on inflows. Edwards (2001b, 25) concludes that these controls "were successful in changing the maturity profile of capital inflows, and of the country's foreign debt. Also, the controls allowed the monetary authority to have greater control over monetary policy. This effect, however, appears to have been confined to the short run, and was not very important quantitatively." In evaluating Chile's experience, one should keep in mind that Chile has been the best performing country in Latin America in recent years. Hence, Chile's experience may provide limited inference about the potential benefits of controls on inflows to countries with more-fragile financial systems.

12.4   Reforming the Financial System: The Challenges

The growing list of proposed reforms is indicative of the emerging consensus that the present financial architecture needs a major overhaul. While it is easy to point out the flaws of the existing system, any fundamental reform will confront a host of challenges. We review briefly some of the general issues involved and illustrate their relevance in understanding the limitations of various proposals.

12.4.1   The Lucas Critique: Political Economy and Coordination Failure

Any significant reform will change agents' behavior in ways that are hard to predict without understanding the fundamental forces explaining sovereign borrowing and default. Some of the relevant fundamentals are determined by the political-economy characterization of emerging markets and by the challenges confronting attempts to deal with coordination failures. A version of the Lucas critique applies; without a fuller understanding of the fundamental forces leading to exposure and crises, suggested reforms may lead to disappointing results, at best, and welfare reduction at worst.[9] We illustrate these considerations by analyzing the potential pitfalls in several proposed reforms.

12.4.2   Debt Maturity Structure

Jeanne (2003) illustrates the importance of understanding the forces leading to vulnerability as a necessary condition for evaluating the welfare effects of changing the international financial architecture. Specifically, he focused on understanding the maturity structure of countries' external liabilities as the solution to an incentives problem. He considered a country attempting to borrow when there is uncertainty about its solvency due to exogenous shocks. The country can enhance its solvency by implementing a costly fiscal adjustment, and it can borrow on a short-term or a long-term basis. This situation imposes a trade-off—when government's solvency deteriorates, short-term debt becomes less expensive or more accessible than long-term debt. This comes with a cost: The government is under more pressure to restore the fiscal situation if its debt has a shorter maturity because it is more vulnerable to a crisis in which creditors do not roll over

---

9. The Lucas critique stresses that economic relationships observed would be modified when policies or economic conditions change. This result follows from the observation that changes in policies affect the incentives and the budget constraints facing economic agents. Hence, new policies would alter the behavior of agents, thereby modifying the observed correlations. If policymakers attempt to take advantage of past statistical relationships, the effects manipulating thought expectations and agents' behavior may cause the relationships to break down (See Lucas 1976). Applications of the Lucas critique include the Phillips curve (illustrating the ineffectiveness of anticipated monetary policy) and the ineffectiveness of temporary changes in taxes.

their claims. This is due to the observation that short-term debt opens the door to self-fulfilling crises in which creditors stop rolling over their loans for an extraneous reason unrelated to the fundamentals. There is a tension, thus, between the disciplinary benefits of short-term debt and the risk of unwarranted rollover crises.

In this context, Jeanne investigates the welfare effect of institutions that facilitate an orderly workout of debt crises (e.g., an international bankruptcy court and officially sanctioned standstills) and of international lender of last resort. These measures are shown to improve welfare but to fall short of the first best. The first best in Jeanne's model is achieved by a crisis-insurance fund, which ex post bails out countries conditional on the ex ante fiscal adjustment and payment of a risk premium.

12.4.3 Transparency and the Feasibility of the Crisis-Insurance Fund Conditional on Ex Ante Adjustment Effort

It is noncontroversial that a minimum level of transparency of financial positions and policies is a necessary condition for financial markets to exist and to operate,[10] yet it is not clear that greater transparency would eliminate the exposure to crises. Setting standards for transparency may encourage creative accounting in which each crisis exposes new loopholes, inducing a change in the required rules of the game. While "transparency creep" is unavoidable, putting too much faith in the importance of transparency may lead some investors to a false sense of security. Indeed, full information does not negate the possibility of crises induced by multiple equilibria.

One of the innovative proposals dealing with reforming the IMF is to insure countries against financial crises only if they met ex ante criteria (see Jeanne 2003; Meltzer 1998). A necessary condition for such a scheme is transparency. In practice, however, verification is costly and fuzzy. Frequently, it takes a major crisis to force the "real books" to open (see the case of Korean's reserves in the 1997 crisis, and the recent Enron fiasco). These practical considerations suggest that it is only in the aftermath of a crisis that we learn the degree to which the ex ante criteria were met, since a crisis may reveal that some of these criteria were met only superficially. It may be hard to verify ex ante if the institutional environment changed enough to warrant the insurance. Hence, costly monitoring and the impossibility to fully verify the depth of the adjustment limit the applicability of this proposal. In these circumstances, we are left with no clean solutions, and there may be no escape from the need to muddle through protracted negotiations in the aftermath of crises.

---

10. For example, greater uncertainty about the net indebtness of a country would lead to thinner markets and may eventually lead to the collapse of voluntary lending (see Kletzer 1984; Calvo 2002; Aizenman and Marion 2002b).

12.4.4   The Use (and Abuse) of International Reserves
         and Vulnerability Indicators

A high short-term debt–international reserves ratio was found to be a vulnerability indicator, signifying exposure to crises (see Rodrik and Velasco 1999). Does it imply that emerging markets would benefit by increasing the cushion of international reserves, signaling thereby they are being a safer borrower? Countries like Chile, Korea, and Taiwan have managed large stocks of international reserves. Does it follow that other countries will benefit from hoarding more international reserves in order to reduce the above-vulnerability index? As the Lucas critique would suggest, a deeper understanding of the economy is needed in order to answer this question.

This point can be illustrated in a model of emerging markets, where there is a conflict between efficiency and political economy considerations. Specifically, countries characterized by sovereign risk, tax-collection costs, inelastic demand for fiscal outlays, and a volatile GDP opt to engage in large external borrowing. Suppose that international reserves are beyond creditors' control (this would be the case if the location and the magnitude of the reserves is not public information, implying also that the partial default repayment is independent of the stock of reserves). In the absence of political-economy considerations, higher borrowing can be shown to be accompanied with a greater accumulation of international reserves (see Aizenman and Marion 2002a). While this adjustment is welfare enhancing, it may do little to prevent a sovereign-debt crisis. Suppose now that there is political uncertainty regarding the identity of the future administration; there is a positive probability that an opportunistic administration will loot the treasury and channel resources toward narrow interest groups. Greater political instability can be shown to reduce the demand for international reserves and to increase borrowing.[11] Hence, the association between external borrowing and international reserves depends critically on political-economy factors. A high short-term debt–reserve ratio may be the symptom of political instability. In these circumstances, a policy that will target a drop in the short-term debt–international reserves ratio, without dealing with the political-economy considerations that determine the prospect of future looting, is welfare reducing. Such a policy does not necessarily reduce vulnerability to crisis, and, in fact, it may increase the probability of a crisis.

This would be the case, for example, if the increase in the stock of re-

---

11. If the present administration is opportunistic, it will loot all liquid resources, hence it will minimize its reserves holdings and maximize borrowing. If the present administration is benevolent, a higher probability of a future opportunistic administration will reduce the present demand for international reserves and will increase borrowing as a way of reducing the resources available for future looting.

serves, triggered by policies, increases the misguided expenditure of opportunistic administrations in the future. This effect is further magnified when the probability of the switch to the opportunistic administration increases with the resources available to such an administration, or when these resources trigger rent-seeking behavior. One may view this example as an illustration of the Lucas critique—policies that are beneficial in the absence of opportunism may backfire and reduce welfare in countries characterized by political polarization and instability.

Similar concerns may apply to the usefulness of vulnerability indicators. These indicators provide information on variables correlated with past crises. Attempts to encourage the dissemination and the use of these indicators in allocating global funds may have mixed results. One doubts the degree to which these indicators will perform in the future when they are out of the sample used to construct them. One may also envision situations in which the introduction of quasi-official indicators provides a false sense of security and in which market participants may attach too much value to these indicators, ignoring other relevant information. It may induce emerging markets to distort the indicators in order to signal their relative soundness. As the previous discussion illustrated, short of deeper reforms, these signals may be misleading and may not indicate a genuine reduction in vulnerability.

12.4.5 Time Inconsistency and Political-Economy Considerations— How Important Is the Choice of Exchange-Rate Regimes?

Crises are frequently the delayed manifestations of political-economy factors. Reforms that ignore these factors run the risk of inducing too optimistic an assessment of countries, which, over time, leads to a large exposure and ultimately to greater vulnerability. The literature on the optimal exchange-rate regimes frequently attaches too much importance to the choice of monetary policy. Beyond the short run, monetary and fiscal policies are intertwined via the intertemporal budget constraints. Indeed, one may argue that a deficient fiscal system may lead to crises independently of the exchange-rate regimes. In these circumstances, the choice of the exchange rate regime will have an impact only on the timing of the ultimate crisis. After all, sovereign risk and exchange-rate risks have different causes. Casting the problem in terms of the "smart" choice of an exchange-rate regime is potentially hazardous, as it obscures the need to challenge the deeper fiscal deficiencies.

These considerations are illustrated in the contrast of the policies undertaken by Brazil and Argentina in the last fifteen years. In the 1980s, both countries were characterized by similar fiscal deficiencies, stemming from their organization as a loose federal system in which the provincial states and municipalities had a significant bargaining power relative to the federal center. In the early 1990s, both countries went through successful exchange-rate-based stabilizations. The nominal anchor, provided by pegging the exchange rate, supported rapid disinflation in both countries. Argentina, however, put a much greater emphasis on the importance of a peg—it adopted a rigid currency board. In contrast, Brazil put greater emphasis on dealing with its fiscal imbalances, thereby reducing the relative power of the provincial states.[12] In addition, Brazil moved over time from a fixed-exchange-rate regime towards discretionary-exchange-rate management, accommodating external adverse shocks with occasional depreciations. As the recent events have painfully illustrated, Brazil's choice allowed it to steer away from a deep crisis, whereas Argentina's choice has led over time to increased vulnerability and ultimately to the recent crisis.

12.4.6   Multiple Equilibria and the International Lender of Last Resort

One possible justification for bailing out countries is the presence of multiple equilibria. Exposure to multiple equilibria is a by-product of the maturity transformation accomplished by financial intermediation in which short-term deposits are used to finance longer-term real projects (see Diamond and Dybvig 1983 for a banking model; Chang and Velasco 1999 for an open economy model of bank and currency runs). In these circumstances, the presence of the lender of last resort is supposed to prevent the bad equilibrium. As Rogoff (1999) discussed, a lender of last resort comes with a hefty cost to the taxpayer. Some may view the fate of Argentina as an example of a country suffering from the adverse consequences of a switch to a bad equilibrium. Supporters of this view point out that conventional measures (e.g., current account, fiscal deficits, etc.) failed to flag out Argentina as a highly vulnerable country in the 1990s. Indeed, Argentina's fiscal measures were comparable to those of "respected" OECD countries. Can we infer from this that a lender of last resort would have prevented the Argentinean crisis?

While it is hard to test this assertion, there are fundamental challenges facing the multiple-equilibria argument. Vulnerability to a crisis may depend on the capacity of an economy to adjust to changing circumstances. This includes the ability of the fiscal system and the labor market to adjust to unforeseen events. More generally, country risk may be determined by the interaction between shocks and the quality of the institutions of conflict management (see Rodrik 1999). In the context of Argentina, the multiple-equilibria interpretation is challenged by the view that Argentina is a quasi-European-style welfare state standing on the shoulders of a very thin tax base. This situation is further exacerbated by the provincial states' bias towards overspending. Hence, one may conclude that there are fundamen-

---

12. While it's premature to conclude that Brazil has accomplished all the adjustments called for under the Fiscal Responsibility Act of 2001, it started the painful process of curbing the biases towards provincial overspending. See Dillinger and Webb (1999) for further details about the reforms.

tal reasons to view Argentina as a risky destination for global capital, even if its fiscal deficits and current-account deficits are comparable to OECD countries.

The insistence of the Argentinean authorities on preserving the currency board, despite the growing strength of the dollar and the occasional real depreciations of Brazilian currency, may be viewed as a manifestation of these risks—viewing the currency board as the main safeguard against inflation runs the hazard of providing a signal that the deeper fiscal problems are still there. Placing too much faith on the currency board as the mechanism for fiscal discipline overlooks the fact that the cost of changing the exchange-rate regime (and of monetary policy, more generally) is much lower than the cost of a fundamental fiscal reform. Hence, a country like Argentina runs the risk of being viewed as fiscally unstable, independently of the realized path of current-account and fiscal deficits. In the long run, according to this view, the fiscal side will determine the strength of the system. Short of resolving fiscal deficiencies, a country like Argentina will find it hard to convince the market that it's a prudent destination for capital.

One may rephrase the above discussion in terms of the rules-versus-discretion literature, where there are gains from delegating monetary policy to a conservative agent. As was illustrated in Rogoff's (1985) seminal work, the optimal commitment to the conservative course depends on the stochastic structure. If the balance of shocks tilts over time toward adverse real shocks, a less conservative course is preferable. The success of Brazil and the failure of Argentina may be viewed as a vivid example of this principle. The success of the structural reform would require also challenging the fiscal deficiencies that determine, in the long run, the course on monetary policy. Hence, the relative success of Brazil is attributed to its success in curbing the bias towards provincial overspending and in a more appropriate use of discretionary-exchange-rate and monetary policy.

12.4.7 Policies Designed to Impose Discipline on the Market— Reserve and Capital-Adequacy Requirements

The introduction of reserve requirements by either borrowers or lenders may impose better discipline on the global financial market. Borrowing will decline and so will default risk, reducing the necessity for continuing bailouts. The introduction of reserve requirements will improve welfare in both the lending and borrowing economies. In these circumstances, the lender's optimal-reserve requirement increases with the expected bailout (see Aizenman and Turnovsky 2002). Indirectly, this policy may reduce the bias in favor of debt and against equity in international lending, identified by Rogoff (1999). But the design of the optimal-reserve requirement in a decentralized world is a delicate matter, and both the optimal lender's reserve requirement and the optimal borrower's requirement have equally attractive and unattractive features. Indeed, without a proper coordination among all lenders, the reserve requirements will reallocate lending from high- to low-reserve countries with few beneficial effects. Hence, the gains of such policies will be determined by the ability of international institutions (e.g., the Bank for International Settlements [BIS], IMF, etc.) to induce all lenders to apply similar policies, driven by the underlying risk factors.

12.5   Concluding Remarks

The global financial market has been shaken throughout the 1990s by a series of major financial crises. Attempts to stabilize the global system have led to large bailouts. This experience suggests that the present system cannot survive indefinitely, since the willingness of taxpayers in the OECD countries to engage in continuing bailouts is approaching its limits. The presumption is that we deal with a second-best situation in which there is no quick fix, but welfare can be enhanced by the proper regulatory changes. While prudent borrowing of emerging-market economies is beneficial, excessive borrowing may be disadvantageous due to existing distortions. In such an environment, one should either reduce the existing distortions, or induce borrowers and lenders to internalize them.

Recent proposals for the new international financial architecture have focused on reform along two margins: reducing the ex ante probability of a crisis and inducing the more-orderly resolution of a crisis. In evaluating the various of proposals, it is important to stress that there are good reasons to support both more-effective crisis management and more-prudent ex ante allocation of credit. As each deals with a different margin, they should complement each other. Specifically, the crisis-management proposals do not address directly the excessive risk undertaken due to moral hazard, as the ex post solvency of some of the resultant projects hinge on bailouts. Similarly, improving the prudential regulations would not eliminate liquidity crises. Hence, the need for more-efficient crisis management and resolution remains a high-priority issue. This is especially due to the growing diversity of lenders, implying that the task of coordinating the resolution of crises is more involved.

Greater global integration increased the responsiveness of financial flows to news. This development is potentially beneficial in good times, but it has adverse consequences when things go wrong. Hence, the darker side of globalization is that financial crises increase the scope for conflicts—the direct stakes are higher. Once the bad news hits the market, the key issue is not only the ultimate distribution of the burden of adjustment between the debtors and creditors, but also the length of time it would take to settle down the dispute. The killer of future cooperation may be the uncertainty regarding the dispute-resolution mechanism, since it exposes creditors to the hazards of long haggling over a shrinking pie. Protracted negotiations will prolong the period in which both domestic and international agents refrain from new investments. This in turn will deepen the recession in the affected countries, increasing the social tension and further increasing losses. The net outcome may be greater temptation for the domestic authorities to embark on populist policies, which tends toward autarky, a trend that will hurt further prospects of trade integration. Hence, the recent crises may be viewed as a test case for the efficiency of the global dispute-resolution mechanism. While one hopes that the direct financial contagion from Argentina to other countries will be limited, one expects that a slow and protracted resolution of the crisis will highlight the inability of the present system to deal efficiently with adverse shocks, thereby reducing future financial flows and putting in jeopardy other vulnerable countries.

The urgency of these issues is illustrated by the willingness of top IMF executives to engage constructively in a debate concerning the future form of the global dispute-resolution mechanism (see Krueger 2001). One expects that only reforms that offer practical solutions will pass the market test and will endure the political process needed to implement them. One doubts the degree to which "clean" ideas, like insurance based only on meeting ex ante conditionality, will survive the time-inconsistency and the transparency challenges. Regulatory enhancements that would use existing institutions would have a greater chance of adaptation. Examples of such interventions are the regulations and supervision undertaken by central banks in the context of domestic banking. One expects a more stringent application of capital and reserve requirements. One expects also a greater role for the BIS and the IMF in coordinating these regulations across countries. Considering the greater weight of nonbank lending and the great increase in the number of institutional investors, one expects reforms dealing with better coordination among creditors and with the formation of international bankruptcy procedures to be vigorously tested by looming crises.

References

Acemoglu, D., and F. Zilibotti. 1998. Was Promotheus unbound by chance? Risk, diversification and growth. *Journal of Political Economy* 105 (4): 709–51.

Aizenman, J. 1989. Country risk, incomplete information and taxes on international borrowing. *The Economic Journal* 99 (394): 147–61.

———. 2003. Capital mobility in a second best world—moral hazard with costly financial intermediation. *Review of International Economics* 11 (1): 1–17.

Aizenman, J., and N. P. Marion. 2002a. International reserve holdings with sovereign risk and costly tax collection. NBER Working Paper no. 9154. Cambridge, Mass.: National Bureau of Economic Research, September.

———. 2002b. Reserve uncertainty and the supply of international credit. *Journal of Money, Credit and Banking* 34 (3): 631–49.

Aizenman, J., and S. Turnovsky. 2002. Reserve requirements on sovereign debt in the presence of moral hazard—on debtors or creditors? *The Economic Journal* 112 (476): 107–32.

Arteta, C., B. Eichengreen, and C. Wyplosz. 2001. When does capital account liberalization help more than it hurts? NBER Working Paper no. 8414. Cambridge, Mass.: National Bureau of Economic Research, August.

Beck, T., R. Levine, and Y. N. Loayza. 2000. Finance and the sources of growth. *Journal of Financial Economics* 58 (1–2): 261–300.

Bekaert, G., C. Harvey, and R. Lundblad. 2001. Does financial liberalization spur growth? NBER Working Paper no. 8245. Cambridge, Mass.: National Bureau of Economic Research, September.

Bhagwati, J. 1968. Distortions and immiserizing growth. *Review of Economic Studies* 35 (4): 481–85.

Bongini, P., S. Claessens, and G. Ferri. 2001. The political economy of distress in East Asian financial institutions. *Journal of Financial Services Research* 19 (1): 5–25.

Brecher, R., and C. Diaz-Alejandro. 1977. Tariffs, foreign capital and immiserizing growth. *Journal of International Economics* 7 (4): 317–22.

Buiter, W. H., and A. C. Sibert. 1999. A contribution to the new international financial architecture. *International Finance* 2 (2): 227–47.

Caballero, R., and A. Krishnamurthy. 2001. International and domestic collateral constraints in a model of emerging market crises. *Journal of Monetary Economics* 48 (3): 513–48.

Calvo, G. A. 2002. Contagion in emerging markets: When *Wall Street* is a carrier. In *Proceedings from the International Economic Association Congress.* Vol. 3, 1–23. http://bsos.umd.edu/econ/ciecrp8.pdf.

Caprio, G., and P. Honohan. 1999. Restoring banking stability: Beyond supervised capital requirements. *Journal of Economic Perspectives* 13 (4): 43–64.

Chang, R., and A. Velasco. 1999. Financial crises in emerging markets. *Facultad Regional Buenos Aires (FRBA)* 84 (2): 4–17.

Cole, H., and M. Obstfeld. 1991. Commodity trade and international risk sharing: How much do financial markets matter? *Journal of Monetary Economics* 28 (1): 2–34.

Corsetti, G., P. Pesenti, and N. Roubini. 1999. Paper Tigers? A model of Asian crisis. *European Economic Review* 43 (7): 1211–36.

De Gregorio, J., S. Edwards, and R. Valdes. 2000. Controls on capital inflows: Do they work? *Journal of Development Economics* 63 (1): 59–83.

Demirgüç-Kunt, A., and E. Detragiache. 1998. Financial liberalization and financial fragility. International Monetary Fund (IMF) Working Paper no. 98/83. Washington, D.C.: IMF, June.

Diamond, D., and P. Dybvig. 1983. Bank runs, deposit insurance, and liquidity. *Journal of Political Economy* 91 (June): 401–19.

Diaz-Alejandro, C. 1985. Goodbye financial repression, hello financial repression. *Journal of Development Economics* 19 (1–2): 1–24.

Dillinger, W., and S. B. Webb. 1999. Fiscal management in federal democracies: Argentina and Brazil. World Bank Macroeconomics and Growth Working Paper no. 2121. Washington, D.C.: World Bank, May. http://www.worldbank.org/html/dec/Publications/workpapers/wps2121/wps2121.pdf.

Dooley, M. 2000. A model of crises in emerging markets. *The Economic Journal* 110 (460): 256–72.

Dooley, M., and I. Shin. 2000. Private inflows when crises are anticipated: A case study of Korea. NBER Working Paper no. 7992. Cambridge, Mass.: National Bureau of Economic Research, November.

Eaton, J., and R. Fernandez. 1995. Sovereign debt. In *Handbook of international economics*. Vol. 3, ed. G. Grossman and K. Rogoff, 2031–77. New York: North Holland.

Edwards, S. 2001a. Capital mobility and economic performance: Are emerging economies different? NBER Working Paper no. 8076. Cambridge, Mass.: National Bureau of Economic Research, January.

———. 2001b. Exchange rate regimes, capital flows and crisis prevention. NBER Working Paper no. 8529. Cambridge, Mass.: National Bureau of Economic Research, October.

Eichengreen, B. 1999. *A new international financial architecture: A practical post-Asia agenda.* Washington, D.C.: Institute for International Economics.

Eichengreen, B., A. Rose, and C. Wyplosz. 1995. Exchange rate mayhem: The antecedents and aftermaths of speculative attacks. *Economic Policy* 21:249–96.

Feldstein, M., ed. 2003. Economic and financial crises in emerging market economies: Overview of prevention and management. In *Economic and financial crises in emerging market economics,* 1–29. Chicago: University of Chicago Press.

Frankel, J. A., and N. Roubini. 2003. Industrial country policies. In *Economic and financial crises in emerging market economies,* ed. M. Feldstein, 155–278. Chicago: University of Chicago Press.

Glick, R., and M. Hutchison. 1999. Banking and currency crises: How common are twins? In *Financial crises in emerging markets,* eds. R. Glick, R. Moreno, and M. Spiegel. New York: Cambridge University Press.

Greenspan, Alan. 1998. Understanding today's international financial system. Speech presented to the 34th Annual Conference on Bank Structure and Competition of the Federal Reserve Bank of Chicago. 7 May, Chicago. http://www.federalreserve.gov/boarddocs/speeches/1998/19980507.htm.

Greenwood, J., and B. Jovanovic. 1990. Financial development, growth, and the distribution of income. *Journal of Political Economy* 98 (5): 1076–1107.

Haggard, S. 2000. *The political economy of the Asian financial crisis.* Washington, D.C.: Institute for International Economics.

Hellmann, T., K. Murdock, and J. E. Stiglitz. 2000. Liberalization, moral hazard in banking and prudential regulation: Are capital requirements enough? *American Economic Review* 90 (1): 147–65.

Jeanne, O. 2003. Debt maturity and the international finance architecture. International Monetary Fund (IMF) Research Department. Manuscript, May. http://www.ifk-cfs.de/papers/Jeanne.pdf.

Johnson, G. H. 1967. The possibility of income losses from increased efficiency or factor accumulation in the presence of tariffs. *Economic Journal* 77 (305): 151–54.

Kaminsky, G. L., S. Lizondo, and C. M. Reinhart. 1998. Leading indicators of currency crises. *IMF Staff Papers* 5 (1): 1–48.

Kaminsky, G. L., and C. M. Reinhart. 1999. The twin crises: The causes of banking and balance-of-payments problems. *American Economic Review* 89 (3): 473–500.

Kohn, M., and N. Marion. 1992. The implications of knowledge-based growth for the optimality of open capital markets. *Canadian Journal of Economics* 25 (4): 865–83.

Kletzer, K. 1984. Asymmetries of information and LDC borrowing with sovereign risk. *The Economic Journal* 94 (374): 287–307.

Krueger, A. 2001. A new approach to sovereign debt restructuring. Presented at the Indian Council for Research on International Economic Relations, 20 December, Delhi, India. http://www.imf.org/external/np/speeches/2001/122001.htm.

Levine, R. 1997. Financial development and economic growth: views and agenda. *Journal of Economic Literature* 35 (2): 688–726.

Lucas, R. E. 1976. Econometric policy evaluation: A critique. In *The Phillips curve and labor markets,* ed. K. Brunner and A. Meltzer, 19–46. Vol. 1 of *Carnegie-Rochester Conferences on Public Policy.* Amsterdam: North-Holland.

Martin, P., and H. Rey. 2002. Financial globalization and emerging markets: With or without crash. NBER Working Paper no. 9288. Cambridge, Mass.: National Bureau of Economic Research, October.

Miller, M. H., and L. Zhang. 2000. Sovereign liquidity crisis: The strategic case for a payment standstill. *Economic Journal* 110 (460): 335–62.

McKinnon, R. 1991. *The order of economic liberalization: Financial control in the transition to a market economy.* Baltimore: Johns Hopkins University Press.

Meltzer, A. 1998. Asian problems and the IMF. Testimony prepared for the Joint Economic Committee, U.S. Congress, 24 February. Washington, D.C.

Obstfeld, M. 1994. Risk-taking, global diversification and growth. *American Economic Review* 85 (December): 1310–29.

Portes, R. 2000. Sovereign debt restructuring: The role of institutions for collective action. Center for Economic Policy Research. Manuscript, March. http://www.stern.nyu.edu/globalmacro/Restructuring.doc?wwwstern≠400760098&CH=131.220.109.149& CK≠HgY2qWMc2U12bX89QNuHBw.

Rodrik, D. 1998. Who needs capital-account convertibility? In *Should the IMF pursue capital account convertibility? Essays in international finance* no. 207, ed. P. Kenen, 55–65. Princeton: Princeton University Press.

———. 1999. Where did all the growth go? External shocks, social conflict, and growth collapses. *Journal of Economic Growth* 4 (4): 358–412.

Rodrik, D., and A. Velasco. 1999. Short-term capital flows. NBER Working Paper no. 7364. Cambridge, Mass.: National Bureau of Economic Research, September.

Rogoff, K. 1985. The optimal degree of commitment to an intermediate monetary target. *Quarterly Journal of Economics* 100 (4): 1169–89.

———. 1999. International institutions for reducing global financial instability. *Journal of Economic Perspectives* 13 (4): 21–42.

Sachs, J. 1995. Do we need an international lender of last resort? Presented at the Frank Graham Memorial Lecture, Princeton University. 20 April, Princeton, N.J.

Soros, G. 1998. *The crisis of global capitalism.* New York: Public Affairs Press.

Williamson, J., and M. Mahar. 1998. A survey of financial liberalization. Princeton Essays in International Finance no. 211. Princeton, N.J.: Princeton University, November.

World Bank. 1998. *Global economic perspective.* Washington, D.C.: World Bank.

Comment   Robert M. Stern

In Aizenman's opening section on financial openness and the occurrence of financial crises, what comes out clearly is the role of weak institutions coupled with political economy considerations that demonstrated the unwillingness or inability of government authorities to take timely and effec-

Robert M. Stern is emeritus professor of economics and public policy at the University of Michigan.

tive actions in dealing with the crises. There is abundant evidence of government macroeconomic and financial mismanagement in the cases especially of Mexico in 1993–1994 and several Asian countries in 1997–1998, including Thailand, Indonesia, Malaysia, South Korea, and Hong Kong. But it is interesting to note that some other Asian countries were apparently less vulnerable to crisis because of their more timely and effective domestic policies. The Philippines, Singapore, and Taiwan are cases in point. Furthermore, China and India were not greatly affected by the crises elsewhere in Asia because of their long-standing capital controls.

While Aizenman is mainly concerned with the broad aspects of the occurrence of financial crises, he devotes less attention to the different responses of governments to the crises and especially to the pace of recovery. Thus, for example, in the case of Mexico, considerable financial assistance was provided by the International Monetary Fund (IMF) and bilaterally by the United States. Moreover, with the onset of the crisis, Mexico moved quickly to float the peso and instituted a severe austerity program with tight monetary and fiscal policies. While income and employment in Mexico contracted considerably, the depreciation of the peso combined with the rapid expansion of the U.S. economy served subsequently to bolster the recovery process so that Mexico was able to finance the repayment of the bailout funds within a fairly short period of time.

The financial management experiences of the Asian countries were, as noted, more diverse. The role of the IMF proved more controversial as to whether it helped the recovery process or made things worse at the time, especially in Thailand, Indonesia, and South Korea. But some countries chose to forgo IMF assistance altogether, as in the cases of Malaysia, which instituted capital controls, and Hong Kong, which tightened its macroeconomic policies and was able to maintain its fixed exchange rate and currency-board arrangement. In retrospect, what is perhaps surprising about the Asian experience, as was the case also for Mexico, is how rapidly the countries were able to recover from the crises, aided especially by their currency depreciations and the significant upturn in the demand for their exports due to the rapid expansion of the U.S. economy in the late 1990s.

The question that emerges for several of the Asian countries noted is the extent to which they have been able to strengthen their financial institutions so that they are now less vulnerable to crises than they were previously. Aizenman intimates that there may be an endogenous improvement in institutions and policies once countries have experienced financial crises. This perhaps can now be tested to see how they are responding to the significant reduction of external demand with an economic slowdown in the United States, continued slow growth in Western Europe, and stagnation in Japan.

When we look at experiences with financial crises outside of Asia, the most noteworthy cases include Russia, Brazil, Turkey, and Argentina. Following the collapse of communism, Russia was saddled with weak financial institutions and fiscal inadequacies. It received considerable IMF financial assistance, which was supported by the United States for political reasons, but this assistance proved unsuccessful, perhaps because it came too late. Russia defaulted on a considerable portion of its debt in August 1998. But since that time, aided by the significant depreciation of the ruble and the upturn in world oil and other commodity prices, Russia introduced financial discipline and strengthened its domestic fiscal and regulatory arrangements. Thus, Russia is in much better macroeconomic shape presently than it had been previously.

In the case of Brazil, the IMF provided substantial assistance designed especially so that Brazil could maintain its exchange rate peg. But this turned out to be unsustainable and raises the question again about the wisdom of IMF policies and advice. Subsequently, Brazil floated its currency and adopted policies of monetary and fiscal restraints. These measures have proven successful on the whole, although there are apparently some concerns currently about the sustainability of the fiscal restraints because of domestic political opposition.

Turkey has received considerable IMF assistance and has been supported politically by the United States because of Turkey's importance as an ally in the Middle East. But it is not clear if Turkey's macroeconomic position is sustainable because of insufficient domestic measures and political uncertainties. In any case, Turkey is so large and important to both U.S. and European interests that there will almost certainly be continued external financial support and encouragement of more effective domestic measures to control inflation and restrain expenditures.

It is well established that the maintenance of the currency-board arrangement in Argentina deprived Argentina of the use of monetary policy for stabilization purposes and exchange rate adjustments for external balance. Argentina was thus especially vulnerable to the Brazilian currency depreciation that occurred. Fiscal inadequacies and inflexible labor-market arrangements made it difficult for Argentina to adjust. Here, also, the IMF provided considerable financial assistance that proved to be ineffective, thereby raising the question once again about whether IMF assistance helped or made matters worse. The Argentine case is sad indeed because of the social consequences of the mismanagement involved on the part of the domestic authorities and the maintenance of the ultimately unsustainable exchange rate arrangement. The IMF has been reluctant to provide further financial assistance under current circumstances, and the United States has remained aloof in contrast to the political interests expressed in the cases of Russia and Turkey.

It appears clear from the foregoing review of country experiences that the first line of defense in dealing with financial crisis calls for the strengthening of domestic institutions and responsible government. At the same time, there is a need for complementary international and bilateral measures to deal with (1) short-term liquidity problems, which are the traditional role of the IMF, and (2) more deep-rooted structural problems. These structural problems may require arrangements for the rewriting of debt contracts and possibly for establishing an international system of bankruptcy procedures applied to nations.

In the final analysis, the question that needs to be answered is how much of a nation's painful adjustment in time of crisis is to be borne by the nation itself or shared with foreign creditors. In part, this may depend on international politics, especially as far as the United States is concerned. Otherwise, the country itself will shoulder most of the burden of adjustment.

Openness and Growth: What's the Empirical Relationship?

Robert E. Baldwin

13.1 Introduction

The manner in which the international economic policies of governments affect the rates of growth of their economies has long been a subject of controversy. This situation continues today. Despite a number of multicountry case studies utilizing comparable analytical frameworks, numerous econometric studies using large cross-country data sets, and important theoretical advances concerning how a country's international economic policies and its rate of economic growth interact, there is still disagreement among economists concerning the nature of the relationship.

There are several reasons for this. A key one is the difference among investigators in the manner they define the issue being studied. Some authors focus on whether there is a causal relationship between such variables as increases in trade or foreign direct investment and increases in growth rates (or between increases in growth and increases in trade or investment), no matter what the reasons for the changes in these economic variables. However, most authors are interested in the effects of differences in government policies on economic growth. The impact of policies affecting the "openness" of a country to trade and investment, or its "inward orientation" or "outward orientation," is the subject of many studies. But, of course, just how broadly one defines such terms greatly affects one's conclusions about a particular country or set of countries. One can interpret openness in narrow terms to include only import and export taxes or subsidies as well as explicit nontariff distortions of trade, or in varying degrees of broadness to

Robert E. Baldwin is Hilldale Professor of Economics, Emeritus, at the University of Wisconsin-Madison and a research associate of the National Bureau of Economic Research (NBER).

cover such matters as exchange-rate policies, domestic taxes and subsidies, competition and other regulatory policies, education policies, the nature of the legal system, the form of government, and the general nature of institutions and culture.

Differences in the quality and detail of the data being analyzed are another source of disagreement among economists on the subject. Those who study trade and growth relationships among developing countries are greatly hampered by the lack of good data even on such matters as levels of import protection, and they often are forced to undertake case studies. While many insights have been revealed from such studies about the nature of the development process and its relationship with trade, some are reluctant to draw broad generalizations from them because of their specificity and the bias that the personal viewpoints of the authors may introduce into the analyses. In contrast, while econometric analyses based on quantitative data concerning trade and growth for a cross-section of countries do permit broad generalizations, these studies are limited by the scope and comparability of available quantitative data. Differences in what investigators regard as appropriate econometric models and tests for sensitivity of the results to alternative specifications that may be based in part on the personal policy predilections of the authors can also result in significant differences in the conclusions reached under such quantitative approaches.

The purpose of this paper is to survey briefly the views of economists and policymakers since around the end of World War II concerning the relationships between economic openness and growth, indicating how and why these views have significantly changed over the last fifty years and pointing out the main reasons for the disagreements. Section 13.2 examines the 1950s and 1960s when import substitution was the dominant growth policy in the developing countries and there was also extensive government intervention in many industrial countries aimed at influencing growth rates. Section 13.3 considers the period from the 1970s into the 1990s, in which the findings from an increasing number of studies of the growth experiences of individual countries caused more and more economists and policymakers to become skeptical about the growth merits of import substitution policies and to begin to advocate more export-oriented, outward-looking trade policies. Section 13.4 briefly outlines some of the new relationships between trade and growth brought out by the so-called new growth literature of the late 1980s and early 1990s which, together with the development of new econometric techniques for dealing with time series data, has stimulated new efforts to unravel the relationships between trade and growth through cross-country statistical analyses. Section 13.5 briefly reviews the major studies of this period, all of which reach the general conclusion that openness is associated with higher growth rates. This conclusion has, however, been recently challenged in a detailed, carefully reasoned critique of these papers by Rodriguez and Rodrik (2001). These authors contend that, in fact, because of various methodological short-comings in these studies, one should conclude that there is very little evidence that trade openness is significantly associated with economic growth. Section 13.5 summarizes the criticisms of the paper by Rodriguez and Rodrik. Section 13.6 concludes with an evaluation of the new studies and the critique by Rodriguez and Rodrik.

13.2   The Widespread Acceptance of Import-Substitution Policies as the Means to Stimulate Economic Growth

As more and more countries obtained their independence from the colonial powers in the period shortly after the end of World War II, a widespread view developed among economists and policymakers that the best way for these countries to develop more rapidly was to stimulate industrialization by adopting import-substitution policies. There seemed to be a number of good reasons for such an approach at the time. The political leaders of the newly independent nations were keenly aware not only that most of the countries from whom they obtained independence had much higher per capita income levels and were much more industrialized, but that their former rulers had imposed economic policies in the past which discouraged industrialization within the new nations. To these new leaders, industrialization seemed to offer the possibility of achieving faster growth, higher per capita income levels, and the attainment of the economic and military power needed for national security.

An economically sensible way of achieving industrialization seemed to be to restrict imports of manufactured goods for which there already was a domestic demand, in order both to shift this demand toward domestic producers and to permit the use of the country's primary-product export earnings to import the capital goods needed for industrialization. There also appeared to be a number of examples where high levels of import protection in the nineteenth and twentieth centuries had contributed positively to industrialization. Although Great Britain had adopted a policy of free trade during its period of rapid growth in the nineteenth century, the United States seemed to industrialize and prosper by imposing high import duties on manufactures for much of the later part of the nineteenth century. Germany and France also adopted protectionist policies during this period, as did Japan after 1900.[1] The impressive degree of industrialization achieved by the Soviet Union in the 1920s and 1930s and by China after 1949 by pursuing inward-looking policies were additional historical examples that impressed the leaders of the newly independent nations.

The so-called infant industry argument first set forth in 1791 by Alexan-

---

1. See O'Rourke (2000) and Clemens and Williamson (2001) for evidence supporting the positive effects of tariffs on growth. Also see Irwin (2002) for some contrary evidence.

der Hamilton (1913), further elaborated by Friedrich List (1856), and accepted by many classical and neoclassical economists as the major theoretically valid exception to the case for worldwide free trade provided economic support for import-substitution policies. John Stuart Mill, who first formalized the argument in economic terms, argued that it takes time for new producers in a country to become "educated to the level of those with whom the processes are traditional" and thus for their unit costs to decline. The infant industry argument maintains that during the temporary period when domestic costs in an industry are above the product's import price, a tariff is a socially desirable method of financing the investment in human resources needed to compete successfully with foreign producers.

Soon after World War II, Raul Prebisch (1950), the secretary general of the United Nations Economic Commission for Latin America and later the founder and secretary general of the United Nations Conference on Trade and Development (UNCTAD), among others argued that the infant industry argument was applicable to the entire manufacturing sector and not just to a single industry. He also claimed that an ongoing secular decline in the prices of primary products (the exports of the less-developed countries) relative to the prices of manufactured goods (the exports of the developed countries) and the low elasticity of demand for primary products made expansion in the production of primary products unattractive. Focusing on producing labor-intensive manufactured goods, for example, clothing, for export purposes also did not appeal to most less-developed countries at this time because of the belief that a balanced industrial structure, such as existed in most developed countries, was necessary to achieve their goal of high per capita income levels and, moreover, because high levels of import duties and other import barriers still existed in the developed countries on most of these goods.

Although most economic leaders of less-developed countries looked favorably on the strategy of import substitution, they also often found themselves backed into such a policy somewhat inadvertently. Because of the shortage of goods these countries suffered during World War II and the economic expansion plans of their new leaders, there was a tremendous demand on their part for both capital goods and consumer goods. This meant that their existing foreign exchange reserves were quickly used up, with current export earnings being unable to fill the gap between demand and supply at existing exchange rates. Consequently, most of these countries felt forced to impose foreign exchange and import controls to conserve their available export earnings and to establish a rationing system for the available foreign exchange to ensure that consumer necessities such as food and medicine, key intermediate inputs such as fuel, and essential capital goods could be imported in sufficient quantities to prevent serious political unrest and still permit the pursuit of their development goals. One consequence was that very high levels of implicit protection were put in place on so-called nonessential manufactured goods.

Import substitution policies actually worked quite well initially. The high prices of imported nonessentials shifted domestic demand for these goods from foreign to local producers with the result that there were significant increases in the output of simple manufactured goods as governments provided domestic producers with the foreign exchange needed to import key intermediate inputs and capital goods. Many manufacturing activities consisted largely of simply assembling the components of goods produced abroad, for example, cars. Since the production of most of these products intensively utilized the type of labor that was relatively abundant in the newly industrializing nations, namely, unskilled labor, the adverse effects on economic efficiency of these early import substitution efforts were not sufficient to offset the growth effects of the import substitution policies. Moreover, in this early period, the overvalued domestic currencies resulting from the tight exchange controls and expansionary production policies not only did not seem to reduce earnings from primary-product exports significantly, but kept import prices of needed capital goods and intermediate inputs relatively low.

As import-substitution policies continued and a number of developing countries extended these policies to cover more and more intermediate inputs and capital goods, the drawbacks of such a policy approach became increasingly apparent. In particular, the hardships imposed on the export sector began to have adverse growth effects. An overvalued currency meant that the number of units of foreign exchange received by exporters remained low while, at the same time, these producers were forced to purchase more and more intermediate inputs and capital goods domestically at high prices. The resulting squeeze on profit margins forced them to curtail export production. The higher skill and technology requirements for the more complex intermediates and capital goods and the lack of large domestic markets needed to achieve efficient levels of production of these goods also worsened the profit outlook for domestic producers. At the same time, aggressive expansionary activities by governments and private businesses fueled greater inflationary pressures, with the result that large government budget deficits and balance-of-payments deficits became commonplace. The ensuing budget and balance-of-payments crises were often met by still tighter controls over exchange rates and imports and more extensive government intervention in the economy. The net outcome was generally a slowing in the growth rate compared to the early period of import substitution.

Given the widespread agreement among economists today that the import-substitution strategy did not work out well for most developing countries, an important question to ask is why so many economists were wrong in their predictions that such an approach would be successful in raising long-run growth rates for these countries. What went wrong with our analytical thinking? In my view, two mistakes we made were an uncritical acceptance of the infant industry argument and a failure to take account of the macroeconomic consequences of such a policy when applied to all manufacturing.[2]

Consider the argument set forth earlier that new producers need to be protected for a temporary period so they can acquire the experience and production skills that will make them as efficient as their long-time foreign competitors. As James Meade (1955) pointed out many years ago, the existence during the early period of production of higher costs than those of foreign competitors is, by itself, an insufficient reason to justify tariff protection on economic efficiency grounds. If unit costs in an industry are low enough after the learning period to yield a discounted surplus of revenues over costs (and thus indicate a comparative advantage for the country in producing the product), it should be possible for firms to raise sufficient funds in the capital market to cover their initial excess of expenditures over revenues. These circumstances are no different from those in which firms go to the capital market for funds to cover the excess of expenditures over receipts during the early stages of production because of the need to purchase indivisible units of physical capital. Imperfections in capital markets may prevent access to capital markets but the existence of market imperfections is quite a different case for government intervention than the infant industry argument.

As Meade (1955) also noted, the key argument on which the infant industry case must rest relates to technological externalities associated with the learning process. For example, consider the matter of acquiring the knowledge about local production techniques needed to compete effectively with foreign producers. An entrepreneur who incurs these costs of discovering the best way to produce a particular good faces the problem that this information may become freely available to other potential local producers, who can utilize it at the same time as the initial firm but without incurring the full costs of the knowledge acquisition. Competition from these other producers could then either drive up factor prices or push down the product's price to levels where the initial firm is unable to recover its costs of gaining this knowledge. Realizing that this outcome is possible, firms will be discouraged from undertaking the initial knowledge-acquisition costs.[3]

The imposition of a temporary protective duty is, however, no guarantee that individual entrepreneurs will undertake additional investment in knowledge acquisition. An import tax raises the domestic price of a prod-

---

2. Also see Krueger (1997).

3. See Baldwin (1969) for a more complete discussion of this point and its policy implications. Hausmann and Rodrik (2002) have also recently discussed the development implications of this externality problem.

uct and, from the viewpoint of the industry as a whole, makes some investments in knowledge more profitable. But individual producers still face the same externality problem as before, namely, that other firms will copy, with little cost to themselves, any new technical knowledge discovered by the firm and drive the product's price down to a level where the initial firm will be unable to recoup its costs of acquiring this knowledge. If there were always some technologically fixed time lag between the introduction of a new, cheaper production technique and the change in product or factor prices caused by the entry of the firms who copy the new production method, a duty would operate to make investment in knowledge acquisition more profitable for the individual firm in the industry. But, to make a point too often ignored in such discussions, the speed with which firms respond to market opportunities is itself a function of the level of profit prospects. A duty will make it worthwhile for firms to incur the costs of acquiring the knowledge discovered by other firms faster and also to move into production more rapidly at high output levels. What is needed, of course, is a subsidy to the initial entrants into the industry for the purpose of discovering the better production techniques.

Up to the post–World War II period when some economists began to extend the infant industry argument to all manufacturing, economists had generally framed this argument for temporary protection in partial equilibrium terms. It focused on a single industry, and it was assumed that the temporary import protection granted had no appreciable effect on such macroeconomic variables as exchange rates, aggregate exports and imports, and monetary or fiscal policies. Early proponents of aggressively protecting large segments of the manufacturing sector did not fully appreciate the implications of their policy suggestions on these macroeconomic variables. They did not, for example, take sufficient account of the adverse effects of import substitution on aggregate exports and, thus, on the foreign exchange earnings so essential for importing the capital goods and essential intermediate inputs needed to permit the expansion of the manufacturing sector. Nor did they realize the extent to which government actions to conserve foreign exchange by limiting imports of luxury consumer goods would make the domestic production of these goods the most attractive for domestic entrepreneurs and thus bias the pattern of production in a direction that the government did not particularly want. They also failed to appreciate the extent of the budget and inflationary pressures that would be generated by the development actions of governments and domestic producers. Indeed, it was the macroeconomic crises associated with unsustainable import deficits for central banks, unmanageable government budget deficits, runaway inflation, and so on that had the greater effect in finally turning most countries away from import-substitution policies than a realization of the serious resource misallocation effects of these policies.

13.3   The Shift to Outward-Oriented Policies

The first group of developing countries to shift from an inward-oriented to an outward-oriented approach to development were located in the Far East, specifically Taiwan, Singapore, and South Korea. (Hong Kong had long pursued open trade and investment policies.) South Korea, for example, was characterized by extensive quantitative controls over trade and international payments from the time it separated from North Korea in 1945 through the end of the Korean War in 1953. Inward-looking actions continued to dominate government development policy after 1953, with an increasingly elaborate multiple exchange rate system being established in the attempt to deal with the problems of a large trade deficit and an over-valued exchange rate.[4] While a large currency devaluation took place in 1961 along with efforts to liberalize the trade and payments system, this liberalization effort ended in 1963 as rapid inflation was fed by excessively expansionary fiscal policies and a poor crop. However, a further liberalization effort begun in 1964 and 1965 was much more successful, so that by 1966 the trade and payments regime was fairly liberal compared with earlier years. The country became increasingly outward oriented as the government adopted other policies that encouraged exports of manufactured goods.

Even though they undertook periodic attempts to liberalize their trade and payments regimes, most other developing countries continued to follow what was basically an import-substitution approach to growth until the 1980s. However, the debt crisis of 1982 convinced many developing-country governments that inward-looking policies were no longer sustainable, particularly for smaller countries. They had borrowed heavily in international markets in order to cope with the trade-deficit problem associated with the import-substitution approach only to find that the high and sustainable growth rates sought still did not materialize and, instead, that they were left with massive international debts they could no longer service. Such traditional adherents to the import-substitution approach as Argentina, Chile, Mexico, Turkey, Ghana, and Uganda began to adopt more outward-looking policies.

While the inability to borrow the funds needed to reestablish their import-substitution regimes and the remarkable growth record of more and more East Asian countries under outward-oriented policies were probably the main immediate reasons for the shift in growth policy, the gradual shift in thinking by economists both in academia and in international organizations such as the World Bank, the International Monetary Fund, and even the United Nations Commission for Latin America in favor of outward-looking over inward-looking policies also was an important factor.

---

4. See Frank, Kim, and Westphal (1975) for a detailed discussion of Korea's development experience during this period.

This change in conventional thinking by economists and policymakers about the best policy approach to promote growth in the developing countries was significantly influenced by a series of detailed country studies together with some cross-country statistical analyses of the import-substitution process and by new theoretical modeling of the interactions between trade and growth. Both the studies of commercial policies in developing countries directed by Little, Scitovsky, and Scott (1970) and by Balassa and Associates (1971) utilized the newly formalized concept of the effective rate of protection to compare import-substitution policies across industries and countries.[5] This concept measures protection on a value-added basis rather than on the basis of the final price of a product and thus takes account of the level of protection on intermediate inputs as well as the final product. It brings out the point that, if a good is exported without any export subsidy but the exporter must purchase protected, domestically produced intermediate inputs, the primary factors involved in the value-added process are actually penalized compared to free trade. Similarly, if there are no duties on the intermediate inputs or they are lower than those on the final product, the primary factors producing the value-added are protected to a greater degree than the rate of protection on the final product indicates.

Both the Little, Scitovsky, and Scott (1970) and Balassa and Associates (1971) studies brought out the fact that the average rate of protection of value-added in manufacturing was extraordinarily high in most developing countries—much higher than nominal rates of protection and often exceeding 100 percent. Moreover, there was great variability among industries and broad sectors that often seemed to make little economic sense. An extreme example was Chile's effective rate of protection in 1961 of 2,884 percent for processed foods in contrast to 300 percent for nondurable consumer goods (Balassa and Associates 1971, 54). Perhaps most important, however, was the degree to which the studies demonstrated the discrimination against exports, mainly agricultural and mineral products. In some countries, there actually were negative rates of protection in these sectors, for example, agriculture in Pakistan and mining and energy in Malaysia (see Balassa and Associates 1971, 54). Both sets of studies recommended reducing the average levels of effective protection and, in particular, reducing the discrimination against exports.

Two other noteworthy studies of developing countries were ones directed by Krueger (1978) and Bhagwati (1978) and by Papageorgiou, Michaely, and Choksi (1991). These studies investigated particular episodes of inward-looking and outward-looking policy actions by considering not only

5. The countries covered by the studies directed by Little, Scitovsky, and Scott (1970) were Argentina, Brazil, India, Mexico, Pakistan, the Philippines, and Taiwan, while those investigated by Balassa and Associates were Brazil, Chile, Mexico, Malaysia, Pakistan, the Philippines, and for comparison, a developed country, Norway.

changes in levels of import protection and export subsidization but the array of macroeconomic policies utilized by governments (e.g., monetary policy, fiscal policy, and especially exchange rate policy) to promote import substitution or deal with its consequences. The Bhagwati-Krueger project focused on the effective exchange rates faced by importers and exporters, that is, the nominal rates for imports and exports corrected for various export subsidies and for import tariffs and nontariff barriers, respectively.[6] Following broad guidelines, the individual country-researchers in the Papageorgiou, Michaely, and Choksi (1991) study were asked to construct an annual index of the degree of trade liberalization.[7] Both these sets of studies reached the same conclusion as the two earlier ones, namely, that import-substitution policies generally do not produce sustainable increases in long-run growth rates and that outward-looking policies are more appropriate for achieving this goal. They also both go into considerable detail about the process of moving from inward-looking to outward-looking policies and, in particular, the sequencing of trade and exchange-rate liberalization and the set of other policies, such as monetary, fiscal, and competition policies, that should accompany the liberalization process.

There were also cross-country econometric studies in the 1970s and 1980s that attempted to test the relationship between trade and economic growth. For example, using information from the country studies that he directed, Balassa and Associates (1978) regressed the growth rate of exports on the growth of output, both including and excluding exports from the measure of output. He found the strongest positive relationship when exports are included as part of output, but he also found a generally significant positive effect when exports are excluded from gross national product (GNP). Krueger (1978, chap. 11) also finds that when the growth of exports was faster the growth of GNP was also faster. She did not find, however, that the extent of trade and exchange rate liberalization independently affects growth. Using data based on the indexes of liberalization in the Papageorgiou, Michaely, and Choksi (1991) study, Kessides (1991) runs a number of regressions relating liberalization and growth. Among his findings are that strong liberalization episodes are associated with higher increases in the rate of gross domestic product (GDP) growth than weaker episodes and that countries with sustained liberalization episodes experienced larger increases in the rates of GDP growth than countries with failed liberalization episodes.

As this brief survey of individual country studies and cross-country sta-

6. This study resulted in published volumes that analyzed Chile, Colombia, Egypt, Ghana, India, Israel, Korea, the Philippines, and Turkey.

7. The countries included in this effort were Argentina, Brazil, Chile, Columbia, Greece, Indonesia, Israel, Korea, New Zealand, Pakistan, Peru, the Philippines, Portugal, Singapore, Spain, Sri Lanka, Turkey, Uruguay, and Yugoslavia. Most studies covered the period from around 1950 to the early 1980s.

tistical analyses of inward-looking versus outward-looking policies indicates, the many differences among researchers, both in the issues examined and in the economic techniques employed, make it difficult to draw many firm conclusions. One generalization that seems warranted is that the import-substitution approach was not successful in promoting appreciably higher growth rates on a long-run, sustainable basis for developing countries that wanted to participate in the global economy. Most countries that used this approach were forced eventually to abandon it because of chronic balance-of-payments and budget deficit problems. Those that have basically stuck with an inward-looking approach over the years (e.g., Pakistan, Burma, and Zimbabwe) have had relatively lower growth rates. In contrast, although many developing countries that switched to outward-looking policies were also often forced to abandon these policies temporarily because of unexpected external events or domestic political pressures related to the adjustment problems involved, those that were able to sustain these policies over long periods seem to have grown more rapidly. Another point that stands out in the various country studies is that outward-looking and inward-looking policies involve much more than just trade and trade policies. For example, a willingness to welcome foreign direct investment, to maintain market-oriented exchange rates, to keep the money supply under fairly tight control, to constrain government budget deficits and corruption, and to control monopolistic behavior by firms and industries all seem to be important components of outward-looking development policies. Attempting to isolate the relative importance on growth of a particular component such as the volume of exports or liberal versus protectionist trade policies does not seem to make much sense, since there are complex interrelationships among these types of policies that make them highly intercorrelated. In his influential review of the various investigations of trade and growth through the early 1990s, Edwards (1993) is especially critical of the early cross-country statistical studies, which he argues are based on overly simplistic theoretical models and also are flawed for various econometric reasons. More recently, Srinivasan and Bhagwati (2001) have also sharply criticized cross-country regression analyses as the basis of determining the relationships between trade openness and growth. In their view, due to the weak theoretical foundations of most of these studies, the poor quality of the databases they must use, and inappropriate econometric techniques utilized in many instances, nuanced, in-depth studies of country experiences are the best approach for understanding the linkage between trade and growth.

13.4 Openness and the New Growth Theory

Under the traditional comparative-statics framework, either in the absence or presence of economic distortions, changes in trade policy lead only to one-time changes in levels of production, although in the real world of economic frictions one might expect to observe the shift to new equilibria taking place only over a number of years. Similarly, trade-policy changes in the standard neoclassical model of exogenous growth bring about changes in the pattern of product specialization but not in the steady-state rate of growth. An important analytical development in the latter part of the 1980s and early 1990s, however, was the significant improvement in endogenous growth theory by such authors as Romer (1986), Lucas (1988), and Grossman and Helpman (1991). Part of this new growth theory focused on the relationships between international trade and growth. One of the models of Grossman and Helpman (chap. 6) illustrates the types of relationships stressed in the new growth theory and, in particular, how trade policy can affect growth rates. To keep the model as simple as possible, they assume that each country is "small" in the sense of facing fixed world prices for the two final goods produced. There are two factors of production, human capital (skilled labor) and unskilled labor whose supplies are fixed. One of the final goods is produced with human capital and a fixed amount of differentiated, nontraded intermediate inputs, while the other is produced with unskilled labor and the same bundle of intermediate inputs. The nontraded intermediate inputs are produced under monopolistically competitive conditions with both factors of production. Constant returns to scale prevail for final and intermediate goods.

Human capital is also involved in the research and development (R&D) activities that create new varieties of intermediate goods. These intermediate inputs are the key to increased productivity: Each final good requires a given aggregate of intermediates but the more varieties there are in this aggregate, the higher output becomes. This captures the idea that dividing tasks into smaller and smaller parts through specialization leads to increasing returns. Another important aspect of the R&D process is that it not only produces new varieties of intermediates but also adds to the stock of knowledge, which is nonappropriable. The greater this stock of knowledge, the less the quantity of human capital needed to produce new varieties of intermediate inputs. Thus, the growth process is endogenous with R&D creating new intermediate inputs that increase the productivity of the needed aggregate of inputs and add to the stock of general knowledge. In turn, the larger stock of knowledge reduces the amount of human capital needed for producing new varieties of intermediates. The equilibrium outcome is a constant rate of growth of factor productivity and a constant rate of output growth in the sectors producing the final goods.

Now consider the effects of a tariff on the imported good. If the country is importing the good that only uses human capital as a direct input, and exporting the good intensively using unskilled labor, the import duty will raise the relative domestic price of the human capital–intensive good and via the Stolper-Samuelson theorem raise the relative wages of skilled labor

(1941). This increase in the price of human capital will lower the level of R&D activity by raising its costs and thus lead to a lower equilibrium growth rate. In contrast, if the country imports the unskilled labor-intensive goods, import protection will lower the relative wages of skilled labor and accelerate the growth rate. Thus, in this model there is no definite answer to whether protection increases or decreases the growth rate. It depends on the pattern of imports and exports. Besides using the concept of increasing returns as the driving force for endogenous growth, Grossman and Helpman (1991) and other growth theorists have introduced such concepts as knowledge spillovers resulting from trade in goods and foreign direct investment as well as the ability to imitate the products of foreign producers as engines of endogenous growth. Import protection generally reduces growth rates under these formulations.

13.5   More Sophisticated Cross-Country Studies, Yet Continued Disagreement

Motivated by the improvements in growth theory, the criticisms of earlier statistical analyses, and the availability of more comprehensive data and new econometric techniques, economists devoted renewed attention in the 1990s to more sophisticated cross-country econometric analyses relating various measures of outwardness or openness to the growth rates of GDP or total factor productivity. Almost all of these studies find a strong positive relationship between outward-looking policies and growth. However, in an important detailed review of the most influential of these studies in which they focus on the effects of policy-induced trade barriers on growth rather than on the growth effects of more general measures of openness, Rodriguez and Rodrik (2001, 316) express skepticism "that there is a strong negative relationship in the data between trade barriers and economic growth, at least for levels of trade restrictions observed in practice"; moreover, they "view the search for such a relationship as futile." A unique feature of the Rodriguez and Rodrik analysis is that they use the various authors' actual data sets in undertaking various tests of the robustness of their results. The rest of this section examines the main studies reviewed by Rodriguez and Rodrik (1999) and considers the criticisms they make of these studies.

As Rodriguez and Rodrik point out, one of the most widely cited statistical investigations of outward orientation and growth is by Dollar (1992). (This paper was not covered in Edwards' 1993 review.) Dollar bases his measure of outward orientation on estimates of the comparative price levels in ninety-five countries of an identical bundle of consumption goods calculated by Summers and Heston (1988). As a means for eliminating that part of the differences in prices among countries due to country differences in the prices of nontradables, Dollar first regresses their price estimates on the level and square of GDP per capita as well as regional dummies and then compares the predicted price levels from this regression with the Summer and Heston prices. The argument is that if factor prices are not equalized, the relative prices of nontradables should vary systematically with differences in relative factor endowments. Since good data on relative factor endowments are not available for most less developed countries, he uses per capita income as a measure of per capita factor availability. Even with this procedure, he still finds significant anomalies for some countries with respect to the degree of trade distortion produced by his comparative price measure. However, when he combine this trade-distortion measure with a measure of the degree of volatility of exchange rates, he finds that the number of anomalies declines substantially.

Trade economists have often explored the possibility of measuring the degree of import protection or export subsidization by comparing domestic prices across countries for specific traded goods. However, this has generally been rejected as an adequate method of measuring trade barriers, since even for physically identical goods for which detailed direct information on levels of protection or subsidization exists, price differences are generally not good measures of differences in the degree of trade distortions. Given this result and the rather rough method used to purge the effects of the prices of nontradables in the Summers and Heston price measures, it is not surprising that Dollar finds that his price indexes do not yield reasonable results for a number of countries. Combining these indexes with a measure of the volatility of exchange rates may give more reasonable results but, as Rodriguez and Rodrik argue, his variability index seems to be more a measure of economic instability at large rather than of trade orientation alone.

To test for the relationship between growth and his measures of outward orientation, Dollar regresses growth in per capita income in ninety-five countries averaged over the period 1976–1985 on his trade-distortion and exchange rate volatility measures as well as on the rate of investment in these countries over the same period. He finds that the higher the level of trade distortion and the greater the exchange rate variability for a country, the lower the rate of per capita GDP growth. Rodriguez and Rodrik not only have some theoretical criticisms of Dollar's trade distortion index as an appropriate measure of trade restrictions but find that the regression results for this index are not very robust to alternative specifications of the growth equation. For example, when dummy variables are added for Latin America, East Asia, and sub-Saharan Africa, the trade distortion measure is not statistically significant. Adding initial per capita income and level of education reduces the explanatory power of this variable even more. Furthermore, when Rodriguez and Rodrik use the latest revision of the Summers and Heston database for the same countries and time period covered by Dollar, the trade distortion index is not significant and has the wrong sign even without the addition of regional dummies. However, the exchange rate variability index continues to be negative and statistically significant under all specifications with both the new and old databases. Thus, while Dollar has shown that exchange rate variability is negatively associated with growth rates, I agree with Rodriguez and Rodrik that he has not demonstrated that outward orientation as one would expect this to be affected by trade policies is significantly related to economic growth in the developing countries he studied.

The next, equally influential study critiqued by Rodriguez and Rodrik is by Sachs and Warner (1995). These authors construct a 0-1 dummy of openness for seventy-nine countries that takes a 0 if any one of the following five conditions holds over the period 1970–1989: average tariff rates are over 40 percent on capital goods and intermediates, nontariff barriers cover 40 percent or more of imports of capital goods and intermediates, the country operates under a socialist economic system, there is a state monopoly of the country's major exports, and the black-market premium on its official exchange rate exceeded 20 percent in the 1980s or 1990s. A value of 0 is viewed as indicating a closed economy, while a value of 1 indicates an open economy. Controlling for such variables as the investment rate, government spending as a fraction of GDP, secondary and primary schooling, and number of revolutions and coups, Sachs and Warner find their openness index to be positively related to the growth rate of per capita GDP in a statistically significant sense.

In reanalyzing the Sachs and Warner data, Rodriguez and Rodrik find that two of the five indicators provide most of this statistical significance: the existence of a state monopoly of the country's major exports and a black-market foreign exchange premium of more than 20 percent. (Neither the measure of tariff levels nor the coverage of nontariff trade barriers is statistically significant when the different indicators of openness are entered separately.) Moreover, they note that the state monopoly variable covers only twenty-nine African countries undergoing structural adjustment programs in the late 1980s and early 1990s, and therefore is virtually indistinguishable from the use of a sub-Saharan Africa dummy. As for the statistical significance of the black-market premium, they argue that this indicator is likely to be a measure of policy failure due to many other reasons besides simply trade policy.

Another paper critiqued by Rodriguez and Rodrik is one by Edwards (1998), the author of the previously mentioned review of the various studies on the trade and growth through the 1980s and early 1990s (i.e., Edwards 1993). One of Edwards' main criticisms in the 1993 paper of the cross-country statistical studies in that period is their failure to test in a systematic way for the robustness of the results obtained. In his 1998 paper, Edwards tries to remedy this shortcoming. He tests the robustness of the extent to which nine different measures of trade policy are related to total factor productivity growth. His nine measures of openness are (a) the Warner-Sachs index just discussed; (b) a subjective World Bank classification of trade strategies; (c) Learner's (1988) index of openness based on the residuals from regressions explaining trade flows; (d) the average black-market premium on a country's official foreign exchange rate; (e) average levels of import tariffs calculated by UNCTAD and taken from Barro and Lee (1994); (f) the average coverage of nontariff trade barriers taken from the same source; (g) a subjective index of trade distortions formulated by the Heritage Foundation; (h) the ratio of taxes on imports and exports to total trade; and (i) a regression-based index of import distortions calculated by Wolf (1993). He regresses these nine different measures of openness on estimates that he calculates of ten-year averages of total factor productivity from 1960 to 1990 for ninety-three developed and developing countries. Controlling for initial per capita GDP in 1965 and the average number of years of education in 1965, he finds that six of the nine measures of openness are statistically significant in the expected direction.

Rather ironically, given Edwards' emphasis on the need to test for robustness by using alternative specifications, Rodriguez and Rodrik find that his results are heavily dependent on the fact that he weighs his regressions by per capita GDP. If one weighs by the log of per capita GDP and uses White's (1980) method of dealing with the heteroscedasticity problem, the number of Edwards' nine openness measures that are significant drops to four out of nine. The four significant openness measures that are significant when White's correction for heteroscedasticity is used are the World Bank's subjective classification of trade regimes, the black-market exchange rate premium, the subjective index of trade distortions calculated by the Heritage Foundation, and the ratio of trade taxes to total trade. With respect to the latter variable, Rodriguez and Rodrik find that recalculating this variable based on more recent data than was not available to Edwards fails to yield a significant sign when introduced into the regression on total factor productivity. They also note that the Heritage Foundation index was calculated for trade restrictions existing in 1996, whereas Edwards' estimates cover the decade of the 1980s. When they calculate a similar index that is based on 1980s data, it is no longer statistically significant in explaining the growth rate of total factor productivity. They also object to the use of this measure as well as the one from the World Bank as being subjective measures that they believe are "apparently highly contaminated by judgement biases or lack robustness to use of more credible information from alternative data sources" (Rodriguez and Rodrik, 2000, 301). Finally, as mentioned earlier, they regard changes in the exchange rate premium as being influenced more by basic macroeconomic policies than trade policies.

Two additional recent papers on the subject are by Frankel and Romer (1999) and by Dollar and Kraay (June 2001). Frankel and Romer directly address the question: Does trade cause growth? Like others, they point out that the ordinary least squares (OLS) regressions of per capita income on the ratio of exports or imports and other variables, which generally find a positive relationship between trade shares and income per person, may not indicate the effect of trade on growth due to the endogeneity of the trade share. Countries whose incomes are high for reasons not related to trade may have high trade ratios. They therefore use geographic characteristics of countries that they believe are not influenced by incomes or government policies and other factors affecting income to obtain instrumental variables estimates of trade's effect on income. Specifically, they include in their trade equation the size of countries, their distance from each other, whether they share a border, and whether they are landlocked. Their main finding is that there is no evidence that OLS estimates overstate the effects of trade. They are careful to point out, however, that this does not mean that changes in trade resulting from policy actions affect growth in the same manner as from their geographic variables, because there are many different mechanisms by which trade can affect income. But they argue (see Frankel and Romer 1999, 395) that the effects of geography-based differences in trade are "at least suggestive about the effects of policy-induced differences."

Rodriguez and Rodrik also critique this paper and argue that the geographically constructed measure by Frankel and Romer may not be a valid instrumental variable. The reason is that geography is likely to be a determinant of income through many more channels than just trade. For example, distance from the equator affects public health and thus productivity through exposure to various diseases. When they include distance from the equator or percentage of land in the tropics, or a set of regional dummies in the Frankel and Romer instrumental variables income regressions, their constructed trade-share variable is no longer statistically significant. However, Frankel and Romer report that when they also include distance from the equator as a control variable there is still no evidence that OLS regressions overstate the influence of trade on income.

The final paper considered here is one by Dollar and Kraay (2003). The unique feature of their regression analysis is its focus on within-country (rather than cross-country) decadal changes in growth rates and changes in the volume of trade. Because of this approach, the authors maintain that their results are not driven by geography or other unobserved country characteristics that influence growth but vary little over time. They also argue that their instrumentation strategy deals with the possibility of reverse causation from growth to trade. Their data consist of 274 observations over three decades from roughly 100 countries.

Dollar and Kraay find a strong and significant positive relationship between changes in trade and changes in growth. Moreover, they believe "that we can at least cautiously ascribe some of the growth effects of trade to underlying trade liberalizing policies that countries have undertaken" (Dollar and Kraay 2003, 151). However, when they introduce institutional factors along with trade as explanatory factors of changes in growth, they find it difficult to disentangle the partial causal effects of institutions and trade separately, using these factors as instruments. They conclude, therefore, "that both trade and institutions are important in understanding cross-country differences in growth rates in the very long run, but the available cross-country variation is not very informative about the relative importance of each" (Dollar and Kraay 2003, 161).

13.6   Conclusions

What are we to conclude from this survey of empirical studies about the relationships between openness and growth, besides the fact that there is disagreement among economists on the matter? As noted in the introductory section, a key reason for the disagreement seems to relate to differences among authors in what they mean by the concept of openness. Rodriguez and Rodrik, for example, focus on the relationship between growth and *trade* openness, as reflected by "policy-induced barriers to international trade" (2001, 264). In appraising the various studies they cover, they consider levels of import duties and measures of the restrictiveness of nontariff barriers to be the most appropriate indicators of trade openness. They are aware, however, of the limitations of the existing measures of these indicators of trade openness. Simple tariff averages weighted by imports tend to underweight the restrictiveness of high tariffs due to the low level of imports. (A tariff so high that there are no imports is a case in point.) Available comprehensive measures of nontariff barriers only measure the number of different types of nontariff trade barriers that a country has introduced and thus do not distinguish between the degrees of restrictiveness of these measures.

In contrast to Rodriguez and Rodrik, most authors both of studies of development episodes in particular countries and of statistical analyses of such periods across a large number of countries study much more than just the effects of trade policies. The country studies led by Bhagwati and Krueger and Papageorgiou, Michaely, and Choksi, for example, specifically focus on exchange rates as well as trade barriers and also examine the monetary, fiscal, and regulatory policies that accompanied market-opening or market-closing episodes. This is why these writers as well as those undertaking cross-country statistical studies describe the effects of the policies they are studying on a country in terms of such broad phrases as its outward orientation and openness in describing the policies they are studying. However, according to Rodriguez and Rodrik: "To the extent that the empirical literature demonstrates a positive causal link from openness to growth, the main operational implication is that governments should dismantle their barriers to trade" (2001, 264).

Most of the authors of this literature would, I think, strongly object to this narrow interpretation of the policy implications of their work. While they generally favor the reduction of high tariff and nontariff barriers in developing countries, these authors also call for other policy changes aimed at eliminating large government deficits, curtailing inflationary monetary policies, maintaining market-oriented exchange rates, increasing competition among domestic firms, reducing government corruption, improving the educational system, strengthening the legal system, and so forth. As the country studies have clearly demonstrated, not only are high tariff levels usually associated with highly restrictive nontariff measures, export subsidies to selected sectors, overvalued exchange rates, large government deficits, extensive rent-seeking and corruption, unstable governments, and so forth; but significant reductions in trade barriers are also accompanied by important liberalization efforts in these nontrade policy areas. The extensive multicolinearity among the policy variables affecting these conditions is the reason that researchers who undertake both cross-country statistical analyses and individual country studies often try to combine various policies into a single index of economic openness or use broad openness measures such as price differences that clearly are affected by much more than just trade policies affecting the individual commodities.

The general strategy followed by Rodriguez and Rodrik in critiquing the various studies involves examining the individual components of the general measures of openness used by the authors to find out if the tariff and nontariff trade components in these measures are by themselves related to economic growth in a statistically significant manner, determining if introducing plausible additional variables not directly related to trade policy changes the significance levels of the trade variables, and exploring whether modifying the econometric techniques followed in a seemingly reasonable manner results in a loss of significance of the trade variables. As the summary of their findings presented in this paper show, they generally find that tariffs and nontariff coverage either are not statistically significant by themselves or lose their significance when other variables are added in the regression equations or different econometric techniques are utilized.

It is quite true that those recommending changes in economic policies in developing countries sometimes make statements implying that just lowering trade barriers will raise growth rates, and we should be grateful to Rodriguez and Rodrik for pointing out that the available empirical evidence does not support this claim. Of course, the quality of the existing data on the restrictiveness of tariffs and nontariff trade barriers is so poor that when better data become available we may find this relationship may indeed hold under certain circumstances. But it is a caricature of the positions of most economists in academia or in governmental institutions to maintain that they fail to realize and recommend the necessity of policy changes beyond just those covering trade to stimulate sustained increases in growth rates. Especially since the Bhagwati and Krueger and Papageorgiou, Michaely and Choksi country studies, economists have emphasized the need, as a minimum, for a stable and nondiscriminatory exchange rate system and the need for prudent monetary and fiscal policies and corruption-free administration of economic policies for trade liberalization to be effective in the long run.

The evidence that a general policy position of openness is preferable to long-run economic growth than an inward-looking policy stance should not be interpreted, however, as implying that no government interventions, such as selective production subsidies or controls on short-term capital movements, are appropriate at certain stages of development. We know from the individual country studies that policymakers in some economies, such as South Korea, in shifting from policies favoring import-substitution policies to an outward-oriented policy approach actively intervened to promote exports. Some authors maintain that they succeeded in spite of these interventionist activities due to the predominance of liberalizing policies, but it may be that some of these government actions actually helped to raise growth rates. In my view, the individual country and cross-country studies support the conclusion that, on balance, general economic openness is much more favorable to growth than a general inward-looking economic approach but that some policies regarded as causing static economic distortions may be appropriate at certain times and under various circumstances. As Rodrik (2002) argues in an introductory essay to a series of country studies he has organized, we urgently need more studies that try give guidance on just what these times and circumstances are. One type of study that should be undertaken more extensively is the careful monitoring of the direct and indirect effects of liberalization measures from the outset of their introduction.

The statistical finding that increases in exports and increased growth are generally positively related in a significant statistical sense also involves the problem of causation. The export increase may be result of trade policy changes, other nontrade policy actions, or forces unrelated to a government's policy actions. As noted earlier, the export increase also may be the consequence of economic growth rather than the cause. Furthermore, the use of exports as an openness measure has the drawback of being a component of GDP, the usual measure of economic growth.

Consequently, as Rodriguez and Rodrik argue, not only does the search for the relationship between trade barriers and growth seem futile, but it does not even seem to make much sense to investigate what the empirical evidence is on this relationship in view of the complex interrelationships between trade policy and other government policies and various macroeconomic variables when one is talking about trade policy actions covering a wide group of goods (e.g., manufactures) rather than a particular industry. Actually, most of the country studies, particularly the later ones, have been concerned with government policies that cover much more than narrowly defined trade barriers to international trade.

It is true that developing countries are often given the policy advice that decreasing trade barriers is a more effective way of achieving higher sustainable rates of growth than tightening trade restrictions. But those giving such advice also emphasize the need, as a minimum, for a stable and nondiscriminatory exchange rate system and usually also the need for prudent monetary and fiscal policies and corruption-free administration of economic policies for trade liberalization to be effective in the long run. It seems to me that the various country studies do support this type of policy advice and that the cross-country statistical studies do not overturn this conclusion. But the recent critiques of these latter studies demonstrate that we must be careful in attributing any single economic policy, such as the lowering of trade barriers, as being a sufficient government action for accelerating the rate of economic growth.

References

Balassa, Bela, and Associates. 1971. *The structure of protection in developing countries.* Baltimore: Johns Hopkins Press.

———. 1978. Exports and economic growth: Further evidence. *Journal of Development Economics* 5:181–89.

Baldwin, Robert E. 1969. The case against infant-industry tariff protection. *Journal of Political Economy* 77 (3): 295–305.

Barro, Robert J., and Jong-Wha Lee. 1994. Data set for a panel of 138 countries. Harvard University, January.

Bhagwati, Jagdish. 1978. *Foreign trade regimes and economic development: Anatomy and consequences of exchange control regimes.* New York: National Bureau of Economic Research.

Clemens, Michael A., and Jeffrey G. Williamson. 2001. A tariff-growth paradox? Protection's impact the world around 1875–1997. NBER Working Paper no. 8459. Cambridge, Mass.: National Bureau of Economic Research, September.

Dollar, David. 1992. Outward-oriented developing economies really do grow more rapidly: Evidence from 95 LDCs, 1976–1985. *Economic Development and Cultural Change* 523–44.

Dollar, David, and Aart Kraay. 2003. Institutions, trade, and growth. *Journal of Monetary Economics* 50 (1): 133–62.

Edwards, Sebastian. 1993. Openness, trade liberalization, and growth in developing countries. *Journal of Economic Literature* 31 (3): 1358–93.

———. 1998. Openness, productivity, and growth: What do we really know? *Economic Journal* 108 (447): 383–98.

Frank, Charles, Jr., Kwang Suk Kim, and Larry E. Westphal. 1975. *Foreign trade regimes and economic development: South Korea*. New York: National Bureau of Economic Research.

Frankel, Jeffrey A., and David Romer. 1999. Does trade cause growth? *American Economic Review* 89 (3): 379–99.

Grossman, Gene M., and Elhanan Helpman. 1991. *Innovation and growth in the global economy*. Cambridge: MIT Press.

Hamilton, Alexander. 1913. *Report on manufactures (1791)*. Rep., U.S. Senate Documents, XXII, no. 172.

Hausmann, Ricardo, and Dani Rodrik. 2002. Economic development as self discovery. Centre for Economic Policy Research (CEPR) Discussion Paper no. 3356. London: CEPR, May.

Irwin, Douglas A. 2002. Did import substitution promote growth in the late nineteenth century? NBER Working Paper no. 8751. Cambridge, Mass.: National Bureau of Economic Research, February.

Kessides, Ioannis N. 1991. Appendix A2. In *Lessons of experience in developing world*, ed. Michael Michaely, Demetris Papageorgiou, and Armeane M. Choksi, 302–17. Oxford: Basil Blackwell.

Krueger, Anne O. 1978. *Foreign trade regimes and economic development: Liberalization attempts and consequences*. Cambridge, Mass.: Ballinger Publishing Co. for National Bureau of Economic Research.

———. 1997. Trade policy and economic development: How we learn. *American Economic Review* 87 (1): 1–22.

Leamer, Edward. 1988. Measures of openness. In *Trade policy and empirical analysis*, ed. Robert E. Baldwin, Chicago: University of Chicago Press.

List, Frederick. 1856. *National system of political economy*. Trans. George-August Matile. Philadelphia: Lippincott.

Little, Ian, Tibor Scitovsky, and Maurice Scott. 1970. *Industry and trade in some developing countries: A comparative study*. Cambridge: Oxford University Press.

Lucas, Robert E. 1988. On the mechanics of economic development. *Journal of Monetary Economics* 22 (1): 3–42.

Meade, James E. 1955. *Trade and welfare*. New York: Oxford University Press.

O'Rourke, Kevin. 2000. Tariffs and growth in the late 19th century. *Economic Journal* 110 (463): 456–83.

Papageorgiou, Demetris, Michael Michaely, and Aremeane M. Choksi. 1991. *Liberalizing foreign trade*. Oxford: Basil Blackwell.

Prebisch, Raul. 1950. *The economic development of Latin America and its principal problems*. Lake Success, N.Y.: United Nations, Department of Economic Affairs.

Rodriguez, Francisco, and Dani Rodrik. 2001. Trade policy and economic growth: A skeptic's guide to the cross-national evidence. In *NBER macroeconomics annual 2000*, ed. Ben Bernanke and Kenneth S. Rogoff, 261–325. Cambridge: MIT Press.

Rodrik, Dani. 2001. The global governance of trade as if development really mattered. Background paper to United Nations Development Program (UNDP) project on Trade and Sustainable Human Development. New York: UNDP.

Romer, Paul M. 1986. Increasing returns and long-run growth. *Journal of Political Economy* 94 (October): 1002–37.

Sachs, Jeffrey, and Andrew Warner. 1995. Economic reform and the process of global integration. *Brookings Papers on Economic Activity*, Issue no. 1:1–118. Washington, D.C.: Brookings Institution.

Srinivasan, T. N., and Jagadish Bhagwati. 2001. Outward-orientation and development: Are revisionists right? In *Trade, development and political economy: Essays in honour of Anne O. Krueger*, ed. Deepak Lal and Richard H. Snape, 3–26. New York: Palgrave.

Stolper, Wolfgang, and Paul Samuelson. 1941. Protection and real wages. *The Review of Economic Studies* 9 (November): 53–73.

Summers, Robert, and Alan Heston. 1988. A new set of international comparisons of real product and price levels: Estimates for 130 countries, 1950–1985. *Review of Income and Wealth* 34 (1): 1–25.

White, Halbert L. 1980. A heteroskedasticity-consistent covariance matrix estimator and a direct test for heteroskedasticity. *Econometrica* 48 (4): 817–38.

Wolf, Holger. 1993. Trade Orientation: Measurement and consequences. *Estudios de Economia* 20 (20): 52–72.

Comment   Simon Commander

The paper provides an elegant and insightful *tour d'horizon* of the main findings of the substantial literature concerned with the relationship between openness and growth.

It takes a critical look at the swings in the intellectual pendulum that first emphasized infant-industry arguments and then gave preference to more open regimes. Throughout, the paper rightly emphasizes the importance of placing trade policy in the context of other policies, including macroeconomic policy and the business environment more generally.

Trade barriers are—at the least—likely to distort resource allocation by shifting relative prices; at the worst, they lead to lower or unsustainable growth. In endogenous growth models, growth should be raised by lower barriers to trade. The size of effect will presumably depend on technology externalities, investment, and learning effects. The elements of the virtuous circle are not broadly in question, although their empirical identification—as the paper indicates—remains more problematic. However, it is quite possible that, depending on initial factor endowments and technology, some countries may have lower growth with lower trade barriers. As Baldwin acknowledges, there may be cases where greater openness can impede growth—say, through initial lack of technological development resulting in specializations that lower growth—but these are ultimately variations around the infant-industry argument.

Over the past twenty years trade opening has, at least in principle, been a central part of the policy talk and, sometimes, conditionality of multilateral lenders—such as the World Bank—when dealing with developing countries (although how hard such conditions have been enforced is another matter). More than a few claims for the positive impact of such measures on performance have been made, whether using cross-country anal-

Simon Commander is director of the Centre for New and Emerging Markets (CNEM) at the London Business School and adviser in the Office of Chief Economist at the European Bank for Reconstruction and Development (EBRD).

ysis or case studies. Yet the results, particularly from the former, have been curiously unsatisfying.

In common with some other recent and skeptical research—principally Rodriguez and Rodrik (2000) and Srinivasan and Bhagwati (2001)—this paper suggests that we can expect relatively small returns to further inquiry into this relationship from cross-country regressions. It suggests that country-level studies may yield more robust conclusions. It would be helpful to understand quite how that would be the case; what sort of empirical strategies could usefully be employed, and how to avoid the standard problem of local detail defying generalization. In this regard, it would surely make sense for focus to be placed on specific episodes of protectionism or liberalization and to try and understand better their consequences.

A significant part of the paper is largely a critique of one particular research strategy—cross-country analysis—and the robustness of its findings. Indeed, it is striking that even some of its most devoted practitioners now acknowledge the relatively meager harvest. Thus, Easterly and Levine (2001), in reviewing more than a decade of empirical work on growth, recently concluded that the residual rather than factor accumulation accounts for most differences in growth across countries but that total factor productivity is still largely a black box. National policies—including the trade regime—do affect growth, but to what extent is unclear, as is the extent to which any positive effect is contingent on consistency with other policies. However, despite the ambiguity of the cross-country empirical results, the fact remains that countries with *significant* and sustained trade barriers have performed relatively poorly.

Why, then, has this literature found this central empirical relationship to be such a bar of soap? This is clearly partly a question of measurement and the quality of data; partly a problem of chronic endogeneity; partly a problem of omitted variables bias; and partly a problem of the inability to disentangle adequately the effect of other—and possibly enabling—policies. Certainly, the data sets used in these cross-country regressions have difficulty in picking up marginal changes in trade regimes, while large-order reforms may simply reflect a response to a wider pathology of problems. Moreover, there are likely to be major problems in identifying the precise weight of trade policies when other significant reforms are being implemented more-or-less contemporaneously. Indeed, perhaps the strongest result that flows from this literature is that the use of trade restrictions (whatever their precise form) tends to be part of a broader pathology of policies that generally limits growth. Fiscal imbalances, multiple exchange rates with black-market premia, and other domestic controls have mostly been observed alongside trade barriers. The causation may be complex, however.

Any robust association between openness and performance appears to be contingent on a number of factors, including country, region, and other attributes. Rodrik (2002) has argued that trade plays a secondary role compared to deeper factors, such as institutions and geography. Obviously, these relationships are not one-way—good institutions generate trade, openness yields better institutions, and so on. However, causality is again difficult to sort out, particularly in cross-country work, not least because of difficulties in measuring institutional performance, let alone the time frame in which changes in institutional performance occur.

The difficulties in pinning down these relationships can be understood from an interesting example. Suppose that openness is also associated with more volatility or income risk—a proposition advanced, inter alia, by Rodrik (1998). (Quite why this should necessarily be the case needs more substantiation). Governments may choose to reduce that volatility through spending programs. Indeed, the argument has been that the growth of transfer programs (or the welfare state) post-1945 in Western Europe was primarily with the objective of lowering citizens' exposure to risk and was—in a political economy sense—a necessary condition for sustaining trade opening. As such, the causality was from openness to government size. However, if we believe Barro and Sala-i-Martin (1995) and others' findings, government size would in due course negatively affect growth. Thus, any positive effect of openness on growth would, to some extent, be offset by this negative effect from size to growth.

How robust has been the hypothesized (positive) association between openness and government size and the (negative) association between government size and growth? Using pooled data with ten-year averages for over 130 countries for the period from the early 1960s to the mid-1990s, it transpires that evidence for government stabilizing through consumption holds only for low-income countries.[1] The finding is not robust for either high- or middle-income countries. Further, the low-income finding could be interpreted in terms of inertia or persistence rather than as the consequence of an active policy of risk mitigation. The negative association between government size to growth seems robust when specifying size in terms of government consumption. However, this is a far from complete measure of government (commonly excluding off-budget items and/or coverage of public enterprises), and if size responds to openness through redistribution (transfers) it would not necessarily capture what we are after. Again, it would seem that work with large cross-country data sets yields ambiguous, if not misleading, results.

That the empirical relationship between openness and performance has not stood up particularly well when using large numbers of pooled observations or countries seems clear. Does this type of approach fare better with smaller samples with, say, more common initial conditions?

---

1. Whether using the standard deviation in the terms of trade as the measure of income volatility or simply the change in the terms of trade, see Commander, Davoodi, and Lee (1997).

The obvious experiment here is the transition countries. All started with common ownership and control regimes, administered prices and trade organized on the basis of Council for Mutual Economic Assistance (CMEA) prescription. These partly mimicked some view of comparative advantage, but with a binding restriction that trade had to be conducted intra-CMEA. Over ten years ago, these barriers came tumbling down, albeit with different degrees of liberalization across country and region. Growth has since varied widely across countries and regions.

How do trade variables fare in explaining comparative performance? "Not very well" seems to be the answer. As usual, these models are sensitive to specification error through omitted variables, high multicollinearity between exogenous variables, and so on. Further, the scale of reform and structural change has meant that it is very difficult to unpick the relative contributions of specific policies to growth; everything is pretty much jumbled up with everything else. Moreover, while most countries—barring the obvious laggards (Uzbekhistan, Belarus, Turkmenistan)—generally have low barriers to trade (import tariffs ranging between 5 and 10 percent), nontrivial other restrictions on trade have commonly been imposed on particular products and sectors generally in response to lobbying by vested interests, while licensing and other restrictions further hold back trade. In short, trade policy on the ground remains quite discretionary. These sorts of things necessarily evade the trade measures often used in cross-country work.

However, there appears to be a strong and positive association between export market growth and growth,[2] and this seems to be closely linked to large-order trade reorientation toward the European Union. Aside from trade in natural resources (a large part of the Russian story), export growth has in turn been associated with prior product upgrading and investment, commonly by foreigners, itself the product of greater openness. By contrast, trade and other investment barriers (e.g., high bribe taxes and the like) limit restructuring, investment (including by foreigners), and quality upgrading. In turn, productivity improvements remain small or absent, as do export opportunities. Clearly, any solutions must necessarily embrace a great deal more than trade policy.

Finally, the transition experience highlights not so much the infant-industry issue, but the problem of declining sectors and whether trade policy can be sensibly used to cushion or smooth restructuring costs—a factor of considerable relevance when job destruction is likely to be large. The welfare costs associated with using trade policy rather than targeted budgetary subsidies would, of course, be larger. The evidence suggests that protection has not been a general policy response for declining sectors.

2. Export market growth being adjusted for the share of exports in GDP; see Christofferson and Doyle (1998).

In short, any review of the growth and openness literature demonstrates that more open trade regimes go hand in hand with good investment climates and other virtuous features, and vice versa. But—as Baldwin's paper confirms—measuring the impact of trade policy and/or openness on growth using cross-country regressions has generally proven a rather unrewarding, and occasionally misleading, exercise. The challenge is to work out at what level of disaggregation such inquiry can best proceed.

References

Barro, R. J., and X. Sala-i-Martin. 1995. *Economic growth*. New York: McGraw-Hill.

Christofferson, P., and P. Doyle. 1998. From inflation to growth: Eight years of transition. *Economics of Transition* 8 (2): 421–51.

Commander, S., H. Davoodi, and U. Lee. 1997. The consequences of government for growth and well-being. *World Bank Working Papers on Governance, Corruption, Legal Reform* 1785 (June). Washington, D.C.: World Bank.

Easterly, W., and R. Levine. 2001. It's not factor accumulation: Stylised facts and growth models. *World Bank Economic Review* 15 (2): 177–219.

Rodriguez, F., and D. Rodrik. 2000. Trade policy and economic growth: A sceptic's guide to the cross-national evidence. In *Macroeconomics annual 2000*, ed. Ben Bernanke and Kenneth S. Rogoff. Cambridge: MIT Press.

Rodrik, D. 1998. Why do more open economies have bigger governments? *Journal of Political Economy* 106 (5): 997–1032.

———. 2002. Institutions, integration, and geography: In search of the deep determinants of economic growth. Paper presented for Analytic Country Studies on Growth, John F. Kennedy School of Government, Harvard.

Srinivasan, T. N., and J. Bhagwati. 2001. Outward orientation and development: Are revisionists right? In *Trade, development, and political economy*, ed. D. Lal and R. Snape, 3–26. London: Palgrave.

Contributors

Joshua Aizenman
Department of Economics
Social Sciences I
University of California
Santa Cruz, CA 95064

Robert E. Baldwin
Department of Economics
University of Wisconsin-Madison
Social Science Building 7321
1180 Observatory Drive
Madison, WI 53706

Drusilla K. Brown
Department of Economics
115 Braker Hall
Tufts University
8 Upper Campus Road
Medford, MA 02155-6722

David L. Carr
Department of Economics
McCabe Hall 121
American University
4400 Massachusetts Avenue, NW
Washington, DC 20016-8029

Simon Commander
London Business School
Regent's Park
London NW1 4SA
England

Jaime de Melo
Université de Genève
Bd. du Pont d'Arve 40
1211 Geneva 4
Switzerland

Alan V. Deardorff
Department of Economics
458 Lorch Hall
University of Michigan
Ann Arbor, MI 48109

Kimberly Ann Elliott
Institute for International
    Economics
1750 Massachusetts Avenue
Washington, DC 20036-1903

Simon J. Evenett
Corpus Christi College
University of Oxford
Oxford OX1 4JF
England

Rod Falvey
School of Economics
Room B71a, Economics &
    Geography Building
University of Nottingham
Nottingham NG7 2RD
England

Harry Flam
Institute for International Economic
  Studies
Stockholm University
Universitetsvägen 10, House A,
  8th Floor
SE-106 91 Stockholm
Sweden

Christopher L. Gilbert
Faculti di Economia
Univertà degli Studi di Trento
Via luama 5
38100 Trento
Italy

Jean-Marie Grether
Université de Neuchâtel
Faculty of Law and Economics
Pierre-à-Mazel 7
CH-2000 Neuchâtel
Switzerland

Carl B. Hamilton
Stockholm School of Economics
Riksdagen
S-100 12 Stockholm
Sweden

Mari Kangasniemi
Poverty Research Unit at Sussex
School of African and Asian Studies
University of Sussex
Falmer, Brighton BN1 9SJ
England

Debayani Kar
Center for Economic and Policy
  Research
1621 Connecticut Avenue,
  NW-Suite 500
Washington, DC 20009

Robert E. Lipsey
National Bureau of Economic
  Research
365 Fifth Avenue, 5th Floor
New York, NY 10016-4309

James R. Markusen
Department of Economics
UCB 256
University of Colorado
Boulder, CO 80309-0256

Keith E. Maskus
Department of Economics
UCB 256
University of Colorado
Boulder, CO 80309-0256

Stephen Redding
Department of Economics
London School of Economics
Houghton Street
London WC2A 2AE
England

J. David Richardson
Department of Economics
347 Eggers Hall
Syracuse University
Syracuse, NY 13244-1090

André Sapir
CP 140
Université Libre de Bruxelles
Avenue F.D. Roosevelt, 50
B-1050 Brussels
Belgium

Robert M. Stern
Department of Economics
University of Michigan
440 Lorch Hall
611 Tappan Street
Ann Arbor, MI 48109-1220

Vanessa Strauss-Kahn
INSEAD
Boulevard de Constance
77305 Fontainebleau Cedex
France

Panos Varangis
Development Research Group
The World Bank
1818 H Street, NW
Washington, DC 20433

Anthony J. Venables
Department of Economics
London School of Economics
Houghton Street
London WC2A 2AE
England

L. Alan Winters
Professor of Economics
School of Social Sciences
University of Sussex
Falmer Brighton BN1 9SN
England

Author Index

Subject Index